EPHESIANS
PAUL'S CONCLUSIVE TREATISE

A New Basic Explanatory Translation

With

A New Extended Interpretive and Expositional Translation

Into

Professional (Non-Ecclesiastical)
Contemporary (Non-Medieval)
American (Non-British)
English

From
The Greek Text

Compared with
William Tyndale's First English Translation (1526)
and
The Authorized King James Version (1611)

Glenn W. Campbell, Th.M., M.A.

Copyright © 2005

© 2005 Glenn W. Campbell. All Rights Reserved.

No part of this book may be reproduced, stored in a retrieval system, or transmitted by any means without the written permission of the author.

First published by AuthorHouse 11/04/05

ISBN: 1-4208-9305-X (sc)
ISBN: 1-4208-9587-7 (dj)

Library of Congress Control Number: 2005909228

Printed in the United States of America
Bloomington, Indiana

This book is printed on acid-free paper.

1663 LIBERTY DRIVE, SUITE 200
BLOOMINGTON, INDIANA 47403
(800) 839-8640
WWW.AUTHORHOUSE.COM

For Sherrie,
Joshua and Niki,
Jessica,
and Caleb

But when Aragorn arose
all that beheld him gazed in silence,
for it seemed to them
that he was revealed to them now for the first time.
Tall as the sea kings of old,
he stood above all that were near,
ancient of days he seemed
and yet in the flower of manhood;
and wisdom sat upon his brow,
and strength and healing were in his hands,
and a light was about him.
And then Faramir cried;
"Behold the King."

J.R.R. Tolkien, *The Lord of the Rings*
Volume 3, *The Return of the King*

PREFACE

This book is a new translation of Paul's *Treatise to the Ephesians*. It is written to and for *professional Christians*, who feel they have not yet found a satisfactory answer to a very important question. It is a question that you may have only just begun to think about, or that you may have been persistently asking yourself and others for years. It is the simple but profound question, "O.K., I'm saved…now what?" If you are looking for an answer to this question, then this book is for you.

In Ephesians, Paul maps out the journey of how we can discover and accomplish the unique and special *lifework* God has assigned to each of us. He will maintain that embarking on this journey is the only way we can ever really find happiness and gain the sense of achievement and significance that all of us – deep down – are searching for. He will show us how we can know for sure that we have invested our lives to make a *valuable and significant contribution* to our fellow human beings in the history of this present era. Moreover, he will also demonstrate that by entering into the quest to find our lifework, we can carry out the even more important endeavor of becoming the Jesus' "apprentices," who He intends to train for leadership. Paul will enable us to realize that Jesus' goal for our divine apprenticeship is and always has been to prepare us and give us the qualifications for a special future role of honorable, personal service as His distinguished, resurrected representatives and leaders in the Kingdom He will found when He returns to earth from heaven.

As Jesus' specially selected recruits, we will learn how to recognize His divine guidance as He directs our lives from heaven in His present role of Commander in Chief over His "Kingdom Apprenticeship Councils." As His apprentices, He will teach us specific ways we can grow in our leadership experience, maturity and wisdom as human beings *right now*. Ultimately, Paul will furnish us with the spiritual equipment required to become familiar with how Jesus orchestrates our present responsibilities, and how He uses them to train us in the interpersonal skills and leadership expertise we will need in order to exercise the authority and administrate the important duties to which He will appoint us during the Kingdom era.

As we grow into our final years of life along this journey, we will learn how to sidestep the disappointment, narrow-mindedness, inflexibility, irritability and even despair that often accompany the lives of a great number of professional Americans during their later years. Instead, we will learn how to leave behind our tendency to become angry, bitter, depressed and cynical as we age, and look forward with an ever-increasing sense of adventure, eager anticipation, enjoyment and gratitude – balanced by a proportional sense of contentment, peace and serenity – as we approach Jesus' Inauguration Day.

On that great Day, Jesus will take up his long awaited role as High King and gather us together with all of His other apprentices who will have accomplished their respective lifeworks within their own historical eras, both past and future. He will then establish us as the unique company that comprises those He will be glad to call His "band of brothers and sisters" – the team of good, gracious and noble members of His Royal Administration. Together with them, we will serve Him as His vice-regents throughout His one-thousand year reign as our future High King over the whole earth.

This special offer is for you. Its time to plunge ahead into the adventure of exploring the answer to the profound question, "O.K., I'm saved…now what?"

Glenn W. Campbell, M.A., Th.M.

Dallas, Texas
September 17, 2005

In Attestation:

Brian Campbell
Jerry Ferguson
Bill Kushnir
Graham McFarlane

ACKNOWLEDGEMENTS

This translation could not have been accomplished without the invaluable help of my wife Sherrie, my son Josh and his wife Niki, my daughter Jessica and my son Caleb. Thanks also must go to my mother Dorothy and my father Ed (who went to be with our Divine Commander in Chief on Christmas Day, now over four years ago), my sister Catherine, and to my mother-in-law Carol Grabein. Special thanks to my two brothers; to Mark, for encouraging me in this effort, and to Brian, who has helped in so many ways – both with helpful suggestions and in freeing up my time by joining GWC Engineering over two years ago to take over many of my duties as Chief Engineering Officer.

To those responsible for never giving up in asking God to awaken me spiritually with His wonderful message of love and forgiveness, I give my thanks: first, to Billy Graham; and then to the Young Life group and the Bible Church in Conroe, Texas, who gave their direction and time; especially to Dave and Betty Anderson, and to Steve and Liz Massey.

I must also acknowledge and thank all my teachers over the years; first at Dallas Seminary – especially to Zane Hodges for giving me a love for the Greek New Testament; and to Norm Geisler, for awakening me to the love of Philosophy; and second, at the University of Dallas – especially to Robert Wood and Dennis Sepper, my guides in the study of Philosophy.

I am also greatly indebted and thankful to the terrific staff at GWC Engineering, and to the dear friends, colleagues and business associates who have given me their encouragement and assistance over the years. Special thanks to Graham McFarlane, Bill Kushnir, Jerry Ferguson and Chris Skinner for proof-reading the manuscript and contributing so many helpful observations, ideas, comments and improvements; and to Jeannette Pittman, Debbie Johnson and Cindy Figer for reading the manuscript and offering valuable and useful suggestions. Thanks also to Phil Blackstone, Rob Brunk, Allen Greenly, Ralph Heffelman, Jim Keton, Leon McCaskill, Russ Medina, Howard Moore, Bruce Noller, Mike Sterlacci, Brad Williams, and all the other members of the Leadership Bible Study Group.

Finally, thanks to all the members of John Dealey's Advisory Council for all of the wisdom and insight they have provided over the last several years; especially to John Dealey, Bob Pierry, Peter Stewart, Jerry Smith, Gene Cooper, Brad Stevens, Mike Hicks, and Chip Harper.

THEME OF THE WORK:

1:18...πεφωτισμένους τοὺς ὀφθαλμοὺς
τῆς καρδίας ὑμῶν εἰς τὸ εἰδέναι ὑμᾶς
τίς ἐστιν ἡ ἐλπὶς τῆς κλήσεως αὐτοῦ,
τίς ὁ πλοῦτος τῆς δόξης τῆς
κληρονομίας αὐτοῦ
ἐν τοῖς ἁγίοις...

1:18...that the eyes of your heart, once they have been enlightened,
would be able to realize what the unique hope of His promising
lifework project for each one of you consists, together with
the vast extent of the wealth of His Inheritance,
which He will bequeath to every one of
His specially selected recruits
who merit it at His
Appearing…

Purpose of the work:

6:17...δέξασθαι, καὶ τὴν μάχαιραν
τοῦ πνεύματος,
ὅ ἐστιν ῥῆμα
θεοῦ...

6:17...and picking up and wielding the sword of the Spirit,
which constitutes the word of God – skillfully, correctly
and meaningfully communicated, as it is accurately
translated, articulated and clearly explained in
public speech, within the comprehensive
context of the contemporary
usage of the language of
those to whom it is
addressed...

CONTENTS

GREEK PRONUNCIATION xiii

INTRODUCTION xv

A NEW BASIC EXPLANATORY TRANSLATION 1

A NEW EXTENDED INTERPRETIVE AND EXPOSITIONAL TRANSLATION 27

    CHAPTER 1 – THE "TOP SECRET" PLAN DECLASSIFIED 29
        NOTES 43

    CHAPTER 2 – TIME TRAVEL: BACK FROM THE FUTURE 81
        NOTES 92

    CHAPTER 3 – RECOGNIZING OPPORTUNITY:
           FAITH IN HIM AND LOVE FOR OTHERS 118
        NOTES 127

    CHAPTER 4 – "DRESSING UP" FOR REAL 139
        NOTES 150

    CHAPTER 5 – ACTOR OF LOVE, FOLLOWER OF LIGHT,
           MASTER OF ETHICAL SKILL 173
        NOTES 189

    CHAPTER 6 – CAREER SPIRITUAL SOLDIERS 222
        NOTES 239

BASIC EXPLANATORY TRANSLATION WITH GREEK TEXT,
    TYNDALE'S VERSION (1526) AND KING JAMES VERSION (1611) 279
        NOTES 330

BIBLIOGRAPHY 335

ENGLISH INDEX 342

GREEK INDEX AND GLOSSARY 357

SCRIPTURE INDEX 366

xi

GREEK PRONUNCIATION[1]

Greek Alphabet and Pronunciation:

A	α	alpha	*a* as in *archon*
B	β	beta	*b* as in *biology*
Γ	γ	gamma	*g* as in *graph*
Δ	δ	delta	*d* as in *demon*
E	ε	epsilon	*e* as in *epigram*
Z	ζ	zeta	*z* as in *adze*
E	η	eta	*e* as in *hey* (*hay*)
Θ	θ	theta	*th* as in *theater*
I	ι	iota	*i* as in *police*
K	κ	kappa	*k* as in *kinetic*
Λ	λ	lambda	*l* as in *logic*
M	μ	mu	*m* as in *metaphor*
N	ν	nu	*n* as in *naphtha*
Ξ	ξ	xi	*x* as in *axiom*
O	ο	omicron	*o* as in *optics*
Π	π	pi	*p* as in *perimeter*
P	ρ	rho	*r* as in *rhinoceros*
Σ	σ, ς	sigma	*s* as in *satire*
T	τ	tau	*t* as in *tactics*
Y	υ	upsilon	*u* as German *ü*
Φ	φ	phi	*ph* as in *Philip*
X	χ	chi	*kh* as in *loch*
Ψ	ψ	psi	*ps* as in *eclipse*
Ω	ω	omega	*o* as in *ocean*

Double Consonants – the letter γ is pronounced like *ng* in *angle* when it comes before γ, κ, ξ, and χ:

γγ	ἄγγελος – *angelos*
γκ	ἄγκυρα – *ankura*
γξ	λάρυγξ – *larunx*
γχ	ἄγχουσα – *anchousa*

Dipthongs – a pair of vowels that make one sound when pronounced. Many English double vowels are pronounced the same way as Greek dipthongs:

αι	as *ai* in *aisle*.
αυ	as *ou* in *house*
ει	as *ei* in *feign*
ευ	as *e* in *met* + *oo* in *moon*
ηυ	as *e* in *hey* + *oo* in *moon*
οι	as *oi* in *foil*
ου	as *oo* in *moon*
υι	as in the word *we*

Breathing Marks – pronouncing "h" at the beginning of a word:

Greek words beginning with a vowel have a breathing mark over them. The smooth breathing mark looks like an apostrophe: ' and does not affect the sound of the vowel. The rough breathing mark looks like a reverse apostrophe: ' and indicates that the word begins with an "h" sound.

Examples:

Smooth breathing mark: The Greek word for "love" is ἀγάπη. It is transliterated *agape* and pronounced *a-gáp-ay*.

Rough breathing mark: The Greek word for "sin" is ἁμαρτία. It is transliterated *hamartia* and pronounced *ha-mar-tí-a*.

---

[1] Adapted from *A New Introduction to Greek*, by Chase and Phillips, pp. 1-3.

INTRODUCTION

This book is a *new extended interpretive and expositional translation* of Paul's *Treatise to the Ephesians*. To make a proper introduction to the reader of what has become a complicated story of the history of the translation of the New Testament over the last two thousand years, it will be beneficial to tell briefly the story of why and how this new translation came into being.

This translation of Paul's final and definitive Treatise to the Ephesians was undertaken at the request of a unique and very special group of professional American Christian business owners, entrepreneurs and CEOs in January 2003, and – with their invaluable friendship, counsel and help – has now reached completion over two years later. These exceptional individuals come from all walks of life, professional experience, diverse ethnic backgrounds and from a broad range of faith groups and denominations (and non-denominations) that exist within the American expression of Christendom.

They are well educated Christians that *sincerely want to know what it is that God wants them to use their lives to accomplish,* in what they acutely realize is the extremely brief period that yet remains to them during the final third or fourth period of their mortal existence. However, since most of them have had less than satisfactory results in getting this question answered to their satisfaction within their own traditional expression of organized Christendom, they have augmented their search for the answer to this question in other ways. They are all leaders, they tend to be driven and they never give up. They have *never stopped searching for the answer* somewhere. It is against this backdrop that we became friends.

Looking back and reflecting upon my life, I now realize that at this, the "two-thirds" point in my own journey through mortality, the gracious gifts and opportunities I have been afforded have brought about a rather unique standpoint from which it became possible for this new translation to emerge. Upon becoming a licensed *Teacher* (B.A.T., Sam Houston State University, 1980), the opportunity to *learn the Greek New Testament* presented itself (Th.M., Dallas Seminary, 1980-1985). Soon after, the prospect of being trained in the *comprehensive scope of the philosophical tradition of world history* followed (M.A., University of Dallas, 1990-1995). In the last ten years, it has been a thrill to teach Philosophy,

Religion, Greek and Mathematics at the University level. During this same decade, it has been an additional challenge as a professional engineer, to found and develop a growing Structural/Civil/Forensic Engineering firm (in Dallas, Texas – the ninth largest city in the U.S., and one of the most economically diverse commercial, marketing, industrial and convention centers in the southwest).

In addition to the professional business leaders and colleagues described above, this translation is intended to *be of help to all other professional American Christians* like them, both men and women, who have chosen the life-path of leadership. It is written to and for those who are business owners, entrepreneurs and CEOs in their own right and others who, in a common or kindred spirit with them, have become leaders in other enterprises or fields of endeavor. Its purpose is to help leaders who have never given up the hope of discovering, becoming engaged in, and ultimately achieving what it is that God has specifically planned for them to accomplish with, in, and through their lives.

Therefore, this translation of Paul's Treatise to the Ephesians from the original Greek Text is a translation into the English used on a daily basis by most American professionals – those who are leaders, entrepreneurs and CEOs in business, politics, law or education in the Late Contemporary Period of our historical era. Accordingly, as will be described in further detail below, every word, metaphor, concept and idea is translated fully, extensively and comprehensively – into what my business friends and colleagues call – *Professional (non-Ecclesiastical), Contemporary (non-Medieval), American (non-British) English.*

PREPARATORY REMARKS – THE FOUR ERAS OF WORLD HISTORY

Before the story of the development of the translational tradition of the English Bible into "professional, contemporary, American English" can begin, a preparatory note may be in order. When one is about to embark into an extended reflection upon the history of the world from the broadest perspective possible, it is helpful to bring the reader "up-to-speed" with the common vocabulary in current circulation. Philosophers and historians are in general agreement that the history of the world is subdivided into four basic periods, commonly referred to as the Ancient, Medieval, Modern, and Contemporary eras.

The Ancient era extends from the beginning of the earliest recorded history through the Church Fathers, Jerome and Augustine (the fourth century A.D.). Accordingly, the period in which the Old Testament was first composed in Hebrew, then translated into Alexandrian Greek, and in which the New Testament was *first written down into the original language* of "common" Greek, is referred to as the Ancient era of history.

The Medieval era begins with Jerome's first translation of the Bible from Hebrew and Greek into "common" Latin (of which more below), as well as the philosophical and theological treatises composed by his contemporary, Augustine (fourth century). It extends through the "Middle Ages," comprising the period culminated by the writings and thoughts of the greatest of all Catholic theologians – Thomas Aquinas (thirteenth century). The Medieval period is the historical era in which the Bible was *translated into Latin,* and then *preserved through being copied repeatedly.*

The Modern era begins with the Renaissance (fourteenth century), continues through the age of world exploration and colonization, and extends through the discovery, development and deployment of modern Science in the Industrial Revolution and its immediate worldwide effects. The emergence of nationalism in the political structures of European countries and the United States, the rise of the modern industrial city founded on the manufacture of goods, and the emergence of modern political economies based on the division of labor and the investment of capital (the beginning of the nineteenth century) signify the climax of the Modern era. This historical period also features the beginning of the English biblical tradition, because the Reformation, the *first translation of the Bible into the English language* and the founding and establishment of America occurred during this era.

The Contemporary era begins suddenly in the middle of the nineteenth century with the surprising, devastating worldwide convulsions and furious wars waged on a scale unparalleled in history. These momentous struggles were the result of complicated, long-term consequences and dilemmas introduced into the sociological dynamics within and between politically nationalized countries by the Industrial Revolution. For America, the beginning of the Contemporary era is marked by our own Civil War (the end of our "age of innocence"). It continues through the periods of upheaval and change produced by World War I, the Great Depression, World War II, the Korean War, the undeclared "Cold War" waged secretly against the post World War II rise of Communist Countries, culminating in the Vietnam War and the rise of Terrorism.

For combatants and non-combatants alike, the conflicts fought during this era have wreaked economic ruin and taxed populations to the point of unprecedented national exhaustion. However, from the perspective of Western Civilized Christendom, it is also true that this era has witnessed the emergence of positive features and tremendous advances in human knowledge, with the resulting improvement in the well-being of humanity. Such advances include the rise of free enterprise as a legitimate, stable, large-scale economic system as well as the rise of nationalism, which resulted in participatory government and its practical requirement to educate the entire populace. Other innovations include the increase in the ability to produce food on a macroscopic scale for consumption by enormous populations, and the rise of the Technology and Information ages, which have resulted in a marked improvement in the development of the medical professions to provide effective relief from the devastations of plague and mass-disease.

Nonetheless, when examined from a worldwide perspective, a disturbing sense of collective anxiety underlies the individual materialistic optimism of the Contemporary era, generated ironically in the political economies of the nations and societies within the historical tradition of Occidental Christendom. Most societies in the contemporary world – both the prosperous and the poor – are marked by a sense of tragedy, disconnectedness, disorientation, frustration, perplexity and a feeling of confused anger, which ranges from bland annoyance to unpredictable outbursts of frenzied rage. A vague awareness of the loss of community due to an overemphasis on individualism, accompanied by a pensive feeling of general shared disillusionment – ranging from mild pessimism, through varying degrees of cynicism, to acute and utmost despair – now plagues many contemporary societies. The Contemporary era is the era in which we now live.

Having thus surveyed the four major eras of world history, we now return to the story that extends from the development of the tradition of biblical translation to the new "professional, contemporary, American English" translation presented here.

THE MAJOR ENGLISH TRANSLATIONS

One might wonder at the apparent audacity (or simply dismiss as superfluous fretting) the notion that anyone should attempt yet *another* translation of the New Testament into the English language. After all, what could one more translation among the plethora of recent, good, scholarly versions possibly accomplish or contribute to the variety offered by the multifaceted historical expression of American Christendom so far?

This is a very good question, because the list of English translations of the Bible is impressive indeed. From the Anglican/Protestant tradition, the major signposts that appear along the long roadway include the following editions (presented in chronological order):

- **The King James Version** (1611). Based on the very first successful translation of the Bible from its original languages into the English language accomplished by William Tyndale in 1526 (of which more

INTRODUCTION

below), the KJV is the preeminent, historically most authoritative, and after 400 years, *still the most popular and best selling* English version of the Bible in English-speaking Christendom today.

- **The Revised Standard Version** (1885). The RSV is the first successful British attempt to produce a translation with the intention of historically updating the language of the KJV (1611) from *late Middle or late Medieval* [Shakespeare's] British English into *Modern* British English, in which British scholars allowed American scholars to participate, but have no significant editorial power.
- **The American Standard Version** (1901). A direct American reaction to the British RSV (1885), which prohibited a rival American translation for fourteen years, the ASV is the first successful attempt performed *exclusively by American scholars* to produce a translation with the intention of historically updating the KJV (1611) from *late Middle or late Medieval British* English into *Modern American* English.
- **The New English Bible** (1970). The NEB is the second successful attempt made in Great Britain to produce a translation with the intention of historically updating the language of the RSV (1885) from *Modern* British English into *Contemporary* British English.
- **The New American Standard Bible** (1971). The NASB, like the NEB (1970), is the second attempt made by exclusively American scholars to produce a translation with the intention of historically updating the language of the ASV (1901) from *Modern American* English into *Contemporary American* English.
- **The New International Version** (1978). The NIV represents the first attempt by "International" English speaking Evangelicals (i.e., Australia, Canada, New Zealand and South Aftrica in addition to Great Britain and America) to recognize the historical fact that the English language has passed beyond the boundaries of Great Britain and America and become an *international language* in the Contemporary era; and to produce an English translation with the intention of *avoiding the use both of Americanisms and Anglicisms* altogether, for an "International" English speaking audience.
- **The New King James Version** (1982). An American reaction to the weakness of literary style of the American English used by the NASB (1971), the NKJV is an attempt to produce a translation that *unifies* the principle of *historically updating* English into *Contemporary American* usage employed by the NASB, together with the principle of *preserving the superior literary style of the British* English compositional structure of the original KJV (1611).

- **The Revised English Bible** (1989). The REB is a British revision designed to simply perform a *second update* to the Contemporary British English of the NEB (1970).
- **The New Revised Standard Version** (1989). The NRSV represents the first attempt to produce a translation that would not only *historically update* the *Modern British* English of the RSV (1885) into *Contemporary American* English, but that would also recognize the *historical aspiration to re-unify Christendom* in an "ecumenical" [Protestant/Catholic/Greek Orthodox] version.

Other translations of note that are significant offshoots from the Anglican/Protestant historical tradition include:

- **The Amplified Bible** (1965). Published by the same American Foundation that later published the NASB (1971), the AB represents that group's first attempt to recognize, isolate, and overcome *specific translational difficulties* from the original languages into contemporary English by *simply mechanically listing* them.
- **The Living Bible** (1956-1971). The Living Bible is the first successful *individual* attempt (representing the lifework of a *single individual* – Kenneth Nathaniel Taylor, an Illinois businessman) since William Tyndale's first translation in 1526 (all authoritative English translations after Tyndale were published by committees or groups of scholars) to *recognize and bridge the gap* of a growing disparity of meaning. This "gap" of meaning between the Modern American English of the ASV (1901) and the much different American English language is emerging rapidly during the Contemporary era. The LB somewhat successfully bridged this gap by *emphasizing understanding the target language* more than understanding the original languages. Taylor used the method of simply *paraphrasing* the *modern* American English of the ASV into and *expanded interpretive restatement* of the ASV into *contemporary* American English.
- **The Good News Bible** (1976). The GNB represents the first deliberate attempt to focus specifically upon *simplifying* an English translation so that it can be understood more easily by the already large and exponentially growing and diverse, yet *minimally educated* people groups produced by the fracturing sociological effects of the Contemporary era upon American society and culture.
- **The New Living Translation** (1996). The NLT is an attempt to provide *legitimacy* and *credibility* to the great popularity of Kenneth Taylor's Living Bible (1971). It attempts to retain its style as an expanded interpretive translation, but goes on to support it as a *legitimate translation* (instead of a paraphrase) with objective scholarship from the original languages rather than the subjective insights based on Kenneth Taylor's

interpretation of the ASV (1901). In addition, the NLT also adopts the principle of *simplification* used by the translators of the GNB (1976), being *deliberately written at a Sixth-Grade* reading level.

The first attempts made by the Catholic Church to actually translate the Bible *from its original languages* (instead of from Latin) into English are, by historical comparison to the Anglican/Protestant tradition, extremely recent. The only two major attempts that have been achieved to date are:

- **The Jerusalem Bible** (1966). A British Catholic attempt, the JB is the first complete Catholic Bible translated into *Contemporary British* English from the *original languages* instead of from the Latin Vulgate.
- **The New American Bible** (1970). The NAB is the first Catholic Bible translated into *Contemporary American* English from the *original languages* instead of from the Latin Vulgate. It has become the most popular American Catholic edition.

The changes, developments and growth spurts that comprise the total sum of the officially recognized biblical tradition of *translation specific to the English language* have occurred in a relatively short historical time frame (only four centuries). However, when one gazes beyond these brief centuries even deeper into the past, it soon becomes evident that the same pattern of continually re-discovering the genuine and authentic meaning of God's divine message to human beings from their own frame of reference and in their own native language *is a recurring quest*.

Therefore, we now turn briefly to this older story in order to put it together with the more recent story of the translation of the Bible into English. From the assembled panorama, we will then be able to glean a more comprehensive perspective of the translational history of the Bible, and formulate the principles of interpretation upon which this extended interpretive and expositional translation is based.

THE TRANSLATION OF THE BIBLE IN HISTORY

THE GREEK SEPTUAGINT

Alexander the Great proved himself to be the greatest military commander in the history of the known world when, in only eleven years near the end of the fourth century B.C., he and his Macedonian army conquered most of the realms that extended over the enormous geographical area surrounding the eastern half of the Mediterranean Sea. Quickly gaining control over Persia, Syria, Palestine, Syria and Egypt, he founded the great ancient port city of Alexandria at the mouth of the Nile River. Alexander's new city soon surpassed Tyre and Carthage as the chief trade center of the Mediterranean world. He then turned eastward and conquered the territories that consist of what is today most of Iraq, Iran, Afghanistan, and northern India. Even after his premature death at the age of thirty-three, these lands became subjugated and consolidated by the Greek dynasties established in them by his main military generals – Ptolemy, Seleucus and Antigonus.

Ptolemy eventually gained control of Egypt, and its preeminent city, Alexandria. Modestly referring to himself thereafter as *Ptolemy Soter* (Greek = Πτολεμαῖος Σωτήρ = "The Warrior-Deliverer"), it was in Alexandria that he consolidated and established the Macedonian Greek language and culture, and founded what was to become the greatest library of the Ancient world. His son *Ptolemy Philadelphus* (Greek = Πτολεμαῖος Φιλάδελφος = "The Warrior-Friend-of-Human-kind") continued his father's work. Since a large Jewish population existed in Alexandria from its earliest years, he commissioned the translation of the Hebrew Old Testament into the Alexandrian Greek language during the third century B.C. for his father's famous library collection.

This first ever translation of the Bible into another language became known as the *Septuagint* (Latin = the "Seventy"), due to the tradition that it was translated by a committee of seventy-two Hellenistic Jews. Although of somewhat uneven quality, overall it is such a good translation, that during the next three hundred years it became used and relied upon by Hellenistic Jews more than the original Hebrew text of the Old Testament. In fact, it had so embedded itself in the Greek culture in Palestine during the time of Christ, that the writers of the New Testament – including Paul – heavily rely upon it, often quoting it directly. The Septuagint translation of the Old Testament continued its respected place in the literature of the eastern Mediterranean Greek culture well into the fourth century.

JEROME – THE LATIN VULGATE

For seven centuries, Greek remained the chief language of the societies conquered by Alexander and consolidated thereafter by the Macedonian dynasties of his leading generals in the eastern half of the Roman Empire. However, by the beginning of the fourth century, the Greek language retained only a tentative hold as the language used in religious, educational, professional and commercial life. Latin had already displaced it as the chief language of politics and law, because Latin emanated from Rome itself – the Empire's political and legal center. By the middle to the end of the fourth century, Greek was finally dying out altogether in the eastern half of the Empire. Latin was replacing it in most aspects of society, except for the Christian religion.

Paradoxically, by this late date, the Roman Empire itself had been in decline for almost 200 years (from the end of the second century onward),

INTRODUCTION

due to the corruption and weakness that had begun to infect the political and legal institutions of the Empire from its very heart, the city of Rome itself. Upon Constantine's conversion to Christianity in 313, he subsequently attempted to reform the Empire by legally recognizing Christianity as an officially tolerated religion. He even went so far as to try to stabilize the Empire by relocating its capital city from Rome to the more centrally located city of Byzantium (which he renamed "Constantinople"). Nevertheless, when Constantine died in 337, the Empire soon re-divided between East and West. Rome promptly re-established itself as the preeminent city of the Western half of the Empire, picked up its corrupt way of life where it had left off, and consequently resumed its own decline.

As Rome's obloquy and ensuing cynicism spread and became rampant throughout the intellectual life of the western Empire by the end of the fourth century, a classical Roman scholar named Sophronius Eusebius Hieronymus, more commonly known as Jerome, traveled from Rome to Antioch in the Eastern Empire, where he experienced a dramatic and renewed transformation in his understanding of Christianity. As a result, he renounced his classical scholarship, including the language of Classical Latin spoken by the corrupt politicians and lawyers in Rome, learned Hebrew, and devoted himself to an exclusive and voracious study of the Bible. Although he returned to Rome for a short period, he was soon forced to leave and return to the East due to his outspoken criticism of the secular clergy in Rome, which by that time had become corrupt itself. Jerome settled in Bethlehem in about 386, and began his most determined and famous project: to re-translate the Bible from Hebrew and Greek into so-called "vulgar" ("common") Latin, the language now commonly spoken by merchants, business people and professionals throughout the Empire. He completed his translation of the Bible into Latin in about 405.

Ironically, the long-term corruption of the political, legal, religious and professional life in Rome had accomplished its diabolical work by that time. The rotted and decaying spirit of the once sturdy and determined citizens of the city of Rome could not remain alive long enough to benefit from Jerome's new translation. By the beginning of the fifth century, the leaders and citizens of Rome, due to their protracted period of moral sickness and the subsequent weakness it produced, allowed their once-famous Imperial City to be besieged, ravaged and sacked by Alaric in 410, only five years after Jerome completed his translation. The devastating event of the fall of the Roman Empire plunged central Europe into what would become appropriately called the "Dark Ages" of the Medieval era, from which it did not emerge for the next thousand years. It is, in fact, from a thirteenth century reference to Jerome's translation of the Bible into the *common* Latin language, not *Classical* Latin, that the "Vulgate" eventually derived its name ("editio vulgata" = "common edition").

THE DARK AGES – THE PETRIFACTION OF LATIN

Following the epic world-catastrophe of the fall of the Roman Empire, the next great crisis in the story of the translation of the biblical text came a thousand years later. After a protracted period of ever-increasing church corruption throughout Europe, the text gradually fell into disuse and an almost mindless cycle of monotonous (albeit fairly accurate) copying and re-copying by hand in the dark, dreary Scriptoria in Medieval monasteries. There is no historical doubt that by the fourteenth century, the living meaning and vitality of the common Latin language of Jerome's translation of the fourth century had become lost or petrified. In fact, except for a scholarly few living in the scattered centers of learning that survived the ubiquitous brutality and ignorance that followed in the wake of the fall of Rome, most people believed that Latin no longer carried any meaning or relevance for their everyday lives. Instead, it had become a mysterious, superstitious, magical "super-language" used only by priests or wizards.

JOHN WYCLIFFE – LATIN INTO ENGLISH

At the end of the fourteenth century, a few courageous individuals undertook the first serious, dedicated life-long projects to resurrect the ossified meaning of the Latin Bible. The first attempt was made in 1377 in England by an Oxford scholar named John Wycliffe (Wyclif), who developed the somewhat dangerous personal custom of translating the Latin Bible verbally in his preaching into the spoken vernacular known as the Middle English "London" dialect (the English dialect used by Chaucer). He no doubt did this so that the people he was addressing could understand what he was saying. The written translation he inspired (the "Wycliffe Bible") was assiduously revised from Wycliffe's somewhat wooden direct-English-from-Latin-translation into a more readable English by his followers (who came to be known as the Lollards), and published four years after his death by his apprentice and most trusted lieutenant, John Purvey, in 1388.

JOHN HUSS – ENGLISH INTO CZECH

Wycliffe's influence immediately spread through these writings to the European continent, where John Huss (Jan Hus) – a Czech scholar, ordained priest, dean of the philosophy faculty and rector of Charles University in Prague – translated Wycliffe's works into the Czech language in Bohemia (1412). Consequently, Huss was excommunicated, tried at the Council of Constance, and burned at the stake by officials of the Roman Catholic Church in 1415. At his execution, Huss asked God to forgive those who condemned him.

However, if that wasn't enough, in order to send a clear message to future would-be translators, the Council also ordered that all of John Wycliffe's writings be burned and his corpse be exhumed (Wycliffe had died when he was fifty-six years old from a stroke, and had been dead and buried for thirty years). Wycliffe's corpse was dug up, his bones were burned and his ashes scattered.

It is of exceptional historical significance that the Polish Pope John Paul II, whose personal name was Karol Józef Wojtyła, speaking as the official chief representative of the Roman Catholic Church, only very recently publicly asked for forgiveness in May 1995 for the Catholic Church's culpability in stake burnings and the religious wars that followed the Protestant Reformation. Further, on December 18, 1999 John Paul II even publicly apologized for the execution of John Huss himself. It is also of interest to note that he also publicly apologized on October 31, 1992 for the unjust condemnation of the Italian philosopher Galileo Galilei that resulted from his trial conducted by the Roman Catholic Church in 1633.

DESIDERIUS ERASMUS – THE RECOVERY, RESTORATION AND REINSTATEMENT OF THE GREEK NEW TESTAMENT AS AUTHORITATIVE OVER THE LATIN NEW TESTAMENT

As a result of Huss' grisly execution, together with the macabre obliteration of Wycliffe's corpse, it seems everybody "got the message" the Roman Catholic Church was sending to those foolhardy enough to consider the very imprudent idea of translating the Word of God into their own common language for just a little over a century. However, this dark cloud of fear could not cast its shadow over all of Europe for long.

In 1466, in a small town in the Netherlands, an illegitimate baby boy named Gerard was born to a Roman Catholic Priest (who, of course, was officially celibate) and a young woman. The young Gerard appeared into this murky late-Medieval world as a sad yet all-too common expression of the corruption in which the Catholic Church had mired itself. When he was seventeen, the Plague claimed both his parents. Renamed Desiderius Erasmus, the young man made it his determined life-goal to reform the corrupt system he knew only all too well, by dedicating his life to the principle that *education* was the only way to restore legitimacy and decency to the Roman Catholic Church.

Therefore, beginning from the University of Paris, Erasmus became a man without a country, restlessly and tirelessly remaining on the move throughout Europe and England, voraciously learning and carefully collecting every scrap of knowledge that one thousand years of intellectual neglect had not allowed to decay into dust. He mastered Latin and Greek, and during the later fifteenth and early sixteenth century, eventually became recognized as the most educated and well-respected scholar in Europe. Erasmus spent decades of tireless detective work carefully sifting through, gathering, collecting, compiling, and editing all of the old Greek manuscripts he could find throughout the dusty libraries in the old monasteries all over Europe. Finally, in 1516, when he was fifty years old, Desiderius Erasmus became the first human being ever to publish the first complete edition of the Greek New Testament, from the relative safety of Basel, Switzerland.

The Reformers, who were Erasmus' own contemporaries, immediately emerged on the scene and wasted no time employing his Greek New Testament as the foundation for their translations of the New Testament into their own vernacular languages. Unlike them however, Erasmus believed that translating the Greek Text into the colloquial languages of the various peoples in Europe was too radical a move. Erasmus was a humanist and an idealist who should be credited by believing – and rightfully so – that the principle of *universal education* would markedly counteract the corruption of the Roman Catholic Church. Unfortunately – like many other scholars since his time – Erasmus slipped into the somewhat naïve and incredibly impractical belief that it was wrong to translate the Bible from its original languages into the common languages of the peoples of Europe. Instead, he believed that the formidable task of *educating all of the people of Europe in Latin* should be undertaken in order for them to understand the Bible. Accordingly, in his several Greek editions, he only produced a new translation of the Greek New Testament into *Latin*.

On balance, the significance of the achievement of Erasmus' lifework cannot be underestimated. The Greek New Testament – published as a unified, available work of literature – existed for the first time in history.

MARTIN LUTHER – THE GREEK NEW TESTAMENT INTO GERMAN

Erasmus' edition of the Greek New Testament quickly found its way into the Universities of northern Europe. Only five years later, in 1521, officials of the Roman Catholic Church charged a thirty-seven year old "upstart" German Augustinian Monk and Theology professor at the University of Wittenberg in the small German kingdom of Saxony, of being guilty of "heresy." They ordered that he be seized and that he should stand "trial" at the "Diet" of Worms ("Worms" was the name of the German town the "Diet" was held in).

A "Diet" was the German word used for what was supposed to be a "formal and official political council meeting convened on a regular basis for the purpose of deliberating upon and deciding governmental legislative policy," but which the Roman Catholic Church had managed to effectively commandeer into being a *de facto* "religious inquisition." The word "heresy," was the Latin word which originally meant "to choose to believe and teach heterodoxy" (the word "heresy" being a Latin transliteration of the Greek noun αἵρεσις from the verb αἱρέω, which means "to physically or mentally grasp, seize, take hold of, or choose;" and the word "heterodox" being a Latin transliteration of the Greek compound noun ἑτερόδοξος from the compound verb ἑτεροδοξέω, which means "to believe and teach erroneous opinions, i.e., opinions that are contrary to the correct ones, i.e., the "orthodox" ones – "orthodox" being a Latin transliteration of the Greek compound noun ὀρθόδοξος from the compound verb ὀρθοδοξέω, which means "to believe and teach correct opinions"). However, by this time in the late Medieval period the word "heresy" had become an inflammatory label hurled by the Church against anyone who had the courage to "publicly point out, enumerate and articulate the corrupt practices of the Roman Catholic Church."

Following the Diet, but before the young professor could be arrested, his political friends led by Frederick the Wise, elector of Saxony, whisked him away and hid him incognito in Wartburg Castle. There, he used the following year to good effect, translating Erasmus' Greek New Testament into the German common language in less than a year, publishing it in 1522 (only six years after Erasmus had first published his Greek New Testament in 1516). When it was finally safe to come out, the young professor emerged from his confinement and grew into middle age by finishing a translation of the Old Testament into German from the Hebrew text during the next twelve years of his life, publishing it in 1534.

Consequently, at age fifty – the same age that Erasmus was when he completed his unique lifework, and almost exactly 1,500 years after Jesus accomplished His divine lifework on the cross – Martin Luther achieved his own significant lifework for God. He became the first human being in over a millennium (since Jerome) to actually *translate* the entire Bible from the languages from Hebrew and Greek – the languages in which it was originally written – into German, the native, living language spoken by a people who lived – and still live today – in a common, day-to-day, lifeworld.

WILLIAM TYNDALE – THE GREEK NEW TESTAMENT INTO ENGLISH

Erasmus' Greek New Testament quickly made its way also into the Universities of Britain. In 1524, the English genius William Tyndale respectfully appealed to the "headquarters" of English Christendom in London itself for permission to accomplish for the English Speaking

Peoples what Luther had accomplished for the Germans. He requested official authorization to translate the New Testament from the Greek original text into the English language. Henry VIII, although only three years older than Tyndale and originally trained for the ministry himself – until his unfortunate older brother Arthur suddenly and inconveniently died and Henry had to change his plans to become King instead, and who had by that time been King of England for fifteen years – refused.

In 1524, the young King had not yet made his famous break with the Roman Church over his "succession problem," caused by the embarrassing but very public fact that God was for some unfathomable reason annoyingly tardy in providing Henry with a male heir to the English Throne. Henry's official interpretation of this awkward circumstance would eventually be that God was perturbed at him for marrying Catherine of Aragon, his dead older brother Arthur's Spanish wife. The problem was complicated by the fact that Catherine was supposed to be the real Queen because Arthur was supposed to be the real King, except for the fact that he had died and bungled everything. Since the established English church was at that time was still officially Catholic and did not permit divorce, the fact that Catherine had borne Henry no male heir left him with an exasperating dilemma.

Tyndale, shocked and frustrated by being legally prohibited from performing his planned translation – Luther's German translation had been completed just two years earlier – set sail for Germany to visit Luther for encouragement and inspiration, where he found both in abundance.

As a result, only four years after Luther translated the Greek New Testament into the German language, William Tyndale became the first human being ever, in the fifteen centuries since its original composition, to translate the New Testament from the original Greek language and publish it in the English language. Remarkably, like Luther, he did it in an extraordinarily short period of time (1525-1526), from the very same small German town (Worms) that had been the location of Luther's trial for heresy by the Catholic Church. When it was finished, he had to smuggle copies of it back into his own country from Germany by ship, where the English Catholic Church, of course, declared it illegal and made every effort to confiscate and publicly burn as many of them as it could.

After spending the next ten years of his life being chased around from hiding place to hiding place in Europe, Tyndale was well into his effort to translate the Old Testament from Hebrew into English as an exile in Brussels (in what is today the country of Belgium). There, he was finally betrayed and seized by officials of the Catholic Church in 1535.

Meanwhile, Henry VIII had also been busy, using his royal time intriguing, plotting, scheming, intimidating, blackmailing, bullying, harassing, punishing, imprisoning, terrorizing, murdering and divorcing his way into successfully becoming the official Head of the Church of His Lord and Savior Jesus Christ in all of England – making his final break with Rome in 1533. As a result, for two whole years, Henry had the authority and the power to protect Tyndale, his British subject. However, not only did Henry not come to Tyndale's rescue, he had in fact sent his own agents to Europe to assist the Catholic Church in his apprehension and arrest.

So, in 1536, Henry VIII, absolute Monarch of the English Speaking Peoples and supreme Head of the Church of England, conspicuously allowed, assisted and probably caused Tyndale to suffer, at the hands of non-English Catholics, their customary method for eliminating people that might threaten their – and therefore, ultimately what Henry perceived to be his own – absolute control. Henry, *after* he had declared an official break between himself and the Roman Catholic Church, turned around to aid them. He did so by permitting Tyndale, his own fellow Englishman, to be tried (as usual), be found guilty of heresy (as usual), be granted the official courtesy of being strangled at the stake (not as usual), before his body was then burned (as usual) by their officials at Vilvoorden – six miles northeast of Brussels. Tyndale's gracious last words were those that reflect the very heartbeat of the main theme of Paul's Treatise to the Ephesians. He simply said, "Lord, open the King of England's eyes" (Eph. 1:18).

Thus, at the age of forty-two, William Tyndale was rewarded by the forty-five year old King of the English Speaking Peoples with execution as a criminal for giving his people perhaps the greatest gift in their entire history – the very first complete translation of the New Testament into the English language from the original Greek texts. Before being cut short by death, he had also translated a significant portion of the Old Testament from Hebrew into English. Despite this tragic outcome, Tyndale had successfully completed his lifework for God.

Ironically, during the eighty years immediately following Tyndale's execution, a flurry of new translations suddenly jumped on the translation "bandwagon" in England. Version after version appeared, all of them competing for ascendancy over Tyndale's first excellent translation. Miles Coverdale completed translating the books of the Old Testament not finished by Tyndale into English (unfortunately, from Latin) in 1535, and they were published in 1537 as the 'Thomas Matthew's Bible'. Commissioned by Henry VIII's secretary, Thomas Cromwell, Coverdale immediately revised that work, and his revision was published as the 'Great Bible' (the modest name chosen by Henry VIII to identify his own version) in 1539.

The 'Geneva Bible,' sponsored by Calvinists and Reformers, was printed outside England in 1560 in Geneva, Switzerland. As a rejoinder to this version, the Bishops of the English Church published their own version in 1568. This version, which became known as the 'Bishops' Bible,' was inferior to the Geneva Bible because it relied heavily on Latin. Accordingly, the Geneva Bible easily won out and quickly became the most popular Bible in England during the reign of Elizabeth I (1558-1603). The final attempt by the Catholic Church to publish an English rival translation to the Geneva Bible was performed in France, and was known as the 'Douay-Rheims' Bible (NT completed in 1582, entire Bible completed in 1609). However, since it too was translated from Latin into English and not from Hebrew and Greek into English, it suffered the same weaknesses – and therefore the same low circulation – as the Bishops' Bible.

THE KING JAMES VERSION

At the climax of the sixteenth century, the several English dialects competing for the collective heart and mind of the British people to become the carrier of their unified voice of literary power and meaning finally found their champion in the English playwright William Shakespeare. Shakespeare produced all of his plays during a brief but brilliant twenty-year period from 1592 until 1613. In 1594, he became a member of the Lord Chamberlain's Men, performing for and writing new plays at the direct request of Henry VIII's fiery redheaded daughter, Queen Elizabeth I. In 1600, Shakespeare wrote his greatest play, *Hamlet*, followed shortly thereafter by the other three of his four most mature works – *Othello, King Lear* and *Macbeth*.

The exceptionally inspired and gifted career of Shakespeare is of great literary significance for the history of the translation of the Bible into the English language. In 1603, Queen Elizabeth died without a male heir. In order to spare her country the certain calamity of Continental or Civil War, she had never married a European sovereign or native English nobleman. Consequently, King James VI of Scotland, the son of Elizabeth's cousin Mary Queen of Scots, was Elizabeth's nearest successor by blood relation. He therefore became the legitimate heir to the English throne. When he traveled south from Scotland to London to take up the throne of England as James I, his first act as the King of England was to at first support, and then ultimately sponsor the idea suggested by the Puritan scholars at Oxford, that as the new King he commission a final, "authorized" English translation of the Bible.

Accordingly, when the official King James translators completed their work seven years later in 1611, they not only relied upon and borrowed heavily from the foundational English of Tyndale's first translation eight decades earlier, but also benefited from the stylistic maturity and power that William Shakespeare achieved with his poetic skill in expressing the English language. As a result, the "King James Version" emerged over time to become the most dynamic, accurate, living yet durable expression of the collective heart, mind and soul of the British People for the next several centuries.

Thus, Tyndale pioneered and Shakespeare matured an authentic and living way of expressing the English language – to the point of defining, and to certain extents even creating – the complex English collective personality. This authentic mode of expression deeply imbedded within the spirit of the English language emerged in the 1611 King James Bible and in the collective works of Shakespeare. Therefore, these two literary masterworks (the King James Bible and the collective works of Shakespeare) effectively became the two pillars of distinctively *English literature* that stabilized the overall structure, spelling, grammar and meaning of the English language for the next three centuries in both Great Britain and America.

In America, the devastation caused by our own Civil War in the middle of the nineteenth century sent the first tremors rippling though the stability of this established English language that all had relied on for generations. These initial tremors increased in speed and volatility over the next one hundred years throughout the Industrial and Economic Revolutions in America. The shock waves produced by the cataclysmic and disorienting events of World War I, the Great Depression and World War II intensified the stresses on American English language and culture. The Technology and Information Revolutions that have recently transpired during the last fifty years have caused further pressures to develop in American English expression.

As a result, the rapid changes caused by the convulsive events experienced in America within only the last fifteen decades have dramatically transformed the English language spoken by the American people into a language that now differs in significant ways from the incomparable and historically extraordinary British English tradition from which it emerged.

THE CONTEMPORARY CONUNDRUM OF MEANING

As summarized above, the Contemporary era in which we live is characterized by a "sense of tragedy, disconnectedness, disorientation, frustration, perplexity, a feeling of confused anger, which ranges from bland annoyance to unpredictable outbursts of frenzied rage," in addition to "a vague awareness of the loss of community due to an overemphasis on individualism, accompanied by a pensive feeling of general shared disillusionment – ranging from mild pessimism, through varying degrees of cynicism, to acute and utmost despair now plagues many contemporary societies" (p. xviii). For well-informed, professional Christians living in America during this era, this pervasive obscure feeling of disorientation from past, future and even present reality gradually surfaces in their lives as a new conundrum – or "puzzle" – of finding activities and relationships that they find to be truly meaningful. Most Americans have trouble trying to "put it all together," or assemble their own life experiences together with those of their forebears, parents, children and descendants into some sort of significant, meaningful, enduring legacy and purpose that possesses an overall, unified sense of stability and continuity.

On one hand, their everyday professional working lives require most Americans to live at an extremely swift pace. Further, they must learn to speak, read, write and become proficient in communicating in the rapidly changing, highly technological and sophisticated American English language. American professionals must keep up with the fluid and complex language of the Contemporary era, because doing so is required to be able to successfully deal with the vastly challenging scientific problems, thorny multifaceted ethical dilemmas and tedious convoluted legal issues that have unavoidably emerged during our time. When philosophers and historians try to comprehend and explain this pressure-packed phenomenon that has recently arisen due to the extremely rapid pace at which the American culture requires its professionals to live, they variously describe this confusing era by using such adjectives as "post-industrial," "post-modern," "technological," "information" and (of course) "contemporary."

On the other hand, contemporary Americans must radically "shift gears" from the fast-paced demands placed upon them by their professional lives when they attempt to engage in meaningful spiritual experiences and communication in their various particular historically determined religious traditions, faith groups and denominational (or non-denominational) relationships within Christendom. As they make the effort to express themselves, listen to others, exchange spiritual ideas, convey religious concepts and understand divine matters and relationships among themselves in some kind of meaningful way, they are confronted with – and can be intimidated and bewildered by – yet another, much older English language that they do not use in their daily professional lives. Further, due to the beauty and tradition of its admittedly marvelous heritage, this older religious English language strongly resists the dramatically changing and evolving contemporary lifeworld, and remains assiduously fastened to its Medieval, Ecclesiastical and British (or other European) origins.

The result of this phenomenon is that in reality, most professional American Christians actually speak, read and write in what are becoming two distinct languages. However, because words in both of these languages read, write and sound like English; most people do not consciously realize they are communicating in two separate languages. The first language with which professional Americans communicate during the main part of their everyday lives and workweek is the complicated, "professional," distinctly American English required to navigate successfully within our fast-paced, disorienting Contemporary era. The second language with which they communicate is the "religious" language they share surrounded by their own particular historically determined expression of Christianity, which emerged and developed its own tradition within the overall history of Christendom.

This second "religious" language is a different language than the first "professional" one. Admittedly, the "religious" English language – to different degrees and extents – uses the "professional" language to carry it and hold it together. Yet despite this, the most important, central concepts of the second "religious" language consist of individual (or combinations of) older words that once had vital, living meanings long ago, but have since become mildly or severely distorted; or in some cases, even petrified.

To complicate things even further, due to the stabilizing effect which tradition produces, these key words of the second "religious" English language are composed of the actual or very similar sounds to the phonemes of all or portions of the original older words from which they came and/or upon which they are based. These older "religious" words come from the following languages, presented roughly in their historical and/or geographical order of development (from oldest to most recent, and from the Ancient Near East westward toward Western Europe):

Hebrew, Greek, Sanskrit, Old Latin, Latin, Vulgar Latin, Medieval Latin, Late Latin, Celtic, Gaelic, Germanic, East Germanic, West Germanic, Old German, Old Norse, Old English, Old Danish, Old Frisian, Old Saxon, Old Irish, Old French, Old North French, Old Low German, Old High German, Low German, High German, Middle High German, Gothic, Middle English, Middle French, Irish Gaelic, Scots Gaelic, Scottish, Icelandic, Irish Dutch, Danish, German, and French.

Moreover, each different religious tradition and/or faith group now spread across the broad range of religious organizations in American Christendom invests the main words of the second English "religious" language with their own specific meanings, which, over time, diverge –

sometimes significantly – from the meanings understood by other groups. These various and different meanings continue to develop within the historical and contextual framework of each group as they consciously or unconsciously derive their current meanings from the plethora of older, archaic languages upon which they relied at their origin. The result of this process is that during the historical development of a multiplicity of religious traditions and groups, the meanings of the words important to each group diverge over time to the extent that they only partially overlap, or in some cases develop in complete isolation from the other groups.

Because of this historical fact, each particular religious tradition or group eventually comes to use words that it has invested at different times, and for various reasons, from their own historical and philosophical frame of reference with what appear to be somewhat artificial or even completely distorted meanings. The origins of the historical circumstances, motivations and controversies eventually become lost to subsequent generations, who simply repeat the words they learned from those who lived during previous generations in their own religious tradition, without realizing or knowing their artificial character. In America, the unwitting result of this historical phenomenon is that the meaning of religious words used by different religious traditions and groups continues to diverge over time, and the gap that separates each religious tradition from the others continues to widen.

This phenomenon explains why intelligent, well-educated, well-informed, well-intentioned and well-meaning professional American Christians can, at a very fundamental level, disagree with each other in spiritual matters in what they are saying, hearing, writing, reading and intending. This occurs because each group is using their own historically embedded yet different versions of the second "religious" language, all the while using words that are spelled and pronounced the same way.

DISTORTION OF MEANING IN THE ENGLISH TRANSLATIONAL TRADITION

Remarkably, only four centuries span the exceedingly valuable English tradition extending from Shakespeare's masterworks and the canon of the King James Version of the Bible to the present day – or almost five centuries, if one begins with Tyndale. Although this is less than half the span of time it took for Latin to petrify during the Medieval era, it is the respectful conviction of this translator that the central message of much of the Greek New Testament has become significantly obscured in the present contemporary professional American era and way of life.

As has been briefly surveyed above, the growing shadow of this eclipse of meaning tends to occur gradually over the centuries in any language, and involves a complicated, multifaceted, sometimes historically prejudiced, but oftentimes simply a miscellaneous process by which the meaning conveyed by a tradition of translation slowly loses its vitality. This process happens as the meanings of words, figures of speech, and the overall structure and complexity of the language itself are transformed into new shapes of meaning over time. As is the case in carefully reflecting upon the history of the translation of meaning in any language, the history of the meaning of most of the present existing English versions of the Bible can be observed to suffer from three main distortions.

OBSOLETE MEDIEVAL LATIN WORDS RE-INVESTED WITH ARTIFICIAL MEANINGS, USUALLY CENTERED AROUND AND RELEVANT ONLY TO ECCLESIASTICAL ORGANIZATION AND CONTROL

First, many of the words allowed to remain in the existing English translations were common professional Latin words used in the fourth century that began to suffer distortion during the Medieval Period from the influence of the ecclesiastical and doctrinal controversies that swirled – sometimes violently – over the meaning of the Latin text. Some sixteen centuries later, the meanings that these words now supposedly bear among the various historically determined religious groups within Christendom have diverged to the extent that they now differ widely, because they have been slowly reinvested with artificial meanings during various centuries whenever a particular distorted meaning was retained by a particular target language.

To an American Christian living in the Contemporary era, these words look like "English" words, because they appear and keep on re-appearing in so many of the English translations. However, in reality they are old Latin words that because they were gradually reinvested with distorted meanings after the Fall of Rome, they in fact still remain distorted – and are therefore misleading. Fortunately, the meaning of ancient Greek texts has to a great extent been restored to us in the Contemporary era, especially since the great lifework of Henry George Liddell and Robert Scott (*Greek-English Lexicon* – First edition published in 1843, through the Ninth edition published in 1940) has now bypassed much of the Medieval smokescreen that later invested fourth century Latin with artificial meanings, thus obscuring it, and made it much more possible to trace and discern the original development of denotative and connotative meanings of the Greek words used in their historical context. This is even more true since the Perseus Digital Library Project has made the entire Greek New Testament, the the central works of the Greek Epics, Classical dramatists, historians and philosophers, as well as the Liddell-Scott *Greek-English Lexicon* available free of charge through the Internet since 1999 (see Bibliography for reference data).

Examples of such Latin words invested with misleading meanings that have survived into our existing English versions – that not only obscure the meaning of the Greek text, but are outmoded in contemporary professional American English usage – are shown in the list below. Many of these words are believed by well-meaning professional Americans to be ecclesiastical words that their own particular historical expression of Christendom knows the "real meaning" of, believing those in all the other religious groups to be misguided or mistaken about them – although their original meaning in fourth century Latin was often not even connected with religious usage. Examples of such words are:

abound, abundant, admonition, bishop, clamor, covenant, doctrine, dominion, Gentile, glorious, glory, grace, habitation, joy, manifest (verb), minister, ministry, ordain, pastor, praise, pray, prayer, predestinate, prince, principality, rejoice, revelation, saint, salvation, sanctified, sanctify, save, slave, supplication, tribulation.

ECCLESIASTICAL INFLUENCES ON BRITISH ENGLISH FROM THE MEDIEVAL AND MODERN ERAS THAT HAVE BECOME OBSOLETE IN PROFESSIONAL AMERICAN ENGLISH IN THE CONTEMPORY ERA (ALSO USUALLY CENTERED AROUND ECCLESIASTICAL ORGANIZATION AND CONTROL)

Second, many theological and doctrinal controversies continued to be battled back and forth within the ecclesiastical and scholarly vocabulary that developed among and between British Catholic, Anglican and Puritan scholars immediately following the first Bible translations by Luther and Tyndale. Furthermore, these controversies arose somewhat apart from the seperately developing common usage of the English language being employed by educated and well-informed Americans in their professional lives during the Colonial Period and the rise of the Modern era (the Industrial Revolution).

Therefore, some of the English words themselves still used today in contemporary translations of the New Testament were never (and never have been) actually *translated*, but only *transliterated* from the Greek original words into their approximate English pronunciations, such as the words in the following list:

air, Amen, anathema, angel, Anti-Christ, aroma, Apocalypse, Apostle, archangel, baptism, Baptist, Bible, blasphemy, call, chaos, charisma, Charismatic, Christ, Christian, cosmos, deacon, diabolical, dialect, dialogue, dogma, dynamic, Epiphany, Episcopalean, Epistle, Eucharist, Evangelical, evangelist, Genesis, Hymn, hypocrisy, hypocrite, idiot, idol, idolater, idolatry, know, liturgy, martyr, mystery, Nazarene, Ode,

INTRODUCTION

panoply, parable, Paraclete, Pentecostal, Peter, Presbyterian, prophecy, Prophet, Psalm, scope, work, zeal, zealous.

Moreover, many of the other words of this type are meaningful only to ecclesiastics and scholars, but are in fact erroneous or misleading concepts since they no longer have any real meaning in the contemporary professional American English language. Examples of such ecclesiastical British English words are those in the following list:

beloved (past ptcp., ME beloven), brethren, calling, Church, commonwealth, conversation (which now means 'to have a dialogue,' not 'to form one's habits to live a certain way'), dispensation, edification, edify, enmity, fullness, impart, long-suffering, preach, predestine, providence, righteousness, will, world.

BRITISH ENGLISH WORDS NEVER TRANSLATED INTO THEIR CONTEMPORARY PROFESSIONAL AMERICAN ENGLISH MEANINGS

Third, other English words that translate many important Greek concepts became ossified in their Old English, Middle English, Germanic or Saxon forms, and never have been freshly translated into their contemporary professional American English equivalents. Thus, although some (though not all) of the words we use in contemporary professional American English are included in the following list, they do not mean the same thing as the Greek word from which they were translated. The Old English form of the word had a different meaning than the contemporary professional American English meaning now bears. Examples of such words are listed below:

beforehand, beseech, bless, blessing, blessed, boast, dwell, dwelling, fellowship, flesh, gird, Gospel, guarantee, holiness, holy, household, Lord, might (meaning 'power,' not 'contingency'), nigh, partaker, quick(en) (meaning "make alive," not "fast"), sin, shew, shod, slay, slain, 'to and fro,' true, trust, truth, twain, unsearchable, utterance, wherewith, wiles, wisdom, word, workmanship, and wrath.

The detailed explanation of the etymology, denotative usage, connotative usage, and the American English translation in specific instances for all of the word groups and categories listed above will be addressed in the extended interpretive and expositional translation, and in the notes at the end of each chapter, as they come up in the translation of the Greek text.

Finally, the grammar and grammatical rules, expressions, and figures of speech used in professional contemporary American English are different from those used by Medieval and Modern British English, and even more different than the figures of speech used in the original Greek language. These various figures of speech will also be addressed in the extended interpretive and expositional translation, and in the notes at the end of each chapter.

PRINCIPLES EMPLOYED FOR TRANSLATING THE GREEK TEXT OF PAUL'S TREATISE TO THE EPHESIANS INTO PROFESSIONAL CONTEMPORARY AMERICAN ENGLISH

The following principles of translation are employed for translating the Greek Text of Paul's Treatise to the Ephesians into professional contemporary American English. These principles are derived from both positive and negative trends observed in the tradition of translation outlined above.

IMPORTANCE OF THE MEANING OF THE ORIGINAL LANGUAGES

The first and most important of these principles is that it is always necessary to preserve the indispensable historical link from any target language to the comprehension of the accurate meanings conveyed by the *original languages* through which God initiated his communication to human beings. The historical fact of the worldwide spiritual renewal that occurred during the Reformation is by far the most significant event that has taken place in the two thousand years of historical Christendom. The Reformation occurred only when the languages of German and English were linked in a true, spiritual and living way with the original Greek language of the New Testament, thus eventually liberating Europe – and later, America – from the distorted traditions of a thousand years that had eventually petrified the Latin language into a impenetrable, mysterious, megalithic myth, to be manipulated by the corrupt and the powerful few, simply as a massive machine to weigh down and enslave the ignorant mass of the European peoples during the Medieval era.

Consequently, the actual Greek Text (from the tradition commonly referred to as the "Majority Text" tradition) is employed as the basis for this translation. It is presented in the third section following the extended interpretive and expositional translation. The most recent, up-to-date and comprehensive edition of the text from this tradition, representing the lifework of another pair of scholars, is *The Greek New Testament According to the Majority Text*, edited by Zane C. Hodges and Arthur L. Farstad (see Bibliography). In addition, extensive use of several Greek Concordances (see Bibliography) are also employed in the translation, foremost to determine distinctively Pauline meanings for important Greek words and concepts, and then progressively wider fields of meaning within the entire New Testament itself.

WORD MEANINGS AS INFORMED BY OLDER GREEK LITERARY TRADITION

During the Medieval era, Latin suffered the cruel misfortune of being twisted and tortured by corrupted human beings into a monster. However, it could only be distorted *after* it had been forcibly separated (by the fall of the Roman Empire) from the living culture in which it was spoken, written and in which it conveyed contextual and historical meaning. The same terrible fate awaits any language – German, English, or even Greek, when it becomes separated from a diligent and deliberate effort to connect its meaning within the overall historical context and literature of the era in which it was spoken and written in great works of literature.

Therefore, the second principle used in this translation is to link it deliberately not only to the original language of the New Testament, but also to the wider context of the literary tradition of the entire Ancient Greek Tradition from which it arose. This is why the great accomplishment of the Greek Lexicon produced as the lifework of the two English friends and scholars Henry George Liddell and Robert Scott in 1843 is so important and is used extensively as a resource in this translation. It serves to provide an actual historical literary background, context, or field of meaning of the development of the life of the Greek language through the various eras of its growth and expansion, from the early epic poets Homer (the composer of the *Iliad* and the *Odyssey*) and Hesiod, who wrote in Ionic Greek; to the Classical period (consisting of the great Tragedians – Aeschylus, Sophocles and Euripides; the Historians – Herodotus, Thucydides and Xenophon; and the Philosophers – Plato and Aristotle), all who wrote in the Athenian, or Attic Greek dialect, up to and including the *koinē* or Hellenistic Greek dialect – the language of Alexander – which eventually became the common (*koinē* = "common") international language of the Eastern Mediterranean, into which the Hebrew Old Testament was translated (the *Septuagint*), and in which the New Testament was written.

For this reason, the *Septuagint* is often consulted to determine the meaning of difficult passages, as well as works by other Greek authors. In cases in which these passages seem to be determinative, the actual passage together with its translation is presented in the notes which follow each of the six chapters of the extended interpretive and expositional translation.

IMPORTANCE OF THE MEANING OF THE TARGET LANGUAGE

The third principle guiding this translation is that the meaning of the *target* language is just as important as the meaning of the *original* language. The benefits gained by understanding the meaning of the original text become truncated if the words into which they are translated are no longer actively used in the culture and lifeworld of the target language. In fact, it appears from a study of the history of translation that the target language is somehow trying to "catch up with" the actual historical needs of those who speak the target language itself. In other words, every tradition of translation in Christendom *eventually begins to lag behind* the actually living, spoken and written target language. All traditions of translation tend to exhibit this tendency to lag behind the target language as it is actually spoken and written, whether the translation lags behind by centuries or decades. It is only when those who speak and read the living contemporary language *recognize* that the language of the translation is lagging behind, that steps should be taken to re-translate it.

Such a pronounced historical "lag" can also be recognized when many different groups of Christian people begin to lose the ability to communicate meaningfully with each other, especially when they all seem to be using the same words. As explained above, what in fact is happening is that each group is in fact speaking two languages. The first is the contemporary professional workweek English language in which they share a large area of agreement, and the second is the historically determined religious language in which they experience difficulty finding agreement with other organized expressions of religion within Christendom. When this occurs, it is the opinion of this translator that the time has come to *re-translate the Greek text into the first language,* i.e., the contemporary professional workweek American English language in which they all find and experience a large area of agreement.

A compelling illustration of this principle in action within recent American history is the story of the *Living Bible*. Its author, Kenneth Nathaniel Taylor, was not a Greek or Hebrew Scholar but an Illinois businessman. In fact, Taylor was not even *translating* from the original Greek texts into English, but only *paraphrasing* the outdated religious language of the ASV (1901). The *Living Bible* was widely received from 1957 through 1971 because of Taylor's facility of paraphrasing the text into meaningful contemporary American English. His skill at paraphrasing demonstrated that he comprehended the subtleties and depths of the meaning of the *target language* – contemporary American English – with the same clarity and accuracy with which scholars understood the original languages of Greek and Hebrew. Further, it exposed the possibility that the religious scholars had spent so much time embedded in the study of the ancient texts that (perhaps) *they* were the ones that had lost meaningful "touch" with the rapidly changing and developing English spoken and written by Americans during the Contemporary era.

Therefore, the third principle used in this translation is that in order to compose a successful translation of a biblical text into a targeted new language, one must embed himself or herself in the life and actual usage of the language used by the group he or she wishes to reach. In other words, one must *comprehend the target language* with the same depth and expertise as he or she *comprehends the original language*. What this implies is that the endeavor of Bible translation is not a static, established fixture of history, but is rather a continual, fluid, dynamic, and above all, *never ending spiritual activity* that is always changing shape, because the target language is always changing shape.

The correlative and equally important principle is that it is necessary to make distinctions between words and concepts in one's own language that are universal, contemporary, living and understood by the informed and "in-touch" majority of people – and those words that have become outdated, fallen out of use, or have little meaning or relevance to the overall society. Words that should be avoided are those that retain only unique – even narrowly "coded" – meanings that make sense only within the isolated groups that use them, consciously or unconsciously, to control and manipulate other people to conform to their own constricted will, viewpoint or perspective of what they believe to be reality.

These reflections upon the importance of the *target language* lead to the fourth principle of interpretation used in this translation.

THE IMPORTANCE OF THE ENGLISH LANGUAGE EMERGING AS THE THIRD INTERNATIONAL LANGUAGE OF WORLD HISTORY

The first truly "international" language of world history was the common *Greek* language. This language was not the Ionic Greek of Homer's Epics; or the Classical Attic Greek of Sophocles, Herodotus, Plato and Aristotle; but rather the *koinē* ("common") Greek language spoken by the soldiers of Alexander's army. His soldiers and the Greek merchants and settlers that followed them soon occupied the vast territories southeast, east and northeast of the Mediterranean Sea they had conquered. Since they were in control – and spoke *koinē* Greek – everyone who wanted to become successful in the new way of life and culture they established in the eastern Mediterranean world soon learned to speak, read and write this language. Due to its vitality, *koinē* Greek quickly became woven into the fabric of the everyday lives of all of the nationalities and peoples living in the eastern Mediterranean world, and thus rapidly became a truly international language. *Koinē* Greek lasted as the first international language of world history for about eight centuries, spanning from Alexander's conquests in the fourth century B.C. to the Fall of Rome in the fifth century A.D. The Old Testament was first translated into *koinē* Greek in the third century B.C., and the New Testament was written in *koinē* Greek in the first century A.D.

The second language that replaced Greek as an international language in world history was *Latin*. However, unlike Greek, its life as an international language was less standardized, less stable and less enduring in its ability to convey accurately the authentic cultural expression of the various European peoples over which it exercised authority.

To begin with, the Classical Latin language written and spoken during the two centuries known as the Golden and Silver Ages in the city of Rome itself *never* became an "international" language. Classical Latin lasted only from the first century B.C. through the first century A.D. It was confined to the highly stylized written prose of epic (e.g., Virgil's *Aeneid*), history (e.g., Julius Caesar) and legal, judicial and political speeches (e.g., Cicero). The Latin language that eventually did replace Greek as an international language is generally known as "vulgar" (i.e., "common") Latin in its spoken form, or "Late" Latin in its written form. This form of Latin began to emerge at the beginning of the second century A.D. in the various regions within the Roman Empire as a distinctly different Latin than the Classical Latin written and spoken only in the city of Rome itself. It did not become an "international" language until the end of the fourth century just before the fall of Rome in the fifth century.

Jerome's translation of the Bible from Hebrew and Greek into Late Latin in the fifth century marks the beginning of its role as a truly "international" language, in the sense that it was the language written and spoken by the common people. However, Late (or common) Latin only lasted as a genuine "international" language for a relatively short period (about four centuries), as it gradually began to diverge into different dialects in each of the separate people groups living in southern Europe. By the ninth century, these dialects eventually formed into completely separate common languages – collectively called the "Romance languages" – of Spanish, Portuguese, French, Italian and Romanian. However, as a result of Charlemagne's concerted effort in the ninth century to preserve Latin as the language of learning (known as the "Carolingian Renaissance"), Latin eventually developed into a "non-natural" standard *legal, educational* language. This is because it was learned and used as a second or third language by speakers of European native languages in an attempt to retain some degree of continuity in law, learning and the Christian religion of Western Europe.

As a result, by the ninth century this artificial standardized Latin, known as "Medieval" or "Ecclesiastical" Latin, ceased to be a *truly international* language, because no one actually spoke it as a genuine language that emerged from or remained as an integral part of his or her own lifeworld. It became a language known only to a select and educated few – mostly church clerics, university dons and the elite nobility who wielded legal authority. This artificial standardized Latin language came to be employed eventually by the Roman Catholic Church to control the life of Europe for the next seven centuries – lasting from the Carolingian Renaissance of the ninth century until the sixteenth century. This period lasted until Erasmus rediscovered, collected and published the Greek New Testament, and Henry VIII broke away from the Roman Catholic Church to form the Church of England. Accordingly, during this period of history, although "Ecclesiastical" Latin paraded itself as the authoritative global language, there was in fact no worldwide "international" language in any authentic, genuine sense.

Due to the daring and astonishing defeat of the Spanish Armada in 1588 by Henry VIII's daughter, Queen Elizabeth I, England rose rapidly to hold the preeminent position of being the most powerful nation in the world for the next four centuries. America abruptly replaced England in that role at the end of World War II in 1945. Since then, America has held the undisputed position of being the most powerful nation in the world for only the last six decades. As a result of the simultaneous rise of the English literary tradition that began with Shakespeare and the publication of the King James Bible at the beginning of the seventeenth century, the English language (British English for three and a half centuries and American English for a little over the last half century) has emerged to become functionally the international language of the contemporary era of world history.

The recent publication of the *New International Version* of the Bible (in 1978, revised in 1984) represents a worthy endeavor to publish a translation of the Bible into "international" English (i.e., Australia, Canada, New Zealand and South Africa in addition to Great Britain and America). It is an attempt to recognize the historical fact that the English language has passed beyond the historical boundaries of Great Britain and America to become an *international language* in the Contemporary era. Its goal is to produce an English translation that *avoids the use of both of Americanisms and Anglicisms* altogether, to address an "international" English speaking audience. Although well motivated, the philosophical viewpoint of language adopted by the NIV remains somewhat artificial, because an authentic language grows from the lifeworld shared by a common people that use it in their everyday lives to communicate with each other.

Therefore, the fourth principle employed in the translation, while cognizant of the historical fact that English has indeed become an international language, is that it is composed deliberately from the standpoint of *American* English usage. It will remain sensitive to the fact that it has been profoundly shaped by the previous international languages of world history – Greek and Latin, as well as by historical British usage – but it will remain distinct from them by reflecting the style, idioms, metaphors and modes of expression currently used in the contemporary lifeworld of professional Americans.

TEACHING AS THE GOAL OF TRANSLATION – THE PRINCIPLE OF AN EXTENDED INTERPRETIVE AND EXPOSITIONAL TRANSLATION VERSUS A WORD-FOR-WORD TRANSLATION

The reasons that this translation of Paul's Treatise to the Ephesians is presented in form of an "extended interpretive and expositional" translation rather than in the form of a "word-for-word" translation are several. First, it is very difficult, if not actually impossible, to transfer the precise and comprehensive meaning conveyed by only one Greek word into exactly one corresponding English word that is its precise and comprehensive equivalent. This is because it is the case in every language that the *connotative* subtleties and inferences of meaning that every word carries along with itself in the living context in which that language is meaningful are often (if not in the majority of cases) more important than the *denotative* meaning of the word as it stands alone and outside of a relationship with other words which accompany it in an overall sentence or complete thought. In such cases, several phrases, clauses, or even sentences in English are required to satisfactorily convey the connotative meanings of the complete thought intended by the Greek sentence.

Second, there are many words in Greek that are "untranslatable," because it is impossible to write down a specific corresponding word in English to convey its meaning, because the Greek word does not "stand for" an objective equivalent concept represented by an English word, but rather a mood, a gradual or sudden shift in emphasis, or whether an abrupt refocusing or a smooth transition is to be used in the direction and pace of a particular literary or logical line of thought or reasoning. In these instances, supplying several words or a complete idiomatic phrase, clause or sentence in English is required.

Third, the figures of speech used in Greek are typically much more compact than those used in contemporary professional American English. Thus, these also must be expanded into an extended interpretive phrase, clause or sentence.

Fourth, the metaphors used by Paul in Ephesians are so highly organized into multiple layers or levels called "vehicles," that many additional sentences are required in English to bring these extended and complicated metaphors into view for the reader.

Fifth, Paul uses what might seem to us to be extremely long sentences. This is because his mind is so well organized, that it can keep track of all of the dependent clauses, prepositional phrases, multiple subjects and objects, participial phrases, etc. that convey the relative importance of the concepts he is presenting – sometimes for several English verses – before he ever introduces a verb into a Greek sentence. Conversely, contemporary professional American English depends upon *word order* to organize and break concepts up into much more simple units that *we call* sentences in order to convey meaning *to us* (usually requiring the subject and the verb be placed very near the beginning of a sentence). Greek, however, is much more flexible, being able to arrange and organize its words by the relative importance of the concepts the author wishes to emphasize and the themes he wishes to accentuate. Although this appears complicated to us, Paul takes advantage of the great flexibility of Greek syntax to arrange his words much more efficiently into what is for him, one complete thought. Sometimes, Paul's line of thought is so complex, that it takes not only extended English sentences, but extended English *paragraphs* to properly organize and place the right amount of proportion and emphasis on the hierarchy of the many concepts he employs. It therefore becomes necessary to "unpack" Paul's highly organized complete thoughts expressed in long Greek sentences, and then "re-package" them into a number of shorter English sentences organized into paragraphs.

Sixth, Paul uses Greek verbs and participles in the *passive* voice much more frequently than is generally recognized as good English writing style in the Contemporary era. Consequently, many of these verbs and participles are translated in the active voice.

Seventh, the historical context of the subject matter of Ephesians is so different from our own, being now separated from it by two thousand years, that extended sentences and paragraphs are sometimes required to amplify and explain in detail what would otherwise be to us a completely foreign concept. The only alternative would be to simply throw the Greek word onto the page as a transliteration, and then put a long footnote at the bottom of the page, which completely defeats the purpose of providing a *translation* of what Paul *means* as he employs Greek to convey his meaning, into the contemporary professional American English words, clauses, sentences and paragraphs he might employ to convey the same *meaning* in English.

Eighth, we often unconsciously or unwittingly bring the theological concepts that we learned from our own historically determined religious tradition or organization with us to the text before we realize that Paul wrote those texts two thousand years ago – the very texts from which those theological concepts were derived, *before* our own historically determined religious tradition ever even existed in Christendom. As such, we are obligated to allow Paul's use of the *koinē*, i.e., "common" Greek, to speak to us *first as "common,"* i.e., not "theological." We should allow Paul to employ the Greek language and its culturally rich context to *teach us* what God is like, rather than behave as if we were trying to compel our own particular theological concepts into the much richer and well thought-out metaphors he regularly employs. It is true that Paul's ultimate goal is in fact to teach us about God, i.e., to teach us "theology." However, he does not want to teach us about God by using the representations, metaphors and vehicles that are familiar *to us* because they come from *our frame of reference*, but rather by using the representations, metaphors and vehicles that are familiar *to him* because they come from *his frame of reference*. Thus, several sentences, and often several paragraphs are required to interpretively *construct the frame of reference itself* that Paul intends to use. This must be done *before* the attempt is then made to translate the particular metaphor Paul chooses as a tool to transfer the meaning from that frame of reference to the desired theological frame of reference or lesson that he wishes to teach to us.

In putting these reflections all together the fifth principle used in this translation emerges, which is that in order to truly and adequately "translate" the Greek text into meaningful English, we must use the literary technique of an *extended interpretive and expositional translation*, through which we allow Paul to teach us about God using his own lifeworld and its frame of reference first. We are then obligated to closely observe and then learn from our own lifeworld how to teach those who live in it what we have learned about God from Paul.

In other words, we must approach the task of *translation* as we would the task of *teaching*. In order to be good *teachers*, we must first be good pupils, or *learners*. We must come to the the text with the attitude that we must first allow Paul to teach us about his world in his own language by learning about his world in his own language. Second, we must then allow him to use that world to teach us about God in its own language. Following that laborious (but very rewarding) task, we must start all over again. Third, we must approach our own contemporary world with the attitude that we will allow our own world to teach us about itself in its own language, i.e, the language that the people within it *actually use* when they speak and write meaningfully to each other. Fourth and finally, it is only then that we can (and therefore must) make the attempt to bridge the gap between Paul's world and our world by "translating," i.e., teaching what we have learned about God from Paul's world in Paul's language to our own world using our own language.

Needless to say, in order to accomplish this conception of what it means to genuinely "translate" the Greek text (i.e., allow Paul to teach us about God by using his own world) into the English language (i.e., when we then allow our world to teach us the way to teach our world what we have learned from Paul about God), requires an interpretive, expositional translation into quite an extended number of English words, phrases, clauses, sentences, and paragraphs.

IMPORTANCE OF LATIN AND BRITISH ENGLISH – THE PRINCIPLE OF PETRIFACTION

The sixth principle used in this translation is that in itself, it is offered as *tentative*, i.e., it is a translation for *this* present moment of the usage of contemporary professional American English only. In other words, it is like buying a new car. Once it is driven it off the lot, it not only has already lost a significant portion of its value, it will also need to be replaced within a few years.

This principle must be consciously kept in view, because once a new translation is accomplished, there will be a tendency to hold onto it, and gradually elevate it to be the "authoritative version." This propensity emerges in the generation for whom the translation is intended, and tends to grow even stronger in the ensuing several generations. This phenomenon is accompanied by a drift to forget or regard the original texts as unimportant, or certainly not as important as the present "authoritative" version. In addition, there is a tendency to resist acknowledging that the spirit and meaning of one's language in the Contemporary era of history will continue to be fluid, keep on changing and moving rapidly ahead. Consequently, one must exercise the conscious effort to keep up with it, or it will leave him or her behind.

ORGANIZATION AND PRESENTATION OF THE TRANSLATION

This translation of Paul's Treatise to the Ephesians into professional, contemporary, American English is organized into three main sections. The first section is a brief, *Basic Explanatory Translation* (only twenty-four pages), consisting of the entire Treatise, presented without break or notes. The second section is an *Extended Interpretive and Expositional Translation*, in which each Chapter is translated as a unit, followed by the notes for each Chapter. The third section consists of the Basic Explanatory Translation with the original *Greek* text, *Tyndale's* translation (1526) and the *King James Version* (1611).

The Basic Explanatory Translation is presented first in order to provide a broad, *synthetic* translation of the entire Treatise that can be read in one sitting, yet supply sufficient detail to briefly and clearly explain Paul's central concepts without break or notes.

The Extended Interpretive and Expositional Translation is presented second in order to provide a more detailed and thorough *analysis* of the meaning of the Treatise. It is presented according to the chapter and verse divisions accepted in the English tradition. As in the NIV, interpretive decisions regarding the the major flow of Paul's thoughts and line of reasoning are arranged in paragraphs rather in a verse-by-verse format, using modern paragraph formation and style. Verses are denoted by the small superscripted number at the beginning of a sentence.

Unlike most translations (and the Basic Explanatory Translation presented in the third section), which italicize the words supplied by the translator that are not in the original text, the use of italics in the Extended Interpretive and Expositional Translation is employed to *emphasize* what this translator judges to be Paul's emphasis in the flow of his reasoning. The Extended Interpretive and Expositional Translation is presented in the Times New Roman font, 11 point type, thus (Ephesians 1:2):

> [2]Accordingly, I greet you all with the sincere hope and expectation that as you read, reflect upon and then put the provisions of this Treatise into action, that the two principal and overarching spiritual character qualities of *graciousness* and *peaceful good-naturedness of spirit* would hallmark your lives. Both of these character qualities come from both God our Father as well as from our present Commander in Chief,[7] Jesus, the High King of the future world. Because of this, you all should aspire to have these two character qualities continually grow throughout the whole process of your training program, to become the predominate spiritual qualities that serve to "bookend" all of the other qualities of personality that should also emerge and eventually become habitual characteristics in your lives and demeanor.

Due to the length and complexity of the notes, the use of footnotes occuring on the same page as the text is not employed. Instead, notes to interpretive decisions made in the Extended Interpretive and Expositional Translation are organized in the form of notes placed at the end of each Chapter. In the translation, reference numbers to the notes appear as superscripted numbers immediately after the word or concept. The notes are supplied as required to clarify, elucidate, justify, or explain the translation further.

Although many sources of information are used in the notes (see Bibiliography for a complete listing), the three primary sources that are most often presented are; first, the entries for Greek words that appear in

INTRODUCTION   xlix

the best Greek-English Lexicon available: the Lexicon produced by Henry George Liddell and Robert Scott, entitled *A Greek-English Lexicon* (see Bibliography). Such entries are often abbreviated to save space, and are denoted by "[LS]" following the endnote entry. Second, because the entries in Liddell-Scott are rendered into modern British English usage and not contemporary professional American English usage, the British English meanings provided by Liddell-Scott must often be adjusted to more accurately reflect contemporary professional American English usage. This is most often accomplished by tracing the denotative and connotative philology of possible English translations through the most up-to-date version of the Merriam-Webster *Unabridged Dictionary*, (see Bibliography). Such entries are also abbreviated to save space, and are denoted by "[W]" following the endnote entry. Third, when the precise meaning of a translation still remains in doubt (many of the words used by Paul in Ephesians are used only once or twice in the New Testament), other passages in the Greek New Testament are consulted when possible. These are accompanied by actual Classical Greek works cited in Liddell-Scott for contextual usage, along with quotations from the Greek *Septuagint* (the first Greek translation of the Hebrew Old Testament – see Bibliography). When used, entries from other Classical Greek works and the *Septuagint* are abbreviated to save space, and are denoted by the Greek author's name or with the accepted abbreviation for the *Septuagint* – "[LXX]" – following the endnote entry.

The third section consists of the Basic Explanatory Translation, followed by the original Greek text, followed by the William Tyndale's first translation of the Greek text into English published in 1526 (in original spelling and grammatical style), followed by the King James Version of 1611 (in original spelling and grammatical style). The new Basic Explanatory Translation is presented in Times New Roman font, 11 point type, with explanatory words supplied in *italics*, thus (Ephesians 1:2):

[2]*May the* graciousness and peacefulness *that come* from God our Father, and *from our* Commander in Chief, Jesus, the High King *of the future world, be given* to you all.

For the reader who is familiar with or has an interest in Greek, the original Greek text is presented immediately below the new Basic Explanatory Translation (a pronunciation guide to assist readers with an interest in learning how to pronounce the Greek words is included on p. xiii). The Greek Text used as the basis for this translation is from the *Greek New Testament According to the Majority Text*, edited by Hodges and Farstad (see Bibliography). The Greek text is presented in the GR Times New Roman Greek Font, in 11 point type, thus (Ephesians 1:2):

²χάρις ὑμῖν καὶ εἰρήνη ἀπὸ θεοῦ πατρὸς ἡμῶν καὶ κυρίου Ἰησοῦ Χριστοῦ.

The first translation of the Greek text into English by William Tyndale in 1526 follows the Greek text for two reasons. First, the verse divisions that are employed in all English versions today were not used by the early editors (e.g., Erasmus) or by Tyndale. Therefore, the texts are presented in paragraph format using Tyndale's paragraph divisions as a guide. His arrangement of paragraphs overall offers a good balance between Paul's extremely long sentences (which are too long for most English readers to follow), and the English tradition of versification of the text, which tends to break up and impede the flow of Paul's line of thought. To assist the reader, the verse divisions now accepted in the English tradition of translation are included in the Basic Explanatory Translation, the Greek text and Tyndale's first translation as small superscripted numbers immediately prior to the sentence that begins the translation of the particular verse.

Second, it has been estimated that approximately eighty percent of Tyndale's words and grammatical construction of English phrases, clauses and overall sentence structure were duplicated by the King James translators. Accordingly, Tyndale's translation of 1526 is presented immediately prior to the King James Version of 1611 to demonstrate the King James Version's dependence on Tyndale's translation published eighty-five years earlier. Tyndale's translation is presented in Georgia font, 10 point type, thus (Ephesians 1:2):

²Grace be with you and peace from God oure father and from the lorde Jesus Christ.

The King James Version of 1611 is presented for reference immediately below Tyndale's translation, in order to provide the reader with an immediate opportunity to compare the new Basic Explanatory Translation to the preeminent translation from the English tradition, as well as to the original Greek text. The KJV appears in the Book Antiqua font, 10 point type, with the interpretive inferential words that were supplied by King James' translators in italics, thus (Ephesians 1:2):

2 Grace *be* to you, and peace, from God our Father, and *from* the Lord Jesus Christ.

EPHESIANS
PAUL'S CONCLUSIVE TREATISE

A New Basic Explanatory Translation

Into

Professional (Non-Ecclesiastical)
Contemporary (Non-Medieval)
American (Non-British)
English

Chapter 1 – The "Top Secret" Plan Declassified

Paul's Conclusive Treatise Commissioned ♦ *The Inauguration Ceremony of the Future Kingdom* ♦ *God's Motive for Including Us in the Kingdom is His Love* ♦ *Kingdom Apprenticeship – Five Benefits God Has Given Us* ♦ *The First Benefit: The Redemption of Resurrection* ♦ *The Second Benefit: God's "Top Secret" Plan Declassified* ♦ *The Third Benefit: He Has Bequeathed Us an Inheritance* ♦ *The Fourth Benefit: He Has Sealed Our Lifework Plan* ♦ *The Fifth Benefit: He Has Paid the Down Payment for Us* ♦ *Paul's Request: Trainees for a Lifework Apprenticeship Council.*

PAUL'S CONCLUSIVE TREATISE COMMISSIONED

I, Paul, High Emissary of Jesus, High King of the future world, appointed by the will of God, am writing this Treatise to you, the specially selected recruits who are in Ephesus, especially to those who have proven themselves trustworthy in their service to the High King of the future world, Jesus:

²May the graciousness and peacefulness that come from God our Father, and from our Commander in Chief, Jesus, the High King of the future world, be given to you all.

THE INAUGURATION CEREMONY OF THE FUTURE KINGDOM

³God, considered especially in His role as the Father of our present Commander in Chief, Jesus, the High King of the future world, is the "Eulogizer;" that is to say, the "Keynote Speaker" at Jesus' Inauguration Day, when the Father will invest Him into His office as High King of the Earth. In this unique role, the Father is the One Whose recognition and commendation of our lives, which He will make in a public speech at the end of history, will matter more than anything else.

Furthermore, our future High King is actually composing the text of this commendation speech right now in the exercise of His present heavenly office. He is compiling its contents concomitant with the spiritual relationship that He has with us and with the Father – as He reports our spiritual progress and accomplishments to Him on a continual and regular basis. Moreover, there will come a day when each of our commendation speeches are finally completed, and our future High King will make the transition from exercising His present responsibilities in heaven as our advocate and helper, to His future role as High King of the world.

⁴Until then, Jesus will execute all of His divine responsibilities in accordance with His divine plan, such that prior to the founding of the organized government of the future world, He will have specially selected, recruited and trained us with the deliberate purpose that we should

personally accompany Him there. He will do this in order to give us distinctive legitimacy, so that we can be unimpaired as we stand directly beside Him to receive our official leadership appointments from God the Father Himself.

GOD'S MOTIVE FOR INCLUDING US IN THE KINGDOM IS HIS LOVE

In view of that future day, and motivated by love, 5God has pre-surveyed and pre-financed us to receive legal adoption as His "sons and daughters" by means of the legal advocacy of Jesus, the High King of the future world. He has legally included us so that we can authentically assist Him in accomplishing His purposes there. His investment in us will ultimately be successful because of the inexorable resolve of His will. 6He has done this so that His graciousness – namely, the incomparable graciousness which He has already demonstrated to us by means of the example of Jesus, the One Whom He loves best – might be finally and conclusively demonstrated in history. At His Appearing, Jesus will finally receive the universal recognition, appreciation and honor He is worthy of in that future, dignified, public ceremony.

KINGDOM APPRENTICESHIP – FIVE BENEFITS GOD HAS GIVEN US

7Because of His love, Jesus is the One Who has bought and secured the following five benefits for us toward that end with the purchase "price" of His own blood.

THE FIRST BENEFIT: THE REDEMPTION OF RESURRECTION

First, God has granted us "redemption" because of Him. He has purchased the right that authorizes us to "redeem" – or "trade in" – our present mortal bodies for our future resurrected bodies, which He will give us to experience the Inauguration of His Kingdom itself.

THE SECOND BENEFIT: GOD'S "TOP SECRET" PLAN DECLASSIFIED

Second, because of Him, God has granted us "forgiveness" from our hopeless indebtedness to Him, which all of us piled up by repeatedly plunging off course and living sidetracked lives. He has forgiven us our enormous debt because of the "riches" of His graciousness. 8He has gone on to "invest" even more of His "riches" in us so that He can "compound" His "interest" in us by making fully available to us the use of two essential leadership skills we will need. The first of these leadership skills is the ability to gain proficiency in all modes of knowledge, especially in ethical competence; and second, in discernment, principally as it relates to the employment of practical and intentional good judgment.

9He has made this investment in us because He has now officially "declassified" and fully briefed us in the contents of the formerly closely guarded Divine Secrets of His ultimate purposes in history, as well as avowing to us His unrelenting resolve to accomplish them. Jesus Himself proposed these specific objectives and resolutions during His recent first visit to the world.

¹⁰God sent Him on that mission to initiate His primary objective to select, recruit and train the right members for the divine government He will found at the fulfillment of history. The High King Himself will head up the comprehensive reorganization of the administration of all authority in that future world under His own leadership. Further, He will accomplish this over the realms of all the administrations of celestial authority that He will redeploy to operate the heavens, as well as over all the administrations of terrestrial authority that He will refound to govern the earth.

THE THIRD BENEFIT: HE HAS BEQUEATHED US AN INHERITANCE

¹¹Third, God has bequeathed His "inheritance" to us along with Jesus. He has included us in the High King's future inheritance, which He pre-surveyed and pre-financed to be consistent with the purposes and proposals He has planned for each role He has worked out for us, and will establish in keeping with the deliberation, counsel and resolution of His "will." ¹²God has included us in the future "estate" of Jesus' Kingdom in order that we, namely those of us who have hoped for the ultimate appearance of the High King of the future world beforehand, might be afforded the privilege to be the first to publicly recognize, appreciate and honor Him at His Appearing.

THE FOURTH BENEFIT: HE HAS SEALED OUR LIFEWORK PLAN

¹³Fourth, His Specially Selecting Spirit has authenticated your lives by officially "sealing" every one of you in precisely the same way that He did Jesus' life. He has authenticated your lives in this way so that you would be able to accomplish your own special and uniquely promising lifework, just as Jesus did. The Spirit performed this validating act when you heard this truthful report – namely, the good news of Jesus' wonderful plan to rescue and deliver you all – and then believed in Him.

THE FIFTH BENEFIT: HE HAS PAID THE DOWN PAYMENT FOR US

¹⁴Fifth and finally, this same Divine Spirit is also the "down payment" of our "inheritance." We can apply and use this down payment in our present lives toward the "redemption" of the "savings account" God has invested in and for each of us. We can therefore add to the initial investment He has made in our lives, so that we might be the first to have the privilege of presenting our transformed lives, which He will have made

valuable and worthy, when we publicly recognize, appreciate and honor Him at His Appearing.

PAUL'S REQUEST: TRAINEES FOR A LIFEWORK APPRENTICESHIP COUNCIL

15It is for this reason that, when I heard about your faith in our Commander in Chief, Jesus, and of the self-sacrificial love that you all have for all of His specially selected recruits, 16I did not stop giving God repeated thanks for you all. I also began to make it my habit to be deliberately mindful and intentionally make inquiry about you all in my requests to Him for information and guidance.

17First, I began to ask God, namely the Father of our Commander in Chief, Jesus, the High King of the future world – Who will preside at His inaugural Appearing – to give you a spirit that would enable you to live *ethically competent lives,* and to *unveil the additional essential information* you need to gain a comprehensive knowledge of Him.

18The second thing I asked Him was that He would enlighten the eyes of your hearts, and that once enlightened, you would be able to realize what the unique hope of His promising *lifework project* for each one of you consists.

Third, I asked Him to give you the capability to appreciate and be motivated by the vast extent of the wealth of the reward of His *inheritance,* which He will bequeath to every one of His specially selected recruits who merit it at His Appearing.

19The fourth thing I asked Him to give you was the *physical, psychological, emotional and spiritual strength* He makes especially available to us who tenaciously persist in believing we can discover and accomplish our lifework for Him. For this quest, I asked Him to give you the sustained dynamic energy you will need, even to the superlative degree of matching the feat achieved by the immense strength 20He demonstrated in the case of our future High King when He raised Him out of death and then seated Him at His right hand in the heavens.

21I know that He has the divine power to help you in this pursuit, because God has appointed Him to the office of having authority over all the angelic regimes and hierarchies of authority, as well as over all sovereign powers and leadership offices established by human governments. His authority exceeds every authoritative title that has ever been conferred – whether angelic or human – not only over both the good as well as the evil angelic forces and human leadership regimes during this historical era, but also over only the good human and angelic leadership hierarchies that will be established in the Kingdom era that is about to come.

22God has not only made all such existing authoritative positions of this era subordinate to our Commander in Chief by placing them under His feet, but He has also given Him headship over all leadership positions that pertain to His "Lifework" or "Kingdom Apprenticeship" Councils. 23These Councils are comprised of the members of His future governmental "body," because they are in fact the fulfilling agency of all the positions that body will eventually consist of, which positions are even now in every way being filled by Him according to His plan.

Chapter 2 – Time Travel: Back from the Future

Time Travel: Our True Future Self Must Rescue Our Sidetracked Present Self from this World's Death Traps ♦ *The Ability of Your Future Valiant Self to Rescue Your Present Vile Self is in Reality God's Gift to You* ♦ *Transformation is Composition: You Are God's Masterpiece* ♦ *Mood of the Masterpiece: Forged into a Peacemaker, Not Petrified into Pretentiousness* ♦ *The Purpose of Peacemaking: God's Building of Harmonious Relationships Into Our Eternal Home.*

TIME TRAVEL: OUR TRUE FUTURE SELF MUST RESCUE OUR SIDETRACKED PRESENT SELF FROM THIS WORLD'S DEATH TRAPS

Most certainly, you all were bound for a never-ending cycle of suffering a premature physical death as well as final spiritual death separated from God due to your repeatedly getting sidetracked, because of failing to set or pursue the right goals in life and on account of constantly missing opportunities. 2You were in this fearful predicament because at one time, you all deliberately conducted your lives according to the misguided philosophical worldview of this present era of civilization, namely – the polytheistic hierarchy of gods who live in the sky under the authority of the sky-god Zeus.

This spiritual being is in fact the very same evil spiritual being who is now incessantly working behind the scenes among the disobedient sons of God, i.e., those in the religious power-regime within Judaism, continually causing them to stir up trouble. 3The reason I know this is that we also – all of us – once displayed the very same public demeanor that they do now. An acrimonious disposition of visceral loathing characterized our conduct, and aggravated us to the point of taking deliberate, persistent and vigorous action against others – even to the extent of using violence.

We were not only motivated utterly by our visceral revulsion of others, but also by irrational hatred of the assumed wrongdoings we supposed were done by everyone else, which in reality was an attitude produced entirely within our own imagination. The result of this despicable frame of mind was that we also became in our deepest nature exactly like certain kinds of contemptible children who are always full of anger, just like the rest of those that now remain in the religious leadership regime within Judaism.

4But God, who is "rich" in mercy, motivated solely by His unimaginably vast love with which He loves us, 5even when we were as good as dead due to our willful persistence in getting sidetracked, brought us back to life, such that it is now possible to actually experience and grow in a living relationship with our future High King. You should never be deluded into thinking that your own initiative has brought about the good things you now enjoy in your Christian lives. Rather, He has rescued all of you from the precipice of suffering a tragic and untimely death because of His graciousness.

6Furthermore, God has raised us up and out of our own limited frame of reference into a new and living relationship with Jesus. Therefore, when we view our lives from this new frame of reference, He has also made it possible for us to avail ourselves of His wisdom and power to live our renewed lives. This divine wisdom and ability to transform our present personalities can only come from a relationship in which God has extended us the privilege of being seated with Jesus, our future High King, as He carries out His present heavenly responsibilities to help us and guide us from His Council Chambers in heaven.

In other words, He has made it possible for our future mature selves, who in reality are already raised and seated with Him, to "travel back in time" – so to speak. In this way, we can transform who we are in our present lives into the mature people we are that are living with Him in what is to us the "future" – from our limited frame of reference; but who in reality we already are – raised and seated with Him – from His eternal frame of reference.

7God has done this for us in order that He might show us the surpassing riches of His graciousness within our own lifetime and in the lifetime of those who will follow us in upcoming historical eras. He has also done this for us so that He can demonstrate His goodness to us even more auspiciously when we are finally physically present with Jesus when He returns to this world to become our High King.

THE ABILITY OF YOUR FUTURE VALIANT SELF TO RESCUE YOUR PRESENT VILE SELF IS IN REALITY GOD'S GIFT TO YOU

8For this reason, it is exclusively due to His graciousness that you all are the ones (of all people!) who have been rescued by Him because of your faith in Him; yet this rescue has in no way been brought about by you at all. Quite to the contrary, it is God's gift to you. 9He has most expressly not done this because of your own endeavors, in order to put a stop to the possibility that anyone might for any reason suppose they had a right to brag that they were somehow able to rescue themselves!

TRANSFORMATION IS COMPOSITION: YOU ARE GOD'S MASTERPIECES

[10]From God's perspective of reality, it is more accurate to say that we are His "masterworks," created by our future High King, Jesus, for the expressed purpose of launching good enterprises. God has in fact prepared these enterprises for us beforehand, so that we can deliberately conduct our lives from the philosophical perspective and subsequent expectation that all we have to do is simply step into them.

MOOD OF THE MASTERPIECE: FORGED INTO A PEACEMAKER, NOT PETRIFIED INTO PRETENTIOUSNESS

[11]As you come to view yourselves from this new standpoint in which you simply recognize and step into the good enterprises that God has prepared for us, you must continually guard yourselves from pride. You can do this by keeping in mind that you were once Barbarians by nature. As such, the leadership regime within Judaism contemptuously labeled you all as "The Uncircumcision," and then condescendingly referred to themselves as "The Circumcision." The consequence of twisting religious symbolism in this way was that they became artificial and pretentious – narcissists, in fact.

[12]During that time, this deluded leadership regime within Judaism excluded all of you from the future High King. They alienated you from citizenship in Israel and made you foreigners to the testamentary provisions of God's Promissory Agreement designed to include you. Because of their contempt, you eventually became fixed in a state in which you were without hope and without God in your lifeworld.

[13]But now you all – who were once extremely remote – have been brought near to God by the future High King, Jesus, by means of the bloody, sacrificial death the High King Himself suffered in your place!

[14-16]Therefore, He is our "Peacemaker!" He is the One who forged a Unity from both you depraved Barbarians and the pretentious leadership regime within Judaism. He effectively demolished the wall of hatred with which that close minded regime screened out all foreign ethnic races and nations – namely, the "Law" of the "Commandments," which that regime had by that time distorted and erected into an overly rigid system of inflexible dogma.

Jesus "put them out of business" by means of the sacrificial death of His own body on the cross. By His sacrifice, what God in fact permanently put to death on the cross was your savage and vicious nature, as well as their narcissism and irrational hatred. He did this so that He might not only create by Himself and for Himself one new kind of peace making human being from the two formerly opposed wicked states of mind, but also that He might reconcile both of them into one future governmental body authentically dedicated to God.

17Now that He has come, the following good news can be announced: "Peace is now immediately available to you all who were once far away from God as well as to those who are near to Him!" 18Now, through Him, we both have a "freeway" to approach the Father by one Spirit.

THE PURPOSE OF PEACEMAKING: GOD'S BUILDING OF HARMONIOUS RELATIONSHIPS INTO OUR ETERNAL HOME

19The result of Jesus' accomplishment is that you all are no longer foreigners and outsiders. Instead, as His specially selected recruits, you are from now on fellow citizens and welcome members to God's home. 20You all are among those who are in fact being "built into a home" upon the "foundation" of God's High Emissaries and Official Spokespersons – the "Cornerstone" being our future High King, Jesus Himself. 21Acting in His role as building superintendent, he is the One upon Whom God's entire "home building project" is being built into an overall shape of harmonious concord according to our Commander in Chief's logical master plan. Under His guidance, it is growing into a very special place where it becomes possible for all people to authentically meet and come to know God. 22Ultimately, He is the One upon Whom the Spirit is assembling you all from a wide assortment of originally dissimilar "materials" into a "house" of congruent relationships. The Spirit's ultimate goal in building this "construction project" of new relationships is to incorporate all of you into becoming an integral part of God's eternal "home."

Chapter 3 – Recognizing Opportunity: Faith in Him and Love for Others

Never Give In To Despair! Digression – Every Circumstance in History is Actually an Opportunity to Achieve Our Lifework ♦ Never Despair! Digression Continued – A Proper Perspective Changes the Stressful Circumstances We Must All Face Into Opportunities to Benefit Others ♦ No Situation Can Ever Defeat Us Our Lifework if We Have Faith in Him and Selfless Love for Others ♦ Paul Asks Jesus to Appear Spiritually in His Lifework Councils Prior to His Kingdom Arrival to Encourage His Apprentices.

NEVER GIVE IN TO DESPAIR! DIGRESSION – EVERY CIRCUMSTANCE IN HISTORY IS ACTUALLY AN OPPORTUNITY TO ACHIEVE OUR LIFEWORK

It is for this reason that I, Paul, have employed the time of my "bondage" here in Rome as an opportunity to compose the "Bond" of this Treatise for the future High King Jesus, for the sake of you former Barbarians –

²[I am compelled to digress for a moment in this Treatise to emphasize that you all have now been fully briefed in the details comprising God's gracious plan to establish His future governmental administration. He specifically gave this task to me for you all, ³namely, making you fully aware of the provisions of His formerly "Top Secret" plan. I have now accurately articulated the provisions of His plan, which He made known to me by means of supernatural revelation, and have concisely delineated its main features above in writing.

⁴Further, the Treatise I have written above contains the special feature that, whenever you all intentionally reread and reexamine its provisions aloud with the motive of discerning its true meaning, you might be enabled by His Spirit to reacquire a complete understanding of the comprehensive perspective of our future High King's "Top Secret" plan that I myself possess.

⁵The comprehensive scope of the provisions contained in this divine plan have never been made known in the history of the world to the degree that they have now been divinely unveiled to His specially selected High Emissaries and Spokespersons by His Spirit.

⁶These provisions specifically stipulate that all of the ethnic races and nations foreign to Judaism – whether they are civilized Greeks or uncivilized Barbarians – are to be, from this point in the history of the world onward, specifically highlighted, recruited and trained to become equal heirs with God's future High King, Jesus. They are to become co-administrators with Him in His future governmental body and equal partners with Him of the promises He has made fully available for them to share with Him during the Kingdom era through the opportunity offered them by this wonderful message.

⁷Because I have received the commission to deliver this message successfully in all its aspects as His special assignment, I have become, in effect, God's "aide-de-camp," which I regard as a gracious gift, granted to me as a unique directive, duly authorized under the auspices of His enacted prerogative.

NEVER GIVE IN TO DESPAIR! DIGRESSION CONTINUED – A CORRECT SPIRITUAL PERSPECTIVE TRANSFORMS THE STRESSFUL CIRCUMSTANCES WE MUST ALL FACE INTO DIVINE OPPORTUNITIES TO BENEFIT OTHERS

⁸God has given this gracious gift to *me* – the very least deserving of all of His specially selected recruits! Amazingly, He assigned me the privilege of being the one He specially selected to announce the wonderful news of the vast and immeasurable riches of the future High King to all of

the ethnic races and nations in the entire world foreign to Judaism, whether they are civilized Greeks or uncivilized Barbarians.

⁹Furthermore, Jesus, the future High King Himself, personally commissioned me to enlighten everyone concerning the provisions of His "Top Secret" plan, containing the details of His future governmental administration, which God has deliberately kept hidden throughout all of recorded history from the beginning of His creation of the world until this present era.

¹⁰God has waited until this historical era to take this initiative of training human beings to achieve mature mastery over the multi-faceted ethical and political skills required to live with and lead others effectively. He will accomplish His divine training program through the specific agency of His Kingdom Apprenticeship Councils.

This is the first time in history that He has made His plan known to the angelic regimes and hierarchies of authority – both good and evil – throughout all of the heavenly realms. ¹¹God previously made this decision to unveil His "Top Secret" plan at this time in history according to His own carefully considered purposes and proposals, which He first deliberated upon and then published and enacted from His Eternal Council, in full collaboration, cooperation and concurrence with the future High King, Jesus, our Commander in Chief.

¹²He is the One through Whom we now have complete freedom of immediate access to His heavenly Council Chambers on the "freeway" He built for us. He built this freeway for us to use in order to approach Him with the full confidence and assurance that He will help, guide, teach and enable us to find and accomplish our lifework, because of His absolute faithfulness and reliability.

¹³And now, I must resume my reason for writing this Treatise to you all.] The reason that I, Paul, am writing this Treatise to you is to ask – or rather, to firmly appeal to you all – that you stop giving in to your dispirited mood and defeatist frame of mind as you think about the various stresses I am going through. You can no doubt see by now that God is the One who is in reality orchestrating my circumstances for your benefit, which you will fully understand and appreciate at our High King's future Appearing.

NO SITUATION CAN EVER DEFEAT US IN ACCOMPLISHING OUR LIFEWORK IF WE HAVE FAITH IN HIM AND SELFLESS LOVE FOR OTHERS

¹⁴For being assigned this gracious privilege, I consistently bend my knees in gratitude in front of the Father of our Commander in Chief, Jesus, the future High King of the earth. ¹⁵You all must maintain this attitude also, because since He is the One Who has appointed every hierarchy of

angels in heaven and every family lineage of human beings upon the earth; He is therefore the One who ultimately controls them all.

¹⁶The riches that He purposes to give you at His Appearing, along with the dynamic spiritual ability He will give you in the deepest part of your psychological and personal inner self during this present life, must motivate you to be strengthened, emboldened and be given confidence by His Spirit.

¹⁷In order to strengthen you with such confidence, our High King is like a divine Explorer, Who is searching for those that have the faith in Him to allow Him to "plant His colony" in their hearts. Like all Pioneers, His desire is to "build a settlement" so that He can "live" and "make His home" there. His ultimate objective is that you would allow Him to become the "governor" of your hearts, having from the very first been founded and rooted there according to the principle of selfless love. ¹⁸He intends to build His divine "colony" in your hearts in order to stretch you – so that you will reach forward with all your strength until you can grasp, together with all of His specially selected recruits, the magnitude of the width and length and height and depth of His building project of supernatural relationships.

¹⁹His purpose in doing this is to enable you to realize, experience and express the selfless love of the High King in your present lives, which surpasses knowledge. His goal is to fully shape and strengthen your personality, so that you can skillfully put into practice God's comprehensive perspective and mature behavior in any situation you may encounter.

PAUL ASKS JESUS TO APPEAR SPIRITUALLY IN HIS LIFEWORK COUNCILS PRIOR TO HIS KINGDOM ARRIVAL TO ENCOURAGE HIS APPRENTICES

²⁰Now, I ask the One Who is more than capable enough to accomplish exceedingly more than we could ask or think, in accordance with the dynamic power with which He energizes us, ²¹namely, the High King, Jesus Himself: May He make Divine Appearances in His Lifework Councils in all generations in era after era. May you all recognize, heartily agree with and live according to the conclusive truths of the provisions and promises presented in this Treatise so far, as I have now reached its midpoint.

Chapter 4 – "Dressing Up" For Real

Molding Ethnically Diverse Egos into Cohesive Teams with Unit Integrity Requires Limiting Petty, Divisive Attitudes ♦ Find a Special Ability God Has Given You to Help Others in Their Lifework and in So Doing, Become Mature Yourself ♦ "Dress Up" Your Mind in the Newly Outfitted Human Being Created by God, Focused on Finding the Truth in Life ♦ Do not Grieve God's Spirit, but Develop Habits that Disarm the Devil's Traps – Lying, Anger, Stealing and Criticism.

MOLDING ETHNICALLY DIVERSE EGOS INTO COHESIVE TEAMS WITH UNIT INTEGRITY REQUIRES LIMITING PETTY, DIVISIVE ATTITUDES

Therefore, through the "Bond" of this Treatise, I respectfully request and expect you all to conduct your lives according to the new philosophical world view presented here in a manner worthy of the lifework to which you have been summoned by our Commander in Chief. ²You should conduct yourselves towards each other without condescension, but rather with an unassuming nature, with gentleness, being tolerant, patient and willing to suffer the emotional pain that inevitably comes when others misunderstand you, maintaining an attitude of being a servant-leader, continually motivated by self-sacrificial love.

³Further, you should strive diligently to guard the *unity* intended by the Spirit through creating and maintaining peace, the bond of union, in your relationships. ⁴You should do this because we all realize that there is but *one* future governmental body and only *one* Spirit that will guide us all during both eras. He has summoned each of you with but *one* single hope of finding and accomplishing the lifework of your present apprenticeship, which leads to your Millennial appointment.

⁵Moreover, there is only *one* Commander in Chief and *one* quest to faithfully follow Him, depicted symbolically throughout the history of God's people by only *one* solemn, public, initiation ceremony of being immersed under water. ⁶In the end, there is only *One* God, Who is the Father of all of us – including Jesus. The Father is therefore the One Who has authority over us all, Who has chosen to act through us all, and Who has assured you that He will always be with you all.

FIND A SPECIAL ABILITY GOD HAS GIVEN YOU TO HELP OTHERS IN THEIR LIFEWORK AND IN SO DOING, BECOME MATURE YOURSELF

⁷Therefore, He has given each one of us the gracious gift of a special spiritual power or ability with which He intends for us to accomplish our lifework, according to the carefully measured gifting of the future High King. ⁸That is why it says in Psalm 68:18:

"When He ascended on high, He led captives into captivity,
And gave gifts to human beings."

⁹Now, what else could the notion that "He ascended" imply except that He first must "descend" from heaven to the "lower regions," namely, the earth? ¹⁰The further implication is that the One Who descended is the One Who ascended above all the heavens, Whose objective for doing so could only be that He might fill all the administrative positions required for His Kingdom.

¹¹Therefore, He has given to some of His specially selected recruits the present apprenticeship office of High Emissary and to others the role of being His Divine Spokespersons. To yet others, He has given the commission of being His Messengers of communicating the Good News, while to others the duty and trust of Guardianship over the spiritual well-being of His new recruits. To still others, He has appointed the meticulous, careful and painstaking responsibility of being the Teachers of His new recruits.

¹²He has given us these abilities in order to equip His specially selected recruits, to enable them to accomplish their own work of service, with the ultimate goal of building the future governmental body of the High King. ¹³He will continue to do this until we all as a historically collected group arrive at "unit integrity" – that is to say, the ability to function interdependently with a seamless team spirit. This team will be capable of operating with full reliance and trust in Him and in each other, and will function with total reliability, complete awareness, understanding and mutual appreciation for the experience and intentions of the Son of God, which is by definition what it means to be mature human beings.

God's goal for us in leading us through this process is that we should finally arrive at the mature stature of the fully mature corporate personality He requires, as measured and determined by our High King Himself. ¹⁴His objective in effecting this transformation is that we should no longer be helpless due to our naïveté, continually confused and having our minds spun around in all directions by others. He wants to make us invulnerable to the kinds of people who pretend to be teachers, but who are only pirates and swindlers, whose only purpose is to deceive us into leading lives that are as erratic, unreliable and volatile as a windstorm. His purpose is to guard us from falling into lifestyles like those of gamblers and dice players, who wrongly believe that mere chance guides their lives.

¹⁵On the contrary, we must grow up to become like Him – the One Who is heading up our training program – in every way; discovering and then speaking what is true, always motivated by self-sacrificial love. ¹⁶It is only by means of this self-sacrificial love that the High King is making His

future governmental body grow into a governmental administration suited for Himself and His purposes.

By means of this love, He is not only training every member of this body to become a vital part of a rational organization structured to function in harmony as a pleasant and enjoyable whole, but is also teaching them to "put it all together" – to find a sense of meaning and significance in their present lives. They are enabled to do this by means of every enlightening contact arranged for them by His Spirit, which He supplies for them from His vast divine resources, but only according to the portion in which He measures out for each one exactly what He has determined that each one needs.

"Dress Up" Your Mind in the Newly Outfitted Human Being Created by God, Focused on Finding the Truth in Life

[17]Accordingly, the Commander in Chief has summoned me as His designated and official lead-witness to make the following official announcement to you all. You all are no longer to conduct your lives according the philosophical schools of thought of any the rest of the ethnic races or nations of the world – whether they are civilized Greeks or uncivilized Barbarians – who follow those philosophical worldviews with futile purposes in their minds.

[18]They continue to become more and more darkened in their intentions through their obstinate refusal to give up their false ways of thinking, to the extent that they are now alienating themselves from the life of God by means of their own willful ignorance and through the callousness of their own hearts. [19]Because they have now sunk into despair on their own, He has given them up to decadence, to every kind of vicious and depraved trade involved in organized crime and to the never-ending insatiability that always accompanies greed.

[20]But you all have not learned this approach to life from the future High King, [21]since you have most certainly heard and obeyed Him and been taught by Him, it follows that the discovery of the truth in life is by means of Jesus also. [22]Bearing this in mind, you must "take off and leave outside" your former way of life – like you would with dirty clothing. That old way of life is depressing – like that of cynical elderly people, who waste themselves away by tenaciously holding onto the vain belief that they were somehow cheated out of what they only imagined they wanted.

[23]Instead, discipline your minds to be continually revived by the Spirit. [24]Like you would with new clothing, adopt the deliberate and daily habit of "dressing up" the newly outfitted and refreshing human being that has been created by God to do what is right and good, totally focused upon the discovery of the truth for your lives.

Do not Grieve God's Spirit, but Develop Habits that Disarm the Devil's Traps – Lying, Anger, Stealing and Criticism

25First of all then, having "taken off and left outside" the "dirty clothing" of falsehood, "you all must tell the truth – each one of you with your fellow human beings" (Zechariah 8:16), because we are members of one another.

26Second, learn to "Be angry, yet do not allow unchecked anger to cause you to fall short of your goals" (Psalm 4:4). Rather, in the same way that God commands the sun to set at the close of every day, so you must also consciously prevent yourselves from harboring the exasperations of your day. 27Neither should you by failing to do so permit the "Slanderer" – the Devil – an opportunity to get you sidetracked.

28Third, he who is a thief, mooch or con artist must stop stealing any more, but rather strive to put his own hands to some kind of laborious but worthwhile occupation. As he does this, he should save up some resources so that he might be able to give or pay a portion of his earnings to those who might have need of temporary assistance – or preferably – provide them with jobs himself.

29Fourth, you all must stop every rotten word from inadvertently spewing out of your mouth. Instead, speak only good, constructive things that are useful and help to build stable and lasting relationships, with the purpose of contributing comments and suggestions that will graciously benefit those who hear what you say.

30Furthermore, you all must stop grieving the Specially Selecting Spirit of God, by Whom you have been officially "sealed" for the Day of "Redemption." 31Rather, you must learn to clear away every form of bitterness, harbored anger, resentment, rage, shouting and blasphemy from your lives, along with every other kind of evil outburst.

32Instead, you must all become effective in providing the most beneficial outcomes for each other, being compassionate and gracious to each other, in exactly the same way that God, by means of the future High King's example, has been gracious to you all.

Chapter 5 – Actor of Love, Follower of Light, Master of Ethical Skill

Live as an "Actor" Portraying the "Role" of God in Your Life, Whose Main "Character" Trait is Self-Sacrificial Love ♦ Be a Leader that Pursues the Light of Truth in Public – With Vulnerability, Mercy, Learning and Consistency ♦ Master Ethically Skillful Disciplines in Life's Relationships – Instead of Going Along With Mindless, Unethical Traditions ♦ Genuinely Bond with Your Spouse by Graciously Offering Yourselves to Each Other in a Spirit of Giving and Sacrifice.

LIVE AS AN "ACTOR" PORTRAYING THE "ROLE" OF GOD IN YOUR LIFE, WHOSE MAIN "CHARACTER" TRAIT IS SELF-SACRIFICIAL LOVE

Third, you must all proceed on to become "actors" that portray the "role" of God in your lives. When you imitate God as an actor would portray a character in this way, you will experience the same thing that only-children often do. After they have been raised in an atmosphere of love and contentment, they frequently go on to imitate their parents' gracious way of life. ²You can do this especially by conducting your lives according to a new philosophical world view based on self-sacrificial love, in exactly the same way that the future High King loved us and surrendered Himself for us as a sacrificial offering to God. God treasured His sacrifice for us in an analgous way to the way we sometimes feel when we are powerfully gripped into reliving a vivid memory of sorrow mixed with gratitude of a special person's sacrifice of themselves for us, when we re-experience the smell of a familiar frangrance with which they were always associated.

³⁻⁴Therefore, precisely because this kind of selfless love is the only form of love that is fitting for His specially selected recruits, you all must stop believing in and practicing the following false forms of so-called "true love:" engaging in sexual intercourse before or outside of marriage; every form of sexually dirty or filthy – and therefore unhealthy – practice, whether in the body or in the soul; erroneously thinking you can "love" material objects, which is nothing but greed; all sexually perverse and violent practices that degrade and injure the other person as well as yourself; holding to old foolish superstitious beliefs that misrepresent God's true nature as one of pettiness or partiality; or the use of insolent humor to belittle others in public. All of these false views of so-called "true love" are wrong. The simple test for the appropriate kind of love is the kind of loving behavior which anyone would consider worthy of gratitude.

⁵You all know it to be obviously true that every one who is a licentious sex addict, or is filthy in body or in mind, or is a greedy miser – who in reality is an idolater – cannot be trusted and therefore will not be given any part of God's inheritance in the Millennial Kingdom by the future High King, who is God Himself.

⁶You must stop being deceived by the empty claims of these false world views. In fact, it was by gradually giving in to these false world views that God became angry with His disobedient sons, namely, those in the leadership regime within Judaism who persist in that religion after they have heard and rejected the good news about Jesus.

⁷Therefore, you all must also stop giving in when you are pressured to enter into partnerships with people who stubbornly persist in staying

immoral or unethical, [8]because although you all used to live in the darkness of stubborn ignorance yourselves, you have now been freed from all that by the Commander in Chief, so that you can enjoy a life of enlightened happiness.

BE A LEADER THAT PURSUES THE LIGHT OF TRUTH IN PUBLIC – WITH VULNERABILITY, MERCY, LEARNING AND CONSISTENCY

Fourth, you must all adopt a philosophy of life in which you conduct yourselves in the same way that young people who are seriously pursuing an education normally do – committed to the enlightened spirit of living a public life of vulnerability, mercy, learning and consistency. [9]You must do so because by living in this way, the Spirit of God will bring about the fruitful results of every form of goodness, justice and the discovery of truth. [10]The additional benefit of these attributes is that by them you will become qualified by our Commander in Chief for future office, because by adopting them you will earn His distinguished confidence.

[11]You all must no longer be shareholders with those who practice the darkness of fearful or stubborn ignorance and suffer the tragic consequences of that way of life, but instead, you must confront people who are like this. [12]It is disgraceful to merely gossip in secret about the evil things such people practice among themselves. [13]Instead, when all such evil things are challenged and refuted by being brought to light in public, it is only then that they are made clearly known and resolved properly. Further, it is only those whose evil is brought to the light of being publicly, justly, and mercifully resolved that can be eventually enlightened themselves. [14]This is the real meaning of the theme found in the writings of Isaiah, God's Spokesman, where he says in effect, "Wake up, you who have fallen asleep at the wheel! Take an exit off of your dark, dead-end road, and the High King will illuminate the way for you!"

MASTER ETHICALLY SKILLFUL DISCIPLINES IN LIFE'S RELATIONSHIPS – INSTEAD OF GOING ALONG WITH MINDLESS, UNETHICAL TRADITIONS

[15]Therefore, see to it that you conduct your lives according to the new philosophical world view set forth in this Treatise, by accurately incorporating its specific principles into every aspect of your lives, no longer living in ethically unskillful ways, but only in ethically skillful ways. [16]The way to accomplish this consistently is to "buy out" every possible opportunity you can find to do good, because the days left in this era will be characterized by much evil. [17]Accordingly, you must all choke down your pride as you decide to bring your senseless habits to an end, and instead find out and pay attention to whatever the will of the Commander in Chief is.

¹⁸As you would do with all of the good things that God provides in life, learn to drink alcoholic beverages graciously, as an expression of your enjoyment of life. You can only do this with self-control and by bringing an end to the futile habit of drinking alcohol excessively, which only ends up wasting the valuable time that God also gives you to use. Fill your lives instead with the skills you need to be gracious and stay focused spiritually.

¹⁹One good way to stay spiritually focused is to learn to sing, either by singing songs accompanied by musical instruments, or by singing other kinds of hymns and spiritual songs or choruses to each other and with each other. Sing and play music enthusiastically and with all your heart, as you would for our Commander in Chief.

²⁰In whatever you do, the key element in remaining spiritually focused is to always be gracious to others and grateful to God in every situation, because He is our Father, and on account of the example provided by our Commander in Chief, Jesus, the High King. ²¹Always show deference, offering help and giving unselfishly to each other out of respect for our High King.

GENUINELY BOND WITH YOUR SPOUSE BY OFFERING YOURSELVES TO EACH OTHER IN A GRACIOUS SPIRIT OF TRUST, GIVING AND SACRIFICE

²²Wives, in your marriages, adopt a cheerful and gracious attitude of deference, offering to help your husbands find their lifework. You should enjoy doing this with him, trusting him and supporting his efforts in a pleasant and agreeable way, with the same positive frame of mind as you would whenever you warmly and gladly assist others for the sake of our Commander in Chief. ²³Do this because our High King has given the husband the responsibility to head up the leadership role between himself and his wife in the same way that God has given Jesus the leadership role in heading up the relationship between Himself and His Lifework Councils. Just as Jesus has the responsibility of being the Liberator of that future governmental body, so also God wants your relationship with your husband to be a liberating experience in your life.

²⁴Therefore, in the same way that His Kingdom Apprenticeship Councils should work together to offer their services to their future High King in following His initiatives to lead their members to find and accomplish their lifework, so you should also in your role as wives offer yourselves to your own husbands in the variety of life events that will occur in your marriage relationship – so that God may employ your augmented power as a couple to enhance and amplify your unique lifework as a woman.

²⁵Husbands, in your marriages, love your wife by generously giving her yourself instead of things. Put her best interests first with a gracious and

gentle disposition, and sacrifice your own ambitions instead of her. Do this for her in the same pleasant and good-natured way that our High King sacrificed Himself for and continues to selflessly love those who are His specially selected recruits in His Lifework Apprenticeship Councils.

26He does this in order that He might get us ready for His special use, by means of "cleansing her in a bath of water," in the same way a shepherd prepares his specially selected and most precious sheep. One specific way in which you husbands can continually "cleanse" your relationship with your wife is to take the initiative to start and lead conversations with her in gracious, loving, well thought-out and positive ways. Wives (or any other human beings for that matter) are never motivated by sarcastic comments or cynical remarks, no matter to what degree those comments may be grounded in what you sincerely believe to be right in your own mind as their husbands. You must do this in the same way that our Commander in Chief did when He set a good example for us as our Teacher during His first visit, always initiating dialogue with people, but also carefully choosing his spoken words with the intention of helping others or training His apprentices to be prepared and ready.

27Moreover, His spoken words that were written down by them will continue to be employed by His Spirit to prepare His specially selected recruits throughout the upcoming era, so that He might officially present her, namely, His historically prepared and completed Kingdom Apprenticeship Councils, to Himself at His own Inauguration Day. On that Day, His well chosen and persuasive speech will have accomplished its fully cleansing effect, having removed from her any spot, stain or wrinkle or any such other defect of moral impurity. She will have become cleansed by obeying His gracious spoken words, so that she can be uniquely special and morally blameless.

28It is for this reason that you husbands ought to be the ones who take loving initiatives in your relationship with your wives in the same way that you do in caring for the health of your own bodies. He who loves his own wife loves himself, 29because nobody ever normally hates or neglects the health of his own physical body, but rather cultivates and cares for it, in precisely the same way that our Commander in Chief cares for His Kingdom Apprenticeship Councils. 30He takes the initiative to care for us in this way because He is training us to become the special members of His future governmental body.

In fact, He regards us with the same intimacy that He wanted Adam to have for Eve, when He "made her out of his flesh and out of his bones." What I mean by using this metaphor from Genesis is that God intends you husbands to cultivate in yourselves the same realization that Adam had when he woke up to discover that God intended him to have a unique, special and intimate relationship with Eve because God had made her out of the very flesh and bones He had drawn from Adam's own chest. ³¹This is why God says in Genesis 2:24 that "A man shall leave his father and mother, in exchange for this new relationship of marriage, namely – that he shall bond to his wife such that both of them come to exist in a relational manner so intimately close that it is as if they are one being."

³²Guided by God's graciousness, living out the relationship of marriage in a spiritually accurate way can be one of the most fulfilling ways in which God accomplishes His "Top Secret" plan in your life as husbands, because as I explained above, it is so similar to the foundational relationship upon which the High King will establish His own relational structure with His Kingdom Apprenticeship Councils.

³³In summary, for those of you who *are* husbands, one of the single most important relationships God is watching and measuring closely is how you conduct your relationship with your wife; You should love your wife as yourself. For those of you who *are* wives, one of the single most important relationships God is watching and measuring closely is your relationship with your husband; You should respect your husband.

Chapter 6 – Career Spiritual Soldiers

Initiate the Skill of Parenting in the Life of Your Family in Gracious, Spiritually Accurate Ways ♦ Perform Your Vocation, Employment, Occupation, Profession or Career in Spiritually Accurate Ways ♦ You Can Prevail Over the Evil Spiritual Forces that Will Attack You in Your Efforts to Be Peacemakers for God Only by Becoming Career Spiritual Soldiers ♦ Strap on The "Sword-Belt" of Discovering Truth, Put On The "Body Armor" of Justice and Lace Up The "Special Forces Boots" for the Long March Required to Be a Peacemaker for God ♦ Protect Yourself with the "Shield" of Faith, Put on the "Helmet" of Rescue to Conquer Your Fear of Leadership and Wield The "Sword" of God's Spoken Words Guided by His Spirit ♦ Maintain an Effective "Command and Control" System of Disciplined Direct Communication with God ♦ Select Friends and Messengers Who Have a Positive, Loving Contented, Cheerful, Faithful and Encouraging Attitude ♦ May the Graciousness of Your Immortal Kingdom Persona Come to Distinguish Your Mortal Personality Also

INITIATE THE SKILL OF PARENTING IN THE LIFE OF YOUR FAMILY IN GRACIOUS, SPIRITUALLY ACCURATE WAYS

Children, obey your parents as you would the Commander in Chief, because this is the right thing for you to do. ²The fifth command of the main Ten Commands of God's Law – recorded in both Exodus 20:12 as well as in Deuteronomy 5:16 – says: "You must honor your father and mother." This is the first command of the Ten that comes with the promise of a reward, namely: ³"in order that your life would go well for you and that you might live a long time in God's 'Promised Land,'" which in reality is the Millennial Kingdom.

⁴Not only should you children be obedient to your parents, but you fathers must also break youselves of your tendency to provoke your children to anger by ignoring them or by dismissing them with a few careless words or critical remarks. As I mentioned above, children (or any other human beings for that matter) are never motivated by sarcastic comments or cynical remarks, no matter to what degree those comments may be grounded in what you sincerely believe to be right in your own mind as their fathers. Instead, set a good example yourselves and cultivate them in following the example of our Commander in Chief. In the same way that he taught His own apprentices, you must with the same gracious manner and demeanor proactively initiate well planned conversations with your children, making it your goal to patiently educate them, warn them of danger and think through how you should reprimand them when necessary – before you do it.

PERFORM YOUR VOCATION, EMPLOYMENT, OCCUPATION, PROFESSION OR CAREER IN SPIRITUALLY ACCURATE WAYS

⁵To those of you who are employees or subordinate officers, I would say this: You must obey your employers, managers or superior officers in whatever business, enterprise, or branch of the civil or military service in which you are presently working, with an attitude of respect, dedication and sincerity of heart, as you would to the High King. ⁶Stop the bad habit of attending to your duties only when you are being watched, like sycophants or brownnosers do. Instead, perform your profession or occupation with the dedication of all your soul, exactly like you would if you were an employee or subordinate officer of the High King Himself, since you now realize that your present vocation, whatever it is, forms an integral part of God's plan for building your lifework.

⁷Approach doing your job with the same good mind-set that you would have if the Commander in Chief Himself was your boss or superior officer instead of your actual human superiors. ⁸You should develop this consistent frame of mind toward your vocational relationships since you now realize that when any of you does a good job in their present vocational life – whatever it is – for the Commander in Chief, that person will receive the reward of a good job from the Commander in Chief during the Kingdom era, regardless of even whether they were a slave or a free person during their mortal lives.

⁹To those of you who are leaders, whether you are employers or superior officers in the civil or military service, I would say this: You must

also perform your responsibilities with the same good mind-set towards your subordinates. Give up the bad habit most leaders fall into of using fear to motivate their subordinates by threatening or intimidating them. You should do this because you now realize that you have the same Commander in Chief in Heaven that they do, and that because He is completely impartial, you will not be able to use your rank or office to gain any kind of favorable treatment when He evaluates your own lives and leadership skills.

You Can Prevail Over the Evil Spiritual Forces that Will Attack You in Your Efforts to Be Peacemakers for God Only by Becoming Career Spiritual Soldiers

[10]Finally, my dear colleagues, I must bring this Treatise to a conclusion by alerting you that you must continually strengthen yourselves spiritually. You must make a habit of doing this by constantly availing yourselves of the Commander in Chief's aid, and of His mastery of the angelic military forces He can and will employ to assist you in your quest to discover and accomplish your lifework. [11]Equip yourselves with the spiritual "body armor," together with its complement of personal weaponry, supplied to you by God. You must do this in order to become strong enough to stand up to the various plots and schemes of the "Predator" – the Devil – to entrap you and destroy your lives. In fact, you must make the decision to become career "spiritual" soldiers.

[12]You must do this because ultimately, the conflicts we must all face in our lives are not actually against 'flesh and blood' human beings, but are in reality against the evil angelic regimes, against the evil angelic hierarchies of authority and against the evil human government regimes that control this present historical era of darkness – or more accurately – against the evil hierarchy of spiritual beings that live in the sky (i.e., the atmosphere of the earth), which in fact manipulate and control those regimes.

[13]For this reason, you all must equip yourselves by taking up and putting on the full spiritual "body armor" and spiritual "military weapons" provided by God, in order that He may make you strong enough to endure this historical era during which limited authority to control and shape events has been temporarily granted to the Evil One. By doing so, you will be able to accomplish your lifework completely, and prevail over him.

Strap on The "Sword-Belt" of Discovering Truth, Put On The "Body Armor" of Justice and Lace Up The "Special Forces Boots" for The Long March Required to Be a Peacemaker for God

[14]You must therefore equip yourselves to never give up by first putting around yourselves the "sword-belt" of the commitment to always discover the truth – especially what is true in your own life – followed by putting on

the "body armor" of being dedicated to do not only what is legally right, but also ethically right.

¹⁵Moreover, be sure you lace up the "military boots" of peace tightly on your feet. You must mentally prepare yourselves for the fact that your life will resemble a long and oftentimes frustrating and tedious march that will be required to achieve God's ultimate objective of bringing His good news into people's lives. The goal of His good news is ultimately to enable people to forgive each other, reconcile with each other and to make living in peacefulness with each other available to people who have formerly lived in hatred and conflict their entire lives.

PROTECT YOURSELF WITH THE "SHIELD" OF FAITH, PUT ON THE "HELMET" OF RESCUE TO CONQUER YOUR FEAR OF LEADERSHIP AND WIELD THE "SWORD" OF GOD'S SPOKEN WORDS GUIDED BY HIS SPIRIT

¹⁶Above all, you must all raise up the "shield" of faith, by which you all, acting together, will be able to extinguish all of the flaming arrow volleys of enticement and temptation to do what is morally wrong that will be incessantly launched by the Evil One against your power to make ethical decisions.

¹⁷In addition, you must put on the "helmet" of rescue to give you the assurance that God will protect you from attacks on your life and from the fears and blackmail that will inevitably come against you in your role of spiritual leadership.

Finally, you must pick up and and become trained in the discipline of wielding the "sword" of the Spirit, which involves gaining experience and eventual mastery of the skillful and appropriate use of the spoken word of God.

MAINTAIN AN EFFECTIVE "COMMAND AND CONTROL" SYSTEM OF DISCIPLINED DIRECT COMMUNICATION WITH GOD

¹⁸You must always maintain direct communication with God – both by means of respectful requests for information and perspective from Him, as well as by lobbying, petitioning and making official appeals to Him to act in your own behalf and in behalf your colleagues. In your communications with God, allow yourself to become sensitive to being directed by the Spirit, who will always guide you with an appropriate sense of proportion, focus you upon what is truly important, lead you to genuine opportunities, enable you to sift out in what is relevant and be sensitive to what time and people you should invest your efforts in, who you should cooperate with, what consequences you should expect, and in what instances you should act – on occasion even to the point of spending sleepless nights in vigilant communication with God, watching with all diligent devotion in

accordance with the lobbying, petitions and applications which concern the best interests of all of His specially selected recruits.

¹⁹I would also ask you to make requests to God and lobby Him for His favor in my behalf also, in order that He might give me good reasoning, sound and persuasive logical arguments, and that I might use the right words whenever I open my mouth to speak in public, that I may do so openly and freely, in order that I might continue to make known God's formerly "Top Secret" plan, namely, the marvelous offer of His Kingdom-inheritance to others. ²⁰I ask you to do this because I need His help especially now, during this period of my confinement and trial, in order that I would be able to speak as a true ambassador should; freely, openly and with with courage and conviction, as it is necessary for me to speak.

SELECT FRIENDS AND MESSENGERS WHO HAVE A POSITIVE, LOVING CONTENTED, CHEERFUL, FAITHFUL AND ENCOURAGING ATTITUDE

²¹⁻²²And now, in order that you all might be made aware of how things are going concerning me – specifically, how I am managing and getting along – Tychicus, my esteemed colleague and faithful envoy in all assignments given him by our Commander in Chief, will bring you all up-to-date about my affairs. I am sending him to you all along with this Treatise for the following purpose, namely, in order that you may know how things are going with us and that he might encourage your hearts, because he is such a positive, loving, contented, cheerful and positive person.

MAY THE GRACIOUSNESS OF YOUR IMMORTAL KINGDOM PERSONA COME TO DISTINGUISH YOUR MORTAL PERSONALITY ALSO

²³My desire for you all, my dear and loyal colleagues, is that your lives would be characterized by peacefulness and selfless love, together with faithfulness – all of which will come from God the Father and our Commander in Chief Jesus, the future High King. ²⁴May the graciousness of our Commander in Chief Jesus, the future High King, be with you in your present lives – Who will ultimately be with all of His dear and loyal colleagues in immortality. May you all recognize, heartily agree with and live according to the truths I have written to you in this, my final and conclusive Treatise.

EPHESIANS
PAUL'S CONCLUSIVE TREATISE

A New Extended Interpretive and Expositional Translation

Into

Professional (Non-Ecclesiastical)
Contemporary (Non-Medieval)
American (Non-British)
English

1

The "Top Secret" Plan Declassified

Paul's Comprehensive, Conclusive Treatise: Its Authentic Commission, Distinguished Service and Guiding Demeanor ♦ *Beginning at the End: The Inauguration Ceremony of the High King and the Kingdom of His Future World* ♦ *God's Motive for Allocating Shares for Us in His Future Kingdom is His Love for Us* ♦ *God's Kingdom Apprenticeship Program: Five Present Benefits that Supply the Capital and Equipment Required* ♦ *The First Benefit: Resurrection – His Guaranteed Return upon the Redemption of His Investment in Us* ♦ *The Second Benefit: God's "Top Secret" Investment Plan Declassified – His Forgiveness of Our Debt, His Deposits into New High Interest Bearing Accounts for Us, and His Offer to Us to Fill New Positions in His Administration* ♦ *The Third Benefit: He Has Bequeathed An Inheritance to Those Who Aspire for It and Qualify for It in Advance* ♦ *The Fourth Benefit: He Has Specially Selected and Sealed Our Life Plan from which We Can Build our New Lifework* ♦ *The Fifth Benefit: He Has Executed the Earnest Money Contract and Paid the Down Payment on Our Inheritance* ♦ *Paul's Planning: His Request that God Recruit Sufficient Trainees to Form a Lifework Apprenticeship Council, Composed of Members Dedicated to Mutually Assist Each Other Recognize and Realize the Lifework of Each.*

PAUL'S COMPREHENSIVE, CONCLUSIVE TREATISE: ITS AUTHENTIC COMMISSION, DISTINGUISHED SERVICE AND GUIDING DEMEANOR

I, PAUL,[1] have been appointed by Jesus, the High King of the future world, to be His High Emissary[2] during the upcoming era of history that will precede its inauguration. He Himself commissioned me to this appointment, in order that I might programmatically articulate the specific provisions of His divine directives within the comprehensive scope of the entirety of God's official program for the immediately upcoming era.

God the Father has entrusted this far-reaching task to Jesus to carry out from His present heavenly office prior to His return to the earth. As such, He has now directed me to complete one of the final but most important tasks of my commission, namely, to put into writing a final, authoritative and definitive Treatise, the purpose of which is to make His master plan for future history absolutely clear to you all, the members of His Lifework Apprenticeship Councils.[3]

To be more precise, His intention in having me write this definitive Treatise is to provide a comprehensive and authoritative guideline for you all to use for spiritual teaching, training, growing, maturing and ultimately progressing to the standpoint from which each one of you might have the opportunity to discover, undertake and accomplish your unique lifework for Him. By doing so, He will employ each one of you during your mortal lives to make a significant, meaningful and valuable contribution to human history. In addition, you will go on to qualify yourselves for special appointment as His colleagues – immortal members of His Kingdom Council – in the governing body through which Jesus will administrate the future worldwide Empire that God will inaugurate for Him upon His return.

As I will explain in this Treatise, becoming qualified for appointment to this Kingdom Council will necessarily entail the difficult and disciplined training program required for developing the character qualities essential for working together harmoniously in such a unique group. In fact, this august assembly will be the first and only one of its kind to ever exist in the history of the world, whose members He will gather together from out of all the generations yet to come, from now until His return. It will be made up of wise, mature and capable leaders, who will have proved themselves trustworthy during their present lives for His use in governing the future world.

The provisions of this Treatise are to be implemented and remain in effect during the upcoming era, in which Jesus will organize and lead all of His Lifework Apprenticeship Councils until His return to take up His role of High Kingship. He has therefore directed me to write this Treatise specifically to you all, the team of recruits He has selected for special service[4] who now live in Ephesus, as a *paradigm* or *prototype* for all of the additional Lifework Apprenticeship Councils that He will bring into existence in the upcoming era.

Consequently, I am addressing this Treatise not only to you novices, but especially to you veterans who have already distinguished yourselves by your dedicated and dependable service to our future High King,[5] Jesus. I am focusing upon you veterans because the significant experience you have gained over the last eleven years[6] (both under my direct supervision of your training for three years, as well as the subsequent development of your leadership skills since then) will prove invaluable in putting the provisions of this Treatise into practice. I expect you to lead the way by implementing its provisions first in and among yourselves, and then among your new recruits and trainees.

2Accordingly, I greet you all with the sincere hope and expectation that as you read, reflect upon and then put the provisions of this Treatise into action, that the two principal and overarching spiritual character qualities of *graciousness* and *peaceful good-naturedness of spirit* would hallmark your lives. Both of these character qualities come from both God our Father as well as from our present Commander in Chief,[7] Jesus, the High King of the future world. Because of this, you all should aspire to have these two character qualities continually grow throughout the whole process of your training program, to become the predominate spiritual qualities that serve to "bookend" all of the other qualities of personality that should also emerge and eventually become habitual characteristics in your lives and demeanor.

BEGINNING AT THE END: THE INAUGURATION CEREMONY OF THE HIGH KING AND THE KINGDOM OF HIS FUTURE WORLD

³I will embark on this Treatise by stating and then briefly explaining my opening theme, and then developing it further in a more programmatic and comprehensive way. My opening theme focuses specifically upon the special, unique event that God the Father, together with our Commander in Chief, Jesus, will share with each other and with us – not at the beginning – but at the *conclusion* of this present upcoming era. That is to say, I think the best perspective to start with is to view the end from the beginning.

At the specific divine ceremony that will in fact culminate this present era, God, considered especially in His unique role of being the Father of our present Commander in Chief, Jesus, the High King of the future world, has chosen for Himself at that formal occasion, the role of being both Jesus' (and our) "Eulogizer," or "Keynote Speaker."[8] Allow me to elaborate on the meaning and significance of the unique relationship that God Father desires to emphasize by choosing the role of being the "Eulogizer" of Jesus (and of us) upon this special occasion.

When Jesus finally returns to the earth from heaven, He must at that time transition from the role of executing His present duties and responsibilities there, and assume His new role and responsibilities here as High King of the future world. Throughout the history of God's people, it has been customary for fathers, during an inheritance ceremony near the end of their lives, to appoint their sons to their respective inherited responsibilities in an official, dignified public speech. In this address, the father recounts the good deeds and meritorious actions of his sons as the basis upon which they are to receive their respective appointments in carrying on the leadership responsibilities over the family estate.[9] The father does this for the explicit purpose of publicly transferring the legitimacy their sons will need in order to rightfully lead and exercise authority over their inherited estates.

In the same way, on the day that God invests Jesus into His new office as High King of the earth, He will also deliver a "Keynote Address," or inaugural speech, acting in His role as Jesus' Father. In this speech, He will recount the superlative goodness and the incomparable merit of the unique and unparalleled sacrificial achievements that Jesus accomplished for our benefit. God will do this to fully endorse and officially establish the *legitimacy* and rightfulness of Jesus' appointment to begin His one thousand year reign[10] as High King of the earth. When God has completed this speech, He will have fully delegated all regal authority and appointment powers to Jesus.

Whereupon, Jesus, acting in His new role as High King, will then begin His own inaugural acceptance speech, in which He will also feature public, enthusiastic affirmation of each of our good, meritorious and self-sacrificial acts performed for His sake. His public recognition of actions that we have done for Him that are worthy of commendation will form the basis of His proclamation of the kingdom-inheritances He will reward each of us with as we begin the performance of our roles and responsibilities in the new world.

The reason that I have chosen this particular theme to begin this Treatise is because its inevitable implications reach into the deepest parts of our lives, and can revolutionize our understanding of who we really are, why we are here, and what our ultimate destiny is. I would like to briefly explain this theme in an introductory way, and then develop its specific features in further detail at the appropriate places in the Treatise that follows.

In the most precise and accurate sense, God is the only eternal being that can be truly comprehended as a "being," because He always "is" everything He is meant to be. In fact, this is what His personal name in the Hebrew Old Testament means. "Yahweh" means "The One Who Always Is."[11] This means that although we customarily call ourselves human "beings," when we say this we are only speaking by way of analogy. This is so because even though we regularly describe ourselves and our activities by who we "are" and what we want to "be," it is actually the case that we *never* "are" all that we could "be" in the complete and final sense. With this in mind, although it might seem a bit awkward at first, it is more accurate to think of God as the only One Who really "is" an actual "being," and to think of ourselves not as human "beings," but rather as human *"becomings."*

It therefore follows that since God is an eternal being, He is actually experiencing the enjoyment of this special reward ceremony in the continual and undiluted clarity of the full and intense reality of meaning, which is always present to Him. Indeed, how could He not? Furthermore, since we are quasi-eternal-temporal (partially eternal, partially temporal) "becomings" (only God is an actual "being," *per se*), God has given us the power to actually enter into the adventure of this eternal experience – which from our perspective still lies in the future – and to "bring" it, as it were, *into our present lives*. We can experience this wonderful transformation by simply allowing Him to "transport," or *mediate*, our future mature personalities (which already exist from His eternal perspective) into our present experience *by faith* – that is to say – by simply believing, or (to state it more precisely) *expecting* that He will do it.

From our frame of reference, we will necessarily experience this divine "conveyance" or *mediation* of our future mature selves into our present immature selves as a *transformational process* or *journey*. This is because, from our limited perspective as quasi-eternal-temporal "becomings," we can only experience the truth of eternal realities as we exercise the expectational power God has given us in order to appropriate His mediation of our mature future selves into our present lives.

It is only through the appropriating process of applying and practicing the spiritual *disciplines* that I will lay out in this Treatise that the Spirit will shape them into spiritual *habits* in our present lives. By forming them into habits, we can cause them to eventually grow within us to the extent that they will be transformed into actual spiritual attitudes, thoughts, demeanors and behaviors that we no longer experience as mediated, external, rigid, foreign and alien to us, but rather as *immediate, internal, familiar* and *at home* in us.

4It is in fact precisely for the supreme goal of this future inaugural event, namely the creation of the most mature government in history – the Millennial Kingdom – that God has made it His priority to especially select[12] us. He has specially selected us in order to deliberately train us to be on the team of His High King's most trusted and confidential associates prior to His founding[13] of any of the organized, civilized governments of the future world.[14] This is a priority for Him, because His desire is that we would be able to stand beside the High King on that great day to receive our millennial appointments of responsibility based on his wise awareness that we will need to begin our leadership duties in a legitimate way.

He knows that our legitimacy to lead others can only come from acquiring an honorable reputation, together with an unassailable résumé of accomplishments that we will have achieved in the course of the execution of our specific apprenticeship assignments. He will give us the opportunity to carry out these assignments under His supervision and direction during the course of our present lives prior to the Kingdom's commencement.

GOD'S MOTIVE FOR ALLOCATING SHARES FOR US IN HIS FUTURE KINGDOM IS HIS LOVE FOR US

⁵God's motive in planning this grand future for you is His *love* for you all. In fact, motivated by that love,[15] God has (astonishingly!) situated you all, the western ethnic races and nations foreign to Judaism that lie north and west of the Mediterranean Sea (who, ironically, might seem at first glance to be the least promising of candidates), at the *very center* of His recruitment efforts for this great inheritance plan. In fact, has He pre-surveyed[16] the geographic spread, range and specific sequence of ethnic and political boundaries through which Jesus, the future High King of the earth, will recruit you, adopt you as His own sons, and then train you to be His own particular brand of mature leaders to hold the offices of His future government. In addition, He has also pre-financed all of the material and human capital that are crucial to assure the growth of His colossal investment in you. Furthermore, because of the inexorable determination and resolve of His will, there can be no doubt that God's momentous plan will ultimately succeed.

⁶In doing this, God's goal is and has always been that the surpassing value of His wonderful love and magnificent graciousness for us should come into full view at His Appearing,[17] – that it should ultimately transpire openly and completely in history. He will bring this about in order that we should have the opportunity and privilege to recognize and then publicly and universally appreciate, acknowledge and honor Him for accomplishing this awe-inspiring plan that He has graciously conferred upon us through the specific agency of Jesus, the One Whom He loves best.

GOD'S KINGDOM APPRENTICESHIP PROGRAM: FIVE PRESENT BENEFITS THAT SUPPLY THE CAPITAL AND EQUIPMENT REQUIRED

⁷By demonstrating how much He loves us through Jesus, the One He loves best, God has made the following five benefits fully available to us. Through the direct agency of our future High King, we can presently possess and make full use of these benefits in our lives *right now*. I will now elaborate on the benefits God's love has secured for us by employing some common business concepts we all use in our everyday experience in commerce and industry, in the following extended economic metaphor.[18]

THE FIRST BENEFIT: RESURRECTION – HIS GUARANTEED RETURN UPON THE REDEMPTION OF HIS INVESTMENT IN US

The first of these benefits we now have because of His love for us is "redemption."[19] When one wishes to make a greater return on the currency in common circulation than loaning it out at interest, one can "invest" it by using it to purchase real estate, stock in a company, or a mutual fund of various company stocks bundled together. They do this with the expectation that it will yield a greater return on their investment in the future. After an extended period of time during which the real estate, stock or fund grows in value, they "redeem" it for a figure much more valuable than the original invested amount.

In the same way, Jesus "purchased" our mutual (but mortal) bodies with the valuable "currency" of the bloody, substitutionary death of His own body on the cross. This "purchase" marked His initial "investment" in us. He then "redeemed" this "investment," for which He received not only a much more valuable immortal, resurrected body of His own, but in addition, secured our actual claim to receive our own future resurrected bodies, in and through which we will perform our duties for Him in His future Kingdom administration.

THE SECOND BENEFIT: GOD'S "TOP SECRET" INVESTMENT PLAN DECLASSIFIED – HIS FORGIVENESS OF OUR DEBT, HIS DEPOSITS INTO NEW HIGH INTEREST BEARING ACCOUNTS FOR US, AND HIS OFFER TO US TO FILL THE NEW POSITIONS IN HIS ADMINISTRATION

The second of these benefits that His love has secured for us is His "forgiveness."[20] Wealthy creditors can and sometimes do "forgive" the debts of people that owe them large amounts of money. When they do this, they release both themselves and the debtor that owes them the money (which often grows to be so large that the pitiful wretch can never hope to repay it) from the emotional anger, guilt and estrangement both of them come to feel over the matter.

In the same way, all of us piled up an enormous "debt" to God by persistently taking willful and deliberate detours, which sidetracked[21] us from finding the right road He planned for us to follow in life. We estranged ourselves from God because we refused to pay the enormous debt we owed him. He was angry with us, and we felt guilty from being hopelessly in debt to Him.

However, Jesus voluntarily "assumed our debt" to God when God unleashed the anger that He harbored toward us upon Jesus, when He died on the cross. Because of this, God can and has "forgiven" our enormous indebtedness to Him, and therefore has released us from the emotional estrangement, anger and resentment that He formerly held against us due to our debt. As a result, Jesus has also released us from our estrangement from God caused by the guilt and fear we felt from being in debt to Him.

Liberation from this emotional estrangement between God and us carries with it several other extremely beneficial consequences. Because God has now removed the emotional barrier between us, He can and now has graciously "deposited" the "riches" of a set of new and unique spiritual abilities into a special "investment account" within our minds. 8Moreover, God has not only "deposited" these new spiritual abilities into an "investment account" in our minds, He also causes these abilities to continue to grow with "compound interest" that result in astonishing "rates of return,"[22] in that we can now grow rapidly in two especially valuable spiritual skills.

The first of these skills in which He enables us to rapidly gain proficiency is in all modes of knowledge, but most especially in the kind of knowledge that makes it possible for us to become competent, then gain mastery, then achieve superior leadership ability in living human life skillfully, especially in the ethical and political arenas.[23]

The second of these skills is that of becoming sensitive to what is most important in other peoples' lives. This new sensitivity enables us to reflect upon what is going on in the lives of others with increasing discernment, and to feel the proper emotions and have the right disposition about them. This sense of balance enables us to gain an understanding from which we can respond and behave toward them from the appropriate perspective and with the right sense of proportion. The result of thinking about others in this way is that we can grow rapidly in our overall comprehension and ability to make sound judgments and decisions and to become proactive, purposeful and intentional in our abilities to plan and then follow through on right courses of action.[24]

9God has given us these two new mental capabilities because He knows we will need them. We will need them because God has now unveiled, and accordingly expects us to comprehend fully, all of the essential specifics of His official plan to recruit and to train us to establish a future just, good and honorable government over the entire world at the end of this present historical era.

This official plan, which I briefly introduced above, has until only very recently been classified by God as "Top Secret."[25] However, at this unique point in this present era, God has commissioned me as His chief Spokesman to *declassify* and make the full scope and extent of this great plan completely clear. He expects nothing less than that I, as well as all of you, should broadcast it, fully explain it, and recruit and train others to do so with the same inexorable determination and resolve with which Jesus Himself intentionally presented it originally to Israel during His first visit to earth from heaven.

¹⁰The overall scope of the plan, in summary, is this: God intends to establish a completely new governmental system and administration[26] immediately following the fulfillment of history as we know it. The main feature of this new government that will radically distinguish it from all of the prior human governments of history will be that the imperfections and inadequacies within all of those former institutions, enterprises, municipalities, states and nations will finally be reconciled and resolved.

God will then reorganize them under the complete and absolute authority of His designated future High King over the entire earth. He will enact, implement and accomplish the scope and extent of His authority through the agency of His organization of resurrected, immortal and mature human administrators, who He recruited, trained, proved and qualified during their mortal lives. Through them, the High King's authority will extend with complete and ubiquitous range throughout not only all the governments that will be newly formed on the earth, but also through this same human administration, throughout the organization of remaining loyal angels and spirits that God has charged with the operation of the Universe.

The Third Benefit: He has Bequeathed An Inheritance to Those Who Aspire for it and Qualify for it in Advance

¹¹The third great benefit that His love has secured for us is that He has granted us the opportunity to be included in this select group of the High King's future administration because He has bequeathed to us a genuine, bona fide "inheritance"[27] in His future Kingdom. Like any well conceived inheritance plan, God, at this unique moment in history, following detailed examination and deliberation over numerous purposes and proposals carefully considered with His High King in their Eternal Council, is now fully and publicly stating, publishing and enacting[28] Their mutually agreed upon "joint venture."

They have pre-surveyed the new worldwide geographical and political scope of the positions and offices that will need to be filled. They have also pre-financed Their treasury department, including the funding of all of the capital resources that the members of the High King's administration will have at their disposal to carry out their assigned responsibilities. Their duties will include building and maintaining the new cities and infrastructures that they will inevitably plan and construct to create His new Society, and promote public commerce and welfare in it. Furthermore, God will execute this inheritance plan with the same thoroughness and justice that have always characterized His actions in accomplishing His purposes throughout history.

¹²God meticulously, deliberately and thoroughly has selected those of us who have placed all our hopes in His inheritance plan before[29] it ultimately appears in history to be His special appointees. To reiterate for a second time what I have already mentioned above, the reason He has done this is that, upon its execution, we should be the first to enjoy the opportunity and privilege to recognize, and then publicly acknowledge, appreciate, celebrate, and honor His designated High King when He finally does appear in history to inaugurate His reign.

THE FOURTH BENEFIT: HE HAS SPECIALLY SELECTED AND SEALED OUR LIFE PLAN FROM WHICH WE CAN BUILD OUR NEW LIFEWORK

¹³God's love has secured a fourth amazing benefit for all of you. When you heard the truthful[30] report that I have outlined above – namely, this wonderful news[31] that is actually able to rescue and then deliver[32] you from a living a meaningless life – and believed it, the Specially Selecting Spirit[33] officially and legally "sealed" each of your inheritance plans. He is the one who uniquely selected each of you for each specific role that God and His High King have planned for the future Kingdom. This supernatural act of sealing[34] your lifework "plans," once officially certified by God in this way, renders it *legally and actually possible* for each of you to read, decipher, comprehend and ultimately "build" your lifework from the sealed "plans" that His Specially Selecting Spirit has issued.

THE FIFTH BENEFIT: HE HAS EXECUTED THE EARNEST MONEY CONTRACT AND PAID THE DOWN PAYMENT ON OUR INHERITANCE

¹⁴The fifth amazing benefit that His love has secured for us is that in addition to the Specially Selecting Spirit being the "seal" on the "plan" of our lifework, the same divine Spirit is also the "earnest money" of the "inheritance"[35] that He has specially designed for each of our lives. Allow me to elaborate further on what it means to represent God's Specially Selecting Spirit as the "earnest money" of God's inheritance plan.

God wants each of us to experience a limited, but still very real and powerful portion of the ultimate supernatural capabilities and personality characteristics that we will ultimately possess in a complete and mature way during the Kingdom Age. The Spirit has therefore enabled us to incorporate and actually put into use *in our present lives* a small portion of our *future supernatural personalities*. For example, once a person places a down payment or earnest money[36] towards a new house or a business they plan to purchase, they then begin to look forward with greater anticipation to the day they can move in. In the same way, God's Spirit has given each of us unique but limited supernatural abilities in our present lives, so that we should look forward with an even greater sense of excitement to the "redemption" of our mortal bodies into our immortal, resurrected bodies on the day He inaugurates His future Kingdom. In addition, these abilities should motivate us to look forward to the "redemption" of the other spiritual "interest bearing accounts"[37] that God has been making into our personalities during our present lives.

Finally, I must again reemphasize for the third time that the reason God has done this is so that we all might be the first to enjoy the opportunity and privilege to recognize, and then publicly acknowledge, appreciate, celebrate, and honor His designated High King when He finally does appear in history to inaugurate His reign.

PAUL'S PLANNING: HIS REQUEST THAT GOD RECRUIT SUFFICIENT TRAINEES TO FORM A LIFEWORK APPRENTICESHIP COUNCIL, COMPOSED OF MEMBERS DEDICATED TO MUTUALLY ASSIST EACH OTHER RECOGNIZE AND REALIZE THE LIFEWORK OF EACH

[15]Now, I must say more about the reason why I am writing this final and comprehensive Treatise of God's Inheritance plan to you Ephesians. The very first time I received news not only of your faith in our Commander in Chief, Jesus, but also of the self-sacrificial love that you all have for all of His specially selected recruits, my eighteen month assignment in Corinth due to the expressed commission of our Commander in Chief from heaven[38] had come to an end. By that time, groups of these recruits had begun to spring up in most of the major metropolitan areas in Asia, Macedonia and Greece. However, at that time, I was returning to Jerusalem to fulfill a solemn promise I had previously obligated myself to God to complete.[39] You recall that because of that obligation, I could not remain among you at that time, even though I desired to do so.

[16]It was then that I began to recognize that Ephesus was the next major city that our Commander in Chief would commission me to teach in for an extended period of time (and in fact, to make it my headquarters for all of Asia).[40] Although I could not begin my stay in Ephesus at that time due to my prior commitment to attend one of Israel's official religious ceremonies in Jerusalem, I was extremely thankful, excited and eager to know that our Commander in Chief had selected Ephesus as my next center of operations.

Realizing this, I knew that I must begin to lay the groundwork for an important and far-reaching enterprise there. I did this by making it a new part of my daily discipline and routine to deliberately think about, reflect upon and begin to plan my overall strategy to help you.[41] I also began to ask and continually seek information, advice and direction[42] from our

Commander in Chief not only about what He would have me do there upon my return, but also about how He should begin preparing your hearts and minds for the things He wanted to accomplish in, among and with you all.

¹⁷As a result of these spiritual reflections, I resolved that I would make it part of my regular schedule to ask God to accomplish the following four things for you in preparation for my return to Ephesus from Jerusalem. First, as I explained above, God – acting in his upcoming specific role as the Father – will be the One who will endorse and authenticate our present Commander in Chief, Jesus, as His designated High King of the earth at His Inaugural Appearing. Accordingly, in anticipation of this wonderful future event, I asked God to give you a unique spiritual ability to gain a comprehensive understanding and appreciation of the full scope of His formerly "Top Secret" but recently unveiled[43] *inheritance plan*. To accompany this understanding I also asked Him to give you the practical, and especially the ethical skills to make good, sound judgments and decisions as you implement its provisions into your lives.[44]

¹⁸The second thing that I continually asked God to give you was a new and unique spiritual ability for the "eyes" of your "heart" to "see." Do not be puzzled – I want to assure you that I am using this mixed metaphor quite deliberately. I know that the "heart" does not actually have "eyes." After all, the "mind" does not have "eyes" either, but like the "eyes," we all know that the rational power of the mind enables us to "see" the truth about things that are not actually visible. However, unlike the mind, the "heart" refers to the *ethical decision-making power of the soul* that remains distinct from the *rational decision-making power of the mind*.

Consequently, the "heart" possesses a unique capability to "see" invisible reality also, but in a different way than the mind does. Since the heart continuously generates the inclinational, moral demeanor and power to make ethical decisions, it enables us to "see" – that is, to *personally realize* – the gravity and finality of the consequences of the future reality that I am explaining to you, and to have the gravity of those consequences change the course of planning and actions for one's life. A further result of this faculty is that ultimately, the ethical decisions made by the heart cannot be successfully masked or concealed from others, as the rational decisions of the mind can.[45]

Because I know this, I asked God to spiritually enable you to realize and act upon what all of us humans, deep down, acutely hope for – that God has given to each of us a special, unique "life purpose," or *"lifework,"*[46] that He alone has designed and planned just for each of us. With this in mind, I asked God to begin to give each of you a realization of what specific and meaningful lifework He has assigned to each of you.

In addition, the third thing I constantly asked God to give you in preparation for my return was a realization and appreciation for just how extraordinarily and *exceedingly valuable* the inheritance He has planned to give us at the future Inauguration Ceremony of the High King really is. The future inheritances He will grant at the beginning of the Kingdom Age are of such surpassing value, that they far outweigh any wealth or riches that any of us could possibly conceive of in our present lives within history. Accordingly, they also bear the unique motivational incentive to encourage each of us to discover and carry out the assigned life project God has specially selected for each of us to accomplish, since doing so is a prerequisite for inheriting the full scope of our assigned responsibilities in His future Kingdom.

19-20 The fourth thing I regularly asked that God supply for you is the exceedingly great reserves of *physical, psychological, emotional and spiritual strength* He makes especially available to us who tenaciously persist in believing we can discover and accomplish our lifework for Him. God is absolutely committed to supporting us and enabling us to realize our lifework. However, because achieving it is most often accompanied by great difficulty, God will supply each of us committed to reaching it with the same kind of enormous strength He exercised in Jesus' case when, upon successfully accomplishing His own lifework for our sake, God raised Him – our future High King – from death.[47] Not only did He do that for Jesus, God then commanded His angels to transport Him from earth through lower heaven to high heaven, at which time God installed Him in His present office of being His Commander in Chief over recruiting His specially selected recruits, and then organizing and training them in His Kingdom Apprenticeship Councils.

21 Keeping this in mind, even though the road to achieving our lifework will be fraught with difficulty, God will always provide us the strength to accomplish it, because it was in exactly this same way that our future High King was promoted by God based upon the merits of Him accomplishing His own lifework. Look at it this way. God rewarded our future High King with His superlative title, which is superior to every ruler or authority[48] or position of power or leadership office, or any other authoritative title ever conferred anywhere or at any time – whether angelic[49] or human – precisely because He completely and fully achieved His own lifework for God. Because of this, God has authorized Him to use the full extent of His authority to accomplish His ends throughout the present historical era[50] as well as in the Kingdom Age which is about to appear. Therefore, God will reward us in a similar way when we believe and appropriate His plan for us to follow our future High King's example.

²²Furthermore, I want you all to realize that pursuing and accomplishing our lifework is such a high priority to God, that He has subordinated every authority structure that now exists or will exist during this present historical era (prior to the inauguration of the Kingdom) to our future High King also. God has done this so that Jesus can accomplish the top priority God has assigned Him in this era, namely, the responsibility of heading up and leading the recruiting, organizing, training and apprenticeship of all of His specially selected future administrators.

When viewed from the perspective of *being apprenticed for future Kingdom service*, His plan is to organize His specially selected recruits into groups, which He has appropriately named "Kingdom Apprenticeship Councils."[51] These Council groups are to consist of dedicated, like-minded teams of His specially selected recruits, whose members mutually focus themselves upon the task of helping each other successfully complete their ethical and spiritual preparation for their future inherited Kingdom responsibilities.

When viewed from the perspective of accomplishing God's *purpose for each of our present lives within history* prior to the High King's return, these Council groups can also be called His "Lifework Councils." From this standpoint, they are to be composed of specialized teams whose members have mutually dedicated themselves to helping each other discover and accomplish their assigned life projects during this present era of history.

²³Moreover, these newly forming "Kingdom Apprenticeship" or "Lifework" Councils are now springing up and growing everywhere, especially in Macedonia, Greece and most recently, Asia. Our Commander in Chief has now commissioned me to help establish His Council group in Rome also. I anticipate that He will continue to employ me to found further Council groups northward and westward for the remainder of my lifetime – and beyond. These specially formed Lifework Council groups are and will continue to be comprised of the members-in-training of our High King's future governmental administrative body.[52]

God's Specially Selecting Spirit will continue to recruit, and our future High King will continue to organize and supervise new Kingdom Apprenticeship Councils throughout the historical period of this present era. He will lead them to eventually locate, recruit, train and comprehensively fill[53] every single Millennial position of service that God and His designated High King have commissioned for His future Kingdom administration. In this way, He will ultimately fill all of the posts of His administration with the competent, qualified appointees who, through the agency of their apprenticeships, will have completed their respective life projects during their present lives, and by doing so, will have achieved spiritual maturity in every respect.

Notes to Extended Interpretive and Expositional Translation
Ephesians Chapter 1

[1] The individual letters used for the extended interpretive and expositional translation and footnotes presented here ("Times New Roman" font) are based on the Latin miniscule letters developed and established during the Carolingian Renaissance in the late eighth century by Charlemagne and his English Court Scholar, Alcuin. This original basic font is known as the "Carolingian miniscule" font, non-italic [the adjective "Carolingian" is derived from Latin "Carolus" referring to Charlemagne = Old French = "Charles the Great" (742?-814), Carolingian king of the Franks (768-814), and emperor of Western Europe (800-814)]. Alcuin (735?-804) was an English churchman and educator, who Charlemagne invited (781?) to his royal court at Aachen to set up a school for his kingdom, where he became the moving spirit behind the Carolingian renaissance. Alcuin encouraged the study and preservation of ancient texts and established the study of the seven liberal arts (the trivium and quadrivium), which became the educational curriculum for medieval Western Europe. Alcuin had been educated at the cathedral school of York in northern Britain by a disciple of Bede (673?-735), who was the first great English historian, and probably the most learned man in Western Europe during his own era. Bede's *Ecclesiastical History of the English Nation*, written in Latin prose, is the indispensable primary source for English history from 597 to 731. The best known of Bede's scientific treatises are those on chronology, in which he established the origin of dating the history of the world, beginning all dates from the birth of Jesus at 0 A.D. (Latin = "Anno Domini" = "in the year of our Lord" [W]), the dating system we still use today – *Columbia Encyclopedia, Sixth Edition, 2001*]. Consequently, the individual letters used to form the English words in this extended interpretive translation of Paul's Treatise to the Ephesians are the characters (developed c. 800 A.D.) currently recognized and used to phonetically pronounce the English language spoken by the great majority of professional Americans in the Contemporary era of our history (c. 2005 A.D.) .

The chapter and verse divisions now commonly accepted and used in our English tradition of the various translations of the Bible (and which will be followed in this translation in order to continue in the English historical tradition), were not used in Paul's original Greek manuscript. Chapter divisions were first introduced into a Latin text in 1205 by Stephen Langton (English Archbishop of Canterbury from 1213-1228, author of the *Magna Carta*, 1215 – see note below). He probably did this in an attempt to aid the English people in memorizing the Bible, in order to resist the edict of the King John (1167-1216, King of England from 1199-1216, younger brother of Richard I – the "Lion Heart" – and last son of Henry II and Eleanor of Aquitaine) that all written copies of the Bible be destroyed (Martin F. Tupper: *Stephan Langton, or The Days of King John*, Guildford, England: Biddles Ltd., 1858 – excellent biography of Stephen Langton, with an insightful perspective on his relationship to Robin Hood and Maid Marian, and to the central role he occupied in the writing of the *Magna Carta*). Verse divisions were first introduced into a Greek edition of Erasmus' Text published by Robert Estienne in 1551 (see note below), and introduced for the first time soon thereafter into the English edition of the New Testament published in Geneva in 1557 (see note below). Although this extended interpretive translation is presented in paragraph format, the chapter and verse divisions accepted in the English tradition of translation will be included to assist the reader as small superscripted numbers immediately prior to the sentence that begins the translation of the particular verse.

[2] ἀπόστολος, ὁ, *messenger, ambassador, envoy*, ὁ μὲν δὴ ἀ. ἐς τὴν Μίλητον ἦν Hdt.1.21; ἐς Λακεδαίμονα τριήρει ἀ. ἐγίνετο **he went off on a mission to Laced.**, Id.5.38.; **b.** commander of a naval force, Hsch. [LS]. Usual translation: "Apostle." Paul uses this word four times in this Treatise (Eph. 1:1, 2:20, 3:5 and 4:11). However, the word "apostle" is merely a transliteration of the Greek word ἀπόστολος and as such, has very little meaning in contemporary professional American English. Denotative meaning: "commissioned messenger, ambassador, envoy or naval commander." Connotative meaning and proposed translation when used by Paul: "High Emissary (of the future High King of the earth)."

[3] Paul does not use the collective name ἐκκλησία for these individual ἅγιοι until Eph. 1:22. See notes at Eph. 1:1 for proposed meaning of the individual term ἅγιος, and at Eph. 1:22 for proposed meaning of the collective term ἐκκλησία.

[4] ἅγιος – usual translation as a plural noun (ἅγιοι): "saints." Paul uses this important word nine of fifteen times with this meaning in this Treatise (1:1, 15, 18; 2:19, 3:8, 18; 4:12, 5:3, 6:18). However, the etymology of the Middle English word "saint" shows that it is merely a transliteration through Old French of the Latin word used to translate the Greek word ἅγιος = *sancire* = to make "sacred" (Middle English). Further study shows that the word "sacred" refers to something that has been set apart, dedicated or devoted exclusively to the service or use of someone, for the purpose of honoring or recognizing that person as unique and special [W]. The usual translation of the word ἅγιος when it is used as an adjective is the word "holy" (used this way 6 times – 1:4, 13; 2:21, 3:5, 4:30, 5:27). Etymological study of the word "holy" shows that is the Old English word for "wholeness" = "*hālig*," from "whole = OE "*hāl*," from which the connotative meaning of the word "health" = OE "*hælth*" is derived [W]. The denotative meaning of ἅγιος in Greek is: "one thing specially selected or separated out from a group of things in order to set it apart for special use." The British translators, who were well trained in Latin, probably used an English transliteration of the Latin word *sancire* to make the English noun "saint," as well as the verb

"sanctify," but used the Old English adjective "wholly" (= "healthy") to translate the principle by which sacrificial animals in the Old Testament had to be selected or marked out for sacrifice. They had to be completely whole, healthy and without and kind of physical defect (whether caused congenitally, by disease, or by injury); i.e., they had to be "wholly," i.e., "healthy," thus unifying the basic notions of the Greek word ἅγιος with the Latin word *sancire* with the Old English word "wholly" ("holy"). To illustrate this philological development, one of the several passages in the Septuagint from which the above line of reasoning can be deduced is Deuteronomy 15:19:

> Deut. 15:19 Πᾶν πρωτότοκον, ὃ ἐὰν τεχθῇ ἐν τοῖς βουσίν σου καὶ ἐν τοῖς προβάτοις σου, τὰ ἀρσενικά, **ἁγιάσεις** κυρίῳ τῷ θεῷ σου· οὐκ ἐργᾷ ἐν τῷ πρωτοτόκῳ μόσχῳ σου καὶ οὐ μὴ κείρῃς τὸ πρωτότοκον τῶν προβάτων σου· 20 ἔναντι κυρίου φάγῃ αὐτὸ ἐνιαυτὸν ἐξ ἐνιαυτοῦ ἐν τῷ τόπῳ, ᾧ ἐὰν ἐκλέξηται κύριος ὁ θεός σου, σὺ καὶ ὁ οἶκός σου. 21 **ἐὰν δὲ ᾖ ἐν αὐτῷ μῶμος, χωλὸν ἢ τυφλὸν ἢ καὶ πᾶς μῶμος πονηρός,** οὐ θύσεις αὐτὸ κυρίῳ τῷ θεῷ σου·

> Deut. 15:19 "From all firstborn animals that shall be born from your herds of cattle and from your flocks of sheep, you shall **specially select and set apart** every male to the Lord your God. You shall do no work with your firstborn calf, nor shall you ever shear your firstborn sheep. 20 You shall eat it year after year (upon sacrificing it first) to the Lord your God at the place that He shall select, you together with those in your household. 21 *But if there is any natural defect in it, e.g., if it is lame or blind, or if it is defective in any other way, e.g., due to an injury or a disease of any kind,* you shall not sacrifice it to the Lord your God" [transl. – GWC].

Thus the word "holy" = "wholly" = "healthy," which describes the *effect* rather than the *cause*. Proposed translation of ἅγιος as a plural noun: "specially selected recruits," as a plural adjective: "specially selected" (High Emissaries – Eph. 3:5), and as a singular adjective: "Specially Selecting (Spirit)" – Eph. 1:13; 4:30).

⁵ χριστός, ή, όν,...*II. of persons, anointed,...2. esp. of the Kings of Israel,* ὁ χ. Κυρίου ib. *1Ki.*24.7, cf. *Ps.*17(18).51; also τῷ χ. μου Κύρῳ *Is.*45.1;...in NT, ὁ χ. *the Messiah, Ev.Matt.*2.4, etc.; ὁ χ. Κυρίου *Ev.Luc.*2.26; *then used as pr. n. of Jesus,* Ἰησοῦς χ. *Ev.Matt.*1.1, etc.; Ἰησοῦς ὁ λεγόμενος χ. ib.16 [LS]. Usual translation: "Christ." Paul uses this important word to refer to Jesus in His future Kingly office 46 times in this Treatise. The word "Christ" is a transliteration of the word **χριστός**, not a translation of it. The Greek word **χριστός** is the translation of the Hebrew word "Messiah" = "Anointed One" = "High King." Although the Greek word for "king" is βασιλεύς, Paul employs the words **χριστός** and βασιλεύς as synonymous terms in 1 Tim. 6:14-15, where he says, "until the appearing of our Commander in Chief (κυρίος), Jesus, the *High King* (**Χριστός**), Whom He [God] will inaugurate as His own invested, happy, and only sovereign *King* over all kings (ὁ **Βασιλεὺς** τῶν βασιλευόντων) and Commander in Chief over all commanders (Κύριος τῶν κυριευόντων)..." The founders of America deliberately crafted our government to exclude the office of a king due to their conviction that it was an inherently corruptible office (from their historical experience of great majority of European kings). However, although the

American government is not based upon the political principles of a consitutional monarchy, Paul clearly indicates in his writings that the government of the future world will be a monarchy characterized by ubiquitous justice and peace, and that Jesus will be High King of that world. Therefore, the proposed translation of χριστός is: "High King of the future world."

[6] Paul does not disclose his own historical situation or circumstances until Eph. 3:1. See note at Eph. 3:1 for a summary of the main events in Paul's life and a chronology of Paul's journeys that provide a contextual setting for this Treatise. For a more detailed chronology of Paul's life, see the extended note on the "helmet" of rescue (from the fear of threats and attacks as leaders) at Eph. 6:17.

[7] κυρίος – Usual translation: "Lord." This important word is used by Paul 28 times in this Treatise, 26 to refer to Jesus in His present leadership role of being our legitimate and authoritative Divine Leader in heaven; and twice to refer to human leaders in Eph. 6:5 and 6:9, in which it could be translated as "leaders, managers, business owners, bosses, entrepreneurs, military officers and civil or political officials." The British word "Lord" has been (and still is) an excellent translation of this word for British law, custom, and culture. However, it is virtually irrelevant in American law, custom and culture. The word "lord" is derived from Old English feudal law, where it referred to the owner of a manor or castle whose chief responsibility was to guard the food grown on the land surrounding the castle, and thus the lives of the serfs that lived on the land surrounding the central castle. Etymologically, the word "lord" is Middle English: *lord, lōverd*, from Old English *hlāford*, from *hlāf* = "bread, loaf" + *weard* = *ward* = "guard, keeper" [W]. In Greek, a κυρίος was the "supreme ruler or leader of a political city-state (and later, a hegemony of several city-states) who held and exercised legitimate, supreme and decisive authority, power, and sovereignty over the people and affairs of that city-state or hegemony" [LS]. For this reason, although it is fairly easy to translate the Greek word κυρίος into the British word "lord," it is rather difficult to translate κυρίος into contemporary professional American English, because as a society we have to a great extent integrated the political concept of division, distribution and thus dilution of power in the cultural expressions of our ways of life, more so in politics and business, and less so in the military. Thus, we do not use the word "lord" in contemporary professional American English (except in the minor compound word "landlord," which carries no meaning of superlative leadership office at all, but refers merely to a person who collects rents from rented real estate). Although Wycliffe translates the Latin word **Dominus** (Jerome's translation for the Greek word κυρίος) as "Lord," it is significant to note that he translates the Latin word **Praeceptor** (Jerome's translation for the Greek word ἐπιστάτης – used only 6 times in the New Testament, all by Luke and all referring to Jesus) as "Commander" ("Comaundoure"), as follows:

> Luke 8:23-24 (original spelling) "And while thei rowiden, he slepte. And a tempest of wynde cam doun in to the watir, and thei weren dryuun hidur and thidur with wawis,

and weren in perel. And thei camen nyy, and reisiden hym, and seiden, **Comaundoure**, we perischen. And he roos, and blamyde the wynde, and the tempest of the watir; and it ceesside, and pesibilte was maad."

Luke 8:23-24 (modern spelling) "And while they rowed, He slept. And a tempest of wind came down into the water, and they were driven hither and thither with waves, and were in peril. And they came night and raised Him and said, **Commander**, we perish! And He rose and blamed the wind and the tempest of water, and it ceased and peaceability was made."

[The Hebrew Old Testament and the Greek New Testament were first translated into "common" Latin by Jerome. Although Jerome translated the Bible into its Latin version c. A.D. 383-A.D. 405, its name ("vulgate") derives from a 13th-century reference to it as the "editio vulgata" (Lat. *vulgata editio* = "common edition"). It is the official Latin version of the Roman Catholic Church – *The Columbia Encyclopedia, Sixth Edition, 2001*. John Wycliffe inspired the first translation of the New Testament into English from the Latin Vulgate in 1388 – *Wikipedia Encyclopedia – 2005*]. In America, we still use the word "Commander" in the title "Commander in Chief," when we refer to the office of the President in his role as the supreme leader of all four branches of the military. Proposed specific translation when referring to Jesus in his present leadership role in heaven: "Commander in Chief;" or more generically, "leader."

[8] εὐλογητός, εὐλογέω, εὐλογία – usual translation: "blessed, bless, blessing." This word group is used by Paul in this Treatise only these three times, all in this one verse (Eph. 1:3). The word "blessing" is an Old English religious term for "consecrating with blood." Its etymology is as follows: Middle English *blessen*, from Old English *bletsian, blētsian, blēdsian*, from *blōd* blood; from the use of blood in consecration or sacrifice (OE "*blōd*" = "blood") [W]. In the above phrase, the Greek adjective εὐλογητός is not in the attributive position, but in the predicate position (i.e., it is an adjective used as a noun; i.e., it is a "predicate nominative"), which means it is in a complete sentence in which the Greek construction does not need the word "is," but in the English translation, the verb "is" must be supplied. Therefore, the translation is: "God (is) blessed..."; or "God (is) the Blessed (One)..." (for other such constructions in which the adjective εὐλογητός is used as a noun, see Rom. 1:25, 9:5 and Mark 14:61). However, the word "blessed" is no longer commonly used in contemporary professional American English, either as an adjective or as a noun. However, interestingly, the transliteration of the noun form of the Greek word εὐλογία is the well known English word, "eulogy," which denotatively means "good word" or "good speech (about someone)." Connotatively, the word "eulogy" is still meaningfully used in contemporary professional American English to refer to the speech given at a formal ceremony (e.g., a banquet or a funeral) in which the person officiating at the ceremony gives a formal speech that recounts the good qualities of another person who is being honored (e.g., at a banquet, usually a living person who has led a life of distinction, or in the case of a funeral, the good qualities in the life of the deceased). Therefore, the proposed translation of the word εὐλογητός when it

is used as a noun is "Eulogizer," perhaps more commonly referred to in professional English as the "Keynote Speaker" (when referring to the person giving the eulogy), and the translation of the noun εὐλογία is "eulogy," or "Keynote Address" (when referring to the speech itself). Proposed translation of this word as a verb (εὐλογέω) in this context is "to deliver a eulogy," which means, "to deliver an official, public, inaugural speech which has the proclamation of rewards for good deeds performed by others as its goal;" and as a noun in this context "inheritance proclamation (given by God at the Inaugural Ceremony of Jesus when He takes up His reign as the future High King of the earth)."

[9] See for example, Genesis Chapter 49, in which Jacob (Israel), at the end of his life, performs such a public ceremony and speech recounting the deeds and thus identifying the spiritual character that will mark the lives of each of his twelve sons (Reuben, Simeon, Levi, Judah, Zebulun, Issachar, Dan, Gad, Asher, Naphtali, Joseph and Benjamin).

[10] See Revelation 20:2, 3, 4, 5, 6, 7; in which the historical duration of the future Millennial Kingdom (see Eph. 5:5, βασιλεία = "kingdom") is specifically disclosed to be 1,000 years [emphatically – 6x!]; thus the use of the Latin word "Millennium:" etymology: from Latin *mille* thousand + *-ennium* years. **1a:** a period of 1000 years, **2a:** the thousand years mentioned in Revelation 20 during which...Christ is to reign on earth...[W]. The adjective "Millennial" (Kingdom) will be used in this translation to refer to the duration of this future Kingdom era.

[11] See Exodus 3:11-15, where God encounters Moses at the burning bush on Mount Horeb to commission him to be His messenger to Pharaoh, in order to rescue Israel out of Egypt. Moses is embarrassed, because he knows that he is obviously speaking to God, but does not know His name. So, in an indirect (and somewhat amusing) way, Moses asks God what His name is. God answers by calling Himself "Yahweh" (Hebrew: יהוה = probably pronounced יָחְוָה = the substantive Qal participle of הוה = היה = "to be"), which comes to mean, "I Am The One Who Is," per the following development:

> Exodus 3:[11] Moses said to God, "Who am I, that I should go to Pharaoh, and that I should bring forth the children of Israel out of Egypt?" [12] He said, "Certainly *I will be with you* (אֶהְיֶה עִמָּךְ = Qal Impf. 1p. sg. = lit. "I will be with you"). This will be the token to you, that I have sent you: when you have brought forth the people out of Egypt, you shall serve God on this mountain." [13] Moses said to God, "Behold, when I come to the children of Israel, and tell them, 'The God of your fathers has sent me to you;' and they ask me, 'What is his name?' What should I tell them?" [14] God said to Moses, " 'I Will Be the One Who Will Be,' " (אֶהְיֶה אֲשֶׁר אֶהְיֶה = Qal Impf. 1p. sg. = lit. " 'I Will Be the One Who Will Be' [with you]") and he said, "You shall tell the children of Israel this: " 'I Will Be' (אֶהְיֶה = Qal Impf. 1p. sg. = lit. " 'I Will Be' [with you]") has sent me to you." [15] God said moreover to Moses, "You shall tell the children of Israel this, " ' "I Am the One Who Is" (יהוה = probably pronounced "Yahweh" = יָחְוָה = the substantive Qal participle of הוה = היה = "to be," which means, "I Am The One Who Is"), the God of your fathers, the God of

Abraham, the God of Isaac, and the God of Jacob, has sent me to you.' *This is my name* forever, and this is my memorial to all generations."

[12] ἐκλέγω – *pick or single out*, Th.4.59, etc.; esp. of *soldiers, rowers*, etc., X.HG1.6.19, Pl.R.535a;...Id.Alc.l.c.; ἐκλελεγμένος *select, recondite*, Diog. Oen.23:--Med., *pick out for oneself, choose*, Hdt.1.199,3.38, D.l.c;...**2**. Lit. Crit., *select*, λ<*>ξεις καλάς D.H.Comp.3;...**II**. *levy taxes or tribute*, χρήματα παρά τινος Th.8.44; τὰς ἐπικαρπίας And. 1.92, cf. IG12.76.8 (Pass., ib.16);...*take toll of*, χαλκοῦς Thphr.Char.6.4. [LS]. Usual translation: "elect," "choose." This word is used by Paul only one time in this Treatise (here, at Eph. 1:4). From an analysis of its usage in context as well as in wider Greek literature, ἐκλέγω means to "single out, select, or choose someone or something for a special purpose." The specific "special purposes" usually in view are three in number: 1) the selection of *funds for business, economic or financial use* (e.g., "levy taxes," "charge a toll or payment"); 2) the selection of *building materials for constructing a building* (e.g.; "I lay in Zion a chief Cornerstone, selected, precious..." – 1 Pet. 2:6) and 3) the selection or singling out of *soldiers and their weapons for military purposes* (e.g., the rigorous training and selection process used by the American Military to select the elite units of its "special forces"). Paul will in fact use these precise three themes of God's "selection" of us as His "specially selected recruits" (see note on ἅγιος at Eph. 1:1) with respect to 1) business, economics and finance, 2) construction and building, and 3) the military and its weaponry; and fully develop them into the three main extended metaphors or "vehicles" through which he will explain the central message of this Treatise.

With respect to the first vehicle, that of *business, economics* and *finance*, what Paul is communicating is that God, considered in the representational image of being an "Investor" or "Venture Capitalist," has selected primarily the western barbarian peoples and ethnic groups located north and west of Judea as those to whom He will entrust the vast wealth of His "investment plan" for their preparation and training to become the future leaders of the Millennial Kingdom, not predominately Israel.

With respect to the second vehicle, that of *construction* and *building*, what Paul is communicating is that God, considered in the representational image of being a "Builder" or "Developer," has invested His vast capital and put it to work by selecting this same group in a monumental enterprise to "build" them into the "superstructure" or main "framework" of the "building" that will consist of the organization of His intimate, trustworthy confidants that will make up the core of His leadership Cabinet during the Millennial Age.

With respect to the third vehicle, that of the *military* and its *weaponry*, what Paul is communicating is that God, considered in the representational image of being a "Military Quartermaster" and the "Commanding Officer" of His vastly expensive and colossal building project will, because of its enormous value, also expend the tremendous effort necessary to select, recruit, organize, train and supply its members with the essential "military equipment" as well as the logistical, strategic and tactical military skills they will need to defend it from the inevitable attacks that will come against it, perpetrated by its bitter evil spiritual enemy, Satan himself.

Although these three main themes overlap each other somewhat in the Treatise, the main development of the extended metaphor of God as our "Investor" or "Venture Capitalist" in the area of business, economics, finance and corporate law comprises Eph. 1:3-2:10. The main symbolic concepts (approx. 37) associated with this first extended economic metaphor are as follows:

- ἐκλέγω = "to single out, select, or choose someone or something for a special purpose, such as levying taxes or charging a toll, the selection of building materials, and the selection of soldiers and their weapons" (1:4),
- κόσμος = "organized system of civilized government, organization, enterprise, or business" (1:4; 2:2, 12),
- προορίζω = "preplan, pre-mark out, pre-survey, pre-finance" (1:5, 11),
- υἱοθεσία = "adoption as a son" (1:5),
- ἀπολύτρωσις = "redemption" (1:7, 14; 4:30),
- πλοῦτος = "wealth, riches" (1:7, 18; 2:7; 3:8, 16), and πλούσιος = "rich" (2:4),
- ἄφεσις = "forgiveness of a debt" (1:7),
- περισσεύω = "to go beyond, abound" – in this context, to "compound" riches, i.e., through "interest" (1:8),
- οἰκονομία = "administration, government, economy" (1:10; 3:2, 9),
- πάροικος = "household member, cabinet member, member of an οἰκονομία" (2:19),
- κληρόω = "inherit" (1:11),
- κληρονομία = "inheritance" (1:14, 18; 5:5),
- συγκληρονόμος = "fellow heir" (3:6),
- σφραγίζω = "seal" (1:13; 4:30),
- ἀρραβών = "earnest money, down payment" (1:14),
- περιποίησις = "that which has been gained through acquisition and saved, savings account" (1:14),
- κλῆσις = "vocation, profession, job, lifework, life project" (1:18; 4:1, 4),
- ἐκκλησία = "Lifework Council, Kingdom Apprenticeship Council" (1:22; 3:10, 21; 5:23, 24, 25, 27, 29, 32),
- σῶμα = "governmental, organizational, administrative or associational body" (1:23; 2:16; 4:4, 12, 16[2x]; 5:23, 38,30),
- σύσσωμα = "fellow member of a governmental, organizational, administrative or associational body" (3:6),
- πληρόω = "fill a job position" (1:23; 4:10),
- παράπτωμα = "get sidetracked" [from one's lifework] (1:7; 2:1, 5),
- ἁμαρτία = "miss an [lifework] opportunity" (2:1),
- ἀναστρέφω = "to have one's public demeanor unwittingly formed for better or for worse by one's habitual public or co-worker associations" (2:3),
- δῶρον = "gift" (2:8); and δωρεάν = "gift" (3:7; 4:7),
- ἔργον = "work, enterprise" (2:9, 10; 4:12; 5:11),
- ξένος = "illegal alien, esp. economically, e.g., one who cannot get a job legally" (2:12, 19),
- πολιτεία = "citizenship, especially in conjunction with its accompanying economic right to work" (2:12),
- συμπολίτης = "fellow-citizen" (2:19),

- δέσμιος = "bond" (3:1; 4:1). Although the denotative meaning of this word is "prisoner" (one who is in "bondage"), it is possible that Paul is using this word as a metaphor for "Bond" in the sense of a "guarantee of the performance of a building contract," such as a Bonding Company might issue.
- συμμέτοχος = "fellow business partner" (3:6; 5:7),
- ἐπιχορηγία = "supply, provision, fortune" [emphatic form of the much more common word χορηγία = "office or λῃτουργία of a χορηγός, one who is wealthy enough to pay for the cost of the public choruses"] (4:16),
- ἐργασία = "work, trade or business in the specific sense of the organized crime surrounding those who, in despair, consign themselves to make a living or to "work" in the spheres of human vice: gambling, prostitution, drug addiction, and the violence that is inevitably committed in organized crime" (4:19),
- κοπιάω = "hard work, so as to make one exhausted by the end of the work day" (4:28),
- ἐργάζομαι = "the honest work of the manual labor of a farmer, rancher, craftsman, or blacksmith," "work at a trade or business to earn an honest living" (4:28),
- χρεία = "to gain the ability to become useful, to provide a service, especially by 'providing a service' in business or 'going into the service' in the military," (4:28, 29),
- ἐξαγοραζω = "buy up, buy out" (5:16)]."

The main section of this Treatise in which Paul uses the extended metaphor of God as our "Builder" or "Developer" in the area of the construction and building of the vital relational structures He will found and build upon throughout this historical era comprises Eph. 2:11-6:9 (see note at Eph. 2:11 for list of main concepts utilized by Paul in this extended metaphor). The main section of this Treatise in which Paul uses the extended metaphor of God as our "Military Quartermaster and Commanding Officer," in the area of the equipping us and training us to defend ourselves throughout this historical era against our spiritual enemy, Satan, comprises Paul's third and final section in Eph. 6:10-20 (see note at Eph. 6:10 for list of main concepts employed by Paul in this extended metaphor).

It is reasonable to ask the question of how Paul could have been so well acquainted and technically competent in such a wide variety of seemingly different worlds of religion, history, economics, business, construction and the military arts. This observation seems even more astounding when one reads Paul's other Treatises, in which he employs other extended metaphors that indicate his intellectual comprehension of even more fields of knowledge (*Romans* = the legal and judicial professions; *Philippians* = an extensive understanding of sociology and politics; *Colossians* = ancient mystery religions; *Galatians* = Jewish religious and legal tradition and practice). How did Paul become so competent in so many fields of human knowledge and experience? It is possible that the answer lies in his training in the religious sect of Pharisaic Judaism. For a discussion of the training and world view involved in becoming a Pharisee, see extended note on Flavius Josephus at Eph. 2:3.

[13] **καταβολή** – usual translation: "foundation." This word is used by Paul only one time in this Treatise (Eph. 1:4). Although "foundation" is a meaning of this

word, the emphasis does not seem to be the symbol of the "foundation" of a building, but rather the concept of the "founding" of a political government [LS]; e.g., the "founding fathers" of the United States. Proposed translation: "founding."

[14] κόσμος – usual translation: "world." This word is used by Paul three times in this Treatise (Eph. 1:4, 2:2 and 2:12). This word does not really refer to our planet, i.e., the "earth" as a planet orbiting the sun. The primary meaning of this word is the "organized governmental system of a state" [LS]. Proposed translation: "organized system of civilized government, organization, enterprise, or business."

[15] ἐν ἀγάπῃ – "motivated by love." Paul uses this important word ten times in Ephesians (1:4, 15; 2:4; 3:17, 19; 4:2, 15, 16; 5:2; 6:23). Tyndale translates this phrase "throwe love" ("through love"), placing it in the middle of verse 4 (see Basic Explanatory Translation), which is better than the KJV "in love;" which indicates more clearly in English that God's motive for "selecting" (see extended note on ἐκλέγω above) us for a special purpose in life is His love for us. Proposed translation for ἀγάπῃ: "self-sacrificial love."

[16] προορίζω – usual translation: "predestine." Paul uses this word twice in this Treatise (Eph. 1:5, 1:11), twice in Romans, and once in 1 Corinthians (a total of 5 times). This is a good example of a common professional Greek word that became ossified into a strict ecclesiastical meaning in British history via Jerome's Latin translation of this word, **praedestino**, which in Latin simply means "to determine beforehand." We no longer use the word "predestine" in contemporary professional American English (if, indeed, we ever did). The Greek word generically means "to determine or plan ahead of time." In order to determine the specific root concept, we must look at the root word ὁρίζω (used 8 times in the NT, and once by Paul in Romans 1:4). The Greek word ὁρίζω means to "*mark out by boundaries, mark out*, βωμὸν ἱδρύσατο καὶ τέμενος περὶ αὐτὸν οὔρισε Hdt.3.142, cf. 6.108, S.Tr.754, E.Hel.1670, IG12.76.54, 42(1).76.19 (Pass., Epid., ii B.C.), etc.; v. infr....*2. trace out as a boundary*, πόρον (*of 10 tracing out the Bosporus*), A.Supp.546 (lyr.)...Att. **law-term**, δισχιλίων ὡρισμένος τὴν οἰκίαν *having the house marked with* ὅροι (cf. ὅρος II) *to secure a claim on it for 2,000 drachmas*, D.31.5; so χωρίον ὡρισμένον Poll.9.9 [LS]. From an analysis of the above contexts in which the word ὁρίζω occurs, two primary fields of meaning emerge. It is used as a term during the planning stages for the development or use of land for the professional task of surveying and setting the legal boundaries of a parcel of land, or as a legal/financial/accounting term, i.e., in the setting of financial boundaries, as in determining the amortization schedule on a loan or mortgage. Proposed translation for **προορίζω**: "preplan, pre-mark out, pre-survey, pre-finance, amortize."

[17] δόξα – usual translation: "glory." This is an important word, used by Paul eight times in Ephesians (Eph. 1:6, 12, 14, 17, 18; 3:13, 16 and 21). However, the

British word "glory" is simply a transliteration of the Latin word "**gloria**," which Jerome used in the Latin Bible to translate the Greek word δόξα. Thus, the word "glory" is not an English word, but an adoption by the English speaking peoples of a transliterated Latin word, and is rarely if ever used in contemporary professional American English.

However, the Greek word δόξα is a common word in that language used to mean (denotatively) "appearance," as in the way something first "appears" to sight before it is subjected to further examination, reflection or evaluation. In the Greek philosophic tradition, the word δόξα is used quite often, and comes to mean (connotatively) "opinion," as opposed to genuine "knowledge," as when we use the English expression, "it *appears* to me that..." meaning "it is my *opinion* that..." The central concept in Ephesians seems to be the denotative use of the word δόξα, e.g., that when God actually "appears" in History, it will be quite a noteworthy, marvelous, and wonderful thing to be able to actually see and observe personally. Proposed translation: "Appearing" or "Appearance (of God in the form of Jesus, the High King of the earth, in future historical reality)."

[18] Paul actually begins the use of economic terminology in an extended metaphor in Eph. 1:4. For a complete list of these economic terms, see the extended note above on the Greek word ἐκλέγω.

[19] ἀπολύτρωσις, εως, ἡ, *ransoming*, αἰχμαλώτων Plu.Pomp.24 (pl.), cf. J.AJ12.2.3, Ph.2.463. **II.** *redemption by payment of ransom, deliverance*, Ev. Luc.21.28, *Ep.Rom.*3.24, al.; of Nebuchadnezzar's recovery, LXX Da.4.30c; in NT, *redemption*, *Ep.Rom.*3.24,al [LS]. The word "redeem, redemption" is still commonly used in contemporary professional American English, mainly as a financial and legal term, as follows: "redeem – Etymology: Middle English *redemen*, modification (perhaps influenced by *demen* to judge, deem) of Middle French *redimer*, from Latin *redimere*, from *red- re-* + *-imere* (from *emere* to take, buy, acquire)...As a transitive verb: **1a:** *to buy back*: REPURCHASE <if a man sell a dwelling house in a walled city, then he may redeem it within a whole year after – Lev. 25:29 (Revised Standard Version)> **b:** *to get or win back* <redeemed his championship status by winning the return bout> **2a:** *to liberate (as from slavery or captivity) by paying a price*: RANSOM <a parley to decide the terms for redeeming captured warriors>...**c:** *to release from blame or debt*...[modification of Late Latin *redimere*, from Latin]...**3a:** *to repossess upon fulfillment of an obligation; specifically: to free (property) from a lien or encumbrance and regain absolute title by payment of an amount secured thereby or by performing the condition securing the same. **b(1):** to remove the obligation of by payment* <the United States Treasury redeems war bonds upon demand> *(2): to convert into something of value* <people who always redeem trading stamps>. As an intransitive verb:... **2:** *to buy back property: regain title by purchase* <rights...must be exercised within forty years from the time at which the proprietor is allowed to redeem > [W]. Paul uses this word a total of seven times: three times in this Treatise (Eph. 1:7, 14; 4:30), and four times in his other

Treatises (Rom. 3:24, 8:23; 1 Cor. 1:30; Col. 1:14). He uses it to refer to Jesus "buying us back" from the two powers that "own" or "have the present power to control" us, e.g., Satan and his hierarchy of wicked angelic beings, and our own unregenerate nature. The currency He uses to "ransom" us, i.e., pay the purchase price for us, is His "blood," i.e., His own substitutionary death on the cross in our place. The result of the purchase is not only a new (regenerate) mind and spirit in our present experience, but most especially a new immortal body that we will receive at the resurrection. N.B. esp. Rom. 8:23: "and not only [the whole creation], but we also who have the firstfruits of the Spirit, even we ourselves groan within ourselves, eagerly waiting for the adoption [namely], the *redemption of our body*."

[20] ἄφεσις, εως, ἡ, ([ἀφίημι]) *letting go, release*, περὶ τῆς τῶν πλοίων ἀφέσεως Philipp. ap. D.18.77, cf. Pl.Plt.273c; καρπῶν PAmh.2.43.9 (ii B. C.); γῇ ἐν ἀφέσει land in private hands, opp. βασιλική, PTeb. 5.37 (ii B. C.), etc. **b.** *of persons, dismissal*: in ritual, λαοῖς ἅ. Apul.Met.11.17; *release*, Plb.1.79.12, IG2.314.21, Ev.Luc.4.18. **2.** c. gen., ἀ. φόνου *quittance from murder*, Pl.Lg.869d: so abs., Hermog.Stat.8; *discharge from a bond*, D.33.3; ἅ. ἐναντίον μαρτύρων ποιήσασθαι Id.45.41; opp. ἀπόδοσις χρημάτων, Isoc.17.29; *exemption from attendance, leave of absence*, Arist.*Ath*.30.6; ἀ. τῆς στρατείας *exemption from service*, Plu.Ages.24; *remission of a debt*, ταλάντου Michel1340 B7 (Cnidus, ii B. C.); χρημάτων IPE12.32B70 (Olbia, iii B. C.); sc. καταδίκης, Inscr.Magn.93c16. **b.** *forgiveness*, *Ev.Marc*.3.29; ἁμαρτιῶν *Ev.Matt*.26.28 [LS]. Paul uses this word only twice in his writings, here in Eph. 1:7 and in Col. 1:14. The main idea of this word is that of being "released, discharged, or exempted" from some sort of negative experience, such as debt, punishment for a crime, military service, etc. In order to understand fully what Paul is intending, we must therefore first solve what kind of negative consequences Paul means when he uses this word, namely: *from what* does Jesus' death on the cross "release, discharge or exempt" us? The word usually used to translate **ἄφεσις** is "forgive(ness)," which is derived from Old English, as follows: etymology: Middle English *foryeven, foryiven, forgeven, forgiven*, from Old English *forgiefan, forgifan* (akin to Old Saxon *fargean* to give, forgive, promise, Old High German *firgeban* to give, forgive, Gothic *fragiban* to forgive), from *for-* + *giefan, gifan* to give--transitive verb: **1:** to cease to feel resentment against on account of wrong committed: give up claim to requital from or retribution upon (an offender): ABSOLVE, PARDON <Father, forgive them, for they do not know what they are doing -- Lk. 23:34 (NCE)> **2a:** to give up resentment of or claim to requital for (an offense or wrong): remit the penalty of <and their sins should be forgiven them -- Mk 4:12 (Authorized Version)> **b:** to grant [financial] relief from: refrain from exacting <forgave his tenants thousands of dollars in back rent> <a loophole in the tax law that forgives all if a taxpayer is out of the U.S. -- Time> [W]. So, the word **ἄφεσις** should be translated, "for both creditor and debtor, to be released from the emotional estrangement, anger and resentment caused by the debtor being hopelessly in debt, resulting from the creditor releasing the debtor from his obligation to pay the

debt." The emphasis seems to be on the deliverance from the *emotional estrangement, anger and resentment*, more than upon the canceling out of the debt, even though both are in view.

[21] παράπτωμα (from παραπίπτω) – usual translation: "sin, trespass;" this important word is used three times by Paul in Ephesians to describe the particular kind of human failure we commonly refer to as "getting off track," or "getting sidetracked" (Eph. 1:7, 2:1 and 2:5). The philological analysis of the Greek words translated "sin" in English serves to illustrate another of the numerous instances in which an English word derived from Latin comes to have a wide, general meaning that dilutes and thus obscures the specific meanings of the original Greek words used in the New Testament. Etymology of the English word "sin" shows it to be derived from Middle English *sinne*, from Old English *synn, syn* [the word used by Tyndale – 1526]; akin to Old Frisian *sende*, Old Saxon *sundia*, Old High German *sunta*, **suntea** and perhaps to Latin *sont-, sons* = "guilty;" probably akin to Latin *est is* [W]. However, the Greek word for the specific legal concept of "guilt" is ἔνοχος from ἐνεχόμενος = lit. "held in, bound by," which clearly infers the connotative meaning of "legally liable to the penalty for, guilt" [LS]. The Greek word for "legal liability" is ὑπόδικος = lit. "under [or subject to] justice." However, Paul does not use the legal concepts of "guilt" or "liability" in Ephesians (as he does in Romans). In Greek, there are seven specific concepts obscured by the generic English word "sin." These are as follows:

a) ἁμαρτία – usual translation: "sin" (Eph. 2:1). This Greek word is the one most often translated "sin." Denotatively, the verb ἁμαρτάνω means to "miss the mark" (especially when throwing a spear) [LS]." Connotatively, ἁμαρτάνω comes to mean "to fail in one's purpose or intention," or "to lose possession or be deprived of one's powers, especially of a physical or metaphysical organ of intention" [LS]. Proposed translation as a verb: fail, lose (as in "lose one's sight," "lose hope," "lose one's mind," etc.), miss (as in "miss" a field goal, "miss" a business opportunity); proposed translation as a noun: "failure," "loss," "missed."

b) ἄνομος = "without law, lawless, unlawful" (Paul does not use this word in Ephesians, but uses it once in Romans).

c) ἔνοχος = "guilt" (not used by Paul in Ephesians, but once in 1 Corinthians).

d) ὑπόδικος = "legal liability"(not used by Paul in Ephesians, but once in Romans).

e) παραβαίνω, παράβασις, παραβάτης = "trespass (v.), trespass(n.), trespasser (n.); transgress (v.), transgression (n.), transgressor (n.)" [LS], or better in contemporary professional American English: "encroach, infringe, intrude (v.), encroachment, infringement, intrusion (n.), intruder (n.)" (not used by Paul in Ephesians, but extensively [5 times] in Romans),

f) ὀφείλω, ὀφείλημα, ὀφειλέτης = lit. "to be in debt, debt, debtor" [LS]. This is the word Jesus uses in the "Lord's Prayer" in Matt. 6:12. The primary denotative meaning of the word is financial = "financial indebtedness," as when we say that a person has too much credit card "debt." Thus, it also means things like "owe," "due." It is used as a legal term to mean "bound," or "penalty." From these denotative meanings the primary connotative use of the word came to be used most often in the moral or ethical sense of "that which one has not, but *ought* to have done" ("ought" being the preterite of "owe"). It is used often in strong expressions of moral or ethical regret and remorse when one sees in hindsight what one ought to have done, as in the expressions, "Oh, I wish I would have...," or, "If only he would have...". Thus, it should probably be translated something like: "Forgive us of the things that we *ought* to have done (for You, Lord, and for others), as we forgive others of the things that they *ought* to have done for us." Paul uses this word only once in Ephesians (Eph. 5:28 – "so *ought* men to love their own wives"); but extensively in Romans and his other Treatises/Letters.

g) The seventh Greek word usually translated "sin" is this word, παραπίπτω, **παράπτωμα,** which Paul uses three times in this Treatise, and extensively (9 times) in Romans. However, in Eph. 2:1, **παράπτωμα** is mistranslated "*trespasses*." But the specific Greek word for "trespass" is **παραβαίνω**, (lit. "stand beside or beyond, walk beside or beyond a boundary" [LS]), and thus, connotatively, **παραβαίνω** refers to the specific legal concept of "legal trespass," as when a person deliberately crosses a legal boundary or property line and walks on or stands on land that does not belong to him and which he does not have permission to walk or stand upon. "Transgress" is derived from Latin, *trans + gressus*, ptcp. of *gredi*, from *grad* = "step," thus to "transgress" means "to step across" [W]. "Trespass" is the French pronunciation of the Latin *transpasser* = "to pass beyond" [W]. The central notion of these two English translations of the Greek word **παραβαίνω** is the notion of encroachment. Thus, good translations for **παραβαίνω** (see above) would be "encroach," "infringe," "intrude."

Now, we must return to a consideration of **παράπτωμα** (from **παραπίπτω**), the word Paul uses here. In Greek, **πίπτω** is the common verb for "to fall," and **παρά** is the normal preposition for "to the side, beside" i.e., as in Geometry, lines that said to be *parallel* are *beside* each other. So, **παραπίπτω** means "to fall to the side (of the road), to fail because one turned aside, to take a detour, to veer 'off course,' to get 'off track,' to get 'sidetracked,'" [LS] (cf. Hebrews 6:6). Proposed translation: "to take a willful and deliberate detour which sidetracks us from taking the right road God plans for us to take in life," or "to veer off course," "to get off track," or "to get sidetracked."

[22] περισσεύω = Usually translated "to go beyond, abound" [LS]. In this context, refers to the financial concept of "compounding" money, i.e., through "interest."

[23] σοφία, Ion. -ιη, ἡ, prop. **A.** *cleverness or skill in handicraft and art*, as in carpentry, τέκτονος, ὅς ῥά τε πάσης εὖ εἰδῇ ς. Il.15.412; of the Telchines, Pi.O.7.53; ἡ ἔντεχνος ς., of Hephaestus and Athena, Pl.*Prt*.32 1d; of Daedalus and Palamedes, X.*Mem*.4.2.33, cf. 1.4.2; *in music and singing*, τέχνῃ καὶ ς. h.Merc.483, cf. 511; *in poetry*, Sol.13.52, Pi.O.1.117, Ar.*Ra*.882, X.*An*.1.2.8, etc.; in driving, Pl. *Thg*.123c; in medicine or surgery, Pi.P.3.54; in divination, S.OT 502 (lyr.);...σημαίνοντες τὴν ς...., ὅτι ἀρετὴ τέχνης ἐστίν Arist.*EN*1141a12... **2.** *skill in matters of common life. sound judgement, intelligence, practical wisdom, etc., such as was attributed to the seven sages, like* φρόνησις, Thgn.790,876,1074, Hdt.1.30,60; ἡ τῶν δεινῶν ς., opp.ἀμαθία, Pl.*Prt*.360d;...**3.** *learning, wisdom*, μείζω τινὰ ἢ κατ' ἄνθρωπον σοφίαν σοφοί Pl.*Ap*.20e;...*freq. in Arist., speculative wisdom*, *EN* 1141a19, *Metaph*. 982a2, 995b12 (pl.), 1059a18; defined as θείων τε καὶ ἀνθρωπίνων ἐπιστήμη, Stoic.2.15; *but also of natural philosophy and mathematics*, ς. τις καὶ ἡ φυσική Arist.*Metaph*.1005b1, cf.

1061b33. **4.** among the Jews, ἀρχὴ σοφίας φόβος Κυρίου LXX Pr.1.7, cf. Jb.28.28, al.; Σοφία, *recognized first as an attribute of God, was later identified with the Spirit of God*, cf. LXX *Pr.*8…[LS]. The word **σοφία**, usually translated "wisdom," conveys a very important concept in Ephesians. Paul uses this word four times in this Treatise (Eph. 1:8, 17, 3:10, and 5:15). However, the basic meaning of the Greek word **σοφία is** not really "wisdom," but rather "achieving mastery or excellence in the exercise of a human skill." The best analysis of the distinction to be drawn between the four most important human abilities for achieving excellence in life (British English: **ἐπιστήμη** = "scientific knowledge;" **φρόνησίς** = "prudence;" **σοφία** = "wisdom;" and **νοῦς** = "intelligence") are explained by Aristotle in his *Nicomachean Ethics*, 1141a10 ff., where he says (ed. J. Bywater, Oxford, 1894; transl. H. Rackham, Cambridge, 1934):

> [2] If then the qualities whereby we attain truth (ἀληθεύομεν), and are never led into falsehood (διαψευδόμεθα), whether about things invariable or things variable, are Scientific Knowledge (**ἐπιστήμη**), Prudence (**φρόνησίς**), Wisdom (**σοφία**), and Intelligence (**νοῦς**), and if the quality which enables us to apprehend first principles cannot be any one among three of these, namely Scientific Knowledge, Prudence, and Wisdom, it remains that first principles must be apprehended by Intelligence. VII. The term Wisdom (**σοφία**) is employed in the arts to denote those men who are the most perfect masters of their art, for instance, it is applied to Pheidias as a sculptor and to Polycleitus as a statuary. In this use then Wisdom merely signifies artistic excellence [= "skill," "competence," "proficiency" – GWC]. [2] But we also think that some people are wise in general and not in one department, not 'wise in something else,' as Homer says in the Margites:
>> Neither a delver nor a ploughman him
>> The Gods had made, nor wise in aught beside.
>
> Hence it is clear that Wisdom (**σοφία**) must be the most perfect of the modes of knowledge. [3] The wise man therefore must not only know the conclusions that follow from his first principles, but also have a true conception of those principles themselves. Hence Wisdom (**σοφία**) must be a combination of Intelligence (**νοῦς**) and Scientific Knowledge (**ἐπιστήμη**): *it* (**σοφία**) *must be the chief kind of knowledge (20) of the most honorable objectives of human life* [italics mine – GWC].

Rather than being linked to the Greek word **σοφία**, the English word "wisdom" has a clear etymological link to the Greek word [ϝ]οἶδα= "to know because one has seen;" through Latin **videre**, into Old English as *"wat"* and *"wit"* as both Liddell-Scott and Webster demonstrate:

Liddell-Scott: εἶδον – always in sense of *see* (so in pres. and aor. 1 Med., *to be seen*, i.e. *seem*): but pf. οἶδα , in pres. sense, *know*. (With ἔ-[ϝ]ιδον, cf. [ϝ]είδομαι, [ϝ]εἶδος, Lat. *videre*; with, cf. Skt. *véda*, Goth. *wait*, OE. *wát* 'know.'

Webster: Main Entry for **wisdom** [from "**wise**:" Middle English, from Old English *wīsa*, from *wīs* = wise]: Inflected Form(s): past *wist* \wist\; past part *wist* present part *witting* present first & third singular *wot* \wät\, usu -äd.+V\ Etymology: Middle English *witen* (1st & 3d singular present *wot*, *wat*, present plural *witen*, past *wiste*, past participle *witen*, *wist* [thus linking *"wisdom"* with *"wizard"* = Middle English *wysard*, from *wys* wise + *-ard* - GWC]), from Old English *witan* (1st & 3d singular present *wāt*, present plural *witon*, past *wiste, wisse*, past participle *witen*); akin to Old High German *wizzan* to know (1st & 3d singular present *weiz*, past *westa, wessa*, past participle *giwizzan*), Old Norse *vita* (1st & 3d singular present *veit*, past *vissa*, past participle *vitathr*), Gothic *witan* to know (1st singular present *wait*, past *wissa*), Latin *vidēre* to see, Greek *[F]eidenai* to know, *[F]oida* I know, *[F]idein* to see, Sanskrit *veda* I know, he knows, *vidyā* knowledge; basic meaning: *"to see."*

> **Historical example from Alfred the Great** (Churchill, Winston S. *A History of the English Speaking Peoples, Volume I – The Birth of Britain*, New York, 1956): As a result of His treaty with the Danish Vikings in 886, Alfred the Great conceptualized his own lands and people as a "State." He refers to his own administrative organization as "King and *Witan*." In the treaty he made with the Danish Vikings, "*Witan*" means "the counselors of the English nation," from the old English word "*wita*" = "one who knows." "*Witan*" is the plural form of "*wita*," and an official organization of political counselors is called a "*witenagemot*." In American English, we still say of leaders that they can keep their "*wits*" in a stressful situation. Also, in a legal court trial, those who "saw" (and thus, those who "know") what really happened are called upon by the court as "*witnesses*," because they are the most reliable sources of information needed to determine the knowledge of what occurred.

Consequently, the English word "wisdom" carries with it the connotation of "knowing" something because one has "seen" it; i.e., it is connected conceptually to the metaphor of "sight" (going all the way back to the meaning of the Greek word [F]οἶδα, which means to "see" something in the sense of "realizing" something). However, the Greek word σοφία is not linked to the notion of human "sight" at all, but rather to the notion of a practiced human "physical skill" (τέχνη) or "soul-skill" (ἀρετή) to such a high level of proficiency that one can be said to be an "ethically or morally skillful person in particular areas of human experience," such as being a good husband or wife, or a good father or mother, etc. Proposed translation: "the kind of knowledge that makes it possible for us to become competent, then gain mastery, then achieve superior leadership ability in living human life skillfully, especially in the ethical and political arenas."

[24] φρόνησις, εως, ἡ, ***purpose, intention***, S.OT664 (lyr.); φρόνησιν λαβεῖν λῴω ἡμῖν Id.Ph.1078. **2. *thought***, ἰδίᾳ φ., opp. λόγος ξυνός, Heraclit. 2; φ. ἔχειν Emp.110.10, cf. Arist.*Metaph.* 1009b18. **3. *sense***, εἴ τις ἄρα τοῖς ἐκεῖ φ. περὶ τῶν ἐνθάδε γιγνομένων Isoc.14.61. **4. *judgment***, κατὰ τὴν ἰδίαν φ. οὐδεὶς εὐτυχεῖ Men. Mon...**II. *practical wisdom, prudence in government and affairs***, Pl. Smp.209a, Arist. *EN*1140a24, 1141b23;...*also attributed to sagacious animals*, Arist.*GA*753a12, HA608a15 [LS]. Therefore, φρόνησις means something like "the ability to not only discern, but also to convert that discernment through the proper use of thinking rationally, into habitually making good decisions, especially those decisions that affect the lives of others in society."

This word is not a main concept in Ephesians, but it is Paul's main theme in his *Treatise to the Philippians*, where he uses it in its verbal form (φρονέω) 11 times, to not only refer to the "ability to grow in the skill of using one's mind to think correctly" but then spiritually transforms it into meaning "the ability to think and then decide to behave toward others exactly like Jesus would have us to" (e.g. Phil. 2:5 – τοῦτο γὰρ **φρονείσθω** [3rd sg pres imperat mid/pass] ἐν ὑμῖν ὃ καὶ ἐν Χριστῷ Ἰησοῦ... "*Let* this *mind be* in you which was also in Jesus, our High King." A more detailed study of the word φρονέω from Philippians shows it to refer to "the ability to always be ready, aware of, sensitive and alive to that which at any given moment is most important in the lives of other people – then to think about, consider, ponder and reflect upon those things with the goal of improving one's skill of discernment – and then believe, feel (actually experience proper emotions with emotional balance), have the right inclinations, dispositions (and predispositions), understand, respond, purpose, intend, and decide to behave toward others from the appropriate perspective and with the right sense of proportion, such that one is always continuing to grow rapidly in their overall comprehension of how Jesus our Commander in Chief would have us conduct our lives with respect to our own context and lifeworld." This word has such a wide, deep field of meaning that Tyndale had difficulty in selecting just the right English word to encompass all of it. He chose the word "prudency" (prudence) to translate it in his 1526 edition, and the word "perceavaunce" (perceivance = perception, discernment) in the 1534 edition.

[25] μυστήριον – Usually translated "mystery." However, "mystery" is not a translation, but simply a transliteration (**μυστήριον** = *"mustērion"* = "mystery"), and as such bears little meaning in contemporary professional American English. However, Paul uses this word to convey a central and important concept in his other writings, and most of all in this Treatise. He uses this word 6 times in Ephesians (Eph. 1:9, 3:3, 4, 9, 5:32 and 6:19), 5 times in 1 Corinthians, and 4 times in Colossians. In ancient Greek usage **μυστήριον** means "divine secret," thus, the "secrets of the gods," that they deliberately withhold from the knowledge of human beings. In this context, it is God's "Top Secret" Plan to recruit and train the members of the barbarian nations, in addition to Israel, to occupy a major role in being incorporated to become significant, essential, good and just leaders through which He will exercise His administrative rule during the period of the Millennial Kingdom. Paul explains why God kept this official divine plan "Top Secret" in 1 Cor. 2:7-8, as follows:

1 Cor. 2:7-8 ἀλλὰ λαλοῦμεν θεοῦ σοφίαν ἐν **μυστηρίῳ**, τὴν ἀποκεκρυμμένην, ἣν προώρισεν ὁ θεὸς πρὸ τῶν αἰώνων εἰς [8]δόξαν ἡμῶν· ἣν οὐδεὶς τῶν ἀρχόντων τοῦ αἰῶνος τούτου ἔγνωκεν, εἰ γὰρ ἔγνωσαν, οὐκ ἂν τὸν κύριον τῆς δόξης ἐσταύρωσαν,

Transl.: [7]But we proclaim everything with respect to God's ***"Top Secret" Plan***, namely (His great plan) to recruit and train us (barbarian peoples) to rapidly gain skillful proficiency in all modes of knowledge but most especially in ethical competence, which had formerly been kept hidden by Him, but which God pre-surveyed and pre-financed in Eternity prior to our own appearance in history, [8]which none of the evil angelic rulers of this historical era could have even fathomed, because if they would have known about it, they wouldn't have crucified our Commander in

Chief, who is soon to return to make His Appearing, (at which time He will justly sentence them to their doom)" [transl. – GWC].

For a more detailed treatment of the specific roles and offices of the organized administrative structure Jesus will implement during the Millennial Kingdom, see *Footsteps of the Messiah – A Study of the Sequence of Prophetic Events*, by Arnold G. Fruchtenbaum, Th.M., Ph.D., Chapter 18: "The Government of the Messianic Kingdom," Chapter 19: "Israel in the Messianic Kingdom" and Chapter 20, "The Gentiles in the Messianic Kingdom" (see Bibliography).

²⁶ **οἰκονομία, ἡ,** *management of a household or family, husbandry, thrift*, Pl.*Ap*.36b, R.498a, X.*Oec*.1.1, Arist.*EN*1141b32, *Pol*.1253b2 sqq.: pl., Pl.*R*.407b; **households,** Arist.*GA*744b18. **2.** *generally, direction, regulation,* Epicur.Ep.1p.29U.; *esp. of a State, administration,* αἱ κατὰ τὴν πόλιν οἱ. Din.1.97; *principles of government,* Chrysipp.Stoic.2.338; τῶν γεγονότων Plb.1.4.3, al.; πολιτικὴ οἱ. Phld.Rh. 2.32 S.;...*3. arrangement,* ἡ περὶ τὸν νοσέοντα οἱ. Hp.Epid.6.2.24;...οἰκονομίαι *proceedings*, IG9(1).226 (Drymaea); τίνα οἰκονομίαν προσαγήγοχας *what steps you have taken,* PCair.Zen.240.10 (iii B. C.);...**5.** *stewardship,* LXX *Is*.22.19, *Ev.Luc*.16.2 [LS]. Usual translation: "dispensation." This word **οἰκονομία** is also an important concept for Paul in this Treatise, because he uses the word three times (Eph. 1:10, 3:2, 3:9), more than in any of the other of his Letters/Treatises (one time in 1 Corinthians and one time in Colossians). The Greek word for "house" is **οἶκος**, for "law," **νόμος**; and thus, the denotative meaning of the word **οἰκονομία** is literally "house-rules," or "laws of the house" = "household" [LS]. This word has also come directly into the English language as a direct transliteration: "**οἰκονομία**" = "*oikonomia*" = "economy." This word and the concepts which it conveys were so important to the Greek mind, that Aristotle wrote a complete Philosophical Treatise on the subject, which he entitled "ΟΙΚΟΝΟΜΙΚΩΝ" (= "OECONOMICA" = "Economics") in the late fourth century B.C. Three summary passages from this work now follow, in order to provide a sense of context to develop an accurate contemporary professional American English translation for this concept (transl. G.C. Armstrong, Cambridge, 1935):

1. On the three character qualities required of the leadership offices for the right administration of an **οἰκονομία** ("government," "household"):	
[1345b][7] τὸν **οἰκονομεῖν** μέλλοντά τι κατὰ τρόπον τῶν τε τόπων, περὶ οὓς ἂν **πραγματεύηται**, **μὴ ἀπείρως ἔχειν**, καὶ τῇ **φύσει** **εὐφυῆ** εἶναι καὶ τῇ **προαιρέσει** **φιλόπονόν τε καὶ δίκαιον**: ὅ τι γὰρ ἂν ἀπῇ τούτων τῶν μερῶν, πολλὰ διαμαρτήσεται περὶ τὴν πραγματείαν ἣν μεταχειρίζεται.	[1345b][7] "**Right administration of a household (or government)** demands in the first place **familiarity with the localities wherein we work**; in the second place, **good natural endowments**; and in the third, an **upright and industrious way of life**. For the lack of any one of these qualifications will involve many a failure in the task one takes in hand."

2. On the four types of **οἰκονομίαι** ("governments," "administrative systems"):	
[1345b][13] **οἰκονομίαι** δέ εἰσι τέσσαρες, ὡς ἐν τύπῳ διελέσθαί τὰς γὰρ ἄλλας εἰς τοῦτο ἐμπιπτούσας εὑρήσομεν, **βασιλική, σατραπική, πολιτική, ἰδιωτική.**	"[1345b][13] Of such **administrations** there are four main types, under which all others may be classified. We have the **administration of a king** (i.e., a kingdom); of the **governors** under him; of a **free state**; and of **a private citizen**."
3. On the four main character qualities required of the personality of the individual leader of an **οἰκονομία** ("government," "household"):	
[1344b][22] εἴδη δὲ τοῦ **οἰκονόμου** τέτταρα ἃ δεῖ ἔχειν περὶ τὰ χρήματα. καὶ γὰρ τὸ **κτᾶσθαι** δυνατὸν χρὴ εἶναι καὶ **φυλάττειν**· εἰ δὲ μή, οὐδὲν ὄφελος τοῦ κτᾶσθαι· τῷ γὰρ ἠθμῷ ἀντλεῖν τοῦτ' ἔστιν, καὶ ὁ λεγόμενος τετρημένος πίθος. ἔτι δὲ καὶ εἶναι **κοσμητικὸν** τῶν ὑπαρχόντων καὶ **χρηστικόν**· τούτων γὰρ ἕνεκα κἀκείνων δεόμεθα.	[1344b][22] "There are four qualities which the head of a **household** must possess in dealing with his property. Firstly, he must have the faculty of **acquiring**, and **secondly** that of **preserving** what he has acquired; otherwise there is no more benefit in acquiring than in baling with a colander, or in the proverbial wine-jar with a hole in the bottom. **Thirdly** and **fourthly**, he must know how to **improve his property**, and how to **make use of it**; since these are the ends for which the powers of acquisition and of preservation are sought."

The notion that emerges from reading Aristotle's ΟΙΚΟΝΟΜΙΚΩΝ for the concept conveyed by the Greek word **οἰκονομία** is that of "the responsible administration of a large, self-sufficient household, estate, city-state or State composed of a hegemony of multiple city-states, consisting not only of the finances, the property, the agriculture, the animals and the people required for it to be self-sustaining, but also including the management skills and character required to manage the whole interpersonal organization well." Later, the word used in a political sense connotatively comes to mean, "administration, government" [LS]. Proposed translation: "administration, government."

[27] **κληρόω** – Usual translation: "inherit." Paul uses this word as a verb only once in the New Testament, here in Eph. 1:11. This verb in its original early use meant to "obtain by lot, be allotted, be assigned" [LS]. Its closely associated verb is **κληρονομέω**, which clearly means "to inherit" = "to obtain by lot (**κληρόω**) but also by law (**νόμος**), thus, to be legally appointed" [LS]. The noun form in Paul's Treatise to the Ephesians is **κληρονομία** (see note on **κληρονομία** at Eph. 1:14). Proposed translation: "inherit," "to obtain an appointment or an estate by legally recognized proceedings."

[28] **πρόθεσις**, εως, ἡ, ([προτίθημι]) *placing in public*; of a corpse, laying it out (cf. προτίθημι 11), Pl.*Lg*.947b, 959a, 959e, D.43.64 [denotative meaning – GWC]. 2. *public notice*, αἱ π. τῶν ἀναγεγραμμένων Arist.Pol.1322a9. 3. *statement of a case*, Id.Rh.1414b8; ὑπέρ τινος τὴν πρόθεσιν ποιήσασθαι Id.Cat. [p. 1481] 11a21; *theme, thesis*, Phld.Rh.1.36, al. S.: generally, *proposition, statement*, D.H.Amm.2.2....**II.** *purpose, end proposed*, ἐπαινῶ σὴν π. SIG22.14 (Magn. Mae., Epist. Darei), cf. Philipp. ap.D.18.167, Arist.APr.47a5, Cleanth.Stoic.

1.131, Plb.5.35.2, Arr. Epict.1.21.2, etc.; π. βίων Adam.Phgn.1.2 [LS]. It therefore seems the main connotative meaning of this word is "to, following sufficient planning and deliberation, assert or publish in public an official case, proposition or statement." Paul uses this word twice in Ephesians: here, and again in Eph. 3:11.

²⁹ προελπίζω, A. *hope for before*, Posidipp.27.8, Them.Or.5.65a; προηλπικότες ἐν Χριστῷ *Ep.Eph.1.12*: generally, *anticipate, expect*, Gal.16.822, Dexipp.Hist.32(h) J., Simp.in Epict.p.50D [LS]. This word clearly means "to hope for before (in time), to look forward to, anticipate, expect something in the future" (**προ** = "before" + ελπίζω = "hope"). In context, Paul clearly means that our proper attitude toward the Millennial Kingdom Age is always to hope for it, look forward to it, and expect it with a sense of eagerness and anticipation in this present era before it arrives. Tyndale translated this word correctly in his 1526 edition ("which before *hoped*"), then for some reason changed to the incorrect translation of "which before *beleved*" (believed) in his 1534 edition. This incorrect translation then set a precedent for the KJV translators to translate this word incorrectly as "who first *trusted*."

³⁰ ἀλήθεια – [ἀλ], ἡ, Dor. ἀλάθεια (also ἀλαθείᾱ B.12.204); ἀλάθεα Alc.57, Theoc.29.1 is neut. pl. of ἀλᾱθής; Ep. (and Farly Att. acc. to Hdn.Gr.2.454) ἀληθείᾱ; Ion. ἀληθείη: **I.** *truth, opp. lie or mere appearance: 1. in Hom. only opp. a lie*, **2.** after Hom. also *truth, reality, opp. appearance*, --with Preps., ἐν τῇ ἀ. Pl.La.183d; ἐπὶ τῆς ἀληθείας καὶ τοῦ πράγματος *in truth and reality*, D.21.72; ἐπ' ἀληθείᾳ *for the sake of truth*, A.Supp. 628, Ar.Pl.891; also, *according to truth and nature*, Theoc.7.44:--μετ' ἀληθείας X.Mem.2.1.27, D.2.4:--κατὰ τὴν ἀ. Isoc.1.2.46, etc.; κατ' ἀλήθειον Arist.*Pol*.1278b33, etc.:--ξὺν ἀληθείᾳ A.Ag.1567:--πρὸς ἀλήθειαν D.S.5.67, etc. **3.** *real* war, opp. exercise or parade, Plb.10.20.4,al.; ἐπ' αὐτῆς τῆς ἀ. Id.1.21.3. **4.** *true event, realization of dream or omen*, Hdt.3.64, Damon ap.Sch.Ar.Pl.1003 [LS]. Paul will use this important word ἀλήθεια 6 times in this Treatise (Eph. 1:13, 4:21, 24, 25, 5:9 and 6:14). He will use it very consistently to mean "the ability to spiritually discover what is real," and in specific context of this Treatise: "to be given the spiritual ability by God to 'discover' one's lifework and then help other people to 'discover' theirs also." This meaning of "dis-cover" or "un-cover" that which was previously hidden from human comprehension comes from the two Greek words that ἀλήθεια is composed from: ἀ, which means the "opposite" or "negative" of something, and λανθάνω (verb) = λῆθος (noun), which means "to conceal, cover-up, to escape notice, to be unknown, unseen, unnoticed." Thus, the root meaning of the word ἀλήθεια is "to un-conceal" (i.e., to "uncover, discover or realize the ultimate reality of") something previously not understood.

It is insightful to explore why the British translators selected the Old English word "truth" to translate ἀλήθεια, when "uncover," "discover," or "realize" would be better English translations. The answer can be deduced from a philological study of the Old English word for "truth." According to Webster, the word "truth" is derived from a very ancient, older word "true," which has the following etymology: "Middle English *trew*, *trewe*, from Old English *trēowe* faithful, trustworthy; akin to Old High German *gitriuwi* faithful, trustworthy, Old Norse *tryggr*, Gothic *triggws* faithful, trustworthy, Old Irish *dreb* certain, Old Prussian *druwis* faith, Lithuanian *drūtas* strong, thick, Sanskrit *dāruna* hard, *dāru* wood--more at TREE" [W].

When we analyze the word for "tree," we find the following etymology from Webster: "Middle English *tre*, tree, from Old English *trēow*; akin to Old Frisian & Old Norse *trē* tree, Old Saxon *trio*, *treo* tree, Old High German *apholtra* apple tree, Gothic *triu* tree, wood, Greek *drys* tree, *dory* spear, Sanskrit *dāru* wood, *dru* tree, branch wood" [W].

Thus, we find that the word "true" and "tree" have the same denotative origin. The question then becomes, how did the word for "tree" develop the connotative meaning of "true" = "that which un-conceals, uncovers or discovers reality" in the English (British) language? The hint lies in comparing the most ancient pronunciation of both words in Sanskrit: *"dāru* = wood, *dru* = tree." Members of the ancient pre-Christian religious order that lived on what is today the Island of Britain were called the "Druid (pl.)." Webster supplies the following etymology and meaning for the word "druid:" "Latin *druides*, *druidae*, plural, from Gaulish *druides*; akin to Old Irish *druī* (plural *druid*) wizard, *daur* oak tree, Welsh *derwen* oak tree, Old English *trēow* tree -- more at TREE. **1a:** often capitalized: a member of a priesthood in ancient Gaul, Britain, and Ireland who are said to have studied the natural sciences, prophesied through priestly sacrifices, and acted as judges and teachers but who later appeared in Irish and Welsh sagas and Christian legends as magicians and *wizards* [see note on σοφία at Eph. 1:8 above for link between the word *"wisdom"* and *"wizard"* = Middle English *wysard*, from *wys* wise + *-ard* – GWC]), **b:** BARD, PROPHET [W]."

Putting all this information together, the following development of meaning seems plausible: The ancient word for "tree" used by the pre-Christian inhabitants of what is today the Island of Britain was the word *"dru."* When the Romans conquered the Island in the first century A.D., they encountered the group of very secret religious leaders, wise men (wysards = "wizards") and bards who were collectively called the "Druid (pl.)," and, being unable to translate the meaning of this word, simply transliterated it into Latin as the word "Druides." Although very secret in the performance of their religious rituals, it is now widely believed that the Druids consulted with the spirits that guided them in circular openings in tree groves in the forests. The Druids would enter these sacred, circular openings in the trees to inquire of the spirits, and ask them to "un-conceal" or "un-cover" the meaning of future events, such as the outcome of battles, the identity of future kings, who should be brought together in royal marriages, etc. These places would then have come to be known as the "places of the un-covering (i.e., 'discovery") of reality," thus uniting the denotative meaning of the word for "tree" (the *"dru"*), with those human beings in spiritual leadership who could communicate within the circle of "trees" to discover the meaning of future reality (the *"Druid"*), and finally with the connotative meaning of the meaning of the unconcealment of reality itself.

[31] εὐαγγέλιον, τό, *reward of good tidings, given to the messenger*, εὐαγγέλιον δέ μοι ἔστω Od.14.152; οὐ...εὐ. τόδε τείσω ib.166; ἀπολήψῃ τὸ εὐ. Plu.Demetr.17: in Att. always in pl., εὐαγγέλια θύειν *to make a thank-offering for good-tidings*, Isoc.7.10, Men. Pk.415; εὐ. θύειν ἑκατὸν βοῦς τῇ θεῷ Ar.Eq.656; ἐβουθύτει ὡς εὐ. X. HG4.3.14; εὐαγγελίων θυσίαι Aeschin.3.160; εὐ. στεφανοῦν, ἀναδῆσαί τινα, *to crown one for good news brought*, Ar.Eq.647, Pl.765; ἐστεφανωμένη ἐπ' εὐαγγελίοις Plu.Sert.11, cf. Supp.Epigr.1.362.7 (Samos, iv B.C.). **II.** *good tidings, good news*, in pl., LXX 2 Ki.4.10, Cic.Att.2.3.1, 13.40.1, Inscr.Prien.105.40 (i B.C.): sg., J.BJ2.17.4, Luc.Asin.26, App.BC3.93, Sammelb.421 (iii A.D.). **2.** in Christian sense, *the gospel*, Ep.Gal.1.11, etc. [LS]. This Greek noun, εὐαγγέλιον, is another example of how a normal Greek word has become ossified into an Old English word that is no longer commonly used in contemporary professional American English. The Greek word εὐαγγέλιον is usually translated, "gospel," or capitalized as "Gospel," especially when referring to the first four books or stories of the life of Jesus in the New Testament; e.g., Matthew, Mark, Luke and John are commonly called the "Gospels." Paul uses this word in its noun form four times in this Treatise (here in Eph. 1:13, and in 3:6, 6:15 and 19), and in its verb form (εὐαγγελίζομαι) twice (Eph. 2:17 and 3:8), where it is usually translated "preach," or "preach the gospel:" εὐαγγελίζομαι,...only in later Gr., LXX *1 Ki.*31.9, *Apoc.10.7*, PGiss. 27.6 (ii A.D.):...*bring good news, announce them*, λόγους ἀγαθοὺς φέρων εὐαγγελίσασθαί τινι Ar.Eq.643, cf. Phryn.Com.44, D.18.323;...Pass., *receive good tidings*, ἐν ᾗ -ίσθη ἡ πόλις ἡμέρᾳ AJA18.323 (Sardes, i B.C.). **II.** *preach or proclaim as glad tidings*, τὴν βασιλείαν τοῦ Θεοῦ Ev.Luc.4.43, etc.; εἰρήνην ὑμῖν *Ep.Eph.*2.17, etc. **2.** abs., *proclaim glad tidings*, πτωχοῖς LXX *Is.*61.1, cf. *Ev.Luc.*4.18, etc.: c. acc., *preach the glad tidings of the gospel to*, τὸν λαόν ib.3.18; κώμας τῶν Σαμαρειτῶν Act.Ap.8.25:--so in *Act., Apoc.*10.7; τινι LXX *1 Ki.*31.9:--Pass., *have the gospel preached to one*, *Ev.Matt.*11.5, *Ep.Hebr.*4.2,6; *also of the gospel, to be preached*, *Ev.Luc.*16.16, *Ep.Gal.*1.11 [LS]. Upon investigation of the philology of the Old English word "gospel," the following results and reflections are offered: Etymology: Middle English, from Old English *godspel, gōdspel* (translation of Late Latin *evangelium*), from *gōd* good + *spell* tale -- more at GOOD, SPELL, EVANGEL...**a**: glad tidings...[W]. The Old English word "glad" is not really accurate, because we commonly use the word "good" to mean "good," (the cause) not "glad," (which is the effect). Thus, we discern that the Old English word *"gōd"* is now easily and commonly translated by the professional American English word "good," which is used quite normally. The Old English word *"spell"* is no longer used in contemporary professional American English in its original meaning: "spell" – Etymology: Middle English, speech, talk, tale, from Old English; akin to Old High German *spel* tale, talk, Old Norse *spjall*, Gothic *spill* tale, talk, Greek *apeilē* boast, threat, Latvian *pal'as* rebuke, abuse **1.a** obsolete: "STORY, TALE" [W]. The Latin word

"evangelium" is of no substantive help because it is only a transliteration of the original Greek word "εὐαγγέλιον" = "evangelium" (the Latin letter "v" is substituted for the Greek letter "υ," the Latin letter "n" is substituted for the first Greek letter "γ," which when combined as a "γγ," the first "γ" is pronounced as a Latin "n," and the Latin letter "m" is substituted for the last Greek letter "ν"). The suggested British words "tidings" and "tale" to translate the Old English word "spell" are also not quite satisfactory, because these two words are also not commonly used in professional American English. The three words that are used very commonly in professional American English to translate the Greek word "ἀγγελία" are the words "message," "report," and the word "news:" ἀγγελία, Ion. and Ep. ἀγγειο-ίη, ἡ, ([ἄγγελος]) *message, tidings, as well the substance as the conveyance thereof*, Il.18.17, Od.2.30, etc.; ἀ. λέγουσα τάδε Hdt.2.114; ἀγγελίην φάτο, ἀπόφασθε, ἀπέειπε, Il.18.17, 9.422, 7.416; φέρειν 15.174; πέμπειν Hdt.2.114; ἐσπέμπειν 3.69; τὰς ἀ. ἐσφέρειν 1.114, 3.77:-ἐμὴ ἀ. *a report of me, concerning me*, Il.19.337; ἀ. τινός *a message about a person or thing*, ἀγγελίην πατρὸς φέρει ἐρχομένοιο *news of thy father's coming*, Od.1.408...[LS].

Therefore, the proposed translation of the noun εὐαγγέλιον are the phrases: "good (or wonderful) news," "good (or wonderful) message," and "good (or wonderful) report," and the proposed translation of the verb εὐαγγελίζομαι are the phrases "to tell or announce good (or wonderful) news, a good (or wonderful) message, or a good (or wonderful) report."

[32] σωτηρία – usual translation: "salvation." The word "salvation" is not often used in professional contemporary American English. More often used are the accurate translations of "rescue, deliverance." Paul uses this noun only one time in all of his writings: here in this Treatise (Eph. 1:13). However, he uses the verb form (σώζω) many times throughout his writings (29 times) and twice in this Treatise; in Eph. 2:5 and 2:8. See note on σώζω at Eph. 2:5.

[33] ἅγιος πνεύματος – usual translation: "Holy Spirit" (Eph. 1:13, 4:30). When used in the New Testament, this phrase refers to the third Divine Person of the Triune Godhead. However, as explained above (see note at Eph. 1:1 on the meaning of the word ἅγιος), "holy" refers to the *effect*, not to the *cause*, which is the activity of the Divine Person appointed with the task of specially selecting His own human recruits for the High King of the future world. Therefore, the proposed translation of this phrase is: "Specially Selecting Spirit," referring to the third Divine Person of the Trinity.

[34] σφραγίζω, Ion. σφρηγίζω, *close or enclose with a seal*, σφραγίζεις λύεις τ' ὀπίσω . . πεύκην (= δέλτον) E.IA38 (anap.);...**2. *authenticate a document with a seal*,** IG9(1).61.78,95 (Daulis, ii B.C.):....τὸ βιβλίον τῆς κτήσεως τὸ ἐσφραγισμένον LXX Je.39(32).11; τὴν παρὰ τοῦ βασιλέως διὰ τῆς θυρίδος ἐσφραγισμένην . . <ἔντευξιν> UPZ53.5 (ii B.C.). **3. *certify an object after examination by attaching a seal*** (cf. Hdt.2.38), μέτροις . . ἐξητασμένοις καὶ ἐσφραγισμένοις ὑπὸ τοῦ οἰκονόμου PRev.Laws 25.10 (iii B.C)...[LS]. Usually translated "seal." Etymology of the word "seal:" Middle English *selen*, from Old

French *seeler,* from *seel,* n. transitive verb: **1:** to confirm or make secure by or as if by a seal: confirm in a particular association...as **a:** to give a character to (a person) such that he may be recognized as belonging to an agent....**2a:** to set or affix an authenticating seal to; also: to formally authenticate: RATIFY **b:** to mark with a stamp usually as an evidence of standard exactness, legal size, weight, or capacity, or merchantable quality **c:** to give under or as if under seal: grant authentically...**d:** to give authenticity to [W]. Thus, the main idea conveyed by the Greek verb σφραγίζω appears to be something like "to make the practice of professions that significantly affect the public health, safety and welfare legally possible by a legitimizing authority or agency, by publicly certifying that individual professionals are competent to practice their particular profession by officially licensing them to practice through the use of the application of their signification by the use of legally defined, publicly displayed stamp or official symbol, granted and regulated by the legitimizing governmental authority." In contemporary American professional life, individual professionals who actively practice within their respective professions (e.g., medicine, law, teaching, architecture, engineering, etc.) must be so certified by such a legitimizing authority, usually the State Government. For example, the following is an excerpt from the Texas Engineering Practice Act, which is administered and enforced by the Texas Board of Professional Engineers:

"**1. THE LAW.** The...engineer's registration law...is cited as the Texas Engineering Practice Act (CHAPTER 1001, TEXAS OCCUPATIONS CODE)...By Legislative intent, in order to protect the public health, safety, and welfare, the practice of engineering is entrusted only to those persons duly licensed and practicing under the Act. Only licensed engineers may call themselves or be otherwise designated as "any kind of an engineer" or use the term "engineer" or any variations thereof as a professional, business, or commercial title, name, representation, claim, asset, or means of advantage or benefit. The Act prohibits unlicensed persons from practicing, offering or attempting to practice engineering; the direct or indirect use of proscribed engineering terms; or the receipt of any fee or compensation or promise of same for performing, offering, or attempting to perform any part of engineering as defined by the Act."

"Licensed engineers must properly identify themselves as such by using one of the following identifications after their name: "Engineer, Professional Engineer, or P.E. *They must affix their official seal to the engineering documents when issued* [italics added; see example of official seal (left) – GWC]; abide by the Act, rules, and standards of conduct and ethics; and maintain their license in an active, unexpired status."

The idea that emerges is, that in the same way that a professional doctor, teacher, lawyer, architect or engineer must be "sealed" by the State government in which they practice their profession, which renders it legally and actually possible for them to heal, teach, practice law, architecture or engineering, so also each individual specially selected recruit must be "sealed" by the "Specially Selecting

Spirit" of God, which renders it legally and actually possible for that recruit to discover and accomplish their unique "lifework" (Greek: κλῆσις = "lifework," see note at Eph. 1:18 for philological analysis of this concept) for God during their present lifetimes, as they experience the supernatural assistance of the Spirit.

[35] κληρονομία – Usual translation: "inheritance," Paul uses this word in this Treatise more than in all of his other writings (three times = Eph. 1:14, 1:18, 5:5), but only one time each in Galatians and Colossians. Thus, his definitive development of this concept is in this Treatise. Literally (denotatively), the word means "appointment (κλῆρος) obtained by law (νόμος); and thus, legal appointment" (see note on the verb form κληρόω at Eph. 1:11) [LS]. Proposed translation: "inheritance," which still conveys a perfectly accurate concept in contemporary professional American English.

[36] ἀρραβών, ῶνος, ὁ, *earnest-money, caution-money, deposited by the purchaser and forfeited if the purchase is not completed*, ἀ. δοῦναί τινος Is.8.20, cf. Arist.*Pol.*1259a12, Stilpoap.D.L.2.118, BGU446.18 (ii A. D.): pl., *deposits required from public contractors*, IPE12.32B34 (Olbia) [LS]. Usually translated "earnest," i.e., "earnest money." The idea seems to be that, unlike the giving of the Spirit during the era of the Old Testament, in which divine powers or abilities were granted to only a few, were given to them fully, were temporary and were given for the purpose of fulfilling a specific role or task requiring supernatural leadership skill, whether physical or psychological (e.g., the craftsmen who constructed the Tabernacle [super-artists], Samson [super-warrior strength], David [super-military commander] King Solomon [super-wise ruler], the Prophets [super-accurate Spokesmen of God's messages], etc.), in the era of the New Testament, the Spirit gives certain specific divine powers to all of His specially selected recruits; but unlike the Old Testament era, they are given only a small portion (ἀρραβών = "down payment") of the divine enablement that will be ultimately granted to them in full measure during the future era of their immortal lives in the Kingdom Age. The consistent feature of all three eras (the Old Testament era, the New Testament era and the era of the future Millennial Kingdom) appears to be that the divine powers of the Spirit are granted to human beings for the purpose of accomplishing a specific role or task requiring *supernatural spiritual leadership*. See Ephesians Chapter 4 for Paul's further development of this supernatural (yet still partial) gifting, granting and enabling power given to God's specially selected recruits for leadership tasks by His Spirit.

[37] περιποίησις, "that which has been gained through acquisition and saved" [LS]. In this context, proposed translation: "interest bearing savings account."

[38] Acts 18:9-11 "Now the Lord (κυρίος) spoke to Paul in the night by a vision, 'Do not be afraid, but speak, an do not keep silent; for I am with you, and no one will attack you to hurt you; for I have many people in this city (Corinth).' And he (Paul) continued there a year and six months, teaching the word of God among them" (approx. 50-51 A.D.).

³⁹ Acts 18:19-21 "And he (Paul) came to Ephesus, and left them (Aquila and Priscilla) there; but he himself entered the synagogue and reasoned with the Jews. When they asked him to stay a longer time with them, he did not consent, but took leave of them, saying, 'I must by all means keep this coming feast in Jerusalem; but I will return again to you, God willing.' And he sailed from Ephesus" (approx. 52 A.D.).

⁴⁰ Acts 19:10 "And this (Paul's teaching the "disciples" daily in the school of Tyrannus) continued for two years, so that all who dwelt in Asia heard the word of the Lord (κυρίος) Jesus, both Jews and Greeks." From Acts 20:31, we know that the total duration of Ephesus as Paul's headquarters was three years, because upon departing from there he commissions the leaders of his Ephesian apprentices as follows: "Therefore watch, and remember that for *three years* I did not cease to warn everyone night and day with tears" (approx. 53, 54, 55 A.D.).

⁴¹ **μνεία** – ἡ, A. = μνήμη, *remembrance*, βίου δὲ τοῦ παρόντος οὐ μνείαν ἔχεις S.El.392, cf. E.Ph.464, Pl.Lg.798b; κατά γε τὴν ἐμὴν μ. dub. in Ael. VH6.1; μνείας χάριν, *freq. in late epitaphs*, IG3.3112, al. **II.** *mention*, περί τινος μνείαν ποιεῖσθαι And.1.100, cf. Aeschin.1.160; περί τινος πρός τινα Pl.Prt.317e; τὴν μνείαν περί τινος ἀποδιδόναι Arist.*PA*58b13; ὅ τι καὶ μνείας ἄξιον Id.*Pol*.1274b17; μ. τινῶν ποιεῖσθαι ἐπὶ τῶν προσευχῶν *Ep.Rom*.1.9 al., cf. Epigr.Gr.983.3 (i B. C.); *reminder*, τινος Pl.Phdr.254a;...[LS]. Usually translated "remembrance," or "mention." The noun **μνεία** is derived from the verb **μνάομαι**. Upon study, it becomes clear that both the verb and the noun forms do not primarily mean "to remember," or "remembrance" in the sense of "to use the mental faculty of memory in order to recall to mind an experience that occurred in previous linear time." This is because Paul says in Romans 1:9 (see above reference) that he "makes mention" of them in his communication with God, but it is clear that when Paul wrote his Letter/Treatise to the Romans, he had not yet been there. This observation is reinforced upon inspection of the use of the verb **μνάομαι**: contr. **μνῶμαι**...**I.** *to be mindful of*, c. gen., οὐ πολέμοιο ἐμνώοντο Il.2.686;...also, *turn one's mind to a thing*, φύγαδε μνώοντο ἕκαστος Il.16.697 [LS]. Metzger also points out that the ancient root of this verb is the sound "**MA**" and that the basic concept conveyed by this root is "to use mental discipline to persistently think about something, i.e., to reflectively think about something." When passages from Aristotle's *Politics* are consulted, it becomes clear that this word **μνεία** means "to, in a disciplined manner, deliberately think about and reflect upon something that is initially indeterminate (vague and incoherent), in order to eventually and accurately comprehend its determinate (specific distinctive) meaning." The following passages from Aristotle's *Politics* are helpful (ed. W. D. Ross, Oxford, 1957; transl. H. Rackham. Cambridge, 1944):

> Arist., *Politics*, Book 3, Section [1274b][17] Δράκοντος δὲ νόμοι μὲν εἰσί, πολιτείᾳ δ' ὑπαρχούσῃ τοὺς νόμους ἔθηκεν· ἴδιον δ' ἐν τοῖς νόμοις οὐδὲν ἔστιν ὅ τι καὶ **μνείας** ἄξιον, πλὴν ἡ χαλεπότης διὰ τὸ τῆς ζημίας μέγεθος.

Transl.: "There are laws of Draco, but he legislated for an existing constitution, and there is nothing peculiar in his laws that is worthy of *mention* (i.c, "deliberate, disciplined reflection so as to gain wisdom from"), except their severity in imposing heavy punishment" [transl. – GWC].

Arist., *Politics* Book 4, Section 1[293b][17]: τελευταῖον δὲ περὶ τυραννίδος εὔλογόν ἐστι ποιήσασθαι **μνείαν** διὰ τὸ πασῶν ἥκιστα ταύτην εἶναι πολιτείαν...

Transl.: "And to complete our study of governmental forms, when we consider a tyranny (a complete monarchy), a good word is to be made in the following Treatise when we come to the appropriate place *to mention* it, *consider* it and *reflect upon* it, even though among of all those forms of government we have considered, this one is usually considered to be a constitutional government the least of all (because our main objective in this Treatise is the pursuit of that which constitutes an ideal constitutional government)" [transl. – GWC].

Thus, the proposed translation for the word μνεία is "to make it a part of one's daily discipline and routine to deliberately and specifically think about and reflect upon something (or someone) in order to formulate specific plans do something about it (or for them)." In so doing, one enables others to discover the ability God has given them to become "creative," and to use this specific gift of creativity from God to be employed in the accomplishment of their lifework.

[42] προσεύχομαι – Usually translated "pray." Paul uses the word προσεύχομαι to describe this vital activity for maintaining the quality of the spiritual life three times in this Treatise: here in Eph. 1:16; and in Eph. 6:18 twice (once as a verb, and once in its noun form – προσευχή). The Greek word προσεύχομαι is a compound word made from two smaller Greek words: **προ** = "before" (or **προς** = "to, towards") + **εὔχομαι** = "to wish, desire, or hope for something to come about in the future." From a study of the Concordance of the *Septuagint* (especially *Daniel* Chapter 9), and the NT, the old common vernacular British translation of this word as the word "pray" is no longer used in professional contemporary American English usage, except for very minor and specific usage in legal documents stating the case in law suits [Webster: Main Entry: **pray** – Etymology: Middle English *preyen, prayen*, from Old French *preier*, from Latin *precari*, from *prec-, prex* request, entreaty, prayer; akin to Old English *gefr[AE]ge* hearsay, report, *fricgan, frignan, frīnan* to ask, inquire, Old High German *frāga* question, *frāgēn* to ask, Old Norse *frētt* question, *fregna* to inquire, find out, Gothic *fraihman* to find out by inquiry, Tocharian A *prak-* to ask, Sanskrit *prās* interrogation, *prcchati* he asks - [W].

Therefore, it is proposed that the Greek word προσεύχομαι be translated as follows: "to make a request to God for divine information, in order to discover sufficient essential facts necessary to make an important spiritual decision in the future, or to seek out God's advice and direction in the process of gaining a spiritual understanding or perspective in order to plan an important course of action for the future."

However, the concomitant interest of "lobbying" or "submitting official petitions" to heaven for our spiritual desires is equally emphasized in the NT (see extensive philology on the Greek concept conveyed by the word δέησις = "to lobby or submit official petitions to God," developed in the note on the word δέησις at Eph. 6:18). Jesus Himself uses this word προσεύχομαι where He gives specific and precise instructions to us on how we should conduct our communication with God, which sensibly, thoughtfully and prudently merge these two emphases of προσεύχομαι = "to seek out information by asking God for His advice and direction in the process of gaining a spiritual understanding or perspective in order to plan an important course of action for the future," and δέησις = "to lobby or submit official petitions to God to act in our behalf;" in Matt. 6:9-13 (traditionally called the Lord's Prayer; imperative verbs shown in bold type):

6:9 Οὕτως οὖν **προσεύχεσθε** ὑμεῖς·
Πάτερ ἡμῶν ὁ ἐν τοῖς οὐρανοῖς,
ἁγιασθήτω τὸ ὄνομά σου,
10 **ἐλθέτω** ἡ βασιλεία σου, **γενηθήτω** τὸ θέλημά σου, ὡς ἐν οὐρανῷ καὶ ἐπὶ γῆς.
11 Τὸν ἄρτον ἡμῶν τὸν ἐπιούσιον **δὸς** ἡμῖν σήμερον·
12 καὶ **ἄφες** ἡμῖν τὰ ὀφειλήματα ἡμῶν, ὡς καὶ ἡμεῖς ἀφήκαμεν τοῖς ὀφειλέταις ἡμῶν·
13 καὶ **μὴ εἰσενέγκῃς** ἡμᾶς εἰς πειρασμόν, ἀλλὰ **ῥῦσαι** ἡμᾶς ἀπὸ τοῦ πονηροῦ.

Basic translation into English is as follows – GWC:

6:9 Therefore, whenever you (all) **make** (your) **requests** (to God), do so in the following manner – say:
"Our Father, the One who is in the heavens,
Make Your Name **special**.
10 **Bring** Your Kingdom.
Bring Your will **into being**, as in heaven, so also upon the earth.
11 **Give** to us this day our daily supply of bread.
12 And **forgive** us our indebtedness in the same way that we forgive those who are indebted to us.
13 And **do not lead** us into temptation, but **guard** us from the Evil One."

The following extended interpretational translation of the above central passage is proposed to show that Jesus' instruction on communication with God is a perfect blending in which the meanings of προσεύχομαι and δέησις merge:

Matt. 6:9 (Jesus speaking:) "You should form the spiritual habit of making daily requests for information, advice and direction from God, organized in your mind according to the following model of discipline, and according to the following order of importance. You should all address God as "our Father," but always be aware that He lives beyond the stars of the universe – nevertheless, that does not diminish His ability to hear and respond to you instantaneously. You should make your requests to God on a daily basis according to the following outline of six regular concerns. The first three concern God's interests because His interests are more important than ours, and thus take priority over ours. The second three concern our interests because God loves us and is interested in providing and sustaining our well being. This form of address will balance the two relational emphases that should frame your relationship with God: first, orienting your lives around His interests and goals as a priority; and second, knowing that He has an intimate concern for your ultimate maturity and best interest, just as a Father would for His son or daughter, but not in a trivial, glib or distant way. Thus, you should approach God with your daily requests according to the following outline:

1. '**Make** Your Name **special** in my life today. Let me always be actually more excited and thrilled knowing that You are pleased with me as You evaluate my decisions and actions today.

2. (v. 10) **Bring** the future High King and His Millennial Kingdom to the earth today. I am actually looking forward with more expectation to the inauguration of the Kingdom than I am with any of the important plans, deals or initiatives that I have planned for today. But if not today, then...

3. Use me and my lifework to **bring** Your will **about** on the earth today in increasingly wider spheres of influence and to greater extents, until such time as your High King does return to set up His Regal Administration.

4. (v. 11) **Provide** for the financial and temporal requirements for myself, my family, and my business and employees today. (Here one should specifically request and "lobby" God to bring success with one's proposals, business initiatives, current projects, collections and other matters that have to do with one's business and financial interests).

5. (v. 12) **Forgive** me of the things I ought to have done for You and for other people but failed to do, (name specifics, as in an official petition). In addition, enable me to forgive those who ought to have done things for me but didn't (name specifics as above); because I realize that You will forgive me by the same measure that I forgive others, and that being released from emotional anger, resentment and bitterness toward others is essential for me to make mature decisions today, in order that my mind may remain unclouded and undistracted, so that I may be able to remain sensitive to and discern divine 'contacts' from You to enable me to gain other slight but unique insights into what Your lifework for me in fact entails.

6. (v. 13) **Prevent** me from encountering situations today that would cause me to be tempted to do unethical or immoral acts. Because I realize that Satan does have an active and detailed plan to destroy my life, I ask that You effectively **shield** and **guard** me from his plans to harm me today.'"

[43] ἀποκάλυψις [κᾰ], εως, ἡ, uncovering, of the head, Phld.Vit.p.38J.; *disclosing, of hidden springs*, Plu.Aem.14: metaph., ἁμαρτίας Id.2.7o f; *revelation,* esp. of *divine mysteries, Ep.Rom.*16.25, etc.; of persons, *manifestation, 2 Ep.Thess.*1.7, etc.; title of the *Apocalypse* [LS]. The Greek word ἀποκάλυψις is made from two Greek words: ἀπο (= "away from") and κάλυψις (noun derived from the verb καλύπτω = "to hide, conceal, cover, veil"). The name of the Greek goddess Καλυψώ (= "Calypso"), from whom Odysseus must escape in Homer's *Odyssey*, is derived from καλύπτω, ('she that conceals')...Od.1.14, Hes.Th.359, etc [LS]. When the two Greek words ἀπο and κάλυψις are combined into the compound word ἀποκάλυψις, the meaning that emerges is "to withdraw a cover or veil from, to uncover, to unveil." In context, the adjective "unveiled" seems the best American English translation here.

[44] σοφίᾳ – Refer to note at Eph. 1:8, where we recall that the Greek word σοφίᾳ does not really mean "wisdom," but rather more something like, "the kind of

knowledge that makes it possible for us to become competent, then gain mastery, then achieve superior leadership ability in living human life skillfully, especially in the ethical and political arenas."

[45] καρδία – usual translation: "heart." The "heart" is one of Paul's most important metaphors. He uses it 52 times in his treatises and letters in the NT, most frequently in Romans (15 times), in the Corinthian letters (16 times) and in this Treatise to the Ephesians (6 times – Eph. 1:18, 3:17, 4:18, 5:19, 6:5, 22). This concept is somewhat difficult to recover in professional American English. Therefore, the following analysis is offered in an attempt to reconstruct this important concept that is absolutely vital to good and effective leadership:

a. The "heart," like the mind, is a spiritual reality. It is a power, but unlike the powers of the mind (memory, attention, and expectation), it cannot be turned "off." It is always "on." The heart can have thoughts, but these thoughts are not advanced, complex concepts or ideas. They might be more properly called "inclinations." Further, they are inclinations to act in ethical or unethical ways. (Gen. 6:5 "every imagination of the thoughts of his heart were only evil continually." Matt. 15:19 "Out of the heart proceed evil thoughts"). This means that when one willfully creates continually impure imaginational images and intentions, he is doing it in his "heart" (Matt. 5:28), and such a person has an "impure heart." Conversely, one can discipline himself to consciously avoid this tendency of the heart, and have a "pure" heart. An impure heart leads to unhappiness, and a pure heart leads to happiness (Matt. 5:8 "Happy are the pure in heart.")

b. God has a "heart." This must mean that His ethical inclinations are to do good only. (Gen. 6:6 – "And it repented the LORD that he had made man on the earth, and it grieved him at His heart.") A good heart experiences grief when it observes moral or ethical evil being done.

c. It is possible for a leader to "harden" his heart. Leaders make leadership decisions with their heart. These decisions are made with the awareness that they are or are not in consonance with divine or ethical authority. Accordingly, to "harden" one's heart means to become resolved to make ethical leadership decisions that defy God's will or laws. This results in a proud, arrogant disposition, and the leader can be said to have a "proud heart." Pride is therefore a "thought of the heart." If this is true, then God can judge the leader by making him more proud, which leads to his greater judgment. (Ex. 7:3-4 "And I [God] will harden Pharaoh's heart... But Pharaoh shall not hearken unto you.")

d. Proud leaders always harden their own hearts (i.e., have proud thoughts against God or His ethical laws) before God continues to harden their hearts. (Ex. 8:15 – "But when Pharaoh saw that there was respite, he hardened his heart, and hearkened not unto them.") To harden one's heart means to allow the inclination of disobedience due to pride to become a fixed resolve of permanent rebellion that guides all future thoughts and decisions of the mind. Therefore, humility (the opposite attitude of arrogance or pride) is also a "thought of the heart."

e. Fear and anxiety are experienced within the heart. Communication with God is a spiritual discipline that brings peace to the heart (Phil. 4: 6-8).

f. Although the mind is a distinct spiritual power that is capable of loving God and other people, the primary spiritual power within the personality that loves is the heart.

Love in this sense means to decide to be loyal to, to trust, to confide in, to be dedicated to (Matt. 22:36-40: "You shall love the Lord you God with all your *heart*, and with all your soul, and with all your mind...and you shall love your neighbor as yourself").

g. This has several implications. First, that as leaders, we are always projecting to others the thoughts of our heart, consciously or unconsciously, whereas we can usually develop the personality skills to either display or mask the thoughts of our minds (Matt. 6:21 "Where your treasure is, there will your heart be also." Matt. 12:34 "Out of the heart the mouth speaks"). Second, the "thoughts of the heart" seem to be prerequisite to the "thoughts of the mind." In other words, in order to think rationally, one must first dedicate himself to be loyal to what is right and good ethically.

h. One believes with the "thoughts of the heart." (Romans 10:10 "For with the heart man believes unto righteousness...").

i. Patience is a "thought of the heart."

SUMMARY. The word "heart" (although suffering decline and misuse) is not yet lost to proper usage in professional American English. Therefore, in order to be rescued and used properly it must be reinvested in our language with its proper meaning. A summary statement of the proposed meaning for the "heart" refers first to the inclinational power, and then to the ethical decision making power of the soul (that remains distinct from the rational decision making power of the mind), in that the heart's ethical decisions cannot ultimately be successfully masked or concealed, as the decisions of the mind can; and so, the personality characteristics of fear or courage, rage or calmness, sorrow or joy, disloyalty or loyalty, hate or love, impatience or patience, unbelief or belief, despair or hope, pride (arrogance) or humility are all "thoughts of the heart." Further, this inclinational and ethical decision-making power of the soul can be strengthened by one asking God to do so.

[46] κλῆσις – usual translation: "calling." This word reflects an important concept for Paul. It is a noun, and it is derived from the verb καλέω = "to call, summon" [LS]. Its adjectival form is the word κλητός = "called, summoned" [LS]. Paul uses this word five times in Ephesians; three times as a noun (Eph. 1:18; 4:1, 4), and two times as a verb (Eph. 4:1, 4). In all of his writings, he uses this word 48 times (32 times as a verb, 9 times as a noun, and 7 times as an adjective). It is probably the most important single concept in the Treatise. Originally, the noun form of this word meant an official "summons," both formal (a "legal summons"), and informal (an "invitation") [LS]. It then came to mean one's "vocation" (Latin = "**vocatio**"), line of work, or life-profession. Paul uses this latter meaning to introduce the specific nuance of a unique and special "lifework," "life purpose," or "life project" that God "summons" or "appoints" each of us to discover and accomplish.

In Ephesians as well as in his other Treatises and letters, Paul uses this word in two ways. He uses it to refer to the specific future leadership roles that God will reward to trustworthy and reliable Christians during the Millennial Kingdom, but he also uses the word to refer to the "lifework" of the Christian in this life by which he becomes qualified for that future role. Thus, sometimes, the concept of "apprenticeship" seems more appropriate. Sometimes both meanings seem to be fused together. After he uses it here in Eph. 1:18, he returns to this theme in the very first topic sentence of the second half of the Treatise (Eph. 4:1), where his objective is to make application of the theological provisions in the first half of the Treatise into everyday life to enable us to discover our "lifework" through those venues.

Not only is the concept that God has a unique and special "lifework" (κλῆσις) for each of us the most important concept in this Treatise, it is also a dominant theme in Paul's other Treatises. He uses the word as a noun (κλῆσις) a total of six other times in five of his other Treatises to refer to the same inclusive concept he uses it to mean in Ephesians (Rom. 11:29; 1 Cor. 1:26; 7:20, Phil. 3:14; 2 Thess. 1:11; 2 Tim. 1:9). For example, in 2 Tim.1:9, when Paul's chief apprentice, Timothy, became discouraged after Paul delegated him to lead the "Lifework Council" (ἐκκλησία) at Ephesus for several years, Paul encouraged him by reminding him of this central truth in the following passage, in which he used the word twice, once as a participle, and once as a noun, as follows:

2 Tim.1:8-11 ⁸Μὴ οὖν ἐπαισχυνθῇς τὸ μαρτύριον τοῦ Κυρίου ἡμῶν μηδὲ ἐμὲ τὸν δέσμιον αὐτοῦ, ἀλλὰ συγκακοπάθησον τῷ εὐαγγελίῳ κατὰ δύναμιν Θεοῦ, ⁹τοῦ σώσαντος ἡμᾶς καὶ **καλέσαντος κλήσει** ἁγίᾳ, οὐ κατὰ τὰ ἔργα ἡμῶν, ἀλλὰ κατ' ἰδίαν πρόθεσιν καὶ χάριν, τὴν δοθεῖσαν ἡμῖν ἐν Χριστῷ Ἰησοῦ πρὸ χρόνων αἰωνίων, ¹⁰φανερωθεῖσαν δὲ νῦν διὰ τῆς ἐπιφανείας τοῦ Σωτῆρος ἡμῶν Ἰησοῦ Χριστοῦ, καταργήσαντος μὲν τὸν θάνατον, φωτίσαντος δὲ ζωὴν καὶ ἀφθαρσίαν διὰ τοῦ εὐαγγελίου, ¹¹εἰς ὃ ἐτέθην ἐγὼ κῆρυξ καὶ ἀπόστολος καὶ διδάσκαλος ἐθνῶν. ¹²Δι' ἣν αἰτίαν καὶ ταῦτα πάσχω, ἀλλ' οὐκ ἐπαισχύνομαι, οἶδα γὰρ ᾧ πεπίστευκα καὶ πέπεισμαι ὅτι δυνατός ἐστι τὴν παραθήκην μου φυλάξαι εἰς ἐκείνην τὴν ἡμέραν.

Transl.: "⁸Consequently, you must stop being ashamed and reticent to execute the tough assignment which I commissioned you to carry out there in Ephesus, of continuing to forthrightly state the case for our Commander in Chief, and for me, His duly bonded agent. On the contrary, you must never give up when you continue to suffer hostility, because whenever you announce His wonderful message as you are empowered by God, opposition from others will inevitably come with it. ⁹He is the One Whose responsibility it is to guard us and rescue us from the dangers we face in this task, because He is *the One Who summoned* (καλέσαντος) us and commissioned us to accomplish the *lifework* (κλήσει) that He has specially selected for us in the first place. This special lifework bears no relation to just any of the professions or vocations we might have easily chosen for ourselves. Unlike those occupations, God deliberately planned a unique lifework for each of us before this historical era ever began. ¹⁰Each one was then officially and graciously assigned to each of us by our future High King, Jesus. Due to the first divine Visit and historical Appearance of our Liberator, Jesus, the future High King of the earth, it has now become possible for Him to liberate each of us by enabling us to discover and openly demonstrate what our lifework is. The reason we don't need to be afraid of those who oppose us is because the central claim of His wonderful message, after all, is that He is the One Who has now put death out of commission, and finally brought out into the light of public view exactly what eternal life and immortality are like. ¹¹As you know, I was assigned the lifework of being His official Envoy, High Emissary and Teacher of all of the ethnic races and nations foreign to Judaism, whether they are civilized Greeks or uncivilized

Barbarians. ¹²In fact, the reason that I myself suffer hostility all the time for this very cause, but am never ashamed or hesitant to speak about Him, is because I have fully realized Who it is that I have placed my confidence in. It is also because I have been persuaded by Him that He is quite able to watch over and guard my life, which I have entrusted to Him to protect until the specific day He has determined that my lifework is accomplished [transl. – GWC]."

Furthermore, the other writers of the New Testament use this word numerous times to convey the same concept. For example, the writer of the *Treatise to the Hebrews* says in Hebrews 11:8-10 that God not only "summoned" (**καλέω**) Abraham to his lifework to be the founder of the nation of Israel during his mortal life, but that his "summons" also included the promise of living in God's future "city" (**πόλις**) that God will build during the Millennial Kingdom, as follows:

Hebrews 11:8-10 ⁸Πίστει **καλούμενος** Ἀβραὰμ ὑπήκουσεν ἐξελθεῖν εἰς τὸν τόπον ὃν ἤμελλε λαμβάνειν εἰς κληρονομίαν. Καὶ ἐξῆλθε μὴ ἐπιστάμενος ποῦ ἔρχεται. ⁹Πίστει παρῴκησεν εἰς γῆν τῆς ἐπαγγελίας ὡς ἀλλοτρίαν, ἐν σκηναῖς κατοικήσας μετὰ Ἰσαὰκ καὶ Ἰακὼβ τῶν συνκληρονόμων τῆς ἐπαγγελίας τῆς αὐτῆς. ¹⁰Ἐξεδέχετο γὰρ τὴν τοὺς θεμελίους ἔχουσαν πόλιν, ἧς τεχνίτης καὶ δημιουργὸς ὁ θεός.

Transl.: "⁸By faith, **when** Abraham **was summoned** (**καλούμενος**) by God to go out to the land which he would receive as an inheritance in the future, he obeyed Him. In fact, he departed when he didn't even know where he was going. ⁹He spent his entire mortal life there by faith – living beside the land that he had been promised, like a foreigner. Moreover, he lived like an Explorer would – in tents – even throughout the lifetimes of his own son Isaac and grandson Jacob, who were to be included as co-inheritors of the same future promise along with him. ¹⁰He did this because he was waiting to receive a city whose foundation had yet to be laid, Whose Architect and Builder is God [transl. – GWC]."

In addition, the word **κλῆσις** is an important word because it is the main root word in the Greek compound word **ἐκκλησία** (translated "Lifework Apprenticeship Council" – see extended note on **ἐκκλησία** at Eph. 1:22 below). Accordingly, it is proposed that Eph. 1:18 serves to encapsulate the central thematic concept of this entire Treatise. Proposed translation: "lifework," "life purpose," "life project," or sometimes (when referring specifically to our mortal lifework), "apprenticeship."

⁴⁷ **νεκρός** – usual translation: "dead" (1:20; 2:1, 5; 5:14). Earliest denotative meaning in Homer: "corpse," especially of a body lying dead as a result of being killed in a military battle. Later came to be used of a person not yet dead, but dying. Connotative meaning: metaphorically, of a living person who is dying or about to die prematurely. Proposed denotative translation: "dead body," "death." Proposed connotative translation: "as good as dead."

⁴⁸ **ἀρχῆς...ἐξουσίας...δυνάμεως...κυριότητος** – usual translation: "rulers," "authorities," "sovereign powers," "leadership offices" (Eph. 1:21, 2:2, 3:10, 6:12). Proposed meaning of this phrase in Ephesians: "the organized spiritual infrastructure or echelon of good angels charged by God with the operation of the universe and who remain loyal to Him under His rule; as well as the separate

organized spiritual echelon of angels who rebelled against God and are under Satan's control." Paul uses this phrase in his Treatises and letters consistently to refer mostly to angelic hierarchies of authority (both good and evil) but he also uses it to refer to human government officials and authoritative leadership offices (both good and evil), as demonstrated in the following passages:

Rom. 8:38-39 Πέπεισμαι γὰρ ὅτι οὔτε θάνατος οὔτε ζωὴ οὔτε **ἄγγελοι** οὔτε **ἀρχαὶ** οὔτε **δυνάμεις** ἐνεστῶτα οὔτε μέλλοντα οὔτε ὕψωμα οὔτε βάθος οὔτε τις κτίσις ἑτέρα δυνήσεται ἡμᾶς χωρίσαι ἀπὸ τῆς ἀγάπης τοῦ Θεοῦ τῆς ἐν Χριστῷ᾽ Ἰησοῦ τῷ κυρίῳ ἡμῶν.

Transl.: "For I am persuaded, that neither death, nor life, nor *angels*, nor *angelic regimes*, nor *sovereign powers*, nor things present, nor things to come, nor height, nor depth, nor any other created thing, will be able to separate us from God's love in the High King, Jesus our Commander in Chief."

1 Cor. 15:24-25: Εἶτα τὸ τέλος, ὅταν παραδῷ τὴν βασιλείαν τῷ Θεῷ καὶ Πατρί, ὅταν καταργήσῃ πᾶσαν **ἀρχὴν** καὶ πᾶσαν **ἐξουσίαν** καὶ **δύναμιν**, δεῖ γὰρ αὐτὸν βασιλεύειν ἄχρι οὗ θῇ πάντας τοὺς ἐχθροὺς ὑπὸ τοὺς πόδας αὐτοῦ.

Transl.: "Then comes the end, when He [Jesus] delivers the Kingdom to God the Father; when He has finally put all evil *angelic regimes* and *hierarchies of authority*, as well as *sovereign powers* established by evil human governments out of commission, because the Scriptures declare that 'He must reign until he has put all his enemies under His feet.'"

Eph. 1:21 καὶ ἐκάθισεν ἐν δεξιᾷ αὐτοῦ ἐν τοῖς ἐπουρανίοις ὑπεράνω **πάσης ἀρχῆς καὶ ἐξουσίας καὶ δυνάμεως καὶ κυριότητος** καὶ **παντὸς ὀνόματος ὀνομαζομένου** οὐ μόνον ἐν τῷ αἰῶνι τούτῳ ἀλλὰ καὶ ἐν τῷ μέλλοντι.

Transl.: "...by seating Him at His right hand in the heavens far above all *angelic regimes* and *hierarchies of authority*, as well as over all *sovereign powers* and *leadership offices* established by human governments, even above *every authoritative title that has ever been conferred* – whether angelic or human – not only over both the good as well as the evil angelic forces and human leadership regimes during this historical era, but also over only the good human and angelic leadership hierarchies that will be established in the Kingdom era that is about to come."

Eph. 2:2 ἐν αἷς ποτε περιεπατήσατε κατὰ τὸν αἰῶνα τοῦ κόσμου τούτου, κατὰ **τὸν ἄρχοντα τῆς ἐχουσίας** τοῦ ἀέρος, τοῦ **πνεύματος** τοῦ νῦν ἐνεργοῦντος ἐν τοῖς υἱοῖς τῆς ἀπειθείας·

Transl.: "You were in this predicament because at one time, you all deliberately conducted your lives according to the misguided philosophical world view of this present era of civilization, namely – the *polytheistic hierarchy of gods* who live in the sky under the *authority* of the *sky-god Zeus*. At the present time, this spiritual being is in fact the very same evil *spiritual being* who is incessantly working behind the scenes among the disobedient sons of God,..."

Eph. 3:10 ἵνα γνωρισθῇ νῦν **ταῖς ἀρχαῖς** καὶ **ταῖς ἐξουσίαις** ἐν τοῖς ἐπουρανίοις διὰ τῆς ἐκκλησίας ἡ πολυποίκιλος σοφία τοῦ Θεοῦ,

Transl.: "God has waited until this historical era to take this initiative so that His training of human beings to achieve the multi-faceted mastery of the political and ethical skills required to live with and lead others effectively, which He will accomplish through the specific agency of His "Kingdom Apprenticeship Councils," might now be made known for the first time to the *angelic regimes* and *hierarchies of authority* – both good and evil – throughout all of the heavenly realms."

Eph. 6:12 Ὅτι οὐκ ἔστιν ἡμῖν ἡ πάλη πρὸς αἷμα καὶ σάρκα, ἀλλὰ πρὸς **τὰς ἀρχάς**, πρὸς **τὰς ἐξουσίας**, πρὸς **τοὺς κοσμοκράτορας** τοῦ σκότους τοῦ αἰῶνος τούτου, πρὸς τὰ πνευματικὰ τῆς πονηρίας ἐν τοῖς ἐπουρανίοις.

Transl.: "...because our fight is not actually against 'flesh and blood' human beings, but is in reality against the evil *angelic regimes,* against the evil *angelic hierarchies of authority*, against the evil *human government regimes* that control this present historical era of darkness, – or more accurately – against the evil *hierarchy of spiritual beings that live in the sky* (i.e., the atmosphere of the earth), which in fact manipulate and control them."

Col. 1:16 ὅτι ἐν αὐτῷ ἐκτίσθη τὰ πάντα τὰ ἐν τοῖς οὐρανοῖς καὶ τὰ ἐπὶ τῆς γῆς, τὰ ὁρατὰ καὶ τὰ ἀόρατα, εἴτε **θρόνοι** εἴτε **κυριότητες** εἴτε **ἀρχαὶ** εἴτε **ἐξουσίαι**· τὰ πάντα δι' αὐτοῦ καὶ εἰς αὐτὸν ἔκτισται,

Transl.: "For all things were created by Him, in the heavens and on the earth, both visible things and invisible things, whether they be *seats of human governmental power* or *leadership offices*, or *angelic regimes* or *hierarchies of authority;* all things were created by Him, and for Him."

Col. 2:10 καὶ ἐστὲ ἐν αὐτῷ πεπληρωμένοι, ὅς ἐστιν ἡ κεφαλὴ πάσης **ἀρχῆς** καὶ **ἐξουσίας**,

Transl.: "...and you all are the those who will have been selected by Him to fill the positions within His government – He Who is in fact the head over all *regimes* and *hierarchies of authority*, be they angelic or human."

Col. 2:15 ἀπεκδυσάμενος **τὰς ἀρχὰς** καὶ **τὰς ἐξουσίας** ἐδειγμάτισεν ἐν παρρησίᾳ θριαμβεύσας αὐτοὺς ἐν αὐτῷ.

Transl.: "...when He had by it [the cross] disarmed the evil *angelic regime* and its *authority structure*, He publicly demonstrated his triumph over them by His resurrection from death."

Tit. 3:1-2 Ὑπομίμνησκε αὐτοὺς **ἀρχαῖς** καὶ **ἐξουσίαις** ὑποτάσσεσθαι πειθαρχεῖν, πρὸς πᾶν ἔργον ἀγαθὸν ἑτοίμους εἶναι, μηδένα βλασφημεῖν, ἀμάχους εἶναι, ἐπιεικεῖς, πᾶσαν ἐνδεικνυμένους πραΰτητα πρὸς πάντας ἀνθρώπους.

Transl.: "Remind them [leaders of the High King's Lifework Councils] to be in subjection to *human government officials* and *authorities*, to be obedient, to be ready for every good work, to speak evil of no one, not to be contentious, to be gentle, showing all humility toward all men."

Paul employs this phrase or portions of it in his Treatise to the Ephesians more than in any other of his writings. As can be seen in the above passages in the context of Ephesians, Paul uses it to refer to all leadership authority structures, both angelic and human, good and evil. In Eph. 2:2, Paul is probably referring to the spiritual hierarchy of powerful demonic beings who disguise themselves as the Greek gods immediately beneath Zeus in authoritative power: Apollo, Athena, and Aphrodite; and perhaps even some of those even slightly lower in power: Artemis, Ares, Dionysus, Poseidon, Hephaestus, Hera, etc.

⁴⁹ ἀρχή – usual translation: "principality, prince" (1:21, 2:2, 3:10, 6:12). Denotative meaning: "sovereign, magistrate, leader, chief, ruler, god." Connotative meaning used most often by Paul in Ephesians: The leader of the rebellious angels – Satan, appearing in Greek polytheism (in disguised form) as Zeus.

⁵⁰ αἰών – usual translation: "world" (1:21; 2:2, 7; 3:9, 11, 21; 6:12). Denotative meaning: "lifetime." Later, came to be used connotatively to refer to a historical period containing the story of the lifetime of a civilized people: "era, epoch, age." Proposed translation: "era, epoch, age."

⁵¹ ἐκκλησία – usual translation: "Church." This extremely important word is used by Paul nine times in this Treatise (Eph. 1:22, 3:10, 21; 5:23, 24, 25, 27, 29, 32). However, one of the strangest anomalies ever to occur in the study of historical philology is that the word "Church" is not a Greek word, nor is it even derived from the Greek word ἐκκλησία, and therefore it is not even a word, concept or idea that appears anywhere in the New Testament.

Rather, the word "Church" is an artificial British word that somehow cemented itself into the tradition of the historical Christendom of the English Speaking Peoples, because it comes from the Old English word "*cirice,*" which, through Old Saxon, Old High German, and finally Gothic, is a transliteration from the Greek pronunciation of the Greek phrase for "the Lord's house," (*kyriakon dōma*) an early reference to the building where early British Christians would meet (Etymology from Webster's Unabridged Dictionary: Middle English *chirche*, from Old English *cirice*; akin to Old Saxon *kirika*, Old High German *kirihha*; all from a prehistoric West Germanic word borrowed from (assumed) Gothic *kyriko* (whence Old Slavic *cruky*), from Late Greek *kyrikon*, alteration of *kyriakon*, short for *kyriakon dōma* = "the Lord's house," from Greek *kyriakon* (neuter of *kyriakos* = "of the lord or master," from *kyrios* = "lord, master," from *kyros* = "power") + *dōma* = "house;" akin to D *kerk*, G *Kierche*, Icel *kirkja*) [W]. Even historically, the Scots converted by John Knox, who eventually became the denomination in Christendom called the Presbyterians, called the building in which they would meet the "Kirk." The translation problem this presents is that the word "Church" (or "Kirk"), which the English speaking world has used for centuries – even millennia – does not accurately translate the meaning of the Greek word ἐκκλησία.

The challenge then becomes to decipher what an accurate translation of the word ἐκκλησία might be into contemporary, professional American English. Literally, the word ἐκκλησία is closely linked to the word κλῆσις (noun) and καλέω (verb), which is the most important concept and/or theme in this Treatise (see note at Eph. 1:18). Denotatively, the word ἐκκλησία means something like "out-of-profession," or perhaps, "those summoned out of their profession (for some other important purpose than the practice of their profession)." In Classical Greek, the ἐκκλησία came to refer to the "legislative assembly," indicating "an assembly of selected professional citizens summoned from out of all the citizens for special organized meetings, the purpose of which was to make political decisions that affected the larger issues of the corporate life of the πόλις (Gk: πόλις = "city-state," most specifically, the πόλις of Athens) than simply the practice of their specific profession" [LS]. Tyndale did not translate the word ἐκκλησία as the word "Church" in either his 1526 or his 1534 edition, but translated it in both editions as "congregacion" (congregation – see basic translation), which is more in line with this classical meaning.

However, the Greek preposition "ἐκ" can have other meanings than "out of." It can be used to intensify the meaning of the root word it is attached to. The root word of ἐκκλησία is κλῆσις = "lifework," "life purpose," life project," or sometimes (when referring specifically to our mortal lifework), "apprenticeship" (again, see note on κλῆσις at Eph. 1:18). Thus, combining the notion of a specially selected assembly of people summoned to meet in order to accomplish an important common purpose or goal, the word ἐκκλησία probably refers to the organization of Christians who have become mutually committed to assist and help each other "out" ("ἐκ" = "out," used connotatively) in order to discover, implement, and accomplish the "lifework," or "apprenticeship" that God has assigned to each of them in preparation for inheriting their future roles in the Millennial Kingdom of Jesus, God's High King.

Thus, the best professional American English word for conveying the concept of an interdependent group of professionally trained people committed to assist each other in giving and receiving wise advice and counsel about extremely important matters that they all share in common is not the word "assembly," but the word "council." Therefore, the proposed translation for the Greek word ἐκκλησία in contexts in which our future Kingdom role is emphasized, are the phrases: "Kingdom Apprenticeship Council," or "Kingdom Council;" and in contexts in which discovering and accomplishing the present role of our lifework during our mortal lives during this era is emphasized, the proposed translation is "Lifework Council."

[52] σῶμα = "governmental, organizational, administrative or associational body" [LS]. Paul uses this important word 9 times in this Treatise (1:23; 2:16; 4:4, 12, 16 [2x]; 5:23, 28, 30). In every context (except for Eph. 5:28 – "so ought husbands to love their own wives as their own *bodies"*), Paul uses this word to refer to the future "governmental body" of Jesus' cabinet ministers with whom He entrusts leadership responsibilities during the Millennial Kingdom, or to refer to the "associational body" of His specially selected recruits who are members of the ἐκκλησία, i.e, His "Lifework Councils."

[53] πληρόω – **I.** c. gen. rei, *fill full of*, λάρνακας λίθων Hdt.3.123, etc.;...Pass., *to be filled full,* τινος of a thing, Hp.VM 20, Pl.R.550d, etc.;...**III.** without any modal case, π. νέας *man ships,* Hdt.1.171, cf. Th.1.29 (Act. and Pass.) (in full πεντηκόντερον π. ἀνδρῶν Hdt.3.41); π. ναυτικόν Th.6.52; πληροῦτε θωρακεῖα *man the breastworks*, A.Th.32:--Med., τριήρη πληρωσάμενος Is.11.48, cf. X.HG5.4.56, etc...[LS]. Paul uses this word 4 times in this Treatise (Eph. 1:23;

3:19; 4:10; 5:18). In two of these contexts (here and in Eph. 4:10), Paul is speaking about Jesus "fully manning the posts" (British usage) of His future government, i.e., in contemporary professional American English, we would say that He is "filling" all of the leadership positions and other job positions of His future government.

2

Time Travel: Back From the Future

Time Travel: God Must Transport Our True Self Living in His Future Kingdom Back in Time to Rescue Our Sidetracked Self from the Death Traps of the Present World ♦ *Warning! Do not Allow the Exhilaration of the Rescue of Your Present Vile Self by Your Future Valiant Self Go to Your Head – The Rescue of Time Travel is God's Gift to You* ♦ *Transformation is in Reality Composition: Our Future Self "Traveling Back in Time" to Transform Our Present Self is Only How We See It – It is More Accurate to Say that God Employs Eternity to Compose Our Life into a Masterpiece* ♦ *Mood of the Masterpiece: Forged by the High King into a Peacemaker, Not Petrified by Hatred into Pretentiousness* ♦ *The Purpose of Peacemaking: To Build God's Building of Harmonious Relationships From All of the Masterpieces He Will Compose in History into what Will Become Our Eternal Home.*

TIME TRAVEL: GOD MUST TRANSPORT OUR TRUE SELF LIVING IN HIS FUTURE KINGDOM "BACK IN TIME" TO RESCUE OUR SIDETRACKED SELF FROM THIS PRESENT WORLD'S DEATH TRAPS

You[1] must never forget that until very recently, you all were as good as dead due to your incessantly getting sidetracked and taking detours from following the right road in life. In addition to this, you all had fallen into the dead-end road of failing to set, pursue or propose the right goals for your lives. For that matter, some of you had neglected yourselves to the point of allowing yourselves to think that your lives had no purpose or meaning at all.

Due to living in this aimless way (in some of your families for generations, and in others for even centuries), the quality of your lives gradually but inevitably deteriorated into a kind of degraded spiritual stupor. The awful result of this protracted condition was that you all merely existed in a kind of fear-filled dream world, in which you thought what was real, was in fact an elaborate illusion. Since you were all trapped in this formidable illusion, you were constantly failing to recognize and repeatedly missing the numerous opportunities[2] provided by God to liberate you and lead you out of it to discover and fulfill your lifework, because it was virtually impossible. On the contrary, living your lives weighed down by this frightful illusion over generations most often led to a never-ending cycle of suffering a tragic and heartbreaking premature physical death, as well as final and horrible spiritual death separated from God.

²The reason you all were failing so miserably in life was because you had allowed yourselves to fall into a sinister and invisible spiritual trap similar to that of a spider's web. This invisible trap has been deliberately woven to capture you and then gradually enervate you with a slow-acting but deadly spiritual poison. You all were drawn into and entrapped by this unseen spiritual web when you permitted yourselves, little by little – often unwittingly – to be gradually but inexorably deceived. You became ensnared as you slowly but inevitably chose to pursue, then practice and finally conduct your whole way of life guided by the philosophical "world view"[3] that pervades this present era of Greco-Roman civilization.

In time, this "world view" produced a "lifeworld," i.e., a value system and a way of thinking that is so gradually infused, it eventually becomes deeply embedded into the corporate mind of an entire society without being noticed or recognized by anyone living in it. This world view, and the now one thousand year old lifeworld it has produced, is in reality a deadly trap, consisting of the cultural, political and historical principles founded upon the religion of the polytheistic hierarchy of gods who live in the sky[4] under the authority of the chief sky-god, Zeus.[5]

The religion of Zeus and the hierarchy of gods under his authority is in actuality an elaborate, carefully crafted and extremely potent deception. It is instigated, maintained and animated by a hierarchy of wicked spiritual beings led by the most powerful of all of God's enemies – the evil archangel Satan himself. Like the spider, the desire of this malevolent archangel and his wicked angelic hierarchy is to progressively devitalize and debilitate you by gradually poisoning your minds. His scheme is to slowly suck away your physical, emotional, mental and spiritual strength, and in the end replace it with only by a vague, hazy, sluggish sense of fatigue, exhaustion and lethargy.

This "spiritual narcosis" is in fact Satan's calculated attempt to desensitize you to the point that you give in to apathy, then to cynicism and ultimately to despair. His aim is to get you to give up trying to climb out of the ditch you have fallen into – or otherwise block you in any way he can from getting back onto the road God has planned for you to follow in life. He never will (because he never can) give up plotting to lead you away from the one true God, because by doing so he thinks he can achieve his prime objective, which is to *prevent you from discovering or accomplishing God's plan for your true lifework.*[6]

Being the mastermind operating behind, within and through the Greek polytheistic religion is only one of Satan's pernicious schemes. He is also the devious spiritual being now active in provoking God's "sons," i.e., the religious and political leadership regime within Judaism, to obstinately refuse compliance[7] with His will. He is the one who is continually blinding and manipulating this regime. He is the motivating force that causes them to stubbornly persist in their rebellion against Jesus, their very own legitimate Divine King, and to hunt down and cruelly oppress His followers. The irony of this historical fact is astonishing!

³The reason it is necessary to remind you of the egregious (and admittedly, oftentimes monstrously insane) behavior I have outlined above, is because I must also continually force myself to remember just how far Jesus' graciousness has brought me back from going down the wrong road in my own life. At one time, I too had become gravely sidetracked into a deplorable, protracted delusion.[8]

You see, I used to be a fanatically dedicated, but ruthlessly driven Pharisee[9] – positioning myself to be the "rising star" in that most ambitious of all the religious sects within Judaism. I was motivated only by my desire to eventually become an influential "insider" in their powerful religious organization. I desperately wanted to be among those who held or aspired to hold the highest ranking positions of authority and prestige in the small circle of elite men who exercised their power from the very pinnacle of the leadership regime within Judaism.

Just like them, I too was once completely ensnared by their sanctimonious attitude and arrogant public demeanor[10] of insolence and cruelty. We who were members inside the upper echelons of that regime eventually fomented our collective state of mind into a permanent, acrimonious disposition of visceral loathing not only of Jesus, but also more specifically of His followers. We allowed this vicious outlook to grip us to the extent that we took deliberate, persistent and vigorous – even violent – action against them. We were motivated in our attempts to destroy them not only by our visceral revulsion of them, but also by our mindless hatred of them, produced by what we keenly (but erroneously) imagined to be all kinds of wrongdoing that we merely supposed them to be guilty of.

Because of this bizarre delusion, we deliberately twisted our own warped vagaries about them even further into pretexts upon which we could press false legal charges against them, so we could hunt them down and imprison them – or worse. I am ashamed to admit that the disgusting result of this delusion was that all of us within the upper leadership regime of Judaism became in our deepest natures just like petty children who are characterized by continual bitterness, rage and anger. In so doing I became exactly like – indeed, worse than – the rest of the intolerant, self-righteous, haughty, narcissists who had perched themselves atop the leadership regime within Judaism.

⁴To summarize, all of us, both you all as well as myself, had fallen into two of the most powerful traps calculated by Satan for this era to lead us away from finding God's lifework for us. You all had been diverted into the clutches of the insidious religion of Greek polytheism, while I had been sidetracked from following the true road of God's intended destiny for Israel into the detour of the rebellion of the counterfeit religion constructed by the leadership regime within Judaism. However, irrespective of the despicable and contemptible person I had turned out to be, *God took the initiative* to find me, reorient me and guide me back to the right road He had planned for my life. He did this solely because of His *great love* for me, and because one of the central characteristics of His love is His "wealth" of *mercy*. If God's love and mercy can put a person as disgracefully sidetracked as I was back on the right road in life, He can do it for you, or for *anyone*.

⁵⁻⁶It is notable to observe from human experience that our willful, obstinate persistence in staying sidetracked on these dead-end roads would have inevitably lead to our premature and meaningless death. Consequently, it must therefore also be true that when God places us back on the right road He has mapped out for us, He will lead us to find a mature and meaningful life. In fact, viewing life from His eternal perspective, He has – so to speak – *already* "made us alive with" our *future* High King in (what from our perspective is) our *present* life experience. Moreover, it is exclusively due to His *graciousness* that you all – like me – have also been rescued[11] by Him from an inevitable, premature and meaningless death that so often characterizes the tragic lives of those who are enslaved within the lifeworld of Greek polytheism.[12]

Allow me to elaborate further on the significance of what it means to "be made alive with" our future High King, since our initial perspective of this experience can often be somewhat limited. As I stated above, whenever God snatches us out of being sidetracked in the distorted "lifeworld" we had become accustomed to for so long, and places us back on what He has planned (and therefore knows to be) the right road for our lives, we experience it – and rightly so – as being "rescued." After we proceed along the right road for a while, we soon begin to perceive that God is there too, "walking" (so to speak) along beside us, calmly and evenly pointing things out, and teaching us His completely new way of thinking and living.[13]

When we reflect upon this fact, it soon begins to dawn on us that if He is with us *now* upon the road, He must have been there when He "rescued" us also (to in effect, "pull us out of the ditch"), even though at that time we could only dimly perceive Him being there, if at all. This realization leads to the conclusion that if this is true, He also can "see" us with perfect clarity wherever we happen to "be" *at any time at all* – on the right life-road as well as when we were living a sidetracked life.

Furthermore, if He knew us and loved us when He rescued us, it implies that He also knew *then* what we would become *now*. He knew *then* that we would soon come to enjoy and appreciate being really "alive" on the right road *now* more than merely existing in the sidetracked dream-world we previously had become so accustomed to. Therefore, it must be true that He also knows *now* that in the future, the person we will eventually become will come to recognize and appreciate being "alive with" Him *even more than the person that we now are* does.

This implies that from His standpoint, He always has been, always is and always will be "alive with" us. The conclusion of this reflective thought process is that if this is true, then the only thing that remains for us to do is to realize that He has made it possible for us to always "be alive with" Him too. The result of comprehending this is that we can *intentionally accelerate* becoming more and more like the real person He has always planned for us *to become* in what we call the "future" (from what is our limited, time-bound frame of reference) but which He knows we in fact *already are* (from His unlimited, eternal frame of reference). We can become in our present lives the person who is "alive with" Jesus, His High King, living together with Him in the Millennial Kingdom Age.

Not only has God made it actually possible for us to "be alive with" our High King in His future *kingly Office* in our present life experience, He has also enabled us to behave as if we were already "resurrected with" and "seated with"[14] our future High King, Jesus, in His present *heavenly Office*. What this means is this: since God is a purely eternal being and we are only quasi-eternal-temporal "becomings" (as I explained earlier), when Jesus assumed His present heavenly Office, He was immediately invested with the divine authority to direct us and give us divine aid in His purpose of guiding each of us into our respective lifework.

Even more than this, God has given Jesus in His resurrected Office the spiritual power of actually transporting, or *mediating*, our future, resurrected, dignified and mature leadership personalities and their corresponding character qualities (which already exist in heaven from God's perspective of reality)[15] into our present apprenticeship experiences. In other words, He made it supernaturally possible for us, by entering into His program of discovering, performing and accomplishing the lifework involved in our respective apprenticeships, to gradually become transformed into the mature, gracious and loving leaders who we in fact *already are* (from His eternal perspective).

Therefore, from His heavenly Office, our Commander in Chief has the power to transform our personalities in this way *as we interact with Him to perform our lifework here and now in preparation for our Millennial appointments.* The unique and supernatural transformational process, in which He enables you to transform your present immature personalities by appropriating your future mature leadership personalities and their corresponding character qualities, is the precise means by which God will rescue, deliver and preserve the significance of accomplishing your unique lifework for Him *right now* – in this present life. Further, since you do not know when Jesus will transition from executing His heavenly responsibilities as our Commander in Chief to His regal responsibilities as the future High King of the world, you should approach your mortal lives as an *opportunity,* accompanied by a *sense of urgency,* to discover, accomplish and complete our lifework for God.

[7]God has established this miraculous transformational relationship whereby our future mature personalities are transported from heaven "back in time" (so to speak, from our temporal perspective), into our present apprenticeship personalities, so that He might show us the surpassing riches of His graciousness throughout all upcoming historical eras. In addition, He has done this in order to demonstrate His goodness to us even more auspiciously when we are finally with Jesus, our future High King, during the age of the Millennial Kingdom. The exceedingly marvelous depth of all of His graciousness will fully appear to us only when we finally arrive at the ultimate destiny of realizing our unique, special leadership roles – when we are actually personally present with our High King Jesus – from the beginning to the end of that wonderful coming era.[16]

WARNING! DO NOT ALLOW THE EXHILARATION OF THE RESCUE OF YOUR PRESENT VILE SELF BY YOUR FUTURE VALIANT SELF GO TO YOUR HEAD – THE RESCUE OF TIME TRAVEL IS GOD'S *GIFT* TO YOU

[8]Because we can be so easily deluded even *after* we have become our High King's apprentices, we are prone to slip back into the erroneous attitude of taking the credit for ourselves whenever God enables us to find and perform our lifework for Him. Therefore, it is necessary for me at this juncture to reemphasize the fact that there is *nothing* about God's great plans for our present apprenticeships or our future Millennial appointments *that is* or *could ever have been* planned, initiated or brought about *by us.* Quite to the contrary, it is exclusively and entirely due to *God's graciousness initiative* that you are the ones (of all people!) who have been rescued *by Him* from living sidetracked lives.

Furthermore, He rescued you not only from living out a futile and meaningless life, but also from suffering a premature and early death. In addition to these two benefits, has given you two more: His irrevocable promise that you will live an eternal, resurrected life with Him in the future world, as well as His divine assistance to transform your present life and personality into that of your resurrected life and personality *right now, in your present lifetime*. Although it is indeed true that He has rescued you because you believed in Him; yet this profound deliverance[17] and its marvelous benefits – both present and future – *have not been or ever could be* brought about by anything that you have done. Rather, the entire rescue mission, together with its marvelous results – beginning, middle and end – is solely and entirely God's *gift* to you all.

⁹I must and will continue to reemphasize that none of us has ever been – or ever will be – rescued by God because of any of our own efforts, endeavors or accomplishments. God *alone* has taken the initiative to rescue us from our foolish self-endangerment and to deliver us safely into the discovery and performance of our lifework for Him *all by Himself*. He has done this in order to put a stop to even the possibility that anyone might for any reason suppose they had the right to brag that they were somehow able to *rescue themselves(!)* – or that they had the slightest grounds to claim any of the credit for the supernatural transformational process He has brought about in our lives so far, and will continue to cultivate until we become spiritually mature people.

TRANSFORMATION IS IN REALITY *COMPOSITION*: OUR FUTURE SELF "TRAVELING BACK IN TIME" TO TRANSFORM OUR PRESENT SELF IS ONLY HOW WE SEE IT – IT IS MORE ACCURATE TO SAY THAT GOD EMPLOYS ETERNITY TO COMPOSE OUR LIFE INTO A MASTERPIECE

¹⁰In order to gain a more accurate perspective of this divine process, think of God as a master-artist, a master-author, a master-composer or a master-builder. From this perspective, we are in fact His "masterworks,"[18] formed and shaped[19] by our future High King, Jesus, for the purpose of becoming the entrepreneurs of good and worthwhile enterprises.[20] The remarkable thing about God's gracious plan for each of us is that He has actually *set us up for success*, by carefully preparing all of our entrepreneurial opportunities beforehand. All we have to do is simply recognize them and then have the faith and courage to step into them.

With this in mind, we should approach our lives as a *mission* or *quest* to discover and then carry out our life projects according to a deliberate philosophical world view[21] that involves a disciplined approach to founding and accomplishing the magnificent enterprises that God has prepared for us.

MOOD OF THE MASTERPIECE: FORGED BY THE HIGH KING INTO A PEACEMAKER, NOT PETRIFIED BY HATRED INTO PRETENTIOUSNESS

11It is for this reason (namely, that it is human nature to tend to gravitate towards taking the credit for things that are in reality God's gifts to us), that you should develop the mental discipline to continually remind yourselves of two things.

The first thing you should make it a habit to remind yourselves of is the degraded and hopeless lives you all used to live, from which God's gracious love has now delivered you. After all, you used to be miserable barbarians – members of the ethnic races and nations completely foreign to Judaism[22] – who were totally enslaved by your natural visceral appetites.

Because of this, you were contemptuously labeled "The Uncircumcised" by the self-righteous and cruel leadership regime within Judaism of which I used to be a part. Remember their error of arrogantly usurping and then supplanting God's true lifework for Israel, and that because they were eager to take the credit for God's gifts to Israel for themselves, they condescendingly named themselves "The Circumcised," as some sort of narcissistic and pretentious badge of pride. Because of this, they failed to realize that the original symbolic act of circumcision itself was merely an artificial[23] object lesson given by God to Israel for a temporary period, whose historical purpose has now been fulfilled.[24]

12The second thing you should make it a habit to remind yourselves of is that during that former time, you were all completely excluded by the leadership regime within Judaism from the realm of their future High King. They deliberately alienated you from legal citizenship within the true lifework and mission of the authentic Israel.

Moreover, because you were foreigners, you were also legally barred by their regime from the testamentary provisions of the Promissory Agreement that God had guaranteed to you through them – both in its stipulations for the historical Kingdom of Israel itself, as well as in its provisions for God's future Millennial Kingdom. This regime ostracized you from God's plans for Israel's legitimate lifework, which eventually left you all utterly devoid of hope and bereft of any regard for God at all in your own deluded lifeworld.

13As a result of living in this former alienated and degraded state of affairs, you had all become extremely remote from the promises spelled out in this Divine Agreement. However, in sharp contrast, you all have now been suddenly brought into a close, privileged and intimate position with breathtaking prospects for your immediate and long-term future! The future High King, Jesus Himself, has given you all the opportunity to be legally eligible to actually inherit all of the benefits of the promises contained in the Divine Agreement formerly offered through Israel. Your eligibility was made possible by means of the bloody capital punishment suffered by the High King Himself, which He subjected Himself to as a legal sacrifice for you all. He did this precisely in order to satisfy God's judicial requirement that His death was the only way to effect restoring you to Him from such an estranged lifeworld.

[14-16]The startling result of His extraordinary peace initiative is that He was *actually successful* – which makes Him our "Peacemaker!"[25] – that is, the Peacemaker between the savage Barbarian mindset and the sanctimonious mindset of the leadership regime within Judaism. His peace initiative secured the specific effect of forming a totally new and unique concord out of both utterly antithetical deluded states of mind outlined above. He forged[26] a new unity from your initially savage state of mind that was wholly enslaved by your natural visceral appetites as brutal Barbarians, and my formerly contemptuous state of mind as a member of the cruel, arrogant, condescending, narcissistic leadership regime within Judaism.

If this is hard to comprehend, try to imagine the following illustration to make it easier to understand. As we all know, building a wall around a city is important as a defensive strategy to protect its inhabitants from a destructive invasion attempt from their enemies. However, in the case of the sanctimonious leadership regime within Judaism, it is as if they built their "wall" around Jerusalem with the *opposite intent* – namely, to "screen out"[27] the rest of the world. This disgraceful, self-centered behavior effectively shut you all out from God's intended purpose for Israel, which originally was that they should *take the initiative* to "reach out" from Jerusalem and become His gracious representatives to you and all other nations in the world of God's goodness, justice and love.

With this in mind, now imagine Jesus being brutally and ruthlessly thrust outside the city wall of Jerusalem to suffer the gruesome form of capital punishment used by the Romans – that of crucifixion – by this very regime. This outrageous scandal resulted from their own deliberate scheme to kill him, all stealthily plotted and carried out against Him *contrary to the central ordinances of their very own Legal Code.* The height of the irony was reached when they openly declared their allegiance to the Roman Caesar on the same day they defiantly forced *their own King*, the High King of the authentic *Israel* – to carry ignominiously His own *Roman* cross![28] This twisted regime actually thought they could not only destroy Him by putting Him to death on a Roman cross, but by doing so, deftly and cleverly sidestep any guilt they knew they would incur by committing treason against their own High King.

Paradoxically, now imagine that what happened instead was that Jesus used His Roman cross as a "battering ram" to demolish[29] the "wall" of the "Law" of the "Commandments" of Judaism itself, which this same close minded Jewish regime had by that time distorted and erected into an overly rigid system of inflexible dogma around Jerusalem's people. By doing this, Jesus in effect "put them out of business"[30] by shattering the delusion that they could use the "Law" to control their own Jewish people, as well as to shut all other people out from what they condescendingly thought to be their privileged status with God.

Moreover, Jesus used His cross as more that a "battering ram" to smash down the wall of proud dogma the leadership regime within Judaism had built up over the centuries and then used to deliberately separate people from God. Imagine now that He also used the cross as new kind of "anvil," in order to forge upon it not some weapon, but instead, *a brand new kind of human "becoming,"* fashioned from the two deformed, hate-making creatures we had become by this point in history. In other words, Jesus forged and invented[31] (for the first time in history!) from these two diametrically opposed kinds of "hate-makers" (if you can imagine that!) a completely transformed new human being like Himself: a Peacemaking Human Being.

The unique feature of reflecting upon the cross as Jesus' "new anvil," is that instead of making weapons (which is the normal function of an anvil), He can and eventually will forge upon this new anvil a unique group of people into the peacemaking governmental "body" of His future Kingdom, dedicated to performing God's purposes and intentions. The only thing in fact, that was finally put to death on the cross, was not Jesus (because He came to life again), but rather *our own inevitable propensity toward hatred*: whether it be the savage and visceral hatred like that of typical Barbarians, or the condescending and selfish hatred like that of the religious leadership regime within Judaism.

[17]In summary, at this unique milestone in history, Jesus has come and effectively restored Israel's original Mission and Lifework through designating and commissioning me to be his High Emissary. His prime directive for my life is that I carry this message of good news to the ethnic races and nations foreign to Judaism that live north and west of the land of Palestine along the northern coast of the Mediterranean Sea. This message of good news[32] can be summed up in the following headline:

BE FORGED INTO A "PEACE-MAKING HUMAN BEING!"
BE DELIVERED *TODAY* FROM THE SAVAGE OR SELF-RIGHTEOUS HATRED THAT HAS ENSLAVED YOU ALL YOUR LIVES!

¹⁸The ultimate promise of this headline is that now, for the first time in history, anyone from both formerly alienated groups – whether they be from any of the ethnic races or nations foreign to Judaism, or whether they be a member from within Judaism – no longer face any man-made "walls" of any kind, human or otherwise. No bodyguards, barricades, blockades or barriers whatsoever can prohibit them from approaching and reaching intimacy with God or with each other. Now, we all have a common "freeway,"[33] built by the Specially Selecting Spirit to not only approach, but gain immediate, intimate contact with the Father; and Jesus is that "Freeway!"

THE PURPOSE OF PEACEMAKING: TO BUILD GOD'S BUILDING OF HARMONIOUS RELATIONSHIPS FROM ALL OF THE MASTERPIECES HE WILL COMPOSE IN HISTORY INTO WHAT WILL BECOME OUR HOME

¹⁹Therefore, those of you who are from any of the ethnic races or nations foreign to Judaism are no longer to be regarded as foreigners or as outsiders to God's household, but instead you are now included as fellow citizens – incorporated as specially selected recruits yourselves – those who are in fact intimate members of God's home.

²⁰Let us now transition to imagining this new unified matrix of relationships organized upon the principles of graciousness and peacefulness as a *large building*.[34] It is as if you Ephesians, as well as all of the other ethnic groups and nations foreign to Judaism that are now forming into Kingdom Apprenticeship Councils on the northern coast of the Mediterranean Sea, are those who are now in fact being built by God into a brand new kind of "home" of harmonious relationships.

Moreover, if you all are to become the integral "superstructure" of this new home of God, you must be built upon a solid and absolutely reliable "foundation." This foundation consists of the fundamental concepts articulated by Jesus' appointed High Emissaries in their speeches and writings, as well as upon the ethical principles of the writings of God's Official Spokespersons and Authors of the Old Testament of authentic Israel. Furthermore, like every solid foundation, the foundation of this marvelous building of relationships that comprise God's home must and in fact does have a "Corner-Foundation-Stone," which is our future High King, namely Jesus Himself. In this image of picturing Jesus as our "Cornerstone," I am referring not only to the foundational writings that record Jesus' life and teachings written by some of His chief apprentices that He appointed to become His High Emissaries, but also to His continued direction of the construction of the superstructure of this enormous building project from heaven.

²¹This entire "home building project"[35] is in the process of being shaped by Him in such a way that the special people who He recruits to be a part of it grow to be harmoniously joined together with other like-minded individuals, who commit themselves to forming close-knit interpersonal frameworks consisting of mature relationships of trust, encouragement and concord. His objective is to structure the corporate voice of the organization rationally and intentionally into a pleasant, agreeable and enjoyable whole.[36] The goal of our Commander in Chief for this building project is that it would grow into a special place where people can authentically meet with each other and with Himself, such that they become transformed into mature human beings.

²²Finally, this building project necessarily entails being specially selected and built by the Spirit into a "house" of relationships that are of such mature quality that you flourish as a consistent group of people along with and alongside many other people of originally diverse backgrounds, who become motivated to have only constructive attitudes and motives toward others.[37] The goal that the Specially Selecting Spirit has for this "house" is that it be transformed into God's spiritual "home," that exists primarily for the sake of providing a harmonious haven where everyone might go to find a place of relational warmth, protection from harm, and growth into spiritual maturity.

Notes to Extended Interpretive and Expositional Translation
Ephesians Chapter 2

[1] Here Paul begins a long Greek sentence that does not conclude until the end of Eph. 2:7. Since the main three verbs of this sentence do not occur until near the end of the sentence (in Eph. 2:5-6, συνεζωοποίησε... καὶ συνήγειρε καὶ συνεκάθισεν = "He *has made us alive with*...and He *has resurrected us with* and He *has seated us with* our future High King, Jesus, in the heavenly places"), it is proposed that the main theme of this section of Eph. 2:1-10 is Paul's explanation of the divine process by which we become spiritually transformed and supernaturally aided in our present lives to discover and accomplish our "lifework" for God. Since the meaning of a complete thought conveyed by a sentence in the English language is so highly dependent on the *word order* of the sentence itself (and not on the inflected prefix and suffix of the form of the word itself, as in Greek), and since most of the meaning is carried by the subject and the

verb of the sentence in any language, it is thus usually required *in English* that the subject and the verb of a sentence be placed close together near its beginning, and that (in the indicative mood) the verb follow in close proximity to the subject of the sentence.

The King James translators in fact did this very thing by moving only one (the first) of the above three verbs in verses 5-6 all the way forward into verse 1 of Chapter 2, as follows: "And you ***hath he quickened*** (συνεζωοποίησε), who were dead in trespasses and sins." No doubt they were simply following the precedent set by Tyndale, who translated this same passage almost a century earlier (1526) as follows: "And ***hath quickened*** you also that were deedd in treaspasse and synne,..." See note at Eph. 2:5-6 below.

[2] ἁμαρτία – usual translation: "sin" (Eph. 2:1). This Greek word is the one most often translated "sin" (see note on παράπτωμα at Eph. 1:7 for a full discussion of other Greek words translated "sin," as well as the derivation of the English word "sin"). Denotatively, ἁμαρτάνω means to "miss the mark (especially when throwing a spear)" [LS]. Connotatively, ἁμαρτάνω means "to fail in one's purpose or intention," or "to lose possession or be deprived of one's powers (especially of a physical of metaphysical organ of intention) [LS]." Proposed translation as a verb: fail, lose (as in "lose one's sight," "lose hope," "lose one's mind," etc.), miss (as in "miss" a field goal, "miss" a business opportunity) [LS]; proposed translation as a noun: "failure," "loss," "missed."

[3] περιπατέω – usual translation: "walk." Paul employs this important philosophical concept seven times in this Treatise (Eph. 2:2, 10; 4:1, 17; 5:2, 8, 15). He uses this word all seven times as deliberately placed literary structural markers that serve to show the reader the organization of his thoughts and line of reasoning. He uses this word the first two times to explain how one is to appropriate what it means to "be made alive with" Jesus, which is the main theme of Eph. 2:1-10. The remaining five times, Paul uses this word in Chapters 4 and 5 to itemize the five main practical life applications of the theological and philosophical themes he develops in the first half of the Treatise (Chapters 1 - 3). The denotative meaning of the word περιπατέω is to "walk around, walk about, walk up and down" [LS] (from πέρι = "around," as in the word "*perimeter*," which means "to measure the distance *around*" something; and πατέω = "to walk"). During the time of Aristotle, περιπατέω came to mean, "walk about while teaching and having philosophical dialogue," to the extent that the followers of Plato and Aristotle eventually came to be called "Peripatetics." Later, the word came to mean a "School" of Philosophy; e.g., a coherent philosophical interpretation of reality according to which one deliberately conducted his or her life: or in other words, a "world view;" viz: ...**3. *school of philosophy, first used of the Academy***, ἀναπεπταμένου τοῦ Πλάτωνος π. Epicur.Fr.171; ἔτη ὀκτὼ κατασχὼν τὸν π. (sc. Σπεύσιππος) Phld. Acad.Ind.p.38 M.; οἱ ἀπὸ τοῦ **Π. *name given to Xenocrates and Aristotle, because their teacher Plato was accustomed to walk about while teaching***, Ammon. in Cat.3.8; οἱ ἐκ τοῦ π. ***the school of***

Aristotle, Luc.Pisc.43; οἱ ἐκ τῶν π. Str.13.1.54; οἱ ἀπὸ τοῦ π. φιλόσοφοι Plu.2.1131; τοῦ Π. προστάς Antig.Car. ap. Ath.12.547d: generally, *any school of philosophy*, ἕτερος π. Phld.Acad.Ind.p.39 M.; αὐτὸς ἴδιον π. κατασκευάσας ib.p.79 M., cf. p.53M. (pl.); οἱ τὸν αὐτὸν Ἀριστοτέλει ἐμβαίνοντες π. Diog.Oen.4 [LS]. With this in mind, the proposed translation of περιπατέω is "to deliberately and intentionally learn, practice and teach others a comprehensive philosophical worldview."

[4] ἀήρ – usual translation: "air" (Eph. 2:2). Refers to the "high air," or the realms of the upper regions of the sky, where the Greek gods travel from Olympus down to the earth to involve themselves in the affairs of humans. Proposed translation: "sky."

[5] **Zeus** – see note at Eph. 1:21.

[6] Prior to writing this Treatise, Paul had spent three years teaching in Ephesus, the conclusion of which was marked by a dangerous riot incited by Ephesian merchants who based their entire industry on the silver shrines and idols they made and sold in conjunction with the worship of Artemis (Acts 19-20). Prior to that, Paul had spent one and a half years teaching in Corinth (Acts 18); and prior to that, he had visited Athens and delivered a speech there in an attempt to persuade the Athenians to turn away from the Greek polytheistic religion of Zeus (Acts 17:16-34). He would therefore have been well acquainted with the Greek religion, and had ample time to reflect upon it and spiritually discern that Satan was in fact the evil spiritual being behind it.

[7] ἀπείθεια, ἡ, – noun form of the verb ἀπειθ-έω, Att. form of ἀπῐθέω (though even Trag. preferred ἀπιστέω, q.v. 11), **A. *to be disobedient, refuse compliance*,** A.*Ag.*1049; opp. πείθομαι, Pl.*Phdr.*271b: freq. c. dat., *disobey*, οὐκ ἀπειθήσας θεῷ E.*Or.*31; ἀ. ἅμα νόμῳ καὶ τῷ θεῷ Pl.*Lg.*741d, etc.; τὰ μεγάλα ἀ. τινί *in* great matters, Id.*R.*538b; ἀ. ταῖς ἐνεχυρασίαις *not to abide by* them, Id.*Lg.*949d: later c. gen., ψαφίσματος *GDI*3705.111 (Cos); ἐντολῶν LXX*Jo.*5.6. **2.** of animals, X.*Cyr.* 7.5.62; of ships, τοῖς οἴαξιν ἀ. D.S.13.46. **3.** of a woman, *refuse compliance*, Aristaenet.2.20 [LS]. The denotative meaning of ἀπειθέω is "to be unpersuaded" (cf. πείθω = "persuade" [LS]). As noted above, a close synonym for the word ἀπείθεια in Greek is ἀπιστία = "unbelief, disbelief, distrust" [LS] (cf. πιστεύω = "believe, trust" [LS]). However, as shown by a study of the above passages, ἀπειθέω comes to be used most often in contexts in which the *effect* of not being persuaded of something, i.e., engaging one's will to *purposely decide to be disobedient* to a law or *to deliberately refuse to comply* with an ordinance that one is not persuaded is correct or right, is emphasized. There are several words available in contemporary professional American English that can accurately convey this concept, such as: "refuse compliance," "defiance," "rebellious" or "insubordinate." Paul is careful to distinguish and be consistent in his usage of the two words ἀπείθεια and ἀπιστία. He uses this word (ἀπείθεια), which means to "refuse compliance," a total of ten times in the NT (the noun ἀπείθεια five

times [Ro. 11:30, 32; here in Eph. 2:2 and 5:6; Col. 3:6] and its verb form ἀπειθέω five times [Ro. 2:8; 10:21; 11:30, 31; 15:31), and the word for "unbelief" a total of seven times in the NT (the noun ἀπιστία five times [Ro. 3:3; 4:20; 11:20, 23; 1 Ti. 1:13] and its verb form ἀπιστέω two times [Ro. 3:3; 2 Ti. 2:13]). Moreover, Paul uses this word to mean "refuse compliance" all ten times, in both its noun (ἀπείθεια) and verb (ἀπειθέω) forms, to exclusively refer to the religious and political leaders within Judaism who deliberately planned the crucifixion of Jesus and continued to actively resist the spread of Christianity (in Ro. 2:8-9, Paul says that Greeks who follow the bad example of defiant Judaism will also be included with them in being punished by God: "upon the Jew first, and also the Greek" (Ιουδαίου τε πρῶτον καὶ Ἕλληνος).

Moreover, the author of the *Treatise to the Hebrews* uses this word four times (Heb. 3:18; 4:6, 11; and 11:31) to exclusively refer to leaders among the Jewish people, who in the history of Israel, "refused to comply" with God's commands. Furthermore, in *Acts*, Luke uses this word only three times, and in all three narratives, he uses it to refer exclusively to the religious leaders of Jewish communities established within the cities in the northern Mediterranean regions of Asia and Macedonia who deliberately "refused to be persuaded" by Paul that Jesus was their Messiah and the legitimate King of Israel (Acts 14:2; 17:5; and 19:9). Proposed translation: "obstinate refusal to comply."

[8] It is probable that Paul intentionally uses the special metaphorical sense of the Greek word **παράπτωμα** (in near context – see Eph. 2:1 – and see note on **παράπτωμα** at Eph. 1:7 for fuller treatment of this concept) for the common human failure of "getting sidetracked" or of "taking a willful detour from the right road" in this Treatise, because he himself was literally on (the wrong) "road" to Damascus (Acts Chapter 9) when Jesus so dramatically stopped him, and then "put him on the right road," so that he could find and accomplish his own lifework. As Saul, Paul thought that the "right road" (lifework) for him was persecuting Christians. However, as the man Saul, he was in reality on the "wrong road." Jesus changed all that and put Paul on the "right road" for his life.

The metaphor of the Christian life portrayed as a "road" or a "journey" (Greek: **ὁδός**) is a major theme used not only by Paul, but also by all of the other writers of the New Testament. For example, all four of the Gospel writers (Matthew, Mark, Luke and John) emphasize this theme by stating at the very beginning of their Gospels that Jesus Himself had to follow the right "road" (prophesied by Isaiah – Isa. 40:3) to accomplish His own lifework for God:

Matt. 3:3 Οὗτος γάρ ἐστιν ὁ ῥηθεὶς ὑπὸ Ἠσαΐου τοῦ προφήτου, λέγοντος, «Φωνὴ βοῶντος· 'Ἐν τῇ ἐρήμῳ ἑτοιμάσατε **τὴν ὁδὸν** Κυρίου, Εὐθείας ποιεῖτε τὰς τρίβους αὐτοῦ.'»

Matt. 3:3 For this (John the Baptist) is the One who was spoken of by Isaiah the prophet, saying, "[I am only] a voice of one crying out in the desert, [as I never stop announcing:] 'Make *the way* (lit. **τὴν ὁδόν** = "the road") of the Lord ready, make His paths straight.'"

Mark 1:2-3 Ὡς γέγραπται ἐν τοῖς προφήταις, «Ἰδοὺ ἐγὼ ἀποστέλλω τὸν ἄγγελόν μου πρὸ προσώπου σου, Ὃς κατασκευάσει **τὴν ὁδόν** ἔμπροσθέν σου· ³Φωνὴ βοῶντος· Ἐν τῇ ἐρήμῳ, ἑτοιμάσατε **τὴν ὁδὸν** Κυρίου, Εὐθείας ποιεῖτε τὰς τρίβους αὐτοῦ.»

Mark 1:2-3 As it is written in the prophets, "Behold, I send my messenger before Your face, who will prepare Your *way* (lit. **τὴν ὁδὸν** = "the road") before You. ³The voice of one crying in the wilderness, 'Make ready *the way* (lit. **τὴν ὁδὸν** = "the road") of the Lord! Make his paths straight!'"

Luke 3:4 ὡς γέγραπται ἐν βίβλῳ λόγων Ἠσαΐου τοῦ προφήτου, λέγοντος, «Φωνὴ βοῶντος ἐν τῇ ἐρήμῳ, Ἑτοιμάσατε **τὴν ὁδὸν** Κυρίου, Εὐθείας ποιεῖτε τὰς τρίβους αὐτοῦ.»

Luke 3:4 As it is written in the book of the words of Isaiah the prophet, "The voice of one crying in the wilderness, 'Make ready *the way* (lit. **τὴν ὁδὸν** = "the road") of the Lord. Make his paths straight.'"

John 1:23 Ἔφη, Ἐγὼ «φωνὴ βοῶντος· Ἐν τῇ ἐρήμῳ, εὐθύνατε **τὴν ὁδὸν** Κυρίου,» καθὼς εἶπεν Ἠσαΐας ὁ προφήτης.

John 1:23 He said, "I am the voice of one crying in the wilderness, 'Make straight *the way* (lit. **τὴν ὁδὸν** = "the road") of the Lord,' as Isaiah the prophet said."

Further, the first three Gospel writers (Matthew, Mark and Luke) also conspicuously emphasize this theme again when Jesus enters Jerusalem for the last time to fulfill the prophecy of Zechariah 9:9 one week before his death on the cross, which is the major accomplishment of His lifework:

Matt. 21:8 Ὁ δὲ πλεῖστος ὄχλος ἔστρωσαν ἑαυτῶν τὰ ἱμάτια ἐν **τῇ ὁδῷ**, ἄλλοι δὲ ἔκοπτον κλάδους ἀπὸ τῶν δένδρων καὶ ἐστρώννυον ἐν **τῇ ὁδῷ**.

Matt. 21:8 A very great multitude spread their clothes on *the road* (lit. **τῇ ὁδῷ** = "the road"). Others cut branches from the trees, and spread them on *the road* (lit. **τῇ ὁδῷ** = "the road").

Mark 11:8 Πολλοὶ δὲ τὰ ἱμάτια αὐτῶν ἔστρωσαν εἰς **τὴν ὁδόν**, ἄλλοι δὲ στοιβάδας ἔκοπτον ἐκ τῶν δένδρων καὶ ἐστρώννυον εἰς **τὴν ὁδόν**.

Mark 11:8 Many spread their garments on *the way* (lit. **τὴν ὁδόν** = "the road"), and others were cutting down branches from the trees, and spreading them on *the road* (lit. **τὴν ὁδόν** = "the road").

Luke 19:36 Πορευομένου δὲ αὐτοῦ ὑπεστρώννυον τὰ ἱμάτια αὐτῶν ἐν **τῇ ὁδῷ**.

Luke 19:36 As He went, they spread their cloaks in *the way* (lit. **τῇ ὁδῷ** = "the road").

John, in one of the most central passages of his Gospel, records one of the last and most important truths Jesus ever said, the very day before He accomplished His own lifework on the cross:

John 14:4-6 "Καὶ ὅπου ἐγὼ ὑπάγω οἴδατε καὶ **τὴν ὁδόν** οἴδατε." ⁵Λέγει αὐτῷ Θωμᾶς, "Κύριε, οὐκ οἴδαμεν ποῦ ὑπάγεις, καὶ πῶς δυνάμεθα **τὴν ὁδὸν** εἰδέναι?" ⁶Λέγει αὐτῷ ὁ Ἰησοῦς, "Ἐγώ εἰμι **ἡ ὁδὸς** καὶ ἡ ἀλήθεια καὶ ἡ ζωή. Οὐδεὶς ἔρχεται πρὸς τὸν Πατέρα εἰ μὴ δι᾽ ἐμοῦ."

John 14:4-6 "And you know where I am going, and you know *the way* (lit. **τὴν ὁδόν** = "the way")." ⁵Thomas said to him, "Lord, we don't know where you are going. How can we know *the way* (lit. τὴν ὁδόν = "the way")?" ⁶Jesus said to him, "I am *the way* (lit. ἡ ὁδὸς = "the way"), the truth, and the life. No one comes to the Father, except through me."

Luke continues this important theme, employing irony by the use of a word-play, in which he deliberately employs the Greek word for "road" (= ὁδός) to represent how Jesus rescues Paul from going down the wrong "road" for his life, and puts him on "Straight Street" – the name of the street in Damascus upon which Jesus has arranged for Paul to meet Ananias – where Jesus not only restores Paul's physical and spiritual sight, but also where He places Paul on the right "road" for his life. Luke records how Jesus stops Paul and physically blinds him, because he is spiritually blind to the fact that he is on the wrong "road" for his lifework, i.e., on the "road" (= ὁδός) to Damascus, to arrest those who are following Jesus in "the Way" (= ἡ ὁδὸς, lit. "The Road"):

Acts 9:1-2: Ὁ δὲ Σαῦλος, ἔτι ἐμπνέων ἀπειλῆς καὶ φόνου εἰς τοὺς μαθητὰς τοῦ Κυρίου, προσελθὼν τῷ ἀρχιερεῖ, ²ᾐτήσατο παρ' αὐτοῦ ἐπιστολὰς εἰς Δαμασκὸν πρὸς τὰς συναγωγάς, ὅπως ἐάν τινας εὕρῃ **τῆς ὁδοῦ** ὄντας, ἄνδρας τε καὶ γυναῖκας, δεδεμένους ἀγάγῃ εἰς Ἰερουσαλήμ.

Acts 9:1-2: But Saul, still breathing threats and slaughter against the disciples of the Lord, went to the high priest, ²and asked for letters from him to the synagogues of Damascus, that if he found any who were of *the Way* (lit. **τῆς ὁδοῦ** = "the Way"), whether men or women, he might bring them bound to Jerusalem.

Acts 9:17 Ἀπῆλθε δὲ Ἀνανίας καὶ εἰσῆλθεν εἰς τὴν οἰκίαν, καὶ ἐπιθεὶς ἐπ' αὐτὸν τὰς χεῖρας εἶπε, Σαοὺλ ἀδελφέ, ὁ Κύριος ἀπέσταλκέ με, ὁ ὀφθείς σοι ἐν **τῇ ὁδῷ** ᾗ ἤρχου, ὅπως ἀναβλέψῃς καὶ πλησθῇς Πνεύματος Ἁγίου.

Acts 9:17 Ananias departed, and entered into the house. Laying his hands on him, he said, "Brother Saul, the Lord, who appeared to you *on the road* (lit. **τῇ ὁδῷ** = "the road") which you came, has sent me, that you may receive your sight, and be filled with the Holy Spirit."

Acts 9:27 Βαρναβᾶς δὲ ἐπιλαβόμενος αὐτὸν ἤγαγε πρὸς τοὺς ἀποστόλους, καὶ διηγήσατο αὐτοῖς πῶς ἐν **τῇ ὁδῷ** εἶδε τὸν Κύριον καὶ ὅτι ἐλάλησεν αὐτῷ, καὶ πῶς ἐν Δαμασκῷ ἐπαρρησιάσατο ἐν τῷ ὀνόματι Ἰησοῦ.

Acts 9:27 But Barnabas took him, and brought him to the apostles, and declared to them how he had seen the Lord *on the road* (lit. **τῇ ὁδῷ** = "the road"), and that He had spoken to him, and how at Damascus he had preached boldly in the name of Jesus.

In fact, throughout the Book of Acts, Luke characteristically and repeatedly (11 times – 3 of these by directly quoting Paul himself following his conversion) refers to Christianity as "The Way" (= ἡ ὁδὸς, "The Road" or "The Journey" that everyone who believes in Jesus should take in life: Acts 2:28, 9:2, 13:10, 16:17, 18:25, 26; 19:9, 23; 22:4, 24:14, 22).

⁹ ἐν οἷς καὶ ἡμεῖς…ὡς καὶ οἱ λοιποί = "among whom we also…just like the rest of them still do now." Paul is describing here his former way of being motivated and driven when he was a part of the religious and political regime within Judaism, as a member of the sect of the Pharisees (Acts 23:6; 26:5-11). Webster

provides the following background on what it meant to be a Pharisee: Etymology: Middle English *pharise*, from Old English *farise*, from Late Latin *pharisaeus*, from Greek *pharisaios*, from Aramaic *perīshayyā*, plural of *perīshā*, lit,. "*separated;*" akin to Hebrew *pārūsh* = "*separated, distinct."* 1. usually capitalized: a member of a school or party among the ancient Jews who were noted for strict and formal observance of rites and ceremonies of the written law and for insistence on the validity of the traditions of the elders, who differed from the Sadducees in traditionalism and in their teachings concerning the immortality of the soul, the resurrection of the body, future retribution, and a coming Messiah, and whose interpretation provided the standard of observance and belief for the great majority of Jews from the 1st century A.D. [W]." The Jewish historian *Flavius Josephus,* who was himself a Jew, a Pharisee and only about three decades younger than Paul, gives three descriptions of the Pharisees in his historical works [Flavius Josephus, A.D. 37-c.A.D. 100, Jewish historian and soldier, b. Jerusalem. Josephus' historical works are among the most valuable sources for the study of early Judaism and early Christianity. Having studied the tenets of the three main sects of Judaism—Essenes, Sadducees, and Pharisees—he became a Pharisee. At the beginning of the war between the Romans and Jews, he was made commander of Galilee, despite the fact that he had opposed the uprising. He surrendered to the Romans instead of committing suicide when the stronghold was taken. He won the favor of the Roman general Vespasian (Titus Flavius Vespasianus) and took his name, Flavius. He lived in Rome under imperial patronage, where he wrote the Greek-language historical works for which he is renowned. He wrote *The Jewish War;* the famous *Antiquities of the Jews,* a history of the Jews from creation to the war with Rome; *Against Apion*, an exalted defense of the Jews; and his autobiography, or *apologia.* *(Columbia Encyclopedia, Sixth Edition. 2001-05)*]. Josephus' first description of the Pharisees in his *The Wars of the Jews,* Book 2, Section 119 and Section 162, as follows (ed. B. Niese, Berlin, 1892; transl. William Whiston, Auburn and Buffalo, 1895):

> [119] For there are three philosophical sects among the Jews. The followers of the first of which are the **Pharisees (Φαρισαῖοι)**; of the second, the Sadducees (Σαδδουκαῖοι); and the third sect, which pretends to a severer discipline, are called Essens ('Εσσηνοι) ...[Josephus then gives an extended, detailed and appreciative description of the pious yet reclusive philosophy and way of life of the Essenes – GWC]...[162] But then as to the two other orders at first mentioned, the **Pharisees** are those *who are esteemed most skillful in the exact explication of their laws* [italics mine – GWC], and introduce the first sect. These ascribe all to fate [or providence], and to God, and yet allow, that to act what is right, or the contrary, is principally in the power of men, although fate does co-operate in every action. They say that all souls are incorruptible, but that the souls of good men only are removed into other bodies, – but that the souls of bad men are subject to eternal punishment. But the Sadducees are those that compose the second order, and take away fate entirely, and suppose that God is not concerned in our doing or not doing what is evil; and they say, that to act what is good, or what is evil, is at men's own choice, and that the one or the other belongs so to every one, that they may act as they please. They also take away the belief of the immortal duration of the soul,

and the punishments and rewards in Hades. Moreover, the ***Pharisees*** *are friendly to one another* (φιλάλληλοί), *and are for the exercise of concord, and regard for the public; but the behavior* (ἦθος = *"custom, manner, disposition, character, outward bearing"* [LS]) *of the Sadducees one towards another is in some degree wild* (ἄγριος = *"savage, wild, fierce, cruel, harsh"* [LS]), *and their conversation* (ἐπιμιξία = *"mixing with others, intercourse, dealings"* [LS]) *with those that are of their own party is as barbarous* (ἀπηνής = *"ungentle, rough, hard, cruel, unpleasant"* [LS]) *as if they were strangers to them* [italics mine – GWC]. And this is what I had to say concerning the philosophic sects among the Jews.

Josephus' gives his second description of the Pharisees in *Antiquities of the Jews,* Book 13, Section 171 (ed. B. Niese, Berlin, 1892; transl. William Whiston, Auburn and Buffalo, 1895):

> [171] At this time there were three sects among the Jews, who had different opinions concerning human actions; the one was called the sect of the Pharisees, another the sect of the Sadducees, and the other the sect of the Essens. Now for the **Pharisees**, they say that some actions, but not all, are the work of fate, and some of them are in our own power, and that they are liable to fate, but are not caused by fate. But the sect of the Essens affirm, that fate governs all things, and that nothing befalls men but what is according to its determination. And for the Sadducees, they take away fate, and say there is no such thing, and that the events of human affairs are not at its disposal; but they suppose that all our actions are in our own power, so that we are ourselves the causes of what is good, and receive what is evil from our own folly. However, I have given a more exact account of these opinions in the second book of the Jewish War.

Josephus' third and most extended description of the Pharisees occurs later in *Antiquities of the Jews,* Book 18, Sections 11 and 12:

> [11] The Jews had for a great while had three sects of philosophy peculiar to themselves; the sect of the Essens, and the sect of the Sadducees, and the third sort of opinions was that of those called **Pharisees**; of which sects, although I have already spoken in the second book of the Jewish War, yet will I a little touch upon them now. [12] Now, for the Pharisees, they live meanly, and despise delicacies in diet; *and they follow the conduct of reason* (λόγος); *and what that prescribes to them as good for them they do; and they think they ought earnestly to strive to observe reason's dictates for practice* [italics mine – GWC]. They also pay a respect to such as are in years; nor are they so bold as to contradict them in any thing which they have introduced; and when they determine that all things are done by fate, they do not take away the freedom from men of acting as they think fit; since their notion is, that it hath pleased God to make a temperament, whereby what he wills is done, but so that the will of man can act virtuously or viciously. They also believe that souls have an immortal rigor in them, and that under the earth there will be rewards or punishments, according as they have lived virtuously or viciously in this life; and the latter are to be detained in an everlasting prison, but that the former shall have power to revive and live again; *on account of which doctrines they are able greatly to persuade the body of the people; and whatsoever they do about Divine worship, prayers, and sacrifices, they perform them according to their direction; insomuch that the cities give great attestations to them on account of their entire virtuous conduct, both in the actions of their lives and their discourses also* [italics mine – GWC].

From the above passages, it is possible to assemble the following general sketch of the depth of Paul's intellectual preparation provided by his training as a member of this sect. From reading both Paul and Josephus' works, we can observe that both men were extremely articulate, that they knew and wrote Greek extremely well, that they had a profound knowledge of the history of their own Jewish people, as well as an understanding of the different philosophical schools of thought that surrounded them, both within Judaism and outside it. They both had extended relationships with the Roman military and political machine, both traveled widely, and both lived in Rome for an extended period of time. Although Josephus understood and appreciated the piety, dedication, and religious devotion of the Essenes, he chose not to adopt their austere and reclusive way of life which did not permit them to have meaningful, genuine contact with the Hellenic or Roman culture and way of life. Josephus has a negative opinion of the behavior of the Sadducees, which from his account, resembles the unethical conduct characteristic of being exposed to a long-corrupted political climate. Along this line, he comments that their behavior toward one another is "in some degree wild," and their "conversation with those that are of their own party is as barbarous as if they were strangers to them."

If the maturity and intellectual depth of Josephus' historical works are an indication of the quality of his education as a Pharisee, and if Paul had a similar education, then like Josephus, Paul would have been rigorously educated in all the detailed aspects of Jewish life, especially in religion, particularly with respect to its interpretation and application to philosophical, historical, political and legal matters, economics, one's vocational and professional life, construction projects, and the organization and operation of the occupying Roman military force. From Josephus' description of the Sadducees, who held greater political power than the Pharisees, it is plausible to understand how Paul could have been influenced by them to develop his extremist, driven, aggressive and even violent attitude toward Jesus' followers before his own conversion. For further development of the psychological dynamic of how Paul might have been negativley influenced by the leadership regime within Judaism, see the extended note on ἀναστρέφω (at Eph. 2:3) immediately below.

[10] ἀναστρέφω – usual translation: "conversation" (Eph. 2:3, KJV), no doubt once again following Tyndale, who translates this word "conversacion." Its denotative meaning in the active voice is to "turn upside down, turn back, turn around, retreat, wheel around." Its denotative meaning in the passive voice is to: "to live in a place, go about in public, to continue an alliance, to be engaged in." The connotative meaning that eventually emerged and then rose to prominence was "the manner of conducting oneself in public affairs, behave in public" [LS]. In the *Nicomachean Ethics* 1103b, Aristotle uses this word in an *ethical sense* to describe the formation of one's professional public demeanor, disposition, or public comportment as we respond to powerful passions, desires and anger. Aristotle's argument is that one's public, social disposition and demeanor is formed to a large extent by those with whom one continually associates, even if

the person remains *passive and unaware* that this or her personality, attitudes and entire worldview is being shaped by the dispositions of those they surround themselves with. Since this is true, Aristotle maintains that one therefore must *actively decide* to select his or her friends and associate with and surround himself or herself with wise, thoughtful people. It is worth quoting Aristotle here, because one can clearly discern in his explanation the union of the active and passive senses of the word ἀναστρέφω. On the formation of "virtue" (ἀρετή = "soul-skill"), which is one of the most important themes of the *Nicomachean Ethics*, Aristotle says (ed. J. Bywater, Oxford, 1894; transl. H. Rackham, Cambridge, 1934):

> "The virtues (ἀρεται)...we acquire by first having actually practiced them, just as we do the arts. We learn an art or craft by doing the things that we shall have to do when we have learnt it: for instance, men become builders by building houses, harpers by playing on the harp. Similarly we become just by doing just acts, temperate by doing temperate acts, brave by doing brave acts...The same is true of the virtues. It is by taking part in transactions with our fellow-men that some of us become just and others unjust; by acting in dangerous situations and forming a habit of fear or of confidence we become courageous or cowardly. And the same holds good of our dispositions with regard to the appetites (better: "desires" = ἐπιθυμίαις), and anger; some men become temperate and gentle, other profligate and irascible, by actually comporting themselves (ἀναστρέφεσθαι = better: "unwittingly being formed in their public demeanor by being bounced back and forth due to public peer pressure between the vice of excess and the vice of defect") in one way or the other in relation to those passions. In a word, our moral dispositions are formed as a result of the corresponding activities. Hence it is incumbent on us to control the character of our activities, since on the quality of these depends the quality of our dispositions. *It is therefore not of small moment whether we are trained from childhood in one set of habits or another; on the contrary it is of very great, or rather of supreme, importance*" [italics mine – GWC].

In Middle English, the word that accurately translated this Greek concept of having one's public behavior permanently formed by those with whom one habitually associated was the word "*conversacioun*." Therefore, Tyndale accurately used the Middle English word "*conversacion*" to translate ἀναστρέφω in 1526. Webster confirms that "conversation" had this meaning in Middle English usage, but that this meaning has since become obsolete, being replaced by the meaning of "having verbal dialogue or discussion with another person," as follows: Etymology: Middle English *conversacioun*, from Middle French *conversation*, from Latin *conversation, conversatio* frequent abode in a place, intercourse, manner of life, from *conversatus* (past participle of *conversari* to associate with) + *-ion-, -io -ion* -- more at CONVERSE **1** obsolete **a:** the action of living or dwelling in a place <for our *conversation* is in heaven--Phil 3:20 (Authorized Version)> **b:** the action of living, associating, or having dealings with others <my long ... *conversation* with him, that continued to his death for twenty-three years--Gilbert Burnet> **c:** manner of living: conduct or behavior <be ye holy in all manner of *conversation*--1 Pet 1:15 (Authorized Version)> **d:** those with whom one associates: social circle: COMPANY <you may know the man by the *conversation* he keeps--Thomas Shelton> **e:** occupation or association especially with an object of study or a subject: close acquaintance or intimacy <experience in business and *conversation* in books--Francis Bacon>...**3 a** (1): oral exchange of sentiments, observations, opinions, ideas: colloquial discourse <in casual *conversation* on the street corner> <we had talk enough but no *conversation*; there was nothing discussed--Samuel Johnson> (2): an instance of *conversational* exchange: TALK, COLLOQUY <had a long *conversation* with his friend> **b** archaic: a meeting or assembly for *conversing* or discussing: (1): a public conference or debate (2): an at home or reception: CONVERSAZIONE **c:** an informal exploratory discussion of an issue by diplomats of two or more governments or by officials or representatives of any institutions or groups <diplomatic *conversations*> <*conversations* among representatives of the colleges, business, and industry--H.D.Gideonse> [W]. Therefore, the proposed translation of ἀναστρέφω is "to have one's public demeanor unwittingly formed for better or for worse by one's habitual public associations."

Paul is clearly admitting that by the time he had reached early adulthood, his own public demeanor had been shaped into an acerbic and disagreeable personality due to his association with the members of the leadership regime within Judaism. Even though this also may be true of us to varying degrees, Paul's emphasis in this passage is that we, like him, can transform our dysfunctional public personalities through God's gracious power and become pleasant, peaceful, loving people.

[11] σώζω – Root verb of the substantive participle σεσωσμένοι. This verb is usually translated "saved," although the word "rescue" is used more commonly to convey this Greek concept in contemporary professional American English. The English word "save" is not the best translation for the word σώζω because in American usage, "save" predominately means "to preserve" (mostly money and information), as in the expressions "I opened a *savings* account at the Bank;" and "Did you *save* your computer files to the back-up disk?" The English word "deliver" is also not the ideal translation for the word σώζω either, because in American usage, "deliver" predominately means "to transport or convey something, usually through an organized distribution system," as in the expressions, "the Post Office does not *deliver* the mail on holidays;" "the Doctor and the ER staff *delivered* her baby at the hospital;" and "Did Fed-Ex *deliver* the package yet?"

The grammatical construction Paul uses is identical in the only two clauses in which he employs it in this entire Treatise: here in Eph. 2:5 and immediately following in close context in Eph. 2:8. Paul's specific identical grammatical construction in both passages is as follows: "χάριτί ἐστε σεσωσμένοι," which translated, is: "[For it is only] by means of [His] graciousness (χάριτί = fem. dat. sing.) [that] you all are (ἐστε = pres ind act 2nd pl) those who have been rescued [by Him] (σεσωσμένοι = perf part mid/pass masc nom pl)]." Thus, the main verb of the clause is not σώζω, but rather ἐστε, which is the second person plural form of the present indicative active verb εἰμί, which should be translated, "you all are." The word σώζω occurs in the participial form σεσωσμένοι, which is a masculine nominative plural perfect passive substantive participle, and should be translated "the ones who have been rescued." Thus, the New King James translation for this clause both here in Eph. 2:5 as well as in Eph. 2:8 ("by grace you have been saved") is slightly misleading, because that translation suggests that the main verb is the word "saved" in the second person plural form of the perfect indicative passive verb "to save" (i.e., "you have been saved"). Rendered into smooth American English, it is therefore proposed that this clause be translated as follows in both Eph. 2:5 and Eph. 2:8: "Because it is only by means of His graciousness that you all are presently enjoying the benefits of being among those who have been rescued by Him from the normal ruinous consequences that usually result from having been misguided for such a long time in going down the wrong road in life."

[12] One need only read Homer's Epics, *The Iliad* and *The Odyssey*, the tragic plays of Aeschylus (N.B. *Agamemnon, Eumenides, Libation Bearers*), Euripides (N.B. *Bacchae, Iphigenia in Aulis*), and Sophocles (N.B. *Antigone, Oedipus Tyrannus, Oedipus at Colonus, Philoctetes*), to gain an understanding of the deception, injustice, cruelty, anger and murder that caused the escalating cycles of revenge which resulted in the numerous early and tragic deaths which the Greeks that lived during these early eras suffered due to their relationships with the envious gods in Greek polytheism that selfishly manipulated them.

[13] See note above at Eph. 2:2 on περιπατέω, which means "to deliberately and intentionally learn, practice and teach others a comprehensive philosophical world view." Because Paul uses this word in close context to "bookend" or "bracket" (Eph. 2:2 and 2:10) this entire section (Eph. 2:1-10), it is reasonable to infer that the central concept it conveys pervades and guides his train of thought throughout the entire section.

[14] συνεζωοποίησε...καὶ συνήγειρε καὶ συνεκάθισεν: These three verbs that occur in verses 5 and 6 are the main three verbs of the single Greek sentence that Paul begins in Eph. 2:1 and concludes at the end of Eph. 2:7. They are all 3rd person singular 1st aorist active indicative in form, and so should be translated, "He has made us alive with...and He has resurrected us with and He has seated us with our future High King, Jesus, in the heavenly (places)." Thus, the phrase – χάριτί ἐστε σεσῳσμένοι – (see analysis in note above at Eph. 2:5) is epexegetical, e.g., it is an explanation following a word or larger part of a text that limits its application or clarifies its meaning [W]. Thus, in Eph. 2:5 and 2:8, being "rescued" from a ruined life is a result of appropriating the benefits of being "made alive with, resurrected with, and seated with" Jesus.

There is an inferential distinction to be observed between the first verb in Eph. 2:5 (συνεζωοποίησε = "He has made us alive with") and the next two verbs in Eph. 2:6 (συνήγειρε καὶ συνεκάθισεν = "He has resurrected us with and He has seated us with"). The first verb occurs by itself, whereas the next two verbs occur in conjunction with each other, and are connected to the phrase "in the heavenly (places)." In Hebrews 10:11-13, the author of that Treatise bases his theological argument that Jesus' present *heavenly Office* and duties (which He exercises during this historical era) are to be distinguished from his *kingly Office* and duties (that He will exercise in the next era of the Millennial Kingdom) by deliberately pointing out that in contrast to the earthly priests of Israel, who had to *remain standing* in the exercise of their priestly office, that in contrast Jesus is a final and Heavenly Priest, because He *"has sat down"* (Heb. 10:12, ἐκάθισεν = 3 p sg 1aor act ind: "He has sat down," cf. Eph. 2:6, συνεκάθισεν = 3 p sg 1aor act ind: "He has seated us with"). The author of Hebrews then points out that the significance of Jesus' *seated position in heaven* is that He is *"waiting"* to *return to the earth* to defeat all his enemies (Heb. 10:13 – "from that time *waiting* until His enemies are made His footstool"). Hebrews 10:11-13 is therefore the climactic conclusion to the theme introduced in Hebrews 1:13, in which the God the Son is told by God the Father to "sit" at His "right hand," until He makes His enemies His footstool; i.e., until He returns to earth to win the final battle against God's enemies and be inaugurated as the High King of the Millennial Kingdom.

This seems to indicate that although God "has made us alive with" Jesus in *all* of His experience following His resurrection; i.e., in His presently heavenly Office as Priest, His future kingly Office as High King, etc.; that He "has seated us with" Jesus during the period of His present heavenly Office as Priest only. This implies that since Jesus' heavenly office as Priest will be accomplished and therefore be completed when He takes up His office as High King during the Millennial Kingdom, that our relationship of being "seated with" Him *will also be completed and the opportunities that were afforded us during that time will also come to an end.* This implies that since during this present historical era, Jesus, from His heavenly Office, has the power to transform our personalities into our future Kingdom personalities as we interact with Him to perform our lifework here and now in preparation for our Millennial appointments, that there will come a time when the period of this historical era – and thus the opportunities for becoming more mature – will be over. The implication of this line of reasoning is that since we do not know when Jesus will transition from executing His heavenly responsibilities as our Commander in Chief to His regal responsibilities as the future High King of the world, that we should approach our mortal lives with a *sense of urgency* to find, accomplish and complete our lifework for God.

See both the extended translation and the basic translation for a proposed theological and philosophical interpretation of the meaning that can be inferred from the above observations and distinctions concerning these three main verbs.

[15] In 2 Corinthians 5:1-4, Paul teaches that in addition to the mortal body in which we presently dwell in this life, we have a superior (albeit temporary) supernatural body with which we are embodied in heaven immediately following our death, which we inhabit until the resurrection of our mortal bodies, at which time the angels of God will fully restore our decayed, mortal bodies into an immortal form

to us, and in which we will then live during the Millennial Kingdom, and following that, in His Eternal Kingdom:

> 2 Cor. 5:1-4 "For we know that if the earthly house of our tent is dissolved (i.e., our temporary mortal body dies, is buried and decays), we have a building from God, a house not made with hands, eternal, in the heavens (God provides us with another more durable body which we employ during our temporary, albeit protracted, lives and relationships in heaven). ²For most assuredly in this (temporary mortal body) we groan (due to illness, injury, and eventually the debilitating diseases of old age), longing to be clothed with our habitation which is from heaven (our more durable body that we will inhabit in heaven when we die); ³so that when we are clothed (in our heavenly body) we will not be found naked (i.e, not exist in heaven as disembodied spirits). ⁴For indeed we who are in this tent (our temporary mortal body) do groan (due to illness, injury, and eventually the debilitating diseases of old age), being burdened (by the pain that results from the aforementioned inevitable decaying process); not that we desire to be unclothed (no one naturally wants to experience death), but that we desire to be clothed (God eventually allows all of us to experience more and more pain involved in the inevitable aging process, so that we will actually desire exchanging our old, worn-out mortal bodies for our immortal heavenly bodies), and that what is mortal may ultimately be swallowed up by life (that our decayed mortal bodies would eventually be reconstructed and transformed into our permanent immortal bodies, at which time we exchange our temporary immortal heavenly bodies for our permanent rebuilt immortal resurrected bodies)."

[16] The end of verse 7 completes the sentence Paul began in Eph. 2:1. He now proceeds on in Eph. 2:8-9 to warn us by making it absolutely clear that this "rescue," i.e., this unique transformational process by which God gradually "transplants" or "transfuses" our future mature personalities into our present immature personalities in this life in order to completely renovate them – is a *gift* from God. In other words, we do not "get better" or "become more mature" based on our own efforts, but only by God's gracious power. Otherwise, we would take the credit for ourselves, become sanctimonious, and thus become disqualified from the kind of loving, self-sacrificial personalities that God will require from those who are the leaders in His coming Kingdom.

[17] σώζω – The phrase in which the word σώζω occurs in Eph. 2:8 (χάριτί ἐστε σεσῳσμένοι) is identical to the phrase Paul uses in Eph. 2:5 (See note at Eph. 2:5 for a grammatical analysis and translation of this phrase in its context).

[18] ποίημα, ατος, τό, ([ποιέω]) **anything made or done**: hence, **I. *work***, π. χρύσεα, χάλκεα καὶ σιδήρεα, Hdt.4.5, 7.84, cf. 2.135; Γλαύκου τοῦ Χίου π. Id.1.25; *of the works of Daedalus...***2. *poem***, Cratin.186, Pl.Phd.60d, Ly.221d; τὰ μετὰ μέτρου π. Isoc.2.7, 15.45; π. εἰς τὰς Μούσας IG7.1773.17 [LS]. The English word "poem" is a transliteration of this Greek word (**ποίημα** = "poiēma" = "poem"). Its etymology is as follows: Middle French *poeme*, from Latin *poema*, from Greek *poiēma, poēma*, from *poiein* to make, do, create, compose – 1: a composition in verse 2: a piece of poetry designed as a unit and communicating to the reader the sense of a complete experience 3: a composition, creation, achievement, experience, or object likened to a poem [W]. As can be seen from the above

philology, this word is much broader and refers to a much wider scope of creative work than just Epic Greek Poetry. Proposed translation of **ποίημα**: "masterwork."

[19] **κτίζω**...*people a country, build houses and cities in it,* κτίσσε δὲ Δαρδανίην Il.l.c.; κ. χώρην, νῆσον, Hdt.1.149, 3.49. **2.** *of a city, found, build,* Θήβης ἕδος ἕκτισαν Od.l.c., cf. Hdt.1.167, 168, Th.6.4, PCair.Zen.169 (iii B.C.); ἀποικίαν A.Pr.815:--Pass., *to be founded,* Σμύρνην τὴν ἀπὸ Κολοφῶνος κτισθεῖσαν *founded by emigrants from Colophon,* Hdt.1.16, cf.7.153, 8.62; **3.** κ. ἄλσος *plant a grove,* Pi.P.5.89; βωμόν *set up an altar,* Id.O.7.42; ἑορτάν, ἀγῶνα, *found, establish it,* ib.6.69, 10(11).25 (Med.);...**4.** *produce, create, bring into being,* γόνῳ τινά A.Supp.172 (lyr.); *bring about,* τελευτήν ib.140 (lyr.), cf. Ch.441 (lyr.); ὁ τὴν φιλίην ἐκτικώς Lyr.Alex.Adesp. l.c.; *of painters,* δένδρεα . . καὶ ἀνέρας ἠδὲ γυναῖκας Emp.l.c.; ἵπποισι τὸν χαλινὸν κτίσας *having invented it,* S.OC715 (lyr.). [LS]. Usually translated "created." Proposed translation: "to create, form, shape, build, invent or forge."

In this second section of his Treatise, Paul transitions his extended metaphor or "vehicle" from that of *economics* to that of a *building* or *construction project* (cf. note at Eph. 1:4). Although there is some overlap, the main portion of this second extended metaphor of God as our "Builder" or "Developer" in the area of the construction and building of the vital relational structures He will found and build upon comprises the middle portion of Ephesians (Eph. 2:10-6:9). The main symbolic concepts (approx. 22) associated with this second extended metaphor which Paul organizes around the theme of "building" are as follows:

- **καταβολή** = "foundation, founding" (1:4),
- **κτίζω** = "to create, form, shape, invent, forge" (2:10, 15; 3:9; 4:24),
- **χειροποίητος** = "made by hand, artificial" (2:11),
- **ποιέω** = "make, forge, build, create, conceive, produce, solve a problem, satisfy a condition (1:16; 2:3, 14, 15; 3:11, 20; 4:16; 6:6, 8, 9),
- **λύω** = "demolish, break up, destroy, put an end to, annul, dissolve (2:24),
- **μεσότοιχος** = "partition wall, dividing wall" (2:14),
- **φραγμός** = "fence, partition, fortification wall, screen wall" (2:14),
- **προσαγωγή** = "freeway" (2:18, 3:12),
- **οἰκεῖος** = "house-hold, home (2:19),
- **ἐποικοδομέω** = "to build up, to build upon" (2:20),
- **θεμέλιος** = "foundation of a building" (2:20) and **θεμελιόω** = to lay the foundation of, found firmly (3:17),
- **ἀκρογωνιαῖος** = "corner foundation stone" (2:20),
- **οἰκοδομή** = "building" (2:21; 4:12, 16, 29),
- **συναρμολογέω** = "to fasten or join together carefully, harmoniously, and logically, as in assembling a ship's outer planking or in laying masonry" (2:21, 4:16),
- **συνοικοδομέω** = "to successfully build a house from a variety of divergent materials" (2:22),
- **κατοικητήριος** = "to build a house into a home" (2:22),
- **κατοικέω** = "to land, plant a Colony, then settle in, then live, and finally adminster and govern a new land" (3:17),

- πλάτος καὶ μῆκος καὶ ὕψος καὶ βάθος = "width and length and height (dimensions of the superstructure of a building) and depth (crucial dimension of the foundation of a building)" (3:18),
- μέτρον = "measure, in both senses of laying out dimensions prior to construction, as well as evaluating and appraising the value of something built after its construction is completed" (4:7, 13, 16).

When this "building" metaphor is extended from the "framework or structure of buildings" to the "interpersonal frameworks or structures involved in collective human relationships," there are an additional two main words that are in concord with the extended metaphor of "building" in this sense (of interpersonal relational frameworks), and these are as follows:

- ἐκκλησία = "Lifework Council, Apprenticeship Council" (1:22; 3:10, 21; 5:23, 24, 25, 27, 29, 32),
- σῶμα = "administrative, organizational, governmental, or associational body" (1:23; 2:16; 4:4, 12, 16 [2x]; 5:23, 30).

See note above at Eph. 2:3 on for an explanation of how it might have been possible for Paul to be so well acquainted with the profession of the construction of buildings that he could use its concepts competently as an extended metaphor to accurately communicate this second major theme of this Treatise.

[20] ἔργον, Dor. ϝέργον *IG*4.800 (vi B. C.), Elean ϝάργον *SIG*9 (vi B.C.), τό: (ἔρδω, OE. **A.** *weorc* (neut.) 'work', Avest. *var[schwa]za-*):-- [p. 683] *work*, Il.2.436, etc.;...esp. in pl., ἄλλος ἄλλοισιν..ἐπιτέρπεται ἔργοις Od. 14.228;...τὰ σ᾽ αὐτῆς ἔργα κόμιζε see to thine own *tasks*, Il.6.490: esp. in the following relations, **1.** in Il. mostly of *works* or *deeds* of war, πολεμήϊα ἔ. Il.2.338, al., Od.12.116;...ἐν τῷ ἔ. during the *action*, Th.2.89, cf.7.71;...τῶν πρότερον ἔ. μέγιστον ἐπράχθη τὸ Μηδικόν Th.1.23; ἔργου ἔχεσθαι to engage in *battle*, ib.49. **2.** of peaceful *contests*, κρατεῖν ἔ. Pi.*O*.9.85; ...also ἔργα θῆκε κάλλιστ᾽ ἀμφὶ κόμαις placed [the reward of] noble *deeds* about his hair, Id.*O*.13.38. **3.** of *works of industry*, **a.** of *tillage, tilled lands*, ἀνδρῶν πίονα ἔ. Il.12.283, etc.; ἔργ᾽ ἀνθρώπων 16.392, Od.6.259; etc.;...Ἔργα καὶ Ἡμέραι [transl. *"Works and Days"*]--the title of Hesiod's *work*; πατρώϊα ἔ. their father's *lands*, Od.2.22; οὔτ᾽ ἐπὶ ἔργα..ἴμεν will neither go to our *farms*, ib. 127, cf. 252;᾽Ἰθάκης..ἔργα *the tilled lands* of Ithaca, 14.344; ἀμφὶ.. Τιταρησσὸν ἔργ᾽ ἐνέμοντο inhabited *lands*, Il.2.751; τὰ τῶν Μυσῶν ἔ. Hdt.1.36; so later, *PBaden* 40.5 (ii A.D.): generally, *property, wealth, possessions*, θεὸς δ᾽ ἐπὶ ἔργον ἀέξῃ Od.14.65 , cf. 15.372. **b.** of women's *work, weaving*, Il.9.390, etc.; ἀμύμονα ἔ. ἰδυίας ib.128; ἔργα ἐργάζεσθαι Od.22.422 , 20.72. **c.** of other *occupations*, θαλάσσια ἔ. *fishing*, 5.67; **a seaman's life,** Il.2.614: periphr., δαιτὸς..ἔργα *works* **of feasting**, 9.228; φιλοτήσια ἔ. Od.11.246;...φίλα ἔργα μελίσσαις, *works* **of flowers,** Theoc.22.42; *works* **of mines**, etc., ἔ. ἀργυρεῖα X.*Vect*.4.5, D.21.167, etc.;...**4.** *deed, action*, ἔργ᾽ ἀνδρῶν τε θεῶν τε Od.1.338; θέσκελα ἔ. Τρώων Il.3.130;...opp. ἔπος, *deed*, not word (v. ἔπος 11.1); opp. μῦθος [transl. *"deed*, not myth" – GWC], Il. 9.443, 19.242, A.*Pr*.1080 (anap.), etc.; opp. λόγος [transl. *"deed*, not logical spoken argument" –

GWC], S.*El*.358, E.*Alc*. 339;...opp. ῥήματα [transl. *"deed*, not articulate, persuasive public speech" – GWC], Id.*OC*873; opp. ὄνομα [transl. *"deed*, not name or reputation" – GWC], E.*IA*128 (anap.), Th.8.78,89; in many phrases, πέπρακται τοὔργον A.*Pr*.75, cf. *Ag*.1346; χωρῶ πρὸς ἔργον S.*Aj*.116; τὸ μὲν ἐνθύμημα χαρίεν.., τὸ δὲ ἔ. ἀδύνατον [the manner of *execution of a deed* – GWC], X.*An*.3.5.12; ἐν ἔργῳ χέρνιβες ξίφος τε ready for *action*, E.*IT*1190;...**II. thing, matter**, πᾶν ἔ...ὑπείξομαι in every *point*, Il.1.294;...μέγα ἔ. a serious *matter*, Od.4.663, Th.3.3. **2.** μέγα ἔ. [transl. "big *deal*" – GWC], like μέγα χρῆμα [transl. "great deed"– GWC],...φυλόπιδος μέγα ἔ. *a mighty call to arms*, 16.208. **III.** Pass., *that which is wrought* or *made*, *work*, οἵ᾽ ἐπιεικὲς ἔργ᾽ ἔμεν ἀθανάτων, of the **arms** ["arms" = "absolutely unique weapons of superior quality" – GWC] of Achilles, Il.19.22 ; ἔ. ʹ Ηφαίστοιο **metal-*work*** [transl. *"works* of Hephaestus" – GWC], Od.4.617; πέπλοι.., ἔργα γυναικῶν [transl. *"woven cloaks...works* of women" – GWC] Il.6.289, Od.7.97,...of a **wall**, Ar.*Av*.1125;of a **statue**, X.*Mem*.3.10.7: in pl., of **siege-*works***, ἔ. καὶ μηχαναί Plb.5.3.6; of a *machine*, Apollod.*Poliorc*.157.4, al., Ath.Mech.15.2, al.; of *public buildings*, Mon.Anc.Gr.18.20; of an **author's *works***, D.H.*Comp*.25; τὸ περὶ ψυχῆς ἔργον ʹ Αριστοτέλους [transl. "...concerning the soul of the *works* of Aristotle" – GWC], *AP*11.354.8 (Agath.). **2.** *result of work*, *profit* or *interest*, ἔργον [χρημάτων] *interest* or *profit* on money, Is.11.42, cf. D.27.10. **IV.** special phrases: **1. ἔργον ἐστί, a.** c. gen. pers., *it is his business*, **his** *proper work*, ἀνδρῶν τόδ᾽ ἐστὶν ἔ. A.*Ch*.673; ὅπερ ἐστὶν ἔ. ἀγαθοῦ πολίτου Pl.*Grg*.517c; of things, φραδέος νόου ἔργα τέτυκται it is *a matter* [better: *"enterprise, endeavor*" – GWC] (which calls) for a wary mind, Il.24.354 [referring to Priam's bold venture to go to the tent of Achilles with much treasure in order to ransom the body of his son Hektor – GWC]; *function*, ἅπερ νεῶν ἄμεινον πλεουσῶν ἔργα ἐστίν [transl. "the *enterprise* which comprises this larger shipyard is better in its *operational function*" – GWC] Th.2.89;...**b.** c. gen. rei, *there is need* of..,καὶ ἐνταῦθα δὴ πολλῆς φυλακῆς ἔ. (ἐστί) [transl. "and there is especially a need for exercising great care in *undertaking the task* (of selecting the appropriate apprentices to promote to higher levels of training)" – GWC] Pl.*R*. 537d;...also c. inf., οὐδὲν ἔ. ἑστάναι there is no *use in* standing still, Ar.*Lys*.424, cf. *Av*.1308;...**c.** c. inf., *it is hard work, difficult to do*, πολὺ ἔ. ἂν εἴη διεξελθεῖν X.*Mem*.4.6.1;...also in gen., πλείονος ἔργου ἐστὶν ἀκριβῶς πάντα ταῦτα ὡς ἔχει μαθεῖν [transl. "it is a great and difficult *endeavor to undertake* having to accurately learn all of these things" – GWC] Pl.*Euthphr*.14b: *it can scarcely happen* that.., ἐκεῖ δ᾽ **ἔργον** ἅμα πάντας ὀργισθῆναι καὶ ἁμαρτεῖν [transl. "it is a *difficult endeavor* to arouse all of the people to anger and make them all go wrong at the same time" – GWC] Arist.*Pol*.1286a35...**4.** ἔ. ποιεῖσθαί τι **to make a matter** *one's* [*most important* – GWC] **business, attend to** it, [καὶ ἰδεῖν ἀκολουθοῦντας τοῖς ἐρωμένοις καὶ **ἔργον** τοῦτο ποιουμένους, transl. "whenever people follow the activities of those who are in love with one another, they observe that they make this relationship with each other their *most important endeavor*" – GWC] Pl.*Phdr*. 232a, X.*Hier*.9.10; so ἐν ἔργῳ τίθεσθαι Ael.*VH*4.15 [LS]. This word is usually translated "work."

Paul uses the word ἔργον four times in this Treatise (Eph. 2:9, 10; 4:12; 5:11). Upon study of the way in which this word is used in Greek (see above philological analysis), it is used to refer to "works" that require significant (even a lifetime of) effort exerted over an extended period of time. Therefore it is proposed that the Greek word ἔργον would be more accurately translated as "enterprise, venture, endeavor, project, undertaking, business, industry, operation."

[21] περιπατέω means "to deliberately and intentionally learn, practice and teach others a comprehensive philosophical world view" – see extended note above on the meaning of this word at Eph. 2:2.

[22] ἔθνος, εος, τό: (ϝέθνος, cf. Il.2.87, 7.115, al.): – **A. *number of people living together, company, body of men*,** ἑτάρων ἔ., ἔ. ἑταίρων, *band* of comrades, Il.3.32, 7.115, etc.; ἔθνος λαῶν *host* of men, 13.495; *of particular tribes,* Λυκίων μέγα ἔ. 12.330; Ἀχαιῶν ἔ. 17.552: pl., ἔθνεα πεζῶν 11.724, cf. 2.91; ἔ. νεκρῶν Od.10.526...**2.** after Hom., *nation, people,* τὸ Μηδικὸν ἔ. (γένος being a subdivision of ἔθνος) Hdt.1.101; ἔ. ἠπειρογενές, μαχαιροφόρον, A.*Pers*.43, 56 (anap.), etc.; τῶν μηδισάντων ἐθνέων τῶν Ἑλληνικῶν Hdt.9.106. b. later, τὰ ἔ. *foreign, barbarous nations,* opp. Ἕλληνες, Arist.*Pol*.1324b10; ἔ. νομάδων, of Bedawîn, *LW*2203 (Syria); at Athens, athletic *clubs of non-Athenians,* IG2.444, al.; in LXX, *non-Jews, Ps*.2.1, al., cf. *Act.Ap*.7.45; *Gentiles,* τῶν ἐθνῶν τε καὶ Ἰουδαίων ib.14.5, etc.; used of *Gentile Christians, Ep. Rom*.15.27...[LS]. Usually translated "Gentile(s)." Thus, **ἔθνος** means "any member of an ethnic race or nation foreign to Judaism." Paul uses this term five times in this Treatise (2:11, 3:1, 6, 8; 4:17). The British word "gentile" is no longer used in contemporary professional American English. Paul used the word "barbarian" as a virtual synonym for this word, in Romans 1:13-14:

> Rom. 1:13-14 Οὐ θέλω δὲ ὑμᾶς ἀγνοεῖν, ἀδελφοί, ὅτι πολλάκις προεθέμην ἐλθεῖν πρὸς ὑμᾶς (καὶ ἐκωλύθην ἄχρι τοῦ δεῦρο), ἵνα τινὰ καρπὸν σχῶ καὶ ἐν ὑμῖν, καθὼς καὶ ἐν τοῖς λοιποῖς **ἔθνεσιν**. [14]Ἕλλησί τε καὶ **βαρβάροις**, σοφοῖς τε καὶ ἀνοήτοις ὀφειλέτης εἰμί.
>
> Rom. 1:13-14 Now I don't desire to have you unaware, brothers, that I often planned to come to you, and was hindered so far, that I might have some fruit among you also, even as among the rest of the **Gentiles**. [14]I am debtor both to Greeks and to **barbarians**, both to the wise and to the foolish.

The etymology of the word "Gentile" is as follows: Middle English ***gentil, gentile***, from Late Latin ***gentilis*** foreigner, heathen, from Latin, member of the same family or ***gens***, fellow countryman, from ***gentilis***, adjective **1a** often capitalized: a person of a non-Jewish nation or of non-Jewish faith; especially: a Christian as distinguished from a Jew--used especially by Jews **b**: HEATHEN, PAGAN [W]. The etymology of the word "Barbarian" is as follows: Latin ***barbarus*** from Greek ***barbaros*** foreign, rude, ignorant; perhaps akin to Sanskrit ***barbara – stammering, non-Aryan*** + English ***-ian* 1:** of or relating to a land, culture, or people alien and usually believed to be inferior to one's own **2:** lacking refinement, gentleness, learning, or artistic or literary culture: marked by a tendency toward brutality, violence, or lawlessness but sometimes displaying a rough vigor or vitality **3**: of or relating to a people or group in a stage of cultural development about midway between savagery and full civilization; also: of or relating to such a stage [W]. Proposed translation: "any member of an ethnic race or nation foreign to Judaism (whether a civilized Greek or an uncivilized Barbarian)."

[23] χειροποίητος, ον, *made by hand, artificial*, opp. αὐτοφυής (natural), σκῆπτρον Hdt. 1.195 [literal, or denotative meaning – GWC]; λίμνη 2.149; ἔργον Pl.Criti.118c; ὁδός X.An.4.3.5; τείχη J.BJ4.10.5; γήλοφος, τέλμα Jul.Or.2.63b, 65c: freq. in LXX *of idols*, Is.2.18, al...[LS]. Proposed translation: "artificial."

[24] περιτομή, ἡ, = *"circumcision"* [LS]. Paul clearly maintains that the religious rite of circumcision is no longer significant in the era of the New Testament, especially with respect to accomplishing one's lifework (**κλῆσις**) for God (Acts 15:1-29; Rom. 2:28-29; 1 Cor. 7:18-20; Gal. 5:6, 6:15; and Col. 3:11). For example, Paul makes this extremely clear in 1 Cor. 7:18-20, as follows:

1 Cor. 7:18-20: [18]Περιτετμημένος τις **ἐκλήθη**? Μὴ ἐπισπάσθω. Ἐν ἀκροβυστίᾳ τις **ἐκλήθη**? Μὴ περιτεμνέσθω. [19]Ἡ περιτομὴ οὐδέν ἐστι καὶ ἡ ἀκροβυστία οὐδέν ἐστιν, ἀλλὰ τήρησις ἐντολῶν θεοῦ. [20]Ἕκαστος ἐν τῇ **κλήσει ᾗ ἐκλήθη**, ἐν ταύτῃ μενέτω.

Transl.: [18]Was anyone *summoned to accomplish their lifework* (**ἐκλήθη**) after they were circumcised? Let him not become uncircumcised. Was anyone *summoned to accomplish their lifework* (**ἐκλήθη**) while they were still uncircumcised? Let him not be circumcised. [19]Circumcision is nothing, and uncircumcision is nothing, but accomplishing God's directives is everything. [20]Let each man stay in the same state to accomplish his *lifework* (**κλήσει**) that he was when *he was summoned* (**ἐκλήθη**) to perform it [transl. – GWC].

[25] εἰρήνη (v. infr.), ἡ, **A.** *peace*, Od.24.486, etc.; ἐπ' εἰρήνης *in time of peace*, Il.2.797; ἔθηκε πᾶσιν εἰ. φίλοις A.Pers.769; εἰ. τἀκεῖθεν τέκνοις *on that side they have peace, have naught to fear*, E.Med.1004; εἰ. γίγνεται *peace is made*, Hdt.1.74: hence later, *a peace, treaty of peace*, ἡ βασιλέως εἰ. IG22.103.24, etc.; εἰ. ποιεῖν Ἀρμενίοις καὶ Χαλδαίοις *make peace between* . . , X.*Cyr*.3.2.12;...εἰ. ἄγειν *keep peace, be at peace*, Ar.*Av*.386, etc.; πρὸς ἀλλήλους Pl.*R*.465b; εἰ. ἄγειν (v.l. ἔχειν) *enjoy peace*, X.*An*.2.6.6; λύειν *break it*, D.18.71; πολλὴ εἰ. τινὸς γίγνεται *profound peace*, Pl. *R*.329c; ἐν εἰρήνῃ λέγειν, τὸν βίον διάγειν, Id.Smp.189b, R.372d; πόλεμον εἰρήνης χάριν [αἱρεῖσθαι] Arist.*Pol*.1333a35; εἰρήνης ἄρξας, = εἰρηναρχήσας, IGRom.3.784, cf. 452. **II.** *the goddess of peace, daughter of Zeus and Themis*, Hes.*Th*.902 ["**Εἰρήνη**" = *"Eirēnē"* = "Irene" – GWC], cf. Pi.O.13.7, B.Fr.3.1, IG3.170, Plu.Cim.13, etc. [LS]. In Hesiod's *Theogony*, "Peace" is the goddess "Irene" ["**Εἰρήνη**" = *"Eirēnē"* = "Irene"], born to the second generation of gods and goddesses from the union of Zeus and his second wife, Themis (lines 895-905 transl. Hugh G. Evelyn-White, 1914):

Hes.*Th*.[885] Ζεὺς δὲ θεῶν βασιλεὺς πρώτην ἄλοχον θέτο Μῆτιν πλεῖστα τε ἰδυῖαν ἰδὲ θνητῶν ἀνθρώπων. ἀλλ' ὅτε δὴ ἄρ' ἔμελλε θεὰν γλαυκῶπιν Ἀθήνην τέξεσθαι, τότ' ἔπειτα δόλῳ φρένας ἐξαπατήσας [890] αἱμυλίοισι λόγοισιν ἑὴν ἐσκάτθετο νηδὺν Γαίης φραδμοσύνῃσι καὶ Οὐρανοῦ ἀστερόεντος...δεύτερον ἠγάγετο λιπαρὴν Θέμιν, ἣ τέκεν Ὥρας, Εὐνομίην τε Δίκην τε καὶ **Εἰρήνην** τεθαλυῖαν, αἳ ἔργ' ὠρεύουσι καταθνητοῖσι βροτοῖσι, Μοίρας θ', ᾗ πλείστην τιμὴν πόρε μητίετα Ζεύς, [905] Κλωθώ τε Λάχεσίν τε καὶ Ἄτροπον, αἵτε διδοῦσι θνητοῖς ἀνθρώποισιν ἔχειν ἀγαθόν τε κακόν τε.

English translation: Hesiod, *Theogony* – [885] "Now Zeus, king of the gods, made Metis his wife first, and she was wisest among gods and mortal men. But when she was about to bring forth the goddess bright-eyed Athena, Zeus craftily deceived her [890] with cunning words and put her in his own belly, as Earth and starry Heaven advised...Next he married bright Themis who bore the Horae (Hours), and Eunomia (Order), Dikē (Justice), and blooming **Eirene** (*Peace*), who mind the works of mortal men, and the Moerae (Fates) to whom wise Zeus gave the greatest honor, [905] Clotho, and Lachesis, and Atropos who give mortal men evil and good to have."

Paul is probably deliberately contrasting Jesus as the true "God of Peace," against the Greek religion, for whom the "goddess of Peace" was Irene. In the stories of the Greek gods, there is in fact no real peace at all between them, but only jealousy, intrigue, strife and conflict. From this analysis, Paul's emphasis is that the goal of the good news of God's inheritance plan for all the barbarian peoples and nations is that they learn to experience living in peace together – without distrust, hatred and violence – in their interpersonal relationships, corporate relationships, and international relationships. He is not referring to an "inner psychological *state of peace* within oneself," but rather to two or more people "*living in peace* with each other," i.e., living together without conflict.

One need only read Winston Churchill's four volume lifework entitled *A History of the English Speaking Peoples* to appreciate just how long, difficult and imperfect a road it has been for Christendom to slowly evolve and establish the relatively stable, *peaceful*, liberal democracies of modern times, compared to the savage periods through which our history has come. An excellent example of such a "peacemaker" in the history of the English Speaking Peoples is Stephen Langton, the Archbishop of Canterbury from 1213-1228. He tirelessly worked behind the scenes to resolve the selfish and wicked policies of King John vs. the English Nobles, when he not only authored the *Magna Carta*, but orchestrated the political arena at the field of Runnymede in June, 1215, in which he effectively used the Nobles to manipulate King John, against his will, to sign this historic document that serves today as one of the foundational documents of living in civilized, peaceful freedom.

[26] ποιέω...Used in two general senses, *make* and *do*. A. *make, produce,* first of something material, as *manufactures, works of art,* etc. (opp. πράττειν, Pl.Chrm.163b), in Hom. freq. of *building,* π. δῶμα, τύμβον, Il.1.608,7.435; εἴδωλον Od.4.796; π. πύλας ἐν [πύργοις] Il.7.339; of *smith's work* [= *"forge"* – GWC], π. σάκος ib.222; ἐν [σάκεϊ] ποίει δαίδαλα πολλά 18.482, cf. 490,573: freq. in Inscrr. on [p. 1428] *works of art,* Πολυμήδης ἐποίfηh' (= ἐποίησε)· Ἀργεῖος SIG5 (vi B.C., cf. Class.Phil. 20.139);...εἵματα ἀπὸ ξύλων πεποιημένα *made from trees,* i.e. of *cotton,* Hdt.7.65;...Med., *make for oneself,* as of *bees,* οἰκία

ποιήσωνται *build them houses*, Il.12.168, cf. 5.735, Od.5.251, 259, Hes.Op.503; [ῥεῖθρον] π., of a river, Thphr. HP3.1.5; also, *have a thing made, get it made*, ὀβελούς Hdt.2.135;...2. *create, bring into existence*, γένος ἀνθρώπων χρύσεον Hes.Op.110, cf. Th.161, 579, etc.; ὁ ποιῶν *the creator*, Pl.Ti. 76c;...*conceive*, παιδίον π. ἔκ τινος Pl.Smp.203b...**3**. generally, *produce*,...Ev.Matt.3.10 (metaph. *in religious sense*, ib.**8**); of men;...**b**. *Math., make, produce*, τομήν, σχῆμα, ὀρθὰς γωνίας, Archim. Sph.Cyl.1.16,38, Con.Sph.12;...**c**. *postulate, imply*, ἡ προσθήκη ἀφαίρεσιν καὶ ἔλλειψιν ποιεῖ Plot.3.9.3 .**d**. π. τὸ πρόβλημα *effect a solution of the problem*, Apollon.Perg.Con.2.49,51; π. τὸ ἐπίταγμα *fulfil, satisfy the required condition*, Archim.Sph.Cyl.1.2,3...[LS]. In Genesis, God created the original pair of human "becomings," but at the cross, God "created" (in the specific sense of "forged") a totally new kind of human "becoming;" namely, He "solved the problem" of how to make a "peaceful and peacemaking human becoming" from two different kinds of totally hateful human creatures: hateful vicious barbarians and hateful sanctimonious members of the leadership regime within Judaism.

²⁷ φραγμός, ὁ, **A**. *fencing in, blocking up*, τῆς ἀκουούσης πηγῆς S.*OT*1387...**II**. *fence, paling*, X.*Cyn*. 11.4, *AP*9.343 (Arch.) *BGU*1119.32 (i B. C.), *Ev.Matt*.21.33, etc.; *hedge*, Aesop.385; *railing* of the bridge over the Hellespont, Hdt. 7.36: *fortification*, ib.142; *of the diaphragm*, Hp.*Flat*.10, Arist.*PA* 672b20;...**2**. metaph., *partition*, *Ep.Eph*.**2.14**., as in διάφραγμα, ατος, τό, **A**. *partition or barrier*, Th.1.133,...**II**. *muscle which divides the thorax from the abdomen, midriff, diaphragm*, Pl.*Ti*.70a, 84d, Gal.*UP*4.14, etc. [LS]. From a study of the above texts, the main notion conveyed by this word seems to be that of setting up a partition with the intention of providing a barrier from something. In the context of Eph. 2:14, the proposed translation of this concept into contemporary American English would be to "screen out."

²⁸ σταυρός, ὁ, **A**. *upright pale or stake*, σταυροὺς ἐκτὸς ἔλασσε διαμπερὲς ἔνθα καὶ ἔνθα πυκνοὺς καὶ θαμέας [transl. – "Outside, he had driven upright stakes side by side continuously, compact and set close together" – GWC] Od.14.11, cf. Il.24.453, Th.4.90, X. *An*.5.2.21; *of piles* **driven in to serve as a foundation**, Hdt.5.16, Th.7.25. **II**. *cross*, **as the instrument of crucifixion**, D.S.2.18, *Ev.Matt*.27.40, Plu.2.554a; ἐπὶ τὸν ς. ἀπάγεσθαι Luc.*Peregr*.34; ς. λαμβάνειν, ἆραι, βαστάζειν;...**b**. *pale for impaling* **a corpse**, Plu.*Art*.17 [LS].

See John 18:28-37; 19:12-22. John is most effective at recreating the *literary irony* of Jesus' illegal Roman crucifixion on a cross as as an ignominious act of hypocrisy, defiance and treason committed deliberately by the religious and political leadership regime within Judaism against the rightful High Kingship of Jesus, as follows (clauses highlighting John's use of literary irony are in *italics*, with brief interpretive comments in brackets – "[ ]" – GWC):

> John 18:28-37 They [the highest officials within the leadership regime of Judaism] led Jesus therefore from Caiaphas [the Jewish High Priest] into the Praetorium [the public place in Jerusalem where the justice of Roman law was supposed to be enacted and enforced]. It was early, *and they themselves didn't enter into the Praetorium, that they*

might not be defiled, but might eat the Passover [hypocrisy – they are concerned about not being "defiled" by contact with the Romans, but not concerned with the treasonous act of deliberately plotting the assasination of their own High King]. ²⁹Pilate therefore went out to them, and said, "What accusation do you bring against this man?" ³⁰They answered him, "If this man weren't an evildoer, *we wouldn't have delivered him up to you*" [evasion – they are lying, they know it, Pilate knows it, and they know that Pilate knows it. Therefore, not only do they implement their carefully planned evasion of Pilate's direct question, but also set in motion their equally well planned political attempt to manipulate Pilate by forcing him "into the corner" of appearing in public to be disloyal to his own Caesar. The irony of the situation is that the only way they can be clever enough to think of and then plot to project political disloyalty upon Pilate, is because they are already actually guilty of this very crime themselves!]. ³¹Pilate therefore said to them, "Take him yourselves, and *judge him according to your law*." [Pilate knows they are lying hypocrites, but he also suspects that they are making a political "gamble" to achieve some object he does not yet perceive, so he "calls their hand."] Therefore the Jews said to him, "It is not *lawful for us* to put anyone *to death*" [they spring the trap on Pilate, he knows they have, but he still does not know what they are scheming], ³²that the word of Jesus might be *fulfilled, which he spoke, signifying by what kind of death he should die* [Jesus has known how it will play out all along – e.g., that He would be killed by crucifixion – the Roman method of execution]. ³³Pilate therefore entered again *into the Praetorium*, called Jesus, and said to him, "Are you the *King of the Jews*?" [Pilate knows his only chance for political survival is to attempt to find out what the Jewish leadership regime is up to by flushing it out of them in a *public setting* – he is well aware that they have planned something against Jesus in secret, and from his perspective, that it has to do with their unwillingness to accept Jesus as their recognized vassal-king to Rome]. ³⁴Jesus answered him, "Do you say this *by yourself*, or did *others* tell you about me?" [Jesus knows that Pilate knows that He is innocent and is merely asking Jesus if He is King to get Him to say "yes, I am," only so Pilate can then publicly confront the Jewish regime with the possibility of their own treason, thus theoretically putting the problem back into their court. Jesus realizes this is a naïve move by Pilate, yet nevertheless, Jesus still gives Pilate the opportunity as a human being to summon the courage to believe in Him as God, which by this point in the political conflict is a pretty tall order, and thus fairly remote possibility]. ³⁵Pilate answered, "I'm not a *Jew*, am I? *Your own nation and the chief priests* delivered you to me. What have you done?" [Pilate now knows that Jesus knows that the whole thing is a deadly charade, and yet that Jesus is also appealing to him as his real authority figure – probably higher than Caesar. But Pilate also knows that only he and Jesus know this, so he becomes evasive himself, thinking that if he sarcastically points out that both he and Jesus are on the same side in that they both know that the Jewish leadership regime is composed of corrupt hypocrites, that perhaps he can find some cynical "common ground" with Jesus. The only problem with Pilate's cynical plan is that he must *recognize* and yet at the same time *deny* Jesus' rightful authority over him, because his question to Jesus about what He has done is really not to find out what Jesus has done – Pilate already strongly suspects if not knows for sure that Jesus is innocent; but it is rather a weak attempt by Pilate to reassert his own authority over Jesus, which he knows at some level is wrong, and therefore he gives in to the temptation to cynically point out the hypocrisy of others and not face his own hypocrisy in evading what he knows the genuine and sincere intent of Jesus' question to him is.] ³⁶Jesus answered, "*My kingdom* is not of this world. *If my kingdom were of this world*, then my servants would fight, that I wouldn't be delivered to the Jews. But now *my kingdom* is not from here." [In claiming that He has a rightful Kingdom – three times – Jesus clearly infers that He is indeed a rightful King – while at the same time unseating Pilate's erroneous assumption that Jesus is merely a vassal-king of Rome, like Herod.] ³⁷Pilate therefore said to him, "Are you a *king* then?" Jesus answered, "You say rightly that *I am a king*. For this reason I have been born, and for this reason I have come into the world…" [thus, the crux question of the entire conflict is finally asked and answered as a historic, public fact. Jesus knows, Pilate knows, and the Jewish regime knows that Jesus in fact claims to be High King over them all, and that His claim is publicly established as a matter of record; making them – and us – responsible in how they – and we – respond to His claim].

John 19:12-22 Pilate was seeking to release him [Jesus], but the Jews cried out, saying, "If you release this man, *you aren't Caesar's friend!* Whoever *makes himself a king speaks against Caesar!*" [the trap set by the Jewish regime in 18:31, and weakly countered by Pilate in 18:33, finally snaps shut on Pilate. Pilate naïvely thought he could force the Jews into a problematic political position of possible treason if Jesus was in fact a Jewish "vassal-king," but instead he finally realizes the ultimate gravity of Jesus' claim: If Jesus is God, then it logically follows that He does have authority over Caesar; but since Pilate is a Roman Governor sworn to allegiance to the highest Roman ruler, if he admits this in public he commits treason himself! Ironically, Pilate is trapped by his own naïveté in trying to play the "treason game." He is clearly not willing to go as far as the Jews by being willing to defy his own king (Caesar) as they are willing to defy theirs (Jesus). Consequently, the only political option left for Pilate is, in an ironic twist, to become the manipulated "vassal" puppet-governor to the Jewish leadership regime – to be used by them only as a "rubber stamp" to allow them to use the Roman legal system and its method of execution in order to politically evade their culpability in using it to kill an innocent man they had to eliminate to retain their own power.] ¹³When Pilate therefore heard these words, he brought Jesus out, and sat down on the judgment seat…He said to the Jews, *"Behold, your King!"* [Pilate vents his exasperation at how he has been publicly outwitted by the Jewish leadership regime with this cynical remark, which although true, is also his admission that he has divested himself of his authority to enforce a just resolution to the false accusation against what he knows to be an innocent man.] ¹⁵They cried out, "Away with him! Away with him! Crucify him!" Pilate said to them, *"Shall I crucify your King?"* [Once again, tragically, Pilate can now only play out the charade of being used as a puppet while still only pretending to be in authority – and knowing that everyone knows it, too. So his only emotional and ethical option to attempt to cling to whatever is left of his shredded dignity is to slip back into his old habit of cynicism.] The *chief priests* answered, *"We have no king but Caesar!"* [The raw motive of the blatant open rebellion of the highest officials within the leadership regime of Judaism is climactically uttered and recorded as an historical fact.] ¹⁶ So then he delivered him to them to be crucified. So they took Jesus and led him away. ¹⁷He went out, *bearing his cross*, to the place…¹⁸where they crucified him…¹⁹Pilate wrote a title also, and put it on the cross. There was written, "JESUS OF NAZARETH, THE KING OF THE JEWS."' ²⁰Therefore many of the Jews read this title, for the place where Jesus was crucified was near the city; and *it was written in Hebrew, in Latin, and in Greek.* ²¹The chief priests of the Jews therefore said to Pilate, *"Don't write, 'The King of the Jews,' but, 'he said, I am King of the Jews.'"* ²²Pilate answered, *"What I have written, I have written."* [The irony John reveals in the petty squabbling over the placard's naked truth that Jesus is the High King of the entire world is played out to the end – and beyond – by the open, defiant rebellion of the corrupt leadership regime within Judaism and the sad, cold cynicism of a hopeless Roman barbarian who only appears to be civilized on the outside; both caught in the sinister and insidious spiritual traps uniquely laid out for each of them by Satan – GWC.]

[29] λύω...**I.** of things, ***unbind, unfasten***, esp. clothes and armour, λῦσε δέ οἱ ζωστῆρα, θώρηκα, Il.4.215, 16.804;...**b.** of men, ***release, deliver***, esp. ***from bonds or prison***, and so, generally, ***from difficulty or danger***, Il.15.22, Od.8.345, 12.53, D.24.206, etc.; **c.** ***of prisoners, release on receipt of ransom, admit to ransom, release***, Il.1.29, 24.137,555, etc.;...**II.** ***dissolve, break up***, λ. ἀγορήν ***dissolve the assembly***, Il.1.305; ἀγορὰς ἠμὲν λύει ἠδὲ καθίζει Od.2.69, etc;...**2.** ***of concrete objects*** λ. τὴν σχεδίην ***break it up***, [= ***"demolish"*** – GWC], Hdt.4.97; [τὴν γέφυραν] X. An.2.4.17; τὴν ἀπόφραξιν ib.4.2.25...**4.** ***undo, bring to naught, destroy***, πολίων κάρηνα Il.9.25; Τροίης κρήδεμνα 16.100, Od.13.388, cf. B.Fr.16.7: generally, ***put an end to***, νείκεα Il.14.205;...**b.** in Prose, λ. νόμους ***repeal or annul laws***, Hdt.3.82, D.3.10, Arist.*Pol.*1269a15;:--Pass., λέλυται πάντα ***all ties are broken, all is in confusion***, D.25.25...**5.** ***break a legal agreement or obligation***, τὸν νόμον Hdt.6.106; τὰς σπονδάς Th.1.23, 78, cf. 4.23, al.; τὰ συγκείμενα Lys.6.41 ; σίς κε τὰς ϝρήτας τάσδε λύση ***whoso breaks this agreement***, Inscr.Cypr.135.29 H. **6.** ***in physical sense, dissolve***, λύθεν, opp. πάγεν, Emp.15.4;...***melt***, παγείσας χιόνας Hdn.8.4.2; τι πυρὶ λ. Hippiatr.52...[LS]. This word accurately describes how Jesus' death on the cross destroyed the oppressive and cruel, counterfeit, twisted, overly rigid system of inflexible dogma that the wicked leadership regime within Judaism had used to control the Jewish people and to shut out all other peoples from the love of God. Proposed translation of **λύω**: "demolish," as when a Contractor must use a "Demolition Plan" to demolish and haul off the rubble from and old, worn out building before he can begin building the new building. To extend Paul's metaphor, it is as if Jesus, acting in the role of a "Demolition Contractor," used His "cross" as a "battering ram" to "demolish" the "walls" (i.e., the counterfeit system of Judaism) of Jerusalem, before He could begin to build His new "Building" (i.e., His "Lifework Councils").

[30] **καταργέω**, [from **κατα** = (opposition to, in the sense of "put out") + **ἀ-εργός** = lit. "no-work" = "un-employed," cf. extended note on **ἔργον** = "work" above; thus to "put out of business," "put out of commission," or "put out of action" – GWC] **A. *leave unemployed* or *idle***, Χέρα E.*Ph.*753; κατηργηκέναι τοὺς καιρούς ***to have missed*** **the *opportunities***, Plb.*Fr.*176; κ. τὴν γῆν ***make*** the ground ***useless, cumber*** it, *Ev.Luc.*13.7. **2. *cause to be idle, hinder* in one's work**, LXX *2 Es.*4.21, *POxy.*38.17 (i A.D.):--Pass., LXX *2 Es.*6.8; ***to be rendered or lie idle***, PFlor.176.7 (iii A.D.), etc. **II. *make of no effect***, *Ep.Rom.*3.3,31, al.:--Pass., ***to be abolished, cease***, ib.6.6, 1 *Ep.Cor.*2.6, etc.; κ. ἀπὸ τοῦ νόμου ***to be set free from...***, *Ep.Rom.*7.2; ***to be parted***, ἀπὸ Χριστοῦ *Ep.Gal.*5.4 [LS]. Usually translated, "put away," "abolish." Proposed translation: "put out of business," "put out of commission," or "put out of action."

³¹ κτίζω – Proposed translation: "to create, form, shape, build, invent or forge." See analysis of this word in the note at Eph. 2:10.

³² εὐαγγελίζομαι – See extended analysis of this word, in both its noun and verb forms, in the note at Eph. 1:13.

³³ προσαγωγή, ἡ, *bringing to*, πρὸς τὴν τῆς τροφῆς π. for the purpose of bringing the food to the mouth, Arist.*PA*687b26; οἰκοδόμῳ εἰς π. πλίνθου PCair.Zen.176.14 (iii B.C.) [denotative meaning – GWC]. **2.** *bringing up*, μηχανημάτων, ὀργάνων, Plb.1.48.2 (pl.), 14.10.9(pl.); ποιεῖσθαι τὴν π., much like our phrase *'to make approaches'*, Id.9.41.1. **3.** *a bringing over, acquisition*, ξυμμάχων Th.1.82; ἐκ π. φίλος *a friend under compulsion*, D.23.174 (ἐκ προαγωγῆς Harp.). **4.** *administering or taking of medicine*, Phld.Ir.p.44 W.(pl.), Dsc.4.148. **II.** *solemn approach, as at festivals or in supplication*, Hdt.2.58(pl.). **2.** *approach, access, introduction to a person, esp. to a king's presence*, X.Cyr.7.5.45, cf. *Ep.Rom.*5.2, *Ep.Eph.***2.18**, etc. [LS]. Paul uses this word only 3 times in the NT: in Rom. 5:2, and twice in this Treatise: here, and in Eph. 3:12. The best American word that captures all of the connotative meanings of "a means of easy and free approach and access to anywhere or to anyone that one desires to see, that formerly involved an arduous, expensive and dangerous journey," is the word, "freeway." For example, Tyndale's translation is "open waye," which is much better than the KJV, which translates this word simply as "access."

³⁴ ἐποικοδομέω = "to build up, to build upon." See note at Eph. 2:22.

³⁵ οἰκοδομή = "building." See note at Eph. 2:22.

³⁶ The Greek word for "being carefully joined together" in verse 21 is συναρμολογουμένη. This word (verb: συναρμολογέω) is only used twice in the NT, both times by Paul in Ephesians: here, and in Eph. 4:16). It is made of three Greek words: συν = "with," ἁρμονία = "harmony" (ἁρμονία, ἡ, ([ἁρμόζω]) *means of joining, fastening*, γόμφοις μιν . . καὶ ἁρμονίῃσιν ἄρηρεν Od.5.248; of a ship, ὄφρ' ἂν . . ἐν ἁρμονίῃσιν ἀρήρῃ ib.361. **2.** *joint, as between a ship's planks*, τὰς ἁ. ἐν ὧν ἐπάκτωσαν τῇ βύβλῳ *caulked the joints with papyrus*, Hdt.2.96; τῶν ἁρμονιῶν διαχασκουσῶν Ar.Eq.533; *also in masonry*, αἱ τῶν λίθων ἁ. D.S.2.8, cf. Paus.8.8.8,9.33.7. **3.** in Anatomy, *suture*, Hp. Off.25, Oss.12; *union of two bones by mere apposition*, Gal.2.737; also in pl., *adjustments*, πόρων Epicur.Fr.250. **4.** *framework*, ῥηγνὺς ἁρμονίαν . . λύρας S.Fr.244; βοός Philostr.Im.1.16; esp. of the *human frame*, ἁρμονίην ἀναλυέμεν ἀνθρώποιο Ps.-Phoc.102;...**c.** *framework of the universe*, Corp.Herm. 1.14. **II.** *covenant, agreement*, in pl., μάρτυροι . . καὶ ἐπίσκοποι ἁρμονιάων Il.22.255. **III.** *settled government, order*, τὰν Διὸς ἁ. A.Pr.551 (lyr.). **IV.** in Music, *stringing*, ἁ. τόξου καὶ λύρας Heraclit.51, cf. Pl.Smp.187a: hence, *method of stringing, musical scale*, Philol.6, etc.;...**2.** generally, *music*, αὐτῷ δὲ τῷ ῥυθμῷ μιμοῦνται χωρὶς ἁ. Id.Po.1447a26. **3.** *special type of scale, mode*, ἁ. Λυδία Pi.N.4.46; Αἰολίς or -ῇς Pratin.Lyr.5, Lasus I, cf. Pl.*R*.398e, al., Arist.*Pol*.1276b8, 1341b35, etc. **b.** *esp.*

the enharmonic scale, Aristox.*Harm*.p.I M., Plu.2.1135a, al. **4.** ἁρμονίαν λόγων λαβών **a** *due arrangement of words, fit to be set to music,* Pl.*Tht*.175e. **5.** *intonation or pitch of the voice,* Arist.*Rh.* 1403b31. **6.** metaph. of persons and things, *harmony, concord,* Pl.*R*.431e, etc. [LS]); and **λόγος** = "the reasonable account of how something works." Thus, the connotative meaning of **συναρμολογουμένη** that emerges is something like, "being harmoniously joined together with other human beings into interpersonal frameworks consisting of mature relationships of trust, encouragement and concord such that the corporate voice of the organization is rationally and intentionally structured into a pleasant, agreeable and enjoyable whole." See note at Eph. 2:11.

[37] The Greek word for "joined together" in verse 22 is **συνοικοδομεῖσθε**. This word (verb: **συνοικοδομέω**) is only used this one time in the NT. It is also made of three Greek words: **συν** = "with," **οἶκος** = "house, home, any place where one might live;" and the verb **δομάω** = **δέμω**, *build,* τεῖχος ἔδειμαν Il.7.436, etc.; τείχη παλαιὰ δείμας E.Rh.232:--Med., ἐδείματο οἴκους *he built him houses,* Od.6.9; ἄστη Pl.Ax.370b. **2.** generally, *construct, prepare,* δ. ἀλωήν h.Merc.87; δ. ὁδόν, Lat. munire viam, Hdt.2.124:--Pass., ἁμαξιτὸς δέδμηται Id.7.200: *metaph. of persons,* δέδμηνται πάσῃ κόσμος᾽ Ἰαονίη Haussoullier MiletP.141 [LS]. Thus, the verb **δομάω** means "to build, construct, or prepare a building or a house." The noun, **δόμος**, through the Latin word **domus**, became the foundational root for forming the British word "domicile" (from which such words as "domestic" and "domesticate" are derived) and the American word "dome," and should be translated as the word "building." Thus, the connotative meaning of **συνοικοδομεῖσθε** that emerges from this analysis might be something like, "to be intentionally built into a mature and complete relationally consistent group of people along with and alongside many others of originally diverse backgrounds, who become motivated to have only constructive attitudes and motives toward others." See note at Eph. 2:11.

3

Recognizing Opportunity:
Faith in Him and Love for Others

Paul's Reason for Writing: Never Give In to Despair! Digression – Every Circumstance in History is Actually an Opportunity God Provides for Us to Achieve Our Lifework ♦ *Never Give In to Despair! Digression Continued – A Correct Spiritual Perspective Transforms Stressful Circumstances We All Face into Divine Opportunities to Benefit Others* ♦ *The Right Frame of Reference: God Has Providentially Planned Not Only History, but Each One of Our Lives Such That There is No Circumstance or Situation That Can Ever Defeat Us in Finding and Accomplishing Our Lifework if Only We Maintain Faith in Him and Selfless Love for Others* ♦ *Paul Asks Jesus to Appear in Marvelous Ways in His Lifework Councils in Order to Encourage His Apprentices Prior to His Physical Appearance as High King at the End of History*

PAUL'S REASON FOR WRITING: NEVER GIVE IN TO DESPAIR! DIGRESSION – EVERY CIRCUMSTANCE IN HISTORY IS ACTUALLY AN OPPORTUNITY GOD PROVIDES FOR US TO ACHIEVE OUR LIFEWORK

With all of these tremendous benefits God has given us in mind, it might have initially struck you all as alarming, inconsistent and even contradictory when you learned that I, Paul, now find myself to be a prisoner in Rome.[1] Your concern and anxiety about these apparently difficult circumstances is precisely why I am writing you. I am taking advantage of this situation to compose this final and comprehensive Treatise[2] of God's plans and purposes for the final era of world history especially to you delivered Greeks and Barbarians[3] in Ephesus for a precise and specific reason.

Before I explain that reason fully, you must understand two things. First, you must know that I regard my present status as a "prisoner" in Rome not as onerous, but rather as instructive, in the following way. I view this "imprisonment" or "bondage," as a providential opportunity God has given me to collect my reflections and thoughts upon the High King Jesus' revealed mission for my life, and to set out this purpose in the form of an organized, culminating Treatise to you all. Because my "bondage" has in fact afforded me the occasion to write out this Treatise, I have come to regard my situation here not as something negative, but ironically as something extremely positive. Rather than using this time to give you an account of my "bondage," I have chosen instead employ it to compose this Treatise as His "Bond,"[4] or "Guarantee." In the same way that a construction bonding company "bonds" a general contractor to guarantee performance of his contract to build a building, the High King has commissioned me to write this Treatise as His "Bond" for His own "building project." It is His "Guarantee" that He will perform His promise to build His "Lifework Councils" in history.

₂Secondly, before I explain further my reason for writing this Treatise to you all, I am compelled to digress at this point and highlight its main themes in a periphrastic review.[5] You have by now – no doubt since you have been listening to this Treatise read aloud – become fully briefed on the details comprising God's gracious plan to establish His future governmental administration,[6] a task which has been given to me for you all. ₃This assignment entails making you fully aware of the provisions of His "Top Secret" Plan[7] to apprentice each of you in a unique "lifework" as preparatory training for the expectation of a future noble role in the administration of His Millennial Kingdom.

The provisions of this plan were unveiled to me directly by Him in a unique, special and supernatural revelatory message,[8] which He commissioned me to write down precisely as He gave it to me. ₄God commissioned me to write this message down because it is important for you all to continually review, reexamine and reflect upon it in order to discipline yourselves to keep the stipulations of His inheritance plan in the forefront of your minds. I of all people, know how easy it is for the day-to-day temptations, distractions and hardships of this present life to cause us to forget the marvelous details of this wonderful plan, and for us to find ourselves getting sidetracked – time after time, it seems – from pursuing God's desire for us to find and achieve our lifework for Him.

But because keeping God's "Top Secret"[9] Plan at the very forefront of our hearts and minds is vital to living each day of our lives with this proper spiritual perspective, He has "built in" to His divine plan a unique, supernatural feature. This special feature is that, whenever you intentionally reread and reexamine the content of this Treatise aloud among yourselves with the motive of discerning its true meaning, God's Specially Selecting Spirit will supernaturally enable you to reacquire a complete discernment and understanding of the provisions of our future High King's "Top Secret" Plan. In fact, He will enable you to do this to the same degree and with the same clarity and comprehensive scope that I myself possess, the one to whom He unveiled it directly and supernaturally! Further, whenever you do this, His Spirit will completely restore a proper spiritual perspective in your hearts and minds, so that you can make renewed progress in accomplishing your lifework.

⁵With this in mind, I think you will agree that this is indeed a unique and special time in the history of all the families of the world that have descended from the original pair of human beings. It is unique in that this is the first time in history that God has in a specially and fully unrestricted way completely and clearly unveiled[10] His central program for our lives to His specially selected High Emissaries and Spokespersons by His Spirit. Further, He commissioned us to write it down so that He can enable any of His other specially selected recruits who seek guidance from His Spirit to understand the provisions of this wonderful message upon reading and studying it.

⁶The provisions of this wonderful message[11] specifically stipulate that the totality of *all of the ethnic races and nations foreign to Judaism – whether they be civilized Greeks or uncivilized Barbarians*[12] – are, from this point in the history of the world onward, to be highlighted, recruited and trained to become fully *equal heirs* with[13] God's future High King Jesus. Moreover, His plan is to train them to become *co-administrators* with[14] Jesus in His future governmental body and *equal partners* with[15] Him of the promises God has made fully available for them to share with Him during the Kingdom era. ⁷Because I have received the commission to deliver this message successfully in all its aspects as His special assignment, I have become, in effect, God's "aide-de-camp," which I regard as a gracious gift, granted to me as a unique directive, duly authorized under the auspices of His enacted prerogative.

Never Give In to Despair! Digression Continued – A Correct Spiritual Perspective Transforms Stressful Circumstances We All Face into Divine Opportunities to Benefit Others

⁸Imagine that! God gave me, who of all people am the *least worthy* of any of His specially selected recruits that have ever or will ever live, this particular gracious gift. It is astonishing that He would have selected me to be His chosen representative to bear this wonderful message[16] of the extraordinarily valuable riches[17] of the future High King's inheritance plan to all of the ethnic races and nations in the entire world foreign to Judaism, whether they are civilized Greeks or uncivilized Barbarians. The reason that my appointment to this high post is so remarkable, is because He deliberately chose me precisely because I alone among all human beings am the most *unworthy person*[18] that could have ever been selected to be given this responsibility.

⁹Consider the supreme irony of this situation: when my name used to be "Saul," I thought that I, more than all people, could "see" spiritual matters clearly because I was a member of the elite religious and political machine perched atop the leadership hierarchy within Judaism. I did not realize that our arrogance and cruelty actually rendered me spiritually "blind." That is why our Commander in Chief had to *blind* me temporarily before I could become truly "enlightened." He showed me that in reality, *I* was the one who had become sidetracked from following His intended plan for authentic Israel, which always has been that they be His messenger of goodness and love to the other non-Jewish – even Barbarian – nations of the world.

He graciously selected me, formerly the most spiritually blind human being in the entire human family, to enlighten[19] everyone else who in like manner has also been blinded to His "Top Secret" plan. This plan not only includes the present founding, formation and administration of His Lifework Councils, but also incorporates His preparation and training of those same conciliar bodies to continue on to become in fact Kingdom Apprenticeship Councils, comprised of the mature human beings that He will eventually appoint to the future governmental body that He will inaugurate in the future Kingdom Age. God has deliberately kept this "Top Secret" plan hidden throughout all recorded history from the beginning of His creation of the world until this present historical era.

¹⁰God has waited until the present historical era to take this initiative so that His divine program of training human beings to achieve mastery over the multi-faceted ethical and political skills required to live with and lead others effectively,[20] which Jesus Himself will accomplish through the specific agency of His Kingdom Apprenticeship Councils, might now be made known for the first time to the angelic regimes and hierarchies of authority – both good and evil – throughout all of the heavenly realms.

First of all, with regard to the evil spiritual regime under Satan's control, it is precisely because the formidable and terrifying grip of the Devil's upper echelon of wicked angelic beings (who exercise their evil authority in the affairs of human beings by gradually corrupting the various governmental regimes of world history up to and including this present era) has been so impenetrable, that God has waited until now to make known to them His comprehensive and final plan through which He will ultimately and decisively defeat them. Furthermore, the superior intelligence of God's plan lies in the fact that He will frustrate and eventually conquer the corrupting influence of these wicked angelic spirits by means of His Special Society of transformed human spirits that they never can or will fully understand, but will always seem to them to have been a total and unexpected surprise.[21]

Secondly, God has made this unique plan known to His own organization of good angels who remain loyal to Him for the first time also. The reason He has done this is because He has determined that those members of Jesus' Kingdom Apprenticeship Councils who become qualified for Kingdom leadership by successfully completing their apprenticeship assignments will be given, among their other duties in His future Kingdom administration, a variety of responsibilities that will require them to periodically exercise authority over certain angelic officers within their own existing long-established hierarchies. God knows that He cannot legitimately place an expectation upon His loyal, high-ranking angelic officers to obey the directives of a new set of superior officers that have not earned their respect – especially since they will be human beings.

[11]Although this incisive strategy was initiated by God the Father Himself, His decision to unveil the provisions of His "Top Secret" plan at this time in history was previously made in concert with His Spirit and His Son in Their Eternal Council. It was only after conducting thorough deliberation and careful consideration of all of Their combined purposes and proposals, followed by meticulous planning in full collaboration, cooperation and concurrence with His Specially Selecting Spirit and His future High King, Jesus, our present Commander in Chief, that God the Father has now fully published, enacted and set into motion the provisions of Their mutually agreed upon "Top Secret" Plan.[22]

[12]In case you are intimidated by the prospect of entering into His divine program of finding your lifework, which will necessarily involve His training you to achieve mastery over the multi-faceted ethical and political skills required to live with and lead others effectively, remember that it has also been enacted that Jesus is the One through Whom we now have complete freedom of access to God to secure the divine help we will all need. In fact, the reason that it is so important for you all to know about the intimate details of God's exhaustive, in-depth, thoroughly prepared plan, formulated in complete and mutual harmony by all three Divine Persons in Their Eternal Council, is so that you would realize that God has sincerely and genuinely offered to all of us the same complete and totally unrestricted freedom of immediate access – a "freeway"[23] – to Himself that our Commander in Chief has always enjoyed. We can use this divine "freeway" any time we want in order to avail ourselves of all the divine help we need during this present era of our apprenticeship, with the full confidence and assurance that He will help, guide, teach and enable us to find and accomplish our lifework for Him. This great privilege has been afforded for us not only because of Jesus' perfect faithfulness in accomplishing His mission on our behalf during His first visit to the earth, but also because of His complete reliability in exercising His present

responsibilities in Heaven as our Representative and Advocate to God the Father, in addition to His roles as our Recruiter, Teacher, Friend and future Companion.

[13]Now, with this extensive review of the main components of God's marvelous inheritance plan in the forefront of your minds – I must return from the above digression to my main idea, which is to tell you my reason for writing this Treatise to you. As I mentioned above, even though you all were no doubt initially surprised and perhaps even shocked when you learned that I, Paul, had been placed under house arrest in Rome, I must ask – or to be frank, I really must insist[24] – that all of you immediately bring to an end the insidious, gloomy, dispirited mood and pervasive defeatist mind-set that I hear you have slipped into and which now seems to have overwhelmed your better selves. You must get a grip on yourselves! You must snap out of this sinister, despondent and fatalistic frame of mind, because if you do not, you stand in danger of easily getting sidetracked and falling into some shameful, cowardly conduct in which you might neglect, give up or even despair of your duty and responsibility to discover and accomplish your lifework for God.[25]

As I explained to you above, the various pressures and resulting stresses[26] that I must face here in my present situation of living under house arrest in Rome are actually not all that bad. In fact, when considered from the proper spiritual perspective, they are but minor inconveniences, and are in reality quite a necessary step for me to endure in order to have the much more precious opportunity of composing this final, definitive, complete and conclusive Treatise on God's inheritance plan for the future world. As I am sure you realize, the wonderful provisions of this Treatise are far-reaching and considerably more important for you and others than for my personal circumstances or me. God's ultimate goal is not my personal safety, but rather your and my *growth in spiritual maturity*, which we will all finally and fully comprehend, appreciate and celebrate at the Appearing[27] of our High King when He returns to inaugurate His Kingdom.

THE RIGHT FRAME OF REFERENCE: GOD HAS PROVIDENTIALLY PLANNED NOT ONLY HISTORY, BUT EACH ONE OF OUR LIVES SUCH THAT THERE IS NO CIRCUMSTANCE OR SITUATION THAT CAN EVER DEFEAT US IN FINDING AND ACCOMPLISHING OUR LIFEWORK IF ONLY WE MAINTAIN FAITH IN HIM AND SELFLESS LOVE FOR OTHERS

[14]I have realized that my present situation of house arrest here in Rome is in reality God's specific mission for me at this moment in my life, in that He has granted me this time as a unique opportunity to write this

conclusive Treatise. Because I recognize this mission to be a gracious privilege given to me by Him, I regularly and consistently go to my knees before the Father of our Commander in Chief, Jesus, the future High King of the earth Himself. I do this to continually express my gratitude to Him, and to tell Him how much I appreciate, revere and love Him for not only salvaging, but for transforming my formerly worthless life into something significant, useful, worthwhile and beneficial to others.

¹⁵In the same way, you all must learn that in order gain the correct spiritual perspective in any set of circumstances, you must evaluate every situation from His frame of reference. After all, acting in His role as our Father, God is the One from Whom every hierarchy of angelic beings who live in heaven as well as every family lineage of human beings that have ever lived or will ever live upon the earth has been appointed.[28] It therefore follows that He is the One Who retains and exercises complete and sovereign control over them, no matter how dismal the circumstances may appear to us or be interpreted by us. He the One Who has assigned to each of them their respective celestial or geographical boundaries, eras, roles and opportunities to know and serve Him, in whatever providential situation that He, in His wise initiative, places them.[29]

¹⁶You must learn to adopt this perpetual attitude of being motivated not by what merely *appears* to be happening to you in your present circumstances, but rather by the *riches* that He purposes to give you at His Appearing. You must do this in order that He might be able to also give you the dynamic spiritual ability in the deepest part of your psychological and personal inner self that you all will need during your present lifetime to be strengthened, emboldened and be made confident by His Spirit whenever you encounter circumstances which appear to be discouraging at first glance.

¹⁷So you see, although the ultimate goal of your training program by the Spirit is serving our High King in His future Kingdom, this training program that I have outlined above has a very important *intermediate* goal for you to attain in during your present lifetime also. This intermediate goal is that you would allow His Spirit to direct and train you to achieve your lifework and gain self-mastery and maturity in all the areas of your personality and character. Because this intermediate goal usually occurs as an initially painful process that you will be somewhat reluctant to embark upon, allow me to use the following illustration to help you understand and then achieve it.

Imagine our High King as an "Explorer," and that your hearts are the "lands" He has mapped out to explore and settle. You must allow Him to not only *land* there, but go on to permit Him to *plant* His heavenly "colony" there, then "settle in," then "live," and finally and ultimately rise to leadership such that He completely and totally "administers and governs" there; that is, in your hearts.[30] This process will only occur at the rate that you allow Him to come to live and continually be "at home" in your hearts through the growth of your faith in and reliance upon Him. As you do, He will always assist you as your Guide, Confidant and Friend as He helps you to make good, wise, prudent and sound decisions.[31] If you allow Him to, He will not only *implant* Himself into your personality and character, but He will go on to *embed*[32] Himself there, with the result that He will guide your thoughts, decisions, and actions such that they are always firmly founded[33] upon and in complete concord with His own selfless love.

[18]This intermediate goal; namely, mastering the skills of following the Spirit by expressing the selfless love of our Commander in Chief in all of your actions and demeanor in every area of this life is of paramount importance. It is important because living a life of selfless love will stretch you to the limit of your capabilities and compel you to reach forward with all of your strength and live your lives by faith. Living by faith involves not only learning to cooperate with and rely upon all of His specially selected recruits now living, but also with those who have lived[34] during this and in past historical eras.

All such remarkable people will, like you all, have dared to envision the comprehensive extent of the "above ground" dimensions, e.g., the "width, length, and height" of the "building" being constructed by our Commander in Chief; i.e., the multi-century, inter-corporate, interpersonal framework of relationships composed of His Lifework Councils. Furthermore, living a life of self-sacrificial love will also enable you to assiduously recognize and profoundly appreciate the superlative value of the "fourth dimension" of reality shared only by two kinds of structures: the "foundation" of a building (to be sure), but more importantly, the *interpersonal* "foundation" which supports the superstructure of His Lifework Councils – specifically, their "depth."

Allow me to explain what I mean. A large building possesses the three above-ground dimensions of width, length and height, which on the surface appear to outline its most striking and remarkable features. Nevertheless, a large building also requires the indispensable fourth dimension of a deep foundation in order to support the superstructure of that building through the centuries of wind and rainstorms that will batter it. In the same way, our Commander in Chief plans to build His Lifework Councils together into an overall interpersonal structure of such marvelous dimensions in the era yet to come, that He preplanned and has already built its stable and enduring foundation over the last two millennia.

This remarkable foundation is composed of His irrevocable Promises to Abraham, Isaac and Jacob, together with His creation, deliverance, and establishment of Israel under His just Laws communicated, written down and preserved by Moses. It goes on to include the founding and extension of His Kingdom under David and Solomon, together with His faithful discipline, exile, and ultimate restoration of Israel, recorded and preserved in the Writings of His Kings and Official Spokespersons. This record is culminated by the teachings of Jesus Himself, our Commander in Chief, recorded and preserved in the Writings and Treatises of His High Emissaries.[35]

[19]It is only by achieving this intermediate goal of learning to express selfless love to others that you will be able to grasp and completely experience the full significance of the love that characterizes our High King. By achieving this goal, you will finally realize that exhibiting divine love for others in this life actually outshines as well as outperforms merely possessing or demonstrating esoteric or encyclopedic knowledge. Accordingly, you will ultimately gain an authentic sense of fulfillment in this present life only by learning to love others selflessly as you follow the leadership of our High King by faith. In reality, what is fulfilling you is God actually enabling you to display the comprehensive range of His divine love for others in your own present experience.

In addition, during the Kingdom era, this sense of initial fulfillment will enable you all to enjoy knowing, working with and serving Him to an even much greater extent as you do so alongside and along with all of His other resurrected specially selected recruits who lived their lives throughout all other eras of history. Like you, they will also have qualified themselves for His distinguished service by living their lives in fidelity to Him during their own eras. He will appoint them along with all of you to share in the thrill of becoming members of the cohesive and like-minded team that will make up His Millennial Ministers in that future wonderful Age.

PAUL ASKS JESUS TO APPEAR IN MARVELOUS WAYS IN HIS LIFEWORK COUNCILS IN ORDER TO ENCOURAGE HIS APPRENTICES PRIOR TO HIS PHYSICAL APPEARANCE AS HIGH KING AT THE END OF HISTORY

[20]And now, I ask Him to show you in concrete and real instances the dynamic power and far-reaching scope with which He can and will place each one of us into more extraordinary and effective action for Him during our present lives. I ask Him to do this because He is more than capable enough to accomplish His purposes and intentions in our lives in ways that exceedingly surpass the meager expectations that we more often than not

feebly anticipate when we ask or make requests from Him. Furthermore, He is able to bring to a successful completion the many things that we uncertainly and indecisively consider, presume, or conceive as possible for Him to achieve through us.

21Further, I ask Him, our future High King, Jesus, that in addition to the superlative physical Appearance He will make when He inaugurates His future Kingdom at the consummation of history, that He would also make special spiritual appearances in magnificent ways even now in and through His Lifework Councils, in all generations and eras of world history yet to be lived until that celebrated future Day.

May you all recognize, heartily agree with and live according to the conclusive truths of the provisions and promises presented in this Treatise[36] so far, as I have now reached its midpoint. I, Paul, acting in my role as the "Bond" of our future High King, guarantee that the provisions stated in the above Treatise will prove true for every generation that acts upon them. Now, I must transition to the task of organizing the specific applications and spheres in which you must all implement these promises and provisions into every aspect and area of your lives.

Notes to Extended Interpretive and Expositional Translation
Ephesians Chapter 3

---

[1] Paul is writing this Treatise from Rome as a "prisoner" (δέσμιος) under house arrest awaiting trial, in approximately 61 A.D. He is writing approximately five or six years after he left his three-year enterprise in Ephesus to return to Jerusalem, where he was subsequently unjustly arrested, confined by Felix and Festus in Caesarea, eventually made his appeal to be tried in Rome (due to his also being a Roman Citizen), traveled there through storm and shipwreck, and placed under house arrest for two years during his trial. He had already written *Galatians* (49 A.D. = 12 years earlier), *1 and 2 Thessalonians* (50 and 51 A.D. = 10 years earlier), *1 and 2 Corinthians* (56 A.D. = 5 years earlier), *Romans* (57 A.D. = 4 years earlier), and probably *Colossians, Philippians,* and *Philemon* either shortly before *Ephesians* or during the same period as *Ephesians*. After his trial in 61 A.D., it is likely that Paul was acquitted and released for a short period (approximately 3 years), before he was recaptured and confined in Rome in 66 and 67 A.D., when he wrote *1 Timothy, Titus* and *2 Timothy* before the Roman Emperor Nero put him to death. These last three letters (commonly called "the Pastoral Epistles") are personal and specific in nature and content. Therefore, Paul's *Treatise to the Ephesians* is probably Paul's last general letter, and represents his most mature and comprehensive spiritual reflections and conclusions concerning Jesus' Plan and Commission for His Kingdom

Apprenticeship Councils for future History prior to His return to earth to take up His High Kingship. In order to provide additional perspective of Paul's divinely intended experiences of suffering and rescue, extending from his personal conversion and supernatural commissioning by Jesus until the writing of this final comprehensive Treatise, the following summaries of this 28 year period now follow:

Summary of Paul's Experiences of Suffering and Divine Rescue, from Acts and from 2 Corinthians 11 (28 years, 35-62 A.D.):
Rescued from continual dangers ("perils") from "rivers, robbers, Jews, city, wilderness, sea, false brothers."
Rescued from continual "hunger and thirst" (probably due to lengthy travels).
Rescued from "cold and nakedness" (no clothing due to being robbed?).
Rescued from 3 overt attempts to bribe him or corrupt him by political officials.
Rescued 6 times from false accusations at bogus "legal" hearings or trials.
Rescued from 11 murder plots/lynch mobs (7 before writing 2 Corinthians 11 and 4 after writing it).
Rescued from serious/permanent injury from being beaten 9 times: 8 times before 2 Corinthians 11 for a total of 312 "stripes" [5 scourgings (5 x 39 = 195 "stripes" from scourges), plus 3 beatings with rods (approx. 3 x 39 (?) = 117 "stripes" from rods)]; and 1 time after it by the Jerusalem crowd.
Rescued from at least 6 imprisonments (Philippi plus at least 2 other imprisonments [Arabia, Syria, Cilicia (?) = 3x total (?)] before 2 Corinthians 11, then 3 imprisonments after it.
Rescued from 4 shipwrecks [the "three shipwrecks" of 2 Corinthians 11, one of them major, involving at least 24 hours clinging to wreckage in the ocean, plus the major shipwreck off Malta on the journey to Rome)].
Rescued from death at least 4 (?) times by being raised to life again [2 Corinthians 11: "deaths often:" stoning at Lystra + 3 (?) other times: scourging(s) (1x?) + beating(s) (1x?) + drowning(s) at sea (1x?)].
Rescued from poverty during his two longest teaching periods by God sending him helpers (Aquilla and Priscilla) to establish and run 2 full-time entrepreneurial businesses to provide for his own living for a total of 4 1/2 years (1 1/2 years in Corinth and 3 years in Ephesus).
Rescued from 1 poisonous (deadly) snake bite on Malta during journey to Rome
Rescued from discouragement by divine visits: Jesus appears and speaks to Paul 8 times (one of those times taking him to heaven – 2 Corinthians 11), God's Spirit speaks directly to Paul or through him 4 times, and an angel appears and speaks to him 1 time.
Rescued from pride for the last 25 years of his life by suffering continuously from a divinely appointed evil spirit ordered by God to "slap him around" (14 years prior to writing 2 Corinthians 11 plus 11 years after writing it).

SUMMARY OF PAUL'S EIGHT MAJOR JOURNEYS, COMPRISING APPROXIMATELY 13,000 MILES, FROM ACTS (28 YEARS, 35-62 A.D.):	
1) Damascus → Jerusalem → Arabia → Damascus → Jerusalem (Jesus sends Saul "to the Gentiles" in "Arabia," most likely to Petra, then Elath, then back to Petra, then perhaps to Gaza, then back to Petra, then back to Damascus, then to Jerusalem = 1,000 total land miles).	3 years: 35-37 A.D. 1,000 miles
2) Jerusalem (1 year) → Tarsus, Syria, Cilicia (disciples send Saul to Tarsus, 4 years) → Antioch (Barnabas brings Saul to Antioch, where Saul and Barnabas then teach 1 year together).	6 years: 38-43 A.D. 1,000 miles
3) Antioch → Jerusalem → Antioch (round trip to Jerusalem to take famine relief gift = 750 land miles) [God's angel puts Herod Agrippa I to death in 44 A.D. for his blasphemy at Tyre and Sidon].	1 year: 44 A.D. 750 miles
4) Antioch → Cyprus → Galatian cities → Antioch ("First Missionary Journey," 2 years = 680 land miles + 620 sea miles, then back to Antioch to teach 1 year = 1,300 total miles).	3 years: 45-47 A.D. 1,300 miles
5) Antioch → Jerusalem → Antioch (round trip to Jerusalem for "Jerusalem Council," 1 year = 750 land miles, then back to Antioch to teach for 1 year).	2 years: 48-49 A.D. 750 miles
6) Antioch → Galatian cities → Macedonia → Achaia (Paul lives and teaches in Corinth 1 1/2 years) → Jerusalem → Antioch ("Second Missionary Journey" = 1,900 land miles + 1,100 sea miles = 3,000 total miles).	3 years: 50-52 A.D. 3,000 miles
7) Antioch → Galatian cities → Ephesus (Paul lives and teaches in Ephesus 3 years) → Macedonia → Achaia → Macedonia → Miletus → Jerusalem ("Third Missionary Journey" = 1,500 land miles + 1,100 sea miles = 2,600 total miles).	5 years: 53-57 A.D. 2,600 miles
8) Jerusalem → Caesarea → Crete → Storm → Malta (Shipwreck) → Sicily → Rome (200 land miles + 2,400 sea miles = 3,000 miles)	5 years: 58-62 A.D. 2,600 miles
Total distance from Damascus to Rome + stay in Rome for 2 years (not counting journeys [?] after Rome until execution by Nero = 7,780 land miles + 5,220 sea miles = 13,000 total miles)	28 years: 35-62 A.D. 13,000 miles

For a more detailed chronology of the specific occasions that God supernaturally rescued Paul during his 28 year period of leadership in which he discovered and accomplished his lifework, see extended note on the "helmet" of rescue (from the fear of threats and attacks) at Eph. 6:17.

[2] If Stephen was stoned (Acts 7) in 33 A.D. when Paul was perhaps 25 years old (in Acts 7:58 Luke describes Paul as a νεανίης = "young man" = approx. age

25[?]), and Paul was converted one year later on the road to Damascus when he was 26 in 34 A.D., then Paul would have been approx. 53 years old at the time he wrote *Ephesians* (61 A.D.). If Paul lived 6 more years after he wrote *Ephesians*, he would have been about 59 years old when Nero put him to death in 67 A.D. If Paul's specific lifework consisted of the period between his conversion at age 26 to the completion of his writings in the New Testament with *2 Timothy* at age 59, this would mean that about 33 years (55 percent) of Paul's total life span was spent in accomplishing his lifework for God. If he wrote *Ephesians* after *Colossians, Philippians,* and *Philemon*, he would have completed about 85 percent of the writings that were an integral part of his lifework. As mentioned above, this would imply that *Ephesians* is Paul's "capstone" Treatise, written approximately 5 years after *Romans* (57 A.D.), and therefore likely represents his most mature and comprehensive thought, being written after his arrest in Jerusalem, period of captivity and trial in Caesarea under Felix and Festus, and his voyage and final shipwreck on his journey to Rome.

³ ἔθνος – Review: Paul introduced the concept of the Ephesians as former "barbarians" in Eph. 2:11 (see note).

⁴ It is likely that Paul is using the Greek word for "prisoner" (δέσμιος – see note above) as a metaphor in the unique sense of a "Bond" or "Guarantee." This idea is suggested by Wycliffe in his translation of this passage into English in 1388 (see Bibliography) as follows (modern spelling): "For the grace of this thing I, Paul, the **bound** of Christ Jesus for you heathen men,…"

⁵ Verse 1 is the subject of a sentence. Paul will not get to the main verb of this sentence (which provides his specific motive or reason) until Eph. 3:13, when he finally provides the first person verb αἰτοῦμαι = "I ask..." to finally form his completed thought. So, the main sentence of the whole of Chapter 3 is, "For this reason (namely, the argument of Chapters 1 through 2), I Paul,...ask that you [Ephesians] stop being dispirited..." Verses 2 through 12 of Chapter 3 then, form a long *periphrasis*, which is an extended digression that serves as a *review* of the central points of the argument of the Treatise contained in Chapters 1 through 2 (see notes below). Paul inserts this protracted digression here in order to remind his readers of the reason that they should "stop being dispirited" (see note at Eph. 3:13).

⁶ οἰκονομία – Review: "administration, government." Paul introduced the concept of the "economy" in Eph. 1:10 (see note).

⁷ μυστήριον – Review: "Top Secret Plan." Paul introduced the concept of the "mystery" in Eph. 1:9 (see note).

⁸ ἀποκάλυψις – Review: "a unique, special and supernatural revelatory message in which God unveils new divine information." Paul introduced the concept that the "mystery" had been supernaturally "unveiled" or "revealed" to him by Jesus in Eph. 1:17 (see note).

⁹ μυστήριον – Review: Eph. 1:9 (see note); 3:3.

¹⁰ ἀπεκαλύφθη (aor ind pass 3rd sg of ἀποκαλύπτω – "it has been unveiled" – cf. Eph. 1:17) τοῖς ἁγίοις ἀποστόλοις αὐτοῦ καὶ προφήταις ("to His specially selected High Emissaries and Official Spokespersons" – cf. Eph. 2:20) ἐν πνεύματι ("by [His] Spirit" – cf. Eph. 2:22). Again, Paul is reviewing concepts introduced previously in near context.

¹¹ εὐαγγέλιον – Review: Paul introduced the theme that the message contained in this Treatise was "good news" in Eph. 1:13 (see extended analysis of this word, in both its noun and verb forms, at Eph.1:13).

¹² ἔθνος – Review: "a member from any of the ethnic races or nations foreign to Judaism – whether they be civilized Greeks or uncivilized Barbarians" – see extended note at Eph. 2:11.

¹³ τὰ συγκληρονόμα – lit. "co-heirship, heirship with" – Paul is purposefully re-emphasizing that we can be "co-heirs" and participate with Jesus in His "inheritance," a theme which he introduced in Eph. 1:11 and 1:14. Paul then asked God that we would come to plan our lives around this concept in Eph. 1:18. Proposed translation: "fully equal heirs." It is well to notice that this was Paul's main theme in his farewell address to the Ephesian leadership in Acts 20:32:

> Acts 20:32 "And now, brethren, I commend you to God and to the word of His grace, which is able to build you up and give you an *inheritance* among all those who have been specially selected."

¹⁴ τὰ σύσσωμα – lit. "co-body-members, body members with" – Paul introduced and explained the concept that the specially selected recruits will become "co-members" in the future governmental "body" through which the High King will enact His administrative will and policy in Eph. 1:23. Proposed translation: "co-administrators with Him in His future governmental body."

¹⁵ τὰ συμμέτοχα – lit. "co-partnership, partnership with" – Paul also emphasizes the fact that we are "fellow-partners" (or "co-partners") with the High King. Proposed translation: "completely equal partners with." The *Epistle to the Hebrews* picks up the term μέτοχοι (Hebrews 1:9) and uses it to emphasize our role of co-rulership with Jesus in the Kingdom, as a fulfillment of Psalm 45:6-7:

> Psalm 45:6-7 [The Father addressing The Son:] "Your throne, O God, is forever and ever; a scepter of righteousness is the scepter of Your Kingdom. You have loved righteousness and hated lawlessness; therefore God, Your God, has anointed You with gladness more than your *companions* (= μέτοχοι)."

¹⁶ εὐαγγελίζομαι – Review: "To announce good news." See extended analysis of this word, in both its noun and verb forms, in note at Eph. 1:13.

¹⁷ πλοῦτος – Paul is re-emphasizing this metaphor of "riches" because he has already used it four times in this Treatise so far to refer to a wide variety of benefits associated with God's future Kingdom. In Eph. 1:7, Paul attributed the

"redemption" and God's "forgiveness" of our getting "side-tracked" from our "lifework" to the "riches of His *graciousness*." In Eph. 1:18, Paul promised that God will grant us the "riches of His *inheritance*, which He will bequeath to His specially selected recruits who merit it at His Appearing." In Eph. 2:4, Paul assured us that because God loves us, He is "rich in *mercy*." And in Eph. 2:7, Paul told us that God desires to show us the "riches of His *goodness* as well as His graciousness."

¹⁸ ἐλαχιστότερος – ...III. from ἐλάχιστος came a new Comp. ἐλαχιστότερος *less than the least*, ἐ. πάντων ἁγίων *Ep.Eph.3.8*: Sup. ἐλαχιστότατος *very least of all*, S.E.M.3.54, 9.406[LS]. Paul is clearly saying that due to the gravity of his offenses against Jesus when he was a Pharisee, he is a primary example of the depth of God's graciousness. Paul says that he believes himself to be "less than the least" of all of God's specially selected recruits. The implication is that there is no moral or ethical failure we can commit that is beyond the reach of God's gracious ability to rescue and restore us to living a productive and meaningful life for Him.

¹⁹ φωτίσαι – aor inf act of φωτίζω, "to enlighten." Paul uses this word twice in Ephesians; here in Eph 3:9 and previously in Eph. 1:18, where he introduced and explained his responsibility to bring "enlightenment" of the specific meaning of the "economy (ἡ οἰκονομία Eph. 1:10) of the mystery" (τοῦ μυστηρίου – Eph. 1:9) as *realizing* one's "lifework" (κλῆσις), motivated by the reward of the "inheritance" (κληρονομία). Eph. 1:18 carries the central theme of this entire Treatise. Proposed translation: "to realize, appreciate and act upon spiritual reality" (see note on the meaning of the noun φῶς at Eph. 5:8).

²⁰ σοφία – Review: "the kind of knowledge that makes it possible for us to become competent, then gain mastery, then achieve superior leadership ability in living human life skillfully, especially in the ethical and political arenas" (see extended note at Eph. 1:8 for analysis of this word).

²¹ ἐκκλησία – Review: Paul introduced and explained the concept that Jesus' "Lifework Councils" will ultimately demonstrate God's σοφία fully, i.e., that through them Jesus will train human beings to the high level of political and ethical skill required for leadership in God's future governmental administration, eventually placing them in positions of authority over the heavenly angelic hierarchy under the leadership of the High King, in Eph. 1:21-2:2 (see notes). The text in which Paul clearly states that Jesus' expectation for His specially selected recruits is that they rapidly grow in their leadership skills in this life because they will be expected to be His administrators during the Kingdom era, even over angels, is in 1 Corinthians 6:1-3, as follows:

> 1 Cor. 6:1-3 Τολμᾷ τις ὑμῶν πρᾶγμα ἔχων πρὸς τὸν ἕτερον κρίνεσθαι ἐπὶ τῶν ἀδίκων, καὶ οὐχὶ ἐπὶ τῶν ἁγίων; ²Οὐκ οἴδατε ὅτι οἱ ἅγιοι τὸν κόσμον κρινοῦσι; Καὶ εἰ ἐν ὑμῖν κρίνεται ὁ κόσμος, ἀνάξιοί ἐστε κριτηρίων ἐλαχίστων; ³Οὐκ οἴδατε ὅτι ἀγγέλους κρινοῦμεν; Μήτι γε βιωτικά!

1 Cor. 6:1-3 "How is it that those of you who have a dispute with each other dare go to trial before those who are clearly unjust in order to legally settle your dispute, instead of having the matter be decided by God's specially selected recruits? ²Don't you realize that as His specially selected apprentices we are supposed to recognize such instances as training opportunities that have been designed by Him in order for us to grow in the kind of maturity that will be required of us to exercise legislative, executive and judicial authority over the governments of the future world? Moreover, if the great privilege of governing the future world during the Kingdom era is to be delegated to you by God Himself, isn't it ridiculous to think that your present lives would not also involve deciding issues of lesser consequence as training exercises? ³Don't you realize that God intends that ultimately, we are to exercise authority over His angelic hierarchy that now operates the affairs of the entire Universe? And since that is true, how much more true it is that we should become proficient in exercising prudent leadership skills during our present lives in preparation for that era!" [transl. – GWC].

²² πρόθεσις – Review: "to, following sufficient planning and deliberation, assert or publish in public an official case, proposition or statement." Paul introduced and explained the concept that God carefully planned the ultimate recruitment of the Barbarian Peoples to fill the inheritance positions within his Kingdom administration in close counsel with Jesus in His Eternal Council with Him before the creation of the world, with a view to its eventually universal publication and enactment, in Eph. 1:11 (see note).

²³ προσαγωγή – Review: "freeway." Paul introduced and explained the concept that Jesus has opened up for His specially selected recruits a new immediate and powerful way of access to God the Father now in their present lives – a "freeway" to approach God – in Eph. 2:18 (see note).

²⁴ αἰτοῦμαι – This sentence began in Eph. 3:1 (see note). Paul concludes his protracted digression in verses 2-12 at this point where he finally returns to his main line of thought by introducing his main verb: "I ask, insist..." (1 p. pres. sing. mid. ind.). αἰτέω – *ask, beg,* abs., Od.18.49, A.*Supp.*341. **2.** mostly c. acc. rei, *ask for, demand,* Il.5.358, Od.17.365, etc.; ὁδὸν αἰ. *ask leave* **to depart,** Od.10.17; αἰ. τινί τι *to ask* **something for one,** 20.74, Hdt.5.17: c. acc. pers. et rei, *ask* **a person** *for* **a thing,** Il.22.295, Od.2.387, Hdt.3.1, etc.; δίκας αἰ. τινὰ φόνου *to demand* **satisfaction from one for...,** Hdt.8.114; αἰ. τι πρός τινος Thgn.556; παρά τινος X.*An.*1.3.16; τὰ αἰτήματα ἃ ᾐτήκαμεν παρ' αὐτοῦ *1 Ep.Jo.*5.15 [LS]. From the context (see note on ἐγκακέω immediately following), Paul is probably not merely "begging" or "politely requesting," and yet he is too gracious to forcefully "demand." A proposed translation that blends and balances both extremes of the meaning of this word perhaps is best expressed in the phrase, "I ask, but to be frank, I really must insist..."

²⁵ ἐγκακέω, *behave remissly* in a thing, ἐνεκάκησαν τὸ πέμπειν they *culpably omitted* to send, Plb.4.19.10, cf. Thd.Pr.3.11, Sm.Ge.27.46: c. part., τὸ καλὸν ποιοῦντες μὴ ἐγκακῶμεν *Ep.Gal.* 6.9: abs., *Ev.Luc.* 18.1, al., cf. BGU1043.3 (iii A. D.); cf. ἐκκακέω [LS]. It seems at first glance that this word means something

like "neglect." However, upon examination of the old British English in Webster, this word is always translated "**faint**:" Etymology: Middle English *faint, feint* (also, *deceitful, feigned*), from Old French, from past participle of *faindre, feindre* to *feign, shirk* -- more at FEIGN **1:** lacking courage and spirit: COWARDLY, SPIRITLESS -- now usually used in the phrase "faint heart" **2:** feeble, dizzy, and likely to faint through or as if through hunger, illness, pain, shock, or emotion. **3 a:** having an appearance of underlying weakness: lacking vigor or strength **b:** performed, acted, or accomplished in a weak, feeble, or hesitant manner: marked by halfhearted forcelessness [W]. This word occurs six times in the NT. It is used once by Jesus in Luke 18:1 ("men ought always to pray and not to *faint*"), and the other five times by Paul in his Treatises. It only occurs once (here) in Ephesians. The word "faint" in American English is not really a good translation, because in our language it does not necessarily carry with it the negative ethical connotation of the British, but retains only the meaning of the physiological effect on the human body, i.e., it merely means "to suddenly lose consciousness, due to shock or loss of blood; to pass out or black out." But the Greek word clearly emphasizes the psychological *cause* of becoming physiologically weak; e.g., becoming weak due to the *cause* of the psychological, moral or ethical flaw of being cowardly, spiritless, lacking endurance or giving up, which the Old British word "faint" is attempting to translate. Consequently, the proposed translation is: "to allow an initial shock of apparently bad news to take hold of one's mind-set such that it causes that person to slip into a pervasive dispirited and defeatist mood, which if left unchecked, eventually leads to the shameful, cowardly or cynical attitude and behavior of neglecting, eventually giving up and even despairing of performing one's rightful duties and responsibilities."

[26] θλῖψις, εως, ἡ, *pressure*, Arist.*Mete*.382a13, Pr.890a2; τῶν νεφῶν Epicur.Ep.2 P.49 U.; ἀντέρεισις καὶ θ. Str.1.3.6; *of the pulse*, Ruf. ap.Orib.8.24.61, cf. Gal.7.306; θ. στομάχου Orib.Fr.42; ὑστερικαὶ θ. Sor.1.42... **3.** metaph., *oppression, affliction*, LXXGe.35.3, al., BGU1139.4 (i B.C.), Act.Ap.14.22 (pl.), al., Vett.Val.71.16 (pl.), POxy.939.13 (iv A.D.) [LS]. This word is usually translated into the British words "affliction" or "tribulation," neither of which is commonly used in contemporary American English. The root notion of "affliction" is "to hit or strike" (Etymology: Middle English *afflicten*, from Latin *afflictus*, past participle of *affligere* to cast down, deject, from *ad-* + *fligere* to strike [W]), and the root notion of "tribulation" is "to experience pressure in the sense of *oppression*" (Etymology: Middle English *tribulacioun*, from Old French *tribulacion*, from Late Latin *tribulation-*, *tribulatio*, from *tribulatus* (past participle of *tribulare* to oppress, afflict, from Latin, to press, from *tribulum* threshing board) + Latin *-ion-, -io -ion*; akin to Latin *terere* to rub: distress or suffering resulting from oppression, persecution [W]). However, the main idea communicated by the Greek word θλῖψις seems to be the psychological meaning of the word "pressure," as in the psychological expression, "being under pressure," which in American English is best translated by the word "stress;" as

the expression "I've been under a lot of pressure lately," is virtually synonymous with the expression, "I've been under a lot of stress lately" ("pressure" being the cause, "stress" being the effect). Proposed translation: "pressures and resulting stresses."

²⁷ δόξα – Review: Paul introduced and explained God's "Appearing" in historical space-time in Eph. 1:6, 1:12 and 1:17 (see note at Eph. 1:6).

²⁸ ὀνομάζω [verb] – A. speak of by name, call *or* address by name, *of persons, πατρόθεν ἐκ γενεῆς ὀνομάζων ἄνδρα ἕκαστον* Il.10.68 **II.** ὀ. τινά τι *call*...**one something**,...παῖδά μ' ὠνομάζετο *called* me *his* son, S.*OT*1021...[better translation into American English: "appoint." In this passage from Sophocles' *Oedipus Tyrannus*, Oedipus is referring to Polybus, the King of Corinth that adopted him and "appointed" Oedipus to be his "son" – GWC]...**b. nominate**, ὀνομασθεὶς εἰς δεκαπρωτείαν *POxy*.1257.1, cf. 1204.4 (iii A.D.) [As a transitive verb, to "name" in the sense of "nominate" in Scottish and British English means the same thing as the American English word "appoint" – **3: to *appoint*** specifically or by name: assign to some purpose: NOMINATE <the king *named* his eldest son to succeed him> <let's *name* an early day for the wedding> [W]. The complete passage and its translation from the *The Oxyrhynchus Papyri* referenced above is helpful, and now follows (*P.Oxy.* 10.1257. "Statement concerning a *dekaprôtos*"):

> Ἐπιμάχου **ὀνομασθέντος** εἰς δεκαπρωτείαν λιβὸς τοπαρχίας τοῦ Ὀξυρυγχίτου νομοῦ παρήλικος ὄντος {καὶ} Θώνιος πατρῳὸς ὢν τοῦ Ἐπιμάχου ἐδιοίκησεν τὰ κατὰ τὴν δεκαπρωτείαν, καὶ τοῦ καιροῦ λήξαντος τῆς παραδόσεως σίτου Θέων ὁ καὶ Πλούταρχος γεν[ό]μενος ὑπομνηματογράφος νυνὶ
>
> English Translation: "What one must possess *who aspires to be appointed* a chief municipal official over a Canal District, in the governed Provinces of Oxyrhynchus, especially over an Agricultural District: He must be of senior age, and one who is of a noble Egyptian ancestry. He must also possess proven management skills over the things that are of concern to a chief municipal official, especially of proportionately distributing the correct and appropriate monthly public allocation of corn provided by the gods. He must also have become rich and presently hold the office of being an official record keeper licensed by Pharaoh's government" [transl. – GWC].

Luke uses the verb ὀνομάζω in his Gospel to refer to Jesus "appointing" the Twelve High Emissaries ["Apostles"], as follows:

> Luke 6:13 καὶ ὅτε ἐγένετο ἡμέρα, προσεφώνησεν τοὺς μαθητὰς αὐτοῦ, καὶ ἐκλεξάμενος ἀπ' αὐτῶν δώδεκα, οὓς καὶ ἀποστόλους **ὠνόμασεν**,
>
> Luke 6:13 When it was day, he called his apprentices [disciples], and from them he chose twelve, whom he also *appointed* to be High Emissaries [apostles].

Proposed translation of ὀνομάζω in this context: "appointed."

²⁹ Paul composes a more definitive statement of this concept of God's historical Providence in his speech to the Athenians in Acts 17:26-27:

> Acts 17:26-27 ἐποίησέν τε ἐξ ἑνὸς αἵματος πᾶν ἔθνος ἀνθρώπων κατοικεῖν ἐπὶ παν τὸ προσώπον τῆς γῆς, ὁρίσας προστεταγμένους καιροὺς καὶ τὰς ὁροθεσίας τῆς κατοικίας

αὐτῶν, ²⁷ζητεῖν τὸν κύριον εἰ ἄρα γε ψηλαφήσειαν αὐτὸν καὶ εὕροιεν, καί γε οὐ μακρὰν ἀπὸ ἑνὸς ἑκάστου ἡμῶν ὑπάρχοντα.

Acts 17:26-27 "He [God] made every nation of human beings from one original pair of human beings, with the intention that they would eventually inhabit the entire surface of the earth, each nation having been appointed and placed both in their own historical eras as well as within the respective geographical boundaries of their homelands by Him, ²⁷in order that they should seek their Divine Leader that led them there, so that in each case they would have the opportunity to reach out for Him and find Him, because during this present era, He has taken the initiative to orchestrate for each nation the most advantageous circumstances to not be far from each one of us" [transl. – GWC].

³⁰ **κατοικέω,** *settle in, colonize,* πόλιν Hdt.7.164;...generally, *inhabit,* τόπους S.*Ph.*40;...etc.:--Pass., *to be dwelt in* or *inhabited,* opp. κατοικίζομαι (to be just *founded*), Arist.*Pol.*1266b2. **2.** abs., *settle, dwell,* ζητοῦσα . . ποῦ κατοικοίης S.*OC*362;...esp. of **non-citizens,** Ἐφέσιοι καὶ οἱ -οῦντες *SIG*352.4 (Ephesus, iv B.C.). cf. 633.67 (Milet., ii B.C.):--pf. and plpf. Pass., *to have been planted* or *settled,* κατὰ κώμας Hdt.1.96, cf.2.102; κ.νῆσον, τὴν μεσόγειαν, Id.4.8, Th.1.120. **II.** *administer, govern,* οἱ τὰς πόλεις – οῦντες Phld.*Rh.*2.225 S.:--more freq. in Pass., κατῴκηνται καλῶς, **of Athens,** S.*OC*1004; ὀρθῶς κ., **of Sparta,** Pl.*Lg.*683a....[LS]. Paul uses this verb only once in this Treatise. He uses it to mean "to allow Jesus to land, plant a Colony, then settle in, then live in, and finally administer and govern in your hearts..." Paul is likely simply pointing out that allowing Jesus to live in our hearts and ultimately control our ethical and life-making decisions is an extended process that is somewhat uncomfortable to us. He is using a metaphor of Jesus as an "Explorer." First, we must allow Him to "land on the beach" of our lives, then "plant His heavenly Colony" there, then progress on to permit Him to "settle in and live there," and finally and ultimately rise to leadership such that He "administers and governs" there (in our hearts; i.e., in our ethical and life-decision making faculties).

³¹ **καρδία** – Review: "heart" = "the inclinational and ethical decision–making power of the soul." See extended note at Eph. 1:18.

³² **ῥιζόω,** *cause to strike root*: metaph., **plant, fix firmly,** ὅς μιν [τὴν ναῦν] λᾶαν θῆκε καὶ ἐρρίζωσεν ἔνερθεν Od.13.163; [νήσους] κατὰ βυσσὸν πρυμνόθεν (s. v.l.) Call.*Del.*35:--Pass., **of trees and plants,** *take root, strike root,* X.*Oec.*19.9, Thphr.*CP*1.2.1:--Med., ἄριστον ῥιζώσασθαι, **of the fig,** Id.*HP*2.5.6; so αἱ πίνναι ἐρρίζωνται, opp. ἀρρίζωτοι, Arist. *HA*548a5; ῥ. ἐπί τινος *AP*6.66 (Paul.Sil.); ὁδὸς βάθροισι γῆθεν ἐρριζωμένος *made fast* or *solid,* S.*OC*1591; **of a bridge,** αἰώνιος ἐρρίζωται *Epigr.Gr.*1078.7 (Adana). **2.** metaph., ἐρρίζωσε τὴν τυραννίδα Hdt.1.64:--Pass., τυραννὶς ἐρριζωμένη ib.60, cf. Pl.*Lg.*839a; ἐξ ἀμαθίας πάντα κακὰ ἐρρ. **have their root** in . . , Id.*Ep.*336b, cf. S E. *Med.*1.271; ἐν ἀγάπῃ ἐρρ. *Ep.Eph.*3.18 [LS]. The main idea of the Greek word ῥιζόω seems to involve both concepts of God being "implanted," as well as growing to such an extent that He is "embedded" in our personality and character. See the Parable of the Farmer

(Sower) in Matthew 13:18-23, where Jesus uses the same symbolic concept in His extended metaphor or parable of the farmer:

> Matt. 13:18-23 "Hear, then, the parable of the farmer. [19]When anyone hears the word of the kingdom, and doesn't understand it, the evil one comes, and snatches away that which has been sown in his heart. This is what was sown by the roadside. [20]What was sown on the rocky places, this is he who hears the word, and immediately with joy receives it; [21]yet he has no *root* (ῥίζαν) in himself, but endures for a while. When oppression or persecution arises because of the word, immediately he stumbles. [22]What was sown among the thorns, this is he who hears the word, but the cares of this world and the deceitfulness of riches choke the word, and he becomes unfruitful. [23]What was sown on the good ground, this is he who hears the word, and understands it, who most assuredly bears fruit, and brings forth, some one hundred times as much, some sixty, and some thirty."

[33] θεμελιόω, *to lay the foundation of, found firmly*, πύργους . . φοίνικι θεμελιώσας X.*Cyr*.7.5.11, cf. IG12(2).11.26 (Mytil.), LXX*Jo*.6.25 (26), *Ep. Hebr*. 1.10, etc.:--Pass., *have the foundations laid*, IG22.1343.15 (i B.C.); ἐπὶ τὴν πέτραν *Ev.Matt*.7.25: metaph., βασιλεία καλῶς θεμελιωθεῖσα D.S.11.68; ἡγεμονία κάλλιστα τεθεμελιωμένη Id.15.1; ἐν ἀγάπῃ τεθ. *Ep.Eph*.3.18; τῇ πίστει *Ep.Col*.1.23 [LS]. Here we think of the "founding" of firm, good decisions and ideas, as well as the symbol of a "foundation;" see Eph. 2:20 and note at Eph. 1:4.

[34] Those specially selected recruits who, though they have died, have written down their observations, reflections and thoughts in valuable historical, philosophical and theological Works for us to use and from which we can profit.

[35] πλάτος καὶ μῆκος καὶ ὕψος καὶ βάθος = "width and length and height and depth." These four dimensions are those commonly used in the planning and construction of buildings. "Width, length and height" are the main quantitative parameters that determine the size of the *above-ground structure* of the building (the relational structure of all of Jesus' "Lifework Councils" during the last 2,000 years of History); whereas "depth" is the crucial design dimension that determines the stability of the building's *foundation* (the relational structure of the 2,000 year era beginning with the families of Abraham, Isaac and Jacob, the formation, deliverance and establishing of the of the Kingdom of Israel, its exile and restoration, as recorded in the writings of Moses, the Historical and Poetic writings, the writings of the Prophets, and the teachings of Jesus recorded by the Apostles) – see Eph. 2:19-22. Jesus Himself uses this same symbolic image of building one's "house" (life) on a solid "foundation" (relationship built upon Jesus' foundational words and teachings) in the Gospel of Matthew 7:24-27, as follows:

> Matt. 7:24-27 "Everyone therefore who hears these words of mine, and does them, I will liken him to a wise man, who built (ᾠκοδόμησεν) his house (οἰκίαν) on a rock. [25]The rain came down, the floods came, and the winds blew, and beat on that house (οἰκίᾳ); and it didn't fall, for it was founded (τεθεμελίωτο) on the rock. [26]Everyone who hears these words of mine, and doesn't do them will be like a foolish man, who

built his house on the sand. ²⁷The rain came down, the floods came, and the winds blew, and beat on that house; and it fell – and great was its fall."

³⁶ ἀμήν, Hebr. Adv. **A.** *verily, of a truth, so be it*...[LS]. Usually translated "amen." Etymology: Middle English, from Old English, from Late Latin, from Greek *amēn*, from Hebrew *āmēn* – **interjection**: used to express solemn ratification (in an expression of faith, in communication with God, or an invocation) or hearty approval (as of an assertion); **noun**: a response especially of ratification, approval, conclusion, or termination <as a sort of amen to that, nine nations quickly recognized the new regime – Time>. Proposed translation: "to recognize, heartily agree with and live according to the conclusive truths presented in a convincing line of reasoning."

4

"Dressing Up" For Real

Because God's Has Tasked Us to Recruit and Mold Diverse, Hostile Ethnic Groups and Nations into Cohesive Groups that Develop Unit Integrity; Sectarianism, Exclusivism and Other Narrow-minded Attitudes of Petty Divisiveness are Fundamentally Counterproductive to His Objectives ♦ *From this Broad-minded Outlook, Identify the Special Ability God Has Given You to Help Others Find and Accomplish Their Lifework, and in the Process, You Will be Transformed by Him into a Fully Mature Human Being* ♦ *Adopt the Conscious Discipline to "Dress Up" Your Mind with the New, Freshly Outfitted Human Being Created by God, Focused on Discovering the Truth About Your Life* ♦ *Do not Grieve God's Spirit, but Consciously Develop Habits of Behavior that Disarm Four Main Traps of the Devil – Lying, Unchecked Anger, Stealing and Criticizing Others.*

BECAUSE GOD HAS TASKED US TO RECRUIT AND MOLD DIVERSE, HOSTILE ETHNIC GROUPS AND NATIONS INTO COHESIVE GROUPS THAT DEVELOP UNIT INTEGRITY; SECTARIANISM, EXCLUSIVISM AND OTHER NARROW-MINDED ATTITUDES OF PETTY DIVISIVENESS ARE FUNDAMENTALLY COUNTERPRODUCTIVE TO HIS OBJECTIVES

Therefore, as the one whose life-mission is to write this official Treatise, which serves as the "Bond"[1] or Guarantee that God will accomplish every provision He offers you, I respectfully request, invite and expect you to intentionally conduct your lives according to the new philosophical world view[2] that I have set out. You must conduct your lives in a manner worthy of the unique lifework[3] to which you have been officially summoned by our Commander in Chief. You must do this in both its aspects of carrying out the apprenticeship that He has assigned to each of you in this present life, as well as in your expectation of being appointed by Him to a unique role of service in His future Millennial Administration.

[2]There are four specific aspects involved in adopting a deliberate demeanor and behavior to reflect public conduct that is worthy for your life of apprenticeship to your lifework. First, you should approach every interaction you have with other people not with *condescension*, but rather with an *unassuming nature*. Second, you should use a *gentle, non-*

aggressive tone and body language with others. Third, you must be able to be *tolerant* and *patient*, and be willing to *suffer the inevitable initial emotional pain* that comes when others do not immediately respond to your wisdom and mature ideas. And fourth, your underlying intention towards others should remain that of a *servant*-leader, whose ultimate goal is to orchestrate ways to help them become mature and successful, as you continue to remain motivated by *self-sacrificial love*.

³It is only this motive of self-sacrificial love that will enable you to keep on diligently striving for the kind of unity that the Spirit of God can and will create among the extremely diverse and hostile barbarian ethnic groups that He intends to recruit for His future government. This bond of union that will bring together such diverse groups is not the status quo of history – namely, continuous cycles of revenge, war and divisiveness – but rather the intentional effort by you all in your leadership roles to establish terms of peace supernaturally between embittered and vengeful factions.

⁴Therefore, sectarianism, exclusivism and all other narrow-minded attitudes of petty divisiveness are fundamentally counterproductive to God's purposes, and should accordingly never characterize your behavior. This is so because – as you should now realize from this Treatise – God intends and is planning but *one future governmental body* through which He will administrate His future worldwide Kingdom to achieve a unified set of objectives. Further, this august body will be guided in that era by a *single Spirit* – the same Spirit that has specially selected each of you and that empowers you now during this present era of your lives. Moreover, you know that the future destiny to which you all have been summoned has but *one single hope* into which each of you have placed your trust. This hope has the power to motivate you to accomplish the *unique lifework* of your present apprenticeship, which in turn will qualify each of you for your future Millennial appointments within that unified governmental body.

⁵In addition, we have all been recruited and solemnly initiated into only *one quest* to faithfully follow only *one* Commander in Chief in exactly the same way, namely, through a *one-time* public ceremony, in which we publicly allow our bodies to be immersed under water.[4] Through this ceremony, we demonstrate our commitment to conduct our lives according to His *unified* set of common teachings He has directed all of us to learn and obey.[5] This ceremony symbolically depicts the *same unified theme* that God has historically required not only from us, but also from *all* those who have made the decision to commit their lives to follow Him in order to accomplish their lifework.

For example, those who lived during the founding of the nation of Israel followed Moses out of Egypt through the waters of the Red Sea[6] into the desert where God led them to Mount Sinai to receive His Laws. Those in Israel who chose to follow Joshua into the land of Canaan to conquer it did so by following God through the waters of the Jordan River.[7] Naaman the Syrian serves as an example of a non-Israelite who demonstrated his decision to follow God by immersing himself in the Jordan River seven times to overcome his leprosy![8] Those who decided to follow Jesus as God's Messiah during His first visit symbolically demonstrated their decision to do so by being publicly immersed under the waters of the Jordan River by John the Immerser[9] or by Jesus' apprentices.[10] Jesus Himself demonstrated His decision to follow God's plan to accomplish His own lifework by publicly allowing John the Immerser to immerse Him in the waters of the Jordan River.[11]

6So you see that even Jesus, our Commander in Chief, obeys the One True God, Who not only has the singular right to exercise His authority over Jesus because He is His Father, but even more so over us all because He is our Father. Jesus has therefore provided the perfect example for us. He has chosen to be included among us because He desires that the Father employ our lives in the same way that the Father used His own life – to reach other people through using us as His delegates; and that we be encouraged by the Father the same way He encouraged Jesus – by assuring us that He is always with us.

FROM THIS BROAD-MINDED OUTLOOK, IDENTIFY THE SPECIAL ABILITY GOD HAS GIVEN YOU TO HELP OTHERS FIND AND ACCOMPLISH THEIR LIFEWORK, AND IN THE PROCESS, YOU WILL BE TRANSFORMED BY HIM INTO A FULLY MATURE HUMAN BEING

7For the purpose of recruiting and training the diverse and hostile ethnic groups and nations north and west of the Mediterranean Sea into cohesive, harmonious organizations, each one of us has been given a special, unique and gracious spiritual power or ability by our Commander in Chief. Further, He has gifted each of us with these various yet distinct divine skills appropriate to His wise, measured[12] assessment of the strengths and weaknesses of our present personalities, as well as the future roles He is planning for us, in order that we may serve Him in His future administration as High King of the earth.

8To prove this, I will make a case that the Psalm 68:18 is the crux passage of the entire Psalm – and that it is in fact a Messianic prediction. Through this Psalm, God's Spirit forecasts that during this present era of history – in which our Commander in Chief governs the world from heaven after ascending back there from here – one of His primary activities is to give distinctive and unique spiritual powers and abilities, graciously and freely, to His specially selected recruits. He does this in order to enable them to recruit others into His divine program. I will quote it as I interpret it, and then explain my interpretation.

First, the interpretation of the quotation itself should read as follows:

"When He ascended on high,
He led captives into captivity,
And gave gifts to human beings."[13]

9Now, the main subject and verb of the above passage is, "He – namely, God – ascended." This leads to the first conclusion of my line of reasoning. If the Psalm says that God "ascended" *from* the earth *to* heaven, what else could that possibly imply except that the Psalm actually prophesies that God must first *make* a visit *to* the earth *from* heaven – namely, that God first had to "descend" from heaven to the "lower regions" – that is to say, the "earth?"

10Second, what is God's *purpose* for "ascending" *from* the earth *back* into heaven, if His ultimate goal is not to live in heaven, but *here on the earth* forever?[14] If this One Divine Being Who descended from the highest heaven is indeed, the One High King Who ascended back to the highest heaven, only to eventually return to His rightful earthly throne; it can only mean that He did so in order to *exercise His authority from heaven temporarily.* The chief task over which He assumed authority in heaven was to *begin filling the positions* of His future Kingdom administration by training His future Ministers in their special and unique apprenticeship roles in present world history.

11It therefore logically follows that He not only has the power and authority to ultimately fill all of the positions that He intends to eventually comprise His Millennial Kingdom administration, but that He also must therefore have the power and authority to freely and graciously give unique, various, supernatural skills and abilities to His specially selected recruits. He therefore intends that we not only employ these skills and abilities during our lifework of apprenticeship to prepare ourselves for these future roles, but also that we use them to recruit and train others for their future roles.

That is why the foremost of these supernatural skills and abilities is given to those in the office of High Emissary, which for the twelve tribes that comprise the nation of Israel, Jesus appointed the original twelve apprentices He personally selected during His first visit (excepting Judas Iscariot, and adding Matthias, of course).[15] When only very few members of Israel responded to God's offer of His inheritance plan through them, Jesus selected me as His High Emissary to recruit His future administrators from all of the ethnic races and nations in the entire world foreign to

Judaism, whether they be civilized Greeks or uncivilized Barbarians (as I previously related above).[16]

The gift of High Emissary is followed by the apprenticeship role of accurately representing God as His legitimate Divine Spokespersons; and next after that, of those who are specially commissioned to be His messengers that enthusiastically announce and communicate His message of Good News. This divine gift must be followed up by those who prove themselves to become trustworthy Guardians, charged with the spiritual care and well-being of those who believe in Him and become new recruits. They must work in harmony with those who are gifted with the talent of being meticulous and careful Teachers, who accept the painstaking responsibility of accurately, reliably and rigorously training His new recruits in the principles and disciplines necessary for growing in the maturity required for their present and future responsibilities to Him.

[12]The High King gives these various supernatural skills and abilities to the ever growing complement of His specially selected recruits for the overall purpose of outfitting them with the full gear and equipment they will need for discovering and accomplishing their own unique lifework of service to Him. This in turn inevitably adds to the eventual comprehensive building of our High King's fully mature and complete governmental body of future High Ministers.

[13]Our Commander in Chief will continue His recruitment, supervision and training program from heaven until such time (known only to Him), that all of us – the formerly excluded and hostile barbarian ethnic groups (scattered across the globe due to being historically ostracized from the eternal life of God by the sanctimoniousness of Judaism) – achieve "unit integrity." This will occur when the full complement of specially selected recruits He has trained to become spiritually mature during the coming historical era can, when He returns (and they all are resurrected), exercise fully authentic and completely functional interdependent reliability upon each other over the vast administration with which He will entrust them as they oversee the new world.

The goal of our training program in this life is that we would *actually experience* a comprehensive understanding of the meaning of the mature experiences of the Son of God Himself, which is, by definition, what it means to become a *fully mature human being.* His purpose for each of us is that we finally arrive at a fully mature human stature, having willingly opened ourselves to being guided completely by the dynamic, gracious power and gifting from the Divine personality of our future High King. In the final analysis, we should make it our own goal to have the total sum of the meaning and significance of our lives measured, evaluated and appraised[17] by Him.

[14]The intentional and deliberate objective of our High King in subjecting us to the painful process of transforming us into fully mature human beings is so that we may cease to act childishly naïve, puerile, gullible and thus *vulnerable* (not considering the consequences of our attitudes, behaviors and actions).[18] His aim is to deliver us from being continually disturbed and confused,[19] and from allowing ourselves to become disoriented by having our minds be spun around in all directions by others.[20] His desire is to make us *invulnerable* to our propensity to let ourselves be carried away by all kinds of people who pretend to be authoritative teachers in spiritual matters, but who are in reality only transient, selfish con artists, pirates[21] or thieving swindlers and scoundrels.[22] He wants to protect us from them, because their only purpose is to deceive us by using cunning, fraudulent schemes[23] to con us into believing unsound opinions, which would eventually cause events in our lives to become as erratic, unreliable and volatile as a windstorm.[24] His purpose is to guard us from falling into the trap of adopting the lifestyle they intend for us, in which we would behave as if the important decisions in life were to be regarded as sheer chance, a gamble or a mere "roll of the dice."[25]

[15]Conversely, the only way for all of us (myself included) to become invulnerable to deception and to guard ourselves from getting sidetracked is to become resolved to continually grow[26] in becoming just like Him – the very One Who is now heading up and is the leader of God's training program.[27] Further, we must intentionally subject ourselves to His training so that we eventually mature to become like Him in every way: in our thoughts, demeanor, attitudes, behavior and public speech. The only avenue to accomplishing these goals, namely – avoiding deception, becoming like Him and discovering and speaking what is true[28] about ourselves, about other people, and about our lifework, is by maintaining a deliberate attitude of self-sacrificial love[29] toward others.

[16]In fact, it is only when we maintain this deliberate attitude of self-sacrificial love that the High King keeps on generating the growth of His future governmental body into that final, completed organizational structure which will ultimately be able to represent Him both in our present lives and throughout the future world in every aspect of His will and policy. Anyone who aspires to become a member of this august body must therefore commit themselves to live their lives according to a philosophical world view based on self-sacrificial love.

It is only that mature band that He will ultimately choose to incorporate into a harmonious, rational organization structured to function in harmony as a pleasant and enjoyable whole,[30] both now and in the future world. It is also only to those that are willing to be continually taught by

Him that He will enable to "put it all together"[31] in their present lives – that is to say, to logically discover the truth about and achieve God's lifework for themselves and others.

He will supply them with the material means they will need for this task through the vast fortune[32] He has at His disposal. Further, He will furnish them with the spiritual insight and encouragement they will need by arranging enlightening personal contacts with other people orchestrated by the Spirit of God, as well as from direct contact with the Spirit of God Himself.[33] During this training process, He will provide them with only the amount of His divine resources He wisely measures out for them, so that they will continue to depend on Him, and not on His immense wealth or on themselves. Each of God's trainees will recognize His provision and special interpersonal contacts because they will have been trained by Him in the habit of being motivated by love in every relationship.

It is in this way that He will lead us to find and accomplish the special and unique lifework that He has measured out[34] for each member who desires to be a part of His team in this life. He will do this because He is the One who will also richly furnish all of the things required for the State which will constitute His future worldwide Kingdom.[35]

ADOPT THE CONSCIOUS DISCIPLINE TO "DRESS UP" YOUR MIND WITH THE NEW, FRESHLY OUTFITTED HUMAN BEING CREATED BY GOD, FOCUSED ON DISCOVERING THE TRUTH ABOUT YOUR LIFE

17It is to this end that I have been enjoined as the one who has been officially summoned by our Commander in Chief as His designated, official, legal lead-witness – to declare[36] the following specific injunction to you all.[37] You all are no longer to conduct your lives according the philosophical schools of thought[38] of any of the rest of the ethnic races or nations of the world – whether they be civilized Greeks or uncivilized Barbarians.[39] You should no longer do this because they hold on to those various philosophical world views motivated by habits of feeling, perceiving and understanding; then formulating purposes, intentions, plans and finally decisions about reality[40] which always prove to be futile and worthless[41] in the end. 18These futile world views slowly but surely cause them to become dulled, enervated and stupefied in their perception and understanding of reality, as well as in their ability to formulate worthwhile purposes and intentions[42] for their lives.

At first, their obtuseness was due to the historical fact that they had been deliberately alienated from legal citizenship in the true lifework and mission of Israel by the corrupt leadership regime within Judaism. However, they now persist in alienating[43] themselves from living the truly vital, authentic and significant lives[44] God desires for them to live due to their own stubborn ignorance, which is the result of the gradual but inevitable process of becoming calloused and indifferent to the welfare of other people[45] and insensitive and dulled in their ethical and moral decision-making faculties.[46]

[19]The inevitable and tragic end of this degrading process is that they eventually sink into despondency and despair[47] on their own. God then reluctantly relinquishes them to become ensnared in every kind of licentious vice involved in the trades of depravity,[48] such as prostitution, and the violence that always accompanies such organized crime rings.[49] Inevitably, the only thing that ends up mattering to them any more is the insatiable greed[50] and arrogant craving and grasping to gain larger and larger shares of loot.

[20]However, in startling contrast, not one of you has ever learned or will ever have acquired the habits[51] of living this degraded way of life – whether it be by study, by practice or by experience – from our future High King. [21]Since it is a fact that you all have most definitely undergone sufficient training and study of Jesus' life and teachings, as well as listened to and heard your teachers with an attitude of obeying Him and His purpose for your lives, it follows that you can be certain that[52] as you continually discover new truths about how to change and discipline your habits of thinking, behaving and living, that the wonderful transformations that will occur in your life will be brought about by Jesus Himself.

[22]The following two images illustrate well how you all can escape from suffering the tragic decay of your minds. First, just as you would "take off" and leave filthy clothing outside[53] before you enter your home, you must also "take off" and leave outside your former lifestyles and habitual ways of viewing things, which were characterized by having your public demeanor, behavior and attitudes unwittingly polluted and sullied by those with whom you formerly associated.[54] Second, you must steer clear of your former lifestyles just as you would avoid being around foolish, acerbic, cynical old folks,[55] who are always complaining to each other about their wasted[56] lives because they think they have been cheated[57] out of what are in reality only empty things that they deluded themselves into believing they wanted out of life.

[23]You must instead resolve to make it your determined habit to relentlessly revive[58] your mental framework and way of feeling, perceiving, understanding, thinking through and then making decisions about reality[59] by consciously depending upon the assistance of the Spirit of God to ascertain the true import of crucial ethical decisions in your life. [24]You must protect your mind from the inevitable decay that comes from allowing false philosophical world views to sully your thoughts.

To continue the illustration of putting on and wearing clothing, in the same way that you deliberately put on and wear certain types of new and beautiful outfits in order to get "dressed up"[60] for different kinds of formal public occasions, you must also adopt the conscious discipline to "dress up" your *mind*. Moreover, you must "dress up" your mind *every day* with the new, bright and freshly outfitted[61] human being that God has created[62] in you in order to do what is good and what is legally and ethically right.[63] As you do so, you will be able to focus[64] your minds totally upon discovering the truth about your life and lifework as God comprehends it.

Do not Grieve God's Spirit, but Consciously Develop Habits of Behavior that Disarm Four Main Traps of the Devil – Lying, Unchecked Anger, Stealing and Criticizing Others.

25In order to become spiritually mature, you must also consciously develop *defensive* mental habits to safeguard your behavior by disarming four main traps Satan will inevitably set for you, which are lying, exploding in unchecked anger, stealing and being critical of other people.

First of all, to continue the above illustration, in the same way that you "take off" and leave filthy clothing outside[65] before you go inside your home, you must "take off" and leave outside your human tendency to evade and not face the truth, by either lying to yourselves or to others. In addition, you must "take off" your predisposition to acquiesce and accept falsehood[66] rather than rigorously find the underlying cause of things and discover what is true. In order to acquire this discipline you must all become committed to the maxim of Zechariah, God's Spokesman, when he said,[67] "Tell each other the truth – each of you with your fellow human beings."[68] You must do this especially in view of the fact that not only are we now fellow colleagues with each other, but also even more so because as His specially selected recruits, we are all destined to become even more intimately trusted associates and members of His future governmental body.

26Second, with regard to handling anger, you must adopt the spirit of David in Psalm 4, where he says, "Acknowledge your feelings of anger, yet do not allow unchecked anger to cause you to miss or fall short[69] of your ultimate goals."[70] To use an illustration from our observation of God's organization of the cosmos, just as the coming of night brings calmness and serenity to the heat and turmoil of the day, so also, as the sun sets at the end of each day, develop the spiritual habit of putting an end to being beside yourself in frustration about the things that have exasperated[71] you that day. 27You must develop this habit of freeing yourself every evening from the exasperating feelings that you will inevitably encounter during each day from certain people and circumstances. You must do this so that you will not inadvertently permit that old deceitful and faultfinding "Slanderer," Satan – who is appropriately named the "Devil"[72] – to have the slightest opening or opportunity[73] to deceive or trap you into a foolish and rash decision or outburst that you will most certainly regret later. You must also avoid such outbursts because they will endanger you by tending to get you sidetracked from focusing on your true lifework for God.

28Third, anyone among you who is taking advantage of others by being a thief, embezzler, con artist, or smuggler[74] must stop stealing. That person should be made to put their own hands to some strenuous or arduous[75] yet worthwhile work or business that involves manual labor[76] – in tending animals, farming, fishing, carpentry or in some other trade or craft. The purpose for doing this is so that they would begin to learn maturity by discovering the value of earning their own living. As they work in this trade, they should be instructed to put some of their earnings aside in a savings account, in order to build some assets. They should do this so that they will be able to give or pay a portion of what they have earned to those who may find themselves in sudden and unexpected need of temporary assistance. It would be even better if they were to reach the point where they could provide lasting employment to others, in order to become part of a larger infrastructure that forms a network of providing services that are useful and helpful to others.[77]

29Fourth, you must prevent the "Slanderer" from manipulating you to your ruin by consciously and deliberately stopping every rotten, foul, disgusting or rancorous[78] thing you might otherwise inadvertently allow yourselves to spew vituperatively out of your mouths about another person in a public setting. On the contrary, you must instead resolve yourselves, with intentional and reflective self-control, to select and speak about only those things that are good about others, namely only those things that tend to build stable and lasting relational structures from groups of otherwise disconnected or even hostile individuals. Make it a careful habit to frame your public speech so that you address others and speak about other people only in constructive[79] ways, in which you make it your objective to ultimately assist or serve those you have in mind in some meaningful way.[80] Learn to orchestrate events such that they not only turn out for the gracious and generous help, encouragement or assistance of those you specifically are focused upon, but also for the benefit of all other people who hear you speak.

30The reason you must arrest and eliminate all of your old bad behavioral habits, attitudes and ways of thinking, speaking and treating others is that when the Specially Selecting Spirit of God observes you continuing to do these things *after He has specially selected you*, it grieves and distresses Him greatly. Remember that He is the same Divine Spirit that specially and intentionally selected[81] each of you for God's future noble and honorable purposes, and that because of this, He is most certainly always watching each of you.

You must always bear in mind the important truth emphasized at the beginning of this Treatise, namely, that the ultimate goal for which the Spirit has officially "sealed" each of you is the exhilarating prospect of the "redemption" of your mortal bodies into resurrected bodies. Remember also that He has also "sealed" you with a view to the "redemption" of all of the other spiritual "interest bearing accounts" in your personalities into which God has been making deposits.[82] Never forget that on the future day that God inaugurates Jesus' Kingdom, it is at that time when He will examine each of our lives, and we will be qualified or disqualified by Him for His High King's Royal Service.

31It is for this reason that all forms of the following thoughts, attitudes, speech and behaviors, like dirty dishes from the table after a meal, must be "cleared away"[83] from your lives. You must "clear away" clinging to a bitter temper of cynical resentment[84] or exploding in impulsive fits of fury or rage that arise from suddenly aroused passions.[85] You must not allow yourselves to slip into a prolonged, settled mood or continuous temperament or disposition of being an acerbic person who has fallen into the habit of harboring anger and holding grudges.[86] You must avoid blowing up in public outbursts of shouting, screaming or shrieking[87] and spouting blasphemous, irreverent speech against God.[88] In addition, you must "clear away" every other kind of disreputable, evil thought, attitude, speech or behavior.

32Instead, you must all become effective in providing whatever services are required that will enable each other to achieve the best and most beneficial outcomes[89] toward accomplishing each person's lifework. As you do this, you must ask for the Spirit's enablement to experience a deep feeling for and an understanding of the misery and suffering of others, as well as a desire to promote its alleviation. This feeling and desire should be accompanied by a sensitive awareness and spiritual consciousness of the personal tragedy that others experience. You should adopt a demeanor of selfless tenderness as you attempt to effectively rescue and assist them to be set free from their dilemmas and predicaments.[90] As you do this, you should always give of yourselves graciously and cheerfully to each other in precisely the same way that God, by means of the example of the life of His future High King, has demonstrated His graciousness to you all.

Notes to Extended Interpretive and Expositional Translation
Ephesians Chapter 4

[1] δέσμιος – This is now the second time Paul has referred to himself using this word. See note at Eph. 3:1 for the extended development of how Paul is using this Greek word for "prisoner" as a metaphor in the unique sense of a "Bond" or "Guarantee."

[2] περιπατέω – Paul has used this verb, περιπατέω, in Eph. 2:2 and 2:10, where it means "deliberately practice a philosophical world view" (see extended note at Eph. 2:2 for philological analysis). He uses this verb now as the main verb of this application section (Chapters 4 and 5), in which it occurs five times and serves as Paul's main outlining verb (4:1, 4:17; 5:2, 5:8 and 5:15) of the section. A brief summary outline of this application section (Chapters 4 and 5) now follows:

a. "Conduct your lives according to this new philosophical world view (περιπατέω) in a manner worthy of the lifework (κλῆσις) to which you have been summoned (καλέω)" [4:1-16].

b. "You must no longer conduct your lives according the philosophical schools of thought (περιπατέω) of the rest of the non-Jewish barbarian nations who follow those philosophical world views (περιπατέω) with futile purposes in their minds" [4:17-31].

c. "You must conduct your lives according to a new philosophical world view (περιπατέω) based on self-sacrificial love (ἀγάπη), exactly as also the future High King has loved (ἀγαπάω) us" [5:1-7].

d. "You must all adopt a philosophy of life in which you conduct yourselves (περιπατέω) as children committed to the enlightened spirit of public vulnerability, mercy, learning and consistency – because the fruit of the Spirit is found in every form of goodness and justice and discovery of truth – thus becoming qualified by our Commander in Chief for future office by means of such character qualities, which are those that earn His distinguished confidence" [5:8-14].

e. "Therefore, see to it that you conduct your lives according to this new philosophical world view (περιπατέω) set forth in this Treatise, by accurately incorporating its specific principles into your lives, no longer living in ethically unskillful ways, but only in ethically skillful ways, buying up every possible opportunity to do good, because the days left in this era will be characterized by much evil" [5:15-21].

[3] "Conduct your lives according to this new philosophical world view (περιπατέω) in a manner worthy of the *lifework* (κλῆσις) to which you have been *summoned* (καλέω)." Paul begins the second half of this Treatise in which his objective is to apply the theological provisions of the first three chapters in the first (Eph. 4:1-16)

of five major specific aspects of common life as the very avenues though which God will enable us to discover our "lifework" (κλῆσις), to which He has deliberately and officially "summoned" (καλέω) each of us as His specially selected recruits. Paul therefore emphasizes the fact that this is the main theme of his Treatise by returning to it to begin the main application section of this Treatise (Chapters 4 and 5), he first introduced in Eph. 1:18, in which he asked God to "enlighten the eyes of your hearts, in order that you might come to realize and accomplish the specific hope of His lifework (κλῆσις) for you." See extended note at Eph. 1:18 for further development of this theme, which in the opinion of this translator, is the most important concept of this Treatise.

[4] βάπτισμα, ατος, τό, **A.** *baptism,* Ev.Matt.3.7, etc.; β. εἰς τὸν θάνατον Ep.Rom.6.4 [LS]. The noun **βάπτισμα** is derived from the verb **βαπτ-ίζω, A.** *dip, plunge,* ξίφος εἰς σφαγήν J.BJ2.18.4; σπάθιον εἰς τὸ ἔμβρυον Sor.2.63:--Pass., of a trephine [**1**: a surgical instrument for cutting out circular sections (as of bone or corneal tissue) – Webster], Gal.10.447; βάπτισον σεαυτὸν εἰς θάλασσαν Plu.2.166a; β. Διόνυσον πρὸς τὴν θάλασσαν ib. 914d:--in Pass., **to be drowned,** Epict.*Gnom*.47; **of ships, sink or disable them,** Plb.1.51.6, 16.6.2 (Pass.); ἐβάπτισαν τὴν πόλιν *flooded* the city, metaph., **of the crowds who flocked into Jerusalem at the time of the siege,** J.BJ4.3.3; β. τινὰ εἰσφοραῖς D.S.1.73; β. τινὰ ὕπνῳ AP11.49 (Even.); ὕπνῳ βεβαπτισμένος Archig. and Posidon. ap. Aët. 6.3:-- Pass., ὡς ἐκ τοῦ βεβαπτίσθαι ἀναπνέουσι Hp.*Epid*.5.63; **to be drenched,** Eub.68: metaph., βεβαπτισμένοι **soaked in wine,** Pl.*Smp*. 176b; ὀφλήμασι βεβ. **over head and ears** in debt, Plu.*Galb*.21; γνοὺς βαπτιζόμενον τὸ μειράκιον **seeing that he was getting into deep water,** Pl.*Euthd*.277d; β. εἰς ἀναισθησίαν καὶ ὕπνον J.*AJ*10.9.4; ὁ τῷ θυμῷ βεβαπτισμένος καταδύεται Ach.Tat.6.19; ψυχή βεβαπτισμένη λύπῃ Lib.*Or*.64.115. **2.** *draw wine by dipping* **the cup in the bowl,** Aristopho 14.5; φιάλαις β. ἐκ . . κρατήρων Plu.*Alex*.67. **3.** *baptize,* [p. 306] τινά Ev.Marc.1.4; ἐν ὕδατι εἰς μετάνοιαν Ev.Matt.3.11:--Pass., βαπτισθήτω ἕκαστος εἰς ἄφεσιν ἁμαρτιῶν Act.Ap.2.38; εἰς Χριστόν Ep.Rom.6.3, etc.:--Med., *dip oneself,* LXX4 Ki.5.14; **get oneself baptized,** Act.Ap.22.16, *1 Ep.Cor*.10.2:--Pass., *perform ablutions, Ev.Luc.* 11.38 [LS]. Thus, the noun "baptism" and the verb "baptize" are not helpful as translations, because they are in reality only transliterations (**βαπτίζω** = *baptizō* = "baptize"). The word is a common noun and verb used in Greek denotatively to mean "dip, immerse, sink, flood, drench, soak in water (or in wine)." Proposed translation: "immersed under water."

[5] See Matthew 28:19-20; Mark 16:15-16.

[6] See Exodus Chapter 14, and 1 Corinthians 10:1-4.

[7] See Joshua Chapter 3.

[8] See 2 Kings Chapter 5. Jesus thinks this story remarkable enough to include it in his public teaching (Luke 4:27).

[9] See Matthew 3:1-12; Mark 1:1-8; Luke 3:1-18; John 1:19-34.

[10] See John 4:1-2.

[11] See Matthew 3:13-17; Mark 1:9-12; Luke 3:21-22.

[12] μέτρον, τό, *that by which anything is measured*: **1.** *measure, rule,* μέτρ' ἐν χερσὶν ἔχοντες Il.12.422; **b. Math.,** *measure, divisor,* Eratosth. ap. Nicom.*Ar.*1.13, etc. **2.** *measure of content,* **whether solid or liquid,** δῶκεν μέθυ, χίλια μ. Il.7.471; also of smaller units, as μ. ἐξαχοίνικον ib.105.40 (ii B.C.); μέτροις καὶ σταθμοῖς *by measure* **and weight,** Decr. ap. And.1.83; **in the widest sense, either** *weight* **or** *measure,* Φείδωνος τοῦ τὰ μ. ποιήσαντος Πελοποννησίοισι Hdt.6.127;...**3.** *any space measured* **or** *measurable, length, size,* **in pl.,** *dimensions,* μέτρα κελεύθου *the length* **of the way,** Od.4.389;...[LS]. Paul uses this important word for "measure" within the context of his second major extended metaphor of God as our "Builder" or "Developer" in the area of the construction and building of the vital relational structures He will found and build upon a total of three times in this Treatise: here in Eph. 4:7, and in Eph. 4:13 and 4:16. Anyone who builds buildings or develops property knows how important it is to not only get the measurements and dimensions of the project correct during the construction phase, but also to continually monitor and measure how much of the building (or apartment complex, etc.) is leased out when it is completed and put into service. In the same way, God not only "measures out" the extent and degree of the divine gifts He gives to us (e.g., the "construction phase"), but what is also implied by this is that after He has given us a gift that He has wisely measured out for each one of us, He follows up by contining to "measure" our progress in how faithfully or well we are putting those gifts into use for Him (e.g. the "placing into service phase"). See follow-up notes at Eph. 4:13 and Eph. 4:16.

[13] Psalm 68:18 in the Septuagint (LXX), reads as follows:

Psalm 68:18 ἀνέβης εἰς ὕψος, ᾐχμαλώτευσας αἰχμαλωσίαν, ἔλαβες δόματα ἐν ἀνθρώπῳ, καὶ γὰρ ἀπειθοῦντες τοῦ κατασκηνῶσαι.

Transl. "You have ascended on high, You have led captives into captivity, You have received gifts among human beings, even from the rebellious, that He [God] might dwell there."

The specific differences between the original text of the Psalm in the Septuagint and how Paul interprets it are four in number, as follows:

1. ἀνέβης (LXX) is 2 p. sing. aor. act. ind. = "*You ascended...*"; vs. Ἀναβὰς (Paul) is 3. aor. act. participle, nom., sing., masc. = "*When He ascended...*"

2. ᾐχμαλώτευσας (LXX) is 2 p. sing. aor. act. ind. = "*You led* [captives] *into captivity...*"; vs. ᾐχμαλώτευσεν (Paul) is 3 p. sing. 1 aor. act. ind. = "*He led* [captives] *into captivity...*"

3. ἔλαβες δόματα ἐν ἀνθρώπῳ (LXX) is 2 p. sing. aor. act. ind. = "*You received* gifts among human beings..."; vs. ἔδωκε δόματα τοῖς ἀνθρώποις (Paul) is 3 p. sing. 1 aor. act. ind. [Second person vs. third person, and Paul uses a completely different verb: δίδωμι = "to give"] = "*He gave* gifts to human beings..."

4. καὶ γὰρ ἀπειθοῦντες τοῦ κατασκηνῶσαι (LXX) = "even from the rebellious, that He [God] might dwell there", vs. Paul, who does not include this last phrase.

In the Psalm, God the Father is addressing God the Son, recounting for Him the comprehensive sequence of important events in His Career. The Psalm prophesies three major events: First, the ascension of the Messiah to heaven following His first Visit to earth; second, the Son being given the authority to confine the devil and his evil angels into captivity in the bottomless pit for 1,000 years (Rev. 20:1-3), and third, the celebration of the Inauguration Banquet and Ceremony that launches the Millennial Kingdom age, when Jesus returns for His second Visit to earth, when He receives gifts and gives gifts to human beings, at the beginning of His 1,000 year reign over the entire earth from Jersualem, His Capital City.

[14] See Revelation Chapters 19 – 22.

[15] Peter (Simon; "Peter" = Πέτρος = "Rocky" is the nickname given to Simon by Jesus), the brothers James and John, sons of Zebedee, nicknamed "Sons of Thunder" by Jesus, Andrew (Peter's brother), Philip, Thomas, Bartholomew (Nathaniel), Matthew, James the son of Alphaeus, Simon the Zealot, Judas the brother of James, and Matthias. See Acts 1:13-26.

[16] See Eph. 3:1-13. See also Rom. 11:13.

[17] μέτρον – "measure" – see note at Eph. 4:7 on the philology and meaning of this word (first "measuring out" in an initial phase of construction, followed by "measuring" in the sense of evaluating performance). Jesus clearly communicates the concepts of both "measuring out" and "giving gifts" to His "servants," and then "measuring" or "evaluating" how they used those gifts, in two of His most noteworthy parables: the Parable of the Talents in Matthew 25:14-31, and the Parable of the Minas in Luke 19:11-26. These two Parables now follow. Note the precision of the similarity of the grammar with regard to the verb δίδωμι = "to give":

> **The Parable of the Talents – Matthew 25:14-31:** "For it is like a man, going into another country, who called his own servants (τοὺς ἰδίους δούλους), and entrusted his goods to them. ¹⁵To one he gave (ἔδωκεν = δίδωμι, 3rd sing. aor. act. = δῶρον [noun] = "gift" [cf. Eph. 2:8; 3:7; 4:7]), five talents, to another two, to another one; to each according to his own ability (ἑκάστῳ κατὰ τὴν ἰδίαν δύναμιν). Then he went on his journey. ¹⁶Immediately he who received the five talents went and traded with them, and made another five talents. ¹⁷In like manner he also who got the two gained another two. ¹⁸But he who received the one went away and dug in the earth, and hid his lord's (τοῦ κυρίου αὐτοῦ) money. ¹⁹Now after a long time the lord (ὁ κύριος) of those servants came, and reconciled accounts with them (συναίρει λόγον μετ' αὐτῶν). ²⁰He who received the five talents came and brought another five talents, saying, 'Lord (Κύριε), you delivered (παρέδωκας) to me five talents. Behold, I have gained another five talents besides them.' ²¹"His lord (ὁ κύριος) said to him, 'Well done, good and faithful servant. You have been faithful over a few things, I will set you over many things. Enter into the joy of your lord.' ²²"He also who got the two talents came and said, 'Lord (Κύριε), you delivered (παρέδωκας) to me two talents. Behold, I have

gained another two talents besides them.' ²³"His lord (ὁ κύριος) said to him, 'Well done, good and faithful servant. You have been faithful over a few things, I will set you over many things. Enter into the joy of your lord.' ²⁴"He also who had received the one talent came and said, 'Lord (Κύριε), I knew you that you are a hard man, reaping where you did not sow, and gathering where you did not scatter. ²⁵I was afraid, and went away and hid your talent in the earth. Behold, you have what is yours.' ²⁶"But his lord answered him, 'You wicked and slothful servant. You knew that I reap where I didn't sow, and gather where I didn't scatter. ²⁷You ought therefore to have deposited my money with the bankers, and at my coming I should have received back my own with interest. ²⁸Take away therefore the talent from him, and give (**δότε** = **δίδωμι** *2nd pl aor imperat act* = **δῶρον** [noun] = "gift" [cf. Eph. 2:8; 3:7; 4:7]), it to him who has the ten talents. ²⁹For to everyone who has will be given (**δοθήσεται** = **δίδωμι** *3rd sg fut ind pass*), and he will have abundance, but from him who has not, even that which he has will be taken away. ³⁰Throw out the unprofitable servant into the darkness outside, where there will be weeping and gnashing of teeth.' ³¹"But when the Son of Man comes at His Appearing (δόξα), and all the holy angels with him, then he will sit on His throne at His Appearing" [δόξα – verse 31 transl. – GWC].

The Parable of the Minas – Luke 19:11-26: As they heard these things, he (Jesus) went on and told a parable, because he was near Jerusalem, and they supposed that the Kingdom of God would be revealed immediately. ¹²He said therefore, "A certain nobleman went into a far country to receive for himself a kingdom, and to return. ¹³He called ten servants of his (δούλους ἑαυτοῦ), and gave (**ἔδωκεν** = **δίδωμι**, *3rd sing. aor. act.* = **δῶρον** [noun] = "gift" [cf. Eph. 2:8; 3:7; 4:7]), them ten minas, and told them, 'Conduct business until I come.' ¹⁴But his citizens hated him, and sent an envoy after him, saying, 'We don't want this man to reign over us.' ¹⁵"It happened when he had come back again, having received the kingdom, that he commanded these servants, to whom he had given (**δεδώκει** = **δίδωμι**, *3rd sg plup ind act*) the money, to be called to him, that he might know (γνοῖ = *3rd sg optative*) what they had gained by conducting business. ¹⁶The first came before him, saying, 'Lord (Κύριε), your mina has made ten more minas.' ¹⁷"He said to him, 'Well done, you good servant! Because you were found faithful in a very little, you shall have authority over ten cities (ἴσθι ἐξουσίαν ἔχων ἐπάνω δέκα πόλεων).' ¹⁸"The second came, saying, 'Your mina, Lord (κύριε), has made five minas.' ¹⁹"So he said to him, 'And you are to be over five cities.' ²⁰Another came, saying, 'Lord, behold, your mina, which I kept laid away in a handkerchief, ²¹for I feared you, because you are an exacting man. You take up that which you didn't lay down, and reap that which you didn't sow.' ²²"He said to him, 'Out of your own mouth will I judge you, you wicked servant! You knew that I am an exacting man, taking up that which I didn't lay down, and reaping that which I didn't sow. ²³Then why didn't you deposit my money in the bank, and at my coming, I might have earned interest on it?' ²⁴He said to those who stood by, 'Take the mina away from him, and give (**δότε** = **δίδωμι** *2nd pl aor imperat act* = **δῶρον** [noun] = "gift" [cf. Eph. 2:8; 3:7; 4:7]), it to him who has the ten minas.' ²⁵"They said to him, 'Lord, he has ten minas!' ²⁶'For I tell you that to everyone who has, will more be given (**δοθήσεται** = **δίδωμι** *3rd sg fut ind pass*); but from him who doesn't have, even that which he has will be taken away from him.'"

¹⁸ **νήπιος** – **A.** *infant, child,* freq. in Hom., νήπιον, οὔ πω εἰδόθ' ὁμοιίου πολέμοιο Il.9.440;...τὸ ν. Pl.*Ax.*366d; ἁρμόττουσα τοῖς ν. [πλαταγή] Arist.*Pol.*1340b30; ἐκ

νηπίου **from** *a child,* **from** *infancy,* [τὸ ἡδὺ] ἐκ ν. ἡμῖν συντέθραπται Id.*EN*1105a2;...*infant* **in law,** *minor,* ἐφ' ὅσον ὁ κληρονόμος ν. ἐστιν *Ep.Gal.*4.1; **of children up to puberty,** αἱ τῶν ν. ἐκλάμψιες Hp.*Epid.*6.1.4 (cf. Herophil. ap. Gal.17(1).826); but of the foetus in its early stage, Hp.*Aph.*4.1 (cf. Gal.17(1).653)...**II.** metaph., **1.** of the understanding, *childish, silly,* Od.13.237; μέγα ν. Il.16.46, cf. Od.9.44; simply, *without foresight, blind,* Il.22.445; ἀνὴρ ν. Heraclit.79, cf. Emp.11.1, Pi.*P.*3.82, A.*Pr.*443, Democr.76, etc.; ν. ὃς . . γονέων ἐπιλάθεται S.*El.*145 (lyr.); οὔτε πρὶν νήπιον, νῦν τ' . . μέγαν **no** *child* **before and now full-grown** (i.e. in mind), Id.*OT* 652 (lyr.); of words, νήπια βάζεις Pi.*Fr.*157; ἀντιτείνειν νήπι' ἀντὶ νηπίων E.*Med.*891; μηδὲν εἴπῃς ν. Ar.*Nu.*105 [LS]. Proposed translation: "naïve, purile, gullible and thus vulnerable (not considering the consequences of our attitudes, behaviors and actions)."

[19] κλυδωνίζω, Suid.: – elsewh. in Pass., **to be** *buffeted, swept by heavy seas,* τὸν κυβερνήτην -ίζεσθαι καὶ ἀστοχεῖν θαλασσομαχοῦντα Vett. Val. 354.26; -ομένη ναῦς Phlp.in APo.381.7: **usu. metaph.,** *to be disturbed, thrown into confusion,* οἱ ἄδικοι κλυδωνισθήσονται LXX Is.57.20;...**to be tossed about,** παντὶ ἀνέμῳ τῆς διδασκαλίας *Ep.Eph.*4.14 [LS]. Proposed translation: "disturbed, confused."

[20] περιφέρω...**III.** Pass., *go round, rotate,* ἐν τῷ αὐτῷ κύκλῳ Pl.*Prm.*138c;...**of argument,** εἰς ταὐτὸ π. ἀεί Pl.*Grg.*517c, cf. *Lg.*659d; εἰς τὰ πρότερα Id.*R.*456b. **2.** *wander about,* X.*Cyn.*3.5;...*to be unstable,* ἡ περιφερομένη εἱμαρμένη Id.*Aem.*27, cf. *Galb.*6; περιφερόμενοι τύπτουσι *at random,* Arist.*Metaph.* 985a14 [LS]. Proposed translation: "to become disoriented by having our minds be spun around in all directions by others." One thinks here of the well-known story of *The Adventures of Pinocchio,* by C. Collodi.

[21] **πλάνης,** ητος, ὁ, *wanderer, vagabond,* ib.1029, E.*IT*417, Isoc.19.6: c. gen., πόντου πλάνητες *roamers of the sea,* Trag.Adesp.100. **2.** πλάνητες ἀστέρες *planets:*...τοὺς ἀστέρας τοὺς ἐνδεδεμένους, τοὺς δὲ π. Arist. *Cael.*290a19 [LS]. To the Ancient Greeks, planets were the "stars" that "wandered," from what astronomers now realize to be the phenomenon of retrograde motion. Proposed translation: "transients, pirates, con artists; those that wander from town to town whose only motive is to swindle or fool people into some confidence scheme to take their money." One thinks here of the "traveling salesman" played by Robert Preston in "The Music Man" (by Meredith Wilson, 1962), whose goal was to sell musical instruments to the naïve parents of the children of a small midwestern town, and then quickly leave town with the profits before he taught the children to play them; or of the "King" and the "Duke" in *Huckleberry Finn,* by Mark Twain.

[22] **πανουργία,** ἡ, *knavery,* A. Th.603, S.Ph.927, Lys.22.16, Pl.*Lg.*747c, Arist.*EN*1144a27: in pl., *villainies,* S.*Ant.*300, Ar.*Eq.*684, etc.[LS]. A "knave" is an Old English word for a "scoundrel, a swindler, or a fraud" [W]. Proposed translation: "scoundrel, swindler, fraud."

[23] **μεθοδεία** or **μεθοδία, ἡ,** *craft, wiliness, Ep.Eph.*4.14: pl., μ. τοῦ διαβόλου ib.6.11. [LS]. The transliteration of this word is the English word "method"

(μεθοδεία = *methodeia* = method). However, the English word "method" has by now lost the negative connotative meaning of the original Greek notion. Craftiness and wiliness are from Old English *cræftig* = strong, skillful, from *cræft* + *-ig -y* 1 dialect chiefly Britain: skillful, clever, ingenious; 2 obsolete: showing skill, skillfully made; 3: adept at deceiving others: cunning, wily, sly [W]. Proposed translation: "to deceive by using skillful, cunning, fraudulent schemes."

²⁴ ἄνεμος [ᾰ], ὁ, *wind*...ἀνέμου κατιόντος μεγάλου *a gale* having come on, Th.2.25;...metaph., ἄνεμος . . ἄνθρωπος *'unstable as the wind,'* Eup.376; φέρειν τιν' ἄρας (sic l.) ἄ. a very wind to carry off, Antiph.195.5 (Lobeck); ἀνέμους θηρᾶν ἐν δικτύοις *try to catch the wind*, and ἀνέμῳ διαλέγεσθαι *talk to the wind*, Zen.1.38; ἀνέμους γεωργεῖν *'plough the sands'*, ib.100. [LS]. When used as a metaphor, the word ἄνεμος seems to convey the notion of unreliability, instability, as well as the idea of extremely rapid and violent change, volatility. Proposed translation: "unreliable, volatile."

²⁵ κυβεία, ἡ, *dice-playing*, Pl.*Phdr*.274d, X.*Mem*.1.3.2, Aen.Tact.5.2, Men.481.10 (pl.), etc. [LS]. Paul seems to be using this word as a metaphor for the incorrect but all-too-common human attitude of living one's life and making major life-decisions based on chance or a gamble, i.e., playing the lottery, gambling in Las Vegas, etc. Proposed translation: "regarding major choices in life as decisions to be made by sheer chance, a gamble or a mere roll of the dice."

²⁶ Paul introduced the concept of the corporate "growth" of the members of the ἐκκλησία into a harmonious, logical "building" or "relational structure" (οἰκοδομή) in Eph. 2:21 (see note). He now returns to this theme here in Eph. 4:15 and 16.

²⁷ κεφαλή – Paul used the term "head" (κεφαλή) in this sense, i.e., "the leader," first in Eph. 1:22.

²⁸ ἀληθεύω, *speak truth*, [p. 64] A.*Th*.562, Hp.*Prog*.15, Pl.*R*.589c; περί τι Id.*Tht*.202b: with neut. Adj., ἀ. πάντα *speak truth* **in all things**, Batr.14; πολλὰ ἀ. X.*An*.4.4.15; τὰς δέκα ἡμέρας ἠλήθευσε he *rightly foretold* . . , ib.5.6.18; ἀ. τοὺς ἐπαίνους *prove their praises true*, Luc.*Ind*.20; τοὔνομα **'make good'**, Them.*Or*.1.4c. **2. of things**, *to be, prove true*, σημεῖα Hp.*Prog*.25...freq. in Arist.:--Act. **of reasoners**, *arrive at truth*, Id.*Metaph*.1062a25...[LS]. Proposed translation: "continuing to discover and speak publicly what is true about ourselves and others." See extended note on ἀλήθεια at Eph. 1:13.

²⁹ Paul is returning to his main theme of "ἐν ἀγάπῃ" = "by means of self-sacrifical love," introduced in Eph.4:2. He will emphasize it here in Eph. 4:15 and 16 (where it occurs twice in close context), and he will return to this theme again in Eph. 5:1.

[30] It is important here to remind ourselves that the Greek word for "being carefully joined together" in verse 16 is **συναρμολογουμένη** (see philological analysis of this word at Eph. 2:21).

[31] **συμβιβάζω**, causal of συμβαίνω, *bring together*: Pass., *to be put together, to be knit together, framed,* ἔκ τινος *Ep.Eph.***4:16**, *Ep.Col.*2.19. **2**. metaph., *bring to terms, reconcile,* Hdt.1.74; ς. τινά τινι *reconcile* one to another, Th.2.29; ς. [τινὰς] εἰς τὸ μέσον, as mediator, Pl.*Prt.*337e: abs., *bring about an agreement,* IG12.57.24. **II.** *put together, compare, examine,* τὰ λεγόμενα Pl.*Hp.Mi.*369d;...**III.** *elicit a logical consequence, infer* (cf. συμβαίνω III.3 b), Arist.*Top.*155a25, *SE*181a22;...Ocell.3.3:--Pass., συμβιβασθέντος *when the conclusion has been drawn,* v.l. in Arist.*SE*179a30. **2.** *teach, instruct,* συμβιβάσω ὑμᾶς ἃ ποιήσετε LXX *Ex.* 4.15; συμβιβάσεις τοὺς υἱούς σου ib.*De.*4.9, cf. *Is.*40.14, *1 Ep.Cor.*2.16 [LS]. Thus, both in the LXX and in Paul, the verb **συμβιβάζω** most likely means something like, "to be able, because of being taught well, to logically conclude the truth about something," or more colloquially, as when we say about a good teacher: "that teacher really enabled me to 'put it all together (in my mind)'."

[32] **ἐπιχορηγία** = "supply, provision, fortune." This word only occurs twice in the NT; here in Eph. 4:16 and in Phil. 1:19. It is the emphatic form of the much more common word **χορηγία** = *office or* λῃτουργία *of a χορηγός, one who is wealthy enough to pay for the cost of the public choruses,* Antipho 2.3.8 (pl.), 5.77 (pl.), Th.6.16 (pl.), etc.: used generally of λῃτουργίαι other than the τριηραρχία, Lys.19.57 (pl.), D.20.19 (pl.), Lex ap. eund. 18.106. **2.** generally, *expense,* Democr.282. **II.** generally, *abundance of external means, fortune,* ἡ ἐκτὸς χ. Arist.*EN*1178a24, cf. *Pol.*1255a14, al.; πολιτικὴ χ. *things necessary to furnish* or *constitute* a state, ib.1326a5: pl., βασιλικαὶ χ. Jul.*Ep.*89b; πρόγονοι καὶ χ. καὶ δόξα *great fortunes,* Lib.*Or.*33.20 [LS]. Proposed translation: "vast fortune from which a benefactor draws in order to invest in other people."

[33] **ἁφή, ἡ,** ([ἅπτω]) *lighting, kindling,* περὶ λύχνων ἁφάς **about lamp-***lighting time,* Hdt.7.215, cf.*PTeb.*88.12 (ii B. C.), D.H.11.33, D.S.19.31, Ath.12.526c. **II.** ([ἅπτομαι]) *touch,* ἐπώνυμον δὲ τῶν Διὸς γέννημ' ἁφῶν (Wieseler for γεννημάτων) τέξεις . . Ἔπαφον A.*Pr.*850. **2.** *sense of touch,* Pl.*R.*523e, cf. Arist.*EN*1118b1, *de An.*424a12;...**3.** *touch of the harp-strings,* metaph., ἐμμελοῦς ἁφῆς καὶ κρούσεως Plu.*Per.*15;...**4. grip, in wrestling,** etc., ἁφὴν ἐνδιδόναι αὑτοῦ Plu.2.86f...**5.** *sand sprinkled over wrestlers, to enable them to get a grip of one another,* Arr.*Epict.*3.15.4; ἁφῇ πηλώσασθαι *IG*4.955 (Epid., ii A. D.). **6. Math.,** *contact of surfaces, etc.,* Arist.*Ph.*227a17, *Metaph.*1014b22, al.; *point of contact,* Euc.*Phaen.*p.16M., al.; *of intersection,* Papp. 988.9, cf. Alex.Aphr. in *Top.*24.16. **7.** in pl., *stripes, strokes,* LXX *2 Ki.*7.14, al...**III.** *junction, point of contact* in the body, Arist.*GC*326b12, 327a12; *ligament,* **Ep.Eph.4:16,** *Ep.Col.*2.19 [LS]. Although the meaning for the word **ἁφή** as "joint" or "ligament" in the anatomy of the human body was first introduced by Tyndale ("the body ys coupled and

knet togedder in every ioynt"), from analysis of the above texts, the meaning of "joint" or "ligament" for the word ἁφή is highly unlikely. While Liddell-Scott attribute this meaning to Aristotle in *On Generation and Corruption*, line 326b12, upon inspection of that text, Aristotle does not mean "joint" or "ligament." In that text Aristotle is criticizing the metaphysical philosophy of Atomism, which claims that reality is composed of "atoms" that are only separable at their points of "contact" (ἁφή). So even in Aristotle's text the word ἁφή means a "point-of-touching" or "point of contact." Thus, due to the great majority (total of 41 occurrences of this word in all Greek texts available) of instances in which the denotational meaning of this word is "touch, grip, or point of contact," from which the connotational meaning of "lighting, kindling" (a lamp, e.g., by 'touching' it with a lighting instrument of some kind), Paul probably is using this word as a metaphor to convey the idea that we are "lighted" (or better in English, "enlightened") when we are "touched" by God's Spirit. This symbolism is completely consistent with the doctrine of how God enlightens people by "touching" them with "divine fire" in the Bible (e.g. Moses and the burning bush in Exodus 3, the Apostles in Acts 2, etc.). Thus, the proposed translation is something like, "the enlightenment that comes from genuinely being *'in touch'* with others, or of authentically coming into *contact* with the Spirit of God."

[34] μέτρον – "measure" – see note at Eph. 4:7 on the philology of this word, but also note at Eph. 4:13 for its primary application.

[35] Ephesians 4:16 is difficult to translate. In addition to the Extended Interpretive and Expositional Translation and the Basic Translation presented here, the following translation is offered as a literal "word-for-word" translation – attempting to follow the word order of the Greek text as close as possible:

> Eph. 4:16 ὁ Χριστός, ἐξ οὗ πᾶν τὸ σῶμα συναρμολογούμενον καὶ συμβιβαζόμενον διὰ πάσης ἁφῆς τῆς ἐπιχορηγίας, κατ' ἐνέργειαν ἐν μέτρῳ ἑνὸς ἑκάστου μέρους, τὴν αὔξησιν τοῦ σώματος ποιεῖται εἰς οἰκοδομὴν ἑαυτοῦ ἐν ἀγάπῃ.
>
> Transl. "The High King, from whom every body member is being incorporated into a rational organization structured to function in harmony as a pleasant and enjoyable whole, and from whom each one is being taught to "put it all together," is, by means of every enlightening contact of provision supplied according to the portion worked out by measure for each one, growing each body member, making them all into the governmental administration for Himself by means of self-sacrificial love."

[36] λέγω – **1. to say, speak**, Hdt., Trag., etc.; λέγε say on, Hdt.; so, λέγοις ἄν Plat.: **of oracles, to say, declare**, Hdt.[LS]. Here, Paul is making an official, legally binding "declaration" of God's specific will to all of the non-Jewish Greek and Barbarian ethnic groups and nations. The word likely has the same force as when the founders of America used it in their "*Declaration* of Independence" from Great Britain.

⁳⁷ μαρτύρομαι...--*call to witness, invoke,* c. acc. pers., Antipho 1.29, S.OC813, etc.; *esp. of the gods,* Ἄρτεμιν, γαῖαν καὶ θεούς, E.Hipp.1451, Ph.626;...c. part., μαρτύρομαι τυπτόμενος *I call you to witness that...,*Ar.Av.1031, cf. E.HF858 (troch.) [LS]. Thus, **μαρτύρομαι** means "to be summoned to testify as an official, legal witness, especially by a divinity."

³⁸ περιπατέω – See note at Eph. 4:1.

³⁹ ἔθνος – "a member from any of the ethnic races or nations foreign to Judaism – whether they be civilized Greeks or uncivilized Barbarians" – see extended note at Eph. 2:11.

⁴⁰ νόος, νόου, ὁ, freq. in later philosophy: **1. mind, as employed in perceiving and thinking,** *sense, wit,* οὐ λῆθε Διὸς πυκινὸν ν. Il.15.461;...νόῳ *prudently,* Od.6.320; παρὲκ νόον *senselessly,* Il.20.133; σὺν νόῳ *wisely,* Hdt.8.86;...νόῳ λαβεῖν τι **to apprehend it,** Hdt.3.51; νόῳ σχεῖν, ἔχειν, *recall, remember,* Id.5.92.ή, Pl.*R.*490a;...**2.** νοῦν ἔχειν **in two senses, a. to have** *sense,* **be** *sensible,* S.*Tr.*553, etc.;...**b.** νοῦν or τὸν ν. ἔχειν **to have** *one's mind* **directed to something,** ἄλλοσ' ὄμμα, θητέρᾳ δὲ ν. ἔχειν S.*Tr.*272;...**3. mind, more widely, as employed in feeling, deciding, etc.,** *heart,* χαῖρε νόῳ Od.8.78;;...ἐκ παντὸς νόου **with all his** *heart and soul,* Hdt.8.97; τῷ νῷ . . κἀπὸ τῆς γλώσσης **in heart as well as tongue,** S.*OC* 936: freq. in phrase κατὰ νόον **according to one's** *mind,* Hdt.1.117, 7.104; εἰ τάδ' ἔχει κατὰ νοῦν κείνῳ S.*OC*1768 (anap.);...**4. mind, resolve, purpose,** ἀγαθῷ νόῳ, i.e. kindly, Hdt.1.60; τί σοι ἐν νόῳ ἐστὶ ποιέειν; **what do you** *intend* **to do?** ib.109; ἡμῖν ἐν ν. ἐγένετο εἰπεῖν Id.9.46; ἐν ν. ἔχειν c. fut. inf., **to intend** . . , Id.1.10 (v.l.): c. pres. inf., ib. 27, Pl.*R.*344d; ποιέειν τι ἐπὶ νόον τινί **to put into his** *mind* **to do** . . , Hdt.1.27;...**5. reason, intellect,** νόου φρενί Xenoph.25,...**II.** *act of mind, thought,* ἡμῖν δ' οὔ τις τοῦδε νόος καὶ μῆτις ἀμείνων Il.15.509;...**2. purpose, design,** νόον τελεῖν τινι Il.23.149; σάφα οἶσθ' οἷος ν. Ἀτρεΐωνος 2.192. **III. sense, meaning of a word,** etc., οὗτος ὁ νόος τοῦ ῥήματος Hdt.7.162;...**meaning of a work of art,** Philostr.*VA*4.28; πολὺς ν. ἐν ὀλίγῃ λέξει συνέσταλται Plu.2.510e; πρὸς τὸν αὐτὸν νοῦν **to the same** *effect,* Str.15.3.7; πρὸς νοῦν οὐδὲν λέγοντες **to the** *point,* Phld.*Mus.*p.96K.; οὐδὲ νοῦν ἔχον *senseless,* Id.*Po.*5.29 [LS]. Proposed translation: "to formulate a philosophical world view motivated by habits of feeling, perceiving, understanding, and reasoned thinking, then go on to resolve purposes, intentions, plans and finally decisions about reality."

⁴¹ ματαιότης, ητος, ἡ, *vanity, purposelessness,* ματαιότης ματαιοτήτων LXX Ec.1.2, cf. Ph.1.426; τῇ μ. ἡ κτίσις ὑπετάγη *Ep.Rom.*8.20; *folly,* ἀνθρώπων Phld.Rh.2.26 S [LS]. Proposed translation: "futile, worthless."

⁴² σκοτόω, *darken, blind,* σκοτώσω βλέφαρα καὶ δεδορκότα S.Aj.85; *stupefy,* Sor.1.125 (Act. and Pass.); *make dizzy,* τὰς ὄψεις Ph.Byz. Mir.2.5: metaph., *Ep.Eph.*4:18:--Pass., *to be in darkness, suffer from vertigo,* like σκοτοδινιάω, Pl.*R.*518a,...Plb.10.13.8; ἕλμινθες -ωθεῖσαι *stupefied,* Herod.Med. ap. Aët. 9.37, cf. Gal.16.657. [LS]. The analysis of the word "stupefy" in Webster is as follows:

Etymology: Middle French *stupefier*, modification (influenced by Middle French -fier -fy) of Latin *stupefacere*, from *stupēre* to be benumbed, be astonished, be stupefied + *facere* to make. **1 a:** to make physically stupid, dull, or insensible, to dull the sensibilities of individuals who must undergo pain **b:** to blunt or deaden the faculties of perception and understanding of [W]. Proposed translation: "to become dulled, enervated and stupefied in one's perception and understanding of reality, as well as in one's purposes and intentions."

[43] The word ἀπηλλοτριόω occurs only three times in the in the New Testament, of which two occurrences are in Ephesians. This word was used by Paul earlier in Eph. 2:18 where he was describing how the non-Jewish barbarian nations had been deliberately "alienated" from legal citizenship within the true lifework and mission of the authentic Israel by the corrupt leadership regime within Judaism.

[44] Greek uses two main words for the English word "life:" ζωή and βίος. The word ζωή refers to qualitative spiritual and emotional life = "verve, vitality, vigor, significance, and finding authentic meaning" – as in the expression, "She makes me come alive," or "now we're really living." The word βίος refers to the quantitative concept of the physiological processes with respect to the natural organism itself = "biological life form."

[45] πώρωσις, εως, ἡ, *process by which the extremities of fractured bones are reunited by a callus*, Hp. Fract.23 (pl.), Art.15, Gal.1.387. [LS]. And, thus, Webster: "**cal·lous**" – Etymology: Middle French *calleux*, from Latin *callosus*, from *callum, callus* callous skin; akin to Sanskrit *kina* callosity, Old Irish *calath* hard, **1:** hardened and thickened having callouses **2a:** hardened in sensibility: feeling no emotion **b:** feeling no sympathy for others: without regard for the feelings or welfare of others: indifferent to the suffering of others [W]. Therefore, the word πώρωσις does not mean "hard," in the denotative physiological sense. Paul is using the word πώρωσις as a metaphor to mean something like: "a tough layer of habits that are gradually built up over time that decrease one's ability to sense or feel things – to disregard and become indifferent to the welfare of other people."

[46] καρδία = "heart;" see the extended note at Eph. 1:18.

[47] ἀπαλγέω, A. put away sorrow for, τὰ ἴδια Th.2.61; ἀ. τὸ πένθος Plu. Cleom.22; τὸ πάθος Procop.Arc.16. **II.** generally, *to be despondent*, ἀ. ταῖς ἐλπίσιν Plb.9.40.4; πρὸς ἐλπίδα D.C.48.37: abs., Plb.1.35.5, ***Ep.Eph.*4:19** [LS]. The word ἀπαλγέω occurs only one time in the NT: here in Eph. 4:19. It does not mean "repentance" (Tyndale – "repentaunce") or "feeling" (KJV). The verb ἀπαλγέω means "to deliberately (and foolishly) choose to give up hope" = "to despair" or "to be despondent." This meaning is very clear in the following passage from Polybius' *Histories*, 1.35.5 (ed. Theodorus Büttner-Wobst after L. Dindorf, Leipzig, 1893; transl. Evelyn S. Shuckburgh, London, 1889):

"Again, we are taught the truth of that saying of Euripides – One wise man's skill is worth a world in arms. For it was one man, one brain, that defeated the numbers which were believed to be invincible and able to accomplish anything; and *restored to confidence a whole city that was unmistakably and utterly ruined, and the spirits of its army which had sunk to the* **lowest depths of despair** (τὸ δὲ προφανῶς πεπτωκὸς ἄρδην πολίτευμα καὶ τὰς **ἀπηλγηκυίας** ψυχὰς τῶν δυνάμεων ἐπὶ τὸ κρεῖττον ἤγαγεν)."

[48] **ἀκαθαρσία** – Lit. "un-cleanness" [in and ethical or moral sense]. See expanded note at Eph. 5:3 for further philological analysis. Proposed translation: "depravity."

[49] **ἐργασία**, Ion. -ιη, Cret. ϝεργασία *Leg.Gort.*8.44, ἡ, ([ἐργάτης]) ***work, business***, ἐργασίην φεύγουσα *h.Merc.*486, etc.;...μὴ γενομένης ἐργασίας **if no *work* was done**, D.27.20;...**3**. generally, ***trade, business***, X.*Mem.*3.10.1; ἐπὶ τῆς ἐργασίας ὧν τῆς κατὰ θάλατταν **engaged in *trade* by sea**, D.33.4; ἡ ἐ. τῆς τραπέζης the **banking *business***, Id.36.6; ἐ. χρυσοχοϊκή, ἀρωματική, *PLond.*3.906.6 (ii A.D.), *PFay.*93.7 (ii A.D.);...**esp. of *a courtesan's trade***, Hdt.2.135, D.18.129; **of sexual *intercourse***, Arist.*Pr.*876a39. [LS]. Paul is probably referring to the organized crime surrounding those who, have given up hope, and in despair, consign themselves to make a living or to "work" in the "businesses" of human vice, e.g.; gambling, prostitution, drug addiction, and the violence that is inevitably committed in organized crime.

[50] **πλεονεξία**, Ion. -ιη, ἡ, ***greediness, assumption, arrogance***, τῶν Σπαρτιητέων ἡ π. Hdt.7.149, cf. And.4.13;...π. συγγενική ***wrong* done to one's kin**, Iamb. *VP*24.108. **2.** *assumption,* αἱ ἐν τῷ πυνθάνεσθαι π. Arist.*SE*175a19. **II.** *advantage*, Isoc.4.183, 15.275, D.23.128;...ἐπὶ πλεονεξίᾳ **with a view to *one's own advantage***, Th.3.84,...**2. a *larger share of*** a thing, τῶν πολιτικῶν δικαίων Arist.*Pol.*1282b29. **3. *gain derived*** from a thing, τὴν ἐπὶ τῶν ἰδίων δικῶν πλεονεξίαν D.21.28;...**III. *excess***, opp. ἔνδεια, Pl.*Ti.*82a. [LS]. Proposed translation: "avarice, insatiable greed."

[51] **μανθάνω**, used by good writers only in pres., as Pl. *Ti.*87b, *Men.*88b.--Hom. uses only the Ep. aor. forms μάθον, ἔμμαθες, ἔμμαθε:--***learn*, esp. *by study*** (but also, ***by practice***, Simon.147, Arist.*EN*1103a32, *Metaph.*1049b31, 980b24; ***by experience***, A.*Ag.*251 (lyr.), Arist.*AP*0.81a40), thrice in Hom., ἔργα κακά Od.17.226, 18.362: οἱ μανθάνοντες ***learners, pupils***, X.*Mem.*1.2.17; μ. τὰ Ὁμήρου ἔπη ***learn by heart***, Id.*Smp.*3.5; μ. βέμβικα Ar.*Av.*1461; μ. τί τινος ***learn from*...**,Pi.*P.*3.80, A.*Pr.*701, S.*OT*575, etc.:...c. inf., ***learn to . .*** , or ***how to . .*** , ll. l.c., Pi.*P.*4.284, A.*Pr.*1068 (anap.);...**II. *acquire a habit of,*** and in past tenses, ***to be accustomed to*** . . , c. inf., Emp.17.9, Hp.*VM*10; τοὺς μεμαθηκότας ἀριστᾶν Id.*Acut.*28; τὸ μεμαθηκός ***that which is usual***, πρότερον ἢ ὕστερον τοῦ μ. Id.*Mul.*2.128; ἀργαὶ μανθάνουσι ***acquire a habit* of idleness**,...*Ep.Ti.*5.13 [LS]. Thus, **μανθάνω** means to always be learning something new (implying that there is always something new to learn) especially by disciplined study, practice and experience; always with a view to *permanent acquisition* of that which is learned in order to transform it into a *disciplined, habitual, consistent* way of thinking,

way of behaving or way of living, to such an extent that it becomes customary. In fact, Jesus calls his "disciples" (= "disciplined ones") the noun form of this word: μαθητής = "learners, pupils, apprentices." In fact, this character quality was the most important criterion for Jesus' selection of His "disciples," i.e., because they were so willing to learn from Him and "discipline" themselves to adopt His way of life. They had developed a life-habit of being learners, and having vulnerable and teachable spirits; they were not and did not act like "know-it-alls."

[52] εἰ, Particle...usu. either in conditions, *if*...**VI.** in citing a fact as a ground of argument or appeal, *as surely as, since,* εἴ ποτ' ἔην γε *if* there was [**as** *there was*], i.e. *as sure as* there was such an one, Il.3.180, al.;...When εἰ is used with γε: γε, enclitic Particle, giving emphasis to the word or words which it follows...**3.** to heighten a contrast or opposition, **a.** after conditional clauses, εἰ μὲν δὴ σύ γ'..., τῷ κε Ποσειδάων γε.. *if* you do so, then *at all events* Poseidon will.., Il.15.49 [LS]. Proposed translation: "Since it is a fact that..., it follows that you can be certain that..."

[53] ἀποτίθημι, *put away, stow away,* δέπας δ' ἀπέθηκ' ἐνὶ χηλῷ Il.16.254, cf. X.*An*.2.3.15;...**II.** Med. (aor. I part. ἀποθησαμένη Hsch.), *put away from oneself, lay aside,* τεύχεα κάλ' ἀποθέσθαι ἐπὶ χθονί Il.3.89; τὴν Σκυθικὴν στολὴν ἀ. *put it off,* Hdt.4.78; ἀ. κόμας *cut it off,* in mourning, E.*Hel.* 367 (lyr., tm.); ἀ. τὸν νόμον *set aside,* i.e. *disregard,* the law, Th.1.77; ἀ. τὰν Ἀφροδίταν *quell* **desire**, E.*IA*558 (lyr.);...[LS]. Paul is using the word ἀποτίθημι to refer to "taking off clothing." The word ἀποτίθημι is also the word used by Luke in Acts 7:58 to describe those that stoned Stephen when they "took off" their cloaks and laid them down at the feet of Saul [Paul]. Paul is using this word as a metaphor to mean that one should adopt a mental discipline to "take off and leave outside" one's former lifestyle and habitual way of viewing things like one should "take off and leave dirty clothing outside" before going indoors.

[54] ἀναστροφή is the noun form of the verb ἀναστρέφω, which Paul used in Eph. 2:3 (see extended note at Eph. 2:3). Proposed translation: "having one's public demeanor, behavior and attitudes formed by one's habitual public associations [deliberately or unwittingly]."

[55] παλαιός, ά, όν, **I.** *old in years,* **1.** mostly of persons, *aged,* ἢ νέος ἠὲ παλαιός Il.14.108; νέοι ἠδὲ παλαιοί Od.1.395;...in bad sense, *a* **dotard** (μωρός [= *"moron"*] Hsch., but σκώπτης [= *"scoffer"*] Suid.), Ar.*Lys*.988. **II.** *of old date, ancient,* **1.** of persons, ξεῖνος π. **an old guest-friend**, Il.6.215, cf. S.*Tr*.263, E.*Alc*.212;...οἱ π. **the ancients**, Th.1.3; π. ἡμερῶν LXX *Da*.7.9. **a.** in good sense, *venerable, held in esteem,* like Lat. *antiquus,* ἄπερ μέγιστα καὶ παλαιότατα τοῖς ἀνθρώποις Antipho 6.4. **b.** in bad sense, *antiquated, obsolete,* κωφὰ καὶ π. ἔπη S.*OT*290. **c.** π. δρᾶμα **a drama which has been previously acted**, *SIG*1078 lxxxvii (Athens, iv B. C.) [LS]. Paul is clearly using this word in a bad sense, and in so doing brings to mind the disagreeable kinds of behaviors that can and often

do characterize elderly people ("old" age). Proposed translation: "foolish, acerbic, cynical old folks."

⁵⁶ **φθείρω**, *destroy* **things**, μῆλα κακοὶ φθείρουσι νομῆες Od. 17.246; φ. τῶν Συρίων τοὺς κλήρους *waste* **them**, Hdt.1.76, cf. X.HG 7.2.11, An.4.7.20;...**4. ruin, spoil**, ποσὶν φθείροντα πλοῦτον ἀργυρωνήτους θ' ὑφάς, of one who treads on rich carpets, A.Ag.949; βαφὰς φθείρουσα τοῦ ποικίλματος, of blood, Id.Ch.1013; *of a poison*, ὧνπερ ἂν θίγῃ, φθείρει τὰ πάντα S.Tr.716;...**3.** *to be morally corrupted*, ἐφθάρη ἡ γῆ ἐναντίον τοῦ θεοῦ LXXGe.6.11, cf. Ho.9.9, al.; ἔστι ἐν' Ἀλεξανδρείᾳ σκηνῶν ἐν τοῖς' Ἀριστοβούλου φθειρόμενος PCair.Zen.37.7 (iii B. C.);...[LS]. Although **φθείρω** does mean to be morally corrupted, the main overtone or connotation of this Greek word is to suffer being "wasted, ruined, or spoiled" (maybe even "poisoned") as a result of being morally corrupted.

⁵⁷ **ἀπάτη**, ἡ, *trick, fraud, deceit*, νῦν δὲ κακὴν ἀπάτην βουλεύσατο Il.2.114, cf. 4.168: in pl., *wiles*, οὐκ ἄρ' ἔμελλες . . λήξειν ἀπατάων, says Athena to Ulysses, Od.13.294, cf. Il.15.31;...2. *guile, treachery*, ἄταν ἀπάτᾳ μεταγνούς A.Supp.111, cf. S.OC230;...ἀ. λεχέων *a being cheated out of the marriage*, S.Ant.630; ἄνευ δόλου καὶ ἀπάτης *'without fraud or covin'*, Hdt.1.69;...[LS]. It appears that the main notion conveyed by **ἀπάτη** is that of being "tricked" or "cheated" out of something.

⁵⁸ **ἀνανεόομαι**,--*renew*, τὸν ὅρκον Th.5.18; τὴν προξενίαν ib.43;...**II.** κἀννεώσασθαι λόγους *revive* them, prob. for καὶ νεώσασθαι, S.*Tr*.396, cf. E.*Hel*.722, Plb.5.36.7.--Act. freq. in LXX, *Jb*.33.24, al.,...Pass., *Ep.Eph.***4.23** [LS]. This word occurs frequently in the LXX (as in Job 33:24 to mean "revive his body from death"). Paul's use of this word here in Eph. 4:23 is the only time this word is used in the NT. Therefore, it probably means something more like "revive" – as in bringing someone near death (from drowning) back to life – than it means "renew."

⁵⁹ **νόος** – see extended philological analysis in note at Eph. 4:17.

⁶⁰ **ἐνδύω** or **ἐνδύνω**...**1. of clothes**, *put on*, ἔνδυνε χιτῶνα Il.2.42; ἔνδυνε περὶ στήθεσσι χιτῶνα 10.21;...pf. ἐνδέδῡκα, *wear*, κιθῶνας λινέους Hdt.2.81, cf. 7.64, 9.22;...metaph., ἐνδυόμενοι τόλμημα Ar.*Ec*.288; also τὸν Ταρκύνιον ἐνδύεσθαι *assume* the person of T., D.H. 11.5; τὸν καινὸν ἄνθρωπον *Ep.Eph.* **4.24**:--Pass., *to be clothed in, have on*, ἐσθῆτα ἐνδεδύσθαι Hp.*Insomn.* 91, cf. Men.432 [LS]. Paul is using the word **ἐνδύω** as a metaphor to mean that in the same way that one must deliberately "put on" and "wear" certain types of new and beautiful outfits in order to get "dressed up" for differing kinds of formal public occasions, so one must also adopt a conscious decision, even disipline, to "dress up" one's mind on a daily basis.

⁶¹ **καινός**, ή, όν, *new, fresh*, ἔργα οὔτ' ὦν κ. οὔτε παλαιά Hdt.9.26; κ. ὁμιλία A.*Eu*.406; κ. λόγους φέρειν **to bring** *news*, [= "to bring a message of something new" – GWC]; ἐκ καινῆς (sc. ἀρχῆς) *anew, afresh*, Th.3.92, Thphr.*CP*5.1.11,

Jahresh.23 *Beibl*.91 (Pamphyl., i A. D.), etc.;...**esp. of *new* dramas**, τραγῳδῶν γιγνομένων καινῶν Aeschin.3.34; briefly τραγῳδοῖς κ. **at the representation of the *new* tragedies**, Docum. ap. D. 18.54;...but κ. κωμῳδία, τραγῳδία, **of a *new style* of drama**, *IG*7.1773 (Thebes, ii A.D.). **2.** *newly-made*, κύλικες, τριήρης, ὀθόνια, οἶνος, *SIG*1026.26 (Cos, iv/iii B. C.), *IG*22.1623.289, *PLond*.2.402v12 (ii B. C.), *Ostr*.1142.4 (iii A. D.). **3.** Adv. -νῶς *newly, afresh,* Alex.240.4. **II.** *newly-invented, novel,* καινότεραι τέχναι Batr.116;...καινὰ ἐπιμηχανᾶσθαι *innovations,* X.*Cyr*.8.8.16 [LS]. Proposed translation: "new, bright and freshly outfitted."

[62] **κτίζω** – "create," see extended philological note at Eph. 2:10.

[63] **δικαιοσύνη, ἡ,** *righteousness, justice,* Thgn.147, Hdt.1.96, al., Pl.*R*.433a, LXX *Ge*.15.6, etc.; δ. δικαστική **legal** *justice,* Arist.*Pol*.1291a27; opp. ἐπιείκεια, Id.*EN*1137a32. **2.** *fulfilment of the Law,* LXX *Is*.26.2, al., *Ev.Matt*.3.15, al. **II.** *justice, the business of a judge,* Pl.*Grg*.464b, 464c (v.l. δικαστική)...[LS]. Proposed translation: "the right thing to do – legally, ethically and morally."

[64] **ὁσιότης, ητος, ἡ,** *disposition to observe divine law, piety,* Pl.*Prt*.329c, Euthphr.14d sq., etc.; πρὸς θεῶν ὁ. *piety towards them,* Plu.Alc.34;...[LS]. The word **ὁσιότης** only occurs twice in the NT: here and in and Luke 2:75. It does not mean "holy" ("holynes" – Tyndale; "holiness" – KJV), which, as explained in the detailed note at Eph. 1:1, is a confused Old English translation of **ἅγιος**. Rather, **ὁσιότης** is most often translated into Latin as the word **"aspecto."** According to Charlton T. Lewis and Charles Short's, *A Latin Dictionary,* aspecto has the following meaning: **aspecto (adsp-** , Ritschl; **asp-**, Lachmann, Fleck., Rib., B. and K., Halm), āvi, ātum, 1, v. freq. a. [id.] , *to look at attentively, with respect, desire,* etc. **I.** Lit. (rare but class.): hicine est Telamon, quem aspectabant, Enn. ap. Cic. Tusc. 3, 18, 39:...Cic. Planc. 42 Illum aspectari, claro qui incedit honore, *is gazed upon*, ast; Lucr. 3, 76: Et stabula aspectans regnis excessit avitis, *and looking back upon* (*with regret*), etc., Verg. G. 3, 228; id. A. 6, 186; 10, 251.--**II.** Trop. **A.** *To observe, regard, pay attention to a thing* jussa principis aspectare, Tac. A. 1, 4.--**B.** Of places as objects, *to look towards, overlook, lie towards* (cf. **specto**) collis, qui adversas aspectat desuper arces, Verg. A. 1, 420: mare, quod Hiberniam insulam aspectat, Tac. A. 12, 32. Therefore, it appears that this word means something like the contemporary American business usage of the concept of **"focus"** = "pay exclusive attention to (with undivided devotion to accomplishing) something."

[65] **ἀποτίθημι** – see extended note on the meaning of this word at Eph. 4:22.

[66] **ψεῦδος, εος, τό:--***falsehood, lie,* ψεύδεα . . ἐτύμοισιν ὁμοῖα Od.19.203 [= "He (Odysseus) knew how to say many false things like they were true sayings" – transl. GWC], Hes.Th.27; ψευδός κεν φαῖμεν Il.2.81; ψεῦδος δ' οὐκ ἐρέει Od.3.20 [Athena giving advice to Telemachos to ask Nestor about his father: 'You yourself must entreat him to speak the whole truth to you. He will not tell you any falsehood; he is too thoughtful' – GWC];...**2.** in Logic, *false conclusion, fallacy,*

συλλογισμὸς τοῦ ψεύδους Arist.*APr*.61b3; συμβαίνει ψ. ib.37a36:--in NT of what is opposed to religious truth, *false doctrine*, *Ep.Rom*.1.25; ποιῶν βδέλυγμα καὶ ψ., i.e. doing what is repugnant to the true faith, *Apoc*.21.27; of *false* anatomical doctrine, τὸ οἴεσθαι . . ψ. ἐστι Sor.1.17...**III.** In Pl. ψεῦδος is freq. opp. ἀληθές, *Grg*.505e, *R*.382d, *Euthd*.272b, al.;...[LS]. Proposed translation: "lying to oneself or others, or giving in to the predisposition to acquiesce and accept falsehood."

[67] Here Paul quotes Zechariah 8:16 from the Septuagint (LXX): λαλεῖτε ἀλήθειαν ἕκαστος πρὸς τὸν πλησίον αὐτοῦ. Transl.: "Tell each other the truth – each of you with your fellow human beings."

[68] **πλησίος** [πέλας] **I.** *near, close to*...Hom.:--absol. *near, neighbouring*, Il., Aesch., etc.:--as Subst. a *neighbour*, ἰδὼν ἐς πλ. ἄλλον Il., etc. **II.** adv. πλησίον, doric πλατίον, πέλας, *near, nigh*, hard by...Hom., Hdt., etc...Eur. 2. with the Art., ὁ πλησίον (sc. ὤν) *one's neighbour*, Theogn., Eur., etc.;...[LS]. Webster gives the following analysis of the word "**neighbor:**" Etymology: Middle English *neighbor, neighebor,* from Old English *nēahgebūr;* akin to Middle Dutch *nāgebuur,* Old High German *nāhgibūr;* all from a prehistoric West Germanic compound whose first element is represented by Old English *nēah* near and whose second element is represented by Old English *gebūr* dweller -- **1a:** one whose house or other place of residence immediately adjoins or is relatively near that of another: one that lives next to or near another **b:** one whose town or district or country immediately adjoins or is relatively near that of another **c(1):** one whose position (as in sitting, standing)...[or] **d:** something located in a position immediately adjoining or relatively near that of another **2a:** a fellow creature; *especially*: a fellow human being <thou shalt love thy neighbor as thyself--*Mt*19:19 (AV)> b: one that evidences true kindness and charity toward his fellowman <proved *neighbor* to the man who fell among the robbers--*Lk*10:36 (RSV)>[W]. In American English, the word "neighbor" is usually used to refer to meaning **1a** above. However, Paul broadens the meaning of the word **πλησίος** in the same way that Jesus emphasizes this word in the Parable of the Good Samaritan (*Luke* 10:36), to refer to one's "fellow human beings."

[69] **ἁμαρτάνω** – Proposed translation as a verb: fall short, fail, lose [as in "lose one's sight," "lose hope," "lose one's mind," etc.), miss (as in "miss" a field goal, "miss" a business opportunity). See extended note at Eph. 2:1 (see note on **παράπτωμα** at Eph. 1:7 for a full discussion of other Greek words translated "sin," as well as the derivation of the English word "sin").

[70] Psalm 4:1-4 [LXX] reads as follows (note well that Paul's theme in Eph.4:17-26, down to the very choice of specific words, emerges from this passage):

Ps. 4:1 Ἐν τῷ ἐπικαλεῖσθαί με **εἰσήκουσέν** [Eph. 4:21] μου ὁ θεὸς τῆς **δικαιοσύνης** [Eph 4:24] μου· ἐν θλίψει ἐπλάτυνάς μοι· οἰκτίρησόν με καὶ **εἰσάκουσον** [Eph. 4:21] τῆς προσευχῆς μου. ("My God, You who are characterized most of all by Your legal demand for goodness and rectitude, when I was unjustly oppressed and I summoned You to help me, You heard me, relieved me from all my cares, had mercy on me and heard my prayer"). ²υἱοὶ **ἀνθρώπων** [Eph 4:24], ἕως πότε **βαρυκάρδιοι** [Eph 4:18]; ἵνα τί **ἀγαπᾶτε** [Eph. 4:16] **ματαιότητα** [Eph 4:17] καὶ ζητεῖτε **ψεῦδος** [Eph 4:25]; διάψαλμα. ("Oh, fellow human beings, how long will you persist in being dullhearted!? For what reason do you continue to love futility and persist in seeking out what is false!? ") ³καὶ γνῶτε ὅτι ἐθαυμάστωσεν κύριος τὸν **ὅσιον** [Eph 4:24] αὐτοῦ· κύριος **εἰσακούσεταί** [Eph. 4:21] μου ἐν τῷ κεκραγέναι με πρὸς αὐτόν. ("Know that the Commander in Chief especially marvels, admires and honors whoever is completely focused upon and dedicated to Him; the Commander in Chief hears me whenever I respectfully and officially summon Him"). ⁴**ὀργίζεσθε καὶ μὴ ἁμαρτάνετε** [Eph 4:26]· λέγετε ἐν ταῖς καρδίαις ὑμῶν καὶ ἐπὶ ταῖς κοίταις ὑμῶν κατανύγητε. διάψαλμα. ("He has told me: 'Acknowledge your feelings of anger, yet do not allow unchecked anger to cause you to miss or fall short of your ultimate goals. The way to avoid unchecked anger is to speak to yourselves and to Me in your heart when you muse upon your beds. As you do this, you must reflect upon your anger with an attitude of contrition'") [Transl. – GWC].

It seems that this text indicates that the proper spiritual discipline is to confess our anger to God over the exasperating events of the day as we lie down to go to bed in the privacy of our own minds – as we reflect upon the events of the day that caused our anger and frustration. Therefore, it is probably not accurate to think that we must not go to bed until we have abandoned our anger, but rather that going to bed with a reflective attitude of contrition towards God is the time during which God will relieve us from our exasperation.

⁷¹ **παροργισμός** – This interesting compound noun is rare in Greek literature, and only occurs once in the NT (here). The Greek preposition **παρά** means "beside," and the Greek noun **ὀργή** means "anger." Literally, the word **παροργισμός** means "beside anger." The closest idea we have in American English is the notion of being "beside ourselves with anger." This notion is most closely expressed by the word "exasperation" (see note at Eph. 6:4 for verb).

⁷² διάβολος, ον, *slanderous, backbiting*, γραῦς Men.878,...**II**. Subst., *slanderer*, Pi. *Fr.*297, Arist.*Top.*126a31, Ath.11.508d; *enemy*, LXX *Es.*7.4, 8.1: hence, = *Sâtân*, ib.1*Chr.*21.1; *the Devil, Ev.Matt.*4.1, etc. [LS]. The proper noun "Devil" is a transliteration of the Greek word **διάβολος**, and is derived from the verb **διαβάλλω**, which originally had the denotative meanings of: **A.** *throw* or *carry over* or *across*, νέας Hdt.5.33,34; in wrestling, Ar.*Eq.*262 codd. **2.** more freq. intr., *pass over, cross*,...Hdt.9.114...**3.** *put through*, τῆς θύρας δάκτυλον D.L.1.118[LS]. However, the verb **διαβάλλω** came to develop the primary connotative meaning of to deliberately "throw words across" at another person, intentionally twisting the meaning of the words with the motive of deceiving, causing enmity, or destroying the other person, as follows: **III.** *set at variance*, ἐμὲ καὶ ʼΑγάθωνα Pl.*Smp.*222c, 222d,...Arist.*Pol.*1313b16; *set against*, τινὰς πρὸς τὰ πάθη, πρὸς τὴν βρῶσιν,; *bring into discredit*, μή με διαβάλῃς στρατῷ S.*Ph.*582; δ. [τινὰ] τῇ πόλει Pl.*R.*566b:--Pass., *to be at variance with*, τινί Id.*Phd.*67e; *to be filled with suspicion and resentment against* another, Hdt.5.35, 6.64;...*to be brought into discredit*, ἐς τοὺς ξυμμάχους Th.4.22;...**IV.**

put off with evasions, δ. τινὰ μίαν (sc. ἡμέραν) ἐκ μιᾶς Sammelb.5343.41 (ii A. D.);...V. *attack* **a man's character,** *calumniate*, δ. τοὺς ᾿Αθηναίους πρὸς τὸν ᾿Αρταφρένεα Hdt.5.96;...*accuse, complain of,* **without implied malice or falsehood,** PTeb.23.4 (ii B. C.): c. dat. rei, *reproach* **a man** *with*, τῇ ἀτυχίᾳ Antipho 2.4.4;...**2.** c. acc. rei, *misrepresent,* D.18.225, 28.1, etc.: *speak or state slanderously,* ὡς οὗτος διέβαλλεν Id.18.20;...**generally,** *give hostile information,* **without any insinuation of falsehood,** Th.3.4. **3.** δ. τι εἴς τινα *lay the blame for a thing on* . ., Procop.Arc.22.19...**VI.** *deceive by false accounts, impose upon, mislead,* τινά Hdt.3.1, 5.50, 8.110;...**VII.** *divert* **from a course of action,** πρὸς τὴν κακίαν τινάς ib.809f;...**IX.** διαβάλλεσθαι ἀστραγάλοις πρός τινα *throw* **against him,** Plu.2.148d, 272f [LS]. Thus, the best translation for **διάβολος** is probably something like "Slanderer," "Deceiver," "Maligner," "Accuser," "Mocker," "Scorner," "Criticizer," "Liar," "Swindler," "Fraud," or even "Predator" or "Con Artist," in the sense of one who deliberately preys upon others with deceitful schemes.

[73] **τόπος,** ὁ, *place, region,...***III.** metaph., *opening, occasion, opportunity,* ἐν τ. τινὶ ἀφανεῖ Th.6.54 (but τρόπῳ is prob. cj.);...μὴ δίδοτε τ. τῷ διαβόλῳ **Ep.Eph.4.27;** δότε τ. τῇ ὀργῇ **leave** *room* **for the wrath (of God), i.e. let God punish,** Ep.Rom.12.19; μὴ καταλείπεσθαί σφισι τ. ἐλέους Plb.1.88.2; μετανοίας τ. οὐχ εὗρε Ep.Hebr.12.17;...**give** *occasion* **to...[LS].** Proposed translation, "opening, opportunity."

[74] **κλέπτω, I.** *to steal, filch, purloin,* Hom., etc.; τῆς γενεῆς ἔκλεψε from that breed Anchises stole, i.e. stole foals of that breed, Il.; σῶμα κλ. to let it down secretly, Eur. **2. in part. act.** *thievish,* κλέπτον βλέπει he has a thief's look, Ar. **II.** *to cozen, cheat, deceive, beguile,* Il., Hes., etc...Hdt. **III.** like κρύπτω, *to conceal, keep secret, disguise,* Pind., Soph., Eur., etc. **IV.** *to do secretly or treacherously,* κλ. σφαγάς *to perpetrate slaughter secretly,* Soph.; κλ. μύθους *to whisper malicious rumours,* id=Soph.; κλέπτων ἢ βιαζόμενος *by fraud* or force, Plat. **2.** *to seize or occupy secretly,* Xen. [LS]. The main idea seems to be stealing in secret ways by thorough practice and habit, such that stealing becomes one's twisted version of a vocation or "work," such as embezzling, being a con artist or a pickpocket, engaging in smuggling, swindling, counterfeiting, etc. as a way to remain lazy and avoid legitimate work.

[75] **κοπιάω,...***to be tired, grow weary,* Ar.Th.795, Fr.318.8, LXX De.25.18 [= refers to the weariness in a soldier who has fought a rear-guard action all day], al.; κ. τὰ σκέλη Alex.147;...κ. ὑπὸ ἀγαθῶν *to be weary of* **good things,** Ar.Av.735; ἐκ τῆς ὁδοιπορίας Ev.Jo.4.6;...**II.** *work hard, toil,* Ev.Matt.6.28, etc.; μεθ᾿ ἡδονῆς κ. Vett.Val.266.6; εἴς τι *1* Ep.Ti.4.10, cf. Ep.Rom.16.6; ἔν τινι *1* Ep.Ti.5.17; ἐπί τι LXX Jo.24.13: **c.** inf., *strive, struggle,* μὴ κοπία ζητεῖν Lyr.Alex.Adesp.37.7 [LS]. The emphasis of this word seems to be to work so hard at a worthwhile, legitimate yet labor-intensive job that one is left exhausted and weary at the end of the day.

⁷⁶ ἐργάζομαι, Il.18.469, etc., Cret. ϝεργάδδομαι *Schwyzer*181v5 [pronunciation: "verg, then = "verk", then = "work" – GWC]: **work, labour,** esp. **of husbandry,** Hes.*Op.*299, 309, Th.2.72, etc.; **but also of all manual labour, of slaves,** ἐ. ἀνάγκῃ Od.14.272; **of quarrymen,** Hdt.2.124, etc.;...ἐ. ἐν τοῖς ἔργοις **in the mines,** D.42.31: c. dat. instr., χαλκῷ **with brass,** Hes.*Op.*151; **also of animals,** βοῦς ἐργάτης ἐργάζεται S. *Fr.*563; **of birds working to get food,** Arist.*HA*616b35;...**of Hephaestus' self-acting bellows,** Il.18.469;...**II.** trans., **work at, make,** ἔργα κλυτά, of Athena, Od. 20.72, cf. 22.422; κηρόν, σχαδόνας, **of bees,** Arist.*HA*627a6,30. **2. do, perform,** ἔργα ἀεικέα Il.24.733; ἔργον ἐπ' ἔργῳ ἐ., **of husbandmen,** Hes.*Op.*382;...Arist.*EN*1121b33;...Od.17.321. **3. work a material,** ὅπλα..οἷσίν τε χρυσὸν ἐργάζετο Od.3.435;...ἐ. θάλασσαν, **of traders,** D.H.3.46; γλαυκὴν ἐ., **of fishers,** Hes.*Th.* 440. **4. earn by working,** χρήματα Hdt.1.24, Ar.*Eq.*840, etc.;...**5. work at, practise,** μουσικήν, τέχνας, etc., Pl.*Phd.*60e,...*Act.Ap.*10.35, *Ev.Matt.*7.23. **6. abs., work at a trade** or **business, traffic, trade,** ἐν [γναφείῳ] Lys.23.2;...those who *trade in* the square, *BCH*8.126 (cf. *Glotta*14.73) [LS]. See extended note on the noun ἔργον, Dor. ϝέργον at Eph. 2:10. Proposed translation: "hard work, manual labor."

⁷⁷ **χρεία: need, want,** χρείας ὕπο A.*Th.*287; ἵν' ἕσταμεν χρείας **considering in what great** *need* **we are,** S.*OT*1443;...ἢ μὴν ἔτ' ἐμοῦ χρείαν ἕξει **will have** *need* **of my help,** A.*Pr.*170 (anap.);...ἀφίκοντο εἰς χρείαν τῆς πόλεως **came to feel** *the need* **of its assistance,** Pl.*Mx.*244d; **2. want, poverty,** S.*Ph.*175 (lyr.), etc.;...**II. business,** ὡς πρὸς τί χρείας; **for what** *purpose?* S.*OT*1174;...**b. esp. military or naval service,** ἡ πολεμικὴ χ. καὶ ἡ εἰρηνική **the employments of war and of peace,** Arist.*Pol.*1254b32; **c.** generally, **business, employment, function,** Id.3.45.2, etc.; ἡ ἐγκεχειρισμένη χ. **the** *duty* **assigned,** *PTeb.*741.11 (iiB.C.);...etc. **d. a business, affair, matter,** like χρέος, Plb.2.49.9, al.;...the *study* of these things, Epicur.*Ep.*1p.29U. **III. use, 1. as a property, use, advantage, service,** χρείης εἵνεκα μηδεμιῆς Thgn.62; χρείαν ἔχειν τοῖς ἀνθρώποις **to be** *of service* **to mankind;**...χρείαν ἔχει εἴς τι **is of** *service* **towards,** Sosip.1.41;...φίλων ἀνδρῶν **services rendered by them,** Pi.*N.*8.42; χρείας παρέχεσθαι **render** *services,* Decr. ap. D.18.84;...παρέχειν χ. to **be** *serviceable, useful,* Aristo Stoic.1.79; **2. as an action, using, use,** κτῆσις καὶ χ. X.*Mem.*2.4.1 [LS]. This word can mean to be in a "state of need" = the notion of "poverty," but that usage seems to be more rare. On the contrary, **χρεία** seems to mean the ability to *become useful* again, to provide a *service*, especially by *employment in business* or in the *military*. Although Paul is not ruling out giving money to people who find themselves in temporary financial need, the *far more important principle* seems to be to learn how to earn money through work, and then *to study the principles of business itself,* so that one can eventually arrive at a position to become part of the larger infrastructure or network that provide jobs for others and pays them to earn a living, rather than simply give them money that supplies only a temporary solution.

78 σαπρός, ά, όν, ([σήπω]) **rotten, putrid,** Hippon.23, Hp.*Oss.*13; of the lungs, **diseased,** Id.*Morb.*1.13; of **bone, carious,** Id.*Fract.*33; **of wood,** etc., **rotten,** ἱστίον Ar.*Eq.*918; βύρσα Id.*V.*38;...esp., **of fish that have been long in pickle, stale, rancid,** τάριχος Ar.*Ach.*1101;...**of withered flowers,** D.22.70. Adv., -ρῶς λούει τὰ βαλανεῖα **so as to leave** one *filthy,* Arr.*Epict.*2.21.14. **II.** generally, *stale, worn out,* ἀρχαῖον καὶ σαπρόν Ar.*Pl.*323; of **clothes,** *PGiss.*26.6 (ii A.D.). Adv., -ῶς περιπατῶ **I am walking about** *in rags,* *BGU*846.9 (ii A.D.). **2. of persons,** γέρων ὢν καὶ ς. Ar.*Pax*698; ὦ σαπρά, **to an old woman,** Id.*Ec.*884, Hermipp. 10;...**5.** metaph., *unsound, bad,* λόγος **Ep.Eph.4.29**; opp. καλός, Vett.Val.36.30, cf. *PSI*4.312.13 (iv A.D.);...τὴν ς. εἱμαρμένην **the** *evil* **fate,** *PMag.Leid.W.*14.38 [LS]. Paul is using the word **σαπρός,** referring to "rotten, foul, disgusting or rancorous" garbage as a metaphor to mean that one should not allow oneself to say "rotten, foul, disgusting or rancorous things."

79 **οἰκοδομὴν** – Paul first introduced the concept of the **ἐκκλησία** as a "building," e.g., a newly forged "structure of mutually constructive relationships," in Eph. 2:20-21 (see note).

80 **χρεία** – See note at Eph. 4:28.

81 **τὸ πνεῦμα τὸ ἅγιον τοῦ θεοῦ** = "Specially Selecting Spirit of God" – See notes at Eph. 1:2 and 1:13.

82 **"sealed (σφραγίζω) for the Day of Redemption (ἀπολυτρώσις)"** – Paul introduced this important theme in Eph. 1:13-14 (see extended notes at Eph. 1:13-14).

83 **ἀρθήτω** – aor impv pass 3rd sg of **αἴρω**...**III.** *lift and take away, remove,* ἀπό με τιμᾶν ἦραν A.*Eu.*847; τινὰ ἐκ τῆς πόλεως Pl.*R.*578e; generally, *take away, put an end to,* κακά E.*El.*942; τραπέζας αἴ. *clear away* **dinner,** Men.273; ἀρθέντος τοῦ αἰτίου Arist.*Pr.*920b11;...[LS]. Paul is using the word **ἀρθήτω** as a metaphor to indicate that one's bad thoughts, attitudes, speech and behaviors must, like dirty dishes from the table after a meal, be "cleared away" from one's life.

84 **πικρία, ἡ,** *bitterness:* **1. of taste,** Thphr.CP6.10.7, Od.32, [p. 1404] LXX Je.15.17, Placit.3.16.2, Dsc.1.61, etc. **2. of temper,** τὴν ἀπὸ τῆς ψυχῆς π. D.21.204, cf. 25.84, Ep.3.33, Arist.VV1251a4, Phld.Ir. p.56W.; ἡ ἐπὶ τοῖς γεγονόσι π. Plb.15.4.11; πρὸς τὸν δῆμον Plu.Ccr. 15; ἡ ἐν τοῖς λόγοις π. D.S.16.88; λόγος π. ἔχων μεμιγμένην χάριτι Plu.Lyc.19. **3. of circumstances,** ἡ τοῦ καιροῦ π. BGU417.5 (ii/iii A. D.) [LS]. Proposed translation: "bitter temper of cynical resentment."

85 **θυμός, ὁ,** **soul, spirit,** as the principle of life, feeling and thought, esp. of **strong feeling and passion** (rightly derived from θύω (B) by Pl.*Cra.* 419e ἀπὸ τῆς θύσεως καὶ ζέσεως τῆς ψυχῆς):... **4.** *the seat of anger,* χωόμενον κατὰ θυμόν Il.1.429; νεμεσιζέσθω ἑνὶ θυμῷ 17.254; θυμὸν ἐχώσατο 16.616, etc.: hence, *anger, wrath,* δάμασον θυμόν 9.496; δακεῖν Id.Nu.1369; θυμῷ χρᾶσθαι

Hdt.1.137, al.; ὀργῆς καὶ θυμοῦ μεστοί Isoc.12.81 (so τὴν ὀργὴν καὶ τὸν θ., i.e. the outward manifestation of ὀ., Phld.Ir.p.90W.); **of horses**, X.Eq. 9.2: pl. (not earlier than Pl., f.l. in S.Aj.718 (lyr.)), *fits of anger, passions*, περὶ φόβων τε καὶ θυμῶν Pl.*Phlb*.40e; οἵ τε θ. καὶ αἱ κολάσεις Id.*Prt*.323e, cf. Arist.*Rh*.1390a11 [LS]. Proposed translation: "exploding in impulsive fits of fury or rage that arise from suddenly aroused passions."

[86] **ὀργή, ἡ,** *natural impulse* or *propensity* (v. ὀργάω II): hence, *temperament, disposition, mood*, κηφήνεσσι κοθούροις εἴκελος ὀργήν Hes.*Op*. 304, cf. Thgn.98,214,964, etc.; ἀστυνόμοι ὀργαί *social dispositions*, S.*Ant*.356 (lyr., cf. σύντροφος 3); ἐπιφέρειν ὀργάς τινι **suit** *one's moods* **to another**, Id.8.83, cf. Cratin.230;...II. **anger, wrath,** ὀργῇ χρῆσθαι **to be in** *a passion*, Hdt.6.85, S.*OT*1241; ὀργὴν ποιήσασθαι Hdt.3.25; ὁ. ἐμποιεῖν τινι **make one** *angry*, Pl.*Lg*.793e; ὀργῆς τυγχάνειν **to be visited with** *anger*, D. 21.175, etc.; ὀργὴν ἄκρος **quick** *to anger*, **passionate**, Hdt.1.73;...[LS]. The words ὀργή and θυμός are synonyms for "anger." It is noteworthy that Homer never uses ὀργή to mean "anger," but only uses θυμός. This would indicate that the difference in meaning between ὀργή and θυμός seems to be that θυμός refers more to a *impulsive, violent outburst of fury* or *rage* that originates from suddenly aroused passion, whereas ὀργή seems to indicate more of a settled, continuous *temperament, disposition*, or habitual *mood* of being an acerbic person who has formed the habit of harboring anger and holding grudges.

[87] **κραυγή, ἡ,** *crying, screaming, shouting*, τίς ἥδε κ.; Telecl.35; κραυγὴν θεῖναι, στῆσαι, E.Or.1510, 1529; ποιεῖν X.Cyr.3.1.4; κραυγῇ χρῆσθαι Th.2.4; κ. γίγνεται Lys.13.71; **rarely of a shout of joy**, PPetr.3p.334 (iii B. C.), *Ev.Luc*.1.42: in pl., Aeschin.1.34, Vett.Val.2.35; κραυγὴ Καλλιόπης, as an instance of bad taste, cited from Dionys.Eleg.(7) by Arist.*Rh*.1405a33 [LS]. Proposed translation: "blowing up in public outbursts of shouting, screaming or shrieking."

[88] **βλασφημία, ἡ,** *word of evil omen, profane speech*, D.25.26; βλασφημίαν ἐφθέγξατο, **at a sacrifice**, E.*Ion*1189; εἴ τις παραστὰς τοῖς βωμοῖς βλασφημοῖ β. πᾶσαν Pl.*Lg*.800c; πᾶσαν β. ἱερῶν καταχέουσι ib.d. **2.** *defamation, slander*, Democr.177, D.10.36, 18.95; β. ποιεῖσθαι εἴς τινα Aeschin. 1.167, cf. *Ep.Eph*.4.31; ὅλας ἁμάξας βλασφημιῶν **whole cart-loads** *of abuse*, Luc.*Eun*....**3.** *irreverent speech against God, blasphemy*, ἡ εἰς τὸ θεῖον β. Men.715: in pl., LXX Ez.35.12, al.; τοῦ Πνεύματος *against* . ., *Ev.Matt*.12.31; πρὸς τὸν θεόν *Apoc*.13.6 [LS]. Proposed translation: "spouting blasphemous, irreverent speech against God."

[89] **χρηστός, I.** *useful, good of its kind, serviceable*, τινι Hdt., Eur.; of victims and omens, *boding good, auspicious*, Hdt.; τελευτὴ χρηστή *a happy* **end** or **issue**, id=Hdt.:--τὰ χρηστά, as Subst., *good services, benefits, kindnesses*, id=Hdt.; χρηστὰ συμβουλεύειν Ar. **2. in moral sense,** *good*, opp. to μοχθηρός, Plat.; τὸ χρηστόν, opp. to τὸ αἰσχρόν, Soph. II. **of men,** *good, a good man and true; generally, good, honest, worthy, trusty*, Hdt., Soph., etc.;--also like χρήσιμος, of

good citizens, *useful, deserving*, Ar., Thuc., etc. **2.** οἱ χρηστοί, like οἱ ἀγαθοί, **Lat. optimates** [= "*optimum, optimize*," – GWC] Xen. [LS]. Proposed translation: "best and most beneficial outcome."

⁹⁰ **εὔσπλαγχνος**, ον, ***with healthy bowels***, Hp.*Prorrh*.2.6. **II.** ***compassionate***, LXX Prec.Man.7, ***Ep.Eph*.4.32**, *1 Ep.Pet*.3.8, PMag. Leid.V.9.3, PMasp.20.11 (vi A.D.) [LS]. This word, which denotatively means "good-bowels" or "good-intestines," is difficult to translate into its connotative meaning, because it rarely occurs in Greek literature, and only two times in the NT (here at Eph.4.32 and I Pet.3.8). Two other texts in which this word occurs are in the LXX, *Ὠδαι* 12:7 and Cairo Papyrus Manuscript 67020. These two texts and their translations now follow. *Ὠδαι* 12:4-7 is a prayer of Manassas to God, and it reads as follows:

> Ωδαι 12:4-7 ὃν πάντα φρίττει καὶ τρέμει ἀπὸ προσώπου δυνάμεώς σου, ⁵ὅτι ἄστεκτος ἡ μεγαλοπρέπεια τῆς δόξης σου, καὶ ἀνυπόστατος ἡ ὀργὴ τῆς ἐπὶ ἁμαρτωλοὺς ἀπειλῆς σου, ⁶ἀμέτρητόν τε καὶ ἀνεξιχνίαστον τὸ ἔλεος τῆς ἐπαγγελίας σου, ⁷ὅτι σὺ εἶ κύριος ὕψιστος, **εὔσπλαγχνος**, μακρόθυμος καὶ πολυέλεος καὶ μετανοῶν ἐπὶ κακίαις ἀνθρώπων.

> Transl.: "You are the One before Whom all are filled with awe and tremble with fear when they are confronted by Your actual powerful Personal Presence, ⁵because You usually keep the magnificence of Your actual appearance concealed. *On those occasions when You reveal* Your thunderous anger towards those who have fallen short of Your goals, they cannot withstand *Your terrifying judgment*. ⁶That is especially why Your official offerings of mercy are so unmeasurable and unsearchable; ⁷since after all, You are the Commander in Chief of the Highest Heaven, it is astonishing that You have such ***concerned compassion***, patience, great mercy and ability to change Your mind and let go of Your emotional anger towards the evil actions *we* human beings do" [transl. – GWC].

Cairo Papyrus Manuscript 67020 is cataloged: "P.Cair.Masp.: Papyrus grecs d'époque byzantine, Catalogue général des antiquités égyptiennes du Musée du Caire document 67020 ["Papyrus Manuscripts in Cairo: Greek Papyrus of the Byzantine Epoch, numbered in the General Catalog of Antiquities in the Egyptian Museum in Cairo as Document 67020]," and reads as follows:

> P.Cair.Masp. 67020: οἶον γὰρ φιλότεκνοι πατέρες ὑμῶν, πάντων τῶν ἀπεριστάτων ἐστὲ πανοίκτιστοι, κειμήλιοι πάσης τῆς ἐπαρχείας, καὶ πενήτων θρεπτῆρες καὶ τυφλῶν καὶ **εὔσπλαγχνοι** δοτῆρες, ἵνα μὴ τῇ λιμῷ ἀνάγχωνται τὰ ἀθλιώτατα αὐτῶν τέκνα. (3.32).

> Transl.: "For if any one among you fathers loves his children, yet leaves any of them unguarded, unprotected or does not provide for them *choosing instead to selfishly spend the money you so treasure upon yourselves rather than to provide for your children*, you are most disgraceful and contemptible, and you yourselves are "treasures" fit only for judgment by the office of the Roman Prefect. Yet *any of you fathers* who feeds or rears or becomes a foster-parent or adoptive parent for those *children* who are poor and blind, ***and who feels and shows concern and compassion*** for them, and provides for them in order to stop their hunger, supplying the things that are necessary for them, they are those *real fathers* that recognize the greatest treasures of all, namely – their children (3:32)" [transl. – GWC].

From the above analysis, this word is usually translated "compassion." Webster provides the following entry for the English word "*compassion*:" Etymology: Middle English *compassioun*, from Middle French or Late Latin; Middle French *compassion*, from Late Latin *compassion-*, *compassio*, from *compassus* (past participle of *compati* to have compassion, from Latin *com-* + *pati* to bear, suffer) + *-ion-*, *-io -ion* -- more at PATIENT: deep feeling for and understanding of misery or suffering and the concomitant desire to promote its alleviation: spiritual consciousness of the personal tragedy of another or others and selfless tenderness directed toward it [W]. Therefore, the best connotative translation for this word is probably that articulated in Webster – which is an emotion so strong that it is accompanied by a powerful feeling of sympathy or empathy inside the chest and stomach. Proposed translation: "deep feeling for and understanding of misery or suffering, and the concomitant desire to promote its alleviation."

5

Actor of Love, Follower of Light, Master of Ethical Skill

Take Up the Attitude of an "Actor," Who Portrays the "Role" of God in the "Production" Entitled "Your Life," Whose Defining Character Quality is Self-Sacrificial Love ♦ *Become a Leader that Pursues the Light of the Discovery of Truth in a Publicly Open Way – In Genuine Vulnerability to God's Cleansing Light, with Sincere Mercy Toward Others, In the Constant Illumination of Learning and by Displaying a Consistent and Clear Life-Message* ♦ *Adopt the Conscious Resolve to Accurately Master Only Ethically Skillful Disciplines and Habits in Every Set of Relationships in Life – Not Unwittingly Follow Mindless, Unethical and Morally Unskillful Customs and Traditions* ♦ *A Primary Relationship in Which You Can Discover and Accomplish Your Lifework is Through Genuinely Bonding with Your Spouse by Graciously Offering Yourselves to Each Other in a Spirit of Trust, Giving and Sacrifice*

TAKE UP THE ATTITUDE OF AN "ACTOR," WHO PORTRAYS THE "ROLE" OF GOD IN THE "PRODUCTION" ENTITLED "YOUR LIFE," WHOSE DEFINING CHARACTER QUALITY IS SELF-SACRIFICIAL LOVE

Not only must you first of all conduct your lives in a manner worthy of the special "lifework" to which each of you have been summoned and gifted by our Commander in Chief, and then secondly cease to allow your lives to be directed by the futile philosophical schools of thought dictated by the rest of the world,[1] you must proceed on to the third life-step of learning how to experience the satisfaction and pleasant contentment that comes only by deliberately imitating God. In other words, you must become like an actor who portrays a part in a play – and the "role" you are "acting" in the "play" of your life[2] – is God Himself.

The remarkable result of "acting" the "role" of God all the time in your lives is that you will experience the same effect that an only-child[3] often does when he or she is raised by his or her parents in an atmosphere of love and contentment.[4] In the same way that actors many times end up taking on the personalities and character qualities of the roles they portray,[5] such children likewise frequently grow up to imitate and act just like the their own fathers and mothers, adopting their loving, cheerful, contented disposition as their own.

[2]The way to accomplish "acting the role" of God is by intentionally resolving to conduct your lives according to a new and comprehensive philosophical world view[6] based on self-sacrificial love[7] for other people. You will be specifically guided in how to do this by following precisely in the same Spirit provided for us by the example of self-sacrifical love that our future High King demonstrated for us when He voluntarily surrendered[8] Himself to the judicial authorities for each one of us, to be officially punished as a criminal in our place, instead of turning us in for the legal punishment each of us rightly deserves, even though He Himself was completely innocent! God highly treasured this act of love by Jesus, namely – His offer of Himself as a sacrifice for us.

The following illustration accurately depicts the way in which God treasures your deeds of self-sacrificial love for others. It is not uncommon for us to be overcome with emotion whenever we catch the smell[9] of the familiar fragrance[10] of a special person, place or activity. The unique smell causes us to be suddenly and emotionally gripped into reliving a vivid and meaningful memory of the past or hope for the future.[11]

The intensity of this experience is especially powerful when the memorable aroma is associated with some special loving person's sacrifice of themselves for us, which can only be described as a feeling of an acute sense of sorrow mixed with overwhelming gratitude. In the same way then, whenever God observes your acts of self-sacrificial love for others, it is as if those acts have a "fragrant aroma" that pleases Him immensely, because they not only cause Him to "remember" (as it were) His supreme pleasure with His own High King's superlative act of self-sacrificial love for us, they also cause Him to "hope" (so to speak) to expect more of such loving deeds from us.

[3-4]A true appreciation of what real, self-sacrificial love is will be the crowning character quality held in common by all of the future High King's Ministers in His Millennial Kingdom. It therefore is also more conspicuously true that this same kind of love is the only fitting behavior for you now in your present apprenticeship roles of being His specially selected recruits as you prepare yourselves for those future positions.

Consequently, you must stop believing and no longer practice any of the false world views that claim to know what "true love" is, and which will incessantly clamor for your attention. These specific false and fraudulent views of so-called "true love" from which you must all disengage yourselves are as follows:

- The false "Romantic" view of "true love" that champions the pornographic ideal of engaging in sexual intercourse outside of the bond of marriage, whether that be in consensual sexual intercourse before marriage, adultery, having a mistress, polygamy, homosexuality or prostitution.[12]

- The false "Criminal" view that "true love" remains unaffected by being dirty, filthy or foul smelling, whether in body or in mind.[13] This is the view promoted by organized crime and by those who blatantly advertize the notion that men can find "true love" in frequenting so-called "men's clubs" or other kinds of "strip-tease joints." Such places are in fact squalid establishments which selfishly use and eventually trap morally weak people into a depraved, degrading business in which making money is the only thing that matters.

- The false "Egoistic" view of "love" that condones infatuation with all forms of so-called material pleasures (e.g., "I *love* money...") that in fact lead only to the insatiable greed and avarice[14] that finally result in the hollow experience of becoming a self-centered miser or materialist.

- The false and degrading "Orgiastic" view that "true love" is merely developing the bad habit of needing to experience base sexual gratification outside of marriage by whatever abnormal – even outrageous and violent – means possible other than the normal act of sexual intercourse within the marriage relationship. Engaging in these degrading practices, such as rape, sadism, masochism or seeking to find sexual pleasure by inflicting or suffering pain, even to the point of committing murder, lead only to deforming the soul and leaving it damaged, distorted, psychopathic and hideously ugly.[15]

- The false "Ethnocentric" view of "love" which holds on to old fables, mythic stories, "old wive's tales" or superstitions that deliberately and obstinately continue to misrepresent God or divine things as petty or trivial. In addition, this view foolishly claims that God should show partiality to those from certain ethnic groups and show prejudice against those from other ethnic groups, rather than be self-sacrificial and loving of all human beings irrespective of their ethnic origin.[16]

- The false "Humorist" view of "love" that excuses the use of insolent, sarcastic, cynical or derisive humor that deliberately makes fun of, ridicules or is used to mock or belittle another person (usually the supposed "loved one") in public, and then defends itself by facetiously claiming (to the supposed "loved one"): "Oh, I was only joking..."[17]

As I emphasized before, all of the false views of so-called "love" listed above are not fitting for you because they are *beneath* you – each of you has been summoned to a much *higher level* of the virtues that should interest and concern you, and to which you should aspire[18] – namely, only and especially the kind of loving behavior that anyone would be grateful to receive.

⁵Therefore, even though you all – above all people – are especially those who know this from past bitter experience, nevertheless I feel compelled to repeat the following summary in order to be doubly emphatic on this important point. No one who sells himself or herself out from the self-sacrificial love of God in exhange for the primary three above mentioned dominant false world views of so-called "love," namely:

- the false "Romantic" view of "true love" that champions the pornographic ideal of engaging in sexual intercourse outside of the bond of marriage;[19]

- the false "Criminal" view that "true love" remains unaffected by being dirty, filthy or foul smelling in body or depraved in mind,[20] or;

- the false "Egoistic" view of "love" that promotes becoming a self-centered miser or materialist[21] – for in truth such a person is actually an idolater, in that he has sunk to the basest and most empty state possible for a human being, in that he has placed his trust for his own life in lifeless objects rather than in the living God –

can or will have any inheritance,[22] position of trust or responsibility whatsoever in the future Millennial Kingdom of the future High King of the earth, who after all, is God Himself.

⁶But you must always consciously resist even one of these ensnaring world views to continue in their persistent power to deceive any of you by their worthless and empty claims. Here I must remind you that it was through their giving in to these three deceptive temptations – and especially through their insatiable greed for material wealth and power – that God's anger has now become historically prolonged against the rebellion of His disobedient sons, i.e., the religious and political leadership regime within Judaism. For the most part, the members of this regime continue to obstinately persist in being blinded and manipulated by Satan to refuse compliance[23] to God's purposes, defy Jesus – their legitimate King – and hunt down and mistreat His followers.

⁷I cannot emphasize enough the spiritual fact that you must concentrate on willfully resisting the peer pressure that both those who are barbaric or those who are self-righteous will continually exert on you to become partners with them[24] in their craftily veiled agendas of resistance to the will and purposes that our future High King has for each of you to reach the fulfillment of your lives, which can be achieved only by discovering and accomplishing your unique lifework for God.

BECOME A LEADER THAT PURSUES THE LIGHT OF THE DISCOVERY OF TRUTH IN A PUBLICLY OPEN WAY – IN GENUINE VULNERABILITY TO GOD'S CLEANSING LIGHT, WITH SINCERE MERCY TOWARD OTHERS, IN THE CONSTANT ILLUMINATION OF LEARNING AND BY DISPLAYING A CONSISTENT AND CLEAR LIFE-MESSAGE

[8]Not only must you first of all conduct your lives in a manner worthy of the special "lifework" to which each of you have been summoned and gifted by our Commander in Chief, then secondly cease to allow your lives to be directed by the futile philosophical schools of thought dictated by the rest of the world, then thirdly learn the life-step of how to imitate God by showing self-sacrificial love for others,[25] you must proceed on to the *fourth* challenge of the philosophical commitment of conducting your lives in the deliberate, never-ending and difficult quest of aggressively pursuing the *enlightenment that comes only from the continual discovery of truth.*[26]

Living your lives in the never-ending pursuit of the light of the discovery of truth requires the following three disciplines.[27] First, you must adopt the habit of allowing the light of truth to shine into your lives by living your lives in a publicly open way, in order to demonstrate your sincere motives, honesty, vulnerability, mercy and legitimacy to be trusted to lead others. Second, you must commit yourselves to learning, gaining knowlege and educating yourselves in every way, with the purpose of pursuing the never-ending project of continually illuminating your mind. Third, like the steady light that comes from the sun as opposed to uneven light reflected by the moon, you must project the light of your public character, knowledge and life-message consistently and with clarity.

The result of living with a publicly vulnerable and merciful spirit, always learning, and then being consistent and clear in your message and actions is that God will give you the power to discern and liberate yourselves and others from all kinds of unforseen dangers. In addition, He will provide you with the freedom to be able to pursue limitless opportunites, to enjoy confidence and success, and to experience true happiness in your relationships with other people and with God.

Living a public life in which you demonstrate continual vulnerablility, mercy, learning and consistency is absolutely necessary in order to overcome the devastating and destructive effects of the kind of psychological and spiritual darkness that leads to fear, then confusion, then lack of confidence, then indecisiveness, ultimately to hopeless despair and finally suffering an untimely and tragic death caused by obstinately clinging to either naïve or willful ignorance.[28] Never forget that before you all learned of the good news of Jesus, God's High King, your lives were characterized by living out the painful, miserable and all-too-brief existence that always accompanies living in fear, confusion, and stubborn, willful ignorance. But that dismal way of life has gladly come to an end, because we can now continually grow in graciousness and be enlightened and guided by our Commander in Chief to lead meaningful and significant lives.

⁹I must pause here for a moment to emphasize that you can know that God is at work in your lives because the results that the Spirit of God brings about are always the same within every person who becomes committed to living in the light of public vulnerability, mercy, learning and consistency, instead of the darkness of fear and confusion or in stubborn, willful ignorance: namely, *goodness* and *justice* and the *continual discovery of what is true* in life. ¹⁰It is only those who live in the light of these spiritual things instead of the darkness caused by their absence whose lives will display the three results of goodness, justice and the continual discovery of what is true in life. They are the unique people who will earn the distinguished confidence of our Commander in Chief because they have been deliberately tested and proved by Him[29] during their lives of apprenticeship. Consequently, they will be the ones who will be qualified[30] to be entrusted with official responsibilities of service to Him both in this present life, and even more importantly, in His future Kingdom.

¹¹It is for this reason that you all must stop allowing yourselves to be pressured into becoming joint share-holders or business partners with[31] those whose lives are characterized by the depraved results that ensue from the darkness of their own fearful confusion or stubborn ignorance and willful persistence in participating in and practicing evil. On the contrary, you must develop the insight and courage to at first discern and then gently *confront* such people who are fearful and confused.

Second, you must go on to publicly and vigorously resist those who willfully persist in their wicked beliefs and practices by challenging them, then examining them and questioning them to gather the facts, and then taking the following further steps as necessary. If required, you must take steps to refute them in public argument by employing convincing proofs, correct them, expose them, shame them, and if necessary, not be afraid to take any appropriate legal actions required to arrest and stop their destructive behavior, convict them, and set right the frivolous and outrageous disputes they cause.[32]

¹² Ultimately, gentle confrontation with those who live in fear and confusion, or boldly and publicly challenging those who choose to live in the darkness of the stubborn, willful ignorance of participating in and practicing evil are the only appropriate ways to face such people. Your tendency will be to merely gossip in secret about the disgraceful things

they practice among themselves, but then do nothing about it. You all must not do this, because it is not honorable and does you no credit to merely blather about the mixed-up, shameful and reprehensible things that are done by such people.

¹³The reason you must deliberately choose to gently confront or boldly and publicly challenge evil people rather than to merely gossip about them in secret is that it is only when such evil beliefs and conduct are publicly confronted, challenged, refuted and then corrected by the light of truth mixed with mercy, that the tragic consequences of the evil practices of darkness can be suitably and properly resolved. The satisfactory resolution of confrontations with evil come about only when the facts of each case and the proof that the matter has been put right have been made clearly and publicly known to all. The additional benefit of dealing with evil in this manner is that whomever's evil is confronted and then brought to the light of being publicly, justly, and mercifully resolved stands a good chance of becoming enlightened to the truth themselves.

¹⁴When this procedure of confrontation and resolution of the dark, fearful, confused, stubborn, ignorant evil actions of people is accomplished mercifully and truthfully, then the authentic meaning of the theme found in the writings of the Isaiah, God's Spokesman, is accomplished – namely, the theme in which he says in several places,[33] "Snap out of it, you who have lapsed into the lethargy of neglecting yourselves and those you love![34] Climb up and out from the darkness of the fearful and confused or stubborn and ignorant beliefs and lifestyle you have unwittingly fallen into that will lead to your tragic and untimely death! If you do this, the High King will not only shine the light of His mercy upon you, He will also illumine your minds into the discovery of the true and consistent way to enjoy a long life filled with happiness!"

ADOPT THE CONSCIOUS RESOLVE TO ACCURATELY MASTER ONLY ETHICALLY SKILLFUL DISCIPLINES AND HABITS IN EVERY SET OF RELATIONSHIPS IN LIFE – NOT UNWITTINGLY FOLLOW MINDLESS, UNETHICAL AND MORALLY UNSKILLFUL CUSTOMS AND TRADITIONS

¹⁵I have now come to setting down the fifth and final set of applications that you all must add to the philosophical standpoint of how you live and view the world in order to complete the implementation of the foundational principles of this Treatise into your lives.[35] To briefly review the four previous main applicational ideas: you must first of all conduct your lives in a manner *worthy* of the special *lifework* to which each of you have been *summoned* and *gifted* by our Commander in Chief, then secondly cease to allow your lives to be directed by the *futile philosophical*

schools of thought dictated by the rest of the world, then thirdly learn the life-step of how to imitate God by *showing self-sacrificial love* for others, then proceed on to the fourth challenge of the philosophical commitment of conducting your lives in the never-ending quest of pursuing the *light* of the *discovery of truth* through the discipline of living a *public life of leadership* in which you demonstrate continual *vulnerablility, mercy, learning* and *consistency*.[36] Fifth therefore, you must be careful to see to it that you precisely and *accurately* conduct the following specific areas, roles and times of your lives according to the ideals of this Treatise, no longer living in ethically and morally unskillful customs and traditions, but only in *ethically* and *morally skillful*[37] *disciplines* and *habits*.

[16]To use another economic illustration, we must be like a merchant who carefully and patiently watches for the specific items of true value he is in search of, and then immediately buys up[38] all of them on those rare occasions when he discovers them for sale.[39] So also, in order to discover and accomplish our lifework for God, we must actively and aggressively *pursue* the things that God wants us to, continually *asking* Him for the spiritual skills and abilities that we must continually *add to,* tenaciously *hold on to,* and become more and more *proficient* in using during our lives, as we *take care* of the people and things of value God has entrusted to us.[40]

Further, as God observes and evaluates our commitment and growth in this pursuit, He will give us a share or portion uniquely suited to us of a larger corporate enterprise involving other people, with whom we must come to learn to work in harmony, balance and the right sense of proportion. Through this corporate enterprise, we must learn to sort through the many things competing for our attention, and "import" only those which are *important* enough into our lives, and disregard those which should be excluded. In addition, among even the important things, God will send a rare number of "super-important" things into our lives of such superlative value that we must recognize them as divine *opportunities* sent from Him and eagerly "bring them into the port" of our lives.

The most valuable of these opportunities will be in recognizing the people that are of such crucial importance that we dedicate ourselves to seeing them as the most *relevant* people in our lives, raising them up to the point that we can *leverage* ourselves and our energies through them. Included in this process is *investing* the money, time and training necessary to cultivate and groom them for the time when these young leaders are ready for us to legitimately transfer power, control and authority over the valuable things and relationships God has entrusted to us – to them. We should transfer that authority through the use of *public symbols* in front of those we place under their leadership, so that they will give recognition to the legitimacy of their new leader's power, control and authority.

Throughout this process, the only people that we should allow to participate with us in our endeavor are those who are willing to follow our example of being *hard workers*, who can learn to work alongside and *cooperate* with us and with each other. The outcomes of the growing sequence of good works that our enterprise performs should continue to expand to the point where the their long-term effects produce a multitude of good and harmonious *consequences* that extend far beyond our direct knowledge or control.

In this way, God will show us a pattern of growth in our enterprise through different *seasons of growth*, in which He will accomplish His divine purposes through us in the course of bringing about renewed cycles of gradual development and maturity. He will always start us out with a period of "*sowing*," follow that by a prolonged period of "*cultivation*" and finally culminate the process in a period of "*reaping*." We must therefore learn to be patient and allow God to bring the natural process of *growth* in our lives to fruition as we progress higher in our maturity to the point at which we become qualified for positions of service to Him in His Kingdom.[41]

The reason I am compelled to alert you to allow yourselves to mature in this way is because during this final era of world history prior to the return of our High King, His archenemy – the Evil One – is very aware that he has but a short time left, and he will consequently attempt to do everything within the considerable scope of the wicked powers remaining to him to thwart and resist your spiritual responsibilites to develop into the mature, gracious and loving human beings our Commander in Chief desires for His present and future service.

17For all these reasons, you must all bring your formerly senseless customs and mindless traditions to an end. Rather, you must all instead continually make a concerted effort to be attentive and listen assiduously to wise counsel and advice that is given in an attempt to dissuade you from taking foolish and precipitous action due to your pride, in order that you might be able to perceive with understanding[42] what our Commander in Chief's purposes and intentions for you are.

18One of the senseless practices you must bring to an end is the bad habit of drinking alcohol to excess.[43] On the contrary, as you would do with all of the good things that God provides in life, learn to drink wine as well as other alcoholic beverages graciously and with a sense of due proportion – as an expression of celebration and of your enjoyment of life. After all, drinking alcohol excessively as a mindless habit is futile, because it causes you to waste so many other valuable things that God has also given you to use – time, money, opportunities, relationships, the ability to behave with self-control and from a measured sense of proportion, and above all the ability to perceive and respond to God's spiritual messages and contacts. It is mainly due to this last reason that you must instead develop the habit of filling your minds and hearts with the spiritual skills of alertness, attentiveness, perceptiveness and discernment.

[19]One effective way to develop the discipline of intentionally filling your minds and hearts with spiritual skills is by *singing*, either individually or as a member of a chorus or a choir. You can do this (or learn to do this) formally or informally by singing the songs written primarily by King David, which he originally composed to be played accompanied by the lyre, but now could be accompanied by other kinds of instruments.[44] You can also learn to sing hymns or choruses and other kinds of spiritual songs. As you learn this skill you should always sing and play to our Commander in Chief with a sincerely grateful attitude, and with the genuine and fervent feeling of all your heart.

[20]Allow me to elaborate on the relationship between developing a perpetually grateful attitude to God and your ability to discern God's will for your lifework. We must always be grateful and openly express our thanks to God for everything He has planned to come into our lives – not only for what we think is good, but also for the things that we do not yet understand, as well as the things we might initially perceive to be negative. The reason we must must never allow ourselves to harbor feelings of anger or resentment toward God is because He is our Father. As our Father, His motives toward us are not only to provide for us as His children, but also to guide the experiences of our lives in such a way as to lead us to become spiritually mature. By giving your thanks to God in the name of our Commander in Chief, Jesus, our future High King, you will develop the discipline of following His example of being grateful to God in the same way that He was when He not only enjoyed, but also suffered everything God assigned Him to endure on our account.[45]

[21]In addition to following the example of Jesus' gratitude to God in all of His experiences, you must also follow His example of subordinating[46] His own wishes, desires and will to God's purposes and intentions for His lifework. Therefore, the only way that each of you will also be able to recognize God's lifework for yourselves is by approaching every relationship you have with each other with an attitude of *deference* and *forbearance* instead of with our disgraceful tendency to presuppose that we are always right and others we encounter or communicate with are always in the wrong. You should be motivated to act in this way towards each other out of a deep sense of admiration and respect for our High King's expectation that you should all follow His own example.

[22]It is important for me at this juncture to apply this principle of developing the spiritual skill of forming a foundationally relational attitude

of showing deference and forbearance to each other in three of the most important relationships in life essential to recognize and fulfill your lifework for God. They are, in the order of importance, the *marriage* relationship,[47] the *parental* relationship,[48] and the *vocational* relationship.[49]

A PRIMARY RELATIONSHIP IN WHICH YOU CAN DISCOVER AND ACCOMPLISH YOUR LIFEWORK IS THROUGH GENUINELY BONDING WITH YOUR SPOUSE BY GRACIOUSLY OFFERING YOURSELVES TO EACH OTHER IN A SPIRIT OF TRUST, GIVING AND SACRIFICE

First, with regard to the marriage relationship, you wives must learn the spiritual skill of adopting a cheerful and gracious attitude of deference and forbearance[50] toward your own husbands, offering to help them find and accomplish their lifework. You should enjoy doing this with him, trusting him and supporting his efforts in a pleasant and agreeable way, with the same positive frame of mind as you would whenever you warmly and gladly assist others for the sake of our Commander in Chief. 23You wives should do this in order to allow God to guide your husbands into implementing their spiritual responsibility to take the lead in actively implementing the loving initiatives God intends for them to perform in your marriage relationship.

God's appointed spiritual training for the husband is that he learn to take up his divinely appointed lifework of becoming your respected and honored leader, of whom you would be proud to be called his wife. You must come to comprehend that this spiritual process that God commands you to go through, although difficult and sometimes protracted, is very much the same spiritual process by which the future High King of the earth never gives up His responsibility to take up His own leadership role of rescuing, forming and developing every one of His specially selected recruits within His Kingdom Apprenticeship Councils into the sprital maturity required to liberate them so that they can recognize and fulfill their lifework. It is in this way that the High King prepares us all for performing future duties that are much higher and nobler than those that concern this life – namely, becoming the distinguished Ministers of His future governmental body through which He will administrate the future world.

24Admittedly, this principle is initially problematic for you wives to readily accept, due to the seemingly preponderant tendency for the majority of males in general and husbands in particular to become passive, pathetic whiners and cowards in most historical eras. That is why it is so necessary at this point for me to reiterate its importance. In precisely the same way that His Lifework Apprenticeship Councils have been subordinated by God to our future High King in order for Him to lead His specially selected recruits which comprise them to gradually realize, and then over time, bring to fruition the unique lifework He has planned for them – over what admittedly is usually a protracted and somewhat rocky relationship – so also you wives should recognize that God is at work in the same way in your marriage relationship with your husband.

Allow me to elaborate. Every event that occurs in your marriage relationship, when discerned from a spiritual perspective, is designed by God to eventually liberate your husbands from their typical historical habit of becoming sidetracked into passive, pusillanimous and spineless male behavior. His goal is to transform your husbands, so that they take up their spiritual responsibilities as true husbands, and become the leaders He intends for them to become, actively and courageously implementing the loving initiatives towards you and your families that our High King desires them to. It is through understanding that the marriage relationship itself consists precisely of this transformational process that our High King can and will lead your husbands to discover and achieve the noble lifework He has planned for them.

However, the only way in which this transformational process can take place is through your deliberate spiritual commitment to relationally offer yourselves to your husbands in the variety of life-events that will occur in you marriage relationship with an attitude of deference and forbearance, just as you would to our High King. If you fail to do this and give in to the strong temptation to keep taking over the leadership initiative in the relationship whenever your husbands fail, they will keep on using your desire to control the relationship as an *excuse to remain passive and pathetically weak*, with the result that you will continue to disrespect them and even hold them in contempt.

So, in order for this process to work, you must by your respect for and faith in the High King, force your husbands to face Him and allow Him to discipline them and transform them into the leader you desire and can come to respect. If you do this, God will lead you wives to discover and accomplish the special and unique lifework He has planned for each of you as a woman. In addition, He will also employ your augmented power as a couple to enhance and amplify your lifework as a married couple.

[25]Now I must address you husbands. As one of the specially selected recruits of our Commander in Chief, a primary spiritual relationship you must continually renovate and keep in good condition in order to find and accomplish your lifework is your relationship with your wife. If you desire to find the special lifework that our future High King has for each of you, you must abandon your tendency to get sidetracked into being a passive, weak male, and instead become committed to becoming a true

husband that takes the lead in your marriage bond. You must become resourceful and actively implement self-sacrificial, loving initiatives in your relationship with your wife.

Allow me to elaborate. You must take as your example our own High King, who in His present role in heaven continues to postpone taking up His rightful throne as King of the Earth, and instead patiently continues to give spiritual gifts and abilities to the specially selected recruits that comprise His Lifework Apprenticeship Councils, in order to slowly but steadily liberate each member within them into discovering and accomplishing the lifework He has planned for each of them. As you reflect upon your own lives, and how *patient* our High King has been every time He has taken a loving initiative to rescue you from the consequences of your own selfishness, or get you back on the right road from getting sidetracked, or give you a unique and special spiritual ability to help others – so also in the same way you husbands must follow His example by taking up your responsibility to patiently and sacrificially originate the loving initiatives to lead your wife by giving of yourselves to her as a habitual way of life over your entire lifetime. If you do this, she will come to respect you and willingly follow your leadership, because she will know that your initiatives toward her will always be guided by self-sacrificial love.

26The spiritually accurate[51] living out of the husband-wife relationship (in which the role of the husband is to lead the relationship with self-sacrificial loving initiatives, and the role of the wife is to respectfully receive and implement those initiatives) is of primary importance for each of them to discover and accomplish their respective lifeworks as His specially selected recruits, for two reasons. First, because the ultimate purpose of our High King in the entire history of the world is and always has been that He might identify, separate out, and specially select a unique group of human beings to set apart for His special use in the administration of His future Kingdom. The problem He has always had with us humans is that we, as it were, have (as I previously explained above) made ourselves spiritually "filthy" without being aware of it – either by adopting the false philosophical world views of the Barbarian nations in leading degraded and hopeless lives, completely enslaved by natural visceral appetites, as you all did in your former lives; or by adopting an arrogant, condescending, cruel and sanctimonious attitude, which I used to do.

On the contrary, in the same way that young King Solomon, in the wisdom of his youth, used the metaphor of how much he enjoyed taking the initiative to bathe his newly-shorn sheep flocks in water to have them be bright and clean, he also continually "cleansed" his own relationship with his first and only true wife by taking the initiative to lead their conversation in humorous, gentle, tender and loving speech.[52]

In similar fashion, just as our Commander in Chief made it His habit to take the initiative to continually "cleanse" the relationships He had with His own apprentices by His encouraging, gentle, yet meaningful and well-considered spoken words, so also you husbands should follow His example by adopting the habit of continually "cleansing" your relationships with your wife by not fearing to initiate kind, gentle, considerate, yet truthful speech[53] in conversation with her. Husbands, it is through this spiritual skill of *taking up the responsibility to initiate loving conversation with your wife* that you will not only continually "cleanse" your relationship with her from misunderstandings, anger, bitterness and even cruelty, but you will also secure both for yourself and your wife the ability to discern the purpose of the lifework that our future High King has for each of you to accomplish.

[27]Allow me to use the illustration of a wedding to explain the second reason why living out your husband-wife relationships in a spiritually accurate manner is of paramount importance in being able to discover and accomplish your lifework as the High King's specially selected recruits. In the same way that you husbands, upon your own wedding day, desired that your bride be presented to you (or as parents, that your daughter be presented to her husband) in a special, dignified, official public ceremony, in which her beauty, loveliness and moral purity might be seen, honored and appreciated[54] by all, so also our Commander in Chief desires that at His own inaugural ceremony, when He finally takes up his rightful throne as High King of the Earth, He might present His own "bride" to Himself in the same distinguished way. In this metaphor, the "bride" of our High King is His fully completed Kingdom Council, composed of the full complement of His resurrected specially selected recruits, who, having qualified themselves for His special Kingdom service by discovering their respective lifeworks and accomplishing them during their apprenticeship in the course of their mortal lives, now as a comprehensive governmental body of mature and wise servants, stand ready for beginning their new lives of service to Him.

In addition, the formal clothing of a wedding has important symbolic meaning. The dress of the bride is white and without any spots, stains wrinkles or other defects, because it represents her moral purity and eagerness to begin her new life with her husband as uniquely his, and to follow his leadership in discovering and creating together the children and the distinctive family that God will give to them. In the same way, our High King, through the process of the severe training involved in their apprenticeships, will have removed all the spots, stains or wrinkles of moral impurity, vice or or any other kind of faults of character from the members of His Kingdom Councils that would have hindered them in accomplishing His will for their future lives spent in unique roles of special service to Him.

In other words, in the same way that the bride should prepare her own life to be morally blameless in order that she, her husband, and their families might enjoy her special, honorable wedding and marriage, so also should you all spend your married life as husband and wife. You should spend your married life together sacrificially loving and giving yourselves to each other with deference and forbearance, in preparation to enjoy the same special, honorable Inaugural Day when the High King returns and we all begin our new life together with Him.

28In fact, a practical and straightforward way for you husbands to ascertain if you are loving your wife to the extent that our Commander in Chief requires you to if you desire His approval and resulting qualification for His eventual Millennial Service, is if you take the initiative to love and care for her with precisely the same measure of utmost care as you love and care for the health, welfare, development and growth of your own selves during your mortal lives.[55] A short but effective maxim for you to memorize would be, "He who loves his wife loves himself."[56] Therefore, it is also true that he who does not love his wife in some area, has to that extent a defect in his life of his own love of what is good and virtuous for himself, and consequently to that same extent disqualifies himself from service to our future High King.

29Moreover, when you reflect upon it, nobody ever makes a habit of harboring sustained abhorrence and ill will towards himself, whether it be his physical or psychological health. Quite to the contrary, observation of normal human behavior shows that we habitually nuture, rear up, cultivate and carefully watch over the physical health and intellectual growth process of our children as well as ourselves.[57] We take care of our own, whether it be our children or our own selves, in that we all desire to be comforted and cared for with tenderness and warmth, as well as vigorously and passionately protected and defended when we are in danger.[58] To come to the point, since our Commander in Chief takes care of those of us whom He has specially selected to become members of His Kingdom Apprenticeship Councils in precisely these same ways, you husbands should imitate Him by showing warmth and tenderness in gently caring for your wife in these same ways also.

30Allow me to develop this theme further by expanding its scope to include the biological metaphor of God's creation of the first woman Eve out of the first man Adam, which speaks directly to the deep level of intimacy with which our Commander in Chief regards the husband-wife relationship as emblematic of His own relationship with His Kingdom Apprenticeship Councils. It speaks to the fact that the husband-wife relationship is a major test case of your behavior that forms a primary basis of His evaluation of your qualifications for service to Him in that future governmental body through which He will rule the earth. As His chosen and specially selected apprentices, He regards us already as members of that future body in the same intimate way that Adam regarded Eve when he first saw her and realized that God had miraculously fashioned her from the deepest part of his physical body – his chest – out of his own skin, muscles, organs and bones, to illustrate to him that she was to be his most intimate and unique companion, helper, and friend.

[31]To prove this, I will make a case that the meaning of the passage in Genesis 2:24 in which God creates Eve for Adam is fulfilled by our Commander in Chief in that He *exchanged* the intimacy of His relationship with His Father for the *new relational intimacy* He desires to have with His own specially selected recruits who are the members of His Kingdom Apprenticeship Councils. Since this is true, each of you husbands should therefore follow His example by *exchanging* the intimate relationship you initially had with your own parents for a new and intimate realtionship with your wife in the same way. I will first quote the passage as I interpret it from the Septuagint, and then explain my interpretation.

The passage itself, in its fulfilled meaning, reads as follows, "A man shall leave his initial relationship with his father and mother and *exchange it for* the following relationship, namely – the bond of marriage – in that he shall take the initiative to bond to[59] his wife such that the two of them come to exist in a relational manner so intimately close and "connected" to each other, that it is as if they are one being."[60] [32]Consequently, *a primary relationship in which God will accomplish His "Top Secret" Plan through His Lifework Councils is by your living out the bonded relationship of marriage in a spiritually accurate way.*

The additional feature of God's "Top Secret" Plan I am emphasizing at this point is that the High King has chosen to *exchange* His relationship with the Father for a new, enduring and intimate relationship with you all who are members of His Kingdom Apprenticeship Councils. It therefore follows that it is only by your comparable display of commitment to *exchange* your relationship with your parents for a lifetime of living together in the mutually bonded, intimate relationship of being married, loving husbands and wives that you will be able to discern and fulfill your respective lifework. By doing this, each of you will become qualified to serve our future High King as His mature representatives when He returns to establish His Kingdom on the earth.

³³To summarize and conclude what we have conveyed so far on the importance of the marriage relationship: For those of you who *are husbands* – the "bottom line" of the foregoing multifaceted and admittedly complicated line of reasoning is that each of you should remember this one simple principle: *You must love your wife in the same way that you love yourself.* And for those of you who *are wives* – the main thing you should remember from the line of reasoning presented above is the following simple principle: *You must respect your husband.*

◆―――――――――――――――――――――――――――――――◆

Notes to Extended Interpretive and Expositional Translation
Ephesians Chapter 5

¹ See a summary of the content of the first two of the total of five *"περιπατέω"* sections previously covered in Chapter 4 (see note and outline at Eph. 4:1).

² **μιμητής**, οῦ, ὁ, *imitator*, τινων ib.1.6.3, cf. Hp.*Vict.*1.22, *1 Ep.Cor.*4.16; οἱ μ. τῶν γραμμάτων *forgers*, Lib. *Ep.*115.4. II. *artist* (cf. μίμησις 11), Pl.*R.*602a, al.; esp. *one who impersonates characters, as an actor or poet*, Arist.*Pr.*918b28, *Po.* 1460a8 [LS]. Proposed translation: "one who deliberately imitates or impersonates; who approaches reality not as oneself, but as an actor portraying a specific role or part in a play."

³ The word most often used in Greek for "child" is the word "**παῖς**," which carries the connotative impersonal meaning of the mere effect of biological parentage only, and therefore is most often translated "offspring, issue." Less often used, (and therefore probably deliberately used by Paul here) is the word **τέκνον**. It is the noun derived from the verb **τίκτω**, which means "to give birth." Thus the word **τέκνον** carries the connotative meaning of the *mutual intimate tenderness and personal feeling and experience of relationship* that exists between mothers and fathers and their "children."

⁴ ἀγαπητός, ή, όν, Dor. ἀγαπ-ατός, ά, όν, *that wherewith one must be content* (cf ἀγαπάω 111), *hence of only children*, μοῦνος ἐὼν ἀ. Od.2.365; Ἑκτορίδην ἀ. Il.6.401, cf. Od.4.817, Sapph. 85, Ar.*Th.*761, Pl.*Alc.*1.131e;...--hence, ἀγαπητόν [ἐστι] *one must be content*, εἰ . . , ἐάν . . Pl.*Prt.*328b, X.*Oec.* 8.16, D.18.220, Arist.*Metaph.*1076a15, etc.; c. inf., *EN*1171a20. **II.** of things, *desirable*, ἤθη X.*Mem.*3.10.5; βίος Pl.*Phlb.*61e (Sup.). **2.** of persons, *beloved*, ἀδελφὲ ἀγαπητέ LXX *To.*3.10: in letters, as a term of address, *Ep.Rom.*12.19, cf. *PGrenf.*2.73, etc. **III.** Adv. -τῶς *gladly, contentedly,* Pl.*Lg.*735d, D.19.219, etc...[LS]. It appears from a study of the above texts that the strong connotative meaning that eventually comes to be emphasized in the adjective ἀγαπητός is the *effect produced in the soul that has been nurtured by the self-sacrificial love of devoted*

parents, namely the experience of *"glad and cheerful contentment"* that comes only by learning to self-sacrificially love other people. This is the main sense in which Aristotle uses this word in the final section of his *Nicomachean Ethics* on the necessity of a society of mature friends to experience "contentment" and happiness. It is also one of the main themes of the Scottish novelist and poet George MacDonald (1824-1905), whom C.S. Lewis credits as the man who posthumously led him from being an atheist to becoming a Christian. Reading Aristotle's view of friendship in the *Nicomachean Ethics* – or more especially MacDonald's novels – will give one a far deeper appreciation of how important the link between *showing self-sacrificial love* and *experiencing glad* and *cheerful contentment* in life is. Proposed translation: "glad and cheerful contentment."

[5] Plato emphasizes the phenomenon of how the human personality eventually takes on as second nature the characteristics of roles it habitually acts out (μιμητής = *"actor,"* see note above) in the *Republic*, Book III, as follows (ed. John Burnet, Oxford, 1903, transl. Paul Shorey, Cambridge, 1969):

> [394e] "This then, Adeimantus, is the point we must keep in view, do we wish our guardians to be good mimics (μιμητικός = "actors") or not? Or is this also a consequence of what we said before, that each one could practise well only one pursuit and not many, but if he attempted the latter, dabbling in many things, he would fail of distinction in all?" "Of course it is." "And does not the same rule hold for *imitation*, (μιμήσεως) that the same man is not able to *imitate* (μιμεῖσθαι) many things well as he can one?" "No, he is not." "Still less, then, will he be able to combine [395a] the practice of any worthy pursuit with the *imitation* (μιμήσεται) of many things and the quality of a *mimic* (μιμητικός); since, unless I mistake, the same men cannot practise well at once even the two forms of *imitation* (μιμήματα) that appear most nearly akin, as the writing of tragedy (τραγῳδίαν) and comedy (κωμῳδίαν)? Did you not just now call these two *imitations* (μιμήματε)?" "I did, and you are right in saying that the same men are not able to succeed in both, nor yet to be at once good rhapsodists and *actors*." "True." "But [395b] neither can the same men be *actors* for tragedies and comedies – and all these are *imitations* (μιμήματα), are they not?" "Yes, *imitations* (μιμήματα)." "And to still smaller coinage than this, in my opinion, Adeimantus, proceeds the fractioning of human faculty, so as to be incapable of *imitating* (μιμεῖσθαι) many things or of doing the things themselves of which the *imitations* (μιμήματά) are likenesses." "Most true," he replied. "If, then, we are to maintain our original principle, that our guardians, released from all other crafts, [395c] are to be expert craftsmen of civic liberty (ἐλευθερίας τῆς πόλεως), and pursue nothing else that does not conduce to this, it would not be fitting for these to do nor yet to *imitate* (μιμεῖσθαι) anything else. But if they *imitate* (μιμῶνται), they should from childhood up *imitate* (μιμεῖσθαι) what is appropriate to them – men, that is, who are brave, sober, pious, free and all things of that kind; but things unbecoming the free man they should neither do nor be clever at *imitating* (μιμήσασθαι), nor yet any other shameful thing (αἰσχρῶν – cf. Eph. 5:4 "αἰσχρότης"), lest from the *imitation* (μιμήσεως) [395d] they imbibe the reality. Or have you not observed that *imitations* (μιμήσεις), if continued from youth far into life, settle down into habits and (second) nature in the body, the speech, and the thought?" "Yes, indeed," said he. "We will not then allow our charges, whom we expect to prove good men, being men, to play the parts of

women and ***imitate*** (**μιμεῖσθαι**) a woman young or old wrangling with her husband, defying heaven, loudly boasting, fortunate in her own conceit, or involved in misfortune [395e] and possessed by grief and lamentation – still less a woman that is sick, in love, or in labor." "Most certainly not," he replied. "Nor may they ***imitate*** (**μιμεῖσθαι**) slaves, female and male, doing the offices of slaves." "No, not that either." "Nor yet, as it seems, bad men who are cowards and who do the opposite of the things we just now spoke of, reviling and lampooning one another, speaking foul words in their cups or when sober [396a] and in other ways sinning against themselves [ἁμαρτάνουσιν; better = "missing the mark, falling short of their goals" – GWC] and others in word and deed after the fashion of such men. And I take it they must not form the habit of likening themselves to madmen either in words nor yet in deeds. For while knowledge they must have both of mad and bad men and women, they must do and ***imitate*** (**μιμητέον**) nothing of this kind." "Most true," he said."

[6] Ephesians 5:1-7 comprises the third of Paul's five "**περιπατέω**" sections (see note at Eph. 4:1 for an overall outline of the **περιπατέω** sections).

[7] Paul's definitive exposition of what it means to "**περιπατεῖτε ἐν ἀγάπῃ**," i.e., "to conduct your lives according to a new and comprehensive philosophical world view based on *self-sacrificial love* for others" is in 1 Cor. 13:4-8, 13, presented and translated below:

> 1 Cor. 13:4-8, 13 [4]'Η ἀγάπη μακροθυμεῖ, χρηστεύεται, ἡ ἀγάπη οὐ ζηλοῖ, ἡ ἀγάπη οὐ περπερεύεται, οὐ φυσιοῦται, [5]οὐκ ἀσχημονεῖ, οὐ ζητεῖ τὰ ἑαυτῆς, οὐ παροξύνεται, οὐ λογίζεται τὸ κακόν, [6]οὐ χαίρει ἐπὶ τῇ ἀδικίᾳ, συνχαίρει δὲ τῇ ἀληθείᾳ· [7]πάντα στέγει, πάντα πιστεύει, πάντα ἐλπίζει, πάντα ὑπομένει. [8]'Η **ἀγάπη** οὐδέποτε πίπτει...[13]νυνὶ δὲ μένει πίστις, ἐλπίς, **ἀγάπη**: τὰ τρία ταῦτα, μείζων δὲ τούτων ἡ **ἀγάπη**."
>
> Transl.: "[4]**Love** suffers long and is kind; **love** doesn't envy. **Love** doesn't brag, is not proud, [5]doesn't behave rudely, doesn't seek its own way, is not provoked, takes no account of evil; [6]doesn't rejoice when wrong is done, but rejoices in the truth; [7]bears all things, believes all things, hopes all things, endures all things. [8]**Love** never fails...[13]But now faith, hope, and **love** remain – these three; but the greatest of these is **love**."

A recent best-selling novel and then motion picture that offers an accurate, true-to-life contemporary portrayal of this kind of love is entitled *A Walk to Remember*, by Nicholas Sparks (1999).

[8] **παραδίδωμι...3. *give up to justice***, etc., ἥντινα μήτε...παραδοῦναι ἐξῆν Antipho 6.42;...***give up a slave to be examined by torture,*** Isoc.17.15, Test. ap. D.45.61:-- Pass., ἐγκλήματι π. dub. l. in D.C.62.27: metaph., σιωπῇ καὶ λήθῃ παραδοθείς D.H.*Pomp.*3 [LS]. The word commonly used in professional American English to mean "give up or hand over a person to justice" is the word "surrender." Proposed translation in this context: "surrender."

[9] **ὀσμή**, ἡ, Att. form of the older **ὀδμή** (v. fin.), ***smell, odour*...II. *the sense of smell*,** = ὄσφρησις, Democr.11, Hsch.--The older form **ὀδμή** (cf. ὄδωδα, ὄζ-ω, odor) is alone used by Hom., Hdt., and Pi.; it occurs also in A.Pr.115 (lyr.), Democr. l. c., and in later Prose [LS]. Proposed translation as a noun: "smell."

[10] εὐωδία, Ion. -ιη, ἡ, *sweet smell*, Hdt.4.75, X.*Smp.*2.3, etc.; esp. of sacrifices, ὀσμή-ίας LXX *Ge.*8.21: metaph. in *Ep.Eph.***5.2**: in pl., Pl.*Ti.* 65a: in pl., also, *fragrant substances*...[LS]. This word is used only 3 times in the NT, all by Paul: here in Eph. 5:2, in 2 Cor. 2:15 and Phil. 4:18. In the other two passages it is also used metaphorically of actions of self-sacrificial love which please God (in the Corinthians' passage, of Paul's proclaiming, teaching and explaining the good news of Jesus to others without cost; and in the Philippians' passage, of their gifts brought to Paul by Epaphroditus to keep him alive during his imprisonment and trial in Rome). Proposed translation: "frangrance, fragrant."

[11] Aristotle's analysis of the connection between the *smell of fragrances* and *reliving experiences* associated with them through *memory* or *hope* is noteworthy. He says (in the *Rhetoric*, Section 1370a-b, W. D. Ross, Oxford, 1959, transl. J. H. Freese, Cambridge, 1926):

> "Now, of desires some are irrational, others rational. I call irrational all those that are not the result of any opinion held by the mind [i.e., 'mental consideration of the results that may follow – the desires arise without anything of the kind; they simply come' – Jebb, Welldon]. Such are all those which are called natural; for instance, those which come into existence through the body – such as the desire of food, thirst, hunger, the desire of such and such food in particular; the desires connected with taste, sexual pleasures, in a word, with touch, ***smell of fragrances*** [ὀσμὴν εὐωδίας – note that Aristotle uses exactly the same phrase as Paul does here – GWC] hearing, and sight. I call those desires rational which are due to our being convinced; for there are many things which we desire to see or acquire when we have heard them spoken of and are convinced that they are pleasant. Further, if pleasure consists in the sensation of a certain emotion, and imagination is a weakened sensation, then both the ***man who remembers and the man who hopes will be attended by an imagination of what he remembers or hopes.*** This being so, it is evident that there is pleasure both for those who remember and for those who hope, since there is sensation. Therefore all pleasant things must either be present in sensation, or past in recollection, or future in hope; for one senses the present, recollects the past, and hopes for the future. Therefore our recollections [whether induced irrationally through the smell of a fragrance, or rationally through the use of the mind – GWC] are pleasant, not only when they recall things which when present were agreeable, but also some things which were not, if their consequence subsequently proves honorable or good; whence the saying: 'Sweet 'tis when rescued to remember pain [Euripides, *Andromeda*, Frag. 133];' and, 'Even his griefs are a joy long after to one that remembers all that he wrought and endured [Homer, *Odyssey,* 15: 400-401].' The reason of this is that even to be free from evil is pleasant. Things which we hope for are pleasant, when their presence seems likely to afford us great pleasure or advantage, without the accompaniment of pain. ***In a word, all things that afford pleasure by their presence as a rule also afford pleasure when we hope for or remember them*** [italics mine – GWC]."

The Gospels make specific note of incidents in which Jesus uses the *smell of fragrances* to teach the pleasure caused by the memory of or hope for *good deeds*. We recall the important incident recorded in the Gospels of Mary anointing Jesus' head and feet with **spikenard** (an extremely expensive and fragrant ointment) at

Simon the Leper's house in Bethany three days prior to Jesus' crucifixion (Matt. 26:6-13, Mark 14:3-9, John 12:1-8). Although all the disciples are indignant and regard Mary's action as a waste of money, Jesus rebukes them and approves of Mary's action, saying:

> "Why do you trouble the woman? For she has done a good work for Me...for in pouring this fragrant oil on My body, she did it for My burial (Matt. 26:10-12);" and, "Let her alone...she has done a good work for Me...she has come beforehand to anoint my body for burial (Mark 14:6-8);" and, "Let her alone; she has kept this for the day of My burial (John 12:7)."

In all three of these passages, the link between fragrance and *memory* of a dear person or event is emphasized. Luke records a similar incident earlier in Jesus' ministry (Luke 7:36-50), when a sinful woman [ἁμαρτωλός = "failure, 'Loser'," – since this woman is probably a prostitute, a good translation might be "slut" – GWC] anoints Jesus' feet at Simon the Pharisee's house. In this passage, the link between the fragrant smell of the ointment and the woman's *hope* seems to be emphasized; namely, her *self-knowledge* of her own moral failure, her desire to be *forgiven*, her *faith* in Jesus to forgive her, her *love* [Gk: ἀγάπη] for Jesus, and Jesus' final *encouragement for her future life*, when He says to her, "Your faith has saved you. Go in peace (Luke 7:50)."

[12] πορνεία, Ion. πορν-είη, ἡ, *prostitution*, Hp.Epid.7.122, etc.; of a man, D.19.200; *fornication, unchastity*, Ev.Matt.19.9: pl., 1 Ep.Cor. 7.2 [LS]. The Greek word "πορνεία" has historically most often been translated into English as the Latin word "**fornication**" (**for·ni·ca·tion:** Etymology: Middle English *fornicacioun,* from Middle French & Late Latin; Middle French *fornication,* from Late Latin *fornication-, fornicatio,* from *fornicatus* (past participle) + Latin *-ion-, -io* -ion. **1:** human sexual intercourse other than between a man and his wife: sexual intercourse between a spouse and an unmarried person: sexual intercourse between unmarried people -- used in some translations (as AV, DV) of the Bible (as in Mt 5:32) for *unchastity* (as in RSV) or *immorality* (as in NCE) to cover all sexual intercourse except between husband and wife or concubine, **2:** sexual intercourse on the part of an unmarried person accomplished with consent and not deemed adultery [W]). The Greek word "πορνεία" has been transliterated historically into English as the word "*porn*," and when combined with the Greek word "γραφή," which means "writing," it became the word "*pornography*" (**por·nog·ra·phy** – Etymology: Greek *pornographos* writing of harlots (from *pornē* harlot + *-graphos* writing) + English *-y* **1:** a description of prostitutes or prostitution **2:** a depiction (as in writing or painting) of licentiousness or lewdness: a portrayal of erotic behavior designed to cause sexual excitement [W]). My own observation is that the word "fornication" is no longer commonly used in contemporary professional American English. Therefore, I propose the (somewhat wooden) translation, "consensual sexual intercourse outside the bond of marriage."

¹³ ἀκαθαρσία, ἡ, A. *uncleanness, foulness, of a wound or sore*, Hp. *Fract*.31, cf. Pl.*Ti*.72c(pl.); ἀγγείων Hp.Epid.6.31. **b.** *dirt, filth*, BGU1117.27 (13 B.C.), etc. **2.** in moral sense, *depravity*, D.21.119. **3.** *ceremonial impurity*, LXX Le.15.3,al. [LS]. The Greek Philosopher Epictetus wrote a treatise entitled *"On Purity"* [Book 4.11], in which he condemns filthiness in the body as well as in the soul. Paul associates filthiness both of body and soul most often with sexual perversion. Proposed translation: "dirty, filthy, foul-smelling" (of an unwashed human body); "depraved" (when used as a metaphor for "un-clean" in an ethical or moral sense).

¹⁴ πλεονεξία – "greed, avarice;" see note at Eph. 4:19 for the analysis of the meaning of this word.

¹⁵ αἰσχρότης...**II.** *filthy conduct, Ep.Eph*.5.4; euphem. for *fellatio*, Sch.Ar.Ra.1308 [LS]. [transl. = euphemism for the Latin word "fellatio" (**fel·la·tio** – Etymology: New Latin *fellation-*, *fellatio*, from Latin *fellatus*, *felatus* (past participle of *fellare*, *felare* to suck) + *-io-*, *-io -ion*: the practice of obtaining sexual satisfaction by oral stimulation of the penis [W]), used in this context in Aristophanes *Frogs*, line 1308, as follows (ed. F.W. Hall and W.M. Geldart, Oxford, 1907, transl. ed. by Matthew Dillon):

> **Dionysus:** What is this phlattothrat? Is it from Marathon, or where did you assemble these songs of a rope-twister?
> **Aeschylus:** Well, to a fine place from a fine place did I bring them, lest I be seen garnering from the same meadow as Phrynichos. But this guy gets them from everywhere, from little whores, Meletus' drinking songs, Carian flute solos, Dirges, dances. This will all be made clear immediately. Someone bring in a lyre. And yet, what need of a lyre for this guy? Where's the girl who clacks the castanets? Hither, Muse of Euripides, for whom these songs are appropriate to sing.
> **Dionysus:** This Muse never did *the Lesbian thing*, oh no..."

The word αἰσχρότης is rare in Greek literature, occurring only once in the NT (here). Two other occurances that prove helpful for understanding its meaning are the passage above, and in Plato's *Gorgias*, section 525a. In Plato's passage, Socrates is speaking with Callicles about how the human soul appears and what happens to it in the afterlife. The full context of the passage is noteworthy because in Ephesians Chapter 4, Paul uses the same metaphor that Socrates employs in this passage – that of using *clothing* as an illustration for *performing ethical or unethical actions in one's life*. Socrates explains to Callicles what he believes, as follows (ed. John Burnet, Oxford 1903, transl. W.R.M. Lamb, Cambridge, 1967):

> **Socrates:** [523a] "Give ear then, as they say, to a right fine story, which you will regard as a fable, I fancy, but I as an actual account; for what I am about to tell you I mean to offer as the truth. By Homer's account, Zeus, Poseidon, and Pluto divided the sovereignty amongst them when they took it over from their father. Now in the time of Cronos there was a law concerning mankind, and it holds to this very day amongst the gods, that every man who has passed a just and holy life departs after his decease [523b] to the Isles of the Blest, and dwells in all happiness apart from ill; but whoever has lived unjustly and impiously goes to the dungeon of requital and penance, which,

you know, they call Tartarus. Of these men there were judges in Cronos' time, and still of late in the reign of Zeus – living men to judge the living upon the day when each was to breathe his last; and thus the cases were being decided amiss. So Pluto and the overseers from the Isles of the Blest came before Zeus with the report that they found men passing over to either abode undeserving. [523c] Then spake Zeus: "Nay," said he, "I will put a stop to these proceedings. The cases are now indeed judged ill and it is because they who are on trial are tried in their clothing, for they are tried alive. Now many," said he, "who have wicked souls are clad in fair bodies and ancestry and wealth, and at their judgement appear many witnesses to testify that their lives have been just. Now, the judges are confounded not only by their evidence [523d] but at the same time by being clothed themselves while they sit in judgement, having their own soul muffled in the veil of eyes and ears and the whole body. Thus all these are a hindrance to them, their own habiliments no less than those of the judged...they must be stripped bare of all those things before they are tried; for they must stand their trial dead. Their judge also must be naked, dead, beholding with very soul the very soul of each immediately upon his death, bereft of all his kin and having left behind on earth all that fine array, to the end that the judgement may be just. Now I, knowing all this before you, have appointed sons of my own to be judges; two from Asia, Minos and Rhadamanthus, [524a] and one from Europe, Aeacus. These, when their life is ended, shall give judgement in the meadow at the dividing of the road, whence are the two ways leading, one to the Isles of the Blest, and the other to Tartarus. And those who come from Asia shall Rhadamanthus try...from these stories, on my reckoning, we must draw some such moral as this: death, as it seems to me, is actually nothing but the disconnection of two things, the soul and the body, from each other. And so when they are disconnected from one another, each of them keeps its own condition very much as it was when the man was alive, the body having its own nature, with its treatments and experiences all manifest upon it....whatever sort of bodily appearance a man had acquired in life, that is manifest also after his death either wholly or in the main for some time. And so it seems to me that the same is the case with the soul too, Callicles: when a man's soul is stripped bare of the body, all its natural gifts, and the experiences added to that soul as the result of his various pursuits, are manifest in it. So when they have arrived [524e] in presence of their judge, they of Asia before Rhadamanthus, these Rhadamanthus sets before him and surveys the soul of each, not knowing whose it is; nay, often when he has laid hold of the Great King or some other prince or potentate, he perceives the utter unhealthiness of his soul, striped all over with the scourge, and a mass of wounds, [525a] the work of perjuries (ἐπιορκία) and injustice (ἀδικία); where every act has left its smirch upon his soul (ψυχή), where all is awry (σκολιός = "twisted, crooked" [LS]) through falsehood (ψεῦδος = "lying, deceit" [LS]) and imposture (ἀλαζονεία = "pretentiousness" [LS]), and nothing straight because of a nurture (τρέφω = "being brought up, reared, education" [LS]) that knew not truth (ἀλήθεια): or, as the result of an unbridled course of fastidiousness (τρυφάω = "licentiousness, being effeminate" [LS]), insolence (ὕβρις = "wanton violence, arising from the pride of strength or from passion, committing a sexual outrage on a person, esp. violation, rape" [LS]), and incontinence (ἀκρατής = "being immoderate, lacking self-control, without command over oneself or one's passions" [LS]), he finds the soul full fraught with disproportion (ἀσυμμετρία = "disproportionate, lack of symmetry, proportion or harmony" [LS], lit. = "unsymmetrical") and **ugliness** (**αἰσχρότης** = ***"ugly, deformed"*** [LS]). Beholding this he sends it away in dishonor (ἄτιμος) straight to the place of custody, where on its arrival it is to endure the sufferings that are fitting."

Although the feminine noun **αἰσχρότης** is rare, the adjective **αἰσχρός** (and the verb **αἰσχύνω** from which it is derived) are used more often: **αἰσχρός**, ά, όν, also ός, όν *APl.*4.151: ([αἶσχος]):--in Hom., **A. *causing shame, dishonouring, reproachful***, νείκεσσεν . . αἰσχροῖς ἐπέεσσιν Il.3.38, etc. Adv. αἰσχρῶς, ἐνένισπεν 23.473. **II.** opp. καλός: **1.** of outward appearance, ***ugly, ill-favoured***, of Thersites, Il.2.216, cf. *h.Ap.*197, Hdt.1.196 (Comp.), etc.; ***deformed***, Hp.*Art.*14 (Sup.); αἰσχρῶς χωλός *with an ugly* lameness, ib.63: **but commonly, 2. in moral sense, *shameful, base***, Hdt.3.155, A.*Th.*685, etc.; αἰσχροῖς γὰρ αἰσχρὰ πράγματ' ἐκδιδάσκεται S.*El.*621; αἰσχρόν [ἐστι], c. inf., Il.2.298, S.*Aj.*473, etc.; αἰσχρόν, εἰ πύθοιτό τις ib.1159; ἐν αἰσχρῷ θέσθαι τι E.*Hec.*806; ἐπ' αἰσχροῖς on the ground of ***base actions***, S. *Fr.*188, E.*Hipp.*511:--τὸ αἰ. as Subst., ***dishonour***, S.*Ph.*476; τὸ ἐμὸν αἰ. my ***disgrace***, And.2.9; τὸ καλὸν καὶ τὸ αἰ. virtue and ***vice***, Arist.*Rh.* 1366a24, etc. Adv., ***shamefully***, S.*El.*989, Pl.*Smp.*183d, etc.: Sup. αἴσχιστα A.*Pr.*959 , S.*OT*367 [LS]. Sophocles employs this word often in his plays to describe the shameful and violent crimes associated with sexual disloyalty: murder, adultery, and plotting the murder of others due to being terrified of suffering retribution for the original heinous acts. Sophocles uses the word **αἰσχρός** in this way multiple times in close context in Electra's speech in which she condemns her mother Clytaemnestra for murdering her husband (Electra's father) Agamemnon, and then living in open adultery with her co-conspirator Aegisthus, who is plotting to kill Clytaemnestra's other two children Orestes and Electra herself in order to prevent retribution for his crime, as follows in lines 558, 586, 593 and 621 (ed. and transl. Sir Richard Jebb, Cambridge, 1894):

> **Electra (accusing her mother Clytaemnestra):** [558] "Then I will speak. You admit that you killed my father (Agamemnon). What statement could be more ***shameful*** (**αἰσχίων**) still than that, [560] whether you did it justly or not? But I will demonstrate to you that you did not justly kill him. No, the persuasion of that wicked man (Aegisthus) with whom you now sleep dragged you to it...[585] For tell me, if you please, what crime it is that you requite by doing the most ***shameless deeds*** (**αἴσχιστα**) of all: sharing your bed with that blood-guilty one (Aegisthus), with whom you first destroyed my father (Agamemnon) and now bear his children [590] while you have cast out the earlier born, the pious offspring (Orestes) of a pious marriage? How can I commend these deeds? Or will you claim that this, too, is recompense for your daughter? No, it is a ***shameful*** (**αἰσχρῶς**) plea, if you so plead, for there is nothing noble in marrying an enemy for a daughter's sake...I know that my behavior is unsuited to my age and inappropriate. But then the enmity I get from you and your [620] behavior compel me with harsh necessity to do this; for ***reprehensible deeds*** are learned from ***reprehensible examples*** (αἰσχροῖς γὰρ αἰσχρὰ πράγματ' ἐκδιδάσκεται)."

Upon consideration of the above passages, the word **αἰσχρότης** means something like "developing the bad habit of needing to experience sexual gratification outside of marriage by whatever abnormal – even outrageous and violent – means possible other than the normal act of sexual intercourse within the marriage relationship (e.g., such as rape, sadism, masochism, seeking to find sexual pleasure by inflicting or suffering pain, even to the point of murder), which results in deforming the soul and leaving it damaged, distorted, psychopathic and hideously ugly."

[16] μωρολογία = lit. "foolish words." This word is also rare in Greek literature, occuring only once in the NT (here in Eph. 5:4). An occurrence that is helpful for understanding its meaning is in Flavius Josephus, *Contra Apionem [= "Against Apion"]*, Book 2, Section 115, as follows (ed. B. Niese, Berlin, 1892, transl. William Whiston, A.M. Auburn and John E. Beardsley, Buffalo, 1895):

> [112] "Nay, this miracle or piety derides us further, and adds the following pretended facts to his former fable; for he says that this man related how, "while the Jews were once in a long war with the Idumeans, there came a man out of one of the cities of the Idumeans, who there had worshipped Apollo. This man, whose name is said to have been Zabidus, came to the Jews, and promised that he would deliver Apollo, the god of Dora, into their hands, and that he would come to our temple, if they would all come up with him, [113]and bring the whole multitude of the Jews with them; that Zabidus made him a certain wooden instrument, and put it round about him, and set three rows of lamps therein, and walked after such a manner, that he appeared to those that stood a great way off him to be a kind of star, walking upon the earth; [114]that the Jews were terribly affrighted at so surprising an appearance, and stood very quiet at a distance; and that Zabidus, while they continued so very quiet, went into the holy house, and carried off that golden head of an ass, (for so facetiously [115]does he write,) and then went his way back again to Dora in great haste." And say you so, sir! as I may reply; then does Apion load the ass, that is, himself, and lays on him a burden of *fooleries* (μωρολογίας) and lies (ψευσμάτων); for he writes of places that have no being, and not knowing the cities he speaks of, he changes their situation; for Idumea borders upon our country, and is near to Gaza, in which there is no such city as Dora; although there be, it is true, a city named Dora in Phoenicia, near Mount Carmel, but it is four days' journey from Idumea. Now, then, why does this man accuse us, because we have not gods in common with other nations, if our fathers were so easily prevailed upon to have Apollo come to them, and thought they saw him walking upon the earth, and the stars with him? for certainly those who have so many festivals, wherein they light lamps, must yet, at this rate, have never seen a candlestick! But still it seems that while Zabidus took his journey over the country, where were so many ten thousands of people, nobody met him...[121]Apion tells a second false and mythic story (πρὸς δευτέραν' Ἀπίωνι μυθολογίαν καταψεύσασθαί), when he mentions an oath of ours, as if we "swore by God, the Maker of the heaven, and earth, and sea, to bear no good will to any foreigner, and particularly to none of the Greeks." Now this liar ought to have said directly that "we would bear no good-will to any foreigner, and particularly to none of the Egyptians." For then his story about the oath would have squared with the rest of his original forgeries, in case our forefathers had been driven away by their kinsmen, the Egyptians, not on account of any wickedness they had been guilty of, but on account of the calamities they were under; for as to the Grecians, we were rather remote from them in place, than different from them in our institutions, insomuch that we have no enmity with them, nor any jealousy of them. On the contrary, it hath so happened that many of them have come over to our laws, and some of them have continued in their observation, although others of them had not courage enough to persevere, and so departed from them again; nor did any body ever hear this oath

sworn by us: Apion, it seems, was the only person that heard it, for he indeed was the first composer of it."

Therefore, in context, it seems that **μωρολογία** ("foolish words") refers to "old fables, mythic stories, 'old wive's tales' or superstitions that deliberately and obstinately continue to misrepresent God or divine things as petty or trivial, or claim that God – or indeed anyone – should show partiality to those from certain ethnic groups and prejudice against those from other ethnic groups, rather than be self-sacrificial and loving of all human beings irrespective of ethnic origin."

[17] εὐτραπελία, ἡ, *ready wit, liveliness*, Hp.*Decent.*7, Pl.*R.*563a; ...*pleasantries*, Demetr.*Eloc.*177; defined by Arist. as πεπαιδευμένη ὕβρις, *Rh.*1389b11, cf. *EN*1108a24; ἡ περὶ τὰς παιδιὰς καὶ τὰς ὁμιλίας εὐ. Plu.*Ant.*43. **2. rarely in bad sense,** = βωμολοχία, *Ep.Eph.*5.4. [derived from:] εὐτράπελ-ος, ον, ([τρέπω]) *easily turning or changing*, of the Athenians, Ael.VH5.13; *nimble*, of apes, Id.NA5.26; in earlier Gr. always metaph., λόγος εὐ. *a dexterous, ready plea*, Ar.V.469 (lyr.). Adv. -λως *dexterously, readily, without awkwardness*, Th.2.41. **2.** *of persons, ready with an answer or repartee, witty*, Arist.*EN*1108a24, 1128a10; εὐ. παρὰ τὰς συνουσίας Plb.23.5.7; τίτθη εὐ. Jul.Or.7.227a: Sup., Plb.9.23.3. **b. in bad sense,** *jesting, ribald*, Isoc.7.49; εὐτράπελόν ἐστι c. acc. et inf., it is ludicrous that..., Plu.2.1062b. **3.** *tricky, dishonest*, v.l. in Pi.P.4.105; εὐ. κέρδη *time-serving arts, of flatterers*, ib.1.92 [LS]. This word is common in Greek literature, but rare in the NT, being used only once (here in Eph. 5:4). From the above texts, it is possible to discern what sort of behavior is being described by this word. In the *Nicomachean Ethics*, Aristotle defines the masculine adjective **εὐτράπελος** as "*wittiness*," which is one of the higher moral virtues with regard to making skillful and pleasant social conversation, being the mean between the vice of defect ("boorishness," Gk: ἄγροικος) and the vice of excess ("buffoonery," Gk: βωμολοχία) as follows (ed. J. Bywater, Oxford, 1894, transl. H. Rackham, Cambridge, 1934):

> "VIII. But life also includes relaxation, and one form of relaxation is playful conversation. Here, too, we feel that there is a certain standard of good taste in social behavior, [1128a] (1) and a certain propriety in the sort of things we say and in our manner of saying them, and also in the sort of things we allow to be said to us; and it will also concern us whether those in whose company we speak or to whom we listen conform to the same rules of propriety. [2] And it is clear that in these matters too it is possible either to exceed or to fall short of the mean. [3] Those then who go to excess in ridicule are thought to be *buffoons* (βωμολοχία) and vulgar fellows, who itch to have their joke at all costs, and are more concerned to raise a laugh than to keep within the bounds of decorum and avoid giving pain to the object of their raillery. Those on the other hand who never by any chance say anything funny themselves and take offence at those who do, are considered *boorish* (ἄγροικος) and morose. Those who jest with good taste are called *witty* (εὐτράπελος) or versatile – that is to say, full of good turns; for such sallies seem to spring from the character, and we judge men's characters, like their bodies, by their movements. [4] But as matter for ridicule is always ready to hand, and as most men are only too fond of fun and raillery, even *buffoons* (βωμολοχία) are called *witty* (εὐτράπελος) and pass for clever fellows;

though it is clear from what has been said that *Wit* (εὐτράπελος) is different, and widely different, from *Buffoonery* (βωμολοχία). [5] The middle disposition is further characterized by the quality of tact, the possessor of which will say, and allow to be said to him, only the sort of things that are suitable to a virtuous man and a gentleman: since there is a certain propriety in what such a man will say (20) and hear in jest, and the jesting of a gentleman differs from that of a person of servile nature, as does that of an educated from that of an uneducated man. [6] The difference may be seen by comparing the old and the modern comedies; the earlier dramatists found their fun in obscenity, the moderns prefer innuendo, which marks a great advance in decorum. [7] Can we then define proper raillery by saying that its jests are never unbecoming to gentlemen, or that it avoids giving pain or indeed actually gives pleasure to its object? Or is it impossible to define anything so elusive? for tastes differ as to what is offensive and what amusing. [8] Whatever rule we lay down, the same will apply to the things that a man should allow to be said to him, since we feel that deeds which a man permits to be ascribed to him he would not stop at actually doing. [9] Hence a man will draw the line at some jokes; for raillery is a sort of vilification, and some forms of vilification are forbidden by law; perhaps some forms of raillery ought to be prohibited also. [10] The cultivated gentleman will therefore regulate his wit, and will be as it were a law to himself. Such then is the middle character, whether he be called 'tactful' or *'witty'* (εὐτράπελος). The *buffoon* (βωμολοχία) is one who cannot resist a joke; he will not keep his tongue off himself or anyone else, if he can raise a laugh, and will say things [1128b] (1) which a man of refinement would never say, and some of which he would not even allow to be said to him. The *boor* (ἄγροικος) is of no use in playful conversation: he contributes nothing and takes offence at everything; [11] yet relaxation and amusement seem to be a necessary element in life [italics mine – GWC]."

However, in his *Rhetoric*, Aristotle clearly seems to use the feminine noun (εὐτραπελία), which Paul uses here, as a synonym for "buffoonery" (βωμολοχία) as shown in his definition of εὐτραπελία as "cultured (or well-bred) insolence," in the section in which he is describing the common characteristics of youth, as follows (W. D. Ross, Oxford, 1959, transl. J. H. Freese, Cambridge, 1926):

"[1389b][1]...All their [youthful] errors are due to excess and vehemence and their neglect of the maxim of Chilon [One of the Seven Wise Men of Greece. The maxim was Μηδὲν ἄγαν, Ne quid nimis, Never go to extremes], for they do everything to excess, love, hate, and everything else. And they think they know everything, and confidently affirm it, and this is the cause of their excess in everything. If they do wrong, it is due to *insolence*, not to wickedness...And they are fond of laughter, and therefore *witty* (εὐτραπελία); *for wit is cultured insolence.* Such then is the character of the young [italics mine – GWC]."

[18] ἀνήκω, *to have come up to* a point, *reach up to,* of persons and things, ἐς μέτρον τινὸς ἀ. Hdt.2.127; αἱμασιὴν ὕψος ἀνήκουσαν ἀνδρὶ ἐς τὸν ὀμφαλόν Id.7.60; ἐς τὰ μέγιστα ἀ. ἀρετῆς [transl. = "virtue is the greatest thing for which one can *reach up (aspire) to"* – GWC], πέρι 5.49; χρήμασι ἀ. ἐς τὰ πρῶτα 7.134; φρενῶν ἐς τὰ ἐμεωυτοῦ πρῶτα οὔκω ἀ. *have* not yet *reached* the highest point I aim at, ib.13;...ἀ. εἰς τὸ ὀξύ *to rise to* a point, Ael.*NA*1.55;...Arist.*EN*1167b4 [transl. = "true politics deals with the friendships between citizens, focusing on

the valuable *interests and concerns* of life" – GWC], (v.l.); τὰ εἰς ἀργυρίου λόγον ἀ. ἀδικήματα which *involve* a money consideration, Din.1.60;...**2. abs., *to be fit or proper, Ep.Eph.*5.4,** *Ep.Col.*3.18; τὸ ἀνῆκον, = τὸ προσῆκον, *Ep.Philem.*8 [LS]. The concept conveyed by the word ἀνήκω seems to be that for God's specially selected recruits, there are many behaviors accepted as normal by the common cultures in which they find themselves in, that are in fact "beneath them," because God has purposed a human personality and character for His specially selected recruits which is superior ("higher") than such demeaning behaviors, and which they must "reach up to" or "aspire to" as "the most valuable interests and concerns of life."

[19] πόρνος – See explanation of this word in note at Eph. 5:3.

[20] ἀκάθαρτος – See explanation of this word in note at Eph. 5:3.

[21] πλεονέκτης – See note at Eph. 5:3 and the explanation of this word in note at Eph. 4:19.

[22] κληρονομία – Paul introduced the vital concept of the Millennial Kingdom as the "inheritance" in Eph. 1:11-18 (see notes on that section in Chapter 1). When a society bases all of its ethical notions self-willingly and self-reflectively on the self-sacrificial love of Christ, it will discover a tremendous prosperity, stability and corporate moral health that endures over many generations. The only alternative is the corporate disease of immorality, that not only destabilizes the present society, but since it cuts off that society from a sense of *inheritance*, posterity or a living legacy, cannot be given any *inheritance* (κληρονομία) in the Millennial Kingdom of God's High King. In other words, a national sense of the reality of the inheritance of the Millennial Kingdom would serve to reverse sexual immorality as a deteriorating societal force. As a valuable by-product it would generate a sense of historical inheritance – or *heritage* – which will build the civilization into a vibrant, stable continuation of generations who believe in providing an inheritance to the next generation, in order they they would continue the building project of missionizing and civilizing the world into the future.

[23] τοὺς υἱοὺς τῆς ἀπειθείας – "the sons who obstinately refuse compliance," cf. extended note at Eph. 2:2.

[24] This word, συμμέτοχοι = "fellow-partners," is used only twice in the New Testament, both by Paul, and both in this Treatise (here in Eph. 5:7, and earlier in Eph. 3:6 – see note). In both contexts, Paul stresses the fact that due to God's "inheritance" (κληρονομία), He has made us eligible to become "completely equal partners with" (συμμέτοχοι) the future High King (μέτοχοι = Hebrews 1:9 as fulfillment of Psalm 45:7 – μετόχους [LXX]).

[25] A summary of the content of the first three of the five "περιπατέω" sections previously covered in Chapter 4 and Eph 5:1-7.

EPHESIANS CHAPTER 5 – ACTOR OF LOVE, FOLLOWER OF LIGHT, MASTER OF ETHICAL SKILL   201

[26] Ephesians 5:8-14 comprises the fourth of Paul's five "περιπατέω" sections (see note at Eph. 4:1 for an overall outline of the περιπατέω sections that encompass Chapters 4 and 5).

[27] φάος, φάεος, τό, Att. contr. φῶς... – *light*, esp. *daylight*... **b. in Poets, freq. in phrases concerning the life of men,** ζώει καὶ ὁρᾷ φ. ἠελίοιο Il.18.61, cf. Od.4.540, etc.; but also εἰς φῶς ἰέναι *to come into the light, i.e. into public*, S.*Ph*.1353; εἰς φῶς λέγειν ib.581; τὸ φῶς κόσμον παρέχει *light* (i.e. *publicity*) **is a guarantee for order**, *X*.Ages.*9.1*...**II. light, as a metaph. for deliverance, happiness, victory, glory, etc.**, καὶ τῷ μὲν φάος ἦλθεν Il.17.615; φόως δ' ἑτάροισιν ἔθηκεν 6.6; ἐπὴν φάος ἐν νήεσσι θήῃς 16.95; ἐν χερσὶ φόως 15.741; [πύλαι] πετασθεῖσαι τεῦξαν φάος 21.538; **esp. in addressing persons**, ἦλθες, Τηλέμαχε, γλυκερὸν φάος Od.16.23...**b. of God**, ὁ θεὸς φ. ἐστί *1 Ep.Jo*.1.5; φ. καὶ ζωή ἐστιν ὁ θεὸς καὶ πατήρ *Corp.Herm*.1.21; **of Christ**, φ. εἰς ἀποκάλυψιν ἐθνῶν *Ev.Luc*.2.32, etc. **2. with reference to *illumination* of the mind**, τῆς ἀληθείας τὸ φῶς E.*IT*1026; φ. ἐν τῷ φιλοσοφεῖν Plu.2.77d, cf. 47c; τὸ φ. τὸ ἐν σοί *Ev.Matt*.6.23; τὸ φ. τῆς ζωῆς *Ev.Jo*.8.12; ἐν τῷ φ. εἶναι *1 Ep.Jo*.2.9; τέκνα φωτός, ὅπλα τοῦ φ., ***Ep.Eph*.5.8**, *Ep.Rom*.13.12 [LS]. Several passages listed above by Liddell-Scott are worthy of study. The first is from Sophocles' play *Philoctetes*, lines 1353 and 581. These lines from Sophocles' play are noteworthy because they clearly convey that the word "light" is used as a metaphor to mean "to come out into the open, into public, with the purpose of exposing one's hidden and wrong motives, so as to return to normal, public corporate life of acceptance and recognition of others; i.e., to become 'vulnerable,' even 'merciful'." A brief background of the story is helpful to provide the context for Sophocles' use of this metaphor. Philoctetes is a Greek warrior who the Greek war-leaders decide to leave marooned on the island of Lemnos during the initial expedition of the Greek army to Troy across the Aegean Sea. They decide to maroon him there because he has been bitten in the foot by the divine serpent of the goddess Chryse, which causes him such pain that his continual loud moaning prevents the Greek leaders from sacrificing in solemn silence to the gods. After ten years of fighting at Troy without achieving victory, the prophet Helenus declares that the Greeks must return to Lemnos to get Philoctetes, because the Gods have ordained that the bow of Heracles (which that demi-god had given to Philoctetes when Heracles went to live with the Gods on Olympus) must be the weapon used to kill Paris, who by stealing Menelaus' wife Helen caused the Trojan War. Further, Helenus prophesies that Philoctetes must himself shoot the lethal arrow, and that he must return willingly. The problem is that Philoctetes bitterly hates the Greek war-leaders for marooning him for ten long years on the lonely island, where he has suffered greatly because the divine wound to his foot festers, is not permitted by the gods to heal and from which he suffers great and continual pain. So, Neoptolemus, the son of Achilleus (who has been recently killed in battle at Troy) is sent by the Greek war-leaders back to the island of Lemnos in order to attempt to persuade Philoctetes to forgive the Greek war-leaders who marooned him there, and come willingly to Troy and kill Paris with his divine bow. The key passage

now follows, as Neoptolemus replies to Philoctetes' initial refusal to give up his hatred for the Greek war-leaders and to return to Troy to help the Greeks win the Trojan War (ed. Sir Richard Jebb, Cambridge, 1898, transl. Robert Torrance, 1966):

"**Neoptolemus**: 1315 I am truly glad to hear you
praise my father (Achilleus) and me; now listen to the benefit
I hope to win from you. Men must endure
the fortunes which are given them by God;
but when they willingly persist in pain,
1320 like you, it is not right for anyone
to pardon them or have compassion on them.
You are too harsh, and will not hear advice;
and if one counsels you with good intentions
you hate him and consider him your foe.
1325 Yet I will speak, and call God as my witness:
so hear my words and write them in your heart.
This suffering is sent on you from heaven
because you once went near to Chryse's serpent,
the secret guardian of her roofless home.
1330 Be certain you will never find relief
from your hard illness while the sun continues
to rise and set again, until you come
of your own will to Troy, where you will find
the children of Asclepius among us,
1335 and they will soothe your illness; then, with me,
and with our bow, you will demolish Troy.
Now I will tell you how I know all this.
We have a Trojan prisoner among us,
Helenus, best of prophets, who declares
1340 that these things shall occur, and furthermore
he says it is ordained that Troy shall fall
this very summer: he will give his life
willingly if his prophecy proves false.
Now that you are aware of this, yield freely.
1345 It is a fair reward to be acclaimed
the noblest of the Greeks, and find your way
to healing hands, and then, when you have captured
sorrowful Troy, to win immortal glory.

Philoctetes: My hateful life, why do you keep me here
instead of letting me go down to Hades?
1350 What shall I do? how can I disobey
his words, when he has counseled me in friendship?
Shall I submit? But then, in my misfortune,
how could I face ***the light*** (εἰς φῶς τάδ' ἔρξας εἶμι; [i.e., how could I return to public life – if I must become vulnerable and give up my bitter anger to do so – GWC])?
Whom could I speak to?
My eyes, who have beheld my many wrongs,

> 1355 how could you ever bear to see me with
> the sons of Atreus, who have ruined me,
> or with that villainous son of Laertes?
> Resentment for the past is not what hurts me,
> but thinking on the pains that I must suffer
> 1360 hereafter: for when men have given birth
> to evil thoughts once, they will soon learn others."

Sophocles uses φῶς in the same way in line 581 earlier in the play, when he deliberately contrasts "light" (φῶς) with "darkness" (σκότος – line 579):

> **Neoptemus:** Who is it that Odysseus is seeking?
> **Spy:** There was a certain man – but tell me first
> who he is; and speak softly when you say it.
> **Neoptolemus:** 575 This is the famous Philoctetes, stranger.
> **Spy:** Ask me no more, but sail from here as quickly
> as possibly you can, and leave this island.
> **Philoctetes:** What is he saying, child? what ***shadowy bargain*** (κατὰ σκότον ποτὲ διεμπολᾷ [= lit. 'what kind of ***dark*** bargain...' i.e., what kind of secret, hidden – and thus made with wrong motives – bargain]) is this man making with you about me?
> **Neoptolemus:** 580 I am not certain yet; but he must speak ***openly***, to my sailors, and to you (δεῖ δ' αὐτὸν λέγειν εἰς φῶς [= lit. 'it is necessary for him to speak into ***the light...'*** i.e., he must speak his agreement in public so as to show his motives to be legitimate – GWC] ὃ λέξει, πρὸς σὲ κἀμὲ τούσδε τε)."

The second example of the use of the word φῶς as a metaphor for "living one's life in a publicly open way" occurs in Xenophon, *The Biography of Agesilaus*, Section 9, Paragraph 1, as follows (Oxford, 1920, transl. Cambridge, 1984):

> "IX.[1] I will next point out the contrast between his behaviour and the imposture ("deceit, false posturing, pretentiousness" [W]) of the Persian king. In the first place the Persian thought his dignity required that he should be seldom seen: Agesilaus delighted to be constantly visible, believing that, whereas secrecy was becoming to an ugly career, ***the light shed lustre on a life of noble purpose*** (τῷ δὲ εἰς κάλλος βίῳ τὸ φῶς μᾶλλον κόσμον παρέχειν). [2] In the second place, the one [the Persian King] prided himself on being difficult of approach: the other [Agesilaus] was glad to make himself accessible to all. And the one [the Persian King] affected ("artificial behavior" [W]) tardiness in negotiation: the other [Agesilaus] was best pleased when he could dismiss his suitors quickly with their requests granted."

The meaning of "living one's life in a publicly open way (to God and others)" also appears to be the primary meaning of the word "light" (φῶς) in 1 John 1:5-10:

> 1 John 1:5-10: ⁵This is the message which we have heard from him and announce to you, that God is ***light***, and in him is no darkness at all. ⁶If we say that we have fellowship with him and walk in the darkness, we lie, and don't tell the truth. ⁷But if we walk in the ***light***, as he is in the ***light***, we have fellowship with one another, and the blood of Jesus Christ, his Son, cleanses us from all sin. ⁸If we say that we have no sin, we deceive ourselves, and the truth is not in us. ⁹If we confess our sins, he is faithful and righteous to forgive us our sins, and to cleanse us from all unrighteousness. ¹⁰If we say that we haven't sinned, we make him a liar, and his word is not in us.

From the above texts, it appears that the first meaning of the metaphorical use of the word "light" is to "live one's life in a publicly open way in order to demonstrate one's sincere motives, honesty, vulnerability, mercy and legitimacy to be trusted to lead others" or more briefly, "to live in a publicly open way, showing sincerity, honesty, vulnerability and mercy." The second metaphorical use of the word "light" refers to the "enlightenment or illumination of the mind that comes through learning and education, and the happiness and freedom that result from no longer living in ignorance." The third meaning for the metaphor of "light" in the New Testament seems to be that of living "consistently." This can be inferred from James 1:17, when James is speaking of God's *consistency* of character. He says, "every good gift and every perfect gift is from above, and comes down from the Father of **lights,** *with whom there is not variation or shadow of turning."*

[28] σκότος, ὁ, more rarely σκότος, εος, τό (v. sub fin.), ***darkness, gloom,*** Od.19.389, Emp.121.4, Pi.Fr.142, etc.; opp. φάος, A.Ch.319 (lyr.), E.Hipp.417, etc.; opp. ἡμέρα, Pl.Def.411b....**2.** in Il. always of the ***darkness of death,*** mostly in the phrase τὸν δὲ ς. ὄσσε κάλυψεν 4.461, al.;...**6.** metaph., σκότῳ κρύπτειν ***hide in darkness*** [= ***hide in fear*** – GWC] S.El.1396 (lyr.), cf. Pi.Frr.42.5, 228; σκότον ἔχειν to be in ***darkness, obscurity*** [= ***confusion*** – GWC];...Id.N.7.13, E.Fr.1052.8; ἀπορία καὶ ς. Pl.Lg.837a; περικαλύψαι τοῖσι πράγμασι σκότον E.Ion 1522: with Preps., διὰ σκότους ἡ ὁδός it is ***dark*** and ***uncertain*** [= ***lack of confidence*** and ***indecisiveness*** – GWC], X.An.2.5.9;...**7.** of a person, Μητρότιμος ὁ ς., like ὁ σκοτεινός, the mystery-man, Hippon.78; also, ***darkness,*** i.e. ***ignorance,*** D.19.226; ***deceit,*** ς. καὶ ἀπάτη Pl.Lg.864c [LS]. From the above texts, it appears that the metaphorical use of the word "darkness" refers to "the fear and confusion, or the stubborn and willful ignorance that results in deceitfulness, lack of confidence, and indecisiveness that eventually lead to an early and tragic death," e.g., as in the case of someone who refuses to learn from their mistakes.

[29] εὐάρεστος, *well-pleasing* [from] ἀρεστός [ᾰ], ή, όν, *acceptable, pleasing,* Semon.7.46, Hdt.1.119,...of persons, *acceptable, approved,* τινί X.*Cyr*.2.3.7[LS]. The passage listed above from Xenophon, *Cyropaedia*, Book 2, Section 3, Paragraph 7 is very helpful in determining the meaning of this word. This passage now follows (Oxford, 1910, transl. Cambridge, 1979):

> "Thus spoke Chrysantas. And after him Pheraulas stood up, who although he was one of the Persian commoners, nevertheless had become a man who had from the beginning earned Cyrus's ***confidence*** (ἀρεστός) and affection, achieved by his own merits (of intelligence and prowess); besides, he was well-favoured in body and a gentleman at heart."

In other texts, the word εὐάρεστος is used in similar contexts – namely, of trials of character held by a king or a nobleman, the goal of which is to select a few qualified people from a group after a test of merit. It therefore probably means something like, "distinguished confidence earned by one after being deliberately tested or proved."

[30] δοκιμάζω...**2.** as a political term, **a.** *approve after scrutiny as fit* **for an office**, Lys.16.3, Pl.*Lg.*759d, Arist.*Ath.*45.3; Pass., *to be approved as fit,* Lys.15.6, etc.; δοκιμασθεὶς ἀρχέτω Pl.*Lg.*765b;...(ii A. D.):...[LS]. The above passage from Aristotle, *Athenian Constitution*, Section 45, Paragraph 3, is noteworthy in clarifying the meaning of this word, as follows (ed. Kenyon, Oxford, 1920, transl. H. Rackham, Cambridge, 1952):

> "The Council also checks the *qualifications* (δοκιμάζει) of the Councillors who are to hold office for the following year, and of the Nine Archons. And formerly it had sovereign power to reject them as *disqualified* (ἀποδοκιμάσαι), but now they have an appeal to the jury-court."

The main idea that emerges from the context of the above passage is that the verb **δοκιμάζω** refers to "proving one's qualifications," or of "becoming qualified" for service in high governmental office.

[31] This word, **συγκοινωνέω**, occurs only three times in the New Testament. It means *to have a joint share of,* τῆς δόξης ταύτης D.57.2; *to be connected with,* τῆς κνήμης Hp.Art.85; ς. τινί τινος *go shares with one* **in a thing**, Alex.162.5. **2.** in NTc. dat., *take part in, have fellowship with,* ταῖς ἁμαρτίαις Apoc.18.4; τοῖς ἔργοις *Ep.Eph.***5.11**; ς. μου τῇ θλίψει *Ep.Phil.*4.14 [LS]. Proposed translation: "become joint share-holders or business partners with."

[32] ἐλέγχω, Od.21.424, etc.:--*disgrace, put to shame*, μῦθον ἐ. *treat* **a speech** *with contempt*, Il.9.522; ἐ. τινά *put* **one** *to shame*, Od. 21.424.--This usage is only Ep. II. *cross-examine, question,* Hdt.2.115, Pl.*Ap.*18d, etc.;...τὰς ἀρχὰς βασάνοις χρώμενοι ἐλεγχόντων Pl. *Lg.*946c: c. acc. et inf., *accuse* **one** *of doing*, E.*Alc.*1058:--Pass., *to be convicted*, Hdt.1.24,117;...**2.** *test, bring to the proof*, ἀνδρῶν ἀρετὰν παγκρατὴς ἐλέγχει ἀλάθεια B.*Fr.* 10.2;...**3.** *prove,* τοῦτο ἐ. ὡς . . Pl.*Phdr.*273b, cf. *Sph.*256c: abs., *bring convincing proof*, ὡς ἡ ἀνάγκη ἐ. Hdt.2.22;...**4.** *refute, confute,* τινά or τι, Pl.*Grg.*470c, al., D.28.2, Luc.*Nigr.*4:--Pass., Pl.*Tht.*162a; χρυσὸς κληῒδας ἐλέγχει *proves that they avail not,* AP5.216 (Paul. Sil.). **b.** *put right, correct, prove by a reductio ad impossibile,* ὅσα ἔστιν ἀποδεῖξαι, ἔστι καὶ ἐλέγξαι τὸν θέμενον τὴν ἀντίφασιν τοῦ ἀληθοῦς Arist.*SE* 170a24; παράδοξα ἐ. Id.*EN*1146a23. **5.** *get the better of,* στρατιὰν ὠκύτατι ἐ. Pi.*P.*11.49, cf. D.P.750, Him.*Or.*1.16. **6.** *expose,* τινὰ ληροῦντα Pl.*Tht.*171d, cf. X.*Mem.*1.7.2, M.Ant.1.17; *betray* **a weakness**, Democr.222. **7.** *decide* **a dispute**, ἀνὰ μέσον τῶν δύο LXX *Ge.* 31.37 [LS]. Usually translated, "rebuke, reprove." The Greek word ἐλέγχω generically conveys the idea expressed by the English word "confront," but it seems specifically to articulate a series of actions along a continuum, extending from "confronting" someone at the level of a "gentle rebuke" at one extreme to the ultimate recourse of "confronting" someone by "taking legal action" against them at the other – see above translation in Eph. 5:11 for the proposed continuum of the different levels of "confronting" someone who is doing wrong.

[33] Passages from Isaiah such as:

Isaiah 26:19: "Your dead shall live; my dead bodies shall arise. Awake and sing, you who dwell in the dust; for your dew is [as] the dew of herbs, and the earth shall cast forth the dead;" and

Isaiah 60:1: "Arise, shine; for your light is come, and the glory of Yahweh is risen on you."

[34] καθεύδω...**A.** *sleep*...**II.** metaph., ***lie asleep, lie idle***, Χερί A. *Ag.*1357; cf. X.*HG*5.1.20, *An.*1.3.11, D.19.303; κ. τὸν βίον ***to be asleep* all one's life**, ***sleep away* one's life**, Pl.*R.*404a; opp. ἐνεργεῖν, Arist.*EN*1157b8 [LS]. Aristotle uses the word **καθεύδω** as a metaphor to mean something like the word "neglect." The above passage from Aristotle, *Nicomachean Ethics*, line 1157b8 now follows (ed. J. Bywater, Oxford, 1894, transl. H. Rackham, Cambridge, 1934):

> "V. It is with friendship as it is with the virtues; men are called good in two senses, either as having a virtuous disposition or as realizing virtue in action, and similarly friends when in each other's company derive pleasure from and confer benefits on each other, whereas friends who ***are asleep*** (**καθεύδοντες**) [i.e., have neglected] their friendship or parted are not actively friendly, yet have the disposition to be so. For separation does not destroy friendship absolutely, though it prevents its active exercise. *If however the absence be prolonged, it seems to cause the friendly feeling itself to be forgotten: hence the poet's remark: 'Full many a man finds friendship end for lack of converse with his friend'" [italics mine – GWC].*

Proposed translation: "to neglect, to lapse into lethargy, to become lethargic."

[35] Ephesians 5:15-21 is the fifth and final of Paul's five "περιπατέω" sections, in which he makes specific applications of the principles articulated in Chapters 1-3.

[36] A summary of the content of the first four of five "περιπατέω" sections previously covered in Chapter 4. See note at Eph. 4:1 for overall outline of the five "περιπατέω" sections.

[37] σοφία – The Greek word **σοφία** does not really mean "wisdom," but rather more something like, "the kind of knowledge that makes it possible for us to become competent, then gain mastery, then achieve superior leadership ability in living human life skillfully, especially in the ethical and political arenas" (see extended note at Ephesians 1:8 for analysis of this word).

[38] ἐξαγοραζω – This word does not mean "redeem." The word for "redeem" is ἀπολύτρωσις (Eph. 1:7, 14, 4:30). The denotative meaning of this word (ἐξαγοραζω) is "to buy out" (or "to buy up") something, as when a person buys every single item for sale in a store so that they are then "out" of it. The following passage from Polybius, *Histories*, Book 3, Chapter 42, Line 2, "The Passage of the Rhone," illustrates this meaning well (Leipzig, 1893, transl. Evelyn S. Shuckburgh, London, 1889):

> "Meanwhile Hannibal had reached the river and was trying to get across it where the stream was single, at a distance of four days' march from the sea. He did all he could to make the natives living by the river friendly to him, and ***purchased from them all***

(ἐξηγόρασε) their canoes of hollow trunks, and wherries, of which there were a large number, owing to the extensive sea traffic of the inhabitants of the Rhone valley."

[39] Here it is profitable to reflect upon two short parables of Jesus recorded in Matthew 13:44-46:

"Again the Kingdom of Heaven is like a treasure hidden in a field, which a man found and hid; and for joy over it he goes and **sells all that he has and buys that field.** Again, the Kingdom of Heaven is like a merchant seeking beautiful pearls, who, when he had found one pearl of great price, went and **sold all that he had and bought it.**"

[40] From a study of the word ἐξαγοραζω, the following four English words are all appropriate connotative translations: "buy out," or "buy up" = "purchase, aquire, obtain, procure." A further study in WEBSTER on these four words is also profitable for discovering the connotative meaning involved in this concept, and now follows:

- **"purchase:"** Etymology: Middle English *purchacen,* from Old French *porchacier, purchacier* to seek to obtain, from *por, pur, pour* for (modification -- perhaps influenced by Latin *per* through -- of Latin *pro* for) + *chacier* to **pursue**, chase -- more at FOR, CHASE. 1. *"to pursue of chase for, to chase after"* (something of value). 2. Once acquiring that thing of value for which one has been chasing, to *"hold on" or "grasp tightly"* to it, so as not to let it go.
- **"acquire:"** Etymology: alteration (influenced by Latin *acquirere*) of earlier *acquere,* from Middle English *aqueren,* from Middle French *aquerre,* from Latin *acquirere,* from *ad-* + *-quirere* (from *quaerere* to seek, gain, obtain, ask). 1. To *search for and ask* for a skill or power by which I can contol something of value which I do not possess until after I have begun an effort to **search for** and **ask** for it. 2. Once finding those who can give or teach me this valuable skill or power I seek, *to expend the life-long sustained effort to become and remain proficient in the use of* this valuable skill or power with which I can control the thing of value.
- **"obtain:"** Etymology: Middle English *obteinen,* from Middle French & Latin; Middle French *obtenir,* from Latin *obtinēre* to take hold of, from *ob-* to, completely + *-tinēre* (from *tenē*re *to hold*)1. To *hold onto* something of value, or a valuable skill, or a valuable power *so completely and comprehensively* that doubt is dispelled and replaced by confidence, certainty and stability. 2. Thus emerges the notion of obtaining a professional *"firm"*, or becoming *"established,"* or becoming *"recognized"* as an expert in a certain valuable field of human endeavor.
- **"procure:"** Etymology: Middle English *procuren* to take care of, bring about, obtain, from Late Latin & Latin; Late Latin *procurare* to obtain, from Latin, to take care of, from *pro-* for, on behalf of + *curare* to take care of -- more at PRO-, CURE. 1. To acquire possession of something of value *for on on behalf of some other party or person.* 2. Once aquiring the thing of value, *protecting and caring for it* for or on behalf of the other person or party (i.e., the concept of "stewardship").

SUMMARY of applications of the verb ἐξαγοραζω: To "buy out" or "buy up:"
1. Pur-chase = to "chase for:" To always be in pursuit of the things that God wants us to be in pursuit of, eventually catch up to them, grasp them, and then "hang on to them for dear life."

2. A(d)-quire = to "ask for and add to" my personality the things of value that God will only give me if I ask for them and then once getting them, develop the spiritual habits required to continue to use them in my life.
3. Ob-tain = to "completely or tenaciously hold on" to those things of value that God wants us to hold on to.
4. Pro-cure = to get possession of something of value in order "to take care of it for" someone else. Implied is the concept of stewardship.

[41] καιρός, ὁ, *due measure, proportion, fitness* καιρὸς δ' ἐπὶ πᾶσιν ἄριστος (which became a proverb = "Observe due measure: and *proportion* is best in all things".) Hes.Op.694, Thgn. 401;...εἰ ὁ κ. ἦν σαφής *the distinction, the point*, E.Hipp. 386; ἡ ἀπορία ἔχει τινὰ κ. *has some point or importance*, Arist.*Metaph*.1043b25; καιροῦ πέρα *beyond measure, unduly*, A.Pr.507;...**III. more freq. of Time,** *exact or critical time, season, opportunity*, Χρόνου κ. S.El. 1292:...κ. τηρεῖν Arist.*Rh*. 1382b11;...καιρῷ Χειμῶνος ξυλλαβέσθαι *co-operate* with the occurrence of a storm, Pl.*Lg*.709c; ἔχει κ. τι *it happens in season*...**b.** *critical times, periodic states*, καιροὶ σωμάτων Arist.*Pol*.1335a41 [LS]. The main connotative meaning that emerges from a study of the word **καιρός** is not "time," but rather "proportion," "due measure," "fitness," "important" or "relevant" (Aristotle); and when applied to time, means "critical timing," "opportune," "investment," "co-operate," "season," "consequence." A further study in WEBSTER of these eight English words is profitable for filling out the connotative meaning conveyed by this concept, and now follows:

• **"proportion:"** Etymology: Middle English *proporcioun*, from Middle French *proportion*, from Latin *proportion-*, *proportio*, from *pro* for + *portion-*, *portio* part, share, portion -- more at FOR, PORTION. 1. That out of our participation in every important or valuable thing or relationship from God, we will only be able to participate in a "part, share, or portion" of it which is appropriate "for" us. We should learn the skill of discerning what that part, share or portion best suited for us is. 2. That the way to tell when when have achieved the right "pro-portion" is when appropriate balance, harmony, or symmetry within the overall whole corporate reality of the valuable thing is reached. 3. That often the way to determine this apportioning is through the use of mathematical proportional models to determine the amount of "portions" or "shares" each member of the group who desires to participate in the value of the whole is to be given. 4. That when things get out of proportion, God is not causing the imbalance and chaos that results.

• **"important:"** Etymology: Middle French, from Old Italian *importante* (verbal of *importare* to be important), from Latin *important-*, *importans*, present participle of *importare* to bring or carry in, convey, cause -- more at IMPORT. 1. There are only a certain number of things that are valuable enough to be worthy of being carried in wagons, trucks, or ships, and being "imported" into a country that does not have them. Such things worthy of "import" are those which are "important."

• **"opportune ("opportunity"):"** Etymology: Middle English, from Middle French *opportun*, from Latin *opportunus*, from the phrase *ob portum* (*veniens*) coming to harbor, from *ob to*, *towards* + *portum*, accusative of *portus* harbor, port -- more at PORT. 1. Very similar to the concept of "importance," there are only a limited number of things that are worthy of being put on a ship, carried accross the sea, and being sailed "towards the port" of the country that does not have these valuable things but desires to "import" them. However, such things of value differ from all "imports" in that these must come on ships, and thus are subject to how God grants good or bad weather for passage of the ship coming from the far country. Therefore, these things are so important that the ship's captain must wait for the best weather to "bring them to port," i.e., he must wait for the most "opportune" conditions of weather, tides, seasons, and timing. In this sense then, these items are of such value that they come into the port of the country that wants them only on certain, rare "opportunities."

• **"relevant" (Aristotle):** Etymology: Medieval Latin *relevant-, relevans,* from Latin, present participle of Latin *relevare* to raise up, lift up 1. That out of the many preliminary matters or things that we may initially consider valuable, that only very few of them turn out to be of crucial importance, and only these are to be "raised up" in our minds through an evaluative process to a level higher than they are, and that only these "raised-up things" are thus "relevant."

• **"invest" ("investment"):** Etymology: Medieval Latin *investire,* from Latin, to clothe, cover, surround, from *in-* in- + *vestire* to clothe, from *vestis* garment. 1. To display legitimate transmission of power, control or authority over valuable things or relationships by one leader to another by publically placing clothing, crowns, rings, or other external ornaments utilized as symbols by the legitimized leader conveying power to the new leader receiving those powers, such that those placed under the control of the new leader give recognition to the legitimacy of the new leader's power, control and authority. 2. Thus, from the above, the introduction of the concept of the appropriate amount of time necessary to prepare the recipient of power, control and authority, to be able to wield it wisely and responsibly. 3. From this concept emerges the modern notion of investing money in people or companies who have demonstrated that over time, they can increase the value of the money invested in them by increasing the value of the product or service they provide.

• **"co-operate:"** Etymology: Latin *operatus,* past participle of *operari* to work, from *oper-, opus* work, labor; plus *co* – with. 1. One must be "at work" to discover God's plan or will for their lifework; they must be a "hard worker." 2. One must also learn to "work with" others to learn God's will for their lifework.

• **"consequence:"** Etymology: Middle English, from Medieval Latin *sequentia* = sequence, from Late Latin, *succession,* state or fact of following, from Latin *sequent-, sequens* (present participle of *sequi* to follow) + *-ia -y + con* = with. 1. That valuable events in one's life can only follow one after another in a sequence, and that one can only begin to see God's providence in his life when he agrees that he must accept or go along "with the sequence." 2. That when this point of view is adopted, one can learn to act in such a way that a positive effect follows from his action, and thus his act becomes valuable because it produces a good "consequence," i.e., it fits in harmony with the sequence of the other actions and events that God has brought into his life. 3. That the long-term effect of living the kind of life in which one becomes proficient at this process increases one's skill and power in acting to the point where the performance of only one action in harmony with God's providence of opportunity can cause thousands of good consequences to follow for thousands of people. 4. That the result of living rightly gives one dignity, i.e., one can rightly be called by others a "person of consequence."

• **"season:"** Etymology: Middle English *sesoun, seisoun,* from Old French *saison, seson,* from Latin *sation-, satio* action of sowing, from *satus* (past participle of *serere* to sow) + *-ion-, -io* -ion -- more at SOW. 1. A period of time whose only importance lies in the natural duration from the sowing of the seed to the time of the harvest, during which there must necessarily be a period of time of care and cultivation for the sown seed; i.e., the "seed-sown" = "season." 2. The derivative concept that in God's ways, the periods of one's life will resemble that of farming and agriculture: a period of "sowing," "cultivation," and "reaping." Implied here is the introduction of the notion of patience, to allow God to bring the natural process of growth to fruition.

SUMMARY of applications of the noun καιρός:
1. **"Pro-portion:"** That out of our participation in every important or valuable thing or relationship from God, we will only be able to participate in a "part, share, or portion" of it which is appropriate "for" us. We should learn the skill of discerning what that part is, and share in the portion best suited for us in an overall harmonious, balanced organization.
2. **"Im-port-ant:"** There are only a certain number of things that are valuable enough to be worthy of being "imported" into our lives. Such things worthy of "import" are those which are "important." Obviously, the application is that to discover our life work we must always be "importing" that which is *genuinely* valuable into our lives: education, training, etc.
3. **"Op-port-une ("opportunity"):"** There are certain things that God wants to "bring into the port" of our lives that are more valuable, and thus far more rare, than the other important, but less valuable things that we ought to "import" into our lives also. These things depend on His timing; i.e., when He thinks that it is best to "bring them into the port" of our lives. In this sense, these items are of such value that they come into our lives only on certain, rare "opportunities," and those with spiritual skill must learn to recognize these opportunities and allow them to "come into port" in order to discover their lifework.
4. **"Re-lev-ant" (Aristotle):** Out of the many preliminary matters or things that we may initially consider valuable, that only very few of them turn out to be of crucial importance, and only these are to be "raised up" in our minds through an evaluative process from the others to a level (or, more accurately, "lever") higher than the others, and that only these "raised-up things" are thus "relevant." These things of crucial importance must be "re-raised," i.e., "re-leveraged" from time to time. This leads to the concept that the most relevant matters in our business are those that we have learned to "leverage" (raise up to importance); e.g., training others, apprenticeships, etc.
5. **"In-vest" ("in-vest-ment"):"** As leaders, we must learn to spend the money, time and training necessary to cultivate and "groom" people in our organizations for a specific time in which we legitimately transfer power, control or authority over valuable things or relationships to them by transferring that authority through the use of symbols in public in front of those placed under the control of the new leader, so that they will give recognition to the legitimacy of the new leader's power, control and authority.
6. **"Co-operate:"** In order to discover our lifework, we must be diligent operators ("hard workers") ourselves, as well as surround ourselves in organizations in which all of our "co-operators" are "hard workers with" us in the common endeavor.
7. **"Con-sequence:"** Valuable events that God brings into our lives can only follow one after another in a sequence, and that we can only see God's providence when we learn that we must go along "with the sequence." When we do this, we can learn which of our actions produce a good "consequence," i.e., fit into harmony with the sequence of the other actions and events that God has brought into our lives. The long-term effect of living our lives proficiently in this process increases our skill and power in acting to the point where we can act in harmony with God's providence of opportunity, such that He can use us to cause thousands of good consequences to follow for thousands of people, with the result that we can rightly earn the dignity of being known as a "person of consequence."
8. **"Sea-son (Seed-sown):"** God will always make the pattern of growth in our lives follow the pattern of farming and agriculture: He will first start us out with a period of "sowing," followed by a period of "cultivation," culminated by a period of "reaping." We

must therefore learn to be patient and learn to allow God to bring the natural process of growth in our lives to fruition.

⁴² συνίημι...II. metaph., *perceive, hear*, freq. in Hom. (who also has Med. in this sense, ἀγορεύοντος ξύνετο Od.4.76); ὣς φάθ᾽, ὁ δὲ ξυνέηκε Il.15.442; εἰ δ᾽ ἄγε νῦν ξυνίει Od.1.271:--Constr., c. acc. rei, ξυνέηκε θεᾶς ὄπα φωνησάσης Il.2.182; ἐμέθεν ξυνίει ἔπος Od.6.289...[In all these passages in Homer, συνίημι means especially "to listen to wise counsel and advice that is given in an attempt to dissuade arrogant leaders from taking foolish and precipitous action due to their pride" – GWC]. 2. *to be aware of, take notice of, observe*, τοὓν Od.18.34 ; τῶν δὲ σὺ μὴ ξύνιε Thgn.1240 (sed leg. ξυνίει): c. acc., Hdt.1.24: folld. by a relat., ξύνες δὲ τήνδ᾽, ὡς . . χωρεῖ S.*Tr.*868 (lyr.): abs., πολλά με καὶ συνιέντα παρέρχεται Thgn.419. 3. *understand*, ξ. ἀλλήλων [LS]. Thus, συνίημι means something like "to deliberately set aside the tendency to face a dilemma with a proud or arrogant attitude, and replace it with the intention of being able to perceive a dilemma and make decisions about it with understanding."

⁴³ μεθύσκω – Paul is not saying that it is wrong to drink wine (οἶνος). He is saying that it is wrong to *drink alcohol excessively*. In Psalm 104:14-15, David rejoices that God "causes grass to grow for the cattle, and vegetation for the service of man, that he may bring forth food from the earth, *and wine that makes glad the heart of man*, oil to make his face shine, and bread which strengthens man's heart." Furthermore, Jesus' first miracle recorded in John 2:1-12 was to create by a miracle between 120 and 180 gallons of "good wine" for a wedding feast in Cana in Galilee. It was common in the ancient world to drink water mixed with wine (usually about 3 parts water to 1 part wine). Paul is here speaking about drinking *unmixed* wine, strong in alcoholic content in excessive amounts, resulting in the state of "drunkenness, intoxication, inebriation" (μεθύσκω, [LS]). An especially noteworthy passage that supplies insight in this regard occurs in the *Odyssey* of Homer, where Odysseus lands on the island of the Cyclops, and because the Greek hero suspects danger from the Cyclops, takes a gift of especially *strong wine* to him. This particular wine was a special gift given to Odysseus by Maro, son of Euanthes, which is so strong in alcoholic content that even when it is mixed with *"twenty parts of water"* it remains quite potent. Homer says it this way through his hero Odysseus (transl. Walter Shewring, Oxford, 1980):

> "With me I had a goat-skin of the dark, sweet **wine**, which Maro, son of Euanthes, had given me, the priest of Apollo, the god who used to watch over Ismarus (3.31) [book 9, line 195]...And he gave me splendid gifts: of well-wrought gold he gave me seven talents, and he gave me a mixing-bowl all of silver; and besides these, **wine**, wherewith he filled twelve jars in all, **wine** sweet and unmixed, a drink divine. (5.59) [line 200]...And as often as they drank that honey-sweet red **wine** he would *fill one cup and pour it into twenty measures of water, and a smell would rise from the mixing-bowl marvellously sweet; then verily would one not choose to hold back* (2.77) [line 205]."

[44] **ψαλμός** ὁ, *twitching* or *twanging* with the fingers, ψαλμοὶ τόξων E.*Ion*173 (lyr.); τοξήρει ψαλμῷ [τοξεύσας] Id.*HF*1064 (lyr.). **II. mostly of musical strings**, πηκτίδων ψαλμοῖς κρέκον ὕμνον Telest.5, cf. Diog.Trag.1.9, Aret.*CA*1.1. **2. the sound of the cithara or harp**, Pi.*Fr*.125, cf. Phryn.Trag.11; ψαλμὸς δ' ἀλαλάζει A.*Fr*.57.7 (anap.); there were contests in τὸ ψάλλειν, *Michel*898.10(Chios, ii B. C.), 913.6 (Teos, ii B. C.). **3. later, song sung to the harp, psalm**, LXX *2 Ki*.23.1, al., *Ep.Eph*.**5.19**; βίβλος ψαλμῶν *Ev.Luc*.20.42 [LS]. Proposed translation: "a spiritual song that is sung individually or in a group, accompanied by a musical instrument or instruments."

[45] **ὄνομα, name**...**IV.** in periphr. phrases, ὄ. τῆς σωτηρίας, = σωτηρία, E.*IT*905;... with the names of persons, periphr. for the person, ὦ φίλτατον ὄ. Πολυνείκους Id.*Ph*.1702. **2.** of persons, ὄχλος ὀνομάτων *Act.Ap*.1.15; ἕτερα ὁ. ἀντ' αὐτοῦ...πέμψαι Wilcken *Chr*.28.19 (ii A.D.); *in Accountancy, both of persons and things* (cf. Lat. *nomen*), Hyp.*Ath*.6,10 (both pl.), *Jahresh*.26 *Beibl*.13 (Ephes., ii A.D.); βαρέσαι τὸ ἐμὸν ὄ. **charge my account**, POxy.126.8 (vi A.D.) [LS]. Proposed translation: "the deliberate assigning or measuring out [of something], and then keeping an account or record of it."

[46] **ὑποτάσσω,**...**place or arrange under, assign**, τινί τι Plb.3.36.7, Plu.*Nic*.23, etc.; ὑ. ὑπὸ τὸ τῆς προδοσίας ὄνομα Plb.18.15.4:--Pass., τὸ ὑποτεταγμένον (sc. ὀστέον) the *inferior* bone, i. e. the ulna, Hp.*Off*.16. **II.** *post in the shelter of*, ὑποτάσσεσθαι τινι Luc.*Par*.49; *draw up behind*, Ael.*Tact*.15.1 (Pass.), Arr. *Tact*.26.7. **2. subject**, ἑαυτοὺς οὐδενί Phld.*Rh*.2.204 S., cf. Plu.*Pomp*.64; *subdue, make subject*, Θηβαΐδα *OGI*654.7 (Egypt, i B. C.), cf. 199.10, al. (Adule, i A. D.); ἔθνη Hdn.7.2.9; αὐτῷ τὰ πάντα *Ep.Phil*.3.21; **πάντα ὑπὸ τοὺς πόδας αὐτοῦ** *Ep.Eph*.**1.22**:--Pass., *to be obedient*, τινι *Ep.Col*. 3.18, al.; ὑποτάγητε τῷ θεῷ *Ep.Jac*.4.7, cf. Arr.*Epict*.3.24.65; ἄγρια θηρία ὑποταγήσεται αὐτῷ Cyran.15; ὑποτάξονται **they will submit**, Hdn.2.2.8; τὸ πλῆθος -όμενον Onos. 1.17, cf. Palaeph.38: abs., κοὐχ ὑποταγεὶς ἐβάδιζεν ὥσπερ Νικίας *dejectedly, timidly*, Phryn.Com.59 (s. v. l.); οἱ ὑποταττόμενοι *subjects*, Plb.3.13.8, etc.; ὑποτεταγμένοι *subordinates*, Phld.*Oec*. p.72 J.; ἐδούλευσας, ὑπετάγης Arr.*Epict*.4.4.33; ὑποτεταγμέναι ἀρεταί **subordinate virtues**, i.e. the **sub-divisions** of the four cardinal (πρῶται]) virtues, *Stoic*.3.64...[LS]. Usually translated "submit" ("submission"), "subject" ("subjection"). Proposed translation: "subordinate" (for both the verb and the noun forms – but see extended note below at Eph. 5:22).

[47] Ephesians 5:22-33.

[48] Ephesians 6:1-4.

[49] Ephesians 6:5-9.

[50] **ὑποτασσεσθε** is the second person plural imperative verb of **ὑποτάσσω** = "You must subordinate yourselves" (see note above at Eph. 5:21). This verb has a wide range of meanings in Greek, both in its denotative and connotative uses, just as

the many words used in English to translate it do. In our Contemporary era, these many possible meanings have become the source of much controversy as to the appropriate behavior in the relationship between husbands and wives. The following philosophical analysis is offered as both an attempted explanation as well as a possible solution to this dilemma.

There can be no doubt that historically, the denotative meaning of this word is to "place under," i.e., "place someone or something under the authoritative subjugation, subjection or subordination of another superior being." For example, Paul uses it this way in this very treatise in Ephesians 1:22, when he says, "*He (God) has subordinated* every authority structure present in history prior to the inauguration of the Kingdom to our future High King..." However, Paul also uses the word in its connotative meaning, as he does in the immediately preceding context (Eph. 5:21), where it means something like, "to follow Jesus' example of voluntarily subordinating or submitting one's will in a relationship to perform the will of the other, which involves an initial attitude of deference and forbearance." What Paul is attempting to accomplish in Eph. 5:22-6:9 is to offer three specific applications for the primary arenas of human relationships in life in which we are to apply the general principle stated in Eph. 5:21, which are foundational relationships in which we must apply it in order to be given spiritual abilities to discover and accomplish our lifework. These are: 1) the *marriage* relation in Eph. 5:22-33; 2) the *parental* relation in Eph. 6:1-4; and 3) the *vocational* relation in Eph. 6:5-9. Here in Eph. 5:22, Paul begins with the marriage relation, and addresses the wives first. He simply says "subordinate yourselves to your own husbands, as [you would subordinate yourselves] to the Commander in Chief". There is no grammatical doubt that the verb "subordinate" [or "submit" – Tyndale and KJV] is in the imperative mood (ὑποτασσεσθε). The vital question then becomes *in what category of being* is this statement of command predicated? Aristotle, in his work entitled, *Categories,* lists and explains that there are ten fundamental "Categories" of Being, and that they are the categories that are required to meaningfully describe or talk about reality, as follows:

1. *Substance* – e.g., the individual soul of a particular human or animal being. Sometimes referred to as "ontological being."
2. *Quantity* – discrete or continuous parts of wholes that can stand in specific relation to other parts, especially the relation of *equality* or *inequality*; e.g., number, lines, surfaces, solids, space, time.
3. *Quality* – attributes of wholes that cannot be compared using the relation of equality, but rather only of *similarity*; e.g., virtue, talent, color, heat, sweetness.
4. *Relation* – that which can be explained only in terms of its correlative and in no other way, e.g., *habit, disposition, perception, knowledge, attitude, father, child, husband, wife, employer, employee, etc.*).
5. *Place* – the location of a quantity.
6. *Time* – the duration of a quantity.

7. *Position* – the vantage point in space from which relation to an object is observed.
8. *State* – the specific condition required for the appropriate action of a relation; e.g., 'shod,' 'armed' (of soldiers); 'financed' (of a home-buyer); 'educated' (of a graduate), etc.
9. *Action* – The specific principle of initiation of motion by a substance within a necessary relation; e.g., that which *makes* hot, or glad.
10. *Affection* – The specific principle of reception of motion by a substance within a necessary relation; e.g., that which is *made* hot, or glad.

Example: By the tenth game of the season (quantity), John Elway (substance) had gained such confidence (state) that he made perfect passes (quality) as he led his team (relation) the length of the field (place) in the final two minutes (time), and won the game by throwing (action) a pass that the wide receiver caught (affection) so close to the corner of the end zone, that it was ruled a touchdown only after the official reviewed the replay from the end zone camera (position).

In the context of this passage (Eph. 5:22-6:9), Paul is speaking here of *relational organization* (Category 4) and the *intitiative of action* or the *affection of action* (Categories 9 and 10), and *not any of the other seven Categories that are often taken for granted as presuppositional grounds for interpreting this passage* (which result in the mis-interpretation of this passage). Paul is not claiming that wives are subordinate in their *substantial ontological* being (husbands are superior beings to wives, as men are to horses), nor *quantitative* being (because men are bigger than women, they are superior to women), nor *qualitative* being (because men are stronger than women, they are superior to women), nor the being *of place* (because a man sits at the head of the table, he is superior to the woman), nor the being *of time* (because God created Adam before Eve in time, the man is superior to the woman), etc. Just as Jesus is in His *ontological* being completely *equal* with God the Father, nevertheless in His experience of *relational organization* within the Trinity He is *submissive* or *subordinate* to the Father. The way in which He is subordinate in His relation to the Father is in the Category of "affection" = "receiving the actions" of the Father (Category 10). The way in which the Father is *superordinate* in His relation to the Son is in the category of "action" = "originating all Divine initiatives" toward the Son (Category 9). In the relationships within the Trinity, God the Father is the Person who lovingly initiates all Divine Actions, and God the Son is the Divine Person who is "affected by" = "receives, obeys, and implements" the Father's initiatives.

For example, just as a running back or a receiver on a football team is *ontologically* equal with the quarterback (they are all athletic human beings), nevertheless they are *relationally* "under" the quarterback in terms of how the various plays in the game of football are organized – the quarterback initiates the play, whether it will be a run or a pass, and the running back and the receiver "receive" the ball, whether as a hand-off or a pass from the quarterback. For another example, just as in a choir all the singers are *ontologically* equal (they are all singing human beings), nevertheless, the sopranos (in this case, mostly women) are organized as *relationally* primary to the altos, tenors and bases, because they carry the melody of the song. So also, a woman, in the relationship of marriage, has been assigned by God the *relational role* of wife. Although she is *ontologically* equal with a man (they are both adult human beings) she is *relationally* to submit or receive his organizational responsibility to initiate the actions in the marriage relation in a loving way – the same way that God the Son relationally submits to and carries out the loving initiatives given Him in His relationship with God the Father. It is appropriate to note here that historically, in many barbarian societies, the wife exercises relational rule over passive males. In other words, barbarian societies exhibit feminization of the male and masculinization of the female, which breaks apart the moral stability of the family as the basic relational building unit of a stable society. The post-Homeric Greek Tragedians, most notably, Sophocles (*Antigone*) and Euripides (*The Bacchae*); as well as the Greek Philosopher Aristotle (*Nicomachean Ethics* and *Politics*) were among the first to reflect on the foundational character of the marriage relation to the maturity of a society.

Although in certain limited contexts within American culture the words "submit" and "subordinate" are still used accurately to convey concepts of *relational organizational structure* (e.g., in the military, and in business and commerce), they have suffered so much ill-usage and caused so much needless misunderstanding in wider American English culture, that the proposed translation of the word ὑποτασσεσθε in this context is: "to develop the spiritual skill of adopting a cheerful and gracious attitude of *deference* and *forbearance*, trusting and supporting others, offering to help and enjoying the opportunity to warmly and gladly assist them in their efforts in a pleasant and agreeable way and with a positive frame of mind."

[51] See Ephesians 5:15.

[52] In Ephesians 5:26, perhaps Paul is alluding to the happy and playful mood depicted in the relationship between Solomon and Shulamith in the *Song of Solomon* 4:2. Perhaps he is reminding the husband of the message of the entire passage of the *Song of Solomon* 4:1-16, that when making love, the husband's role is to take the playful, loving intitiative in speech, in action and in tenderness. In the lovemaking scene in the *Song of Solomon* 4:2, Solomon says to Shulamith, "Your teeth are like a newly shorn flock, which have come up from the washing, where every one of them has twins. There is not one of them that is sad." Solomon had many flocks of sheep, which required washing. In the poetic metaphor, Solomon is comparing his wife's teeth, shown in laughter, with his fond and humorous memories of washing his newly-shorn sheep. The fact that Solomon can see all of her teeth in their lovemaking means that the nature of their conversation is humorous. She is more than smiling. She is laughing. She is a happy person. She responds to his sense of humor. He has a sense of humor to

which she responds. Their sexual relationship is not "serious and grave." It is extremely playful and fun.

[53] ῥῆμα, ατος, τό, ([ἐρῶ]) *that which is said or spoken, word, saying,* Archil.50, Thgn.1152, Simon.37.14,92 (where perh. it = ῥήτρα 11.2), Pi. (v. infr.), etc.; in Prose first in Hdt. (s.v.l.), ὁ νόος τοῦ ῥ. 7.162; τὰ λεγόμενά τινων [ῥήματα] 8.83; τοῦ Πιττακοῦ . . περιεφέρετο τοῦτο τὸ ῥ. Pl.*Prt.*343b; τὸ δόγμα τε καὶ ῥ. Id.*R.*464a; opp. ἔργματα, Pi.N.4.6; opp. ἔργον, Th.5.111; opp. τὸ ἀληθές, Pl.*Phd.*102b: prov., ῥήματα ἀντ' ἀλφίτων *'fine words* **butter no parsnips'**, ap.Suid.; ῥήματα πλέκων Pi.N.4.94; ῥήματα θηρεύειν *catch at one's words,* And.1.9; ῥ. ἱπποβάμονα, ῥ. μυριάμφορον, Ar.Ra.821, Pax 521; ῥήματος ἐχόμενον *depending on the word,* Pl.*Lg.*656c; τῷ ῥ. τῷ τόδε προσχρώμενοι the word τόδε, Id.*Ti.*49e; τῷ ῥ. λέγειν, εἰπεῖν, *say in so many words,* Id.*R.* 340d, *Grg.*450e, cf. *Tht.*166d; κατὰ ῥῆμα ἀπαγγεῖλαι *word for word,* Aeschin.2.122 [LS]. Study of the word ῥῆμα throughout the Septuagint, which is the word Paul deliberately uses in this verse in Eph. 5:26, indicates that it means, "to communicate skillfully and accurately using public speech, with the intent of bringing the matter spoken about into actual real existence," and so should be translated in this context as "the skill of initiating kind, gentle, considerate, yet truthful speech, with the goal of cleansing the hurt or wound caused by earlier harsh speech." Thus, the meaning of ῥῆμα is different than the word λόγος, which Paul uses four times in this letter to refer to the "rational, logical use of the mind to truthfully use words to accurately reflect, describe or communicate reality."

[54] ἔνδοξος, ον, ([δόξα]) *held in esteem* or *honour, of high repute,* πρός τινος by one, X.*Oec.*6.10 codd. (Sup.); -ότατοι ποιηταί Id.*Mem.*1.2.56; πόλις -οτέρα εἰς τὰ πολεμικά ib.3.5.1; νέοι πλούσιοι καὶ ἔ. Pl.*Sph.* 223b; μὴ πλουσιώτερος ἀλλ' -ότερος Isoc.1.37; ὀλίγοι καὶ ἔ. ἄνδρες Arist.*EN*1098b28 [= *"distinguished"* – GWC], cf. Epicur.*Sent.*7, etc. **2.** of things, *notable,* πράγματα Aeschin.3.231, cf. Diod.Com.2.21; *generally approved,* τὸ καλόν, = τὸ ἔ., Epicur.*Fr.*513; *glorious,* ταφαί Plu.*Per.*28; ἡδὺ καὶ ἔ. καὶ ὠφέλιμον Id.2.99f. Adv.-ξως, freq. in Inscrr., *SIG*442.7 (Erythrae, iii B. C.), etc., cf. *Vit.Philonid.*p.12C., Plu.*Alc.*1, etc.: Comp. -οτέρως, τὰ ἔνδοξα ἐ. λέγειν Hermog.*Id.*1.9; also στῆλαι ἔχουσαι ἐπιγραφὰς-ξως *conspicuously* **placed**, *Sammelb.*6152.22 (i B. C.): Sup. -ότατα, ἐβουλεύσασθε D.18.65 [LS]. Proposed translation in this context: "special, dignified, distinguished public recognition, in which one's attributes and virtue are conspicuously seen, honored and appreciated."

[55] σῶμα...**2.** *the living body,* Hes.Op.540, Batr.44, Thgn.650, Pi.O.6.56, P.8.82, Hdt.1.139, etc.;...τὸ ς. σῴζειν or -εσθαι *save one's life,* D.22.55, Th.1.136;...περὶ τοῦ ς. ἀγωνίζεσθαι *for one's life,* Lys.5.1; ἔχειν τὸ ς. κακῶς, ὡς βέλτιστα, etc., to be in a bad, a good state of *bodily health,* X.*Mem.*3.12.1, 3.12.5 [LS]. Proposed translation in this context: "health, welfare, development and growth of one's own self during one's mortal life."

[56] In his analysis of human friendship, Aristotle confirms the truth that one must love himself rightly before he can love others rightly. Thus, even though the vague notion of "self-love" is often misunderstood as synonymous with "selfishness," and therefore regarded as something pejorative, a correct understanding of self-love as the love of what is virtuous and good for oneself is required before one can actually love another properly, by desiring what is good and virtuous for them also. Aristotle says it this way in his *Nicomachean Ethics*, 1166a1-34 and 1168a28-1169b2 (ed. J. Bywater, Oxford, 1894, transl. H. Rackham. Cambridge, 1934):

> [1166a1-34](1)IV. "The forms which friendly feeling for our neighbors takes, and the marks by which the different forms of friendship are defined, seem to be derived from the feelings of regard which we entertain for ourselves. A friend is defined as (a) one who wishes, and promotes by action, the real or apparent good of another for that other's sake; or (b) one who wishes the existence and preservation of his friend for the friend's sake...Friendship is defined by one or other of these marks. [2] But each of them is also found in a good man's feelings towards himself (and in those of all other men as well, in so far as they believe themselves to be good; but, as has been said, virtue and the virtuous man seem to be the standard in everything). [3] For the good man is of one mind with himself, and desires the same things with every part of his nature. Also (a) he wishes his own good, real as well as apparent, and seeks it by action (for it is a mark of a good man to exert himself actively for the good); and he does so for his own sake (for he does it on account of the intellectual part of himself, and this appears to be a man's real self). Also (b) he desires his own life and security, and especially that of his rational part. [4] For existence is good for the virtuous man; and everyone (20) wishes his own good: no one would choose to possess every good in the world on condition of becoming somebody else (for God possesses the good even as it is), but only while remaining himself, whatever he may be; and it would appear that the thinking part is the real self, or is so more than anything else. [5] And (c) the good man desires his own company; for he enjoys being by himself, since he has agreeable memories of the past, and good hopes for the future, which are pleasant too; also his mind is stored with subjects for contemplation. And (e) he is keenly conscious of his own joys and sorrows; for the same things give him pleasure or pain at all times, and not different things at different times, since he is not apt to change his mind. It is therefore because the good man has these various feelings towards himself, and because he feels towards his friend [in this context – his wife – GWC] in the same way as towards himself (for a friend is another self), that friendship also is thought to consist in one or other of these feelings, and the possession of them is thought to be the test of a friend..."

> [1168a28-1169b2] VIII. "The question is also raised whether one ought to love oneself or someone else most. We censure those who put themselves first, and 'lover of self' is used as a term of reproach. And it is thought that a bad man considers himself in all he does, and the more so the worse he is – so it is a complaint against him for instance that 'he never does a thing unless you make him' – whereas a good man acts from a sense of what is noble, and the better he is the more he so acts, and he considers his friend's interest, disregarding his own. [2] But the facts do not accord with these theories; nor is this surprising. [1168b] (1) For we admit that one should love one's best friend most; but the best friend is he that, when he wishes a person's good, wishes it for that person's own sake, even though nobody will ever know of it. Now this

condition is most fully realized in a man's regard for himself, as indeed are all the other attributes that make up the definition of a friend; for it has been said already that all the feelings that constitute friendship for others are an extension of regard for self. Moreover, all the proverbs agree with this; for example, 'Friends have one soul between them,' 'Friends' goods are common property,' 'Amity is equality,' 'The knee is nearer than the shin.' All of these sayings will apply most fully to oneself; for a man is his own best friend. Therefore he ought to love himself most. So it is naturally debated which of these two views we ought to adopt, since each of them has some plausibility. [3] Now where there is a conflict of opinion the proper course is doubtless to get the two views clearly distinguished, and to define how far and in what way each of them is true. So probably the matter may become clear if we ascertain what meaning each side attaches to the term 'self-love.' [4] Those then who make it a term of reproach call men lovers of self when they assign to themselves the larger share of money, honors, or bodily pleasures; since these are the things which most men desire and set their hearts on as being the greatest goods, and which accordingly they compete with each other to obtain. Now those who take more than their share of these things are men who indulge (20) their appetites, and generally their passions and the irrational part of their souls. But most men are of this kind. Accordingly the use of the term 'lover of self' as a reproach has arisen from the fact that self-love of the ordinary kind is bad. Hence self-love is rightly censured in those who are lovers of self in this sense. [5] And that it is those who take too large a share of things of this sort whom most people usually mean when they speak of lovers of self, is clear enough. For if a man were always bent on outdoing everybody else in acting justly or temperately or in displaying any other of the virtues, and in general were always trying to secure for himself moral nobility, no one will charge him with love of self nor find any fault with him. [6] Yet as a matter of fact such a man might be held to be a lover of self in an exceptional degree. At all events he takes for himself the things that are noblest and most truly good. Also it is the most dominant part of himself that he indulges and obeys in everything. But (a) as in the state it is the sovereign that is held in the fullest sense to be the state, and in any other composite whole it is the dominant part that is deemed especially to be that whole, so it is with man. He therefore who loves and indulges the dominant part of himself is a lover of self in the fullest degree. Again (b), the terms 'self-restrained' and 'unrestrained' denote being restrained or not by one's intellect, and thus imply that the intellect is the man himself. [1169a] (1) Also (c) it is our reasoned acts that are felt to be in the fullest sense our own acts, voluntary acts. It is therefore clear that a man is or is chiefly the dominant part of himself, and that a good man values this part of himself most. Hence the good man will be a lover of self in the fullest degree, though in another sense than the lover of self so-called by way of reproach, from whom he differs as much as living by principle differs from living by passion, and aiming at what is noble from aiming at what seems expedient. [7] Persons therefore who are exceptionally zealous in noble actions are universally approved and commended; and if all men vied with each other in moral nobility and strove to perform the noblest deeds, the common welfare would be fully realized, while individuals also could enjoy the greatest of goods, inasmuch as virtue is the greatest good. Therefore the good man ought to be a lover of self, since he will then both benefit himself by acting nobly and aid his fellows; but the bad man ought not to be a lover of self, since he will follow his base passions, and so injure both himself and his neighbors. [8] With the bad man therefore, what he does is not in accord with what he ought to do, but the good man does what he ought, since intelligence always chooses for itself that which is best, and the good man obeys his intelligence. [9] But it is also true that the virtuous man's conduct is often guided by the interests of his friends and of his country, and that he will if necessary (20) lay down his life in their behalf. For he will surrender wealth and power and all the goods that men struggle to win, if he can secure nobility for himself; since he would prefer an hour of rapture to a long period of mild enjoyment, a year of noble life to many years of ordinary existence, one great and glorious exploit to many small successes. And this is doubtless the case with those who give their lives for others; thus they choose great nobility for themselves. Also the virtuous man is ready to forgo money if by that means his friends may gain more money; for thus, though his friend gets money, he himself achieves nobility, and so he assigns the greater good to his own share. [10] And he behaves in the same manner as regards honors and offices also: all these things he will relinquish to his friend, for this is noble and praiseworthy for himself. He is naturally therefore thought to be virtuous, as he chooses moral nobility in preference to all other things. It may even happen that he will surrender to his friend the performance of some achievement, and that it may be nobler for him to be the cause of his friend's performing it than to perform it himself. [11] Therefore in all spheres of praiseworthy conduct it is manifest that the good man takes the larger share of moral nobility for himself. [1169b] (1) In this sense then, as we said above, it is right to be a lover of self, though self-love of the ordinary sort is wrong."

[57] ἐκτρέφω, **bring up from childhood, rear up**, Hdt.1.122, A.*Ch*.750, etc.; ἐξέφυσε κἀξέθρεψέ με S.*OT*827; ἐκτεθραμμένοι σκύμνοι λεόντων **true-bred**..., E.*Supp*.1222; **of plants**, τὸ ἐκτρέφον τὴν ῥίζαν Hdt. 1.193; ἐκτρέφει ἡ γῆ τὸ σπέρμα X.*Oec*.17.10; ποταμοῦ πνεῦμα τραχύτερον ἐκθρέψαντος Plu.2.357d:-- Med., **rear up for oneself**, τινά h.*Cer*. 166; ἤνεγκα κἀξέσωσα κἀξεθρεψάμην, **says the παιδαγωγός**, S.*El*.13, cf. *Fr*.387, Pl.*Lg*.929a:--Pass., εἴ σοί τις υἱός ἐστιν ἐκτεθραμμένος Ar.*Nu*.796; ἐγένου τε καὶ ἐξετράφης Pl.*Cri*.50e, cf. *Lys*.19.8. II. Med., of **pregnant animals, nourish**, [ζῷα] μεγάλα ἐντὸς ἐκθρέψωνται Pl.*Ti*.91d:--Act., **bring to birth**, τὰ κυήματα Arist.*GA*773a34 [LS]. This word is only used twice in the New Testament – both by Paul – and both of them in this Treatise. The other passage in which Paul uses this word is Ephesians 6:4, where in context the word clearly means "to rear, bring up, properly raise and educate children."

[58] θάλπω, fut. -ψω Orph.*Fr*.258, Alciphr.2.4: fut. Med. in pass. sense θάλψομαι Id.3.42:--**heat, soften by heat**, Od.21.179, al.:--Pass., ἐτήκετο κασσίτερος ὣς . . θαλφθείς Hes.*Th*.864, cf. S.*Tr*.697: metaph., **to be softened, deceived**, αἴ κε μὴ θαλφθῇ λόγοις Ar.*Eq*.210. II. **heat, warm, without any notion of softening**, καῦμ' ἔθαλπε (sc. ἡμᾶς) S. *Ant*.417; θερμὴ ἡμᾶς ἀκτὶς θ. Ar.*Av*.1092; **keep warm**, χλανιδίοις ἐρειπίοις θάλπουσα καὶ ψύχουσα *Trag.Adesp*.7: prov., θ. τὸν δίφρον, **of an idle life**, Herod.1.37; θ. τὰς κοχώνας Id.7.48; τὴν βαίτην θάλπουσαν εὖ ib.129:--Pass., Hp.*Aff*.4; θάλπεσθαι τοῦ θέρους **to be warm in summer**, X.*Cyr*.5.1.11; τῷ πυρὶ θάλψομαι Alciphr.3.42: metaph., ἔτι ἀλίῳ θάλπεσθαι **to be alive**, Pi.*N*.4.14. **2. warm at the fire, dry**, θάλπεται ῥάκη S.*Ph*.38, cf. E.*Hel*.183 (lyr.). **3. hatch**, ᾠά *Gp*.14.1.4: so abs., sit, ib.3; θ. ἐπὶ τῶν νοσσῶν, ἐπὶ τῶν ᾠῶν, LXX*De*. 22.6. III. metaph., **of passion, heat, inflame**, ἣ Διὸς θάλπει κέαρ ἔρωτι

A.*Pr*.590, cf. S.*Fr*.474 (Pass.);...**2. comfort**, ὕπνος . . θάλπει κέαρ B.*Fr*.3.11, cf. *Fr*.16.2, *Com.Adesp*.5.16D.; **cherish, foster**, ἄλλον θάλπε φίλον Theoc.14.38; ὡς ἐὰν τροφὸς θάλπῃ τὰ ἑαυτῆς τέκνα *1* **Ep.Thess.2.7**; τὴν ἑαυτοῦ σάρκα ***Ep.Eph*.5.29**; τὸ ἀσθενοῦν Alciphr.2.4; θ. καὶ τρέφειν P*Masp*.6 *B*132 (vi A.D.); τὴν πόλιν θ. **tend** it **with fostering care**, *OGI*194.5 (Egypt, i B.C.). **3.** ἐμὲ οὐδὲν θ. ἡ δόξα **I** *care* nothing for glory, Alciphr.2.2; ἐμὲ οὐδὲν θ. κέρδος Aristaenet.1.24. **IV.** intr., *to be full of heat, vigorous*, Arist.*Pr*.879a33; θάλψαι τρεῖς ποίας *to live* three summers, *AP*7.731 (Leon.) [LS]. This word also is only used twice in the New Testament – both by Paul – once here and once in 1 Thessalonians 2:7. In the Thessalonians passage, the contextual meaning emphasizes the "gentleness with which a nurse cares for a child:" Paul says, "We were gentle in the midst of you, as when a nurse ***warmly cares for and gently comforts*** her own children."

⁵⁹ **προσκολλάω**, *glue on or to*, τι πρός τι Hp.Art.33:--Pass., generally, *to be stuck to, stick or cleave to*, Pl.*Phd*.82e, Lg.728b; ὑπὸ τοῦ αἵματος προσκολληθῆναι τὴν ῥομφαίαν αὐτοῦ τῇ δεξιᾷ J.*AJ*7.12.4; *of a snail*, τοῖς θαμνίσκοις π. Dsc.2.9; *of a* **husband**, π. τῇ γυναικί *Ev.Matt*.19.5, cf. LXX *Ge*.2.24, *MEv.Marc*.10.7, ***Ep.Eph*.5.31**; τοῖς ἐπαοιδοῖς LXX *Le*.19.31; ψυχαὶ π. θεῷ Ph.Fr.51 H [LS]. The word "cleave" in American English has come to mean "cut" or "sever," instead of "stick to" or "glue to." Perhaps the best contemporary American expression to use here would be "bond to."

⁶⁰ Paul is quoting Genesis 2:24. Below is the Greek text of the entire passage (Genesis 2:18-25) from the Septuagint of which Genesis 2:24 is the crucial verse, followed by an English translation. Note especially the use of the symbols of both "flesh" and "bones" (Paul uses the phrase "of His flesh and of His bones" in the immediately preceding verse of Ephesians 5:30 because he is thinking of this entire passage from Genesis) to connote a "special, unique and lasting bond of intimacy:"

Gen. 2:18-25 Καὶ εἶπεν κύριος ὁ θεός Οὐ καλὸν εἶναι τὸν ἄνθρωπον μόνον· ποιήσωμεν αὐτῷ βοηθὸν κατ' αὐτόν. ¹⁹καὶ ἔπλασεν ὁ θεὸς ἔτι ἐκ τῆς γῆς πάντα τὰ θηρία τοῦ ἀγροῦ καὶ πάντα τὰ πετεινὰ τοῦ οὐρανοῦ καὶ ἤγαγεν αὐτὰ πρὸς τὸν Αδαμ ἰδεῖν, τί καλέσει αὐτά, καὶ πᾶν, ὃ ἐὰν ἐκάλεσεν αὐτὸ Αδαμ ψυχὴν ζῶσαν, τοῦτο ὄνομα αὐτοῦ. ²⁰Καὶ ἐκάλεσεν Αδαμ ὀνόματα πᾶσιν τοῖς κτήνεσιν καὶ πᾶσι τοῖς πετεινοῖς τοῦ οὐρανοῦ καὶ πᾶσι τοῖς θηρίοις τοῦ ἀγροῦ, τῷ δὲ Αδαμ οὐχ εὑρέθη βοηθὸς ὅμοιος αὐτῷ. – ²¹καὶ ἐπέβαλεν ὁ θεὸς ἔκστασιν ἐπὶ τὸν Αδαμ, καὶ ὕπνωσεν· καὶ ἔλαβεν μίαν τῶν πλευρῶν αὐτοῦ καὶ ἀνεπλήρωσεν σάρκα ἀντ αὐτῆς. ²²καὶ ᾠκοδόμησεν κύριος ὁ θεὸς τὴν πλευράν, ἣν ἔλαβεν ἀπὸ τοῦ Αδαμ, εἰς γυναῖκα καὶ ἤγαγεν αὐτὴν πρὸς τὸν Αδαμ. ²³**καὶ εἶπεν Αδαμ Τοῦτο νῦν ὀστοῦν ἐκ τῶν ὀστέων μου καὶ σὰρξ ἐκ τῆς σαρκός μου· αὕτη κληθήσεται γυνή, ὅτι ἐκ τοῦ ἀνδρὸς αὐτῆς ἐλήμφθη αὕτη.** ²⁴**ἕνεκεν τούτου καταλείψει ἄνθρωπος τὸν πατέρα αὐτοῦ καὶ τὴν μητέρα αὐτοῦ καὶ προσκολληθήσεται πρὸς τὴν γυναῖκα αὐτοῦ, καὶ ἔσονται οἱ δύο εἰς σάρκα μίαν.** ²⁵καὶ ἦσαν οἱ δύο γυμνοί, ὅ τε Αδαμ καὶ ἡ γυνὴ αὐτοῦ, καὶ οὐκ ᾐσχύνοντο.

Transl.: ¹⁸"Yahweh God said, "It is not good that the man should be alone; I will make him a helper suitable for him." ¹⁹Out of the ground Yahweh God formed every animal of the field, and every bird of the sky, and brought them to the man to see what he would call them. Whatever the man called every living creature, that was its name. ²⁰The man gave names to all cattle, and to the birds of the sky, and to every animal of the field; but for man there was not found a helper suitable for him. ²¹Yahweh God caused a deep sleep to fall on the man, and he slept; and he took one of his ribs, and closed up the flesh in its place. ²²He made the rib, which Yahweh God had taken from the man, into a woman, and brought her to the man. ²³*The man said, "This is now bone of my bones, and flesh of my flesh. She will be called Woman, because she was taken out of Man."* ²⁴*Therefore a man will leave his father and his mother, and will join with his wife, and they will be one flesh.* ²⁵They were both naked, the man and his wife, and were not ashamed."

Also note that Paul quotes the text precisely but changes only one word: the first word of verse 24 (Paul uses the preposition ἀντὶ instead of the preposition in the Septuagint – ἕνεκεν – see word studies below) in order to emphasize his interpretational emphasis upon a ***deliberate exchange of relational intimacy*** (ἀντὶ) instead of the meaning of the original text: "for this purpose" (ἕνεκεν). In other words, Paul wants to emphasize that in the same way that Jesus *exchanged* his relational intimacy with His Father for the new relational intimacy He desires to have with His specially selected apprentices organized into His Kingdom Apprenticeship Councils, the husband should *exchange* his initial initimacy with his parents for a new relational intimacy with his wife. A comparison of the meanings of the prepositions ἀντὶ (= "in exchange for" = Paul) and ἕνεκεν (= "for the purpose of" = LXX) now follows:

ἀντὶ...3. *to denote exchange, at the price of, in return for,* σοὶ δὲ θεοὶ τῶνδ' ἀντὶ χάριν . . δοῖεν Il.23.650; νῆσον ἀντὶ χρημάτων παρέλαβον *for money paid,* Hdt.3.59; ἀντ' ἀργυρίου ἀλλάξασθαι Pl.*R.* 371d;...δοίην ἀντ' ἀνιῶν ἀνίας *grief for grief,* Thgn.344; ἀντ' ἀγαθῶν ἀγαθοῖσι βρύοις A.Supp.966:--hence ἀνθ' ὧν *wherefore,* A.Pr.31, S.OT264, Th.6.83, *Ev.Luc.*12.3; ἀντὶ τούτου *therefore,* *Ep.Eph.*5.31; but ἀνθ' ὧν also for ἀντὶ τούτων ὅτι..., *because,* S.Ant. 1068, Ar.Pl.434;...also ἀνθ' ὧν ὅτι ἦτε...*instead of being as you were*..., LXX De.28.62 [LS]. Proposed translation: "in exchange for."

ἕνεκεν – 1. *on account of,* Τρώων πόλιν . . ἧς εἵνεκ' ὀϊζύομεν κακὰ πολλά Il.14.89, etc.;...τοῦδ' ἕνεκα *for this,* ib.110; ὧν ἕ. *wherefore,* 20.21; τίνος ἕ. βλάβης; A.Fr.181; παῖσαι ἄνδρας ἕνεκεν ἀταξίας X.*An.* 5.8.13 στεφανοῦσθαι ἀρετῆς ἕνεκα Aeschin.3.10; *for the sake of,* τοῦ ἕ.; Pl.*Prt.*31c b; τῶν δὲ εἵνεκα, ὅκως . ., or ἵνα . ., Hdt.8.35,40; κολακεύειν ἕ. μισθοῦ X.*HG*5.1.17; διὰ νόσον ἕ. ὑγιείας *by reason of* sickness *for the sake of* health, Pl.*Ly.*218e, cf. *Smp.*185b; τὸ οὗ ἕ. the final cause [= *"purpose, goal or end of something"* – GWC], Arist.*Ph.*194a27, *Metaph.*983a31 [this is the famous passage in the *Metaphysics* in which Aristotle articulates the four causes of any reality: the formal, the material, the instrumental, and the final cause, i.e., the purpose, goal or end of something – GWC]; τὸ οὗ ἕνεκεν Id.*Ph.*243a3, *Metaph.*1059a35 [LS]. Proposed translation: "for the purpose of."

6

Career Spiritual Soldiers

A Second Important Relationship in Which You Can Discover and Accomplish Your Lifework is by Initiating the Skill of Parenting in the Life of your Family in Gracious, Spiritually Accurate Ways ♦ A Third Important Relationship in Which You Can Discover and Accomplish Your Lifework is in Your Vocation – By Performing your Job, Employment, Occupation, Profession or Career in Spiritually Accurate Ways ♦ You Can Prevail Over the Evil Spiritual Forces that Will Attack You in Your Efforts to Bring God's Good News and Peace to Others Only by Equipping Yourselves to Become Career Spiritual Soldiers ♦ Strap on The "Sword-Belt" of The Discovery of the Truth ♦ Put On The "Body Armor" of Justice ♦ Tightly Lace Up The "Special Forces Boots" for the Long March Toward the Ultimate Goal of Being a Peacemaker ♦ Protect Yourself from Inevitable Indiscriminate Spiritual Attacks with the "Shield" of Faith ♦ Put on the "Helmet" of Rescue in order to Overcome Your Fear of the Inevitable Threats and Attacks that Will Come Against You in Your Leadership Role ♦ Like a Master Swordsman, You Must Skillfully Wield The "Sword" of God's Spoken Commands, Declarations, Promises and Principles as You are Guided by His Spirit ♦ The Spiritual Weaponry We Need to Fight the Evil One Will Only be as Effective as Our "Command and Control" System of Maintaining Direct Communication with God ♦ Since Encouragement Comes From Contented, Cheerful, Faithful and Loving People – Make Sure You Choose Friends and Messengers that Possess Such an Attitude ♦ May the Graciousness of Your Immortal Kingdom Persona Come to Distinguish Your Mortal Personality Also

A SECOND IMPORTANT RELATIONSHIP IN WHICH YOU CAN DISCOVER AND ACCOMPLISH YOUR LIFEWORK IS BY INITIATING THE SKILL OF PARENTING IN THE LIFE OF YOUR FAMILY IN GRACIOUS, SPIRITUALLY ACCURATE WAYS

While a primary relationship through which one can discover and accomplish their lifework for God is the marriage relationship, a second important relationship through which one can do so is the *family relationship*, in which the responsibilities of *parenting* are carried out in spiritually accurate ways.

Children, I will begin with you all, by telling you that you are never too young to begin to discover what it is that God wants you to do with your life. To do that, and make the most of what He has planned for each of you, you must all start out by obeying your parents. God has given your parents the responsibility to teach you and guide you in His laws and principles. Like Joseph, Ruth, Samuel, David, Esther, Daniel, Mary and Timothy did when they were children – and even Jesus Himself did when He was a boy – you should also eagerly involve yourselves in the ethical and spiritual training our Commander in Chief has given your parents to accomplish in each of your lives. You should do this because obeying your parents is the first of the many right roads you must learn to recognize and take in order to find the special lifework God has planned for each of you to achieve.

2As the fifth command of the main Ten Commands of God's Law – recorded in both Exodus 20:12 as well as in Deuteronomy 5:16 – says: "You must honor your father and mother."[1] This is the first command of the Ten that comes with the promise of a reward to those who obey it. This promise is as follows: 3"In order that your life would go well for you and that you might live a long time in God's Promised Land." Children, the important part of the promise is not necessarily that you will live a long time to a ripe old age in this mortal life, but rather that you would readily discover and accomplish the good lifework that God has planned for you in this present life, so that your life living in the "Promised Land" of His coming Kingdom will be the one that you truly enjoy for an extremely long time.[2]

4Not only must you children be obedient to your parents, but you fathers must develop the conscious habit of putting a stop to the unwitting behavior of provoking[3] your children to anger by ignoring them or by dismissing them with a few careless words or critical remarks. It will be your tendency to fall into the bad habit and trap of unwittingly *reacting* to their childish mistakes, foolishness, silliness and false starts with the wrong behavior of snapping at them, annoying and irritating them with sarcasm or cynicism, or by exasperating them by making fun of them in public. As I mentioned above, children (or any other human beings for that matter) are never motivated by sarcastic comments or cynical remarks, no matter to what degree those comments may be grounded in what you sincerely believe to be right in your own mind as their fathers.

Instead, you should never react to their immature behavior at all, but rather proactively set a good example for them to follow yourselves. You must consciously adopt the new habit of cultivating and rearing your children up from even their earliest childhood years[4] by following the example of our Commander in Chief. In the same way that he taught His own apprentices, you must with the same gracious manner and demeanor take opportunities to initiate well planned conversations with your children, making it your goal to patiently train, teach and educate them. Warn them of danger when it is required and do not be afraid to reprimand them when they are foolish, quarrelsome or petulant. However, take the time to think through how you should reprimand them when necessary – before you do it.[5]

A THIRD IMPORTANT RELATIONSHIP IN WHICH YOU CAN DISCOVER AND ACCOMPLISH YOUR LIFEWORK IS IN YOUR VOCATION – BY PERFORMING YOUR JOB, EMPLOYMENT, OCCUPATION, PROFESSION OR CAREER IN SPIRITUALLY ACCURATE WAYS

[5]In addition to the marriage relationship and family relationships, a third important relationship through which you can discover and accomplish your lifework for God is the *vocational* relationship, by carrying out the responsibilities involved in performing your job, employment, occupation, profession or career in spiritually accurate ways.

First, I would address those of you who are employees in the various fields of private enterprise or subordinate officers in the departments of the military or civil service.[6] You all should follow policies and procedures, and then act in compliance with and faithfully carry out the orders and directives of your leaders, managers or superior officers within your businesses, companies, corporations, enterprises, departments, outfits, units, or divisions. You must do so with an attitude of respect, a sense of duty and a manner of being candid, direct and straightforward. Perform your work with dedication and with an energetic and enthusiastic demeanor and a "can-do" spirit of thoroughness, behaving in exactly the same way that you would if you were under the personal command of the High King Himself.

[6-8]You must all steer clear of the tendency to succumb to the pernicious peer pressure of pretending to be enthusiastic about your job or occupation and perform your assigned tasks only when your leaders, managers or superior officers are watching you, but then the moment they leave the office or are not around, you stop doing your work and become apathetic, shiftless and lazy. Rather, you must come to the realization that your real "Boss" or "Superior Officer" is the High King Himself, and that He is always watching the way you comport yourself and how you perform your work. Because He is God, He not only can always see what you are doing, but He also always knows your attitude and hidden motives as you do it. The reason He is so interested in your attitude and conduct when you are at work is because He knows that if you are shiftless and lazy in your present job, you will also behave that way if He were to give you tasks to perform for Him in the Kingdom. I can assure you that He has no interest in employing apathetic, incompetent subordinates in His Kingdom.

For this reason, you must adopt a new and good mindset about how you perform your work *now* – in whatever job or occupation or branch of the military or civil service in which you are presently engaged – and realize that your "Boss" or "Commanding Officer" is in reality the Commander in Chief Himself. Therefore, do a good job in whatever enterprise in which you are presently employed, because God is observing and carefully assembling His own completely accurate version and evaluation of your résumé or dossier that He will use as a part of the basis of your Statement of Qualifications for your position of service to Him when He returns to earth to establish His Kingdom.

Furthermore, since He is completely impartial, if you have done a good job in your mortal lives, being motivated to do whatever you were asked to do in your earthly vocation for Him, He will certainly recognize and rightly reward you with a good job in serving Him during the Kingdom era, no matter what kind of unjust blame you may have endured, or what appropriate recognition you may not have received from your human superiors during your mortal career.

[9]Not only must those of you who are subordinates at work behave as though you were working directly for our Commander in Chief, but those of you who have been given the privilege of being leaders, entrepreneurs, business owners, bosses, managers, military officers and political or civil officials must relate with your subordinates as Jesus would have you to. You must avoid the peculiar tendency those in leadership positions have of adopting the bad habit of using fear to motivate their subordinates by threatening or intimidating them in order to secure their obedience. As leaders in your relationships with your subordinates, you must realize that you will all encounter this dangerous tendency to become a sanctimonious, demanding narcissist.

Those of you who are leaders must realize that no matter how high you climb or how superior you come to think you are, you all have a Commander in Chief, who because of His position at the right hand of God the Father in Heaven, out-ranks all of you. Therefore you must learn the new habit of conducting yourselves in the same way that I just outlined that your employees and subordinates should behave in their attitude and conduct toward our Commander in Chief.

In other words, although you may have over the course of your career actually become the *"Chief"* of your organization – whether that be the *Chief* Executive Officer or the Police *Chief* or Fire *Chief* or the Chairman of the Joint *Chiefs* of Staff or even the *Chief* Justice of the Supreme Court – in your leadership roles you are all still subordinate officers of Jesus, our One Supreme *Commander in Chief*, and consequently you are all in reality working for Him, and not for your own selves or your own private or political agendas. Likewise, just as He is doing with your subordinates, God is also observing you and carefully assembling His own completely accurate version and evaluation of your résumé or dossier that He will use as a part of the basis of your Statement of Qualifications for your position of service to Him when He returns to earth to establish His Kingdom.

Now I know that as leaders, you all have become proficient to different extents at the public knack of blustering and bullying your way out of your mistakes and failures by trying to get those to whom you are accountable to accept at face value your excuses and justifications in an attempt to explain away your misconduct by pretending to have sincere, good and genuine motives through the practiced use of your facial expressions and demeanor.[7] However, be assured that there will come a Day when you must face our Commander in Chief and give Him an account of the leadership responsibilities with which He entrusted you during your mortal lives, and that since He is God, there is no disguise, façade, mask, or act with which you can possibly "fake Him out."

Because of this, you all might as well take immediate action and formulate conscious spiritual steps to shed yourselves of and then guard yourselves against this wicked tendency. You must instead approach your leadership roles as *a position of trust*, and consequently begin to behave as one of His trusted subordinate officers, doing so with an attitude of respect, a sense of duty, a manner of being candid, direct and straightforward, with an energetic and enthusiastic demeanor and a "can-do" spirit of thoroughness, just as I instructed your own employees or subordinate officers to do.

YOU CAN PREVAIL OVER THE EVIL SPIRITUAL FORCES THAT WILL ATTACK YOU IN YOUR EFFORTS TO BRING GOD'S GOOD NEWS AND PEACE TO OTHERS ONLY BY EQUIPPING YOURSELVES TO BECOME CAREER SPIRITUAL SOLDIERS

[10]Having completed the main declaration and application of this comprehensive Treatise concerning the central plan and purpose of our High King of His divine program to recruit, train and fill all of the leadership positions He requires for the just, wise and good administration of His future worldwide Kingdom, it remains only for me to conclude this Treatise with the military metaphor that our Commander in Chief has instructed me to employ to adequately represent its main themes in summary.

The reason that I have saved this particular metaphor until the end of this Treatise is because it is the most important one for you all to realize and remember – namely, that during the remaining years of this present evil era of spiritual darkness prior to the coming of God's Kingdom, the evil spiritual being – Satan, whose is appropriately named the "Slanderer," which is what the word "Devil" means[8] – together with the retinue of wicked spiritual beings that he has been allowed to marshal under his command, will take every initiative in their power to wage war against all of you who have become our High King's specially selected recruits. He will do this in a protracted attempt to impede and frustrate each of you in your apprenticeship and training program towards finding and accomplishing your unique lifework for God. He will plot, intrigue, and try to kill you, destroy you, or use a variety of different schemes of continually attacking you to wear you down. His goal is to bring about your eventual failure and total ruin.

Therefore, my dear and loyal colleagues, associates, fellows, and future kings,[9] you must finally learn to regard and discipline yourselves as *career spiritual soldiers* in a spiritual war that will never end until your death, or until our High King returns for us. Moreover, in precisely the same way that a career soldier never stops his continual training regimen, so too you must also continually be engaged in the training required to never stop advancing in your spiritual strength and rank, knowing that you will be enabled to achieve this by our Commander in Chief, as you make it your goal to gain mastery[10] of the vast array of spiritual military forces[11] He will continually place at your disposal.

[11]I must now return to the illustration I used earlier in this Treatise of "taking off and putting on clothing,"[12] and expand upon it with specific application to military arms as an extended metaphor that will be quite helpful both to summarize and to explain how each of you may gain mastery in using all of the spiritual forces our Commander in Chief has placed at your service. You remember that in the same way that you "put on" and "wear" certain types of new and attractive outfits for differing kinds of formal public occasions, so I instructed you also to deliberately "dress up" your mind every morning with the new, fresh and newly-outfitted human being that has been created, founded and built by God, focused on discovering the truth about your lifework.

In addition, I am now forewarning you that you must not only learn how to "dress up" your mind, as it were, for the duties of a civil servant, you must also learn how to "put on" the body armor and become skilled in the use of the personal weaponry of a soldier[13] that God has issued to each of you as your own spiritual "equipment." It is absolutely necessary for you to do this if you would become disciplined enough, strong enough and skilled enough to stand up to the wide-ranging variety of plots, schemes, stratagems, maneuvers, feints, ambushes, snares and booby traps[14] that the "Predator" – namely, the Devil – will set for you as you set out on the right road to accomplish your lifework. You must do this, because I can assure you that he is relentless, he is ruthless, and he will never give up stalking you. His ultimate intention is to kill you – which is precisely why you must learn to become proficient in the disciplined use of this spiritual military equipment God is issuing to each of you.

12You must learn to spiritually discipline your minds according to this military metaphor, because ultimately, the conflicts[15] we must all face in our lives are not actually against other 'flesh and blood' human beings – who because they deceive us, defraud us, oppose us, resist us, confront us, defy us, or openly and violently attack us, seem on the surface of things to be the only enemies we will face in life. In reality, in every single case, our actual enemy is the "Slanderer," i.e., the Devil himself, together with the wicked angels and evil spiritual beings who have declared their loyalty to him. He he has deliberately ordered these evil spiritual beings into a wicked organization, with a chain of command consisting of formidably authoritative and powerful evil spiritual political and military forces[16] that make it their unrelenting and merciless objective to covertly, clandestinely and stealthily infiltrate, influence, manipulate and then eventually control the existing hierarchies of the human leaders in all of the various kingdoms, countries, nations, and governments on earth, as well as every other form of organization, institution or enterprise during this present era of world history.

It is in fact this wicked organization of evil spiritual beings under the leadership of the Devil that ultimately manipulates and causes human beings to suffer the devastating and destructive effects of psychological and spiritual darkness. His goal is to lead us first into an initial state of perpetual pride or fear, then confusion, then lack of confidence, then indecisiveness and lastly to hopeless despair. At any point along this descent, he attempts to manipulate us to the point of initiating the violence that leads to the untimely and tragic deaths caused by crime, revenge and war, which we allow him to bring about by obstinately clinging to our own naïve or willful spiritual ignorance.[17]

Even though you may wonder why it seems that God has not yet destroyed this evil army of spiritual beings whose only objective is to torture and devastate the human race, when viewed from a balanced spiritual perspective, He has in reality placed them under fairly strict controls. During this historical era, they have in fact been restricted by God to live only in the sky, that is, in the atmosphere above the earth, where He rigorously controls the scope and the limits of the degree to which He allows them to exercise their wicked powers.[18]

For those evil spirits who on occasion dare to exceed that scope or go beyond those limits, He confines them to the deepest parts of the Ocean,[19] where He no longer permits them to practice their evil powers. God permits those evil spirits remaining in the sky (including the Devil), only on rare occasion, to travel across the Universe to His Council Chambers in Heaven itself for various limited purposes in either individual or corporate human affairs, which under His wise and providential control, ultimately work out for our education and training toward becoming more spiritually mature and wise human beings.[20]

[13]For this reason, namely the realization that all of our conflicts during this era are ultimately against the Devil and his evil spiritual forces, I must reiterate that it is imperative (although you may at first be reluctant) that each of you come to regard yourselves as a *career spiritual soldier*. Because of this, you all must eventually equip yourselves by picking up and putting on the complete complement of spiritual "body armor" and personal military weapons with which God has supplied you, with the full resolve to wear it into the inevitable spiritual battles that the Devil and his evil organization of spirits will instigate and relentlessly wage against you for the rest of your mortal lives.

You must, despite your reluctance, resolve to pick it up, wear it, and learn to wield it skillfully. It is by means of wearing it and using it that God will enable you to become strong enough to make a spiritual stand, successfully resist the Evil One, and then fight on during this era in which God has allowed the Evil One and his angels to exercise a considerable amount of their combined wicked powers. It is only then, after you have resisted, endured, overpowered, defeated and become victorious over these evil spirits, and with God's help, you have accomplished all that He has asked you to do, that He will invite you to stand with our Commander in Chief when He finally triumphs over the Devil and establishes His reign as High King of the earth.

STRAP ON THE "SWORD-BELT" OF THE DISCOVERY OF THE TRUTH

[14]Therefore, in order to never give up and keep on fighting[21] against the Evil One, it is imperative that you first securely fasten around yourselves the spiritual "sword-belt"[22] of the never-ending commitment to discover the truth in your life. The military sword-belt is designed as the overall foundation of the uniform, because it is used not only to suspend the sword, but also to carry all of the other battle gear and equipment during the long marches inevitable in any military campaign. In view of this, it serves as an accurate spiritual symbol to help you remember that you must "hang on" with total dedication to your foundational commitment to orient everything else in your lives around discovering not only your own true[23] lifework for God, but to also help others do the same.

PUT ON THE "BODY ARMOR" OF JUSTICE

The second essential element of God's spiritual equipment you must "put on" is the "body armor"[24] of justice – that is, of always doing what is morally and ethically the right thing to do. Symbolically, the reason you must fasten this particular piece of equipment over your chest is because the function of body armor is to protect your *heart* from injury during battle.

As you remember, my specific request to God detailed earlier in this Treatise is that God would open the "eyes of your heart" to realize that He has summoned each of you to accomplish a special and unique lifework.[25] It therefore follows that the Devil and his wicked spirits will attempt to spiritually wound you in your "heart," (which, as you recall, is the ethical and moral decision making power of the soul to determine right from wrong, that remains distinct from the rational decision making power of the mind). If the Devil can get you to decide to do something ethically or morally wrong, he can and will eventually use that decision to try to destroy you.[26]

TIGHTLY LACE UP THE "SPECIAL FORCES BOOTS" FOR THE LONG MARCH TOWARD THE ULTIMATE GOAL OF BEING A PEACEMAKER

[15]The third vital step in equipping yourselves for spiritual battle is to think of yourselves as putting on high-top military boots[27] instead of shoes, paying particular attention to lace up your boots tight, double-knot them at the top, and then cut off the excess lacing, like those who are members of the "special forces" do. The reason it is important for you to imagine wearing spiritual "special forces" boots instead of shoes is because our Commander in Chief is sending you on a special *mission*, which involves a *lengthy march* over a protracted spiritual "trail," filled with jungle that has spiritual "briars and thorns" as well as spiritual "swamps and mud-pits."

This special mission (which requires – so to speak – a life-long military "march" through difficult spiritual terrain) is to continue carrying the message of good news[28] that Jesus' pioneering mission from heaven to earth was and still is a *peace initiative*, which, because He was successful in His mission, makes Him our "Peacemaker!" I would remind you here of this important theme I elaborated upon earlier in this Treatise,[29] namely, that God has given us the mission to represent Jesus as our "Peacemaker" by actively encountering and becoming His "peacemakers" (despite the obvious dangers) between savage barbarian states of mind that are wholly enslaved by their natural visceral appetites, as well as sanctimonious, arrogant states of mind projected by those who are contemptuous, cruel, condescending narcissists. Such an arduous mission will require tremendous patience and endurance on your part, because it will entail extended periods of time for such deluded cultures and states of mind to give up their mindless hatreds that in many cases are deeply embedded into their culture, and in some cases, are centuries old.

A simple rule of thumb to remember on this long, wearying march of what will sometimes seem to be a never-ending cacophony of griping, complaining, pettiness, disagreements, quarrels, clashes, acrimony, conflict, hatred, bitterness, spitefulness, hostility and animosity – is that you must never by *reacting* to these mindless quarrels fall into the trap of behaving or even allowing yourself to think like those who are burdened by such things. You must never go into a situation of conflict from which – due to your own reactions caused by your failure to be proactive and plan ahead – you walk away leaving the situation worse than you found it. Instead, you must adopt the attitude that when you go into a situation in which hostility is inevitable, you will intentionally develop a pre-planned strategy beforehand to *proactively* orchestrate the situation or the personalities involved into a more favorable outcome that when you first encountered it.

Protect Yourself from Inevitable Indiscriminate Spiritual Attacks with the "Shield" of Faith

[16]The fourth and most important piece of your spiritual equipment as a collective group of specially selected recruits is the "shield" of faith that our Commander in Chief has issued to each one of you. The specific type of battle shield I am referring to in this illustration is the large, rectangular shield used by the Romans, which is shaped like a door and covers the entire body;[30] not the smaller battle shield used by the Greeks, which is circular in shape and covers only the upper body. The reason I am referring to the larger Roman shield is because it is designed specifically with the purpose of being used by a large number of infantry soldiers acting in concert as a unit to be interlocked together to form a large, impenetrable wall against long range arrow-volleys, unlike the smaller, circular Greek shield which is designed for individual hand-to-hand combat.

You all – each and every one of you – must not only find the initial courage to pick up your own "shield of faith," but you must go on to develop the endurance to continually keep them raised up in front of yourselves and your loved ones – acting as a group – to form an interlocked and impenetrable wall. It is only as a united group that you will be capable of protecting yourselves and each other from all of the flaming[31] arrow-volleys[32] that the Evil One will continue to indiscriminately launch at you from long range, and be able to eventually extinguish them.

Allow me to elaborate on how the Devil will actually pursue his relentless "long-range" and indiscriminate assaults on all of you. You see, Satan, at the very core of his being, is actually a coward, because he knows that he is doomed to lose the final war of this evil era when Jesus, our Commander in Chief, returns from High Heaven with his angelic armies to finally defeat him, judge him and confine him, and then establish His own good and just reign as our High King. Now since the Devil is a coward, he fears our undying faith in the Millennial Kingdom, because he knows that upon its arrival, he is doomed. Therefore, his preferred way of attacking our faith is like that of a terrorist – from long range (because he fears to confront us at close range) and indiscriminately (due to the cruelty of his nature). So, he will continue to shoot volleys of "flaming arrows" not only at us, but also at our families, loved ones, and those under our spiritual care whose faith is not as strong as ours.

Just as we must never allow the fatigue that is bound to set in by holding up such a heavy shield of protection not only over ourselves, our families, and those who are dear to us, but also over those we know who are weak in faith, so also we must continually shield them with our own faith through requests to God for divine information, or by officially lobbying God to use His spiritual power in our behalf;[33] through encouragement, and through our own spiritual vigilance to recognize and protect them from Satan's spiritual "fiery arrow volleys."

These spiritual "fiery arrow volleys" will not only include the random hardships and physical suffering seemingly caused by war, diseases, plagues, financial misfortune and ruin, poverty, violent destructive storms and other natural or economic catastrophes,[34] but also the numerous spiritual temptations of pride, narcissism, envy, lust, passion, immorality, sorcery, gluttony, laziness, discouragement, bitterness, resentment, anger, revenge, cynicism, greed, suicide, murder, theft, fear, terror, despair, lying, fraud, deceit and treachery; which ultimately can destroy one's faith in God and in His coming Kingdom, because they focus one's human desires upon the wicked things that are the only things this evil era has to offer.[35]

PUT ON THE "HELMET" OF RESCUE TO OVERCOME YOUR FEAR OF THE INEVITABLE THREATS AND ATTACKS THAT WILL COME AGAINST YOU IN YOUR LEADERSHIP ROLE

[17]The fifth important piece of armor you must have the courage to take up and put on your head is the "helmet" of rescue. You must do this so that you can overcome the fear of physical danger you will experience from the threats and attacks that will inevitably come against you as you

perform your leadership role in accomplishing your lifework.[36] In battle, the helmet is designed to protect the head. You will recall that three times in this Treatise I have employed the metaphor of "headship" as specific symbolic representation referring to the legitimate and authoritative *leadership roles* given by our Commander in Chief to each of His specially selected recruits in order to enable us to fulfill our lifework for Him.

Hence, it is incumbent upon me to remind you all that the Devil and the evil spiritual beings under his control will attack our "headship," that is, our specific "spiritual role of leadership" during the course of our lifework. We must not give in to fear, disillusionment, discouragement or cynicism when these viscious attacks upon our spiritual leadership roles occur, because God will provide the spiritual protection – the "helmet" of rescue – we will need to endure such attacks. What this means is that God will *temporally rescue* us from such attacks as we perform our leadership responsibilities in this present life for as long as He has determined for us to do so, in order that we might fulfill our lifework.

For example, over the course of endeavoring to carry out my own lifework in the leadership responsibilities involved in being our Commander in Chief's appointed High Emissary, God has rescued me from numerous attempts on my life, in addition to countless other covert and overt attacks upon my leadership role. Even in what might seem to be the suffering of a premature death by many of the spiritual leaders that have gone before us (John the "Immerser," Stephen, the High Emissary James the brother of John, and even Jesus Himself), God's promise to rescue us still applies to that ultimate deliverance we will all enjoy during the resurrection when He will reward each of us with our respective leadership roles serving Jesus, our High King, when He returns to earth to establish His future Kingdom.

LIKE A MASTER SWORDSMAN, YOU MUST SKILLFULLY WIELD THE "SWORD" OF GOD'S SPOKEN COMMANDS, DECLARATIONS, PROMISES AND PRINCIPLES AS YOU ARE GUIDED BY HIS SPIRIT

Now, to complete this summary of your employment of the spiritual body armor and weaponry given to you by God, I must tell you that even though the "shield" of faith is the most important spiritual weapon upon which you must always rely, nevertheless the sixth and final weapon you must additionally learn to develop the courage to skillfully wield against the Devil and his organization of evil spirits if you desire to successfully accomplish your lifework for God, is the "sword"[37] of God's Spirit. Wielding this spiritual "sword" constitutes the skillful and appropriate use in your public speech of all of God's pledges, promises, guarantees, ethical principles, certifications, decrees and sworn oaths recorded in the Bible. You must learn to always incorporate His principles as you speak in public situations, consciously obeying the guidance of His Spirit at the same moment you are formulating your thoughts as you speak.

Allow me to elaborate further upon the use of the symbol of the "sword" as a spiritual weapon. Unlike the shield, which is useful in defending ourselves against arrow-volley attacks that are intended to wound us at random and with the indiscriminate cruelty of being launched from long range, when our enemy the Devil realizes that he cannot injure us in this way by attacking our faith, he will ultimately attempt a more deadly and close range assault with his wicked "sword" of personal temptation and enticement, studying us and attempting to attack us at our most vulnerable spiritual points.

Any warrior who desires to become a skillful swordsman must first apprentice himself to diligently study sword-craft under the personal spoken instruction and training of other experienced masters. He must then discipline himself to continual practice in order to improve and eventually perfect his comprehensive skill in all the offensive and defensive maneuvers and combinations required to become victorious in the mortal combat that sword-fighting ultimately entails.[38] Accordingly, you all must in that same way come to realize and subject yourselves to being trained by God's Spirit with a view to learning from Him how to *master the use of all of your spoken words* – in public and private situations, and in formal and informal contexts – such that you always communicate the words God would have you speak skillfully, correctly and meaningfully.

This skill necessarily includes that you be able to accurately translate, articulate and clearly explain His words in your public speech within the comprehensive context of the contemporary usage of the language of those to whom it is addressed. You should do so in a manner that always provides yourself and others with the same spiritual graciousness, assurance, confidence, firmness, poise, cool-headed steadiness and the proper balanced sense of proportion that is in complete harmony with all that God has communicated through the abundant supply of His spoken pledges, promises, guarantees, ethical principles, certifications, decrees and sworn oaths recorded in the Bible.

The reason you must train yourselves to always and only speak under the conscious direction of God's Spirit in complete harmony with these spoken declarations of God is because they alone have effective legal power in the spiritual realm. In fact, God has given them to you to use in order to defend yourselves from the whole host of wicked temptations in both thoughts and speech that evil spirits will deliberately direct at you at close range, always in personal attacks, usually when you are outnumbered, alone and physically, emotionally or spiritually weak, and which may include the assaults of the Devil himself.

I need only remind you that even Jesus, our Commander in Chief Himself, defended Himself in precisely this way under the direction of God's Spirit when the Devil tempted Him in the desert, by answering each temptation in complete harmony with God's previous decrees spoken by Moses in the desert and which Moses faithfully recorded in the Book of Deuteronomy. In the first temptation, when the Devil tempted Him to deliver Himself from the fear of dying from physical starvation, Jesus replied with the words of Deuteronomy 8:3, "It is written, 'Man shall not live by bread alone, but by every spoken decree[39] that proceeds from the mouth of God.'"[40]

Next, the Devil tempted Jesus to overcome the deep emotional pain of suffering the lack of recognition and appreciation by His own people in their indifferent reception of Him as their true Messiah by twisting one of God's promises in Psalm 91:11-12 in an devious attempt to incite Jesus to pull a miraculous "Superman" stunt that would gain Him only shallow, superficial recognition. Jesus again replied in harmony with the direction of God's Spirit from Deuteronomy 6:16 when He said to Satan, "It is written, 'you shall not tempt Yahweh your God.'"[41]

Finally, the Devil in one last challenge tempted Jesus by offering Him the very thing Satan knew that Jesus most deeply spiritually desired, namely, absolute Kingship over the entire world. The Devil offered Jesus what was in fact legitimately His by Divine Promise and Right, but on the condition that He place Himself under the authority and premature timing of Satan rather than under the authority and predetermined timing of God. Jesus replied under the direction of the Spirit again, this time using Deuteronomy 6:13, saying to the Devil, "Get behind me, Satan. For it is written, 'You shall worship Yahweh your God, and serve Him only.'"[42]

THE SPIRITUAL WEAPONRY WE NEED TO FIGHT THE EVIL ONE WILL ONLY BE AS EFFECTIVE AS OUR "COMMAND AND CONTROL" SYSTEM OF MAINTAINING DIRECT COMMUNICATION WITH GOD

[18]As I conclude the final summary of this Treatise through employing this image of the complete necessity that you appropriate these six indispensable components of God's spiritual "body armor," I must reiterate and reemphasize that you will only be successful in using them to discover and accomplish your lifework for God against the inevitable attacks that will assail you from the Devil and his evil spirits, only if you *maintain your "Command and Control" system of continual communication directly with God*.[43] Such direct communication with God involves always taking

the time and effort required to make your requests known to Him, asking Him for the information you need as well as for His Divine perspective, in order that you may discover the sufficient essential facts and outlook necessary for you to make important spiritual decisions, or to seek out His advice and direction in the process of gaining the spiritual understanding you are in need of in order to plan the important courses of action that will affect future endeavors that you undertake for Him.[44]

However, you must not only ask God for information, His perspective and advice. You must also not be afraid to lobby and petition Him – that is to say – to confidently and officially promote or urge Him to employ is great power to influence those subordinate to Him who hold angelic or human political, legal or military powers – whether good or evil – in order to positively affect the outcome of your efforts in favor of the specific spiritual interests that are important to you, including making official application for a desired office or position for yourself or others that would promote goodness and justice.[45]

In initiating such deliberate communications with Him, whether they be requests for divine information or officially lobbying Him to use His spiritual power in your behalf, you must be mindful to always do so as you are directed by His Spirit. You can be assured that the Spirit Who specially selected each one of you will always guide you by giving you an appropriate sense of proportion, the discernment to determine what is really relevant in any dilemma, the ability to invest your time and efforts only in the important events, people or opportunities with which the Spirit of God presents you, and by cooperating only with those who demonstrate their dedication to God by being willing to share in the hard work of sowing, cultivating and reaping the spiritual consequences and lessons that result from your joint initiatives.[46]

Furthermore, you must continue in your vigilance during times of spiritual attack from the Evil One, that at times will require staying awake all night and watching[47] with absolute confidence, firm patience, persistence, diligence and devotion.[48] During such times, you should make certain that your requests and petitions are in conformity with the lobbying, petitions and applications made to God by all of His specially selected recruits that concern realizing their best interests.

[19]I would also request that when you communicate with God, that you continue to ask Him that He would supply me with the information and insight that I need. In addition, please continue to lobby and petition Him in my behalf to influence those who have political control over my situation, and that He might give me the ability to always think intelligently, use good reasoning, speak with a clear mind and equip me with the best logical use of words in public speaking, whether the public

forum be teaching, a public address, a debate or my own legal defense.[49] Moreover, please ask that He might give me the best opportunities possible to speak openly, freely and confidently in public;[50] and when I do, that He would enable me to use precisely the right words to accurately and eloquently communicate His marvelous good news[51] of His formerly concealed but now openly unveiled "Top Secret" plan of His Kingdom Inheritance (which I articulated in the first half of this Treatise) to the specific needs of my audience, such that they can come to comprehend it fully and clearly.

20It is for this reason, namely, my chief duty and responsibility to spiritually recognize and engage in every opportunity to freely articulate this good news of God's offer of His Kingdom Inheritance Plan – whether in public teaching, public speeches, public debates, or legal proceedings resulting from my unjust arrest in Jerusalem – that I have come to be unjustly imprisoned in Rome as a consequence. However, what I have discerned has actually occurred is that I am in reality being transported by the Spirit to accomplish the commission that I received directly from our Commander in Chief Himself when I was first imprisoned in Jerusalem after my stay in Ephesus. It was during that period of confinement that He instructed me to represent Him as His chief ranking Ambassador in Rome,[52] and in that capacity to act as His lead Negotiator,[53] in order to negotiate the "Peace Initiative"[54] of our future High King to the organized world of this present era of history, by placing me directly in its Imperial Capital City.

It is with this perspective in mind that I respectfully request that you continue to ask God that He would supply me with the information and insight that I need. Please continue to petition Him in my behalf to influence those who have political control over my situation, in order that I might be able to spiritually discern the most favorable opportunities in which I should speak freely and openly in public. I must continue to do this in order to faithfully accomplish the divine commission I received directly from our Commander in Chief four years ago when I was in Jerusalem.

SINCE ENCOURAGEMENT COMES FROM CONTENTED, CHEERFUL, FAITHFUL AND LOVING PEOPLE – MAKE SURE YOU CHOOSE FRIENDS AND MESSENGERS THAT POSSESS SUCH AN ATTITUDE

21-22And now, to close this Treatise, I would like to touch upon a few personal matters that are especially important for me to tell you about because of our mutual long-term friendship. I have appointed Tychicus to perform the absolutely vital assignment of carrying and delivering this

Treatise to you all. I have chosen him because I know him to be a loving, glad, cheerful and contented person,[55] as well as a dear and loyal colleague, associate, fellow, and future king,[56] who has proven himself as a faithful envoy in all matters that our Commander in Chief has entrusted to him.

I have instructed him also to personally bring you up-to-date in everything that is going on here in Rome concerning my present condition, including my specific living circumstances during this temporary period of confinement under Roman "house arrest," and how I am getting along. I selected him because I want him to fully brief you concerning my relatively good condition here in Rome, and also especially because his personal optimism and cheerful spirit will further encourage and hearten you about my situation, so that you will not be unjustifiably depressed about how I am doing. As I mentioned to you earlier, I want you to realize that things here are really not that bad at all![57]

MAY THE GRACIOUSNESS OF YOUR IMMORTAL KINGDOM PERSONA COME TO DISTINGUISH YOUR MORTAL PERSONALITY ALSO

[23]As I close, my parting personal request to God for you all as my dear and loyal colleagues, associates, fellows, and future kings under the future reign of our High King is and will always be that you would excel in your spiritual skill during your present role in this life as His "peacemakers," and that you all would continue in the spiritual skills of self-sacrificial love, along with that of unfailing faithfulness to our Commander in Chief, Jesus. Furthermore, I have complete confidence that you all will be supplied with every spiritual ability you will need from God, Who, because He is ultimately the Father of us all, can and will enable you to accomplish your unique lifework for Him.

[24]Finally, remember the most important spiritual quality that should characterize the rest of your mortal lives – the same one that I introduced this entire Treatise with – namely, that as the dear and loyal colleagues, associates, fellows, and future kings of our present Commander in Chief, Jesus, the future High King of the Earth, your entire lives and demeanor as His apprentices would be marked by the *graciousness* that, like Him, will be the primary and distinctive characteristic of your immortal[58] personality in His Kingdom.

May you all recognize, heartily agree with and live your lives according to the conclusive truths I have written to you in this, my final and conclusive Treatise.[59]

Notes to Extended Interpretive and Expositional Translation
Ephesians Chapter 6

[1] The text of the Fifth Commandment in Exodus and Deuteronomy from the Septuagint read as follows:

Exodus 20:12 – τίμα τὸν πατέρα σου καὶ τὴν μητέρα, ἵνα εὖ σοι γένηται, καὶ ἵνα μακροχρόνιος γένῃ ἐπὶ τῆς γῆς τῆς ἀγαθῆς, ἧς κύριος ὁ θεός σου δίδωσίν σοι.

Deuteronomy 5:16 – τίμα τὸν πατέρα σου καὶ τὴν μητέρα σου, ὃν τρόπον ἐνετείλατό σοι κύριος ὁ θεός σου, ἵνα εὖ σοι γένηται, καὶ ἵνα μακροχρόνιος γένῃ ἐπὶ τῆς γῆς, ἧς κύριος ὁ θεός σου δίδωσίν σοι.

Paul is closely quoting both of these passages. The striking feature that should be noted is that in both passages, the promise in the original context is made exclusively to the children of Israel, because the Exodus passage translates, "in order that it might go well for you, and in order that you might live a long time *in the good land which the Lord your God is giving to you*;" and the Deuteronomy passage translates similarly, "in order that it may go well for you, and in order that you may live a long time *in the land which the Lord your God is giving to you*." In Ephesians, Paul leaves this last phrase out, which in the English tradition has been typically translated to universalize the promise to be translated something like, "in order that you may live a long time *on the earth*" ("live longe on the erthe" – Tyndale, 1526; "live long on the earth" – KJV, 1611).

However, in both passages in the Pentateuch, the emphasis is not so much on the individual long length of one's personal life, as it is in living in God's specially Promised "Good Land" (which becomes the Kingdom of Israel) for many generations. Accordingly, although it is not wrong to live a long mortal life of 70 or 80 years (Psalm 90:10), it is far more important to accomplish one's lifework for God, even if that means living only a short time in this life, so that one can enjoy a long and meaningful life of service to the High King when He returns to His own "Promised Land," i.e., the Millennial Kingdom. For example, when Stephen is stoned to death by the leadership regime within Judaism in Acts 7:54-60, he dies as a young man, but his lifework for God is accomplished. In that passage, Paul (then Saul), witnesses Stephen's stoning and condones it. In Acts 7:58, Luke is careful to point out that Paul (Saul) is still a "young man" (**νεανίης** [νέος] **I.** *a young man, youth,* with ἀνήρ, Od.; so, παῖς νεηνίης Hdt.; alone, like νεανίσκος, Soph., Eur., etc. **2.** *youthful, i. e. in good sense, impetuous, brave, active,* Eur., Ar., etc.; *or in bad sense, hot-headed, headstrong,* Eur., Dem. [LS]). A reasonable guess for an approximate age for Paul in 33 A.D. would be that he may have been about 25 years old. If this is true, then in 61 A.D., when Paul writes *Philippians*, he would have been only about 53 years old. However, by that time he is convinced that the majority of his lifework for God has been accomplished, and that he is ready, and even prefers to go and "be with the High King," because he says in Philippians 1:20-25:

> Phil. 1:20-25 – "according to my earnest expectation and hope, that I will in no way be put to shame, but with all boldness, as always, now also the High King will be magnified in my body, whether by life, or by death. ²¹For to me, the only reason for continuing to live in this present life is to serve the High King, and to die is gain. ²²But if I live on in the flesh, this will bring fruit from my work; yet I don't make known what I will choose. ²³But I am in a dilemma between the two, having the desire to depart and be with the High King, which is far better. ²⁴Yet, to remain in the flesh is more needful for your sake. ²⁵Having this confidence, I know that I will remain, yes, and remain with you all, for your progress and joy in the faith."

Furthermore, when Paul writes *2 Timothy* six years later in 67 A.D., he may have been only about 59 years old, yet he knows his execution under Nero's regime is imminent ("the time of my departure has come"); and that he has "finished the race" (i.e., accomplished his lifework for God), because he says in 2 Tim. 4:6-8:

> 2 Tim. 4:6-8 – "For I am already being offered, and the time of my departure has come. ⁷I have fought the good fight. I have finished the course. I have kept the faith. ⁸From now on, there is stored up for me the crown of righteousness, which the Commander in Chief, the righteous Judge, will give to me on that day; and not to me only, but also to all those who have loved His appearing."

Two other examples of people who accomplish their lifework for God but die young are or Commander in Chief Jesus Himself (age 33) and His cousin, John the "Immerser" (age 30).

² The duration of the Millennial Kingdom is 1,000 years (see note at Eph. 1:3).

³ παροργίζω, fut. -ιῶ LXX *De*.32.21*:--provoke to anger,* Arist.*Ath.* 34.1, LXX 3 Ki.16.13,33, Ph.1.682, ***Ep.Eph*.6.4.** II. Pass., *to be or be made angry*, Thphr.HP9.16.6, prob. in Str.7.2.1; τι πρός τινας v. l. in D.26.17 [LS]. The passage in Aristotle's *Athenian Constitution* (34:1) is helpful, as follows (ed. Kenyon, Oxford, 1920; transl. H. Rackham, Cambridge, 1952):

> XXXIV. So the people speedily took the government out of these men's hands; and in the sixth year after the dissolution of the Four Hundred, in the archonship of Callias of the deme of Angele, after the occurrence of the naval battle at Arginusae, it came about first that the ten Generals to whom victory in the naval battle was due were all condemned by a single vote, some of them not even having been in the engagement at all and the others having escaped on board a ship not their own, the people being completely deceived through the persons who ***provoked their anger (παροργίζω).***

Proposed translastion: "provoke one to anger" (see note at Eph. 4:26 for noun).

⁴ ἐκτρέφω – "to rear, bring up or properly raise and educate children." See note at Eph. 5:29 on the spiritual metaphor of rearing and cultivating someone through patient education.

⁵ For those who have perhaps experienced growing up as children in a dysfunctional family, God's graciousness is capable of spiritually healing and transforming the psychological and spiritual damage, bad habits and "blind spots"

that may have formed because of such a prolonged negative experience. See Eph. 3:14-21, in which Paul elaborates on the theme that the right frame of reference from which we can finally make sense out of a formerly confused life is when we realize that God has providentially planned each one of our lives such that there is no circumstance or situation that can ever defeat us in finding and accomplishing our lifework for Him if only we maintain faith in Him and selfless love for others.

[6] δοῦλος – This word clearly means "slave." In the Greek world during this time, common labor was provided by slaves. However, in the development of civilization in the History of the English Speaking Peoples, slavery has been declared illegal by the British in 1833 and by the United States in 1865 following the Civil War. Therefore, this word must be translated with its philosophical equivalent of "subordinate worker or laborer." The word most commonly used in private enterprise for this position is the word "employee." In the military or civil service departments (police department, fire department, etc.), the most common phrase is "subordinate officer."

[7] προσωπολημψία is made from two Greek words: πρόσωπον, which means (denotatively) "the face, especially the countenance or projection of attitude or mood by using one's face," and so (connotatively) "putting up a front or façade," or even "putting on a mask" (προσωπεῖον), or "playing a dramatic part in a play" [LS]; and the word λῆψις, which means "accepting or receiveing" something [LS]. Accordingly, although the translation of "showing partiality" is fairly good, the more precise meaning of προσωπολημψία is something like "unwittingly or deliberately accepting at face value the false intentions of someone who is trying to deceive you or others by pretending to have sincere, good and genuine motives through practiced deceitful use of his facial expressions and demeanor."

[8] See note at Eph. 4:27 on the various meanings of the word διάβολος = "*diabolos*" (transliteration) = "Devil."

[9] ἀδελφός [ᾰ], (ἀ- copul., δελφύς, Arist.*HA*510b13; cf. ἀγάστωρ) properly, *son of the same mother*: **I.** as Subst., ἀδελφός, ὁ, *brother*, Hom., etc.; ἀδελφοί *brother and sister*, E.*El*.536; so of the Ptolemies, θεοὶ ἀδελφοί Herod.1.30, *OGI*50.2 (iii B. C.), etc.; ἀπ' ἀμφοτέρων ἀδελφεός Hdt.7.97: prov., χαλεποὶ πόλεμοι ἀδελφῶν E.*Fr*.975: metaph., ἀ. γέγονα σειρήνων LXX *Jb*.30.29. **2.** *kinsman,* ib.*Ge*.13.8, al.; *tribesman, Ex*.2.11, al. **3.** *colleague, associate,* PTeb.1.12, *IG*12 (9).906.19 (Chalcis); *member of a college,* ib.14.956. **4.** *term of address, used by kings, OGI*138.3 (Philae), J.*AJ*13.2.2, etc.; generally, LXX *Ju*.7.30; *esp. in letters,* P*Par*.48 (ii B. C.), etc.:*--as a term of affection, applicable by wife to husband,* LXX *To*.10.12, P*Lond*.1.42.1 (ii B. C.), etc. **5.** *brother (as a fellow Christian), Ev.Matt*.12.50, *Act.Ap*.9.30, al.; of other religious communities, e.g. Serapeum, P*Par*.42.1 (ii B. C.), cf. *PTaur*.1.1.20. **6.** metaph., of things, *fellow,* ἀνὴρ τῷ ἀ. προσκολληθήσεται, of Leviathan's scales, LXX *Jb*.41.8 [LS]. Proposed translation: "esteemed colleague, dear colleague, associate, fellow, future king."

[10] κράτος – Although the denotative meaning of this word is simply "power," its two main connotative meanings in this military context include military authority or the concept of military "rank," as well as the concept of the "mastery" of the military arts [LS]. This verse implies that one can increase in spiritual "rank," or level or spiritual maturity (i.e., Abel, Enoch, Noah, Abraham, Sarah, Isaac, Jacob, Joseph, Moses, Joshua, Caleb, Rahab, Samuel, David, Job, Ruth, Daniel, Mary, John the "Immerser" – cf. *Hebrews 11*).

In this third and last section of his Treatise, Paul transitions his extended metaphor or "vehicle" from that of a *building* or *construction* project to that of a the *military* and its *weaponry*; with God considered as a "Military Quartermaster" and "Commanding Officer" who will defend His vastly expensive and colossal "building project." Because of the enormous value of this "building project," it is reasonable that God would expend the tremendous effort to select, recruit, organize, train and supply its members with the essential "military" equipment and skills required to defend it from the inevitable attacks of its bitter evil spiritual enemy, the Devil (cf. note at Eph. 1:4). Although there is some overlap, the main portion of this third extended metaphor of God as our "Military Quartermaster" and "Commanding Officer" in the area of training us to conduct ourselves with spiritual military discipline comprises the third and last portion of Ephesians (Eph. 6:10-6:20). The main symbolic concepts (approx. 17) associated with this third "military" extended metaphor are as follows:

- ἅγιος = "specially selected recruit," (1:1, 15, 18; 2:19, 3:8, 18; 4:12, 5:3, 6:18),
- κύριος = "Commander in Chief" (used by Paul 28 times in this Treatise, 26 to refer to Jesus in His present leadership role; and twice to refer to human leaders in Eph. 6:5 and 9, in which it could be translated as "leaders, managers, business owners, bosses, entrepreneurs, military officers and civil or political officials"),
- ἐκλέγω = "the selection or singling out of soldiers and their weapons for military purposes" (1:4),
- ᾐχμαλώτευσεν αἰχμαλωσίαν = "He led captives into captivity," referring to the prophecy in Psalm 68:18 (see note at Eph. 4:8),
- κράτος = "military authority and its corresponding rank, that are earned and awarded as a result of mastering ascending levels of the practice of the military arts" (6:10),
- ἰσχύς = "military forces" (6:10),
- πανοπλία = "soldier's military equipment, including his equipment belt, body armor, helmet, shield, boots, and sword" (6:11, 13),
- μεθοδεία = "stratagems, maneuvers, feints, ambushes, snares and booby traps" (4:14, 6:11),
- πάλη = "military fight, battle" (6:12),
- περιζωσάμενοι = "to deliberately put a military sword-belt and sword upon one's own body for the purpose of preparing for combat" (6:14),
- θώραξ = "breastplate, chain-mail covering the chest, body armor, chest-armor, bullet-proof vest" (6:14),
- ὑποδέω = "to put on heavy gauge, sandal-type boots, probably including 'greaves,' i.e., armor plates strapped on to protect the leg and shin below the knee; to put on high-top military boots" (6:15),

- θυρεός = "oblong, rectangular, curved (Roman) shield, shaped like a door, covering the body from head to foot and designed to be used by a unit of infantry soldiers to be interlocked together to form a large, impenetrable wall against long range arrow-volleys" (6:16),
- βέλος = "arrow volleys" + • πεπυρωμένα = perf part mid/pass neut nom pl of the verb πυρόω = in context, "flaming," = "flaming arrow volleys" fired from the wicked angelic armies of the Evil One (6:16),
- περικεφάλαιος = "that which goes around the head," and so in a military context = "helmet" (6:17),
- μάχαιρα = "as a weapon, short combat sword used by infantry," (6:17).

See note above at Eph. 2:3 for an explanation of how it might have been possible for Paul to be well acquainted with the military profession, such that he could use its concepts competently as an extended metaphor to communicate accurately this third major theme of his Treatise.

[11] ἰσχύς – Although the denotative meaning of this word also is simply "power," its main connotative meaning in this military context is in the notion of the tactical use and movements in the employment of blocks of soldiers in battles, i.e., military "forces" [LS]. Proposed translation: "(tactical) spiritual (angelic) military forces."

[12] ἐνδύω – See notes at Eph. 4:22-24 on the meaning of the spiritual metaphor of "taking off and putting on clothing."

[13] πανοπλία, Ion. -ιη, ἡ, *suit of armour of a* ὁπλίτης, i.e. *shield, helmet, breast plate, greaves, sword, and lance*; from ὁπλίτης, ὁ, *heavy-armed foot-soldier, man-at-arms, who carried a pike* ([δόρυ]) *and a large shield* ([ὅπλον]); from ὅπλον, τό, *the large shield, from which the men-at-arms took their name of* ὁπλῖται [LS]. Proposed translation: "body armor, together with its complement of personal weaponry."

[14] μεθοδεία – See note at Eph. 4:14 on the meaning of the spiritual metaphor of "methods."

[15] πάλη [ᾰ] (A), ἡ, *wrestling*, Il.23.635; ἢ πὺξ ἠὲ πάλῃ ἢ καὶ ποσίν Od. 8.206: κρατέων πάλα Pi.*O*.8.20; νικᾶν πυγμὴν καὶ π. E.*Alc*.1031. cf. Hp.*Acut.(Sp.)*62, Th.1.6, Pl.*Lg*.795b, Plu.2.638d, Antyll. ap. Orib. 6.28.3;...etc. **2.** generally, *fight, battle*, ἅπτειν πάλην τινί A.*Ch*.866 (anap.); π. δορός E.*Heracl*.159 [LS]. Proposed translation: "conflict."

[16] ἀρχάς...ἐξουσίας...κοσμοκράτορας...πνευματικὰ τῆς πονηρίας. See notes at Eph. 1:21 and Eph. 2:2 on the historical manifestation of these wicked spiritual beings organized into evil forces during Paul's historical era as the Greek polytheistic hierarchy of gods under the authority of Zeus, etc.; and the counterfeit religious leadership regime within Judaism deliberately manipulated by Satan into intentionally plotting the crucifixion of Jesus.

[17] **σκότος** – See note at Eph. 5:8 on the meaning of the metaphor of spiritual "darkness."

[18] See the Book of Daniel, especially Chapter 10.

[19] For example, read the story of the Gadarene demoniac in Luke 8:26-39. In verse 31, the many demonic spirits that possess the poor man beg Jesus that He not cast them out and send them to the ἄβυσσος (transliteration = *"abyss"*). The meaning of this Greek word is as follows: **ἄβυσσος, ov,** *bottomless, unfathomed,* πηγαί Hdt.2.28; ἄτης ἄβυσσον πέλαγος A.*Supp*.470; χάσματα E.*Ph*.1605; λίμνη Ar.*Ra*.137: generally, *unfathomable, boundless,* πλοῦτος A.*Th*.948; ἀργύριον Ar. *Lys*.174 ; φρένα Δίαν καθορᾶν, ὄψιν ἄβυσσον A.*Supp*.1058. **II.** ἡ ἄ. *the great deep*, LXX *Ge*.1.2, etc.: *the abyss, underworld*, *Ev. Luc.*8.31, *Ep.Rom*.10.7, *Apoc*.9.1, etc.; *the infinite void, PMag.Par.* 1.1120, cf. *PMag.Lond*.121.261 [LS]. Paul uses this word in Romans 10:7, quoting Deuteronomy 30:12-14, where he seems to use it to refer to the deepest parts of the Ocean. In the *Book of Revelation*, the word ἄβυσσος is used seven times to refer to the place where God has confined super-wicked spirits during the period of this historical era. In context, the *abyss* seems to be in the deepest parts of the earth even below the bottom of the deepest Oceans. God allows these super-wicked spirits to come out of the abyss during the seven-year period of the Tribulation to torment evil men, and then He re-confines them there together with Satan and all of the evil angels during the 1,000 year period of the Millennial Kingdom.

[20] For example, see the Book of Job (esp. Chapters 1 and 2). Especially noteworthy also is 2 Corinthians 12:1-10, where Paul recounts that in about 42 A.D., during his early 3 year ministry in Syria and Cilicia (Gal. 1:21), God transported him to heaven to unveil to him the divine revelation of His plan for Paul's life and for the future. Because of this great privilege, Paul says in 2 Cor. 12:7-9 that:

> 2 Cor. 12:7-9 Καὶ τῇ ὑπερβολῇ τῶν ἀποκαλύψεων ἵνα μὴ ὑπεραίρωμαι, ἐδόθη μοι σκόλοψ τῇ σαρκί, ἄγγελος Σατᾶν ἵνα με κολαφίζῃ, ἵνα μὴ ὑπεραίρωμαι. ⁸Ὑπὲρ τούτου τρὶς τὸν κύριον παρεκάλεσα ἵνα ἀποστῇ ἀπ' ἐμοῦ. ⁹Καὶ εἴρηκέν μοι "'Αρκεῖ σοι ἡ χάρις μου, ἡ γὰρ δύναμίς μου ἐν ἀσθενείᾳ τελειοῦται."
>
> Transl.: ⁷Now because of the superlative nature of the divine revelations [shown to me by God when He transported me to heaven fourteen years ago], He therefore afterwards gave me a spiritual "thorn" in my body that causes me chronic and continual pain, that is to say, one of *Satan's angels*, for the purpose of hitting me and slapping me around, in order to stop me from my tendency to become proud and arrogant. ⁸This evil spiritual being has continued to cause me such chronic pain that I have begged the Commander in Chief on three separate occasions that He remove it from me. ⁹However, each time He has replied to me, "My grace is sufficient for you, because My kind of power can only make you spiritually mature through your weakness" [transl. – GWC].

Since Paul wrote 2 Corinthians in 56 A.D. (when he was about 48 years old), and God gave him this evil spirit fourteen years previous to that (about 42 A.D. when

Paul was about 34 years old), and Paul is now writing this final Treatise to the Ephesians in 61 A.D. (he is about 53 years old), it would imply that Paul has been suffering chronic pain from this evil spiritual being for approximately the last *nineteen years* of his life!

²¹ **στῆτε** is the 2 pl. impv. of the verb ἵστημι = "stand fast," "stand firm". It begins a long Greek sentence that Paul will continue through the entire six components of military body armor and weaponry, and will include all of his instructions on maintaining communication with God in verses 18 and 19. He does not complete the sentence until the end of verse 20. Proposed translation "never give up."

²² **περιζωσάμενοι** (is a masc nom pl aor part mid of the verb περιζώννυμαι). In this context, this word means "to deliberately put a military sword-belt and sword upon one's own body for the purpose of preparing for combat." A first example of this meaning can be clearly seen in Appian's narrative of Hannibal's strategy in the Battle of Cannae against the Romans, as follows (*The Foreign Wars – Hannibal,* Chapter 4, Section 20 – ed. L. Mendelssohn, Leipzig, 1879; transl. ed. Horace White, New York, 1899):

> Hann. 4.20 – ἄνδρας τε πεντακοσίους Κελτίβηρας ἐπὶ τοῖς μακροῖς ξίφεσιν ὑπὸ τοῖς χιτῶσιν ἄλλα ξίφη βραχύτερα **περιέζωσεν**, οἷς ἔμελλεν αὐτὸς ὅτε δέοι χρῆσθαι σημανεῖν.
>
> Transl.: Hann. 4.20 – "With them were placed [by Hannibal] 500 Celtiberians who had, in addition to the long swords at their ***sword-belts***, short daggers under their garments. These they were not to use till he himself gave the signal."

A second example is Flavius Josephus' account of King Saul attempting to arm the youth David in his upcoming battle against the giant Goliath, as follows (*Antiquities of the Jews – Book 6, Line 184,* ed. B. Niese, Berlin, 1892; transl. ed. William Whiston, A.M. Auburn and Buffalo, 1895) – note the other words used for pieces of armor in this passage:

> 6.184 – Σαοῦλος…"ἄπιθι," φησί "πρὸς τὴν μάχην." καὶ περιθεὶς αὐτῷ τὸν αὐτοῦ **θώρακα** καὶ **περιζώσας** τὸ **ξίφος** καὶ **περικεφαλαίαν** ἁρμόσας ἐξέπεμψεν. ὁ δὲ Δαβίδης βαρυνόμενος ὑπὸ τῶν **ὅπλων** … τίθησιν οὖν τὰ **ὅπλα** καὶ…Γολίαθον ἐπορεύετο.
>
> Transl.: 6.184 – "…Saul…said, "Go thy way to the fight." So he [Saul] put about him [David] his *breastplate* (θώρακα), and ***girded on*** (**περιζώσας**) his *sword* (ξίφος), and *fitted the helmet to his head* (περικεφαλαίαν), and sent him away. But David was burdened with his *armor* (ὅπλων)…Accordingly he laid by the *armor* (ὅπλα), and…went towards Goliath."

The third example comes from Aristotle's *Politics,* Section 1324b, describing the militaristic basis of the laws of the Macedonians, as follows (ed. W. D. Ross, Oxford, 1957; transl. H. Rackham, Cambridge, 1944):

> 1324b – ἦν δέ ποτε καὶ περὶ Μακεδονίαν νόμος τὸν μηθένα ἀπεκταγκότα πολέμιον ἄνδρα **περιεζῶσθαι** τὴν φορβειάν.

Transl.: 1324b – "at one time there was also a law in Macedonia that a man who had never killed an enemy must wear his halter instead of a *sword-belt*".

²³ Paul has used the word ἀληθείᾳ five times before in Ephesians. In context of the specific emphasis of this Treatise, Paul is referring to the "truthful report of God's Inheritance Plan" (see extended note at Eph. 1:13 on the meaning of this word), with special emphasis upon the gradual "uncovering" or "discovering" of what our specific lifework is for God. It includes the notion of speaking the "truth" to others so that we can help them "discover" their lifework for God also (see notes at Eph. 4:21, 24, and 25). In Eph. 5:9, it means, "the ability to continually learn and discover what is true in life" (e.g., especially with regard to one's lifework).

²⁴ θώραξ – "*breastplate, chain-mail covering the chest*" [LS]. Perhaps the best translation into American English would be either "body armor" or "bullet-proof vest."

²⁵ The purpose of this piece of armor is clearly to protect the "heart." See extended note at Eph. 1:18 on the meaning of "**καρδία**" = "*heart*" = "the moral and ethical decision making power of the soul." It is likely that Paul is alluding back to Eph. 1:18, which appears to be the central theme verse of this entire Treatise:

> Eph. 1:18 πεφωτισμένους τοὺς ὀφθαλμοὺς τῆς **καρδίας** ὑμῶν εἰς τὸ εἰδέναι ὑμᾶς τίς ἐστιν ἡ ἐλπὶς τῆς **κλήσεως** αὐτοῦ, τίς ὁ πλοῦτος τῆς δόξης τῆς κληρονομίας αὐτοῦ ἐν τοῖς ἁγίοις,
>
> Transl.: "so that the eyes of your *heart*, having been enlightened, would be enabled to see what the hope of His *lifework* is for each of you, and what the riches of the appearing of His inheritance for His specially selected recruits entails."

²⁶ Some examples of people who, because of a failure to make the right moral or ethical decision in their "heart," permanently injured their own lives are:

- **Esau** (Genesis 27:41): "So Esau hated Jacob because of the blessing with which his father [Isaac] blessed him, and Esau said *in his heart*, 'The days of mourning for my father are at hand, then I will kill my brother Jacob.'"
- **Pharaoh** (Exodus 14:5): "Now it was told the King of Egypt that the [Israelite] people had fled, and *the heart of Pharaoh* and his servants was turned against the people; and they said, 'Why have we done this that we have let Israel go from serving us?'"
- **Samson** (Judges 16:16-17): "And it came to pass, when she [Delilah] pestered him [Samson] daily with her words and pressed him, so that his soul was vexed to death, ¹⁷that he *told her all his heart*..."
- King **Saul** (1 Samuel 28:5, 7): "When Saul saw the army of the Philistines, he was afraid, and *his heart trembled greatly*...⁷Then Saul said to his servants, 'Find me a woman who is a medium, so that I may go to her and inquire of her.'"
- King **Solomon** (1 Kings 11:4, 6): "For it happened, when Solomon was old, that his wives *turned away his heart* after other gods; and *his heart was not perfect with Yahweh his God*, as was the *heart of David* his father. ⁵For Solomon went after

Ashtoreth the goddess of the Sidonians, and after Milcom the abomination of the Ammonites. ⁶*Solomon did that which was evil* in the sight of Yahweh."
- **Judas** (John 13:2): "After supper, the *devil having already put into the heart* of Judas Iscariot, Simon's son, to betray him..."
- **Ananias** and **Sapphira** (Acts 5:1-5): "But a certain man named Ananias, with Sapphira, his wife, sold a possession, ²and kept back part of the price, his wife also being aware of it, and brought a certain part, and laid it at the apostles' feet. ³But Peter said, 'Ananias, why has *Satan filled your heart* to lie to the Holy Spirit, and to keep back part of the price of the land? ⁴While you kept it, didn't it remain your own? After it was sold, wasn't it in your power? How is it that you have conceived this thing *in your heart*? You haven't lied to men, but to God.' ⁵Ananias, hearing these words, fell down and died. Great fear came on all who heard these things."

On the other hand, for those who have experienced Satan's spiritual attacks and who have perhaps experienced moral or ethical failure, God's graciousness is capable of rescuing, spiritually healing and transforming the psychological and spiritual damage, bad habits and "blind spots" that may have resulted from such breakdowns. See Eph. 3:8-13, in which Paul clearly states that he believes himself to be "less than the least" of all of God's specially selected recruits. The implication is that if God's grace can rescue and restore Paul from his offenses against God, there is no moral or ethical failure we can commit that is beyond the reach of God's gracious ability to rescue and restore us to living a productive and meaningful life for Him.

In fact, when we reflect on the ethical and moral failures of both Paul and Peter, who eventually became Jesus' chief High Emissaries, it becomes clear that Jesus' communication to God in their behalf was the cause of their rescue and restoration from Satan's plotting their failure behind the scenes.

First, in John 8:44, Jesus clearly states that the Devil was the active agent manipulating the Pharisees in their opposition to Him:

John 8:44 "You [Pharisees – John 8:13] are of your father the devil (διάβολος), and the desires of your father you want to do. He was a murderer from the beginning, and does not stand in the truth because there is no truth in him. When he speaks a lie, he speaks from his own resources, for he is a liar and the father of it."

It therefore follows that since Paul was a Pharisee before his conversion (Acts 23:6; 26:5; Phil. 3:5), that the Devil was the active agent manipulating him in his persecution of Christians (Acts 7:58; 8:1,3; 9:1-2 26:9-11). However, when the "chief priests, scribes, elders *and Pharisees*" (Matt. 27:41 [MT]) mocked Jesus when He was crucified, Luke records that Jesus prayed for them as follows:

Luke 23:34 "Then Jesus said, 'Father, forgive them, because they do not realize what they are doing."

In fact, Luke also records that Stephen also petitioned Jesus to forgive Paul when Paul assisted those who stoned Stephen to death, as follows:

Acts 7:57-8:1 "Then they [the high priest's leadership council – Acts 6:15-7:1] cried out with a loud voice, stopped their ears, and ran at him [Stephen] with one accord; ⁵⁸and they cast him out of the city and stoned him. And the witnesses laid down their clothes at the feet of a young man named Saul [Paul]. ⁵⁹And they stoned Stephen as he was calling on God and saying, 'Lord Jesus, receive my spirit.' ⁶⁰Then he knelt down and *cried out with a loud voice, 'Lord, do not charge them with this sin.'* And when he had said this, he fell asleep. ⁸:¹Now Saul [Paul] was consenting to his [Stephen's] death."

Second, Luke records that Jesus knew that Satan would cause Peter to deny Jesus during His own trial and crucifixion, but that Jesus, knowing this, prayed (see note on δέησις = "to submit official petitions to God which, in effect, politically lobby Him to act in our behalf," at Eph. 6:18) for Peter, as follows:

Luke 22:31-34 "And the Lord said, 'Simon, Simon! Indeed, Satan (ὁ Σατανᾶς) has asked for you, that he may sift you like wheat. ³²But I have prayed (ἐδεήθην = "officially petitioned God on your behalf") for you, that your faith should not fail; and when you have returned to Me, strengthen your brothers.' ³³But he [Peter] said to him [Jesus], 'Lord, I am ready to go with you, both to prison and to death.' ³⁴Then he replied, 'I tell you, Peter, the rooster will not crow this day before you will deny three times that you know Me.'"

Accordingly, for those who have perhaps experienced moral or ethical failure due to being manipulated by evil spiritual forces under Satan's control, it follows that just as there was hope for Paul and for Peter, there is also hope for them of being fully restored to usefulness to accomplish their lifework for Jesus. In order to bring such a restoration about, they should not delay in asking God for forgiveness and help, and enlist the aid of their loved ones to make specific petitions to God to help them recover also.

²⁷ ὑποδέω, late Gr. ὑποδεσ-δέννω Gloss., Dosith.p.435 K.:--*bind or fasten under*, ἀμαξίδας ὑ. τῇσι οὐρῇσι, of long-tailed sheep, Hdt.3.113. **II.** *esp.* **underbind the feet, i. e. shoe, because the ancient sandals or shoes were bound on with straps,** [καμήλους] ὑ. καρβατίναις Arist.*HA*499a29, cf. Plu.Pomp.24, Paus.10.25.4;...-- mostly in Med., *bind under one's feet, put on shoes,* Ar.*Av*.492 [for the purpose of going to work – GWC] (anap.), Pl. *Smp*.220b; ὑποδουμένη *as I was putting on my shoes,* Ar.Ec.36, cf. Thphr.Char.10.14; ὑποδεῖται, *for the purpose of going away* [i.e., going on a long journey – GWC], Pherecr.153.4 (hex.);...**III.** in Med. and Pass., also, c. acc., **1.** *of that which one puts on,* κοθόρνους ὑποδέεσθαι Hdt.1.155, cf. 6.125;...**b**:--so in pf. Pass., ὑποδήματα, βλαύτας ὑποδεδεμένος, *with shoes, slippers on one's feet,* Pl.*Grg*.490e, Smp.174a; ἁπλᾶς ὑποδέδενται D. 54.34: abs., ὑποδεδεμένοι ἐκοιμῶντο *with their shoes* [better: **"boots"** – GWC] *on,* X.*An*.4.5.14 [in this passage from Xenophon's *Anabasis*, he is describing the **boots used by soldiers** on the long march of a military expedition – GWC]; ὥσπερ ὑποδεδ. Arist.*PA*687a28...ὑποδησάμενοι τοὺς πόδας ἐν ἑτοιμασίᾳ τοῦ εὐαγγελίου *Ep.Eph*.6:15 [LS]. The Roman and Greek soldier's armor usually included heavy gauge, sandal-type boots, that included "greaves," which were armor plates that were strapped on to protect the leg and shin below the knee. The equivalent equipment in the American Armed Forces are *high-top military boots*. In the Special Forces (Navy "SEALS"), soldiers prepare themselves for long missions by lacing up their boots tight, double-knotting them, and then cutting off the

excess lacing to make sure their boots will not come off in the jungles or being sucked off by walking through mud – see books by Navy SEAL Commander Richard Marcinko.

[28] εὐαγγελίον – See extended analysis of this word, in both its noun and verb forms, in note at Eph. 1:13.

[29] εἰρήνη – See note on the central theme of "peacefulness" in this Treatise at Eph. 2:14.

[30] θυρεός, ὁ, ([θύρα]) *stone put against a door* to keep it shut, Od.9.240, 313. **II.** *oblong shield (shaped like a door), PSI*4.428.36 (iii B.C.), Inscr. ap. Plu.*Pyrrh.*26, Callix.2; **hence, of the Roman** *scutum* **(opp. ἀσπίς,=** *clipeus*), Plb.2.30.3, 6.23.2, D.H.4.16, cf.*Ep.Eph.***6.16**, Apollod. *Poliorc.*163.2, Arr.*Tact.*3.2, etc. [LS]. An analysis of the various Greek and Latin technical terms used for different kinds of shields now follows:

"SCUTUM (θυρεός), the Roman shield worn by the heavy-armed infantry after 340 B.C., instead of being round like the Greek CLIPEUS was adapted to the form of the human body, by being made either oval or of the shape of a door (θύρα), which it also resembled in being made of wood or wicker-work, and from which consequently its Greek name was derived...The shield is curved so as in part to encircle the body. The terms *clipeus* and *scutum* are often confounded; but that they properly denoted different kinds of shields is manifest from the passages of several ancient writers (Liv. viii. 8; Plut. *Rom.* 21). In like manner Plutarch distinguishes the Roman θυρεὸς from the Greek ἀσπὶς in his life of T. Flaminius (p. 688, ed. Steph.). **In** *Eph.* **vi. 16 St. Paul uses the term θυρεὸς rather than ἀσπὶς or σάκος, because he is describing the equipment of a Roman soldier"** [*A Dictionary of Greek and Roman Antiquities.* William Smith, LLD. William Wayte. G. E. Marindin. Albemarle Street, London. John Murray. 1890].

"CLIP'EUS also CLIPEUM (ἀσπίς, σάκος), the large shield used by the Greeks and the Romans, which was originally of circular shape... The heroes of the *Iliad* carry a shield which is round (iii. 347; v. 453), and large enough to cover the whole man... *Turning from the Iliad to the representations and texts of later times, we observe no shields which, like those of heroic times, protect the whole of the warrior's body: they usually cover him from the neck to the knees.* Besides the circular or Argive shield, we frequently find represented an oval shield with a strong rim and apertures in the middle of each side (κεγχρώματα, Eur. *Phoen.* 1386), through which to watch the enemy. This is known as the Boeotian shield" [*A Dictionary of Greek and Roman Antiquities.* William Smith, LLD. William Wayte. G. E. Marindin. Albemarle Street, London. John Murray. 1890].

It is noteworthy to observe that there were two distinct and different types of shields that were well known in the Ancient world. Paul uses the word for the larger shield, called the **θυρεός** (= Latin: **scutum**), which was rectangular in shape, covered the entire body, and was slightly curved in the horizontal direction to make it partially cylindrical in shape when held vertically (perhaps an eighth of a cylinder), so that it could protect the soldier's body from frontal assaults as well as attacks coming at him at an angle from either side. It was designed to be used by a large number of infantry soldiers acting in concert as a unit to be interlocked together to form a large, impenetrable wall against long range arrow-volleys. Paul does not use the word for the smaller shield, called an ἀσπίς (= Latin: **clipeus**), which was round in shape (like a disc), only covered the body from the neck to the knees, and was designed to be used in individual hand-to-hand combat with either a spear or a sword.

[31] πυρόω – In context, "flaming" [LS] arrow-volleys (see note below), fired from the wicked angelic armies of the Evil One.

[32] βέλος, εος, τό, *missile,* esp. *arrow, dart*, freq. in Hom.; of the piece of rock *hurled* by the Cyclops, τόντονδε βαλὼν β. Od.9.495; of an ox's leg *thrown* by one of the suitors at Ulysses, 20.305; of a stool, 17.464; ὑπὲκ βελέων **out** *of the reach of darts, out of shot*, Il.4.465;...**5. engine of war**, Ph.*Bel.*82.8: pl., *artillery*...[LS]. Proposed translation: "arrow-volley."

[33] See note on the meaning of communication with God ("prayer") at Eph. 6:18.

[34] See the Book of Job Chapters 1 and 2, in which Job's hardships are in reality caused by the Devil. A poignant contemporary example of this type of Satanic "long-range" and indiscriminate attack would be not only the immediate loss of thousands of innocent lives lost in the terrorist attack on the Twin Towers of the World Trade Center in New York City on September 11, 2002, but would also include the thousands of jobs lost due to the economic "ripple effects" that resulted from the attack. For example, airline employees have become embittered as a result of the hardships in the travel industry precipitated by the attack, not to mention the thousands who lost jobs in the hotel and hospitality business.

[35] A few examples are:

- **Abraham's** and **Sarah's** weak faith in God's promised procreation of a child allowed the tragic incident in which Abraham bore Ishmael by Hagar (Genesis 18);
- **Lot** allowed his weak faith (manifested as greed and materialism for Sodom and Gomorrah) to destroy his wife and two daughters (Genesis 19);
- **Isaac's** weak faith (favoritism for his son Esau over his son Jacob because of Isaac's gluttony) allowed the tragedy of the selfish personality of his son Esau to develop;
- **Moses** lapse of faith (anger and frustration) at Meribah when he hit the rock with his staff rather than simply speaking to it as God told him to do, prevented him from leading Israel into the Promised Land of Canaan (Numbers 20);
- **Joshua's** lapse of faith (overconfidence) allowed 36 men to be killed in the first battle of Ai (Joshua 7:5);
- **King Saul's** lapse of faith (desire to know the future from a witch through sorcery) resulted not only in his own tragic death through suicide, but also in the tragic deaths of his good son Jonathan, his other two sons and his armor-bearer (ironically, in which long-range archery played a part: 1 Samuel 31);

- **King David's** heartbreaking lapse of faith (his lust for **Bathsheba**) resulted in the tragic death of her innocent and valiant husband **Uriah** (ironically, also by long-range archery conspired by David: 2 Samuel 11), as well as the death of the young and innocent child conceived as a result of David's sexual union with Bathsheba;
- The tragic life of treachery, rebellion and early death of David's son **Absalom** as a result of his father David's failure of faith (2 Samuel 18);
- The death of seventy thousand innocent Israelites due to a plague of judgment from Yahweh when **King David's** faith failed and he foolishly took a census of the people (2 Samuel 24);
- The civil war in Israel that resulted between Solomon's sons **Jeroboam** and **Rehoboam** because of **King Solomon's** failure of faith in allowing his many wives to turn him into an idolater in his old age (1 Kings 11-12);
- The failure of faith by the leaders of the Lifework Council at **Corinth**, in a perversion of the observation of the Lord's Supper, caused many members there to fall ill and some to die (1 Corinthians 11:30).

[36] περικεφαλαίος [ᾰ], α, ον, *round the head*: hence, **II.** Subst. περικεφαλαία, ἡ, *covering for the head, helmet, cap*, Call.Com.1 D., Aen. Tact.24.6, PPetr.3p.328 (iii B. C.), etc.; π. σιδηρᾶ περιηργυρωμένη IG 11(2).161 B77 (Delos, iii B. C.), cf. 22.1478.16, 12(5).647.30 (Ceos), Plb.3.71.4, J.AJ6.9.4, Antyll. ap. Orib.6.36.3 [LS]. περικεφαλαία – lit. "that which goes around the head," and so in a military context = "helmet." Paul only uses this word twice in the NT: here in Eph. 6:17, and in a similar context in 1 Thessalonians 5:8. In the context of 1 Thessalonians 5:1-10, Paul is explaining the future return of Jesus to the earth. He refers to Jesus' return as the "hope of rescue," and in context, means "the hope of your ultimate rescue and deliverance from conflict that involves sharing in the High King's reign on earth during the Millennial Kingdom." The Greek Text is as follows: [1 Thess. 5:8]...ἐνδυσάμενοι θώρακα πίστεως καὶ ἀγάπης καὶ περικεφαλαίαν ἐλπίδα σωτηρίας. The proposed English translation is: "putting on the body armor of faith and self-sacrificial love and putting on your heads the helmet of the hope of your rescue [and ultimate deliverance from conflict that involves sharing in the High King's reign on earth during the Millennial Kingdom]." The noun σωτηρία has only been used once by Paul in Ephesians (1:13 – in which it meant, "this wonderful news that is actually able *to rescue all of you from a living a meaningless life*), and the verb σωζω twice (Eph. 2:5 and 2:8 – see note at Eph. 2:5). Furthermore, the concept of "headship" as the "legitimate authoritative leadership role given to us by Jesus in order to enable us to fulfill our lifework" has been stressed by Paul in this Treatise three times (Eph. 1:22, 4:15 and 5:23).

Therefore, what Paul intends is a reminder that evil spiritual beings will attack our "heads" = "headship" = "spiritual role of leadership" during the fulfillment of our specific lifework, and that *we must not give in to fear, disillusionment, discouragement or cynicism* when these threats and attacks upon our spiritual leadership role occurs. We must not yield to fear, because God has given us the spiritual protection (the "helmet") that we will need to endure such attacks, with the result that God will *temporally rescue* us from such attacks on our leadership in this life for as long as He has determined in order that we might accomplish our lifework. As leader of Jesus' High Emissaries, Paul was temporally rescued by God from at least eleven recorded deliberately planned attempts on his life, plus many other kinds of threats and attacks that he does not count (see Gal. 1:15-19, 1 Cor. 11:23-33 and Acts 13-28, and note at Eph. 3:1).

A summary of the chronology of at least thirty four specific occasions in which God supernaturally rescued Paul from death, physical violence, riots, permanent physical injury, false accusations, sham trials, political or ethical corruption, natural dangers, poverty, and his own weaknesses (discouragement and pride), during the 28 year period of his leadership role in which he discovered and accomplished his lifework now follows:

●──────────────────────────────●
1. Jesus rescues Paul from living a sidetracked and wasted life of hurting other people as a self-righteous Pharisee, by personally appearing to him (as he is traveling to Damascus to arrest and imprison more of Jesus' disciples), speaking to him, blinding him for three days and then healing him (Acts 9:3-19):

³...suddenly a light from the sky shone around him (Paul). ⁴He fell on the earth, and heard a voice saying to him, "Saul, Saul, why do you persecute me?" ⁵He said, "Who are you, Lord?" The Lord said, "I am Jesus, whom you are persecuting. ⁶But rise up, and enter into the city, and you will be told what you must do."...⁹He (Paul) was without sight for three days, and neither ate nor drank... ¹⁷...Ananias...entered into the house (where Paul was). Laying his hands on him, he said, "Brother Saul, the Lord, who appeared to you in the way which you came, has sent me, that you may receive your sight, and be filled with the Holy Spirit." ¹⁸Immediately...scales fell from his (Paul's) eyes, and he received his sight. He arose and was baptized. ¹⁹He took food and was strengthened.

●──────────────────────────────●
2. In Damascus, Paul is given spiritual strength with the result that he is able to successfully prove from the Scriptures in public debate that Jesus is Israel's Messiah, such that all who hear him are amazed, but do not harm him (Acts 9:20-22):

²⁰Immediately in the synagogues he proclaimed the Christ, that he is the Son of God. ²¹All who heard him were amazed, and said, "Isn't this he who in Jerusalem made havoc of those who called on this name? And he had come here intending to bring them bound before the chief priests!" ²²But Saul increased more in strength, and confounded the Jews who lived at Damascus, proving that this is the Christ.

●──────────────────────────────●
3. Paul goes to the temple in Jerusalem to ask God what He should do next. Jesus appears to him and warns him to leave Jerusalem, since the Jews nor the disciples will welcome him (Acts 22:17-21):

¹⁷It happened that, when I (Paul) had returned to Jerusalem, and while I prayed in the temple, I fell into a trance, ¹⁸and saw him (Jesus) saying to me, "Hurry and get out of Jerusalem quickly, because they will not receive testimony concerning me from you." ¹⁹I said, "Lord, they themselves know that I imprisoned and beat in every synagogue those who believed in you. ²⁰When the blood of Stephen, your witness, was shed, I also was standing by, and consenting to his death, and guarding the cloaks of those who killed him." ²¹He said to me, "Depart, for I will send you out far from here to the Gentiles."

●──────────────────────────────●
4. Paul obeys Jesus' warning, not seeking public legitimacy from the Apostles at that time (34 A.D.), but goes on a three year missionary journey to Arabia and is protected by God from Aretas IV (Gal.1:15-19):

¹⁵But when it was the good pleasure of God, who separated me from my mother's womb, and called me through his grace, ¹⁶to reveal his Son in me, that I might preach him among the Gentiles, I didn't immediately confer with flesh and blood, ¹⁷nor did I go up with respect to (seeking to gain legitimacy from) those who were apostles before me in Jerusalem, but I went away into Arabia. Then I returned to Damascus. ¹⁸Then after three years I went up to Jerusalem to visit Peter, and stayed with him fifteen days. ¹⁹But of the other apostles I saw no one, except James, the Lord's brother.

During the time of Paul's three year Arabian missionary journey (Paul converted in 34 A.D., so Arabian journey approx. 35-37 A.D.), Damascus was ruled by Aretas IV, a Nabataean King (Nabataeans were an Arab tribe, and so were true "Arabians"') whose capital city was Petra, a city carved into a natural fortress-like canyon, located in the mountain range south of the Dead Sea just east of the valley running from the Dead Sea southwestward to the north end of the Gulf of Aqaba (Wadi el-'Araba), at the economic and religious center of the busy Arabian caravan trade routes. From Petra, Aretas IV controlled the main commercial routes which passed through it to the port city of Gaza in the west, to Damascus in the north, to the port city of Elath on the Red Sea in the south, and across the desert to the Persian Gulf in the east; ruling over the enormous region of (modern) South Palestine, most of Jordan, Northern Arabia, and Damascus. Aretas IV's daughter was married to Herod Antipas, who put her away in favor of Herodias (Herod Antipas was tricked by Herodias into beheading John the Baptist when John the Baptist confronted them with committing adultery against Aretas IV's daughter). Aretas IV's long reign of 58 years (9 B.C - 49 A.D.) no doubt stabilized the whole Arabian region to such a degree that it would have been a good first choice for Paul to extensively evangelize. This is supported by the *Columbia Encyclopedia*, which says that Petra was "an early seat of Christianity, (although) it was conquered by the Muslims in the 7th century A.D." [*Columbia Encyclopedia, Sixth Edition, 2001* and *Encyclopedia Britannica, 1911*]. If Paul traveled from Jerusalem to evangelize the major Arabian cities along the major caravan trade routes, it is likely that he would have gone down the old "King's Highway" to the capital city of Petra, then perhaps south to Elath, then back to Petra, then perhaps west to Gaza, then back to Petra, then probably back north up the "King's Highway" to Damascus, where he then escaped from the Aretas' governor's plot to kill him, then traveled to Jerusalem, comprising a total journey of approximately 1,000 miles.

●──●

5. Paul returns to Damascus. After three years evangelizing Arabs that Jesus is Israel's Messiah, no Arabian converts are recorded, but Paul has enraged not only the Jews, but also the Arabs (since he probably preached in Aretas IV's capital city and religious center of Petra) so much that they plot to kill him with the complicity of Aretas IV's governor (an Arab), but Paul escapes over the city wall by being lowered by a rope in a basket (Acts 9:23-27, 2 Cor. 11:32-33):

²⁷But Barnabas...declared...how he (Paul) had seen the Lord on the road (to Damascus), and that He (Jesus) had spoken to him (Paul), and how at Damascus he had preached boldly in the name of Jesus...²³When many days were fulfilled (including Paul's initial preaching in Damascus, his Arabian missionary journey – probably to Petra for sure, Aretas IV's capital city and center of religion, and probably also to Gaza on the Mediterranean Sea and to Elath on the Red Sea – then returning to Damascus, the northern frontier city of Aretas IV's Arabian kingdom, for a total of three years in all since his conversion), the Jews (in Damascus) conspired together to kill him (Paul), ²⁴but their plot became known to Saul. They watched the gates both day and night that they might kill him, ²⁵but his disciples took him by night, and let him down through the wall, lowering him in a basket. (Paul in Galatians, nor Luke in Acts, makes mention of any Arabian converts

during this journey, although Paul does have "disciples" whom he teaches and who protect him from danger in Damascus. However, he had no doubt angered many unbelieving Arabs as well, and the Jews plotted to kill him in complicity with them, because in 2 Cor. 11:32-33 Paul adds the following details to the story in Acts 9:23-27: "In Damascus the governor under Aretas the king (the governor of Damascus would no doubt have been an Arab appointed by the Arabian King Aretas IV) guarded the city of the Damascenes desiring to arrest me. 33Through a window I was let down in a basket by the wall, and escaped his hands."

●──●

6. In Jerusalem, Grecian Jews plot to kill Paul, but he is rescued by disciples and sent to safety in his home town of Tarsus (Acts 9:28-30):

28He (Paul) was with them (Barnabas and the other Apostles) going in and going out at Jerusalem, 29preaching boldly in the name of the Lord. He spoke and disputed against the Grecian Jews, but they were seeking to kill him. 30When the brothers knew it, they brought him down to Caesarea, and sent him out to Tarsus.

These events occurred in approx. 38 A.D. = 1 year (?). It seems probable that the total time it would have taken Paul to make his escape from Aretas IV's Arabian governor at Damascus, then make the trip to Jerusalem (150 miles) + "going in and going out at Jerusalem," and "preaching boldly in the name of the Lord," and "disputing against the Grecian Jews" long enough for them to get angry enough to "seek to kill him," + the trip from Jerusalem to Caesarea (60 miles) + the trip north from Caesarea to Tarsus (320 miles by sea, or 450 miles by land) would take the better part of a year.

●──●

7. Paul, protected by God from the oppression in Judea, evangelizes in Syria and Cilicia for four years, no doubt using his home city of Tarsus for his headquarters (Galatians 1:21-23), until Barnabas is sent from Jerusalem to Antioch, where he finds that the Lord has converted so many Greeks there, that Barnabas goes to Tarsus and gets Paul to come to Antioch to help him teach them all. Together, Barnabas and Paul then teach the new converts in Antioch for one year (Acts 11:19-26):

Gal. 1:21 Then I (Paul) came to the regions of Syria and Cilicia (Tarsus being centrally located between Syria and Cilicia). 22I was still unknown by face to the assemblies of Judea which were in Christ, 23but they only heard: "He who once persecuted us now preaches the faith that he once tried to destroy." 24And they glorified God in me (it is uncanny that neither Paul in Galatians nor Luke in Acts record any converts resulting from Paul's four year ministry in Syria and Cilicia with his headquarters in Tarsus – especially since Luke is such a careful chronicler of conversions in Acts, as shown in the following passage in which he records that the Lord was with the Cyprians and Cyrenaicans who preached to Greeks in Antioch with many conversions, at the same time that Paul is preaching in Syria and Cilicia – see Item 21 below for an interpretive guess as to why this is so).

Acts 11:19 They therefore who were scattered abroad by the oppression that arose about Stephen (in Judea) traveled as far as Phoenicia, Cyprus, and Antioch, speaking the word to no one except only to Jews. 20But there were some of them, men of Cyprus and Cyrene, who, when they had come to Antioch, spoke to the Greeks, preaching the Lord Jesus. 21The hand of the Lord was with them, and a great number believed and turned to the Lord. 22The report concerning them came to the ears of the assembly which was in Jerusalem. They sent out Barnabas to go as far as Antioch, 23who, when he had come, and had seen the grace of God, was glad. He exhorted them all, that with purpose of heart they would remain near to the Lord. 24For he was a good man, and full of the Holy Spirit and of faith, and many people were added to the Lord. 25Barnabas went out to Tarsus to look for Saul. 26When he had found him, he brought him to Antioch. It happened, that even for a whole year they were gathered together with the assembly, and taught many people. The disciples were first called Christians in Antioch.

Paul stays in Syria and Cilicia for approx. 39-42 A.D = 4 years, after which Barnabas comes from Antioch and gets Paul, and they both go back to Antioch in order to teach the "many" Greeks who had been converted to Jesus there by "men from Cyprus and Cyrene" for one year (43 A.D.). Consequently, the total distance of Paul's journeys from Jerusalem to Tarsus (approx. 380 miles), plus his journeys through Syria and Cilicia (500 miles ?), plus his journey with Barnabas from Tarsus to Syrian Antioch (120 miles) takes 5 years and comprises approx. 1,000 miles.

8. Paul and Barnabas carry money collected in Antioch to Jerusalem for a famine prophesied by Agabus, and are protected from Herod. They return to Antioch and are commissioned by the Specially Selecting Spirit to go on Paul's "First Missionary Journey" (Acts11:27-30, 12:25, 13:1-3):

Acts 11:27 Now in those days, prophets came down from Jerusalem to Antioch. ²⁸One of them named Agabus stood up, and indicated by the Spirit that there should be a great famine over all the world, which also happened in the days of Claudius. ²⁹The disciples, as anyone had plenty, each determined to send relief to the brothers who lived in Judea; ³⁰which they also did, sending it to the elders by the hands of Barnabas and Saul...(After Herod was dead – see Item 9 below)...Acts 12:25 Barnabas and Saul returned from Jerusalem (to Antioch), when they had fulfilled their service, also taking with them John whose surname was Mark...Acts 13:1 Now in the assembly that was at Antioch there were some prophets and teachers: Barnabas, Simeon who was called Niger, Lucius of Cyrene, Manaen the foster-brother of Herod the tetrarch, and Saul. ²As they served the Lord and fasted, the Holy Spirit said, "Separate Barnabas and Saul for me, for the work to which I have called them." ³Then, when they had fasted and prayed and laid their hands on them, they sent them away.

The round trip from Syrian Antioch to Jerusalem is approx. 750 miles. The total time to collect the gift for the prophesied famine, take it to Jerusalem, return to Antioch, and prepare to set out on the (traditionally-called) "First Missionary Journey" would have taken the better part of a year (44 A.D.). The famine itself actually occurs two years later, in 46 A.D.

9. King Herod kills the Apostle James, the brother of the Apostle John, by beheading him in order to increase his political favor, then arrests and puts Peter in prison, intending to kill him too. But the disciples pray for Peter, and God sends an angel to rescue Peter by miraculously breaking him out of jail. Later, an angel of God puts Herod to death for his arrogance (Acts 12:1-23):

¹Now about that time, Herod the king stretched out his hands to oppress some of the assembly. ²He killed James, the brother of John, with the sword. ³When he saw that it pleased the Jews, he proceeded to seize Peter also...put him in prison, and delivered him to four squads of four soldiers each to guard him...but constant prayer was made by the assembly to God for him. ⁶The same night when Herod was about to bring him out...⁷Behold, an angel of the Lord stood by him, and a light shone in the cell. He struck Peter on the side, and woke him up, saying, "Stand up quickly!" His chains fell off from his hands. ⁸The angel said to him, "Put on your clothes, and tie on your sandals." He did so. He said to him, "Put on your cloak, and follow me." ⁹He went out, and followed him...¹⁰When they were past the first and the second guard, they came to the iron gate that leads into the city, which opened to them by itself. They went out, and passed on through one street, and immediately the angel departed from him. ¹¹When Peter had come to himself, he said, "Now I truly know that the Lord has sent out his angel and delivered me out of the hand of Herod, and from everything the Jewish people were expecting." ¹²...he came to the house...where many were gathered together and were praying. ¹³When Peter knocked at the door of the gate...(and) When they had opened, they saw him, and were amazed...²¹On an appointed day, Herod dressed himself in royal clothing, sat on the throne, and gave a speech (to the people of Tyre and

Sidon)....²²The people shouted, "The voice of a god, and not of a man!" ²³Immediately an angel of the Lord struck him, because he didn't give God the glory, and he was eaten by worms, and he died.

Herod Agrippa I was the grandson of Herod the Great (who was the Herod that the wise men came to, after which he tried to kill Jesus when Jesus was an infant), and the nephew of Herod Antipas (d. after A.D. 39), tetrarch of Galilee and Peraea, who was the Herod who married the Arab King Aretas IV's daughter, but then put her away in favor of Herodias (Herod Antipas was tricked by Herodias into beheading John the Baptist when John the Baptist confronted them with committing adultery against Aretas IV's daughter), and who was ruling at the time of Jesus' death. The eldest son of the executed Aristobulus (Herod the Great's firstborn son and older brother of Herod Antipas), Herod Agrippa I was a man of some ability. Out of friendship Caligula made him king (A.D. 39) of Philip's (third son of Herod the Great) tetrarchy; later he was made (A.D. 41) ruler of South Syria and of Palestine east and west of the Jordan. Herod Agrippa I was strongly pro-Jewish, and he built extensively at Berytus (modern Beirut). He is the Herod who put the Apostle James to death, imprisoned the Apostle Peter, blasphemed after giving a speech to the people of Tyre and Sidon, and as a result was killed by God's angel (44 A.D.) [*Columbia Encyclopedia, Sixth Edition, 2001 and Encyclopedia Britannica, 1911*].

•───•

10. Luke has called Paul by his given name of "Saul" up through setting out on the (traditionally-called) "First Missionary Journey." Luke now changes Saul's name to "Paul." This is significant. Some major spiritual change has occurred in Paul, because although he has evangelized and preached Jesus now for approx. eleven years since his own conversion, and has had much spiritual success at apologetics, Luke has never yet recorded that Paul has ever converted a single person to Jesus. Paul's first recorded conversion of another person happens at the first place Paul lands (Cyprus). This event also marks the first time since Paul's conversion that Luke says that Paul is "filled with the Holy Spirit," and it is the first time that Luke records that another human being (Sergius Paulus) "believes" in Jesus when Paul speaks (this is the only other person in the NT, other than the Apostle Paul, whose name is also "Paul." I think the significance of this is that Paul names himself after his first convert, as a reminder to himself that it is only when he is "in the Spirit" that he is able to lead someone to Jesus. After this, Paul sails north to Galatia, and after giving his first sermon to a non-Jewish audience in Pisidian Antioch, Luke says that "as many as were appointed to eternal life believed" (the second time Luke records that the result of Paul's speech is people "believing" – only this time it is a group, not just one person. God not only delivers Paul from the "persecution," of the Jews in this city, but more importantly, He has delivered Paul from fruitlessness (Acts 13:4-52):

⁴So, being sent out by the Holy Spirit...they sailed to Cyprus... ⁵When they were at Salamis, they proclaimed the word of God in the synagogues of the Jews... They had also John (Mark) as their attendant. ⁶When they had gone through the island to Paphos, they found a certain sorcerer, a false prophet, a Jew, whose name was Bar Jesus, ⁷who was with the proconsul, Sergius Paulus, a man of understanding. The same summoned Barnabas and Saul, and sought to hear the word of God. ⁸But Elymas the sorcerer (for so is his name by interpretation) withstood them, seeking to turn aside the proconsul from the faith. ⁹But Saul, who is also called Paul, filled with the Holy Spirit, fastened his eyes on him, ¹⁰and said, "Full of all deceit and all cunning, you son of the devil, you enemy of all righteousness, will you not cease to pervert the right ways of the Lord? ¹¹Now, behold, the hand of the Lord is on you, and you will be blind, not seeing the sun for a season!" Immediately there fell on him a mist and darkness. He went around seeking someone to lead him

by the hand. ¹²Then the proconsul (Sergius Paulus), when he saw what was done, believed, being astonished at the teaching of the Lord. ¹³Now Paul and his company set sail from Paphos, and came to Perga in Pamphylia. John (Mark) departed from them and returned to Jerusalem. ¹⁴But they, passing through from Perga, came to Antioch of Pisidia. They went into the synagogue on the Sabbath day, and sat down. ¹⁵After the reading of the law and the prophets, the rulers of the synagogue sent to them, saying, "Brothers, if you have any word of exhortation for the people, speak." ¹⁶Paul stood up, and beckoning with his hand said, "Men of Israel, and you who fear God, listen. ¹⁷The God of this people Israel chose our fathers, and exalted the people when they stayed as aliens in the land of Egypt, and with an uplifted arm, he led them out of it. ¹⁸For about the time of forty years he put up with them in the wilderness. ¹⁹When he had destroyed seven nations in the land of Canaan, he gave them their land for an inheritance, for about four hundred fifty years. ²⁰After these things he gave them judges until Samuel the prophet. ²¹Afterward they asked for a king, and God gave to them Saul the son of Kish, a man of the tribe of Benjamin, for forty years. ²²When he had removed him, he raised up David to be their king, to whom he also testified, 'I have found David the son of Jesse, a man after my heart, who will do all my will.' ²³From this man's seed, God has brought salvation to Israel according to his promise, ²⁴before his coming, when John had first preached the baptism of repentance to all the people of Israel. ²⁵As John was fulfilling his course, he said, 'What do you suppose that I am? I am not he. But behold, one comes after me the sandals of whose feet I am not worthy to untie.' ²⁶Brothers, children of the stock of Abraham, and those among you who fear God, the word of this salvation is sent out to you. ²⁷For those who dwell in Jerusalem, and their rulers, because they didn't know him, nor the voices of the prophets which are read every Sabbath, fulfilled them by condemning him. ²⁸Though they found no cause for death, they still asked Pilate to have him killed. ²⁹When they had fulfilled all things that were written about him, they took him down from the tree, and laid him in a tomb. ³⁰But God raised him from the dead, ³¹and he was seen for many days by those who came up with him from Galilee to Jerusalem, who are his witnesses to the people. ³²We bring you good news of the promise made to the fathers, ³³that God has fulfilled the same to us, their children, in that he raised up Jesus. As it is also written in the second psalm [Ps. 2:7], 'You are my Son. Today I have become your father.' ³⁴"Concerning that he raised him up from the dead, now no more to return to corruption, he has spoken thus: 'I will give you the holy and sure blessings of David.' ³⁵Therefore he says also in another psalm [Ps. 16:10], 'You will not allow your Holy One to see decay.' ³⁶For David, after he had in his own generation served the counsel of God, fell asleep, and was laid with his fathers, and saw decay. ³⁷But he whom God raised up saw no decay. ³⁸Be it known to you therefore, brothers, that through this man is proclaimed to you remission of sins, ³⁹and by him everyone who believes is justified from all things, from which you could not be justified by the law of Moses. ⁴⁰Beware therefore, lest that come on you which is spoken in the prophets: ⁴¹'Behold, you scoffers, and wonder, and perish; For I work a work in your days, A work which you will in no way believe, if one declares it to you.'" ⁴²So when the Jews went out of the synagogue, the Gentiles begged that these words might be preached to them the next Sabbath. ⁴³Now when the synagogue broke up, many of the Jews and of the devout proselytes followed Paul and Barnabas; who, speaking to them, urged them to continue in the grace of God. ⁴⁴The next Sabbath almost the whole city was gathered together to hear the word of God. ⁴⁵But when the Jews saw the multitudes, they were filled with jealousy, and contradicted the things which were spoken by Paul, and blasphemed. ⁴⁶Paul and Barnabas spoke out boldly, and said, "It was necessary that God's word should be spoken to you first. Since indeed you thrust it from you, and judge yourselves unworthy of eternal life, behold, we turn to the Gentiles. ⁴⁷For so has the Lord commanded us, saying, 'I have set you as a light of the Gentiles, That you should be for salvation to the uttermost parts of the earth.'" ⁴⁸As the Gentiles heard this, they were glad, and glorified the word of God. As many as were appointed to eternal life believed. ⁴⁹The Lord's word was spread abroad throughout all the region. ⁵⁰But the Jews urged on the devout women of honorable estate, and the chief men of the city, and stirred up a persecution against Paul and Barnabas, and threw them out of their borders. ⁵¹But they shook off the dust of their feet against them, and came to Iconium. ⁵²The disciples were filled with joy with the Holy Spirit.

11. Violent Gentiles and Jews attempt to stone Paul and his companions to death at Iconium, but Paul becomes aware of their plot and they flee to safety in other cities in Asia (Acts 14:1-6):

¹It happened in Iconium that they (Paul and his companions) entered together into the synagogue of the Jews, and so spoke that a great multitude both of Jews and of Greeks believed. ²But the disobedient Jews stirred up and embittered the souls of the Gentiles against the brothers. ³Therefore they stayed there a long time, speaking boldly in the Lord, who testified to the word of his grace, granting signs and wonders to be done by their hands. ⁴But the multitude of the city was divided. Part sided with the Jews, and part with the apostles. ⁵When some of both the Gentiles and the Jews, with their rulers, made a violent attempt to insult them and to stone them, ⁶they became aware of it, and fled to the cities of Lycaonia, Lystra, Derbe, and the surrounding region.

12. At Lystra, Paul is stoned (to death) by Jews who follow him there from Antioch and Iconium, but he immediately comes back to life (Acts 14:19-20):

¹⁹But some Jews from Antioch and Iconium came there (Lystra), and...they stoned Paul, and dragged him out of the city, supposing that he was dead. ²⁰But as the disciples stood around him, he rose up, and entered into the city. On the next day he went out with Barnabas to Derbe.

Lystra to Derbe is a journey of approx 80 miles! Derbe is the endpoint of the (traditionally-called) "First Missionary Journey." After evangelizing there, Paul and Barnabas return by the same route (Lystra, Iconium, Pisidian Antioch, Perga, Attalia) back to Syrian Antioch. The total trip comprises about 680 land miles + 620 sea miles = approx. 1,300 total miles, and takes approx. 2 years (45-46 A.D.). They then stay in Antioch "a long time" with the disciples (Acts 14:28 = approx. one year; 47 A.D.). Paul and Barnabas must then make the round trip to Jerusalem to solve the doctrinal conflict over whether the Gentile Christians have to live according to the Law of Moses (750 miles round trip, and another one year, 48 A.D.). After staying and teaching in Antioch for another extended period (Acts 15:30-35, one year, 49 A.D.), Paul determines to return to visit the Galatian cities of the "First Missionary Journey," this time, over the land route through his home town of Tarsus. This is the beginning of the (traditionally-called) "Second Missionary Journey," in which Paul ends up being directed by the Spirit to go on to Macedonia (Philippi, Thessalonica, Beroea), then ultimately to Achaia (Athens, Corinth).

13. At Philippi, Paul delivers a young girl by casting a fortune-telling demon out of her, depriving her wicked owners of using her any longer to make money. They incite a riot against Paul. He and Silas are unjustly arrested, beaten and thrown in prison. Paul and Silas pray and sing hymns in their prison cell, and God rescues them by a "great" earthquake that unhinges the prison's cell doors. Paul then not only saves the jailer's life (by keeping him from committing suicide), but persuades him and his family to believe in Jesus and receive the gift of eternal life. Then, after being careful to preserve his political integrity as a Roman Citizen according to law, Paul leaves Philippi and travels on to Thessalonica (Acts 16:16-40):

¹⁶It happened, as we were going to prayer, that a certain girl having a spirit of divination met us, who brought her masters much gain by fortune telling. ¹⁷(She) cried out, "These men are servants of the Most High God, who proclaim to us the way of salvation!" ¹⁸...Paul, becoming greatly annoyed, turned and said to the spirit, "I charge you in the name of Jesus Christ to come out of her!" It came out that very hour. ¹⁹But when her masters saw that the hope of their gain was gone, they seized Paul and Silas, and dragged them into the marketplace before the rulers. ²⁰When they had brought them to the magistrates, they said, "These men, being Jews, are agitating our city, ²¹and set forth customs which it is not lawful for us to accept or to observe, being Romans." ²²The

multitude rose up together against them, and the magistrates tore their clothes off of them, and commanded them to be beaten with rods. 23When they had laid many stripes on them, they threw them into prison, charging the jailer to keep them safely, 24who, having received such a charge, threw them into the inner prison, and secured their feet in the stocks. 25But about midnight Paul and Silas were praying and singing hymns to God, and the prisoners were listening to them. 26Suddenly there was a great earthquake, so that the foundations of the prison were shaken; and immediately all the doors were opened, and everyone's bonds were loosened. 27The jailer, being roused out of sleep and seeing the prison doors open, drew his sword and was about to kill himself, supposing that the prisoners had escaped. 28But Paul cried with a loud voice, saying, "Don't harm yourself, for we are all here!" 29He called for lights and sprang in, and, fell down trembling before Paul and Silas, 30and brought them out and said, "Sirs, what must I do to be saved?" 31They said, "Believe in the Lord Jesus Christ, and you will be saved, you and your household." 32They spoke the word of the Lord to him, and to all who were in his house. 33He took them the same hour of the night, and washed their stripes, and was immediately baptized, he and all his household. 34He brought them up into his house, and set food before them, and rejoiced greatly, with all his household, having believed in God. 35But when it was day, the magistrates sent the sergeants, saying, "Let those men go." 36The jailer reported these words to Paul, saying, "The magistrates have sent to let you go; now therefore come out, and go in peace." 37But Paul said to them, "They have beaten us publicly, without a trial, men who are Romans, and have cast us into prison! Do they now release us secretly? No, most assuredly, but let them come themselves and bring us out!" 38The sergeants reported these words to the magistrates, and they were afraid when they heard that they were Romans, 39and they came and begged them. When they had brought them out, they asked them to depart from the city. 40They went out of the prison, and entered into Lydia's house.

14. In Thessalonica, Paul is protected by Jason and other Christians from angry, jealous Jews who get wicked men to incite a riot. They rescue Paul by sending him on to nearby Beroea. (Acts 17:5-10):

5But the disobedient Jews gathered some wicked men from the marketplace, and gathering a crowd, set the city in an uproar. Assaulting the house of Jason, they sought to bring them out to the people. 6When they didn't find them, they dragged Jason and certain brothers before the rulers of the city, crying, "These who have turned the world upside down have come here also, 7whom Jason has received. These all act contrary to the decrees of Caesar, saying that there is another king, Jesus!" 8The multitude and the rulers of the city were troubled when they heard these things. 9When they had taken security from Jason and the rest, they let them go. 10The brothers immediately sent Paul and Silas away by night to Beroea.

15. Thessalonican Jews follow Paul to Beroea. He is protected and escorted to Athens (Acts 17:13-15):

13But when the Jews of Thessalonica had knowledge that the word of God was proclaimed by Paul at Beroea also, they came there likewise, agitating the multitudes. 14Then the brothers immediately sent out Paul to go as far as to the sea, and Silas and Timothy still stayed there. 15But those who escorted Paul brought him as far as Athens.

16. Jesus tells Paul that he will stay for an extended time in Corinth (1 1/2 years) because he will convert many people there. Jesus then providentially brings Aquila and Priscilla to Corinth, with whom Paul goes into the tent-making business in order to earn his own living. Paul's apprentices do not take money either (Acts 18:1-3, 9-11):

1After these things (Paul's speech to the Athenians, to which only a few respond), Paul departed from Athens, and came to Corinth. 2He found a certain Jew named Aquila, a man of Pontus by race, who had recently come from Italy, with his wife Priscilla, because Claudius had commanded all the Jews to depart from Rome. He came to them, 3and because he practiced the same trade, he lived with them and worked, for by trade they were tent makers...9The Lord said to Paul in the night by a vision, "Don't be afraid, but speak and don't be silent; ¹⁰for I am with you, and no one will attack you to harm you, for I have many people in this city." ¹¹He (Paul) lived there (Corinth) a year and six months, teaching the word of God among them.

In 2 Cor. 11:7 and 12:14-16, Paul proves his sincerity by pointing out to the Corinthians that he never took money from them during the one and one-half years he lived in Corinth and taught them, because he made his own living in the tent-making business with Priscilla and Aquila:

2 Cor. 11:7 Or did I commit a sin...because I preached to you God's good news free of charge?...12:14...(when) I...come,...I will not be a burden to you; for I seek not your possessions, but you...(When I was there before), I did not myself burden you...(Further),...¹⁷did I take advantage of you by anyone of them whom I have sent to you?

●───●

17. At the end of his stay in Corinth, God protects Paul again, using a Roman official (Gallio) to perceive the Jews' envious motive and dismiss their complaint against him (Acts 18:12-16):

¹²But when Gallio was proconsul (a Roman government official) of Achaia, the Jews with one accord rose up against Paul and brought him before the judgment seat, ¹³saying, "This man persuades men to worship God contrary to the law." ¹⁴But when Paul was about to open his mouth, Gallio said to the Jews, "If indeed it were a matter of wrong or of wicked crime, it would be reasonable that I should bear with you; ¹⁵but if they are questions about words and names and your own law, look to it yourselves. For I don't want to be a judge of these matters." ¹⁶He (Gallio) drove them from the judgment seat.

Corinth is the endpoint of the (traditionally-called) "Second Missionary Journey." After Paul stays in that city for 1 1/2 years, he travels by sea to Ephesus for a short time, then again by sea travels on to Jerusalem to fulfill a vow, then goes back to Antioch. In total, this journey takes 3 years (50-52 A.D.), and Paul travels approx. 1,900 land miles + 1,100 sea miles = 3,000 total miles.

●───●

18. During Paul's three years in Ephesus, God provides for him the same way that He did in Corinth, by sending Aquila and Priscilla there also, where once again Paul earns his own living with them through the business of the tent-making trade (Acts 18:18, 24; 19:1; 20:31, 35).

18:18 Paul...took his leave...and sailed from there (Corinth) for Syria, with Priscilla and Aquila with him...(They) came to Ephesus, and he left them (Priscilla and Aquila) there; but he himself...set sail from Ephesus (for Jerusalem)...²⁴Now a certain Jew named Apollos...came to Ephesus...he spoke and taught accurately the things concerning Jesus, although he knew only the baptism of John...when Priscilla and Aquila heard him, they took him aside, and explained to him the way of God more accurately...(Apollos then went to Corinth)...19:1...Paul (then) came (back) to Ephesus ...reasoning daily in the school of Tyrannus...for two years. (After Paul visited Macedonia and Achaia again following the Ephesian riot – see Item 16 below – he spoke to the Ephesian leaders on his way back to Jerusalem, saying)... 20:31 "Therefore...remember...that for a period of three years (when I lived in Ephesus)...you...know that these hands ministered to my necessities, and to those who were with me (Priscilla and Aquila). ³⁵...I gave you an example, that so laboring you ought to help the weak, and to remember the words of the Lord Jesus, (who)...said, 'It is more noble to give than to receive.'

Paul spends "some time" in Antioch, then leaves again on what will become the (traditionally-called) "Third Missionary Journey." His target city is Ephesus, where he will spend a total of three years, his longest tenure in any city. He begins the trip by once again visiting all of the Galatian cities of the first missionary journey "in order" (Tarsus, Derbe, Lystra, Iconium, Pisidian Antioch), and then heading due west to

Ephesus, staying there for three years. After the Ephesian riot, Paul leaves Ephesus and again goes through Macedonia (Philippi, Thessalonica, Beroea) ending up once again at Corinth in Achaia after he has written both Corinthian letters. After spending three months there, a Jewish plot to kill him at sea is discovered, so Paul returns by land through Macedonia. After meeting with the Ephesian leadership at Miletus, Paul once again sails to Jerusalem. In total, this journey takes approx. 5 years (53-57 A.D.), and Paul travels approx. 1,500 land miles + 1,100 sea miles = 2,600 total miles.

19. In Ephesus, Paul and his companions are rescued by a city official from being lynched by a rioting mob in the theater, who have been incited to irrational mob-anger against Paul and his companions by Demetrius, a greedy pagan silversmith, who is angry with Paul because he has converted so many of the Ephesians from Artemis-worship to Christianity that they no longer buy silver idols and trinkets surrounding the worship of Artemis (Acts 19:23-40).

[23]About that time there arose no small stir concerning the Way. [24]For a certain man named Demetrius, a silversmith, who made silver shrines of Artemis, brought no little business to the craftsmen, [25]whom he gathered together, with the workmen of like occupation, and said, "Sirs, you know that by this business we have our wealth. [26]You see and hear, that not at Ephesus alone, but almost throughout all Asia, this Paul has persuaded and turned away many people, saying that they are no gods, that are made with hands. [27]Not only is there danger that this our trade come into disrepute, but also that the temple of the great goddess Artemis will be counted as nothing, and her majesty destroyed, whom all Asia and the world worships." [28]When they heard this they were filled with anger, and cried out, saying, "Great is Artemis of the Ephesians!" [29]The whole city was filled with confusion, and they rushed with one accord into the theater, having seized Gaius and Aristarchus, men of Macedonia, Paul's companions in travel. [30]When Paul wanted to enter in to the people, the disciples didn't allow him. ...When the town clerk had quieted the multitude, he said, "You men of Ephesus...you ought to be quiet, and to do nothing rash. [37]For you have brought these men here, who are neither robbers of temples nor blasphemers of your goddess. [38]If therefore Demetrius and the craftsmen who are with him have a matter against anyone, the courts are open, and there are proconsuls. Let them press charges against one another. [39]But if you seek anything about other matters, it will be settled in the regular assembly. [40]For indeed we are in danger of being accused concerning this day's riot, there being no cause. Concerning it, we wouldn't be able to give an account of this commotion."

20. Paul leaves Ephesus, goes to Macedonia, and writes and delivers 2 Corinthians (56 A.D.) before he re-visits Corinth again. In it, he deliberately recounts and enumerates his sufferings and miraculous deliverances in order to prove to the Corinthians the legitimacy of his divine "lifework" as being Christ's chief Apostle ("High Emissary") to the Gentiles (Barbarian ethnic groups living north and west of the Mediterranean Sea – 2 Cor. 11:23-27). At the point of writing this passage, Paul is not even half way through the (traditionally-called) "Third Missionary Journey." He still faces the journey from Macedonia to Corinth, the trip back to Jerusalem, his arrest, escaping murder plots, and 2 years of imprisonment, hearings and trials in Jerusalem and Caesarea, the long Mediterranean storm and shipwreck off Malta on the voyage to Rome, 2 years of further imprisonment in Rome, his release and further travels (back to Antioch?, then on to Spain?), his re-imprisonment, trial, and martyrdom by Nero in Rome:

[23]Are they servants of Christ? (I speak as one beside himself) I am more so; in labors more abundantly, in stripes above measure, in prisons more abundantly, in deaths often. [24]Five times from the Jews I received forty stripes minus one. [25]Three times I was beaten with rods. Once I was stoned. Three times I suffered shipwreck. I have been a night and a day in the deep. [26]I have been

in travels often, perils of rivers, perils of robbers, perils from my countrymen, perils from the Gentiles, perils in the city, perils in the wilderness, perils in the sea, perils among false brothers; 27in labor and travail, in watchings often, in hunger and thirst, in fastings often, and in cold and nakedness.

SUMMARY OF PAUL'S EXPERIENCES OF RESCUE THROUGH 56 A.D.: "labors:" establishing and running at least two full-time tent-manufacturing businesses with Priscilla and Aquila to provide for his own living: 1 ½ years in Corinth and 3 years in Ephesus = 4 ½ total years recorded in Acts + "stripes," approx. 312 total (?), see below + "prisons," Philippi plus several others [Arabia, Syria, Cilicia (?), maybe 3x total (?)] + "deaths often" (note plural noun, and adjective "often") undoubtedly one time from being stoned at Lystra, plus being killed at least several other times from: scourging(s) (1x?) + beating(s) (1x?) + drowning(s) at sea (1x?) = approx. 4x total (?) + 5 scourgings 5 x 39 = 195 "stripes" from scourges + 3 beatings with rods approx. 3 x 39 = 117 "stripes" from rods + 3 "shipwrecks" one of them involving at least 24 hours clinging to wreckage in the ocean; "a night and a day in the deep" + "travels:" 1 journey from Damascus to Jerusalem, then Arabia, then back to Damascus, then Jerusalem = 3 years and 1,000 miles, 1 journey from Jerusalem to Tarsus (plus Syria and Cilicia) to Antioch = 6 years and 1,000 miles, 1 round trip from Antioch to Jerusalem (famine gift trip) = 1 year and 750 miles, 1 trip through Galatia ("First Missionary Journey") = 2 years and 1,300 total miles (680 land miles + 620 sea miles), second round trip from Antioch to Jerusalem ("Jerusalem Council") = 1 year and 750 miles, 1 trip through Galatia, Asia to Philippi, Thessalonica, Boerea, Athens, Corinth ("Second Missionary Journey"), then back through Ephesus to Jerusalem to Antioch = 3 years and 3,000 total miles (1,900 land miles + 1,100 sea miles), 1 trip through Galatia to Ephesus, then after 3 years there, on to Macedonia (on his way to Corinth) = 4 years and 1,000 total miles (850 land miles + 150 sea miles) at the time Paul writes 2 Corinthians from Macedonia; + "perils:" "rivers, robbers, Jews (at least 7 murder plots/lynch mobs so far: at Damascus, Jerusalem, Iconium, Thessalonica, Beroea, Corinth and Ephesus), city, wilderness, sea, false brothers" + "hunger and thirst" + "cold and nakedness" = TOTAL of 2 entrepreneurial businesses, 3 imprisonments, being killed 4 (?) times and raised to life again, 8 scourgings/beatings, 1 stoning, 3 shipwrecks (1 of them major), 6 1/2 major journeys comprising a total of 8,800 miles (6,930 land miles + 1,870 sea miles): 1) Damascus → Jerusalem → Arabia → Damascus (1,000 miles), 2) Jerusalem → Tarsus → Antioch (1,000 miles), 3) Antioch → Jerusalem → Antioch (750 miles), 4) Antioch → Galatian cities → Antioch (1,300 miles), 5) Antioch → Jerusalem → Antioch (750 miles), 6) Antioch → Galatian cities → Asia → Macedonia → Achaia → Jerusalem → Antioch (3,000 miles), 7) (halfway) Antioch → Galatian cities → Ephesus → Macedonia (1,000 miles – Paul writes 2 Corinthians from Macedonia), and escaping from 7 murder plots/lynch mobs over a total time period of 22 years (34-56 A.D.) If Stephen was stoned in 33 A.D. when Paul was 25, and Paul was converted on the road to Damascus when he was 26 in 34 A.D., then Paul is approx. 48 years old at the time of this writing, and he still has 11 years until he is put to death by Nero when he is 59 years old (i.e., he has completed 22/33 years or 2/3 of his "lifework" at this point in his life since his conversion). He has, at this point, written less than half of his total contribution to the NT: *Galatians, 1* and *2 Thessalonians* (49-51 A.D.); and *1* and *2 Corinthians* (56 A.D.). He has yet to write his most mature Treatises: *Romans* (57 A.D.); *Ephesians, Philippians, Colossians, Philemon* (61 A.D.); *1 and 2 Timothy and Titus* (66-67 A.D.).

21. In addition to all of the sufferings and miraculous rescues Paul enumerates in 2 Cor. 11:23-27 (see Item 20 above), he goes on in 2 Cor. 12:7-9 to relate that he has been suffering from one of Satan's evil spirits for the last fourteen years. Ironically, this evil spirit was given to Paul by God in order to "rescue" him from being proud. Although Paul was growing spiritually for the first eight years after his conversion, he still suffered from (and would have for the rest of his life, if not for the continual presence of this evil spirit) the worst bane of being a Pharisee: a tendency to be arrogant:

[4]Now because of the superlative nature of the divine revelations (shown to me by God when He transported me to heaven fourteen years ago), He therefore afterwards gave me a spiritual "thorn" in my body that causes me chronic and continual pain, that is to say, one of Satan's evil angels, for the purpose of hitting me and slapping me around, in order to deliver me from my tendency to become proud and arrogant. This evil spiritual being has continued to cause me such continual pain that I have begged the Commander in Chief on three separate occasions that He remove it from me, but each time He has replied to me, 'My grace is sufficient for you, because My kind of power can only make you spiritually mature through your weakness.' Most gladly therefore I will rather boast in my weaknesses, that the power of the High King may rest on me. [10]Therefore I take pleasure in weaknesses, in injuries, in necessities, in persecutions, in distresses, for the High King's sake. For when I am weak, then am I strong."

Since Paul wrote 2 Corinthians in 56 A.D. (when he was about 48 years old), and God gave him this evil spiritual being fourteen years previously (about 42 A.D., the last year of his four years in Tarsus, just before Barnabas came to Tarsus to bring him to Antioch, when Paul was about 34 years old), it would imply that Paul will suffer pain from this evil spiritual being for the last eleven years of his life, for a total of 25 years (14 + 11 = 25 years). It also implies that God made Paul fruitful in his lifework only after gave Him this evil spiritual being (a full eight years after his conversion!) My interpretive guess of this textual evidence is that Paul, although a great debater and apologist for Christianity during his first eight years of preaching (3 years Arabia + 1 year Damascus → Jerusalem → Tarsus + 4 years in Tarsus, Cilicia, Syria), still tended to be proud (Greek: ὑπεραίρω = "to be lifted up with pride" [LS]), and as a result was unfruitful (no converts to Jesus – just making unbelieving Jews, Arabs, and Greeks angry enough to plot to kill him). Immediately after God gives Paul the evil spirit to plague him, Barnabas comes to get him to take him to Antioch to teach all of the recent Greek converts who have come to faith as a result of the evangelistic efforts of the "men from Cyprus and Cyrene." Soon after this, Paul sets out on his "First Missionary Journey" and he renames himself from Saul to Paul after his first recorded convert (Sergius Paulus), which happens at the very first place he lands (Cyprus). See Item 10 above.

22. Paul is rescued again from a Jewish plot to kill him at sea (Acts 20:2-3):

[2]When he (Paul) had gone through those parts (Macedonia), and had encouraged them with many words, he came into Greece. [3] When he had spent three months there, and a plot was made against him by Jews as he was about to set sail for Syria, he determined to return through Macedonia.

23. While Paul is in Jerusalem, the Asian Jews (who hate Paul) recognize him and incite a riot of other Jews who don't know Paul to unlawfully beat him and try to kill him. God not only protects Paul by using a Roman military officer to rescue him, but he allows Paul to speak to the entire Jewish crowd, giving them one last chance to accept Jesus as their Messiah (Acts 21:27-40):

²⁷...the Jews from Asia, when they saw him (Paul) in the temple (in Jerusalem), stirred up all the multitude and laid hands on him, ²⁸crying out, "Men of Israel, help! This is the man who teaches all men everywhere against the people, and the law, and this place. Moreover, he also brought Greeks into the temple, and has defiled this holy place!"...³⁰All the city was moved, and the people ran together. They seized Paul and dragged him out of the temple. Immediately the doors were shut. ³¹As they were trying to kill him, news came up to the commanding officer of the regiment that all Jerusalem was in an uproar. ³²Immediately he took soldiers and centurions, and ran down to them. They, when they saw the chief captain and the soldiers, stopped beating Paul. ³³Then the commanding officer came near, arrested him, commanded him to be bound with two chains, and inquired who he was and what he had done. ³⁴Some shouted one thing, and some another, among the crowd. When he couldn't find out the truth because of the noise, he commanded him to be brought into the barracks. ³⁵When he came to the stairs, it happened that he was carried by the soldiers because of the violence of the crowd;...³⁷...Paul...asked the commanding officer, "May I say something to you?...I am a Jew, from Tarsus in Cilicia...I beg you, allow me to speak to the people." ⁴⁰When he had given him permission, Paul, standing on the stairs, beckoned with his hand to the people. When there was a great silence, he (Paul) spoke to them in the Hebrew language...

24. Paul delivers himself from Roman scourging by informing the Roman military officer of his Roman citizenship (Acts 22:24-30):

²⁴...the (Roman) commanding officer commanded him (Paul)...to be examined by scourging, that he might know for what crime they (the Jews) shouted against him. ²⁵When they had tied him up with thongs, Paul asked the centurion..., "Is it lawful for you to scourge a man who is a Roman, and not found guilty?"...The commanding officer came and asked him (Paul), "Tell me, are you a Roman?" He said, "Yes." ²⁹The commanding officer...was afraid when he realized that he was a Roman, because he had bound him. ³⁰...on the next day, ...he freed him (Paul) from the bonds...

25. Paul rescues himself from a bogus trial before the Jewish religious regime's council by shrewdly using his awareness of their own contentious divisiveness to trigger a doctrinal argument among themselves (Acts 23:6-10):

⁶...(W)hen Paul perceived that the one part (of the Jewish council) were Sadducees and the other Pharisees, he cried out in the council, "Men and brothers, I am a Pharisee, a son of Pharisees. Concerning the hope and resurrection of the dead I am being judged!" ⁷When he had said this, an argument arose between the Pharisees and Sadducees, and the assembly was divided. ⁸For the Sadducees say that there is no resurrection, neither angel, nor spirit; but the Pharisees confess all of these. ⁹A great clamor arose, and some of the scribes of the Pharisees part stood up, and contended, saying, "We find no evil in this man. But if a spirit or angel has spoken to him, let's not fight against God!" ¹⁰When a great argument arose, the commanding officer, fearing that Paul would be torn in pieces by them, commanded the soldiers to go down and take him by force from among them, and bring him into the barracks.

26. Jesus appears to Paul and promises that He will deliver him safely to Rome (Acts 23:11):

¹¹The following night, the Lord (Jesus) stood by him (Paul, while he was still kept prisoner in the Roman barracks), and said, "Cheer up, Paul, for as you have testified about me at Jerusalem, so you must testify also at Rome."

This marks the conclusion of Paul's seventh major journey (the traditionally-called "third missionary journey"), in which he traveled from Antioch through the Galatian cities to Ephesus, which he made his headquarters for the evangelization of Asia for three years, then revisited the cities of Macedonia and Achaia, then returned over the land route through Macedonia and Miletus to Jerusalem, comprising a total of five years (53-57 A.D.), and traveling a total of approximately 2,600 miles (1,500 land miles + 1,100 sea miles).

27. Paul is rescued by his own sister's son (his nephew!), who overhears a serious conspiracy made by over forty Jews to murder Paul. Paul's nephew has the courage to inform the Roman commanding officer, Claudius Lysias, who then sends Paul to safety in Caesarea under the jurisdiction of the Roman governor Felix (Acts 23:12-24):

[12]...(T)he Jews banded together, and bound themselves under a curse, saying that they would neither eat nor drink until they had killed Paul. [13]...(M)ore than forty people...made this conspiracy. [14]They came to the chief priests...and said, "We have bound ourselves...(to) kill...Paul. [15]...(Y)ou with the council inform the commanding officer that he should bring him down to you tomorrow, as though you were going to judge his case more exactly. We are ready to kill him before he comes near." [16]But Paul's sister's son heard of their lying in wait, and he...told Paul. [17]Paul summoned one of the centurions, and said, "Bring this young man to the commanding officer, for he has something to tell him."...[19]The commanding officer...asked him privately, "What is it that you have to tell me?" [20]He said, "The Jews have agreed to ask you to bring down Paul tomorrow to the council, as though intending to inquire somewhat more accurately concerning him. [21]Therefore don't yield to them, for more than forty men lie in wait for him...(to) kill...him..." [22]...(T)he commanding officer...(charged) him, "Tell no one that you have told these things to me." [23]He called...two of the centurions, and said, "Prepare two hundred soldiers to go as far as Caesarea...at the third hour of the night." [24]He asked them...to bring him (Paul) safely to Felix the governor.

28. Paul is rescued by Felix, the Roman governor, from false accusations of the Jewish leadership regime. He knows that the Roman military commander who was at the scene, Claudius Lysias, is the only reliable witness to refute the false Jewish allegations (Acts 24:1-23):

[1]After five days, the high priest, Ananias, came down with certain elders and an orator, one Tertullus. They informed the governor against Paul...(falsely accusing him of being a political insurrectionist and profaning the temple.) [9]The Jews also joined in the attack, affirming that these things were so. [10]When the governor had beckoned to him to speak, Paul answered...(Paul successfully defends himself by confronting Ananias and the Jewish regime, because they cannot prove their false allegations). [22]But Felix, having more exact knowledge concerning the Way, deferred them, saying, "When Lysias, the commanding officer, comes down, I will decide your case." [23]He ordered the centurion that Paul should be kept in custody, and should have some privileges, and not to forbid any of his friends to serve him or to visit him.

29. Paul is delivered from the corruption of Felix's attempt to gain a bribe from Paul in exchange for his freedom, but he must suffer two more years of custody (Acts 24:24-27):

[24]But after some days, Felix came with Drusilla, his wife, who was a Jewess, and sent for Paul, and heard him concerning the faith in Christ Jesus. [25]As he reasoned about righteousness, self-control, and the judgment to come, Felix was terrified, and answered, "Go your way for this time, and when it is convenient for me, I will summon you." [26]He hoped that way that money would be given to him by Paul, that he might release him. Therefore also he sent for him more often, and talked with him. [27]But when two years were fulfilled, Felix was succeeded by Porcius Festus, and desiring to gain favor with the Jews, Felix left Paul in bonds.

30. Paul saves himself from the corruption of the Roman governor Festus by his own Roman citizenship to appeal to be tried in Rome by Caesar. Paul already knows that Jesus has commissioned him to go to Rome (see Item 25 above), and so he shrewdly uses his knowledge of Roman law to accomplish the means for transporting himself

there, to deliver himself from the persistent corruption of the petty Roman officials in Judea (Acts 25:1-12):

¹Festus therefore, having come into the province, after three days went up to Jerusalem from Caesarea. ²Then the high priest and the principal men of the Jews informed him against Paul, and they begged him, ³asking a favor against him, that he would send for him to Jerusalem; plotting to kill him on the way. ⁴However Festus answered that Paul was kept in custody at Caesarea, and that he himself was about to depart shortly. ⁵"Let them therefore," said he, "that are in power among you go down with me, and if there is anything wrong in the man, let them accuse him." ⁶When he had stayed among them more than ten days, he went down to Caesarea, and on the next day he sat on the judgment seat, and commanded Paul to be brought. ⁷When he had come, the Jews who had come down from Jerusalem stood around him, bringing against him many and grievous charges which they could not prove, ⁸while he said in his defense, "Neither against the law of the Jews, nor against the temple, nor against Caesar, have I sinned at all." ⁹But Festus, desiring to gain favor with the Jews, answered Paul and said, "Will you go up to Jerusalem, and there be judged of these things before me?" ¹⁰But Paul said, "I am standing before Caesar's judgment seat, where I ought to be tried. I have done no wrong to the Jews, as you also know very well. ¹¹For if I have done wrong, and have committed anything worthy of death, I don't refuse to die; but if none of those things is true that these accuse me of, no one can give me up to them. I appeal to Caesar!" ¹²Then Festus, when he had conferred with the council, answered, "You have appealed to Caesar. To Caesar you will go."

●━━━●

31. Festus realizes he has really bungled the situation badly and seriously endangered his own career, because he now faces sending an innocent man to Rome for trial with no legal charge to place against him, which is flagrantly against Roman law and which would spell the end of his career as a chief Roman law enforcement officer. So, with disguised flattery, he invites Agrippa to hear Paul, all the while planning to appeal to Agrippa's vanity to get Agrippa to formulate a charge against Paul so he can claim that the legal charges against Paul are Agrippa's – not his own. Paul delivers himself once again from this bogus attempt by Festus to manipulate the corrupt and immoral King Agrippa (whose is living in incestuously with his own sister Bernice) to take responsibility for formulating Paul's accusation, or for entering into intrigue with the Jews so they can murder Paul. Agrippa, living in open immorality himself, is not so easily tricked and dodges both Festus' attempt to make him responsible for charging Paul or for becoming complicit with the Jews plotting the murder of an innocent man (Acts 25:26 – 26:32):

²³...(W)hen Agrippa and Bernice had come with great pomp, and they had entered into the place of hearing with the commanding officers and principal men of the city, at the command of Festus, Paul was brought in. ²⁴Festus said, "King Agrippa, and all men who are here present with us, you see this man, about whom all the multitude of the Jews petitioned me, both at Jerusalem and here, crying that he ought not to live any longer. ²⁵But when I found that he had committed nothing worthy of death, and as he himself appealed to the emperor I determined to send him. ²⁶Of whom I have no certain thing to write to my lord. Therefore I have brought him forth before you, and especially before you, king Agrippa, that, after examination, I may have something to write. ²⁷For it seems to me unreasonable, in sending a prisoner, not to also specify the charges against him" (this is obviously a bogus excuse, since Festus knows very well why Paul appealed to Caesar – to keep from getting murdered by the Jews on the way to Jerusalem on a false pretext of a change of venue, which Felix and Festus both know is against Roman law in Paul's case. He knows he must send a reasonable accusation with Paul to Rome or he will expose himself to the political danger of sending Paul for trial with no charge, or a frivolous charge, against him. Festus is trying to get Agrippa to take the political responsibility for charging Paul with a crime and extricate himself from bungling the matter). 26:1...Then Paul...made his defense. ²"I think myself happy, King Agrippa, that I am to make my defense before you this day concerning all the things whereof I am

accused by the Jews, ³especially because you are expert in all customs and questions which are among the Jews (this is an ironic but somewhat gentle public rebuke of Agrippa, since the Jewish law prohibits incest, which Agrippa and his sister Bernice are openly practicing). Therefore I beg you to hear me patiently"...Paul then gives his usually polite but practiced and effective sincere testimony, aimed precisely at converting Agrippa to Jesus by identifying himself as just a co-sinner along with Agrippa, reasoning that if Jesus was merciful to Paul himself, He would certainly accept Agrippa's faith also. Paul also however, points out his own repentance and moral integrity since his own conversion, and the injustice of his own arrest, which he knows both Agrippa and Festus are fully aware of: "¹⁹Therefore, King Agrippa, I...declared...throughout all the country of Judea, (aimed at Agrippa) and also to the Gentiles (aimed at Festus), that they should (and so also should you both) repent and turn to God, doing works worthy of repentance. ²¹For this reason the Jews seized me in the temple, and tried to kill me." At this point, Festus interrupts Paul and disingenuously accuses him of being crazy, because Festus knows that Paul is getting dangerously close to the subject that Festus unlawfully entertained the suggestion by the Jewish leadership regime that Paul be sent back to Jerusalem for trial, knowing full well that they would murder him on the road. Both men, knowing their guilt, decide to end the interview and then convince themselves of their innocence when they both know of their own guilt: ³⁰The king rose up with the governor, and Bernice, and those who sat with them. ³¹When they had withdrawn, they spoke one to another, saying, "This man does nothing worthy of death or of bonds" (disguised sincere comment but really disingenuous – what Festus really means is: "Don't get the idea that I was really serious when I thought about sending Paul back to Jerusalem, and also don't get the idea that I was trying to get you to take the fall by inventing a charge against this innocent man!") ³²Agrippa said to Festus, "This man might have been set free if he had not appealed to Caesar" (disguised sincere comment but really disingenuous – what he really means is: "I know I need your political alliance to stay alive around here myself, and I appreciate that fact and will pretend to be polite to you, but you are not going to get me to be the fall guy for making up some false accusation to justify your own intrigue with the Jewish leadership – which you bungled – with the result that you now have to send an innocent man for trial in Rome with no legal accusation – or for that matter, back to Jerusalem – when you and I both know that the Jews are only using us to murder him and then make us, or worse, make ME, take the political heat by blaming his murder on me, and then you Romans would remove me as an incompetent king who can't keep public order! I'm not going to fall into your trap!").

Herod Agrippa II (d. c.100 A.D.), was the son of Herod Agrippa I (the Herod who put the Apostle James to death with the sword, imprisoned the Apostle Peter, and was killed by God's angel for blasphemy), the great-grandson of Herod the Great (the Herod that tried to kill Jesus when Jesus was an infant), and the grand-nephew of Herod Antipas (the Herod who committed adultery with Herodias and beheaded John the Baptist). He received only the northern part of his father's (Herod Agrippa I's) kingdom, and that not until c.52 A.D. (7 years before Paul's hearing before Festus in 59 A.D.). He was a poor ruler and alienated his subjects. His sister, the daughter of Herod Agrippa I, was Bernice. A very beautiful woman, she was often involved in intrigue. After her first husband died, she was married to her uncle Herod of Chalcis. After his death (A.D. 48) she lived in incest with her brother, Herod Agrippa II, causing some scandal. Her third husband was the Cilician king Polemon II, whom she abandoned, returning to Herod Agrippa II. She and her brother sided with Rome in its struggle with Judea. The emperor Titus apparently planned to marry her, but the Romans' great dislike of the Jews forced him to withdraw from the match [*Columbia Encyclopedia, Sixth Edition, 2001* and *Encyclopedia Britannica, 1911*].

32. God delivers not only Paul, but all the crew (276 people in all) on the ship carrying him to Rome, from a terrible storm on the Mediterranean Sea. God sends an angel to tell Paul that all their lives will be saved, but the ship will be lost. They land on the Island of Malta (Acts 27:9-28:1):

27:9...(T)he voyage was now dangerous...Paul admonished them...But the centurion gave more heed to the master...of the ship than to...Paul...(Then) there beat down...a tempestuous wind, which is called Euroclydon. ¹⁵When the ship was caught, and couldn't face the wind, we gave way to it, and were driven along....²⁰When neither sun nor stars shone on us for many days, and no small tempest pressed on us, all hope that we would be saved was now taken away. ²¹When they had been long without food, Paul stood up in the midst of them, and said, "Sirs, you should have listened to me...²²Now I exhort you to cheer up, for there will be no loss of life among you, but only of the ship. ²³For there stood by me this night an angel, belonging to the God whose I am and whom I serve, ²⁴saying, 'Don't be afraid, Paul. You must stand before Caesar. Behold, God has granted you all those who sail with you.' ²⁵Therefore, sirs, cheer up! For I believe God... ⁴¹(T)hey ran the vessel aground...(and it) began to break up by the violence of the waves...So it happened that they all escaped safely to the land. 28:1 When we had escaped, then we knew that the island was called Malta.

•──•

33. God delivers Paul from the poisonous bite of a deadly snake (Acts 28:2-6):

²...The natives...kindled a fire, and received us all, because of the...rain, and...cold. ³But when Paul had gathered a bundle of sticks and laid them on the fire, a viper came out because of the heat, and fastened on his hand...(H)e shook off the creature into the fire, and wasn't harmed...(W)hen they (the natives)...saw nothing bad happen to him, they changed their minds, and said that he was a god.

•──•

34. Paul arrives safely at Rome, and is delivered from trial because no one shows up from Jerusalem to accuse him of anything (Acts 28:21-31):

²¹They (the Jews at Rome) said to him (Paul), "We neither received letters from Judea concerning you, nor did any of the brothers come here and report or speak any evil of you...²³When (Paul) testif(ied) about...Jesus...²⁴Some believed...and some disbelieved. ²⁵When they didn't agree among themselves...the Jews departed...³⁰Paul stayed two whole years in his own rented house, and received all who went in to him, ³¹preaching the Kingdom of God, and teaching the things concerning the Lord Jesus Christ with all boldness, without hindrance.

Paul's journey to Rome took him from Jerusalem to Caesarea where he remained imprisoned for over two years, then westward past Crete across the Mediterranean Sea through storm and shipwreck to land on Malta, eventually traveling to Rome for another two year imprisonment during his trial, comprising a total of five years (58-62 A.D.), and traveling a total of approximately 2,600 miles (200 land miles + 2,400 sea miles).

•──•

Even in those cases in the above chronology in which God's spiritual leaders were not temporally rescued, but seem to suffer a premature death (John the "Immerser," Jesus Himself, Stephen, James the Brother of John, Peter, Paul, etc.) the promise still applies to the ultimate deliverance they will enjoy in their resurrected bodies in their respective leadership roles serving Jesus, the High King, when He returns to establish His future Kingdom. A unique example of this observable fact occurs in Acts 12, in which the High Emissary James, the brother of John, is executed by Herod with a sword, but when Herod arrests Peter intending to do the same to him, the angel of God miraculously rescues Peter from jail in order for him to continue his lifework for a few more years, until he also is ultimately crucified (..."Concerning the manner of Peter's death, we possess a tradition – attested to by Tertullian at the end of the second century...and by Origen [in Eusebius, "Hist. Eccl.," II, i] – that he suffered crucifixion. Origen says: 'Peter was crucified at Rome with his head downwards, as he himself had desired to suffer'" [*The Catholic Encyclopedia*]).

For a summary of these main events and a chronology of the journeys of Paul, see note above at Eph. 3:1.

[37] μάχαιρα...**2.** as a weapon, *short sword, dagger*, Pi.*N*.4.59, Hdt.6.75, 7.225, Lys.13.87, etc.; an assassin's weapon, Antipho 5.69; used by jugglers, Pl.*Euthd*.294e (pl.), etc.; later, *sabre*, opp. the straight sword ([ξίφος]), X.*Eq*.12.11, cf. *HG*3.3.7, *Cyr*.1.2.13, *Ev.Matt*.26.52, etc.; οἱ ἐπὶ τῆς μ., of a bodyguard, Arr.*Epict*.1.30.7; but, ἐπὶ μ. τασσόμενοι possessing power of life and death (*jus gladii*), *Cat.Cod. Astr*.8(4).173; μ. ἱππική *cavalry sabre*, IG11(2).161 *B*99 (Delos, iii B. C.) [LS]. There are three types of "swords" distinguished in Greek. The type of "sword" mentioned most often in the NT is described by this word, **μάχαιρα**. It is used 3 times by Paul, 4 times by John in the *Apocalypse* and 29 times total. The second type of sword mentioned in the NT is the **ῥομφαία, ἡ**, A. *large, broad sword*, used by the Thracians, ὀρθὰς ῥ. βαρυσιδήρους ἀπὸ τῶν δεξιῶν ὤμων ἐπισείοντες Plu.*Aem*.18, cf. Phylarch. *Fr*.57 J., Arr.*Fr*.103J.: generally, *sword*, LXX *Ge*.3.24, al., *Ev.Luc*.2.35, *Apoc*.6.8, Jul.*Ep*.89b; **of the sword of Goliath**, LXX *1 Ki.* 17.51, J.*AJ*6.12.4 [LS]. This word (**ῥομφαία**) is not used by Paul, but is used once by Luke and 6 times by John in the *Apocalypse*, for a total of 7 times. Jerome's translation for both words (**μάχαιρα** and **ῥομφαία**) into Latin is the word **gladius**. The third word used for "sword" in Greek is **ξίφος**. This word is not used in the NT, but is the word used most often for a "sword" in other Greek literature.

The **μάχαιρα** originally was medium-length (blade approx. 18 in. long) variable width (approx. 1.5 in. near the handle, widening to approx. 2 in. toward the tip, then curving to a pointed tip at the end) bladed weapon of uniquely Greek design, having only one edge, and was curved slightly forward. Although Liddell-Scott translate this word as "cavalry sabre," the modern cavalry sabre, although having only one edge like the **μάχαιρα**, is a longer, thinner cutting weapon (approx. 36 in. long x 1 in. wide), has a hilt guard to protect the hand, maintains a uniform width along its length and is curved backward instead of forward. Unlike the **μάχαιρα**, the **ξίφος** was a straight, double-edged sword, slightly longer (approx 24 in.) than the **μάχαιρα** that had a hilt guard to protect the hand in combat. Although Xenophon states that the **ξίφος** was more conventional among Greek armies of his time, he recommended the **μάχαιρα** for cavalry, "μάχαιράν μεν μᾶλλον ἢ ξίφος ἐπαίνουμεν" (Xenophon, *On Horsemanship* 12:11). His reasoning concurs with the general practice of arming cavalry with curved swords through the ages. Greek art along with Xenophon's further commentary suggests that the sword he intended for the cavalry was wider than the more modern sabre [*Wikipedia Encyclopedia, 2005*]. The **ῥομφαία** refers to a sword that is larger, longer (approx. 36 in.) and broader in its blade than either the **μάχαιρα** or the **ξίφος**. In the Septuagint, it is the word used to refer to the sword of Goliath, as follows:

1Regn 17:51 καὶ ἔδραμεν Δαυιδ καὶ ἐπέστη ἐπ' αὐτὸν καὶ ἔλαβεν τὴν **ῥομφαίαν** αὐτοῦ καὶ ἐθανάτωσεν αὐτὸν καὶ ἀφεῖλεν τὴν κεφαλὴν αὐτοῦ.

1 Samuel 17:51 So David ran and stood over him [Goliath], and drew his [Goliath's] ***great sword*** and killed him and cut off his head.

Although a comparison of the uses of the word **μάχαιρα** and **ῥομφαία** in the NT suggests that the **ῥομφαία** is in fact somewhat larger than the **μάχαιρα**, it also appears that they are used as synonyms of each other. Jerome makes no distinction between them, because he translates both terms with the Latin word **gladius**, which refers to the short infantry sword used by the Romans, and which was also commonly used in the Mediterranean world when Paul wrote this Treatise.

It therefore appears that there is no significant distinction to be drawn in this passage between the word "sword" (infantry weapon) and "sabre" (cavalry weapon), or between the size of the sword (short vs. long). It appears that Paul is simply using the word **μάχαιρα** as a general equivalent term for the common Roman **gladius**, which was the medium-length, double-edged stabbing sword without a hilt guard used by infantrymen in close personal combat. The spiritual implication is that when the Devil realizes that he cannot injure us using long-range attacks on our faith, he will ultimately attempt a more deadly and close range assault with his wicked "sword" of personal temptation and enticement, studying us and attempting to attack us at our most vulnerable spiritual points.

[38] E.g., the story of the training of the Spaniard master-swordsman Inigo Montoya in Morgenstern's classic adventure story entitled *The Princess Bride*.

[39] In Matthew 4:4, Jesus quotes the Septuagint text of Deuteronomy 8:3, which uses the Greek word **ῥῆμα,** as follows:

Deut 8:3 – οὐκ ἐπ' ἄρτῳ μόνῳ ζήσεται ὁ ἄνθρωπος, ἀλλ' ἐπὶ παντὶ **ῥήματι** τῷ ἐκπορευομένῳ διὰ στόματος θεοῦ ζήσεται ὁ ἄνθρωπος.

Deut 8:3 [transl.] – "A human being shall not live only on bread, but instead, a human being shall live on every ***spoken word*** that has proceeded from the mouth of God."

Study of the word **ῥῆμα** throughout the Septuagint, which is the word Paul deliberately uses in this verse in Eph. 6:17, indicates that it means, "to communicate skillfully and accurately using public speech, with the intent of bringing the matter spoken about into actual existence." It should be translated in this context as "God's spoken pledges, promises, guarantees, certifications, decrees and sworn oaths." The meaning of the word **ῥῆμα** is therefore different than the meaning of the word **λόγος**, which Paul uses four times in this letter to refer to the "rational, logical use of the mind to truthfully use words to accurately reflect, describe or communicate reality" – see note on **ῥῆμα** at Eph. 5:26.

[40] See Matthew 4:1-4.

[41] See Matthew 4:5-7 and Psalm 91:11-12.

[42] See Matthew 4:8-11.

[43] See note at Eph. 6:14 on the Greek sentence beginning with the imperative verb στῆτε ("stand firm," "never give up"). Paul links one's communication directly with God [i.e., "prayer"] fundamentally to the use of the spiritual "body armor" he lists in Eph. 6:14-17. This culminating sentence begins in Eph. 6:14 and continues through the end of verse 20. The degree to which one communicates with God is the emphatic requirement for comprehending all of the symbolic elements of the extended "military" metaphorical vehicle. See following notes on the vital spiritual balance between the Greek concepts of προσεύχομαι and δέησις, which are the two most important concepts of Eph. 6:18.

[44] προσεύχομαι – "to make a request to God for divine information, in order to discover sufficient essential facts necessary to make an important spiritual decision in the future, or to seek out God's advice and direction in the process of gaining a spiritual understanding or perspective in order to plan an important course of action for the future" (see extended note at Eph. 1:16 for full analysis and meaning of this word).

[45] δέησις – εως, ἡ, *entreaty*, Lys.2.15 (pl.), Isoc.8.138 (pl.), Pl.*Ep.*329d (pl.), etc.; δέομαι δ' ὑμῶν . . δικαίαν δέησιν D.29.4; δεήσεις ποιεῖσθαι *Ev.Luc.* 5.33, cf. Wilcken *Chr.*41 ii 12 (iii A.D.). **2.** *written petition*, CPHerm.6.10, J.*BJ*7.5.2, Ph.2.586, *PGen.*16.10 (iii A.D.). **II.** *want, need*, Antipho Soph.11; ἐν ἐπιθυμίαις τε καὶ δεήσεσιν Pl.*Erx.*405e; κατὰ τὰς δεήσεις *according to their needs*, Arist.*Pol.*1257a23; δεήσεις εἰσὶν αἱ ὀρέξεις Id.*Rh.*1385a22 [LS]. Of the 12 times Paul uses this word in his Letters and Treatises, he uses it most often in his Treatise to the Philippians (4 times – 1:4(2x), 19; 4:6). He uses this word twice in Ephesians, both times in this verse in close context. It is usually translated "prayer (6x)," "supplication (5x)," or "making request" (1x). However, the Greek word most often translated "prayer" in the sense of "to ask or make a request to God" is the word προσεύχομαι, which means "to seek out God's information, advice and direction in the process of gaining a spiritual understanding or perspective in order to plan an important course of action for the future," (see note at Eph. 1:16 for an extended philological analysis of the word προσεύχομαι). Consequently, the translations "prayer" or "making request" are somewhat inaccurate translations for the Greek word δέησις. In addition, from a study of the above passages listed in Liddell-Scott, the old common vernacular British translation for this word as "supplication" is no longer used in professional contemporary American English ["supplication:" Webster Main Entry: **sup·pli·cat** Variant(s): *or* **sup·pli·cate** Etymology: *supplicat* from Latin, he makes supplication, 3d singular present indicative of *supplicare;* from the wording of the petition; *supplicate* from Medieval Latin *supplicatus,* from Latin *supplicatus,* past participle of *supplicare*: SUPPLICATION; *specifically*: a formal written petition for a degree or for incorporation at an English university – [W]. The question then arises as to how it should best be translated.

The Greek word δέησις is derived from the earlier Greek word δεῖ, which means: *there is need* (the sense of *moral obligation*, prop. belonging to χρή, is later, S.Ph.583, etc.): **I.** c.acc.pers.et inf., *it is needful for one to do, one must*, once in Hom., τί δὲ δεῖ πολεμιζέμεναι..' Ἀργείους *why need the Argives fight?* Il.9.337;...II. c. gen. rei, *there is need of*,...τί δεῖ τῆς ἀρετῆς; Arist.*Pol*.1309b10...[LS]. Upon inspection of the above passage from Aristotle's *Politics* [1309][b10], the concept of **δεῖ** = "that which is politically necessary," or "that which ought to be done in political considerations" is extremely helpful (ed. W. D. Ross, Oxford, 1957, transl. Benjamin Jowett, New York, 1941):

> Arist.*Pol.* [1309a][33] τρία δέ τινα χρὴ ("required") ἔχειν τοὺς μέλλοντας ἄρξειν τὰς κυρίας ἀρχάς ("fill the highest offices," lit. "to govern in the highest positions of leadership" – GWC), πρῶτον μὲν φιλίαν ("loyalty") πρὸς τὴν καθεστῶσαν [35] πολιτείαν ("constitution"), ἔπειτα δύναμιν μεγίστην τῶν ἔργων τῆς ἀρχῆς ("the greatest administrative capacity;" lit.: "the greatest dynamic ability in the enterprise of governing" – GWC), τρίτον δ' ἀρετὴν ("virtue") καὶ δικαιοσύνην ("justice") ἐν ἑκάστῃ πολιτείᾳ ("government") τὴν πρὸς τὴν πολιτείαν ("governments")· εἰ γὰρ μὴ ταὐτὸν τὸ δίκαιον ("justice") κατὰ πάσας τὰς πολιτείας ("governments"), ἀνάγκη καὶ τῆς δικαιοσύνης ("justice") εἶναι διαφοράς. ἔχει δ' ἀπορίαν, ὅταν μὴ συμβαίνῃ ταῦτα [40] πάντα περὶ τὸν αὐτόν, πῶς χρὴ ["required" – supplied by GWC] ποιεῖσθαι τὴν αἵρεσιν: [1309b][1] οἷον εἰ στρατηγικὸς μέν τις εἴη, πονηρὸς δὲ καὶ μὴ τῇ πολιτείᾳ ("constitution") φίλος ("not a friend"), ὁ δὲ δίκαιος ("just") καὶ φίλος ("loyal"), πῶς **δεῖ** [*"required"* – GWC] ποιεῖσθαι τὴν αἵρεσιν; ἔοικε δὲ **δεῖν** [*"ought"* = *"is it not necessary for us"* – GWC] βλέπειν εἰς δύο, τίνος πλεῖον μετέχουσι πάντες καὶ τίνος ἔλαττον: διὸ ἐν στρατηγίᾳ μὲν [5] εἰς τὴν ἐμπειρίαν μᾶλλον τῆς ἀρετῆς ("virtue") ἔλαττον γὰρ στρατηγίας μετέχουσι, τῆς δ' ἐπιεικείας πλεῖον, ἐν δὲ φυλακῇ καὶ ταμιείᾳ τἀναντία· πλείονος γὰρ ἀρετῆς ("virtue") **δεῖται** (*"required"*) ἢ ὅσην οἱ πολλοὶ ἔχουσιν, ἡ δὲ ["since this" – GWC] ἐπιστήμη κοινὴ πᾶσιν."

Benjamin Jowett's translation of this important passage is as follows [with proposed supplemental translation additions by GWC]:

> [1309a][33] There are three qualifications required (χρὴ) in those who have to fill the highest offices (ἄρξειν τὰς κυρίας ἀρχάς [= lit. "to govern in the highest positions of leadership" – GWC]) – (1) first of all, loyalty (φιλίαν) to the established [35] constitution (πολιτείαν); (2) the greatest administrative capacity (δύναμιν μεγίστην τῶν ἔργων τῆς ἀρχῆς [= lit.: "the greatest dynamic ability in the enterprise of governing" – GWC]); (3) virtue (ἀρετὴν) and justice (δικαιοσύνην) of the kind proper to each form of government (πολιτείᾳ); for if what is just (δίκαιον) is not the same in all governments (πολιτείαν), the quality of justice (δικαιοσύνης) must also differ. There may be a doubt, however, when [40] all these qualities do not meet in the same person, how the [required = χρὴ – GWC] selection is to be made; [1309b][1] suppose, for example, a good general is a bad man and not a friend to the constitution (πολιτείᾳ), and another man is loyal (φίλος) and just (δίκαιος), which should [**δεῖ** = *"is it required that"* – GWC] we choose? In making the election ought we not [**δεῖν** = *"is it not necessary for us"* – GWC] to consider two points? what qualities are common, and what are rare. Thus in the choice of a general, [5] we should regard his skill rather than his virtue (ἀρετῆς); for few have military skill, but many have virtue (ἀρετῆς). In any office of trust or stewardship, on the other hand, the opposite rule should be observed; for more virtue (ἀρετῆς) than ordinary *is required* (δεῖται) in the holder of such an office, but the [ἡ δὲ = "since this" – GWC] *necessary* (δεῖται –

supplied by BJ) knowledge [ἐπιστήμη; i.e., ἀρετῆς = "virtue" – GWC] is of a sort which all men ["*ought to*" = δεῖται – supplied by GWC] possess."

Therefore, it is proposed that the word δέησις be translated, "to lobby or submit an official legal or political petition, that is, to promote or urge official political influence from those who hold greater political, legal or military powers in order to affect the outcome of their decisions in favor of the interests that the lobbying party believes are right and necessary, and therefore ought to be enacted, including to make official application for a desired office of position based on meeting the necessary qualifications." Therefore, in this context, it is proposed that δέησις be translated: "to submit official petitions to God which, in effect, politically lobby Him to act in our behalf to accomplish some good action that we realize is necessary and ought to be done, but in which we also recognize we are in need of His divine power and assistance to accomplish."

[46] καιρός – "proportion, investment, that which is important, opportunity, co-operating with hard workers, knowing that what is valuable comes from the patience involved in sowing, cultivating and reaping, etc." e.g., Paul is re-emphasizing the theme he developed in Eph. 5:15-17. See the detailed development of this important concept in the note at Eph. 5:16.

[47] ἀγρυπνέω, pf. ἠγρύπνηκα Hp.Prog.2:--*lie awake, pass sleepless nights*, Thgn.471, Hp.l.c., Pl.*Lg*.695a, etc.; opp. καθεύδω, X.*Cyr.* 8.3.42; ἀγρυπνεῖν τὴν νύκτα *to pass a sleepless night*, Id.HG7.2.19, Men.113; οἱ -οῦντες sufferers from insomnia, Dsc.4.64. 2. metaph., *to be watchful*, LXX *Wi*.6.15, *Ev.Marc*.13.33, *Ep.Eph*.**6.18**; ὑπὲρ τῶν ψυχῶν *Ep.Heb*.13.17; ἐπὶ τὰ κακά LXX *Da*.9.14: c. inf., μηθέν σε ἐνοχλήσειν PGrenf.2.14a3. 3. c.acc., *lie awake and think of,* τινά PMag.Par.1.2966 [LS]. There are two words for "be watchful" in Greek. One of them is this word, ἀγρυπνέω (occurs 6x in the NT), and the other is γρηγορέω (occurs 23x in the NT). Paul always uses ἀγρυπνέω to mean "spending a sleepless night communicating with and petitioning God, and remaining vigilant to watch for God's answer (2 Cor. 6:5, 11:27)." Jesus uses this word twice (Mark 13:33 and Luke 21:36) as a synonym for γρηγορέω when He teaches His disciples that they should not sleep but remain "on watch" during the night that He communicated with God all night in the Garden of Gethsemane immediately prior to His arrest, trial and crucifixion. Therefore, Paul in this context is probably teaching that there are certain spiritual "crucial and important times of opportunity" (καιρός) in which we must be sensitive to the Spirit, that will involve the necessity to stay awake all night communicating with God in order to overcome evil spirits attempting to harm us or other specially selected recruits during times when we or they are spiritually weak or vulnerable. Of course, the most noteworthy example of this is Jesus' communicating with God most of the night in Gethsemane, which gave Him the spiritual strength to endure His unjust trial and crucifixion successfully the next day. A second example might be Shakespeare's interpretation of King Henry V's night of communication with God in his historical play of that name, in which he portrays the noble King spending

most of the night petitioning God prior to the Battle of Agincourt on the following morning, in which the English won a miraculous victory against the French against overwhelming odds. A third historical example might be General George Patton's request to the 3rd Army Chaplain during the night of December 23, 1944, that God would improve the bad weather forecasted for his necessary assault on the German armies from the south the next day during the Battle of the Bulge, so that he might have adequate air support during the assault:

> "On Dec. 16, 1944, a strong German force, commanded by Marshal von Rundstedt, broke the thinly held American front in the Belgian Ardennes sector. Taking advantage of the foggy weather and of the total surprise of the Allies, the Germans penetrated deep into Belgium, creating a dent, or "bulge," in the Allied lines and threatening to break through to the N Belgian plain and seize Antwerp. An American force held out at Bastogne, even though surrounded and outnumbered. The U.S. 1st and 9th armies, temporarily under Field Marshal Montgomery, attacked the German salient from the north, while the U.S. 3d Army [under Patton] attacked it from the south...Popular lore of the Battle of the Bulge evokes images of surprised Allied commanders, Gen. George S. Patton's wheeling Third Army, gallantry at Bastogne, *and **answered prayer** for good weather that brought the wrath of Allied air power on German forces... "Inoperable" flying weather closed in on the entire battle area from 19 until 23 December. During this period, the German penetration expanded to a 50-mile bulge – its maximum depth. Saint Vith was evacuated; but Bastogne, although surrounded, still held.* **Patton summoned Army Chaplain James H. O'Neil to "get God on our side for a change" and to pray for good weather.** *The chaplain complied. On 23 December the skies cleared; Chaplain O'Neil earned a medal* [Italics mine – GWC]. Allied air and ground power were ready to strike. Allied ground movements had secured the flanks of the penetration and blunted its expansion westward. Rested and ready, Allied air forces attacked. In the next five days, they flew more than 16,000 sorties. The Allied effort maintained air supremacy to the point that the Luftwaffe did not significantly hinder a single Allied ground movement or operation during the battle. The Allied air forces constructed a layered defense that Luftwaffe pilots had to negotiate just to get into the "battle area." First, in response to heavy Luftwaffe attacks on bombers on 23 December, Eighth Air Force heavy bombers carpet-bombed the German forward bases around Frankfurt on 24 December. The Eighth's fighters engaged the Luftwaffe's airborne fighters and strafed their airfields daily." [Sources: *Columbia Encyclopedia, Sixth Edition, 2001*; Aerospace Power Journal – Winter 1989; "Air Power in the Battle of the Bulge: A Theater Campaign Perspective," Col William R. Carter; USAF Danny S. Parker, "Battle for the Ardennes, May 1940 and December 1944," Strategy and Tactics 71 (November-December 1978): 38.]

[48] προσκαρτερήσει – fem. nom. noun, from προσκαρτερ-έω, Dor. ποτι-*IG*42(1).63.4 (Epid., ii B.C.):--*persist obstinately in*, τῇ πολιορκίᾳ Plb.1.55.4, D.S.14.87; τῇ προφορᾷ Phld. *Rh*.1.158 S.; τῇ προσευχῇ *Act.Ap*.1.14: abs., X.*HG*7.5.14, Ph.*Bel*. 101.9, LXX*Nu*.13.21(20), J.*BJ*6.1.3, Ach.Tat.1.10; καίπερ ἀχθόμενοι τῇ καθέδρᾳ π. J.*AJ*5.2.6. **2.** *adhere firmly to* a man, *be faithful to* him, τινι Plb.23.5.3, *Act.Ap*.8.13, 10.7; **of servants,** *remain in* one's *service*, D.59.120; of a κοσμητής, *IG*22.1028.84. **b.** *remain in attendance* at a law-court, τῷ βήματι, τῷ κριτηρίῳ, *PHamb*.4.7 (i A.D.), *POxy*.261.12 (i A.D.). **c.** *devote oneself to* an

office or occupation, τῇ στρατηγίᾳ ib.82.4 (iii A.D.); τῇ ἑαυτῶν γεωργίᾳ *PAmh*.2.65.3 (ii A.D.). **3.** Pass., ὁ προσκαρτερούμενος χρόνος time *diligently employed*, D.S.2.29. **4.** *wait for* a person, Φιλέᾳ *POxy.* 1764.4 (iii A.D.): abs., ἂν Ἐτέαρχος παραγένηται *PSI*5.598.7 (iii B.C.) [LS]. Proposed translation: "patience, persistence, diligence and devotion."

[49] λόγος, ὁ, verbal noun of λέγω (B), *the word or that by which the inward thought is expressed*...III. **explanation, 1.** *plea, pretext, ground*, with personal subject, εἶχον ἄν τινα λ. I (i.e. my conduct) would have admitted of an *explanation*, Pl.*Ap*.31b; τὸν ὀρθὸν λ. the true *explanation*, ib.34b. **b.** *plea, case*, in Law or argument...**2.** *statement of a theory, argument*, οὐκ ἐμεῦ ἀλλὰ τοῦ λ. ἀκούσαντας prob. in Heraclit.50; λόγον ἠδὲ νόημα ἀμφὶς ἀληθείης *discourse* and reflection on reality,...οὐ γὰρ ἂν ἀκούσειε λόγου ἀποτρέποντος Arist.*EN*1179b27; λ. καθαίρων Aristo Stoic.1.88; λόγου τυγχάνειν to be *explained*, Phld.*Mus*.p.77 K.; ὁ τὸν λ. μου ἀκούων my *teaching*, *Ev.Jo*.5.24; ὁ προφητικὸς λ., collect., of NT prophecy, *2 Ep.Pet*.1.19: pl., ὁκόσων λόγους ἤκουσα Heraclit.108; οὐκ ἐπίθετο τοῖς ἐμοῖς λ. Ar.*Nu*.73; **of arguments leading to a conclusion** ([ὁ λ.]), Pl. *Cri*.46b; τὰ Ἀναξαγόρου βιβλία γέμει τούτων τῶν λ. Id.*Ap*.26d; λ. ἀπὸ τῶν ἀρχῶν, ἐπὶ τὰς ἀρχάς, Arist.*EN*1095a31;...**c. in Logic, proposition, whether as premiss or conclusion**, πρότασίς ἐστι λ. καταφατικὸς ἢ ἀποφατικός τινος κατά τινος Arist.*APr*.24a16. **d.** *rule, principle, law*, as embodying the result of λογισμός, Pl.*Cri*.46b, cf. c; ἡδονὰς τοῖς ὀρθοῖς λ. ἑπομένας **obeying right principles**, Id.*Lg*.696c; προαιρέσεως [ἀρχὴ] ὄρεξις καὶ λ. ὁ ἕνεκά τινος *principle* **directed to an end**, Arist.*EN*1139a32; **of the final cause**, ἀρχὴ ὁ λ. ἔν τε τοῖς κατὰ τέχνην καὶ ἐν τοῖς φύσει συνεστηκόσιν Id.*EN*1140a10; ὀρθὸς λ. **true principle**, **right** *rule*, ib.1144b27, 1147b3, al.; κατὰ λόγον **by rule, consistently**, ὁ κατὰ λ. ζῶν Pl.*Lg*.689d, cf. *Ti*.89d; τὸ κατὰ λ. ζῆν, opp. κατὰ πάθος, Arist.*EN*1169a5; κατὰ λ. προχωρεῖν **according to plan**, Plb.1.20.3. 3. **law, rule of conduct**, ᾧ μάλιστα διηνεκῶς ὁμιλοῦσι λόγῳ Heraclit.72; πολλοὶ λόγον μὴ μαθόντες ζῶσι κατὰ λόγον Democr.53; δεῖ ὑπάρχειν τὸν λ. τὸν καθόλου τοῖς ἄρχουσιν **universal principle**, Arist.*Pol*.1286a17;...**5.** *reason, ground*,... λόγον ζητοῦσιν ὧν οὐκ ἔστι λ. *proof*, Arist. *Metaph*.1011a12;...**6. term expressing** *reason*, λ. τῆς πολιτείας Pl.*R*.497c; ψυχῆς οὐσία τε καὶ λ. **essential definition**, Arist.*PA*642a22, cf. *Metaph*.993a17...**7.** *reason, law* exhibited in the world-process,...esp. in Stoic Philos., **the divine** *order*, τὸν τοῦ παντὸς λ. ὃν ἔνιοι εἱμαρμένην καλοῦσιν Zeno Stoic.1.24; λ. ib.142 K., al...**1.** *thinking, reasoning*, τοῦ λ. ἐόντος ξυνοῦ, opp. ἰδία φρόνησις, Heraclit. 2; κρῖναι δὲ λόγῳ . . ἔλεγχον **test by** *reflection*, Parm.1.36; *reflection, deliberation* (cf. VI.3),...ὁ λ. or λ. αἱρέει *reasoning* **convinces**, Id.3.45,6.124;...τὸ μὲν δὴ νοήσει μετὰ λόγου περιληπτόν **embraced by thought with** *reflection*, ἐπιστήμη ἐνοῦσα καὶ ὀρθὸς λ. **scientific knowledge and right** *process of thought*, Id.*Phd*.73a; πᾶς λ. καὶ πᾶσα ἐπιστήμη τῶν καθόλου Arist.*Metaph*.1059b26; τὸ λόγον ἔχον Id.*EN*1102b15, 1138b9, al.: in sg. and pl., contrasted by Pl. and Arist. as *theory, abstract reasoning* with outward experience, sts. with depreciatory emphasis on the former, εἰς τοὺς λ.

καταφυγόντα Pl.*Phd.*99e πᾶς λ. καὶ πᾶσα ἀπόδειξις **all reasoning and demonstration**, Id.*Metaph.*1063b10; **2. reason as a faculty**, Arist. *EN* 1102b26; **also of the *reason* which pervades the universe**, θεῖος λ. [Epich.] 257; **b. *creative reason***, ἀδύνατον ἦν λόγον μὴ οὐκ ἐπὶ πάντα ἐλθεῖν Plot.3.2.14; **V. *continuous statement, narrative*** (whether fact or fiction), *oration*, etc. (cf. λέγω (B) 11.2), **4. *speech*, delivered in court, assembly, etc.**, χρήσομαι τῇ τοῦ λ. τάξει ταύτῃ Aeschin.3.57, cf. Arist.*Rh.*1358a38;...**3. *discussion, debate, deliberation***, πολλὸς ἦν ἐν τοῖσι λ. Hdt.8.59; μεταβαίνων ὁ λ. εἰς ταὐτὸν ἀφῖκται **our debate**, Arist.*EN*1097a24; **b. *right of discussion* or *speech***, ἢ 'πὶ τῷ πλήθει λ.; S.*OC* 66; λ. αἰτήσασθαι **ask *leave to speak***, Arist.*EN*1095b21, hence, ***time allowed for a speech***;...**c. *dialogue*, as a form of philosophical *debate***, ἵνα μὴ μαχώμεθα ἐν τοῖς λ. ἐγώ τε καὶ σύ Pl. *Cra.*430d; **d. *section, division* of a dialogue or treatise** ἐν τοῖς πρώτοις λ. Arist.*PA*682a3;...**VIII. *thing spoken of, subject-matter*** (cf. 111.1 b and 2), τὸν ἐόντα λ. the **truth of the** *matter*, ib.95,116; **IX. *expression, utterance, speech* regarded formally**, τὸ ἀπὸ [ψυχῆς] ῥεῦμα διὰ τοῦ στόματος ἰὸν μετὰ φθόγγου λ., opp. διάνοια, Pl.*Sph.*263e; ***intelligent utterance***, opp. φωνή, Arist.*Pol.*1253a14; in pl., *eloquence*, Isoc.3.3,9.11; τὴν ἐν λόγοις εὐρυθμίαν Epicur.*Sent.Pal.*5p.69 v. d. M.; λ. ἀκριβής **precise** *language*, Ar.*Nu.*130 (pl.), cf. Arist.*Rh.* 1418b1; **X. the *Word* or *Wisdom* of God, personified as his agent in creation and world-government**, ὁ παντοδύναμός σου λ. LXX *Wi.*18.15;...**in *NT* identified with the person of Christ**, ἐν ἀρχῇ ἦν ὁ λ. *Ev.Jo.*1.1 , cf. 14, *1 Ep.Jo.*2.7, *Apoc.*19.13; ὁ λ. τῆς ζωῆς *1 Ep.Jo.*1.1 [LS]. Proposed translation in this context: "the ability to always think intelligently and speak with a clear mind, use good reasoning, and be equipped with the best logical use of words in public speaking, whether the public forum be teaching, a public address, a debate, or a legal defense."

[50] παρρησία, ἡ, ([πᾶς, ῥῆσις]) *outspokenness, frankness, freedom of speech*, claimed by the Athenians as their privilege [LS]. Proposed translation: "to speak openly, freely and confidently in public."

[51] εὐαγγέλιον – See extended analysis of this word, in both its noun and verb forms, in note at Eph. 1:13.

[52] See Acts 23:11: "But the following night, the Lord stood by Him [Paul] and said, 'Be of good cheer, Paul, for as you have testified for me in Jerusalem, so also you must bear witness at Rome.'" It can be deduced from this passage that Jesus commissioned Paul to go to Rome immediately after Paul's arrest in Jerusalem, which occurred directly after his three-year stay in Ephesus, or about 57 A.D. Paul then spent approximately two years in various confinements in Palestine, appearing in official hearings before Felix, Festus, and King Agrippa (Acts Chapters 23 – 26), at the culmination of which he used his legal prerogative as a Roman citizen to appeal to Caesar. He then voyaged to Rome, was shipwrecked on Malta, and finally arrived in Rome in about 59 or 60 A.D., where he was confined under "house-arrest" for two years. It is from Rome that Paul wrote this final and climatic Treatise to the Ephesians in about 61 A.D.,

approximately four years after Jesus had directly commissioned him to go to Rome.

[53] πρεσβεύω, **I.** prop. of age, **1.** intr., ***to be the elder*** or ***eldest***, S.*OC*1422; hence, **b.** ***take the first place, be best***, S.*Ant.*720; **c.** gen., ***rank before, take precedence of others***, π. τῶν πολλῶν πόλεων Pl.*Lg.*752e...**2.** trans., ***place as oldest*** or ***first, put first in rank***, πρῶτον . . πρεσβεύω θεῶν Γαῖαν A.*Eu.*1: **hold the first place**, Παλλὰς . . ἐν λόγοις π. A.*Eu.* 21;...**II.** ***to be an ambassador*** or ***serve as one***, IG12.135.5; ἀπὸ Κορίνθου Hdt.5.93;...**b. at Rome, act as legatus**, Plu.*Sull.*4. **2.** c. acc. objecti, π. εἰρήνην ***negotiate*** **peace**, And.3.23, Isoc.4.177, D.19.134, etc.; π. ὑπὲρ τουτωνὶ τὰ βέλτιστα ib.189; π. πολλὰ καὶ δεινά ibid.:-- Pass., τὰ αὐτῷ πεπρεσβευμένα **his *negotiations,*** ib.20; πολλὰ καὶ δεινὰ πεπρεσβεῦσθαι ib.240. **3.** Med., ***send ambassadors***, ἐς χωρία, ἐς τὴν Θουρίαν, Th.2.7, 6.104; πρεσβεύεσθαι παρά τινας Id.4.41, etc.; πρός τινας Id.1.126; ἐς Ααкεδαίμονα περὶ καθόδου Id.3.85 .**b. *go as ambassador,*** Id.5.39 [LS]. Proposed translation in this context: "Lead Negotiator."

[54] See Eph. 2:14-22 for the further elaboration of Jesus role as God's chief "Peace-maker." See Eph. 6:15 for further elaboration on our role to represent Him as His "peace-makers."

[55] ἀγαπητὸς – see note at Eph. 5:1.

[56] ἀδελφὸς – see note at Eph. 6:10.

[57] See Acts 28:30-31: "Then Paul lived two whole years in his own rented house (in Rome: approx. 60-62 A.D.), and received all who came to him, preaching the Kingdom of God and teaching the things which concern the Commander in Chief, Jesus, the future High King of the earth, with all confidence, no one forbidding him."

[58] ἀφθαρσίᾳ – In the NT, this word is only used by Paul. He uses it eight times, and in every case, he always uses it to refer to the incorruption of the human body that we will enjoy in the resurrected, immortal state (Rom. 2:7; 1 Cor. 15:42, 50, 53, 54; Eph. 6:24; 2 Tim. 1:10; Tit. 2:7). Proposed translation: "immortality."

[59] ἀμήν – See note at Eph. 3:21.

EPHESIANS
Paul's Conclusive Treatise

A New Basic Explanatory Translation

Into

Professional (Non-Ecclesiastical)
Contemporary (Non-Medieval)
American (Non-British)
English

With

The Greek Text

Compared with

**William Tyndale's
First English Translation** (1526)

and

**The Authorized
King James Version** (1611)

Ephesians: Paul's Conclusive Treatise
Basic Explanatory Translation
With Greek Text, Tyndale's Version (1526) and King James Version (1611)

Introductory Notes and Legend:	
The basic translation into contemporary professional American English is presented first, the Greek Text second, William Tyndale's first translation of the Greek text into English (1526) third and the King James Version (1611) fourth. The text was first grouped into its chapter units by Stephen Langton in a Vulgate edition in 1205.[1] Verse labels were first introduced in a Latin translation of Erasmus' Greek text by Robert Estienne[2] in 1551.[3] These chapter and verse designations were published for the first time in English by Conrad Badius in Geneva in 1557,[4] and have since become accepted in the English tradition of translation. However, the verses that are employed in all English versions today were not used by the early editors (e.g., Erasmus) or by Tyndale, the first English translator. Therefore, the texts will be presented in paragraph format using Tyndale's paragraph divisions as a guide, since his arrangement of paragraphs overall present a good balance between Paul's extremely long sentences (which are too long for most English readers to follow), and the English tradition of versification of the text, which tends to break up and impede the flow of Paul's line of thought. To assist the reader, the verse divisions now accepted in the English tradition of translation will be included in the Basic Translation, Tyndale's first translation and the Greek text as small superscripted numbers immediately prior to the sentence that begins the translation of the particular verse, in the following format:	
²*May* graciousness *be given* to you all, together with peacefulness, from God our Father, and from our Commander in Chief, Jesus, the High King *of the future world*.	Basic Explanatory Translation into contemporary professional American English, with explanatory words in *italics*, thus: *May, be given, of the future world*; Times New Roman font, 11 point.
²Χάρις ὑμῖν καὶ εἰρήνη ἀπὸ Θεοῦ Πατρὸς ἡμῶν καὶ Κυρίου Ἰησοῦ Χριστοῦ.	Greek Text, GR Times New Roman font, 11 point, w/ English paragraph titles in italics,[5] thus: *Paul Greets*...
²Grace be with you and peace from god oure father, and from the lorde Jesus Christ.	Tyndale's First English Edition (1526)[6] transl. from the 3rd ed. (1522) of Erasmus' Greek Text,[7] with original spellings [*f*→s, v↔u] and original paragraph divisions, Georgia font, 10 point.
2 Grace *be* to you, and peace, from God our Father, and *from* the Lord Jesus Christ.	King James Version (1611),[8] with supplied words in *italics*, thus: *be, from*; with original spellings [*f*→s, v↔u], Bookman Antiqua font, 10 point.

Paul's Treatise to the Ephesians

Chapter 1 – The "Top Secret" Plan Declassified

Paul's Conclusive Treatise Commissioned ♦ *The Inauguration Ceremony of the Future Kingdom* ♦ *God's Motive for Including Us in the Kingdom is His Love* ♦ *Kingdom Apprenticeship – Five Benefits God Has Given Us* ♦ *The First Benefit: The Redemption of Resurrection* ♦ *The Second Benefit: God's "Top Secret" Plan Declassified* ♦ *The Third Benefit: He Has Bequeathed Us an Inheritance* ♦ *The Fourth Benefit: He Has Sealed Our Lifework Plan* ♦ *The Fifth Benefit: He Has Paid the Down Payment for Us* ♦ *Paul's Request: Trainees for a Lifework Apprenticeship Council.*

PAUL'S CONCLUSIVE TREATISE COMMISSIONED

I, Paul, High Emissary of Jesus, High King *of the future world,* appointed by the will of God, *am writing this Treatise to you,* the specially selected recruits who are in Ephesus, especially to those *who have proven themselves* trustworthy in *their service to* the High King *of the future world,* Jesus:

²*May the* graciousness and peacefulness *that come* from God our Father, and *from our* Commander in Chief, Jesus, the High King *of the future world, be given* to you all.

ΠΡΟΣ ΕΦΕΣΙΟΥΣ

Paul Greets the Saints in Ephesus

ΠΑΥΛΟΣ, ἀπόστολος Ἰησοῦ Χριστοῦ διὰ θελήματος Θεοῦ, Τοῖς ἁγίοις τοῖς οὖσιν ἐν Ἐφέσῳ καὶ πιστοῖς ἐν Χριστῷ Ἰησοῦ·

²Χάρις ὑμῖν καὶ εἰρήνη ἀπὸ Θεοῦ Πατρὸς ἡμῶν καὶ Κυρίου Ἰησοῦ Χριστοῦ.

The epistel of paul to the Ephesians.

The fyrst Chaper.

Paul an apostle off Jesu Christ by the will off God.

To the saynctes at Ephesus, and to them whiche beleve on Jesus Christ.

²Grace be with you and peace from God oure father, and from the lorde Jesus Christ.

THE EPISTLE OF PAUL
the Apostle to the Ephesians.
CHAP. I.

1 *After the salutation,* 3 *and thankesgiving for the Ephesians,* 4 *he treateth of our Election,* 6 *and Adoption by grace,* 11 *which is the true and proper fountaine of mans salvation.* 13 *And because the height of this mysterie cannot easily be atteined unto,* 16 *he praieth that they may come* 18 *to the full knowledge, and* 10 *possession thereof in Christ.*

P aul, an Apostle of Jesus Christ by the will of God, to the Saincts which are at Ephesus, and to the faithfull in Christ Jesus:

2 Grace *be* to you, and peace from God our Father, and *from* the Lord Jesus Christ.

The Inauguration Ceremony of the Future Kingdom

³God, *considered* especially *in His role as the* Father of our *present* Commander in Chief, Jesus, the High King *of the future world, is* the "Eulogizer;" *that is to say, the "Keynote Speaker" at Jesus' Inauguration Day, when the Father will invest Him into His office as High King of the Earth. In this unique role, the Father is* the One Whose recognition and commendation of our *lives, which He will make in a public speech at the end of history, will matter more than anything else.*

Furthermore, our future High King *is actually composing the text of this* commendation speech *right now in the exercise of His present* heavenly office. *He is compiling its contents concomitant with the spiritual relationship that He has with us and with* the Father – *as He* reports our spiritual progress and accomplishments *to Him on a continual and regular basis.* Moreover, there will come a day when each of our commendation speeches are finally completed, *and our future* High King *will make the transition from exercising His present responsibilities in heaven as our advocate and helper, to His future role as High King of the world.*

⁴*Until then, Jesus will execute all of His divine responsibilities* in accordance with *His divine plan, such that* prior to the founding of the organized government *of the future world*, He will have specially selected, recruited and trained us *with the deliberate purpose that we should personally* accompany Him *there. He will do this in order* to give us distinctive *legitimacy, so that we can be* unimpaired *as we stand* directly beside Him *to receive our official leadership appointments from God the Father Himself.*

GOD'S MOTIVE FOR INCLUDING US IN THE KINGDOM IS HIS LOVE

In view of that future day, and motivated by love, ⁵God has pre-surveyed *and pre-financed* us to receive legal adoption as His "sons *and daughters*" by means of *the legal advocacy of* Jesus, the High King *of the future world*. He has legally included us so that we can authentically assist Him in accomplishing His purposes *there*. *His investment in us will ultimately be successful* because of the inexorable resolve of His will. ⁶He has done this so that His graciousness – namely, the *incomparable* graciousness which He *has already* demonstrated to us by means of the *example of Jesus, the* One Whom He loves best – might be finally and conclusively demonstrated *in history*. At His Appearing, *Jesus will finally receive the universal* recognition, appreciation and honor *He is worthy of in that future, dignified, public ceremony.*

To the Praise of His Glory

³Εὐλογητὸς ὁ Θεὸς καὶ Πατὴρ τοῦ Κυρίου ἡμῶν Ἰησοῦ Χριστοῦ, ὁ εὐλογήσας ἡμᾶς ἐν πάσῃ εὐλογίᾳ πνευματικῇ ἐν τοῖς ἐπουρανίοις ἐν Χριστῷ, ⁴καθὼς ἐξελέξατο ἡμᾶς ἐν αὐτῷ πρὸ καταβολῆς κόσμου, εἶναι ἡμᾶς ἁγίους καὶ ἀμώμους κατενώπιον αὐτοῦ ἐν ἀγάπῃ ⁵προορίσας ἡμᾶς εἰς υἱοθεσίαν διὰ Ἰησοῦ Χριστοῦ εἰς αὐτόν, κατὰ τὴν εὐδοκίαν τοῦ θελήματος αὐτοῦ, ⁶εἰς ἔπαινον δόξης τῆς χάριτος αὐτοῦ ἐν ᾗ ἐχαρίτωσεν ἡμᾶς ἐν τῷ ἠγαπημένῳ,

³Blessed be God the father of oure lorde Jesus Christ, which hath blessed us with all maner of spirituall blessinges in hevenly thynges by Christ, ⁴acordynge as he had chosen us in hym throwe love, before the foundacion of the worlde was layde, that we shulde be sayntes, and without blame in his sight. ⁵And ordeyned us before unto him silfe that we shulde be chosen to heyres throwe Jesus Christ, accordynge to the pleasure of his will, ⁶to the prayse of his glorious grace, where with he hath made us accepted in the beloved.

3 Blessed *be* the God and Father of our Lord Jesus Christ, who hath blessed us with all spirituall blessings in heavenly |*Or, things*| places in Christ:

4 According as he hath chosen us in him, before the foundation of the world, that wee should bee holy, and without blame before him in love:

5 Having predestinated us unto the adoption of children by Jesus Christ to himself, according to the good pleasure of his will:

6 To the praise of the glorie of his grace, wherein he hath made us accepted in the beloved.

KINGDOM APPRENTICESHIP – FIVE BENEFITS GOD HAS GIVEN US

⁷*Because of His love, Jesus is* the One Who *has bought and secured the following five benefits for us toward that end* with the purchase "price" of His own blood.

THE FIRST BENEFIT: THE REDEMPTION OF RESURRECTION

First, God has granted us "redemption" because of Him. *He has purchased the right that* authorizes *us to "redeem" – or "trade in" – our present mortal bodies for our future resurrected bodies, which He will give us to experience the Inauguration of His Kingdom itself.*

THE SECOND BENEFIT: GOD'S "TOP SECRET" PLAN DECLASSIFIED

Second, because of Him, God has granted us "forgiveness" from *our hopeless indebtedness to Him, which all of us piled up by repeatedly plunging off course and* living sidetracked lives. *He has forgiven us our enormous debt* because of the "riches" of His graciousness. ⁸*He has gone on to "invest" even more of His "riches" in us so that* He can "compound" His "interest" in us by *making fully available to us the use of two essential leadership skills we will need. The first of these leadership skills is the ability to gain proficiency in* all *modes of* knowledge, *especially in* ethical competence; and *second,* in discernment, *principally as it relates to the employment of* practical and intentional good judgment.

⁹*He has made this investment in us because* He has now *officially* "declassified" *and* fully briefed us *in the contents of the formerly closely guarded* Divine Secrets of His *ultimate* purposes *in history,* as well as *avowing to us* His unrelenting resolve *to accomplish them.* Jesus Himself proposed *these specific* objectives and resolutions *during His recent first visit to the world.*

¹⁰*God sent Him on that mission to initiate His primary objective to select, recruit and train the right members for* the divine government *He will found* at the fulfillment of history. The High King Himself will head up the comprehensive reorganization *of the administration* of all *authority in that future world under His own leadership.* Further, He will accomplish this over *the realms of* all *the administrations of celestial authority that He will redeploy to operate* the heavens, as well as over all *the administrations of terrestrial authority that He will refound to govern* the earth.

THE THIRD BENEFIT: HE HAS BEQUEATHED US AN INHERITANCE

¹¹*Third, God* has bequeathed His "inheritance" to us along with Jesus. *He has included us in the High King's future inheritance,* which He pre-surveyed *and pre-financed to be* consistent with the *purposes and* proposals *He has planned* for each role He has worked out for us, and *will*

establish in keeping with the deliberation, counsel and resolution of His "will." ¹²*God has included us in the future "estate"* of Jesus' Kingdom in order that we, *namely* those *of us* who have hoped for *the ultimate* appearance *of* the High King *of the future world* beforehand, *might be afforded the privilege* to be *the first* to publicly *recognize, appreciate and* honor Him at His Appearing.

THE FOURTH BENEFIT: HE HAS SEALED OUR LIFEWORK PLAN

¹³*Fourth*, His Specially Selecting Spirit *has authenticated your lives by officially* "sealing" every one of you *in precisely the same way that He did Jesus' life. He has authenticated your lives in this way so that you would be able to accomplish your own special and uniquely promising lifework, just as Jesus did. The Spirit performed this validating act* when you heard this truthful report – *namely,* the good news of Jesus' wonderful plan to rescue and deliver you all – and then believed in Him.

THE FIFTH BENEFIT: HE HAS PAID THE DOWN PAYMENT FOR US

¹⁴*Fifth and finally, this same* Divine Spirit is also the "down payment" of our "inheritance." *We can apply and use this down payment in our present lives* toward the "redemption" of the "savings account" *God has invested in and for each of us. We can therefore add to the initial investment He has made in our lives,* so that we *might be the first to have the privilege of presenting our transformed lives, which He will have made valuable and worthy,* when we publicly *recognize, appreciate and* honor Him at His Appearing.

⁷ἐν ᾧ ἔχομεν τὴν ἀπολύτρωσιν διὰ τοῦ αἵματος αὐτοῦ, τὴν ἄφεσιν τῶν παραπτωμάτων, κατὰ τὸν πλοῦτον τῆς χάριτος αὐτοῦ ⁸ἧς ἐπερίσσευσεν εἰς ἡμᾶς ἐν πάσῃ σοφίᾳ καὶ φρονήσει ⁹γνωρίσας ἡμῖν τὸ μυστήριον τοῦ θελήματος αὐτοῦ, κατὰ τὴν εὐδοκίαν αὐτοῦ ἣν προέθετο ἐν αὐτῷ ¹⁰εἰς οἰκονομίαν τοῦ πληρώματος τῶν καιρῶν, ἀνακεφαλαιώσασθαι τὰ πάντα ἐν τῷ Χριστῷ, τὰ ἐπὶ τοῖς οὐρανοῖς καὶ τὰ ἐπὶ τῆς γῆς· ἐν αὐτῷ, ¹¹ἐν ᾧ καὶ ἐκληρώθημεν προορισθέντες κατὰ πρόθεσιν τοῦ τὰ πάντα ἐνεργοῦντος κατὰ τὴν βουλὴν τοῦ θελήματος αὐτοῦ, ¹²εἰς τὸ εἶναι ἡμᾶς εἰς ἔπαινον δόξης αὐτοῦ τοὺς προηλπικότας ἐν τῷ Χριστῷ· ¹³ἐν ᾧ καὶ ὑμεῖς, ἀκούσαντες τὸν λόγον τῆς ἀληθείας, τὸ εὐαγγέλιον τῆς σωτηρίας ὑμῶν, ἐν ᾧ καὶ πιστεύσαντες ἐσφραγίσθητε τῷ Πνεύματι τῆς ἐπαγγελίας τῷ Ἁγίῳ, ¹⁴ὅς ἐστιν ἀρραβὼν τῆς κληρονομίας ἡμῶν, εἰς ἀπολύτρωσιν τῆς περιποιήσεως, εἰς ἔπαινον τῆς δόξης αὐτοῦ.

⁷By whom we have redempcion thorow his blud, that is to saye the forgevenes of synnes, accordynge to the riches of his grace ⁸which grace he shed on us oboundantly in all wisdom, and prudency. ⁹And hath openned unto us the mistery of his will acordynge to his pleasure, and purposed the

same in hymsilfe ¹⁰to have it declared when the tyme were full come, that all thynges, botthe thynges which are in heven, and also the thynges which are in erthe, shulde be gaddered togedder, even in Christ: ¹¹that is to saye in hym in whom we are made heyres, and were therto predestinate accordynge to the purpose of hym which worketh all thinges after the purpose of his owne will, ¹²that we shulde be unto the prayse off his glory, which before hoped in Christ.

¹³In whom also ye (after that ye hearde the worde off trueth, I mean the gospell of youre health, wherin ye beleved) were sealed with that holy sprete of promes, ¹⁴which is the ernest off oure inheritaunce, to redeme the possession purchased unto the laude of his glory.

7 In whom wee have redemption through his blood, the forgivenesse of sinnes, according to the riches of his grace;

8 Wherein hee hath abounded toward us in all wisedome and prudence:

9 Having made knowen unto us the mysterie of his will, according to his good pleasure, which he had purposed in himselfe:

10 That in the dispensation of the fulnesse of times, he might gather together in one all things in Christ, both which are in |†Gr. *the heavens*| heaven, and which are on earth, *even* in him:

11 In whom also we have obteined an inheritance, being predestinated according to the purpose of him who worketh all things after the counsell of his owne will:

12 That we should be to the praise of his glorie, who first |Or, *hoped*| trusted in Christ.

13 In whom ye also *trusted*, after that ye heard the word of trueth, the Gospel of your salvation: in whom also after that yee beleeved, yee were sealed with that holy Spirit of promise,

14 Which is the earnest of our inheritance, untill the redemption of the purchased possession, unto the praise of his glorie.

PAUL'S REQUEST: TRAINEES FOR A LIFEWORK APPRENTICESHIP COUNCIL

¹⁵It is for this reason that, when I heard about your faith in our Commander in Chief, Jesus, and of the self-sacrificial love that you all have for all of His specially selected recruits, ¹⁶I did not stop giving *God* repeated thanks for you all. I also *began to make it my habit* to be *deliberately* mindful *and* intentionally make inquiry about you all in my requests to Him for information and guidance.

¹⁷*First, I began to ask* God, namely the Father of our Commander in Chief, Jesus, the High King *of the future world – Who will preside* at His *inaugural* Appearing – to give you a spirit *that would enable you* to live

ethically competent lives, *and* to unveil *the additional essential information you need to gain* a comprehensive knowledge of Him.

18*The second thing I asked Him was* that He would enlighten the eyes of your hearts, *and that once enlightened,* you would be able to realize what the *unique* hope of His *promising* lifework *project for each one of you* consists.

Third, I asked Him to give you the capability to appreciate and be motivated by the vast extent of the wealth *of the reward of* His inheritance, which He will bequeath to every one of His specially selected recruits *who merit it* at His Appearing.

19*The fourth thing I asked Him to give you was the physical, psychological, emotional and spiritual* strength *He makes especially available* to us who *tenaciously persist in* believing *we can discover and accomplish our lifework for Him. For this quest, I asked Him to give you* the sustained dynamic energy *you will need, even to the superlative degree of matching* the feat achieved by the immense strength 20He demonstrated in the case of our *future* High King when He raised Him out of death and then seated Him at His right hand in the heavens.

21*I know that He has the divine power to help you in this pursuit, because God has appointed Him to the office of having authority* over all *the angelic* regimes and hierarchies of authority, as well as over all *sovereign* powers and leadership offices *established by human governments. His authority* exceeds every authoritative title that has ever been conferred – *whether angelic or human –* not only over *both the good as well as the evil angelic forces and human leadership regimes during* this historical era, but also over *only* the *good human and angelic leadership hierarchies that will be established in the Kingdom* era that is about to come.

22*God* has *not only* made all *such existing authoritative positions of this era subordinate to our Commander in Chief by* placing them under His feet, but *He* has also given Him headship over all *leadership positions* that pertain to His "Lifework" *or* "Kingdom Apprenticeship" Councils. 23*These Councils are* comprised *of the members of His future governmental* "body," *because they are in fact* the fulfilling *agency* of all *the positions that body will eventually consist of, which positions* are *even now* in every way being filled by Him *according to His plan.*

Paul Prays for the Ephesians' Spiritual Perception

15Διὰ τοῦτο κἀγώ, ἀκούσας τὴν καθ' ὑμᾶς πίστιν ἐν τῷ Κυρίῳ Ἰησοῦ καὶ τὴν ἀγάπην τὴν εἰς πάντας τοὺς ἁγίους, 16οὐ παύομαι εὐχαριστῶν ὑπὲρ ὑμῶν, μνείαν ὑμῶν ποιούμενος ἐπὶ τῶν προσευχῶν μου, 17ἵνα ὁ Θεὸς τοῦ Κυρίου ἡμῶν Ἰησοῦ Χριστοῦ, ὁ Πατὴρ τῆς δόξης, δώῃ ὑμῖν πνεῦμα σοφίας καὶ ἀποκαλύψεως ἐν ἐπιγνώσει αὐτοῦ, ¹⁸πεφωτισμένους τοὺς ὀφθαλμοὺς τῆς καρδίας ὑμῶν εἰς τὸ εἰδέναι ὑμᾶς τίς ἐστιν ἡ ἐλπὶς τῆς κλήσεως αὐτοῦ καὶ τίς ὁ πλοῦτος τῆς δόξης τῆς κληρονομίας αὐτοῦ ἐν τοῖς ἁγίοις ¹⁹καὶ τί τὸ ὑπερβάλλον μέγεθος τῆς δυνάμεως αὐτοῦ εἰς ἡμᾶς τοὺς πιστεύοντας κατὰ τὴν ἐνέργειαν τοῦ κράτους τῆς ἰσχύος αὐτοῦ ²⁰ἣν ἐνήργησεν ἐν τῷ Χριστῷ ἐγείρας αὐτὸν ἐκ τῶν νεκρῶν, καὶ ἐκάθισεν ἐν δεξιᾷ αὐτοῦ ἐν τοῖς ἐπουρανίοις ²¹ὑπεράνω πάσης ἀρχῆς καὶ ἐξουσίας καὶ δυνάμεως καὶ κυριότητος καὶ παντὸς ὀνόματος ὀνομαζομένου οὐ μόνον ἐν τῷ αἰῶνι τούτῳ ἀλλὰ καὶ ἐν τῷ μέλλοντι. ²²Καὶ πάντα ὑπέταξεν ὑπὸ τοὺς πόδας αὐτοῦ, καὶ αὐτὸν ἔδωκε κεφαλὴν ὑπὲρ πάντα τῇ ἐκκλησίᾳ, ²³ἥτις ἐστὶ τὸ σῶμα αὐτοῦ, τὸ πλήρωμα τοῦ τὰ πάντα ἐν πᾶσι πληρουμένου.

¹⁵Wherfore even I (after that I hearde of the fayth which ye have in the lorde Jesu, and love unto all the saynctes) ¹⁶cease not to geve thankes for you, makynge mencion off you in my prayers, ¹⁷that the God off oure lorde Jesus Christ, and the father off glory, myght geve unto you the sprete of wisdom, and open to you the knowledge of hymsilfe ¹⁸and lighten the eyes of youre myndes, that ye myght knowe what thynge that hope is, whereunto he hath called you, and howe glorious the riches of his inheritaunce is apon the saynctes, ¹⁹and what is the excedynge greatnes off his power to uswarde, which beleve accordynge to the workynge off that his mighty power, ²⁰which he wrought in Christ, when he raysed hym from deeth, and sett hym on his right honde in hevenly thynges, ²¹above all rule, power, and might, and dominacion, and above all names that are named, nott in this worlde only, but also in the worlde to come. ²²And hath put all thynges under his fete, and hath made hym above all thynges, the heed of the congregacion, ²³which is his body, and the fulnes of hym, that filleth all in all thynges.

15 Wherefore I also, after I heard of your faith in the Lord Jesus, and love unto all the Saints,

16 Cease not to give thankes for you, making mention of you in my prayers,

17 That the God of our Lord Jesus Christ the Father of glorie, may give unto you the spirit of wisedome and revelation |*Or, for the acknowledgment*| in the knowledge of him:

18 The eyes of your understanding being inlightned: that yee may know what is the hope of his calling, and what the riches of the glorie of his inheritance in the Saints:

19 And what *is* the exceeding greatnesse of his power to us-ward who beleeve, according to the working |†*Gr. of the might of his power*| of his mightie power:

20 Which he wrought in Christ when he raised him from the dead, and set him at his owne right hand in the heavenly *places*,

21 Farre above all principalitie, and power, and might, and dominion, and every name that is named, not onely in this world, but also in that which is to come:

22 And hath put all things under his feete, and gave him to be the head over all things to the Church,

23 Which is his body, the fulnesse of him that filleth all in all.

◆───◆

Chapter 2 – Time Travel: Back from the Future

Time Travel: Our True Future Self Must Rescue Our Sidetracked Present Self from this World's Death Traps ♦ *The Ability of Your Future Valiant Self to Rescue Your Present Vile Self is in Reality God's Gift to You* ♦ *Transformation is Composition: You Are God's Masterpiece* ♦ *Mood of the Masterpiece: Forged into a Peacemaker, Not Petrified into Pretentiousness* ♦ *The Purpose of Peacemaking: God's Building of Harmonious Relationships Into Our Eternal Home.*

TIME TRAVEL: OUR TRUE FUTURE SELF MUST RESCUE OUR SIDETRACKED PRESENT SELF FROM THIS WORLD'S DEATH TRAPS

M ost certainly, you all were bound for *a never-ending cycle of suffering a premature physical death as well as final spiritual* death *separated from God* due to *your repeatedly* getting sidetracked, *because of* failing to set or pursue *the right* goals *in life* and *on account of constantly* missing opportunities. ²*You were in this fearful predicament because* at one time, you all deliberately conducted your lives according to the *misguided* philosophical worldview of this *present* era of civilization, namely – the polytheistic hierarchy of gods *who live* in the sky under the authority of the sky-god Zeus.

This spiritual being is in fact the *very same evil* spiritual being *who is now incessantly* working *behind the scenes* among the disobedient sons *of God, i.e., those in the religious power-regime within Judaism, continually* causing them to stir up trouble. ³*The reason I know this is that* we also – all of us – once displayed the *very same* public demeanor that they do now. An *acrimonious* disposition of visceral loathing characterized our conduct, *and* aggravated us to the point of taking deliberate, *persistent and vigorous* action *against others – even to the extent of using violence.*

We were not only motivated utterly by our *visceral revulsion of others,* but also *by irrational hatred of the assumed wrongdoings we supposed were done by everyone else, which in reality was an* attitude *produced entirely within our own* imagination. *The result of this despicable frame of mind was that* we also became *in our deepest* nature exactly like *certain kinds of contemptible* children who are *always* full of anger, just like the rest *of those that now remain in the religious leadership regime within Judaism.*

You Are Saved by Grace Through Faith

2 Καὶ ὑμᾶς ὄντας νεκροὺς τοῖς παραπτώμασι καὶ ταῖς ἁμαρτίαις, ²ἐν αἷς ποτε περιεπατήσατε κατὰ τὸν αἰῶνα τοῦ κόσμου τούτου, κατὰ τὸν ἄρχοντα τῆς ἐχουσίας τοῦ ἀέρος, τοῦ πνεύματος τοῦ νῦν ἐνεργοῦντος ἐν τοῖς υἱοῖς τῆς ἀπειθείας· ³ἐν οἷς καὶ ἡμεῖς πάντες ἀνεστράφημέν ποτε ἐν ταῖς ἐπιθυμίαις τῆς σαρκὸς ἡμῶν, ποιοῦντες τὰ θελήματα τῆς σαρκὸς καὶ τῶν διανοιῶν, καὶ ἦμεν τέκνα φύσει ὀργῆς ὡς καὶ οἱ λοιποί·

The .ij. Chapter.

¹And hath quickened you also that were deedd in treaspasse and synne, ²in the which in tyme passed ye walked, acordynge to the course of this worlde, and after the governer, that ruleth in the ayer, the sprete that worketh in the children off unbelefe, ³amonge the which we also had oure conversacion in tyme past, in the lustes of oure flesshe, and fullfilled the will of the flesshe and of the mynde: and were naturally the children of wrath, even as wel as wother.

CHAP. II.

1 By comparing what we were by 3 nature, with what we are 5 by grace: 10 He declareth, that wee are made for good workes; and 13 beeing brought neere by Christ, should not live as 11 Gentiles, and 12 forreiners in time past, but as 19 citizens with the Saints, and the family of God.

A nd you *hath hee quickned* who were dead in trespasses, and sinnes,
2 Wherein in time past ye walked according to the course of this world, according to the prince of the power of the aire, the spirit that now worketh in the children of disobedience:
3 Among whom also we all had our conversation in times past, in the lusts of our flesh, fulfilling | †Gr. *the wills* | the desires of the flesh, and of the minde, and were by nature the children of wrath, even as others:

◆─────────────────────────────◆

⁴But God, who is "rich" in mercy, *motivated solely* by His *unimaginably* vast love with which He loves us, ⁵even when we were as good as dead *due to our willful persistence* in getting sidetracked, brought us back to life, *such that it is now possible to actually experience and grow in a living relationship with our future High King. You should never be deluded into thinking that your own initiative has brought about the good things you now enjoy in your Christian lives.* Rather, He has rescued all of you *from the precipice of suffering a tragic and untimely death* because of *His* graciousness.

⁶Furthermore, God has raised us up and out of *our own limited frame of reference into a new and living relationship* with Jesus. *Therefore, when we view our lives from this new frame of reference,* He has also made it possible for us to avail ourselves of His wisdom and power to live our renewed lives. *This divine wisdom and ability to transform our present personalities can only come from a relationship in which God has extended us the privilege of being* seated with Jesus, our *future* High King, *as He carries out His present* heavenly *responsibilities to help us and guide us from His Council Chambers* in heaven.

In other words, He has made it possible for our future mature selves, who in reality are already raised and seated with Him, to "travel back in time" – so to speak. In this way, we can transform who we are in our present lives into the mature people we are that are living with Him in what is to us the "future" – from our limited frame of reference; but who in reality we already are – raised and seated with Him – from His eternal frame of reference.

⁷*God has done this for us* in order that He might show us the surpassing riches of His graciousness within our own lifetime and in the lifetime of those who will follow us in upcoming *historical* eras. *He has also done this for us so that He can* demonstrate His goodness to us even more auspiciously *when we are finally physically present* with Jesus *when He returns to this world to become our* High King.

⁴ὁ δὲ Θεός, πλούσιος ὢν ἐν ἐλέει, διὰ τὴν πολλὴν ἀγάπην αὐτοῦ ἣν ἠγάπησεν ἡμᾶς, ⁵καὶ ὄντας ἡμᾶς νεκροὺς τοῖς παραπτώμασι συνεζωοποίησε τῷ Χριστῷ — χάριτί ἐστε σεσωσμένοι — ⁶καὶ συνήγειρε καὶ συνεκάθισεν ἐν τοῖς ἐπουρανίοις ἐν Χριστῷ Ἰησοῦ, ⁷ἵνα ἐνδείξηται ἐν τοῖς αἰῶσι τοῖς ἐπερχομένοις τὸν ὑπερβάλλοντα πλοῦτον τῆς χάριτος αὐτοῦ ἐν χρηστότητι ἐφ' ἡμᾶς ἐν Χριστῷ Ἰησοῦ.

⁴But God which is rich in mercy thorow the greate love wherwith he loved us, ⁵even when we were deed by synne, hath quickened us with Christ (For by grace are ye saved) ⁶and with him hath raysed us uppe, and with hym hath made us sitte in heevenly thynges, thorowe Jesus Christ, ⁷For to shewe in tymes to come the excedynge ryches of his grace, in kyndnes to uswarde, thorowe Christ Jesus.

4 But God who is rich in mercie, for his great love wherewith hee loved us,
5 Even when wee were dead in sinnes, hath quickned us together with Christ, (by grace ye are saved)
6 And hath raised *us* up together, and made *us* sit together in heavenly places in Christ Jesus:

7 That in the ages to come, hee might shew the exceeding riches of his grace, in *his* kindnesse towards us, through Christ Jesus.

THE ABILITY OF YOUR FUTURE VALIANT SELF TO RESCUE YOUR PRESENT VILE SELF IS IN REALITY GOD'S GIFT TO YOU

⁸For this reason, *it is exclusively due to His* graciousness that you all are the ones *(of all people!)* who have been rescued *by Him* because of *your* faith *in Him;* yet this *rescue has in* no way *been brought about* by you *at all. Quite to the contrary,* it is God's gift *to you.* ⁹He has most expressly not *done this* because of *your own* endeavors, in order to *put a stop to the possibility that* anyone might *for any reason suppose they had a right to* brag *that they were somehow able to rescue themselves!*

TRANSFORMATION IS COMPOSITION: YOU ARE GOD'S MASTERPIECES

¹⁰From God's perspective of reality, *it is more accurate to say that* we are His "masterworks," created by our *future* High King, Jesus, for the expressed purpose of *launching* good enterprises. God has *in fact* prepared *these enterprises for us* beforehand, so that we can deliberately conduct our lives from the philosophical perspective *and subsequent expectation that all we have to do is simply step into them.*

⁸Τῇ γὰρ χάριτί ἐστε σεσῳσμένοι διὰ τῆς πίστεως· καὶ τοῦτο οὐκ ἐξ ὑμῶν, Θεοῦ τὸ δῶρον· ⁹οὐκ ἐξ ἔργων, ἵνα μή τις καυχήσηται. ¹⁰Αὐτοῦ γάρ ἐσμεν ποίημα, κτισθέντες ἐν Χριστῷ Ἰησοῦ ἐπὶ ἔργοις ἀγαθοῖς οἷς προητοίμασεν ὁ Θεὸς ἵνα ἐν αὐτοῖς περιπατήσωμεν.

⁸For by grace are ye made safe throwe fayth, and that not off youre selves: For it is the gyfte of God, ⁹and commeth not of workes, lest eny man shulde bost hymsilfe. ¹⁰For we are his worckmanshippe, created in Christ Jesu unto good workes, unto the which god ordeyned us before, that we shulde walke in them.

8 For by grace are ye saved, through faith, and that not of your selves: *it is* the gift of God:

9 Not of workes, lest any man should boast.

10 For wee are his workemanship, created in Christ Jesus unto good workes, which God hath before |*Or, prepared*| ordeined, that we should walke in them.

MOOD OF THE MASTERPIECE: FORGED INTO A PEACEMAKER, NOT PETRIFIED INTO PRETENTIOUSNESS

¹¹*As you come to view yourselves from this new standpoint in which you simply recognize and step into the good enterprises that God has prepared for us, you must continually guard yourselves from pride.* You can do this by keeping in mind that you were once Barbarians by nature. As such, *the leadership regime within Judaism contemptuously* labeled *you all as* "The Uncircumcision," *and then condescendingly* referred *to themselves as* "The Circumcision." *The consequence of twisting religious symbolism in this way was that they* became artificial *and pretentious – narcissists, in fact.* ¹²During that time, *this deluded leadership regime within Judaism* excluded all of you from the *future* High King. They alienated you from citizenship in Israel and *made you* foreigners to the testamentary provisions of *God's* Promissory Agreement *designed to include you.* Because *of their contempt,* you *eventually* became *fixed in a state in which you* were without hope and without God in your lifeworld.

¹³But now you all – who were once extremely remote – have been brought near *to God* by the *future* High King, Jesus, by means of the bloody, *sacrificial death* the the High King *Himself suffered in your place!*

Brought Near by the Blood of Christ

¹¹Διὸ μνημονεύετε ὅτι ὑμεῖς ποτε τὰ ἔθνη ἐν σαρκί — οἱ λεγόμενοι ἀκροβυστία ὑπὸ τῆς λεγομένης περιτομῆς ἐν σαρκὶ χειροποιήτου — ¹²ὅτι ἦτε ἐν τῷ καιρῷ ἐκείνῳ χωρὶς Χριστοῦ, ἀπηλλοτριωμένοι τῆς πολιτείας τοῦ Ἰσραὴλ καὶ ξένοι τῶν διαθηκῶν τῆς ἐπαγγελίας, ἐλπίδα μὴ ἔχοντες καὶ ἄθεοι ἐν τῷ κόσμῳ. ¹³Νυνὶ δὲ ἐν Χριστῷ Ἰησοῦ ὑμεῖς οἵ ποτε ὄντες μακρὰν ἐγγὺς ἐγενήθητε ἐν τῷ αἵματι τοῦ Χριστοῦ.

¹¹Wherfore remember that ye beynge in tyme passed gentyls in the flesshe, and were called uncircumcision off them which are called circumcision in the flesshe, which circumcision is made by hondes: ¹²Remember I saye, that ye were att that tyme with outen Christ, and were reputed aliantes from the commenwelth of Israhel, and were fremed from the testamentes of promes, and had no hope, and were without god in this worlde. ¹³but nowe in Christ Jesu, ye whych a whyle agoo were farre off, are made neye by the bloude off Christ.

11 Wherefore remember that ye *being* in time passed Gentiles in the flesh, who are called uncircumcision by that which is called the Circumcision in the flesh made by hands,
12 That at that time yee were without Christ, being aliens from the common wealth of Israel, and strangers from the covenants of promise, having no hope, and without God in the world.

13 But now in Christ Jesus, ye who sometimes were far off, are made nigh by the blood of Christ.

---

¹⁴⁻¹⁶Therefore, He is our "Peacemaker!" *He is* the One who forged a Unity from both *you depraved Barbarians and the pretentious leadership regime within Judaism.* He effectively demolished the wall of hatred *with* which *that close minded regime* screened out *all foreign ethnic races and nations – namely,* the "Law" of the "Commandments," *which that regime had by that time distorted and* erected into an *overly rigid system* of inflexible dogma.

Jesus "put them out of business" by means of *the sacrificial death of* His own body *on the cross. By His sacrifice,* what God in fact permanently put to death on the cross was *your savage and vicious nature, as well as their narcissism and irrational* hatred. *He did this* so that He might *not only* create by Himself and for Himself one new kind of peace making human being from the two *formerly opposed wicked states of mind, but also* that He might reconcile both *of them* into one *future governmental* body *authentically dedicated* to God.

¹⁷Now that He has come, the *following* good news can be announced: "Peace is *now immediately available* to you all who were *once* far away *from God* as well as to those who are near *to Him*!" ¹⁸Now, through Him, we both have a "freeway" to approach the Father by one Spirit.

Christ Is Our Peace and Cornerstone

¹⁴Αὐτὸς γάρ ἐστιν ἡ εἰρήνη ἡμῶν, ὁ ποιήσας τὰ ἀμφότερα ἓν καὶ τὸ μεσότοιχον τοῦ φραγμοῦ λύσας, ¹⁵τὴν ἔχθραν, ἐν τῇ σαρκὶ αὐτοῦ, τὸν νόμον τῶν ἐντολῶν ἐν δόγμασι καταργήσας, ἵνα τοὺς δύο κτίσῃ ἐν ἑαυτῷ εἰς ἕνα καινὸν ἄνθρωπον, ποιῶν εἰρήνην, ¹⁶καὶ ἀποκαταλλάξῃ τοὺς ἀμφοτέρους ἐν ἑνὶ σώματι τῷ Θεῷ διὰ τοῦ σταυροῦ, ἀποκτείνας τὴν ἔχθραν ἐν αὐτῷ. ¹⁷Καὶ ἐλθὼν εὐηγγελίσατο εἰρήνην ὑμῖν τοῖς μακρὰν καὶ τοῖς ἐγγύς. ¹⁸Ὅτι δι' αὐτοῦ ἔχομεν τὴν προσαγωγὴν οἱ ἀμφότεροι ἐν ἑνὶ Πνεύματι πρὸς τὸν Πατέρα.

¹⁴For he is oure peace, whych hath made off both wone, and hath broken doune the wall in the myddes, that was a stoppe bitwene us, ¹⁵and hath also put awaye thorowe his flesshe, the cause of hatred (thatt is to saye, the lawe of commaundementes contayned in the lawe written) for to make of twayne wone newe man in hymsilfe, so makynge peace: ¹⁶and to reconcile both unto god in one body throwe his crosse, and slewe hattred therby: ¹⁷and cam and preached peace to you which were a farre of, and to them that were neye. ¹⁸For thorowe hym we bothe have an open waye in, in one sprete unto the father.

14 For hee is our peace, who hath made both one, and hath broken downe the middle wall of partition betweene us:

15 Having abolished in his flesh the enmitie, *even* the Lawe of Commandements *conteined* in Ordinances, for to make in himselfe, of twaine, one newe man, so making peace.

16 And that he might reconcile both unto God in one body by the crosse, having slaine the enmitie | *Or, in himselfe* | thereby,

17 And came, and preached peace to you, *which were* afar off, and to them that were nigh.

18 For through him wee both have an accesse by one Spirit unto the Father.

THE PURPOSE OF PEACEMAKING: GOD'S BUILDING OF HARMONIOUS RELATIONSHIPS INTO OUR ETERNAL HOME

[19]The result *of Jesus' accomplishment is that* you all are no longer foreigners and outsiders. Instead, *as His* specially selected recruits, *you are from now on* fellow citizens and *welcome* members to God's home. [20]*You all are among* those who are *in fact* being "built into a home" upon the "foundation" of *God's* High Emissaries and Official Spokespersons – the "Cornerstone" being our *future* High King, Jesus Himself. [21]*Acting in His role as building superintendent, He is* the One upon Whom *God's* entire "home building project" is being built into *an overall* shape of harmonious concord according to our Commander in Chief's logical master plan. *Under His guidance,* it is growing into a very special place *where it becomes possible for all people to authentically meet and come to know God.* [22]*Ultimately, He is* the One upon Whom the Spirit is assembling you all from a wide assortment of originally dissimilar "materials" into a "house" of congruent relationships. *The Spirit's ultimate goal in building this "construction project" of new relationships is to* incorporate *all of you* into becoming an integral part of God's eternal "home."

[19]Ἄρα οὖν οὐκέτι ἐστὲ ξένοι καὶ πάροικοι, ἀλλὰ συμπολῖται τῶν ἁγίων καὶ οἰκεῖοι τοῦ Θεοῦ, [20]ἐποικοδομηθέντες ἐπὶ τῷ θεμελίῳ τῶν ἀποστόλων καὶ προφητῶν, ὄντος ἀκρογωνιαίου αὐτοῦ Ἰησοῦ Χριστοῦ, [21]ἐν ᾧ πᾶσα οἰκοδομὴ συναρμολογουμένη αὔξει εἰς ναὸν ἅγιον ἐν Κυρίῳ, [22]ἐν ᾧ καὶ ὑμεῖς συνοικοδομεῖσθε εἰς κατοικητήριον τοῦ Θεοῦ ἐν Πνεύματι.

[19]Nowe therfore ye are no moare strangers and foreners: but citesyns with the saynctes, and of the housholde of god: [20]and are bilt apon the foundacion of the apostles and prophetes, Jesus Christ beynge the heed cornerstone, [21]in whom every bildynge coupled togedder, groweth unto an

holy temple in the lorde, ²²in whom ye also are bilt togedder, and made an habitacion for god in the sprete.

19 Now therefore yee are no more strangers and forreiners; but fellowcitizens with the Saints, and of the household of God,

20 And are built upon the foundation of the Apostles and Prophets, Jesus Christ himselfe being the chiefe corner stone,

21 In whom all the building fitly framed together, groweth unto an holy Temple in the Lord:

22 In whom you also are builded together for an habitation of God thorow the Spirit.

―――◆―――――――――――――――――――――――――――――――◆―――

Chapter 3 – Recognizing Opportunity: Faith in Him and Love for Others

Never Give In To Despair! Digression – Every Circumstance in History is Actually an Opportunity to Achieve Our Lifework ♦ Never Despair! Digression Continued – A Proper Perspective Changes the Stressful Circumstances We Must All Face Into Opportunities to Benefit Others ♦ No Situation Can Ever Defeat Us Our Lifework if We Have Faith in Him and Selfless Love for Others ♦ Paul Asks Jesus to Appear Spiritually in His Lifework Councils Prior to His Kingdom Arrival to Encourage His Apprentices.

NEVER GIVE IN TO DESPAIR! DIGRESSION – EVERY CIRCUMSTANCE IN HISTORY IS ACTUALLY AN OPPORTUNITY TO ACHIEVE OUR LIFEWORK

I t is for this reason that I, Paul, *have employed the time of my "bondage" here in Rome as an opportunity to compose* the "Bond" *of this Treatise* for the *future* High King Jesus, for the sake of you *former* Barbarians –

²[*I am compelled to digress for a moment in this Treatise to emphasize that* you all have now been fully briefed *on the details comprising* God's gracious *plan to establish His future* governmental administration. *He specifically* gave this *task* to me for you all, ³namely, making you fully aware of *the provisions of His formerly* "Top Secret" Plan. *I have now accurately articulated the provisions of this plan*, which He made known to me by means of *supernatural* revelation, and have concisely delineated its main features above in writing.

⁴*Further, the Treatise I have written above contains the special feature* that, whenever you all intentionally reread *and reexamine its provisions* aloud with the motive of discerning its true meaning, you might be enabled by His Spirit to reacquire a complete understanding of the comprehensive perspective of our *future* High King's "Top Secret" Plan that I myself possess.

⁵*The comprehensive scope of the provisions contained in this divine plan* have never been made known *in the history of the world to the degree that they have* now *been* divinely unveiled to His specially selected High Emissaries and Spokespersons by *His* Spirit.

⁶*These provisions specifically stipulate that all of the* ethnic races and nations foreign to Judaism – whether they are civilized Greeks or uncivilized Barbarians – are to be, *from this point in the history of the world onward, specifically highlighted, recruited and trained to become* fully equal heirs with God's *future* High King Jesus. They are to become co-administrators with *Him in His future governmental* body and equal partners with *Him* of the promises He has made fully available for them to share with Him during the *Kingdom* era *through the opportunity offered them* by this wonderful message.

⁷*Because I have received the commission to deliver this message successfully in all its aspects as His special assignment, I* have become, *in effect, God's* "aide-de-camp," *which I regard as* a gracious gift, granted to me *as a unique directive, duly authorized under the auspices of* His enacted prerogative.

Revelation of the Mystery

3 Τούτου χάριν ἐγὼ Παῦλος, ὁ δέσμιος τοῦ Χριστοῦ Ἰησοῦ ὑπὲρ ὑμῶν τῶν ἐθνῶν — ²εἴ γε ἠκούσατε τὴν οἰκονομίαν τῆς χάριτος τοῦ Θεοῦ τῆς δοθείσης μοι εἰς ὑμᾶς, ³ὅτι κατὰ ἀποκάλυψιν ἐγνώρισέ μοι τὸ μυστήριον, καθὼς προέγραψα ἐν ὀλίγῳ, ⁴πρὸς ὃ δύνασθε ἀναγινώσκοντες νοῆσαι τὴν σύνεσίν μου ἐν τῷ μυστηρίῳ τοῦ Χριστοῦ, ⁵ὃ ἑτέραις γενεαῖς οὐκ ἐγνωρίσθη τοῖς υἱοῖς τῶν ἀνθρώπων, ὡς νῦν ἀπεκαλύφθη τοῖς ἁγίοις ἀποστόλοις αὐτοῦ καὶ προφήταις ἐν Πνεύματι, ⁶εἶναι τὰ ἔθνη συγκληρονόμα καὶ σύσσωμα καὶ συμμέτοχα τῆς ἐπαγγελίας αὐτοῦ ἐν τῷ Χριστῷ διὰ τοῦ εὐαγγελίου, ⁷οὗ ἐγενόμην διάκονος κατὰ τὴν δωρεὰν τῆς χάριτος τοῦ Θεοῦ, τὴν δοθεῖσάν μοι κατὰ τὴν ἐνέργειαν τῆς δυνάμεως αὐτοῦ.

The .iij. Chapter.

¹For this cause I Paul the servaunt of Jesus am in bondes, For youre sakes which are gentyles. ²Yf ye have hearde of the ministracion of the grace of god which is geven me to youwarde: ³For by revelacion shewed he this mistery unto me, as I wrote above in feawe wordes, ⁴wherby, when ye rede ye maye knowe myne understondynge in the ministery of Christ, ⁵which mistery in tymes passed was nott opened unto the sonnes of men as it is nowe declared unto his holy apostles and prophetes by the sprete: ⁶that the gentyls shulde be inheritours also, and of the same body, and partakers off his promis that is in Christ, be the meanes of the gospell, ⁷whereof I am made a minister, by the gyfte of the grace of god geven unto me, after the workynge of his power.

CHAP. III.

5 The hidden mysterie, 6 that the Gentiles should be saved, 3 was made knowen to Paul by revelation: 8 And to him was that grace given, that 9 he should preach it. 13 He desireth them not to faint for his tribulation, 14 and praieth, 19 that they may perceive the great love of Christ toward them.

For this cause I Paul, the prisoner of Jesus Christ for you Gentiles,

2 If ye have heard of the dispensation of the grace of God, which is given me to you-ward:

3 How that by revelation hee made knowen unto me the mysterie, (as I wrote |*Or, a little before*| afore in few words,

4 Whereby when ye reade, ye may understand my knowledge in the mysterie of Christ.)

5 Which in other ages was not made knowen unto the sonnes of men, as it is now reveiled unto his holy Apostles and Prophets by the Spirit,

6 That the Gentiles should be fellow heires, and of the same body, and partakers of his promise in Christ by the Gospel:

7 Whereof I was made a Minister, according to the gift of the grace of God given unto mee, by the effectuall working of his power.

NEVER GIVE IN TO DESPAIR! DIGRESSION CONTINUED – A CORRECT SPIRITUAL PERSPECTIVE TRANSFORMS THE STRESSFUL CIRCUMSTANCES WE MUST ALL FACE INTO DIVINE OPPORTUNITIES TO BENEFIT OTHERS

[8]*God* has given this gracious gift to me – the very least *deserving* of all of His specially selected recruits! *Amazingly, He assigned me the privilege of being the one He specially selected* to announce the wonderful news of the vast and immeasurable riches of the *future* High King to all of the ethnic races or nations *in the entire world* foreign to Judaism, whether they are civilized Greeks or uncivilized Barbarians.

[9]Furthermore, Jesus, the *future* High King *Himself, personally commissioned me* to enlighten everyone concerning *the provisions of His* "Top Secret" Plan, *containing the details* of *His future* governmental administration, which God has been deliberately kept hidden throughout all of recorded history from the beginning of His creation *of the world* until this present era.

[10]God *has waited until this historical era to take this initiative of training human beings to achieve mature* mastery over the multi-faceted ethical and political skills required to live with and lead others effectively. *He will accomplish His divine training program* through the specific agency of His Kingdom Apprenticeship Councils.

This is the first time in history that He has made *His plan* known to the *angelic* regimes and *hierarchies of* authority – *both good and evil* – throughout all of the heavenly realms. ¹¹*God previously made this decision to unveil His "Top Secret" plan at this time in history* according to *His own carefully considered* purposes *and proposals*, which He *first deliberated upon and then* published and enacted from *His* Eternal Council, in *full collaboration, cooperation and concurrence* with the *future* High King, Jesus, our Commander in Chief.

¹²*He is the One* through Whom we *now* have complete freedom of immediate access *to His heavenly Council Chambers* on the "freeway" *He built for us. He built this freeway for us to use in order to approach Him* with the full confidence and assurance *that He will help, guide, teach and enable us to find and accomplish our lifework,* because of His absolute faithfulness and reliability.

¹³And now, *I must resume my reason for writing this Treatise to you all.*] The reason that I, *Paul, am writing this Treatise to you is to* ask – *or rather, to firmly appeal to you all* – that you stop *giving in to* your dispirited mood *and defeatist frame of mind as you think* about the various stresses I am going through. *You can no doubt see by now that God is the One who is in reality orchestrating my circumstances* for your benefit, which you *will fully understand and appreciate at His High King's future* Appearing.

Purpose of the Mystery

⁸Ἐμοὶ τῷ ἐλαχιστοτέρῳ πάντων ἁγίων ἐδόθη ἡ χάρις αὕτη, ἐν τοῖς ἔθνεσιν εὐαγγελίσασθαι τὸν ἀνεξιχνίαστον πλοῦτον τοῦ Χριστοῦ, ⁹καὶ φωτίσαι πάντας τίς ἡ οἰκονομία τοῦ μυστηρίου τοῦ ἀποκεκρυμμένου ἀπὸ τῶν αἰώνων ἐν τῷ Θεῷ τῷ τὰ πάντα κτίσαντι διὰ Ἰησοῦ Χριστοῦ, ¹⁰ἵνα γνωρισθῇ νῦν ταῖς ἀρχαῖς καὶ ταῖς ἐξουσίαις ἐν τοῖς ἐπουρανίοις διὰ τῆς ἐκκλησίας ἡ πολυποίκιλος σοφία τοῦ Θεοῦ, ¹¹κατὰ πρόθεσιν τῶν αἰώνων ἣν ἐποίησεν ἐν Χριστῷ Ἰησοῦ τῷ Κυρίῳ ἡμῶν, ¹²ἐν ᾧ ἔχομεν τὴν παρρησίαν καὶ τὴν προσαγωγὴν ἐν πεποιθήσει διὰ τῆς πίστεως αὐτοῦ. ¹³Διὸ αἰτοῦμαι μὴ ἐκκακεῖν ἐν ταῖς θλίψεσί μου ὑπὲρ ὑμῶν, ἥτις ἐστὶ δόξα ὑμῶν.

⁸Unto me the lest of all sayntes is this grace geven, thatt I shulde preache amonge the gentyls the unsearchable ryches off Christ, ⁹and to geve light to all men, that they myght knowe what is the felyshippe of the mistery, which from the begynnynge of the worlde hath bene hid in God which made all thynges thorowe Jesus Christ, ¹⁰to the intent, that nowe unto the ruelars and powers in heven myght be knowen by the congregacion the manyfolde wisdom of god, ¹¹accordynge to the eternall purpose, which he purposed in Christ Jesu oure lorde, ¹²by whom we are bolde to drawe neye in that trust, whiche we have by fayth on hym.

¹³Wherfore I desire, that ye faynt not because of myne adversities which I suffre for you: which is youre prayse.

8 Unto mee, who am lesse then the least of all Saints, is this grace given, that I should preach among the Gentiles the unsearchable riches of Christ;

9 And to make all men see, what is the fellowship of the mysterie, which from the beginning of the world, hath bene hid in God, who created all things by Jesus Christ:

10 To the intent that now unto the principalities and powers in heavenly places, might be knowen by the church, the manifold wisedome of God,

11 According to the eternall purpose which he purposed in Christ Jesus our Lord:

12 In whom we have boldnesse and accesse, with confidence, by the faith of him.

13 Wherefore I desire that yee faint not at my tribulations for you, which is your glory.

NO SITUATION CAN EVER DEFEAT US IN ACCOMPLISHING OUR LIFEWORK IF WE HAVE FAITH IN HIM AND SELFLESS LOVE FOR OTHERS

¹⁴For *being assigned* this gracious *privilege, I consistently* bend my knees *in gratitude* in front of the Father of our Commander in Chief, Jesus, the *future* High King *of the earth.* ¹⁵*You all must maintain this attitude also, because since He is the One* Who has appointed every hierarchy *of angels* in heaven and every family lineage *of human beings* upon the earth; *He is therefore the One who ultimately controls them all.*

¹⁶ The riches *that He purposes to give you* at His Appearing, *along with the* dynamic *spiritual* ability He will give you *in the deepest part of your psychological and personal* inner self *during this present life,* must *motivate you* to be strengthened, *emboldened and be given confidence* by His Spirit.

¹⁷*In order to strengthen* you *with such confidence, our* High King *is like a divine Explorer, Who is searching for those that have* the faith *in Him to allow Him to* "plant His colony" in their hearts. *Like all Pioneers, His desire is to* "build a settlement" *so that He can* "live" *and* "make His home" *there. His ultimate objective is that you would allow Him to become the* "governor" *of your hearts, having from the very first* been founded and rooted *there according to the principle of* selfless love. ¹⁸*He intends to build His divine* "colony" *in your hearts* in order to stretch you – so that you will reach forward with all your strength until you can grasp, *together* with all of His specially selected recruits, *the magnitude of* the

width and length and height and depth *of His building project of supernatural relationships.*

¹⁹*His purpose in doing this is to enable you* to realize, *experience and express* the selfless love of the High King *in your present lives,* which surpasses knowledge. *His goal is to* fully *shape and strengthen your personality,* so that you *can skillfully put into practice* God's comprehensive *perspective and mature behavior* in any *situation you may encounter.*

Appreciation of the Mystery

¹⁴Τούτου χάριν κάμπτω τὰ γόνατά μου πρὸς τὸν Πατέρα τοῦ Κυρίου ἡμῶν Ἰησοῦ Χριστοῦ, ¹⁵ἐξ οὗ πᾶσα πατριὰ ἐν οὐρανοῖς καὶ ἐπὶ γῆς ὀνομάζεται, ¹⁶ἵνα δώῃ ὑμῖν, κατὰ τὸν πλοῦτον τῆς δόξης αὐτοῦ, δυνάμει κραταιωθῆναι διὰ τοῦ Πνεύματος αὐτοῦ εἰς τὸν ἔσω ἄνθρωπον, ¹⁷κατοικῆσαι τὸν Χριστὸν διὰ τῆς πίστεως ἐν ταῖς καρδίαις ὑμῶν, ἐν ἀγάπῃ ἐρριζωμένοι καὶ τεθεμελιωμένοι, ¹⁸ἵνα ἐξισχύσητε καταλαβέσθαι σὺν πᾶσι τοῖς ἁγίοις τί τὸ πλάτος καὶ μῆκος καὶ βάθος καὶ ὕψος, ¹⁹γνῶναί τε τὴν ὑπερβάλλουσαν τῆς γνώσεως ἀγάπην τοῦ Χριστοῦ, ἵνα πληρωθῆτε εἰς πᾶν τὸ πλήρωμα τοῦ Θεοῦ.

¹⁴For this cause I bowe my knees unto the father of oure lorde Jesus Christ, ¹⁵which is father over all thatt ys called father In heven and in erth, ¹⁶that he wolde graunt you acordynge to the ryches of his glory, thatt ye maye be strenghted with myght by his sprete in the inner man, ¹⁷that Christ maye dwell in youre hertes by fayth, that ye beynge roted and grounded in love, ¹⁸myght be able to comprehende wyth all sayntes, what ys thatt bredth and length, deepth and heyth: ¹⁹and to knowe what is the love off Christ, which love passeth knowledge: that ye might be fulfilled with all manner of fulnes which commeth off God.

14 For this cause I bow my knees unto the Father of our Lord Jesus Christ,

15 Of whom the whole family in heaven and earth is named,

16 That he would grant you according to the riches of his glory, to bee strengthened with might, by his Spirit in the inner man,

17 That Christ may dwell in your hearts by faith, that yee being rooted and grounded in love,

18 May be able to comprehend with all Saints, what *is* the breadth, and length, and depth, and height:

19 And to know the love of Christ, which passeth knowledge, that yee might bee filled with all the fulnesse of God.

EPHESIANS CHAPTER 3 – RECOGNIZING OPPORTUNITY: FAITH IN HIM AND LOVE FOR OTHERS

PAUL ASKS JESUS TO APPEAR SPIRITUALLY IN HIS LIFEWORK COUNCILS PRIOR TO HIS KINGDOM ARRIVAL TO ENCOURAGE HIS APPRENTICES

20Now, *I ask* the One Who is more than capable enough to accomplish exceedingly more than we could ask or think, in accordance with the dynamic *power* with which He energizes us, 21namely, the High King, Jesus *Himself:* May He make Divine Appearances in *His* Lifework Councils in all generations in era after era. *May you* all recognize, heartily agree with and live according to the conclusive truths *of the provisions and promises presented in this Treatise so far, as I have now reached its midpoint.*

20Τῷ δὲ δυναμένῳ ὑπὲρ πάντα ποιῆσαι ὑπερεκπερισσοῦ ὧν αἰτούμεθα ἢ νοοῦμεν, κατὰ τὴν δύναμιν τὴν ἐνεργουμένην ἐν ἡμῖν, 21αὐτῷ ἡ δόξα ἐν τῇ ἐκκλησίᾳ ἐν Χριστῷ Ἰησοῦ εἰς πάσας τὰς γενεὰς τοῦ αἰῶνος τῶν αἰώνων. Ἀμήν.

20Unto hym that ys able to do excedynge aboundantly, above all that we axe or thynke, accordynge to the power thatt worketh in us, 21be prayse in the congregacion by Jesus Christ, thorowe out all generacions from tyme to tyme. Amen.

20 Now unto him that is able to do exceeding abundantly above all that wee aske or thinke, according to the power that worketh in us,
21 Unto him be glory in the Church by Christ Jesus, throughout all ages, world without end. Amen.

◆━━◆

Chapter 4 – "Dressing Up" For Real

Molding Ethnically Diverse Egos into Cohesive Teams with Unit Integrity Requires Limiting Petty, Divisive Attitudes ♦ *Find a Special Ability God Has Given You to Help Others in Their Lifework and in So Doing, Become Mature Yourself* ♦ *"Dress Up" Your Mind in the Newly Outfitted Human Being Created by God, Focused on Finding the Truth in Life* ♦ *Do not Grieve God's Spirit, but Develop Habits that Disarm the Devil's Traps – Lying, Anger, Stealing and Criticism.*

MOLDING ETHNICALLY DIVERSE EGOS INTO COHESIVE TEAMS WITH UNIT INTEGRITY REQUIRES LIMITING PETTY, DIVISIVE ATTITUDES

Therefore, *through* the "Bond" *of this Treatise,* I respectfully request and expect you all to conduct your lives according to the *new* philosophical world view *presented here* in a manner worthy of the lifework to which you have been summoned by our Commander in Chief. 2*You should conduct yourselves towards each other without* condescension, *but rather* with an unassuming nature, with gentleness, *being* tolerant, patient and willing to suffer the emotional pain *that inevitably comes when others misunderstand you, maintaining an attitude of being* a servant-leader, *continually motivated* by self-sacrificial love.

³*Further*, you should strive diligently to guard the unity *intended* by the Spirit through *creating and* maintaining peace, the bond of union, *in your relationships.* ⁴*You should do this because we all realize that there is but* one *future governmental* body and *only* one Spirit *that will guide us all during both eras. He* has summoned each of you with but one single hope *of finding and accomplishing* the lifework of your present apprenticeship, *which leads to* your Millennial appointment.

⁵*Moreover, there is only* one Commander in Chief *and* one *quest to* faithfully *follow Him, depicted symbolically throughout the history of God's people by only* one *solemn, public, initiation ceremony of* being immersed under water. ⁶*In the end, there is only* One God, *Who is* even the Father of all of us – *including Jesus. The Father is therefore the One* Who *has authority* over us all, *Who has chosen to act* through us all, and *Who has assured you that He will always be* with you all.

Walk in Unity

4 Παρακαλῶ οὖν ὑμᾶς ἐγώ, ὁ δέσμιος ἐν Κυρίῳ, ἀξίως περιπατῆσαι τῆς κλήσεως ἧς ἐκλήθητε, ²μετὰ πάσης ταπεινοφροσύνης καὶ πραότητος, μετὰ μακροθυμίας, ἀνεχόμενοι ἀλλήλων ἐν ἀγάπῃ, ³σπουδάζοντες τηρεῖν τὴν ἑνότητα τοῦ Πνεύματος ἐν τῷ συνδέσμῳ τῆς εἰρήνης. ⁴῝Εν σῶμα καὶ ἓν Πνεῦμα, καθὼς καὶ ἐκλήθητε ἐν μιᾷ ἐλπίδι τῆς κλήσεως ὑμῶν· ⁵εἷς Κύριος, μία πίστις, ἓν βάπτισμα, ⁶εἷς Θεὸς καὶ Πατὴρ πάντων, ὁ ἐπὶ πάντων καὶ διὰ πάντων καὶ ἐν πᾶσιν ἡμῖν.

The .iiij. Chapter.

¹I therfore which am in bondes for the lordes sake exhorte you, thatt ye walke worthy off the vocation wherwith ye are called, ²in all humblenes of mynde, and meknes, and longe sufferynge, forbearinge one another thorowe love, ³and that ye be dylygent to kepe the unitie of the sprete in the bonde of peace, ⁴beynge one body, and one sprete, even as ye are called in one hope of youre callynge. ⁵Let ther be but one lorde, one fayth, one baptim: ⁶one god and father of all, which is above all, thorowe all, and in us all.

CHAP. IIII.

1 *He exhortethh to unitie,* 7 *and declareth that God therefore giveth diverse* 11 *gifts unto men, that his Church might be* 13 *edified, and* 16 *growen up in Christ.* 18 *He calleth them from the impuritie of the Gentiles.* 24 *To put on the new man.* 25 *To cast of lying, and* 29 *corrupt communication.*

I therefore the prisoner |*Or, in the Lord*| of the Lord, beseech you that yee walke worthy of the vocation wherewith ye are called,

2 With all lowlinesse and meeknesse, with long suffering, forbearing one another in love.
3 Endevouring to keepe the unitie of the Spirit in the bond of peace.
4 *There is* one body, and one spirit, even as yee are called in one hope of your calling.
5 One Lord, one Faith, one Baptisme,
6 One God and Father of all, who is above all, and through all, and in you all.

FIND A SPECIAL ABILITY GOD HAS GIVEN YOU TO HELP OTHERS IN THEIR LIFEWORK AND IN SO DOING, BECOME MATURE YOURSELF

⁷Therefore, He has given each one of us *the* gracious gift *of a special spiritual power or ability with which He intends for us to accomplish our lifework,* according to the *carefully* measured gifting of the future High King. ⁸That is why it says in Psalm 68:18:

"When He ascended on high, He led captives into captivity,
And gave gifts to human beings."

⁹Now, what else could the notion that "He ascended" imply except that He first must "descend" *from heaven* to the "lower regions," namely, the earth? ¹⁰*The* further *implication is that* the One Who descended is the One who ascended above all the heavens, *Whose objective for doing so could only be* that He might fill all *the administrative positions required for His Kingdom.*

Each Believer Has a Spiritual Gift

⁷Ἑνὶ δὲ ἑκάστῳ ἡμῶν ἐδόθη ἡ χάρις κατὰ τὸ μέτρον τῆς δωρεᾶς τοῦ Χριστοῦ. ⁸Διὸ λέγει,

«Ἀναβὰς εἰς ὕψος ᾐχμαλώτευσεν αἰχμαλωσίαν
Καὶ ἔδωκε δόματα τοῖς ἀνθρώποις.»

⁹Τὸ δὲ «Ἀνέβη,» τί ἐστιν εἰ μὴ ὅτι καὶ κατέβη πρῶτον εἰς τὰ κατώτερα μέρη τῆς γῆς ¹⁰Ὁ καταβάς, αὐτός ἐστι καὶ ὁ ἀναβὰς ὑπεράνω πάντων τῶν οὐρανῶν, ἵνα πληρώσῃ τὰ πάντα.

⁷Unto every one of us is geven grace acordinge to the measure of the gyft of Christ. ⁸wherfore he sayth: He is gone uppe an hye, and hath ledde captivitie captive, and hath geven gyftes unto men. ⁹That he ascended: what meaneth it, butt that he also descended fyrst into the lowest parties of the erth? ¹⁰He that descended, is even the same also that ascended uppe, even above all hevens, to fulfill all thynges.

7 But unto every one of us is given grace, according to the measure of the gift of Christ.

8 Wherefore he saith: *Psal. 68.18.* When he ascended up on high, he led | Or, a multitude of captives | captivitie captive, and gave gifts unto men.

9 (Now that he ascended, what is it but that hee also descended first into the lower parts of the earth:

10 He that descended, is the same also that ascended up far above all heavens, that he might | Or, fulfill | fill all things.)

---

¹¹Therefore, He has given to some *of His specially selected recruits* the *present apprenticeship* office of High Emissary and to others the role of being His Divine Spokespersons. To yet others, *He has given* the commission of being His Messengers of communicating the Good News, while to others the duty and trust of Guardianship over the spiritual well-being of His new recruits. To still others, *He has appointed* the meticulous, careful and painstaking responsibility of being the Teachers of His new recruits.

¹²*He has given us these abilities* in order to equip His specially selected recruits, to enable them to accomplish their own work of service, with the *ultimate* goal of building the *future governmental* body of the High King. ¹³*He will continue to do this* until we all *as a historically collected group* arrive at "unit integrity" – *that is to say, the ability to function interdependently with a seamless team spirit. This team will be capable of operating with full reliance and trust in Him and in each other, and will function with total* reliability, complete awareness, understanding *and mutual appreciation for the experience and intentions* of the Son of God, *which is by definition what it means* to *be* mature human beings.

God's goal for us in leading us through this process is that we should finally arrive at the mature stature of the fully *mature corporate personality He requires,* as measured and determined by our High King Himself. ¹⁴*His objective in effecting this transformation* is that we should no longer be helpless due to our naïveté, continually confused and having our minds spun around in all directions *by others. He wants to make us invulnerable to the kinds of people who pretend to be* teachers, but who are only pirates and swindlers, *whose only purpose is to deceive us into leading lives that are as erratic, unreliable and volatile as a* windstorm. *His purpose is to guard us from falling* into *lifestyles like those of gamblers and* dice players, *who wrongly believe that mere chance guides their lives.*

¹¹Καὶ αὐτὸς ἔδωκε τοὺς μὲν ἀποστόλους, τοὺς δὲ προφήτας, τοὺς δὲ εὐαγγελιστάς, τοὺς δὲ ποιμένας καὶ διδασκάλους, ¹²πρὸς τὸν καταρτισμὸν

Ephesians Chapter 4 – "Dressing Up" For Real

τῶν ἁγίων εἰς ἔργον διακονίας εἰς οἰκοδομὴν τοῦ σώματος τοῦ Χριστοῦ, ¹³μέχρι καταντήσωμεν οἱ πάντες εἰς τὴν ἑνότητα τῆς πίστεως καὶ τῆς ἐπιγνώσεως τοῦ Υἱοῦ τοῦ Θεοῦ, εἰς ἄνδρα τέλειον, εἰς μέτρον ἡλικίας τοῦ πληρώματος τοῦ Χριστοῦ, ¹⁴ἵνα μηκέτι ὦμεν νήπιοι, κλυδωνιζόμενοι καὶ περιφερόμενοι παντὶ ἀνέμῳ τῆς διδασκαλίας, ἐν τῇ κυβείᾳ τῶν ἀνθρώπων, ἐν πανουργίᾳ, πρὸς τὴν μεθοδείαν τῆς πλάνης,

¹¹And the very same, made some Apostles, some prophetes, some Evangelistes, some Shepperdes, some Teachers: ¹²that the sainctes might have all thynges necessary to worke and minister withall, to the edifyinge of the body of Christ, ¹³tyll we everychone (in the unitie of fayth, and knowledge of the sonne of god) growe uppe unto a parfayte man, after the measure of age which is in the fulnes off Christ: ¹⁴Thatt we henceforth be no moare chyldren waverynge and caryed with every wynde of doctryne, by the wylynes of men and craftynes, wherby they laye a wayte for us to deceave us.

11 And he gave some, Apostles; and some, Prophets: and some, evangelists: and some, Pastors, and teachers:

12 For the perfecting of the Saints, for the worke of the ministerie, for the edifying of the body of Christ:

13 Till we all come |*Or, into the unitie*| in the unity of the faith, and of the knowledge of the Son of God; unto a perfect man, unto the measure of the |*Or, age*| stature of the fulnesse of Christ:

14 That we hencefoorth be no more children, tossed to and fro, and carried about with every wind of doctrine, by the sleight of men, *and* cunning craftinesse, whereby they lye in waite to deceive:

◆───◆

¹⁵On the contrary, we must grow up to become like Him – the One Who is heading up *our training program* – in every way; discovering and then speaking what is true, *always motivated* by self-sacrificial love. ¹⁶It is only by means of this self-sacrificial love that the High King is making His *future governmental* body grow into a governmental administration *suited* for Himself *and His purposes.*

By means of this love, He is not only training every member of this body to become a vital part of a rational organization structured to function in harmony as a pleasant and enjoyable whole, *but is* also teaching them to "put it all together" – *to find a sense of meaning and significance in their present lives. They are enabled to do this* by means of every enlightening contact *arranged for them by His Spirit, which He supplies for them* from His vast divine resources, *but only* according to the portion in which He measures out for each one *only exactly what He has* determined *that each one needs.*

¹⁵ἀληθεύοντες δὲ ἐν ἀγάπῃ αὐξήσωμεν εἰς αὐτὸν τὰ πάντα, ὅς ἐστιν ἡ κεφαλή, ὁ Χριστός, ¹⁶ἐξ οὗ πᾶν τὸ σῶμα συναρμολογούμενον καὶ συμβιβαζόμενον διὰ πάσης ἁφῆς τῆς ἐπιχορηγίας, κατ' ἐνέργειαν ἐν μέτρῳ ἑνὸς ἑκάστου μέρους, τὴν αὔξησιν τοῦ σώματος ποιεῖται εἰς οἰκοδομὴν ἑαυτοῦ ἐν ἀγάπῃ.

¹⁵Butt lett us folowe the trueth in love, and in all thynges growe in hym which is the heed, that ys to saye Christ, ¹⁶in whom all the body ys coupled and knet togedder, in every ioynt, wherewith one ministreth to another (acordynge to the operacion as every parte hath his measure) and increaseth the body, unto the edyfyinge of itsilfe in love.

15 But |*Or, being sincere*| speaking the trueth in love, may grow up into him in all things, which is the head, *even* Christ:
16 From whom the whole body fitly ioyned together, and compacted by that which every ioynt supplyeth, according to the effectuall working in the measure of every part, maketh increase of the body, unto the edifying of it selfe in love.

◆─────────────────────────────◆

"DRESS UP" YOUR MIND IN THE NEWLY OUTFITTED HUMAN BEING CREATED BY GOD, FOCUSED ON FINDING THE TRUTH IN LIFE

¹⁷Accordingly, the Commander in Chief *has summoned me* as *His designated and official* lead-witness to make the *following official* announcement *to you all.* You all are no longer to conduct your lives according the philosophical schools of thought of any the rest of the ethnic races or nations of the world – whether they are civilized Greeks or uncivilized Barbarians – who follow those philosophical worldviews with futile purposes in their minds.
¹⁸They continue to become *more and more* darkened in their intentions *through their obstinate refusal to give up their false ways of* thinking, *to the extent that they are now* alienating themselves from the life of God by means of their own willful ignorance and through the callousness of their own hearts. ¹⁹Because they have now sunk into despair on their own, He has given them up to decadence, to every kind of vicious and depraved trade *involved in organized crime and to the never-ending insatiability that always accompanies* greed.
²⁰But you all have not learned this *approach to life* from the *future* High King, ²¹since you have most certainly heard *and obeyed* Him and been taught by Him, it follows that the discovery of the truth in life is by means of Jesus *also*. ²²*Bearing this in mind,* you must "take off and leave outside" your former way of life – *like you would with dirty clothing.* That old way of life is *depressing* – like that of cynical elderly people, who

waste themselves away by tenaciously holding onto the vain belief that they were somehow cheated out of what they only imagined they wanted.

[23]Instead, *discipline* your minds to be *continually* revived by the Spirit. [24]*Like you would with new clothing, adopt the deliberate and daily habit of* "dressing up" the newly outfitted *and refreshing* human being that has been created by God to do what is right and good, totally focused upon the discovery of the truth *for your lives.*

Put on the New Man

[17]Τοῦτο οὖν λέγω καὶ μαρτύρομαι ἐν Κυρίῳ, μηκέτι ὑμᾶς περιπατεῖν καθὼς καὶ τὰ λοιπὰ ἔθνη περιπατεῖ ἐν ματαιότητι τοῦ νοὸς αὐτῶν, [18]ἐσκοτισμένοι τῇ διανοίᾳ, ὄντες ἀπηλλοτριωμένοι τῆς ζωῆς τοῦ Θεοῦ, διὰ τὴν ἄγνοιαν τὴν οὖσαν ἐν αὐτοῖς, διὰ τὴν πώρωσιν τῆς καρδίας αὐτῶν, [19]οἵτινες ἀπηλγηκότες ἑαυτοὺς παρέδωκαν τῇ ἀσελγείᾳ εἰς ἐργασίαν ἀκαθαρσίας πάσης ἐν πλεονεξίᾳ. [20]Ὑμεῖς δὲ οὐχ οὕτως ἐμάθετε τὸν Χριστόν, [21]εἴ γε αὐτὸν ἠκούσατε καὶ ἐν αὐτῷ ἐδιδάχθητε, καθώς ἐστιν ἀλήθεια ἐν τῷ Ἰησοῦ, [22]ἀποθέσθαι ὑμᾶς, κατὰ τὴν προτέραν ἀναστροφήν, τὸν παλαιὸν ἄνθρωπον τὸν φθειρόμενον κατὰ τὰς ἐπιθυμίας τῆς ἀπάτης, [23]ἀνανεοῦσθαι δὲ τῷ πνεύματι τοῦ νοὸς ὑμῶν, [24]καὶ ἐνδύσασθαι τὸν καινὸν ἄνθρωπον τὸν κατὰ Θεὸν κτισθέντα ἐν δικαιοσύνῃ καὶ ὁσιότητι τῆς ἀληθείας.

[17]This I saye herfore, and testifie in the lorde, that ye henceforth walke not as wother gentyls walke, in vanities off their mynde, [18]blynded in their understondynge, beynge straungers from the lyfe which is in god, thorowe the ignorancy that is in them, because of the blyndnes off their hertes: [19]which beynge past repentaunce have geven themselves unto wantannes, to worke all manner of unclennes even with gredynes. [20]But ye have not so learned Christ, [21]Yf so be ye have hearde off hym, and are taught in hym, even as the trueth is in Jesu: [22]so as concernynge the conversacion in tyme past, laye from you that olde man, which is corrupte thorowe the deceavable lustes, [23]and be ye renued in the sprete off youre myndes, [24]and put on that newe man, which after a godly wyse, is shapen in ryghtewesnes, and true holynes.

17 This I say therefore and testifie in the Lord, that yee henceforth walke not as other Gentiles walke in the vanitie of their minde,

18 Having the understanding darkened, being alienated from the life of God, through the ignorance that is in them, because of the |*Or, hardnesse*| blindnesse of their heart:

19 Who being past feeling, have given themselves over unto lasciviousnesse, to worke all uncleannesse with greedinesse.

20 But ye have not so learned Christ:

21 If so be that ye have heard him, and have bene taught by him, as the trueth is in Jesus,

22 That yee put off concerning the former conversation, the olde man, which is corrupt according to the deceitful lusts:
23 And bee renewed in the spirit of your minde:
24 And that yee put on that new man, which after God is created in righteousnesse, and | *Or, holines of trueth* | true holinesse.

DO NOT GRIEVE GOD'S SPIRIT, BUT DEVELOP HABITS THAT DISARM THE DEVIL'S TRAPS – LYING, ANGER, STEALING AND CRITICISM

²⁵First of all then, having "taken off and left outside" *the "dirty clothing" of* falsehood, "you all must tell the truth – each one of you with your fellow human beings" *(Zechariah 8:16),* because we are members of each other.

²⁶*Second, learn to* "Be angry, yet do not *allow unchecked anger to cause you to* fall short of your goals" *(Psalm 4:4). Rather, in the same way that God commands* the sun to set *at the close of every day,* so you must also *consciously* prevent yourselves from harboring the exasperations *of your day.* ²⁷Neither should you *by failing to do so* permit the "Slanderer" – the Devil – an opportunity *to get you sidetracked.*

²⁸*Third,* he who is a thief, *mooch or con artist* must stop stealing any more, but rather strive to put his own hands to some *kind of* laborious but worthwhile occupation. *As he does this,* he should save up some resources so that he might be able to give or pay a portion of his earnings to those who might have need *of temporary assistance – or preferably – provide them with jobs himself.*

Do Not Grieve the Spirit of God

²⁵Διὸ ἀποθέμενοι τὸ ψεῦδος, «λαλεῖτε ἀλήθειαν ἕκαστος μετὰ τοῦ πλησίον αὐτοῦ,» ὅτι ἐσμὲν ἀλλήλων μέλη. ²⁶«Ὀργίζεσθε καὶ μὴ ἁμαρτάνετε»· ὁ ἥλιος μὴ ἐπιδυέτω ἐπὶ τῷ παροργισμῷ ὑμῶν, ²⁷μηδὲ δίδοτε τόπον τῷ διαβόλῳ. ²⁸Ὁ κλέπτων μηκέτι κλεπτέτω, μᾶλλον δὲ κοπιάτω, ἐργαζόμενος τὸ ἀγαθὸν ταῖς χερσίν, ἵνα ἔχῃ μεταδιδόναι τῷ χρείαν ἔχοντι.

²⁵Wherfore putt awaye lyinge, and speake every man truth unto his neghbour, for as moche as we are members one off another. ²⁶Be angry, but synne nott: lett not the sonne goo doune apon your wrathe, ²⁷geve no place unto the backbyter, ²⁸let hym that stole steale no moare, but let hym rather laboure with his hondes some good thinge, that he maye have to geve unto hym that nedeth.

25 Wherefore putting away lying, speake every man truth with his neighbour: for we are members one of another.
26 Be ye angry, and sinne not, let not the Sunne go down upon your wrath:

EPHESIANS CHAPTER 4 – "DRESSING UP" FOR REAL   311

27   Neither give place to the devill.

28   Let him that stole, steal no more: but rather let him labour, working with *his* handes the thing which is good, that he may have |*Or, to distribute*| to give to him that needeth.

❖―――――――――――――――――――――――――――❖

²⁹*Fourth,* you all must stop every rotten word from *inadvertently* spewing out of your mouth. Instead, speak only good, constructive *things that are* useful *and help* to build stable and lasting relationships, with the purpose of contributing *comments and suggestions* that will graciously benefit those who hear what you say.

³⁰Furthermore, you all must stop grieving the Specially Selecting Spirit of God, by Whom you have been *officially* "sealed" for the Day of "Redemption." ³¹*Rather,* you must *learn to* clear away every *form of* bitterness, *harbored* anger, *resentment*, rage, shouting and blasphemy *from your lives, along* with every *other kind of* evil outburst. ³²Instead, you must all become *effective in providing the most* beneficial *outcomes* for each other, being compassionate and gracious to each other, in exactly the same way that God, by means of the *future* High King's *example*, has been gracious to you all.

²⁹Πᾶς λόγος σαπρὸς ἐκ τοῦ στόματος ὑμῶν μὴ ἐκπορευέσθω, ἀλλ᾽ εἴ τις ἀγαθὸς πρὸς οἰκοδομὴν τῆς χρείας, ἵνα δῷ χάριν τοῖς ἀκούουσι. ³⁰Καὶ μὴ λυπεῖτε τὸ Πνεῦμα τὸ Ἅγιον τοῦ Θεοῦ, ἐν ᾧ ἐσφραγίσθητε εἰς ἡμέραν ἀπολυτρώσεως. ³¹Πᾶσα πικρία καὶ θυμὸς καὶ ὀργὴ καὶ κραυγὴ καὶ βλασφημία ἀρθήτω ἀφ᾽ ὑμῶν, σὺν πάσῃ κακίᾳ. ³²Γίνεσθε δὲ εἰς ἀλλήλους χρηστοί, εὔσπλαγχνοι, χαριζόμενοι ἑαυτοῖς, καθὼς καὶ ὁ Θεὸς ἐν Χριστῷ ἐχαρίσατο ἡμῖν.

²⁹Let no filthy comunicacion procede out of youre mouthes: butt thatt whych is good to edefye withall, when nede ys: that it maye have faveour with the heares. ³⁰And greve not the holy sprete off God, by whome ye are sealed unto the daye of redempcion. ³¹Let all bitternes, fearsnes and wrath, rorynge and cursyd speakynge, be put awaye from you, with all maliciousnes. ³²be ye courteouse one to another, and mercifull forgevynge one another, even as God for Christes sake forgave you.

29   Let no corrupt communication proceede out of your mouth, but that which is good |*Or, to edifie profitably*| to the use of edifying, that it may minister grace unto the hearers.

30   And grieve not the holy Spirit of God, whereby yee are sealed unto the day of redemption.

31   Let all bitternes, and wrath, and anger, and clamour, and evil speaking, be put away from you, with all malice,

32   And bee ye kinde one to another. tender hearted, forgiving one another, even as God for Christs sake hath forgiven you.

Chapter 5 – Actor of Love, Follower of Light, Master of Ethical Skill

Live as an "Actor" Portraying the "Role" of God in Your Life, Whose Main "Character" Trait is Self-Sacrificial Love ♦ *Be a Leader that Pursues the Light of Truth in Public – With Vulnerability, Mercy, Learning and Consistency* ♦ *Master Ethically Skillful Disciplines in Life's Relationships – Instead of Going Along With Mindless, Unethical Traditions* ♦ *Genuinely Bond with Your Spouse by Graciously Offering Yourselves to Each Other in a Spirit of Giving and Sacrifice.*

LIVE AS AN "ACTOR" PORTRAYING THE "ROLE" OF GOD IN YOUR LIFE, WHOSE MAIN "CHARACTER" TRAIT IS SELF-SACRIFICIAL LOVE

T *hird,* you must all *proceed on* to become "actors" *that portray the "role"* of God *in your lives. When you imitate God as an actor would portray a character in this way, you will experience* the same *thing* that only-children *often do. After they have been raised in an atmosphere* of love *and contentment, they frequently go on to imitate their parents' gracious way of life.* ²*You can do this especially* by conducting your lives according to a new philosophical world view based on self-sacrificial love, in exactly the same way that the future High King loved us and surrendered Himself for us as a sacrificial offering to God. *God treasured His sacrifice for us in an analgous way to the way we sometimes feel when we are powerfully gripped into reliving a vivid memory of sorrow mixed with gratitude of a special person's sacrifice of themselves for us, when we re-experience* the smell of a *familiar* frangrance *with which they were always associated.*

³⁻⁴Therefore, precisely because this kind of *selfless love is the only form of love that* is fitting for *His* specially selected recruits, you all must stop believing in and practicing the *following false forms of so-called "true love:"* engaging in sexual intercourse before or outside of marriage; every form of sexually dirty or filthy – and therefore unhealthy – practice, *whether in the body or in the soul*; erroneously thinking you can "love" material objects, which is nothing but greed; all sexually perverse and violent practices *that degrade and injure the other person as well as yourself*; holding to old foolish superstitious beliefs *that misrepresent God's true nature as one of pettiness or partiality*; or the use of insolent humor to belittle others in public. *All of these false views of so-called "true love"* are wrong. *The simple test for the appropriate kind of love is*

the kind of loving behavior which anyone would consider worthy of gratitude.

⁵You all know *it to be obviously true* that every one who is a licentious sex addict, or is filthy *in body or in mind*, or is a greedy miser – who *in reality* is an idolater – *cannot be trusted and therefore* will not be given any part of God's inheritance in the *Millennial* Kingdom by the *future* High King, who is God *Himself.*

Walk in Love

5 Γίνεσθε οὖν μιμηταὶ τοῦ Θεοῦ, ὡς τέκνα ἀγαπητά, ²καὶ περιπατεῖτε ἐν ἀγάπῃ, καθὼς καὶ ὁ Χριστὸς ἠγάπησεν ἡμᾶς καὶ παρέδωκεν ἑαυτὸν ὑπὲρ ἡμῶν προσφορὰν καὶ θυσίαν τῷ Θεῷ εἰς ὀσμὴν εὐωδίας. ³Πορνεία δὲ καὶ πᾶσα ἀκαθαρσία ἢ πλεονεξία μηδὲ ὀνομαζέσθω ἐν ὑμῖν, καθὼς πρέπει ἁγίοις, ⁴καὶ αἰσχρότης καὶ μωρολογία ἢ εὐτραπελία, τὰ οὐκ ἀνήκοντα, ἀλλὰ μᾶλλον εὐχαριστία. ⁵Τοῦτο γάρ ἐστε γινώσκοντες ὅτι πᾶς πόρνος ἢ ἀκάθαρτος ἢ πλεονέκτης, ὅς ἐστιν εἰδωλολάτρης, οὐκ ἔχει κληρονομίαν ἐν τῇ βασιλείᾳ τοῦ Χριστοῦ καὶ Θεοῦ.

The .v. Chapter.

¹Be ye counterfeters of god as dere children, ²and walke in love even as Christ loved us, and gave hymsilfe for us, an offerynge and a sacrifyce of a swete saver to god. ³So that fornicicion, and all unclennes, or coveteousnes, be not once, named amonge you, as it becommeth saynctes: ⁴nether filthynes nether folishe talkyng, nether gestinge, which are not comly: but rather gevynge of thankes. ⁵For this ye knowe, that no whormonger, other unclene person, or coveteous person, (which is the worshipper off ymages) hath eny inheritaunce in the kyngdom of Christ, and of god.

CHAP. V.

2 *After generall exhortations, to love, 3 to flie fornication, 4 and all uncleannesse, 7 not to converse with the wicked, 15 to walke warily, and to be 18 filled with the spirit, 22 he descendeth to the particular dueties, how wives ought to obey their husbands, 25 and husbands ought to love their wives, 32 even as Christ doth his Church.*

Be ye therefore followers of God, as deare children.
2 And walke in love, as Christ also hath loved us, and hath given himselfe for us, an offering and a sacrifice to God for a sweet smelling savour:

3 But fornication and all uncleannesse, or covetousnesse, let it not be once named amongst you, as becommeth Saints:

4 Neither filthinesse, nor foolish talking, nor iesting, which are not convenient: but rather giving of thankes.

5 For this ye know, that no whoremonger, nor uncleane person, nor covetous man who is an idolater, hath any inheritance in the kingdome of Christ, and of God.

---

⁶You must stop being deceived by the empty claims *of these false world views*. *In fact,* it was by *gradually giving in to* these *false world views* that God became angry with His disobedient sons, *namely, those in the leadership regime within Judaism who persist in that religion after they have heard and rejected the good news about Jesus.*
⁷Therefore, you all must *also* stop *giving in when you are pressured to* enter into partnerships with *people who stubbornly persist in staying immoral or unethical,* ⁸because *although* you all used to live in the darkness *of stubborn ignorance yourselves, you have now been freed from all that* by the Commander in Chief, *so that you can enjoy a life of* enlightened *happiness.*

⁶Μηδεὶς ὑμᾶς ἀπατάτω κενοῖς λόγοις, διὰ ταῦτα γὰρ ἔρχεται ἡ ὀργὴ τοῦ Θεοῦ ἐπὶ τοὺς υἱοὺς τῆς ἀπειθείας. ⁷Μὴ οὖν γίνεσθε συμμέτοχοι αὐτῶν. ⁸Ἦτε γάρ ποτε σκότος, νῦν δὲ φῶς ἐν Κυρίῳ.

⁶Lett no man deceave you with vayne wordes. For thorow soche thynges commeth the wrath off God upon the chyldren of unbelefe. ⁷Be not therfore companions with them. ⁸Ye were once dercknes, but are nowe light in the lorde.

6 Let no man deceive you with vaine words: for because of these things commeth the wrath of God upon the children of |Or, unbeliefe| disobedience.
7 Bee not yee therefore partakers with them.
8 For yee were sometimes darkenesse, but now *are ye* light in the Lord:

BE A LEADER THAT PURSUES THE LIGHT OF TRUTH IN PUBLIC – WITH VULNERABILITY, MERCY, LEARNING AND CONSISTENCY

Fourth, you must all adopt a philosophy of life in which you conduct yourselves *in the same way that* young people *who are seriously pursuing an education normally do – committed to the* enlightened *spirit of living a public life of vulnerability, mercy, learning and consistency.* ⁹*You must do so* because *by living in this way,* the Spirit *of God* will bring about the fruitful *results of every form of* goodness, justice and the discovery of truth. ¹⁰*The additional benefit of these attributes is that by them* you will become qualified by our Commander in Chief for *future* office, *because by adopting them you will earn* His distinguished confidence.

EPHESIANS CHAPTER 5 – ACTOR OF LOVE, FOLLOWER OF LIGHT, MASTER OF ETHICAL SKILL   315

¹¹You all must no longer be shareholders with those who practice *the darkness of fearful or stubborn ignorance* and *suffer* the *tragic consequences of that way of life*, but instead, you must confront *people who are like this*. ¹²It is disgraceful to merely gossip in secret about the *evil* things *such people* practice among themselves. ¹³Instead, when all such *evil* things are challenged *and refuted* by being brought to light *in public, it is only then that* they are made clearly known *and resolved properly. Further, it is only* those whose evil is brought to the light *of being publicly, justly and mercifully resolved* that can be enlightened *themselves*. ¹⁴This is the real *meaning of the theme found in the writings of the Isaiah, God's Spokesman, where* he says *in effect,* "Wake up, you who have fallen asleep at the wheel! Take an exit off of your *dark, dead-end road*, and the High King will illuminate the way for you!"

Walk in Light

Ὡς τέκνα φωτὸς περιπατεῖτε – ⁹ὁ γὰρ καρπὸς τοῦ Πνεύματος ἐν πάσῃ ἀγαθωσύνῃ καὶ δικαιοσύνῃ καὶ ἀληθείᾳ – ¹⁰δοκιμάζοντες τί ἐστιν εὐάρεστον τῷ Κυρίῳ. ¹¹Καὶ μὴ συγκοινωνεῖτε τοῖς ἔργοις τοῖς ἀκάρποις τοῦ σκότους, μᾶλλον δὲ καὶ ἐλέγχετε. ¹²Τὰ γὰρ κρυφῇ γινόμενα ὑπ᾽ αὐτῶν αἰσχρόν ἐστι καὶ λέγειν. ¹³Τὰ δὲ πάντα ἐλεγχόμενα ὑπὸ τοῦ φωτὸς φανεροῦται, πᾶν γὰρ τὸ φανερούμενον φῶς ἐστι. ¹⁴Διὸ λέγει,

Ἔγειρε, ὁ καθεύδων,
Καὶ ἀνάστα ἐκ τῶν νεκρῶν,
Καὶ ἐπιφαύσει σοι ὁ Χριστός."

Walke as Children of light. ⁹For the frute of the sprete is, in all goodnes, rightewesnes, and trueth. ¹⁰Accept thatt which is pleasynge to the lorde: ¹¹and have no fellishippe with the unfrutfull workes of dercknes: butt rather rebuke them. ¹²For it is shame even to name those thynges which are done of them in secrete: ¹³but all thinges when they are rebuked of the light, are manifest. For whatsoever is manifest, that same is light. ¹⁴Wherfore he sayth: awake thou that slepest, and stond up from deeth, and Christ shall geve the light.

    Walk as children of light,
9 (For the fruite of the spirit is in all goodnesse and righteousnesse and trueth.)
10 Proving what is acceptable unto the Lord:
11 And have no fellowship with the unfruitfull workes of darknesse, but rather reprove them.
12 For it is a shame even to speake of those things which are done of them in secret.
13 But all things that are |Or, discovered| reprooved, are made manifest by the light: for whatsoever doth make manifest, is light.

14 Wherefore hee saith: *Esai.60,1*. Awake thou that sleepest, and arise from the dead, and Christ shall give thee light.

◆───◆

MASTER ETHICALLY SKILLFUL DISCIPLINES IN LIFE'S RELATIONSHIPS – INSTEAD OF GOING ALONG WITH MINDLESS, UNETHICAL TRADITIONS

[15]Therefore, see to it that you conduct your lives according to the new philosophical world view *set forth in this Treatise, by* accurately *incorporating its specific principles into every aspect of your lives,* no longer *living* in ethically unskillful ways, but *only* in ethically skillful ways. [16]*The way to accomplish this consistently is to* "buy out" *every possible* opportunity *you can find to do good,* because the days *left in this era* will be *characterized by much* evil. [17]Accordingly, you must all choke down your pride as you decide to bring your senseless habits to an end, and instead find out and pay attention to whatever the will of the Commander in Chief *is.*

[18]*As you would do with all of the good things that God provides in life, learn to drink alcoholic beverages graciously, as an expression of your enjoyment of life. You can only do this with self-control and by* bringing an end *to the futile habit of* drinking alcohol excessively, which *only* ends up wasting *the valuable time that God also gives you to use.* Fill *your lives* instead with *the skills you need to be gracious and stay focused* spiritually.

[19]*One good way to stay spiritually focused is to learn* to sing, either by singing songs accompanied by musical instruments, or by *singing other kinds of* hymns and spiritual songs or choruses to each other *and with each other.* Sing and play music enthusiastically and with all your heart, as you would for our Commander in Chief.

[20]*In whatever you do, the key element in remaining spiritually focused is to always be gracious to others and* grateful to God in every situation, because *He is our* Father, and on account of the example provided by our Commander in Chief, Jesus, the High King. [21]*Always* show deference, *offering help and giving unselfishly* to each other out of respect for our High King.

Walk in Wisdom

[15]Βλέπετε οὖν πῶς ἀκριβῶς περιπατεῖτε, μὴ ὡς ἄσοφοι, ἀλλ᾽ ὡς σοφοί, [16]ἐξαγοραζόμενοι τὸν καιρόν, ὅτι αἱ ἡμέραι πονηραί εἰσι. [17]Διὰ τοῦτο μὴ γίνεσθε ἄφρονες, ἀλλὰ συνιέντες τί τὸ θέλημα τοῦ Κυρίου. [18]Καὶ μὴ μεθύσκεσθε οἴνῳ, ἐν ᾧ ἐστιν ἀσωτία, ἀλλὰ πληροῦσθε ἐν Πνεύματι, [19]λαλοῦντες ἑαυτοῖς ψαλμοῖς καὶ ὕμνοις καὶ ᾠδαῖς πνευματικαῖς, ᾄδοντες καὶ ψάλλοντες ἐν τῇ καρδίᾳ ὑμῶν τῷ Κυρίῳ, [20]εὐχαριστοῦντες πάντοτε

ὑπὲρ πάντων ἐν ὀνόματι τοῦ Κυρίου ἡμῶν Ἰησοῦ Χριστοῦ τῷ Θεῷ καὶ Πατρί, ²¹ὑποτασσόμενοι ἀλλήλοις ἐν φόβῳ Θεοῦ.

¹⁵Take hede therfore that ye walke circumspectly: not as foles: but as wyse, ¹⁶redemynge the tyme: for the dayes are evyll: ¹⁷wherfore, be ye nott unwyse, but understonde what the will of the lorde is, ¹⁸and be not dronke with wyne, wherin is excesse: but be fulfilled with the sprete, ¹⁹speakynge unto youreselves in psalmes, and ymmes, and spretuall songes, syngynge and playinge to the lorde in youre hertes, ²⁰gevynge thankes allways for all thynges in the name of oure lorde Jesu Christ to god the father: ²¹submittynge youreselves one to another in the feare of god.

15 See then that yee walke circumspectly, not as fooles, but as wise,
16 Redeming the time, because the dayes are evill.
17 Wherefore be ye not unwise, but understanding what the will of the Lord is.
18 And bee not drunke with wine, wherein is excesse: but bee filled with the Spirit:
19 Speaking to your selves, in Psalms, and Hymns, and Spirituall songs, singing and making melodie in your heart to the Lord,
20 Giving thankes alwayes for all things unto God, and the Father, in the Name of our Lord Jesus Christ,
21 Submitting your selves one to another in the feare of God.

◆━━━◆

GENUINELY BOND WITH YOUR SPOUSE BY OFFERING YOURSELVES TO EACH OTHER IN A GRACIOUS SPIRIT OF TRUST, GIVING AND SACRIFICE

²²Wives, *in your marriages,* adopt *a cheerful and gracious attitude of* deference, *offering* to help your husbands *find their lifework. You should enjoy doing this with him, trusting him and supporting his efforts in a pleasant and agreeable way, with the same positive frame of mind* as *you would whenever you warmly and gladly assist others* for the sake of our Commander in Chief. ²³*Do this* because *our* High King *has given* the husband *the responsibility* to head up *the leadership role between himself and* his wife in the same way that *God has given Jesus the leadership role in* heading up *the relationship between Himself and* His Lifework Councils. *Just as Jesus has the responsibility of being* the Liberator of that *future governmental* body, *so also God wants your relationship with your husband to be a liberating experience in your life.*

²⁴Therefore, in the same way that His Kingdom Apprenticeship Councils *should work together to offer their services* to their future High King in following *His initiatives to lead their members to find and accomplish their lifework,* so you should also in your role as wives offer yourselves to your own husbands in *the variety of life* events that *will*

occur in your marriage relationship – so that God may employ your augmented power as a couple to enhance and amplify your unique lifework as a woman.

Husbands and Wives Depict Christ and the Church

²²Αἱ γυναῖκες, τοῖς ἰδίοις ἀνδράσιν ὑποτάσσεσθε, ὡς τῷ Κυρίῳ, ²³ὅτι ἀνήρ ἐστι κεφαλὴ τῆς γυναικὸς ὡς καὶ ὁ Χριστὸς κεφαλὴ τῆς ἐκκλησίας, καὶ αὐτός ἐστι Σωτὴρ τοῦ σώματος. ²⁴Ἀλλ' ὥσπερ ἡ ἐκκλησία ὑποτάσσεται τῷ Χριστῷ, οὕτω καὶ αἱ γυναῖκες τοῖς ἰδίοις ἀνδράσιν ἐν παντί.

²²Wemen submit youreselves unto youre awne husbandes, as unto the lorde: ²³For the husbande is the wyves heed, even as Christ is the heed off the congregacion, and the same is the saveoure off the body. ²⁴Therfore as the congregacion is in subieccion to Christ, lykwyse let the wyves be in subieccion to their husbandes in all thinges.

22 Wives, submit your selves unto your own husbands, as unto the Lord.

23 For the husband is the head of the wife, even as Christ is the head of the Church: and he is the saviour of the body.

24 Therefore as the Church is subject unto Christ, so let the wives *bee* to their owne husbands in every thing.

---

²⁵Husbands, *in your marriage,* love your wife *by generously* giving her yourself *instead of things.* Put her best interests first with a gracious and gentle disposition, and sacrifice your own ambitions instead of her. Do this for her in the same *pleasant and good-natured* way that our High King sacrificed Himself for *and continues to selflessly love those who are His specially selected recruits in* His Lifework Apprenticeship Councils.

²⁶*He does this* in order that He might get us ready for His special use, by means of "cleansing *her* in a bath of water," *in the same way a shepherd prepares his specially selected and most precious sheep. One specific way in which you husbands can continually "cleanse" your relationship with your wife is to take the initiative to start and lead conversations with her in gracious, loving, well thought-out and positive ways. Wives (or any other human beings for that matter) are never motivated by sarcastic comments or cynical remarks, no matter to what degree those comments may be grounded in what you sincerely believe to be right in your own mind as their husbands. You must do this in the same way that our Commander in Chief did when He set a good example for us as our Teacher during His first visit, always* initiating dialogue *with*

people, but also carefully choosing his spoken words *with the intention of helping others or training His apprentices to be prepared and ready.*

27*Moreover,* His spoken words *that were written down by them will* continue to be employed by His Spirit to prepare His specially selected recruits throughout the upcoming era, so that He might officially present her, namely, *His historically prepared and completed* Kingdom Apprenticeship Councils, to Himself *at His own Inauguration Day. On that Day, His well chosen and persuasive speech will have accomplished its fully cleansing effect,* having removed from her any spot, stain or wrinkle or any such other defect *of moral impurity.* She will have become cleansed by obeying His *gracious* spoken words, so that she can be uniquely special and morally blameless.

25Οἱ ἄνδρες, ἀγαπᾶτε τὰς γυναῖκας ἑαυτῶν, καθὼς καὶ ὁ Χριστὸς ἠγάπησε τὴν ἐκκλησίαν καὶ ἑαυτὸν παρέδωκεν ὑπὲρ αὐτῆς, 26ἵνα αὐτὴν ἁγιάσῃ, καθαρίσας τῷ λουτρῷ τοῦ ὕδατος ἐν ῥήματι, 27ἵνα παραστήσῃ αὐτὴν ἑαυτῷ ἔνδοξον τὴν ἐκκλησίαν, μὴ ἔχουσαν σπίλον ἢ ῥυτίδα ἤ τι τῶν τοιούτων, ἀλλ' ἵνα ᾖ ἁγία καὶ ἄμωμος.

25Husbandes love youre wyves, even as Christ loved the congregacion, and gave himsilfe for it, 26to sanctifie it, and clensed it in the fountayne of water thorowe the worde, 27to make it unto hymselfe, a glorious congregacion withoute spot, or wrynckle, or eny soche thynge: but that it shulde be holy and without blame.

25 Husbands, love your wives, even as Christ also loved the Church, and gave himselfe for it:
26 That he might sanctifie and cleanse *it* with the washing of water, by the word,
27 That hee might present it to himselfe a glorious Church, not having spot or wrinkle, or any such thing: but that it should bee holy and without blemish.

28It is for this reason that you husbands ought to *be the ones who* take loving initiatives *in your relationship* with your wives in the same way that you do in caring for the health of your own bodies. He who loves his own wife loves himself, 29because nobody ever *normally* hates *or neglects* the health of his own physical body, but rather cultivates and cares for it, in precisely the same way that our Commander in Chief *cares for* His Kingdom Apprenticeship Councils. 30*He takes the initiative to care for us in this way* because He *is training us to become* the special members of His *future governmental* body.

In fact, He regards us with the same intimacy that He wanted Adam to have for Eve, when He *"made her* out of his flesh and out of his bones." *What I mean by using this metaphor from Genesis is that God intends you husbands to cultivate in yourselves the same realization that Adam had when he woke up to discover that God intended him to have a unique, special and intimate relationship with Eve because God had made her out of the very flesh and bones He had drawn from Adam's own chest.* ³¹*This is why God says in Genesis 2:24 that* "A man shall leave his father and mother, in exchange for *this new relationship of marriage,* namely – that he shall bond to his wife such that both *of them come to* exist in a relational manner *so intimately close that it is* as *if they are* one being."

³²*Guided by God's graciousness, living out the relationship of marriage in a spiritually accurate way can be one of the most fulfilling ways in which God accomplishes His* "Top Secret" *plan in your life as husbands,* because as I explained above, *it is so similar to the foundational relationship* upon which the High King will establish *His own relational structure with His* Kingdom Apprenticeship Councils.

³³In summary, for each of you *who are husbands,* one of the single most important *relationships God is watching and measuring closely is how you conduct your relationship with your wife;* You should love your wife as yourself. For *those of* you *who are* wives, *one of the single most important relationships God is watching and measuring closely is your relationship with your husband;* You should respect your husband.

²⁸Οὕτως ὀφείλουσιν οἱ ἄνδρες ἀγαπᾶν τὰς ἑαυτῶν γυναῖκας ὡς τὰ ἑαυτῶν σώματα. Ὁ ἀγαπῶν τὴν ἑαυτοῦ γυναῖκα ἑαυτὸν ἀγαπᾷ. ²⁹Οὐδεὶς γάρ ποτε τὴν ἑαυτοῦ σάρκα ἐμίσησεν, ἀλλ' ἐκτρέφει καὶ θάλπει αὐτήν, καθὼς καὶ ὁ Κύριος τὴν ἐκκλησίαν. ³⁰Ὅτι μέλη ἐσμὲν τοῦ σώματος αὐτοῦ, ἐκ τῆς σαρκὸς αὐτοῦ καὶ ἐκ τῶν ὀστέων αὐτοῦ. ³¹«Ἀντὶ τούτου καταλείψει ἄνθρωπος τὸν πατέρα αὐτοῦ καὶ τὴν μητέρα, καὶ προσκολληθήσεται πρὸς τὴν γυναῖκα αὐτοῦ, καὶ ἔσονται οἱ δύο εἰς σάρκα μίαν.» ³²Τὸ μυστήριον τοῦτο μέγα ἐστίν, ἐγὼ δὲ λέγω εἰς Χριστὸν καὶ εἰς τὴν ἐκκλησίαν. ³³Πλὴν καὶ ὑμεῖς οἱ καθ' ἕνα, ἕκαστος τὴν ἑαυτοῦ γυναῖκα οὕτως ἀγαπάτω ὡς ἑαυτόν, ἡ δὲ γυνὴ ἵνα φοβῆται τὸν ἄνδρα.

²⁸So ought men to love their wyves, as their awne bodies. He that loveth his wyfe, loveth hymsylfe. ²⁹For no man ever yet, hated his awne flesshe: Butt norysshith, and cherisith itt: even as the lorde doth the congregacion: ³⁰for we ar members of hys body, off his flesshe, and of his bones. ³¹For this cause shall a man leave father and mother, and shall continue with hys wyfe, and two shalbe made one flesshe. ³²This is a grett secrete, but I speake bitwene Christ and the congregacion. ³³Neverthelesse do ye so that every one off you love hys wyfe truely even as hymsylfe. And lett the wyfe se that she feare her husbande.

28 So ought men to love their wives, as their owne bodies: hee that loveth his wife, loveth himselfe.

29 For no man ever yet hated his owne flesh: but nourisheth and cherisheth it, even as the Lord the Church:

30 For we are members of his body, of his flesh, and of his bones.

31 For this cause shall a man leave his father and mother, and shall be ioyned unto his wife, and they two shalbe one flesh.

32 This is a great mysterie: but I speake concerning Christ and the Church.

33 Nevertheless, let every one of you in particular, so love his wife even as himself, and the wife *see* that she reverence her husband.

Chapter 6 – Career Spiritual Soldiers

Initiate the Skill of Parenting in the Life of Your Family in Gracious, Spiritually Accurate Ways ♦ *Perform Your Vocation, Employment, Occupation, Profession or Career in Spiritually Accurate Ways* ♦ *You Can Prevail Over the Evil Spiritual Forces that Will Attack You in Your Efforts to Be Peacemakers for God Only by Becoming Career Spiritual Soldiers* ♦ *Strap on The "Sword-Belt" of Discovering Truth, Put On The "Body Armor" of Justice and Lace Up The "Special Forces Boots" for the Long March Required to Be a Peacemaker for God* ♦ *Protect Yourself with the "Shield" of Faith, Put on the "Helmet" of Rescue to Conquer Your Fear of Leadership and Wield The "Sword" of God's Spoken Words Guided by His Spirit* ♦ *Maintain an Effective "Command and Control" System of Disciplined Direct Communication with God* ♦ *Select Friends and Messengers Who Have a Positive, Loving Contented, Cheerful, Faithful and Encouraging Attitude* ♦ *May the Graciousness of Your Immortal Kingdom Persona Come to Distinguish Your Mortal Personality Also*

INITIATE THE SKILL OF PARENTING IN THE LIFE OF YOUR FAMILY IN GRACIOUS, SPIRITUALLY ACCURATE WAYS

Children, obey your parents as *you would* the Commander in Chief, because this is *the* right *thing for you to do.* ²*The fifth command of the main Ten Commands of God's Law – recorded in both Exodus 20:12 as well as in Deuteronomy 5:16 – says:* "You must honor your father and mother." *This is* the first command *of the Ten that comes* with *the* promise *of a reward, namely,* ³"in order that *your life* would go well for you and that you might live a long time in *God's Promised* Land,'" which in reality is the Millennial Kingdom.

⁴*Not only should you children be obedient to your parents, but you* fathers must also break youselves *of your tendency to* provoke your children to anger *by ignoring them or by dismissing them with a few careless words or critical remarks. As I mentioned above, children (or any*

other human beings for that matter) are never motivated by sarcastic comments or cynical remarks, no matter to what degree those comments may be grounded in what you sincerely believe to be right in your own mind as their fathers. Instead, *set a good example yourselves and* cultivate them in *following the example of* our Commander in Chief. *In the same way that he taught His own apprentices, you must with the same gracious manner and demeanor proactively initiate well planned conversations with your children, making it your goal to* patiently educate *them,* warn them of danger *and think through how you should reprimand them when necessary – before you do it.*

Filial Honor and Fatherly Nurture

6 Τὰ τέκνα, ὑπακούετε τοῖς γονεῦσιν ὑμῶν ἐν Κυρίῳ, τοῦτο γάρ ἐστι δίκαιον. ²«Τίμα τὸν πατέρα σου καὶ τὴν μητέρα,» ἥτις ἐστὶν ἐντολὴ πρώτη ἐν ἐπαγγελίᾳ, ³«ἵνα εὖ σοι γένηται καὶ ἔσῃ μακροχρόνιος ἐπὶ τῆς γῆς.» ⁴Καὶ οἱ πατέρες, μὴ παροργίζετε τὰ τέκνα ὑμῶν, ἀλλ' ἐκτρέφετε αὐτὰ ἐν παιδείᾳ καὶ νουθεσίᾳ Κυρίου.

The .vj. Chapter.

¹Chyldren obey youre fathers and mothers in the lorde: for so is it right. ²Honoure father and mother, that is the fyrst commaundement that hath eny promes, ³that thou mayst be in goode estate, and lyve longe on the erthe. ⁴Fathers, move not youre chyldren to wrath: butt brynge them uppe with the norter and informacion off the lorde.

CHAP. VI.

1 *The duetie of children towards their parents,* 5 *Of servants towards their masters.* 10 *Our life is a warfare,* 12 *Not onely against flesh and blood, but also spiritual enemies.* 13 *The complete armor of a Christian,* 18 *and how it ought to be used.* 21 *Tychicus is comended.*

Children, obey your parents in the Lord: for this is right. 2 Honour thy father and mother, (which is the first commandement with promise,)

3 That it may bee well with thee, and thou maiest live long on the earth.

4 And *yee* fathers, provoke not your children to wrath: but bring them up in the nourture and admonition of the Lord.

◆─────────────────────────────◆

PERFORM YOUR VOCATION, EMPLOYMENT, OCCUPATION, PROFESSION OR CAREER IN SPIRITUALLY ACCURATE WAYS

⁵*To those of you who are* employees or subordinate officers, I would say this: You must obey your employers, managers or superior officers in whatever business, enterprise, or branch of the civil or military service in

which you are presently working, with an attitude of respect, dedication and sincerity of heart, as *you would* to the High King. ⁶Stop *the bad habit of* attending to your duties only when you are being watched, like sycophants or brownnosers *do*. Instead, perform *your profession or occupation* with *the dedication of all* your soul, exactly like you would if you were an employee or subordinate officer of the High King Himself, since *you now realize that your present vocation, whatever it is*, forms *an integral part of* God's plan *for building your lifework.*

⁷*Approach doing your job* with the same good mind-set that you would have if the Commander in Chief *Himself was your boss or superior officer* instead of your actual human *superiors*. ⁸*You should develop this consistent frame of mind toward your vocational relationships since* you now realize that when any of you does a good job *in their present vocational life – whatever it is – for the Commander in Chief,* that person will receive *the reward of a good job* from the Commander in Chief *during the Kingdom era, regardless of even* whether they were a slave or a free *person during their mortal lives.*

Servants, Masters, and the Master

⁵Οἱ δοῦλοι, ὑπακούετε τοῖς κυρίοις κατὰ σάρκα μετὰ φόβου καὶ τρόμου, ἐν ἁπλότητι τῆς καρδίας ὑμῶν, ὡς τῷ Χριστῷ, ⁶μὴ κατ' ὀφθαλμοδουλείαν ὡς ἀνθρωπάρεσκοι, ἀλλ' ὡς δοῦλοι τοῦ Χριστοῦ ποιοῦντες τὸ θέλημα τοῦ Θεοῦ ἐκ ψυχῆς, ⁷μετ' εὐνοίας δουλεύοντες ὡς τῷ Κυρίῳ καὶ οὐκ ἀνθρώποις, ⁸εἰδότες ὅτι ἐάν τι ἕκαστος ποιήσῃ ἀγαθόν, τοῦτο κομιεῖται παρὰ τοῦ Κυρίου, εἴτε δοῦλος εἴτε ἐλεύθερος.

⁵Servauntes be obedient unto youre carnall masters, with feare and trymblynge, in synglenes of youre hertes, as unto Christ: ⁶not with service in the eyesight as men pleasars: butt as the servauntes of Christ, doynge the wyll off god from the herte ⁷with good will, even as though ye served the lorde, and not men. ⁸And remember that whatsoever good thynge eny man doeth, thatt shall he receave agayne off the lorde, whether he be bonde or fre.

5 Servants, bee obedient to them that are your masters according to the flesh, with feare and trembling, in singlenesse of your heart, as unto Christ:

6 Not with eye service as menpleasers, but as the servants of Christ, doing the will of God from the heart:

7 With good will doing service, as to the Lord, and not to men:

8 Knowing that whatsoever good thing any man doeth, the same shall he receive of the Lord, whether he be bond or free.

⁹*To those of you who are* leaders, *whether you are employers or superior officers in the civil or military service,* I would say this: You must also perform *your responsibilities* with the same *good mind-set* towards your subordinates. Give up *the bad habit most leaders fall into of using fear to motivate their subordinates* by threatening or intimidating them. You should do this because you now realize that you have the same Commander in Chief in Heaven that they do, and that because He is completely impartial, *you will not be able to use your rank or office to gain any kind of favorable treatment when He evaluates your own lives and leadership skills.*

⁹Καὶ οἱ κύριοι, τὰ αὐτὰ ποιεῖτε πρὸς αὐτούς, ἀνιέντες τὴν ἀπειλήν, εἰδότες ὅτι καὶ ὑμῶν αὐτῶν ὁ Κύριός ἐστιν ἐν οὐρανοῖς, καὶ προσωποληψία οὐκ ἔστι παρ' αὐτῷ.

⁹and ye masters, do even the same thynges unto them, puttynge awaye threatenynges: and remember thatt even youre master also is in heven, nether is ther eny respecte off persone with hym.

9 And ye masters, do the same things unto them, |*Or, moderating*| forbearing threatning: knowing that |*Some reade, both your, and their master*| your master also is in heaven, neither is there respect of persons with him.

♦―――――――――――――――――――――――――――――――――――――♦

YOU CAN PREVAIL OVER THE EVIL SPIRITUAL FORCES THAT WILL ATTACK YOU IN YOUR EFFORTS TO BE PEACEMAKERS FOR GOD ONLY BY BECOMING CAREER SPIRITUAL SOLDIERS

¹⁰Finally, my dear colleagues, *I must bring this Treatise to a conclusion by alerting you that* you must *continually* strengthen yourselves *spiritually. You must make a habit of doing this by constantly availing yourselves of the* Commander in Chief's aid, and of His mastery of the angelic military forces He can and will employ to assist you *in your quest to discover and accomplish your lifework.* ¹¹Equip yourselves with the *spiritual* "body armor," together with its complement of personal weaponry, *supplied to you* by God. *You must do this* in order to become strong enough to stand up to the various plots and schemes of the "Predator" – the Devil – *to entrap you and destroy your lives. In fact, you must make the decision to become career "spiritual" soldiers.*

¹²*You must do this* because ultimately, the conflicts *we must all face in our lives* are not *actually* against 'flesh and blood' *human beings,* but *are in reality* against the *evil angelic* regimes, against the *evil angelic hierarchies of* authority and against the *evil human* government regimes that control this present historical era of darkness – *or more accurately –*

against the evil *hierarchy of* spiritual beings *that live* in the sky (i.e., the atmosphere of the earth), *which in fact manipulate and control those regimes.*

¹³For this reason, you all must *equip yourselves* by taking up and putting on the full spiritual "body armor" and spiritual "military weapons" *provided* by God, in order that He may make you strong enough to endure this historical era during which *limited authority to control and shape events has been temporarily granted* to the Evil One. *By doing so,* you will be able to accomplish *your lifework* completely, and prevail *over him.*

Put on the Panoply of God

¹⁰Τὸ λοιπόν, ἀδελφοί μου, ἐνδυναμοῦσθε ἐν Κυρίῳ καὶ ἐν τῷ κράτει τῆς ἰσχύος αὐτοῦ. ¹¹Ἐνδύσασθε τὴν πανοπλίαν τοῦ Θεοῦ πρὸς τὸ δύνασθαι ὑμᾶς στῆναι πρὸς τὰς μεθοδείας τοῦ διαβόλου. ¹²Ὅτι οὐκ ἔστιν ἡμῖν ἡ πάλη πρὸς αἷμα καὶ σάρκα, ἀλλὰ πρὸς τὰς ἀρχάς, πρὸς τὰς ἐξουσίας, πρὸς τοὺς κοσμοκράτορας τοῦ σκότους τοῦ αἰῶνος τούτου, πρὸς τὰ πνευματικὰ τῆς πονηρίας ἐν τοῖς ἐπουρανίοις. ¹³Διὰ τοῦτο ἀναλάβετε τὴν πανοπλίαν τοῦ Θεοῦ, ἵνα δυνηθῆτε ἀντιστῆναι ἐν τῇ ἡμέρᾳ τῇ πονηρᾷ, καὶ ἅπαντα κατεργασάμενοι στῆναι.

¹⁰Finally, my brethren be stronge in the lorde, and in the power of his myght. ¹¹Put on the armour of god, that ye maye stonde stedfast agaynst the crafty assautes off the devyll. ¹²For we wrestle not agaynst flesshe and bloud: but agaynst rule, agaynst power, and agaynst worldy ruelars of the darcknes of this worlde, agaynst spretuall wickednes in hevenly thynges.

¹³For this cause take unto you the armoure off god, that ye maye be able to resist in the evyll daye, and to stonde perfect in all thinges.

10 Finally, my brethren, be strong in the Lord, and in the power of his might.
11 Put on the whole armour of God, that ye may be able to stand against the wiles of the devill.
12 For wee wrestle not against flesh and blood, but against principalities, against powers, against the rulers of the darknes of this world, against |Or, wicked spirits| spiritual wickedness in |Or, heavenly| high places.
13 Wherefore take unto you the whole armour of God, that yee may be able to withstand in the evill day, and |Or, having overcome all| having done all, to stand.

STRAP ON THE "SWORD-BELT" OF DISCOVERING TRUTH, PUT ON THE "BODY ARMOR" OF JUSTICE AND LACE UP THE "SPECIAL FORCES BOOTS" FOR THE LONG MARCH REQUIRED TO BE A PEACEMAKER FOR GOD

¹⁴You must therefore equip yourselves to never give up by *first* putting around yourselves the "sword-belt" of *the commitment to always discover the* truth – *especially what is true in your own life – followed* by putting on the "body armor" of *being dedicated* to do not only what is legally right, but also ethically right.

¹⁵Moreover, be sure you lace up the "military boots" of peace tightly on your feet. *You must mentally* prepare *yourselves for the fact that your life will resemble a long and oftentimes frustrating and tedious march that will be required* to achieve *God's ultimate objective of* bringing *His* good news *into people's lives. The goal of His good news is ultimately to enable people to forgive each other, reconcile with each other and to make living in* peacefulness *with each other available to people who have formerly lived in hatred and conflict their entire lives.*

¹⁴Στῆτε οὖν περιζωσάμενοι τὴν ὀσφὺν ὑμῶν ἐν ἀληθείᾳ, καὶ ἐνδυσάμενοι τὸν θώρακα τῆς δικαιοσύνης, ¹⁵καὶ ὑποδησάμενοι τοὺς πόδας ἐν ἑτοιμασίᾳ τοῦ εὐαγγελίου τῆς εἰρήνης,

¹⁴Stonde therfore and youre loynes gyrd aboute with veritie, havynge on the brestplate of rightewesnes, ¹⁵and shood with shewes prepared by the gospell of peace.

14 Stand therefore, having your loynes girt about with trueth, and having on the breast-plate of righteousnesse:
15 And your feete shod with the preparation of the Gospel of peace.

PROTECT YOURSELF WITH THE "SHIELD" OF FAITH, PUT ON THE "HELMET" OF RESCUE TO CONQUER YOUR FEAR OF LEADERSHIP AND WIELD THE "SWORD" OF GOD'S SPOKEN WORDS GUIDED BY HIS SPIRIT

¹⁶Above all, you must all raise up the "shield" of faith, by which you all, *acting together,* will be able to extinguish all of the flaming arrow volleys of *enticement and temptation to do what is morally wrong that will be incessantly launched* by the Evil One *against your power to make ethical decisions.*

¹⁷In addition, you must put on the "helmet" of rescue *to give you the assurance that God will protect you from attacks on your life and from the fears and blackmail that will inevitably come against you in your role of spiritual leadership.*

EPHESIANS CHAPTER 6 – CAREER SPIRITUAL SOLDIERS

Finally, you must pick up and and become trained in the discipline of wielding the "sword" of the Spirit, which involves *gaining experience and eventual mastery of the skillful and appropriate use of* the spoken word of God.

[16]ἐπὶ πᾶσιν ἀναλαβόντες τὸν θυρεὸν τῆς πίστεως, ἐν ᾧ δυνήσεσθε πάντα τὰ βέλη τοῦ πονηροῦ τὰ πεπυρωμένα σβέσαι· [17]καὶ τὴν περικεφαλαίαν τοῦ σωτηρίου δέξασθαι, καὶ τὴν μάχαιραν τοῦ Πνεύματος, ὅ ἐστι ῥῆμα Θεοῦ,

[16]Above all take to you the shelde of fayth, wherwith ye maye quenche all the fyrie dartes of the wicked. [17]and take the helmet of heelth, and the swearde of the sprete, which is the worde of god,

16 Above all, taking the shielde of faith, wherewith yee shall bee able to quench all the fierie darts of the wicked.

17 And take the helmet of salvation, and the sword of the Spirit, which is the word of God:

◆───◆

MAINTAIN AN EFFECTIVE "COMMAND AND CONTROL" SYSTEM OF DISCIPLINED DIRECT COMMUNICATION WITH GOD

[18]You must always maintain direct communication *with God* – both by means of respectful requests for information and perspective *from Him*, as well as by lobbying, petitioning and making official appeals *to Him to act in your own behalf and in behalf your colleagues.* In your communications with God, *allow yourself to become sensitive to being* directed by the Spirit, *who will* always *guide you* with an appropriate sense of proportion, focus you upon what is truly important, lead you to genuine opportunities, enable you to sift out in what is relevant and be sensitive to what time and people you should invest your efforts in, who you should cooperate with, what consequences you should expect, and in what instances you should act – on *occasion* even to the point of spending sleepless nights in vigilant communication *with God,* watching with all diligent devotion in accordance with the lobbying, petitions and applications which concern *the best interests of* all of His specially selected recruits.

[19]I would also ask you to make requests *to God and lobby Him for His favor* in my behalf also, in order that He might give *me good reasoning, sound and persuasive logical arguments, and that I might use the right* words whenever I open my mouth *to speak in public,* that I may do so openly and freely, in order that I might continue to make known *God's* former "Top Secret" plan, namely, the marvelous news *of His Kingdom-Inheritance to others.* [20]*I ask you to do this because I need His help especially now,* in my confinement, in order that with Him, I would be able

to speak as a true ambassador should; freely, openly and with with courage and conviction, as it is necessary for me to speak.

¹⁸διὰ πάσης προσευχῆς καὶ δεήσεως προσευχόμενοι ἐν παντὶ καιρῷ ἐν Πνεύματι, καὶ εἰς αὐτὸ τοῦτο ἀγρυπνοῦντες ἐν πάσῃ προσκαρτερήσει καὶ δεήσει περὶ πάντων τῶν ἁγίων, ¹⁹καὶ ὑπὲρ ἐμοῦ, ἵνα μοι δοθῇ λόγος ἐν ἀνοίξει τοῦ στόματός μου ἐν παρρησίᾳ γνωρίσαι τὸ μυστήριον τοῦ εὐαγγελίου ²⁰ὑπὲρ οὗ πρεσβεύω ἐν ἁλύσει, ἵνα ἐν αὐτῷ παρρησιάσωμαι ὡς δεῖ με λαλῆσαι.

¹⁸and praye allwayes with all maner prayer and supplicacion: and that in the sprete: and watch therunto with all instance and supplicacion for all saynctes, ¹⁹and for me, that uttraunce maye be geven unto me, that I maye open my mought boldly, to utter the secretes of the gospell, ²⁰whereof I am a messenger in bondes, that therin I maye speake frely, as it becommeth me to speake.

18 Praying alwayes with all prayer and supplication in the spirit, and watching thereunto with all perseverance, and supplication for all Saints,

19 And for mee, that utterance may be given unto me, that I may open my mouth boldly, to make knowen the mysterie of the Gospel:

20 For which I am an ambassador | Or, in a chaine | in bonds, that | Or, thereof | therein I may speake boldly, as I ought to speake.

◆━━━━━━━━━━━━━━━━━━━━━━━━━━━━━━━━━━━━━━━◆

SELECT FRIENDS AND MESSENGERS WHO HAVE A POSITIVE, LOVING CONTENTED, CHEERFUL, FAITHFUL AND ENCOURAGING ATTITUDE

²¹⁻²²And now, in order that you all might be made aware of *how* things *are going* concerning me – specifically, how I am managing *and getting along* – Tychicus, my esteemed colleague and faithful envoy in *all assignments given him by our* Commander in Chief, will bring you all up-to-date *about my affairs. I am sending* him to you all *along with this Treatise* for the following purpose, *namely*, in order that you may know how things are going with us and that he might encourage your hearts, *because he is such a positive, loving, contented, cheerful and positive person.*

Paul's Greeting of Grace

²¹Ἵνα δὲ εἰδῆτε καὶ ὑμεῖς τὰ κατ' ἐμέ, τί πράσσω, πάντα ὑμῖν γνωρίσει Τυχικὸς ὁ ἀγαπητὸς ἀδελφὸς καὶ πιστὸς διάκονος ἐν Κυρίῳ, ²²ὃν ἔπεμψα πρὸς ὑμᾶς εἰς αὐτὸ τοῦτο, ἵνα γνῶτε τὰ περὶ ἡμῶν καὶ παρακαλέσῃ τὰς καρδίας ὑμῶν.

²¹But that ye maye also knowe what condicion I am in, and what I do, Tichicus my deare brother and faythfull minister in the lorde, shall shewe

EPHESIANS CHAPTER 6 – CAREER SPIRITUAL SOLDIERS 329

you off all thynges, ²²whom I sent unto you for the same purpose, that ye myght knowe what case I stonde in, and that he myght comfort youre hertes.

21 But that yee also may know my affaires, *and* how I doe, Tychicus a beloved brother, and faithfull minister in the Lord, shall make knowen to you all things.

22 Whom I have sent unto you for the same purpose, that yee might know our affaires, and that he might comfort your hearts.

MAY THE GRACIOUSNESS OF YOUR IMMORTAL KINGDOM PERSONA COME TO DISTINGUISH YOUR MORTAL PERSONALITY ALSO

²³My desire for you all, my *dear and loyal* colleagues, is that your lives would be characterized by peacefulness and selfless love, together with faithfulness – *all of which will come* from God the Father and our Commander in Chief Jesus, the *future* High King. ²⁴*May* the graciousness of our Commander in Chief Jesus, the *future* High King, *be* with *you in your present lives – Who will ultimately be with* all *of His dear and loyal colleagues* in immortality. *May you* all recognize, heartily agree with and live according *to the truths I have written to you in this, my final and conclusive Treatise.*

²³Εἰρήνη τοῖς ἀδελφοῖς καὶ ἀγάπη μετὰ πίστεως ἀπὸ Θεοῦ Πατρὸς καὶ Κυρίου Ἰησοῦ Χριστοῦ. ²⁴Ἡ χάρις μετὰ πάντων τῶν ἀγαπώντων τὸν Κύριον ἡμῶν Ἰησοῦν Χριστὸν ἐν ἀφθαρσίᾳ. Ἀμήν.

²³Peace be with the brethren, and love with fayth from god the father, and from the lorde Jesu Christ. ²⁴Grace be with all them which love oure lorde Jesus Christ in puernes. Amen. Sent from Rome unto the Ephesyans by Tichicus.

23 Peace *be* to the brethren, and love, with faith from God the Father, and the Lord Jesus Christ.

24 Grace be with all them that love our Lord Jesus Christ |*Or, with incorruption*| in sincerity. Amen.

Written from Rome unto the Ephesians by Tychicus.

Notes to Basic Explanatory Translation
with
Greek Text,
Tyndale's Version (1526)
and
King James Version (1611)

[1] *Wikipedia Encyclopedia*, en.wikipedia.org/wiki/Bible#Chapters_and_verses. See extended historical note on Stephen Langton at Eph. 1:1 of Extended and Interpretive Expositional Translation (from a biography of Stephen Langton by Martin F. Tupper written in 1858 – see Bibliography).

[2] *Wikipedia Encyclopedia*, en.wikipedia.org/wiki/Robert_Estienne (and see note below).

[3] *Hapanta ta tés kainés diathékés. Nouum Iesu Christi D. N. Testamentum. Cum duplici interpretatione, D. Erasmi, & Veteris interpretis: Harmonia item Euangelica, & copioso Indice.* [Geneva]: Robert Estienne, 1551. This edition was the first New Testament to divide the text into the verses we use today. It consists of two Latin texts in parallel columns on either side of Erasmus' Greek text. An excellent photographic image of the first two pages of the Gospel of John from this text can be viewed at the following webpage:

http://www.smu.edu/bridwell/publications/ryrie_catalog/xi_3.htm.

From *Formatting the Word of God: the Charles Caldwell Ryrie collection*: 1998 (see Bibliography).

[4] *The Nevve Testament of our Lord Iesus Christ. Conferred diligently with the Greke, and best approued translations.* Geneva: Conrad Badius, 1557. This edition was the first English version of the New Testament to be published with verse divisions placed into the text that we use today. An excellent photographic image of the first page of the Epistle to the Philippians from this text can be viewed at the following webpage:

http://www.smu.edu/bridwell/publications/ryrie_catalog/xi_4.htm.

From *Formatting the Word of God: the Charles Caldwell Ryrie collection*: 1998 (see Bibliography).

[5] *The Greek New Testament According to the Majority Text, 2nd Edition.* Hodges, Z. C., Farstad, A. L., & Dunkin, W. C. (see Bibliography). The development of the Greek Text is briefly traced as follows:

EPHESIANS – INTRODUCTORY NOTES AND LEGEND 331

The Original Manuscript

The original manuscript of Paul's Treatise was written in continuous Greek prose, using only uncial (capital) letters, with no accent marks or spaces between the words. The text shown to the right is an example of such a text. It is the Greek translation of Esther 2:3–8 from the Codex Sinaiticus, written in the late fourth or early fifth century (source: Plate XXII. The S.S. Teacher's Edition: The Holy Bible. New York: Henry Frowde, Publisher to the University of Oxford, 1896; from the Wikimedia Commons website*).

For example, Paul's original manuscript of Eph. 1:1–14 probably looked something like the uncial manuscript shown below (this text is a computer font facsimile of the script shown at right – which would have been similar in appearance to the common uncial Greek letters used during the time Paul wrote his original treatise – computer font "Sinaiticus," developed by Ralph Hancock**).

In order to get an idea of just how difficult it can be to translate this text into contemporary professional American English, the reader should keep in mind that after Paul's initial greeting in verses 1–2, all of what we recognize today as verses 3–14 is *one Greek sentence:*

---

*   http:// commons.wikimedia.org/wiki/Image:Codex_sinaticus.jpg
** www.users.dircon.co.uk/~hancock/antioch.htm

ΠΡΟΣΕΦΕΣΙΟΥΣ

ΠΑΥΛΟΣΑΠΟΣΤΟΛΟΣΙΗΣΟΥΧΡΙΣΤΟΥΔΙΑΘΕΛΗΜΑ
ΤΟΣΘΕΟΥΤΟΙΣΑΓΙΟΙΣΤΟΙΣΟΥΣΙΝΕΝΕΦΕΣΩΚΑΙΠΙ
ΣΤΟΙΣΕΝΧΡΙΣΤΩΙΗΣΟΥΧΑΡΙΣΥΜΙΝΚΑΙΕΙΡΗΝΗΑΠΟ
ΘΕΟΥΠΑΤΡΟΣΗΜΩΝΚΑΙΚΥΡΙΟΥΙΗΣΟΥΧΡΙΣΤΟΥΕΥ
ΛΟΓΗΤΟΣΟΘΕΟΣΚΑΙΠΑΤΗΡΤΟΥΚΥΡΙΟΥΗΜΩΝΙΗΣ
ΟΥΡΙΣΤΟΥΟΕΥΛΟΓΗΣΑΣΗΜΑΣΕΝΠΑΣΗΕΥΛΟΓΙΑΠ
ΝΕΥΜΑΤΙΚΗΕΝΤΟΙΣΕΠΟΥΡΑΝΙΟΙΣΕΝΧΡΙΣΤΩΚΑΘ
ΩΣΕΞΕΛΕΞΑΤΟΗΜΑΣΕΝΑΥΤΩΠΡΟΚΑΤΑΒΟΛΗΣ
ΚΟΣΜΟΥΕΙΝΑΙΗΜΑΣΑΓΙΟΥΣΚΑΙΑΜΩΜΟΥΣΚΑΤΕ
ΝΩΠΙΟΝΑΥΤΟΥΕΝΑΓΑΠΗΠΡΟΟΡΙΣΑΣΗΜΑΣΕΙΣΥΙΟ
ΩΕΣΙΑΝΔΙΑΙΗΣΟΥΧΡΙΣΤΟΥΕΙΣΑΥΤΟΝΚΑΤΑΤΗΝΕ
ΥΔΟΚΙΑΝΤΟΥΘΕΛΕΜΑΤΟΣΑΥΤΟΥΕΙΣΕΠΑΙΝΟΝΔ
ΟΞΗΣΤΗΣΧΑΡΙΤΟΣΑΥΤΟΥΕΝΗΕΞΑΡΙΤΟΣΕΝΗΜΑ
ΣΕΝΤΩΗΓΑΠΗΜΕΝΩΕΝΩΕΧΟΜΕΝΤΗΝΑΠΟΛΥΤ
ΡΩΣΙΝΔΙΑΤΟΥΑΙΜΟΤΟΣΑΥΤΟΥΤΗΝΑΦΕΣΙΝΤΩΝ
ΠΑΡΑΠΤΩΜΑΤΩΝΚΑΤΑΤΟΝΠΛΟΥΤΟΝΤΗΣΧΑΡΙ
ΤΟΣΑΥΤΟΥΗΣΕΠΕΡΙΣΣΕΥΣΕΝΕΙΣΗΜΑΣΕΝΠΑΣΗΣ
ΟΦΙΑΚΑΙΦΡΟΝΗΣΕΙΓΩΡΙΣΑΣΗΜΙΝΤΟΜΥΣΤΗΡΙΟΝ
ΤΟΥΩΕΛΗΜΑΤΟΣΘΥΤΟΥΚΑΤΑΤΗΝΕΥΔΟΚΙΑΝΑΥ
ΤΟΥΗΝΠΡΟΕΘΕΤΟΕΝΑΥΤΩΕΙΣΟΙΚΟΝΟΜΙΑΝΤΟΥ
ΠΛΗΡΩΜΑΤΟΣΤΩΝΚΑΙΡΩΝΑΝΑΚΕΦΑΛΑΙΩΣΑΣ
ΘΑΙΤΟΠΑΝΤΑΕΝΤΩΧΡΙΣΤΩΤΑΕΠΙΤΟΙΣΟΥΡΑΝΟΙ
ΣΚΑΙΤΑΕΠΙΤΗΣΓΗΣΕΝΑΥΤΩΕΝΩΚΑΙΕΚΛΗΡΩΘΗ
ΜΕΝΠΡΟΟΡΙΣΘΕΝΤΕΣΚΑΤΑΠΡΟΘΕΣΙΝΤΟΥΤΑΠΑ
ΝΤΑΕΝΕΡΓΟΥΝΤΟΣΚΑΤΑΤΗΝΒΟΥΛΗΝΤΟΥΘΕΛΗ
ΜΑΤΟΣΑΥΤΟΥΕΙΣΤΟΕΙΝΑΙΗΜΑΣΕΙΣΕΠΑΙΝΟΝΔΟ
ΞΗΣΑΥΤΟΥΤΟΥΣΠΡΟΗΛΠΙΚΟΤΑΣΕΝΤΩΧΡΙΣΤΩΕ
ΝΩΚΑΙΥΜΕΙΣΑΚΟΥΣΑΝΤΕΣΤΟΝΛΟΓΟΝΤΗΣΑΛΗ
ΘΕΙΑΣΤΟΕΥΑΓΓΕΛΙΟΝΤΗΣΣΩΤΗΡΙΑΣΥΜΩΝΕΝ
ΩΚΑΙΠΙΣΤΕΥΣΑΝΤΕΣΕΣΦΡΑΓΙΣΩΗΤΕΩΠΝΕΥ
ΜΑΤΙΤΗΣΕΠΑΓΓΕΛΙΑΣΤΩΑΓΙΩΟΣΕΣΤΙΝΑΡΡΑΒΩ
ΝΤΗΣΚΛΗΡΟΝΟΜΙΑΣΕΜΩΝΕΙΣΑΠΟΛΥΤΡΩΣΙΝΤΗ
ΣΠΕΡΙΠΟΙΗΣΕΩΣΕΙΣΕΠΑΙΝΟΝΤΗΣΔΟΞΗΣΑΥΤΟΥ

As the original text was copied over the centuries, the editors eventually copied the Greek text into miniscule (lower–case) letters, separated the words by inserting spaces between them, and added accent marks to aid in the pronunciation of the words. Such a copied Greek text eventually came to look something like the one shown below (same passage as above – Eph. 1:1–14):

ΠΡΟΣ ΕΦΕΣΙΟΥΣ

ΠΑΥΛΟΣ, ἀπόστολος Ἰησοῦ Χριστοῦ διὰ θελήματος Θεοῦ, τοῖς ἁγίοις τοῖς οὖσιν ἐν Ἐφέσῳ καὶ πιστοῖς ἐν Χριστῷ Ἰησοῦ· Χάρις ὑμῖν καὶ εἰρήνη ἀπὸ Θεοῦ Πατρὸς ἡμῶν καὶ Κυρίου Ἰησοῦ Χριστοῦ. Εὐλογητὸς ὁ Θεὸς καὶ Πατὴρ τοῦ Κυρίου ἡμῶν Ἰησοῦ Χριστοῦ, ὁ εὐλογήσας ἡμᾶς ἐν πάσῃ εὐλογίᾳ πνευματικῇ ἐν τοῖς ἐπουρανίοις ἐν Χριστῷ, καθὼς ἐξελέξατο ἡμᾶς ἐν αὐτῷ πρὸ καταβολῆς κόσμου, εἶναι ἡμᾶς ἁγίους καὶ ἀμώμους κατενώπιον αὐτοῦ ἐν ἀγάπῃ προορίσας ἡμᾶς εἰς υἱοθεσίαν διὰ Ἰησοῦ Χριστοῦ εἰς αὐτόν, κατὰ τὴν εὐδοκίαν τοῦ θελήματος αὐτοῦ, εἰς ἔπαινον δόξης τῆς χάριτος αὐτοῦ ἐν ᾗ ἐχαρίτωσεν ἡμᾶς ἐν τῷ ἠγαπημένῳ, ἐν ᾧ ἔχομεν τὴν ἀπολύτρωσιν διὰ τοῦ αἵματος αὐτοῦ, τὴν ἄφεσιν τῶν παραπτωμάτων, κατὰ τὸν πλοῦτον τῆς χάριτος αὐτοῦ ἧς ἐπερίσσευσεν εἰς ἡμᾶς ἐν πάσῃ σοφίᾳ καὶ φρονήσει γνωρίσας ἡμῖν τὸ μυστήριον τοῦ θελήματος αὐτοῦ, κατὰ τὴν εὐδοκίαν αὐτοῦ ἣν προέθετο ἐν αὐτῷ εἰς οἰκονομίαν τοῦ πληρώματος τῶν καιρῶν, ἀνακεφαλαιώσασθαι τὰ πάντα ἐν τῷ Χριστῷ, τὰ ἐπὶ τοῖς οὐρανοῖς καὶ τὰ ἐπὶ τῆς γῆς· ἐν αὐτῷ, ἐν ᾧ καὶ ἐκληρώθημεν προορισθέντες κατὰ πρόθεσιν τοῦ τὰ πάντα ἐνεργοῦντος κατὰ τὴν βουλὴν τοῦ θελήματος αὐτοῦ, εἰς τὸ εἶναι ἡμᾶς εἰς ἔπαινον δόξης αὐτοῦ τοὺς προηλπικότας ἐν τῷ Χριστῷ· ἐν ᾧ καὶ ὑμεῖς, ἀκούσαντες τὸν λόγον τῆς ἀληθείας, τὸ εὐαγγέλιον τῆς σωτηρίας ὑμῶν, ἐν ᾧ καὶ πιστεύσαντες ἐσφραγίσθητε τῷ Πνεύματι τῆς ἐπαγγελίας τῷ Ἁγίῳ, ὅς ἐστιν ἀρραβὼν τῆς κληρονομίας ἡμῶν, εἰς ἀπολύτρωσιν τῆς περιποιήσεως, εἰς ἔπαινον τῆς δόξης αὐτοῦ.

As the need became more acute to comprehend the complexity of Paul's thought in languages which relied on *word order* instead of *inflected prefixes and suffixes* to communicate meaning, punctuation marks (commas, semicolons, dashes, etc.) were added. The Greek Text used as the basis for *this translation* is from the *Greek New Testament According to the Majority Text*, edited by Hodges and Farstad, and published by Thomas Nelson, Inc. in 1985. An excellent summary of the history of the Majority Text tradition is presented in the "Introduction" to this edition of the Greek New Testament.

[6] William Tyndale was the first person to translate the Greek New Testament into the English language in its entirety. Tyndale published the first English edition in 1526, using Erasmus' 3rd edition of the Greek Text, published in 1522. Tyndale's translation was upbeat, optimistic and written in good common English style. His translation was so good that it more heavily influenced the King James Version than all the other translations made into English from 1537 – 1611 combined. Tyndale's translation included the chapter divisions used today, but did not use the verse divisions. Instead, he translated the text into interpretive paragraphs. An excellent photographic image of the first page of the Gospel of John from this text can be viewed at the following webpage:

> webpage http://www.wlb–stuttgart.de/referate/theologie/tynbl.html

From the Württembergische Landesbibliothek Stuttgart (see Bibliography). Tydale's text presented here is from *The New Testament – The Text of the Worms Edition of 1526 in Original Spelling, edited by* W. R. Cooper and published by The British Library in 2000 (see Bibliography).

[7] Tyndale translated the New Testament into English from the 3rd edition of the Greek Text published in 1522 by Erasmus of Rotterdam. An excellent photographic image of the first page of the Gospel of Matthew from Erasmus' 1516 edition (*Novvm instrumentu[m] omne*, edited, translated, and annotated by Erasmus of Rotterdam, 2 pts, Basel: Johann Froben, March 1516 – Greek in the left column, with Latin translation in the right column; no verse divisions in the text) can be viewed at the following webpage:

> http://www.smu.edu/bridwell/publications/ryrie_catalog/5_2.htm.

From *Formatting the Word of God: the Charles Caldwell Ryrie collection:* 1998 (see Bibliography).

[8] *The Holy Bible, conteyning the Old Testament, and the New.* Imprinted at London: By Robert Barker...,1611 (the first edition of the King James Bible of 1611), in the Annenberg Rare Book and Manuscript Library. In the 1611 King James Version, verses were introduced into the English text, which practically resulted in the loss of Tyndale's interpretive placement of paragraphs. Even though the King James translators followed Tyndale's 1526 translation very closely, because each "verse" begins with a capital letter and punctuation marks are placed at the end of each verse, the interpretation of the main idea and Paul's central argument or theme becomes more difficult to decipher. Excellent photographic images of this entire Bible can be viewed at the following webpage (*Ephesians* from PagePosition 1429-1434):

> http://dewey.library.upenn.edu/sceti/printedbooksNew/index.cfm?TextID=kjb ible&PagePosition=1429

From the Schoenberg Center for Electronic Text and Images, University of Pennsylvania Library (see Bibliography). The text of the King James Version of 1611 presented here is from the above referenced volume (see Bibliography).

BIBLIOGRAPHY

Aeschylus. *Oresteia*. Translated by Richmond Lattimore. Chicago: University of Chicago Press, 1953.

Alighieri, Dante. *The Divine Comedy*. Vol. 1: *Inferno*, Vol. 2: *Purgatorio*, Vol. 3: *Paradiso*. John D. Sinclair, tsl. New York: Oxford University Press, 1961.

Appian. *The Foreign Wars*. L. Mendelssohn. Leipzig: Teubner, 1879. Made available through the Perseus website (see below).

———. *The Foreign Wars*. transl. Horace White. New York: The MacMillan Company, 1899. Made available through the Perseus website (see below).

Aquinas, Thomas. *Summa Contra Gentiles*. Books One through Four. New York: Doubleday, 1957.

———. *Summa Theologica* in *The Basic Writings of Saint Thomas Aquinas*, Vols. I & II. Edited by Anton C. Pegis. New York: Random House, 1945.

———. *Treatise on Happiness*. Passages from the Summa Theologica, translated by John A. Oesterle. Notre Dame, Indiana: University of Notre Dame Press, 1983.

Aristophanes. *Aristophanes Comoediae*, ed. F.W. Hall and W.M. Geldart, vol. 2. F.W. Hall and W.M. Geldart. Oxford. Clarendon Press, Oxford. 1907. Made available through the Perseus website (see below).

———. *Frogs*. Matthew Dillon. Made available through the Perseus website (see below).

Aristotle. *Aristotle's Ethica Nicomachea*. ed. J. Bywater, Oxford, Clarendon Press, 1894. Made available through the Perseus website (see below).

———. *Aristotle's Politica*. ed. W. D. Ross, Oxford, Clarendon Press, 1957. Made available through the Perseus website (see below).

———. *Ars Rhetorica*. Aristotle. W. D. Ross. Oxford. Clarendon Press. 1959. Made available through the Perseus website (see below).

———. *Athenaion Politeia*, ed. Kenyon. Oxford. 1920. Made available through the Perseus website (see below).

———. *Athenian Constitution*. Aristotle in 23 Volumes, Vol. 20, translated by H. Rackham. Cambridge, MA, Harvard University Press; London, William Heinemann Ltd. 1952. Made available through the Perseus website (see below).

———. *Categories.* E. M. Edghill, tsl., in The Basic Works of Aristotle, Richard McKeon, ed. New York. Random House. 1941.

———. *Economics.* Aristotle in 23 Volumes, Vol. 18. translated by G.C. Armstrong. Cambridge, MA, Harvard University Press; London, William Heinemann Ltd. 1935. Made available through the Perseus website (see below).

———. *Metaphysics.* 2 vols. H. Tredennick, tsl. Cambridge: Harvard University Press, 1989.

———. *Nicomachean Ethics.* Aristotle in 23 Volumes, Vol. 19, translated by H. Rackham. Cambridge, MA, Harvard University Press; London, William Heinemann Ltd. 1934. Made available through the Perseus website (see below).

———. *Nichomachean Ethics.* W. D. Ross, tsl. In The Basic Works of Aristotle. Edited by Richard McKeon. New York: Random House, 1941.

———. *On the Soul.* J. A. Smith, tsl. in The Basic Works of Aristotle. Richard McKeon, ed. New York: Random House, 1941.

———. *Politics.* Aristotle in 23 Volumes, Vol. 21, translated by H. Rackham. Cambridge, MA, Harvard University Press; London, William Heinemann Ltd. 1944. Made available through the Perseus website (see below).

———. *Politics.* Benjamin Jowett, tsl. In The Basic Works of Aristotle. Edited by Richard McKeon. New York: Random House, 1941.

———. *Rhetoric.* Aristotle in 23 Volumes, Vol. 22, translated by J. H. Freese. Aristotle. Cambridge and London. Harvard University Press; William Heinemann Ltd. 1926. Made available through the Perseus website (see below).

Brown, Francis; Driver, S. R.; Briggs, Charles A. *A Hebrew and English Lexicon of the Old Testament.* Oxford: Clarendon Press, 1980.

The Catholic Encyclopedia. Made available through the following website: http://www.newadvent.org/cathen/

Chase, Alston H.; Phillips, Jr., Henry. *A New Introduction to Greek,* Third Edition. Cambridge, Mass. & London, U.K.: Harvard University Press, 1997.

Churchill, Winston S. *A History of the English Speaking Peoples, Volume I – The Birth of Britain; Volume II – The New World; Volume III – The Age of Revolution; Volume IV – The Great Democracies.* New York: Dodd, Mead & Company, 1956.

Columbia Encyclopedia, Sixth Edition. New York: Columbia University Press, 2001-05; New York: Bartleby.com, 2001-2005. Made available through website: http://www.bartleby.com/65/

BIBLIOGRAPHY

Douglas, J. D., ed. *The New International Dictionary of the Christian Church.* Grand Rapids, Michigan: Zondervan Publishing House, 1974.

Euripides. *The Bacchae.* Philip Vellacott, tsl. In Euripides - The Bacchae and Other Plays. London, England: Penguin Books, 1973.

Formatting the Word of God: the Charles Caldwell Ryrie collection: an exhibition at Bridwell Library, Perkins School of Theology, Southern Methodist University, October 1998 through January 1999. Edited by Valerie R. Hotchkiss & Charles C. Ryrie; in collaboration with Duane Harbin, David Price, Page A. Thomas, Decherd Turner, Eric Marshall White. Dallas, TX: Bridwell Library, 1998. Made available through website: http://www.smu.edu/bridwell/publications/ryrie_catalog.

Fruchtenbaum, Arnold G. *Footsteps of the Messiah* – A Study of the Sequence of Prophetic Events. Tustin, California: Ariel Ministries Press, 1983.

Hancock, Ralph. *The Greek New Testament*, Third Edition of the UBS (United Bible Societies), from the 26th and 27th editions of the Greek New Testament published by Nestle and Aland [NOVVM TESTAMENTVM. Textus secundum III. editionem UBS, omnino cum XXVI. et XXVII. editionibus Novi Testamenti Graece, Nestle et Aland editoribus, concors, praeter minutias interpunctionis]. Greek text and Greek fonts made available for research purposes in electronic format at the website: http://www.users.dircon.co.uk/~hancock/antioch.htm.

―――. *The Greek Septuagint* [Basic Greek text from BIBLIA GRAECA IVXTA LXX INTERPRETES: Totus fere textus cum Vetere Graeca versione congruit, discrepantes tamen versiones librorum Judicum et Tobit ponuntur: Codicis Alexandrini versio sub littera A, Codicis Vaticani versio sub littera B et Codicis Sinaitici versio sub littera S. Adaeque producuntur binae versiones librorum Susannae, Danielis, atque libri qui inscribitur Bel et Draco: textus Vetus Graecus sub nota LXX, et versio Theodotionis]. Greek text and Greek fonts made available for research purposes in electronic format at the website: http://www.users.dircon.co.uk/~hancock/antioch.htm.

Hodges, Z. C., Farstad, A. L., & Dunkin, W. C. *The Greek New Testament According to the Majority Text,* 2nd Edition. Nashville: Thomas Nelson Publishers, 1985. Greek text and Greek fonts published by T. Nelson made available for research purposes in electronic format through licensed program at the website: http://www.libronix.com.

Homer. *The Iliad.* transl. by Martin Hammond. New York: Penguin Books, 1987.

―――. *The Odyssey.* transl. by Walter Shewring. Oxford, New York: Oxford University Press, 1980.

Josephus, Flavius. *Flavii Iosephi Opera – Antiquitates Judaicae.* B. Niese. Berlin. Weidmann. 1892. Made available through the Perseus website (see below).

———. *Flavii Iosephi Opera – Contra Apionem*. B. Niese. Berlin. Weidmann. 1892. Made available through the Perseus website (see below).

———. *Flavii Iosephi Opera – De bello Judaico libri* vii. B. Niese. Berlin. Weidmann. 1892. Made available through the Perseus website (see below).

———. *The Works of Flavius Josephus – Against Apion*. transl. ed. William Whiston, A.M. Auburn and John E. Beardsley. Buffalo. 1895. Made available through the Perseus website (see below).

———. *The Works of Flavius Josephus – Antiquities of the Jews*. transl. ed. William Whiston, A.M. Auburn and Buffalo. John E. Beardsley. 1895. Made available through the Perseus website (see below).

———. *The Works of Flavius Josephus – The Wars of the Jews*. transl. ed. William Whiston, A.M. Auburn and Buffalo. John E. Beardsley. 1895. Made available through the Perseus website (see below).

The Holy Bible, conteyning the Old Testament, and the New. Imprinted at London: By Robert Barker..., 1611. In Annenberg Rare Book and Manuscript Library. BS185 1611 .L65. Text of Ephesians taken from photographic images from the Schoenberg Center for Electronic Text and Images, University of Pennsylvania Library, and made available on the following webpage: http://dewey.library.upenn.edu/sceti/printedbooksNew/index.cfm?TextID=kjbible.

The King James Bible. Philadelphia. A. J. Holman Co. 1901.

Lewis, C. S. *Abolition of Man*. New York: MacMillan Publishing Co., Inc., 1955.

———. *Mere Christianity*. New York: MacMillan Publishing Co., Inc., 1960.

———. *Miracles*. New York: MacMillan Publishing Co., Inc., 1960.

———. *The Screwtape Letters*. New York: MacMillan Publishing Co., Inc., 1982.

———. *Surprised by Joy*. New York: Harcourt Brace Jovanovich Publishers, 1955.

Lewis, Charlton T., Ph.D. and Short, Charles, LL.D. *A Latin Dictionary*. Founded on Andrews' edition of Freund's Latin dictionary revised, enlarged, and in great part rewritten by Lewis and Short. Oxford. Clarendon Press, 1879. Referenced from Perseus website (see below).

Liddell, Henry George; Scott, Robert. *A Greek-English Lexicon*. Revised and augmented throughout by Sir Henry Stuart Jones, with the assistance of Roderick McKenzie. Oxford: Clarendon Press, 1940 (usually referenced from Perseus website – see below).

Merriam-Webster Unabridged Dictionary, through licensed website:

http://unabridged.merriam-webster.com/ copyright © 2004 by Merriam-Webster, Inc.

Metzger, Bruce M. *Lexical Aids for Students of New Testament Greek.* Princeton, New Jersey: Bruce M. Metzger, 1980.

Nestle, Eberhard; Nestle, Erwin; Aland, Kurt, eds. *Novum Testamentum Graece.* 25th ed. New York: American Bible Society, 1963.

Nestle, Eberhard; Nestle, Erwin; Aland, Kurt; Black, Matthew; Martini, Carlo M.; Metzger, Bruce M.; Wikgren, Allen, eds. *Novum Testamentum Graece.* 26th ed. Stuttgart: Deutsche Bibelstiftung, 1979.

The New King James Bible. Nashville: Thomas Nelson, Inc., 1979.

The New Testament – The Text of the Worms Edition of 1526 in Original Spelling. Transl. by William Tyndale. Ed. W. R. Cooper. London. The British Library, 2000.

The Oxyrhynchus Papyri. P.Oxy. 10.1257. "Statement concerning a dekaprôtos." Duke Data Bank of Documentary Papyri. Made available through the Perseus website (see below).

P.Cair.Masp.: Papyrus grecs d'époque byzantine, Catalogue général des antiquités égyptiennes du Musée du Caire document 67020. Duke Data Bank of Documentary Papyri. Made available through the Perseus website (see below).

Perseus Digital Library Project. Ed. Gregory R. Crane. 1999. Tufts University. References to the Greek New Testament (eds. Brooke Foss Westcott, Fenton John Anthony Hort – see below), *A Greek-English Lexicon by Liddell and Scott* (see above), Greek, Latin and English Classics, including major works consulted for philological research in the Perseus Website Collection of Greek Texts and their English Translations provided by the website: http://www.perseus.tufts.edu.

Plato. *Ion.* Lane Cooper, tsl. in *Plato: The Collected Dialogues.* Edith Hamilton and Huntington Cairns, ed. Princeton, New Jersey: Princeton University Press, 1989.

———. *Meno.* W. K. C. Guthrie, tsl. in *Plato: The Collected Dialogues.* Edith Hamilton and Huntington Cairns, ed. Princeton, New Jersey: Princeton University Press, 1989.

———. *Phaedo.* Hugh Tredennick, tsl. in *Plato: The Collected Dialogues.* Edith Hamilton and Huntington Cairns, ed. Princeton, New Jersey: Princeton University Press, 1989.

———. *Phaedrus.* R. Hackforth, tsl. in *Plato: The Collected Dialogues.* Edith Hamilton and Huntington Cairns, ed. Princeton, New Jersey: Princeton University Press, 1989.

———. *Phaedrus*. C. J. Rowe, tsl. Teddington House, Church Street, Warminster, Wiltshire, England: Aris & Phillips Ltd., 1986.

———. *Platonis Opera – Gorgias*, ed. John Burnet. Oxford University Press. 1903. Made available through the Perseus website (see above).

———. *Platonis Opera – Republic*, ed. John Burnet. Oxford University Press. 1903. Made available through the Perseus website (see above).

———. *Plato in Twelve Volumes, Vol. 3 – Gorgias*, translated by W.R.M. Lamb. Cambridge, MA, Harvard University Press; London, William Heinemann Ltd. 1967. Made available through the Perseus website (see above).

———. *Plato in Twelve Volumes, Vols. 5 & 6 – Republic*, translated by Paul Shorey. Cambridge, MA, Harvard University Press; London, William Heinemann Ltd. 1969.

———. *Republic*. Translated by G. M. A. Grube, revised by C. D. C. Reeve. Indianapolis, Indiana: Hackett Publishing Company, Inc., 1992

———. *Republic*. Translated by W. H. D. Rouse, in *Great Dialogues of Plato*. Eric H. Warmington and Philip G. Rouse, editors. New York: Mentor Books, 1956.

———. *Socrates' Defense (Apology)*. Hugh Tredennick, tsl. in *Plato: The Collected Dialogues*. Edith Hamilton and Huntington Cairns, ed. Princeton, New Jersey: Princeton University Press, 1989.

———. *Symposium*. Michael Joyce, tsl. in *Plato: The Collected Dialogues*. Edith Hamilton and Huntington Cairns, ed. Princeton, New Jersey: Princeton University Press, 1989.

———. *Symposium*. Sir Kenneth Dover, ed. Cambridge: Cambridge University Press, 1980.

Polybius. *Historiae*. Theodorus Büttner-Wobst after L. Dindorf. Leipzig. Teubner. 1893. Made available through the Perseus website (see above).

———. *Histories*. Evelyn S. Shuckburgh, translator. London, New York. Macmillan. 1889. Reprint Bloomington 1962. Made available through the Perseus website (see above).

Robertson, A. T. *A Grammar of the Greek New Testament in the Light of Historical Research*. New York: Hodder & Stoughton, 1914.

Smith, William, LLD., Wayte, William. *A Dictionary of Greek and Roman Antiquities*. G. E. Marindin. Albemarle Street, London: John Murray. 1890. Made available through the Perseus website (see above).

Sophocles. *The Electra of Sophocles*. Edited with introduction and notes by Sir Richard Jebb. Sir Richard Jebb. Cambridge. Cambridge University Press. 1894. Made available through the Perseus website (see above).

———. *The Philoctetes of Sophocles*. Edited with introduction and notes by Sir Richard Jebb. Sir Richard Jebb. Cambridge. Cambridge University Press. 1898. Made available through the Perseus website (see above).

———. *The Women of Trachis and Philoctetes*. A new translation in verse by Robert Torrance. Houghton Mifflin. 1966. Made available through the Perseus website (see above).

Sparks, Nicholas. *A Walk to Remember*. New York. Warner Books, Inc. 1999.

Tupper, Martin F. *Stephan Langton, or The Days of King John*. Guildford, England: Biddles Ltd., 1858.

Westcott, Brooke Foss and Hort, Fenton John Anthony. *The New Testament in the Original Greek*. New York: Harper and Brothers, 1882. Made available through the Perseus Website (see above).

Wigram, George V. *The Englishman's Greek Concordance of the New Testament, Ninth Edition*. Grand Rapids, Michigan: Zondervan Publishing House, 1977.

Wikipedia, *The Free Encyclopedia*. Made available through the following website: http://en.wikipedia.org.

Württembergische Landesbibliothek Stuttgart. From webpage http://www.wlb-stuttgart.de/referate/theologie/tynbl.html.

The Wycliffe New Testament (1388), An Edition in modern spelling with an introduction, the original prologues and the Epistle to the Laodiceans. Transl. by John Wycliffe. Edited for the Tyndale Society by W. R. Cooper. London: The British Library, 2002.

Xenophon. *Xenophontis opera omnia, vol. 5 – Agesilaus*. Oxford, Clarendon Press. 1920 (repr.1969). Made available through the Perseus Website (see above).

———. *Xenophontis opera omnia, vol. 4 – Cyropaedia*. Oxford, Clarendon Press. 1910 (repr. 1970). Made available through the Perseus Website (see above).

———. *Xenophon in Seven Volumes, 5 and 6 – Cyropaedia*. Harvard University Press, Cambridge, MA. William Heinemann, Ltd., London. vol. 5: 1983; vol. 6: 1979. Made available through the Perseus Website (see above).

———. *Xenophon in Seven Volumes, 7 – The Biography of Agesilaus*. Harvard University Press, Cambridge, MA. William Heinemann, Ltd., London. 1984. Made available through the Perseus Website (see above).

ENGLISH INDEX

A

A History of the English Speaking Peoples by Winston Churchill, 58, 111
A Walk to Remember, by Nicholas Sparks, 191
Abel, 242
Abraham, 49, 75, 137, 242, 250, 257
Absalom, 251
abyss, ἄβυσσος, 244
accept (at face value), λῆψις, to accept, to receive; *see* προσωποληµψία, 241
account; ὄνοµα, [lit. 'name'] the deliberate assigning, measuring out and keeping account or record of [something] (5:20); 182, 212
accuse (in positive sense = confront, legally accuse), 178, 205
Accuser (in negative sense = the Slanderer), 167; *see* Slanderer, Devil
acquire [A(d)-quire = search and ask for], 180, 207
actor; µιµητής, impersonator, imitator (5:1); 173, 189, 190-191
administration, 37, 50, 60, 119, 121, 130
adoption; υἱοθεσία, legal adoption as a son (1:5); 34, 50
adultery, 175, 196, 222
Aeschylus, 103
age (era, epoch), 41, 78
Agincourt, 273
Agrippa I, 129, 256
Agrippa II, 266, 276
Ai, 250
air (sky, atmosphere of the earth), 82, 94
Alcuin, 43
Alfred the Great, 58
alien, illegal; ξένος, [economically, one who cannot get a job legally] (2:12, 19); 50, 88, 91
alienated; ἀπηλλοτριόω, to be alienated [from legal citizenship or status] (2:18; 4:18); 90, 145, 160
alive with (to be made)... raised with (to be), and seated with (to be);

συνεζωοποίησε... καὶ συνήγειρε καὶ συνεκάθισεν, He has made us alive with...and He has resurrected us with and He has seated us with (2:5-6), 85, 103-104
amen; ἀµήν, public recognition and wholehearted agreement to live according to the conclusive truths of a convincing line of reasoning (3:21; 6:24); 127, 138, 238, 277
Ammonites, 247
amortize (pre-finance), 34, 52
Ananias (High Priest), 265
Ananias (husband of Sapphira), 247
Ananias (of Damascus), 97, 252
Ancient era, xvi-xvii, xxii, xxxiii, xxxv, xxxix, xli, 43,
angel(s), 128, 129, 255, 267, 268
anger (exploding in impulsive fits of fury or rage), 149, 169
anger; ὀργή, temperament, disposition, or habitual ascerbic mood of harboring anger and holding grudges (4:31); 149, 170
announce good news; εὐαγγελίζοµαι, bring a wonderful message (2:17; 3:8); 90, 116, 120, 131
Anointed One, 45
Aphrodite, 78
Apollo, 77, 197, 211
Apostle, *see* High Emissary
Appearing, δόξα, Appearance[of God] (1:6, 12, 14, 17, 18; 3:13, 16, 21); 34, 38, 39, 40, 41, 52, 123, 124, 127, 135
Appian, 245
appoint; ὀνοµάζω, to appoint, to name, to nominate (3:15); 124, 135
appointed, 61, 135
appreciation, expressed publicly; ἔπαινον, to recognize and then publicly and universally appreciate, acknowledge and express honor [to someone] (1:6, 12, 14); 34, 38, 39
Archbishop of Canterbury, 43, 111
Ares, 78

English Index

Aristophanes, 194
Aristotle, 59, 60, 61, 68, 93, 100, 108, 158, 190, 198, 199, 205, 206, 208, 209, 210, 213, 215, 217, 221, 240, 245, 272
arm (for battle); περιζωσάμενοι, to deliberately put a military sword-belt and sword upon one's body for the purpose of preparing for combat (6:14); 229, 245
arrow-volley, βέλος, (6:16); 231, 250
Artemis, 78, 94, 261
artificial, 88, 106, 110
Ashtoreth, 246
ask, αἰτοῦμαι, (3:13); 123, 130, 133
aspire to; ἀνήκω, to rise to a higher level, to aspire to (5:4); 175, 199-200
associates, e.g., take on the public behavior and demeanor of those with whom one associates, 83, 100
Athena, 77, 111, 163, 164, 168
Athenian Constitution (by Aristotle), 205, 240
Athens, 79, 94, 109, 136, 162, 258, 259, 262
authority(ies), 41, 46, 66, 72, 76, 77, 82, 113, 114, 121, 132, 133, 153, 154, 209, 210, 213, 228, 242, 243
authority; ἐξουσία, [angelic] hierarchy of authority (1:21, 2:2, 3:10, 6:12); 41, 75, 82, 121, 228, 243
avarice (greed), 146, 161, 175, 194

B

baptism, *see* immersion
Barbarian(s), *see* race
Bathsheba, 251
Battle of the Bulge, 274
battle; πάλη, military fight, battle (6:12); 228, 243
Bede, 43
beside onself (with anger = exasperated), 147, 166
beside; παρά, to the side, beside; 56, 166
biological life form, βίος, 173
birth; τίκτω, to give birth, 189
bitterness; πικρία, bitter mood of cynical resentment (4:31); 149, 169
blasphemy; βλασφημία, spouting blasphemous, irreverent speech against God (4:31); 149, 170

bless, blessed, blessing; *see* eulogy
blood; αἷμα, [lit. 'blood'] death by capital punishment (1:7, 2:13); 35, 89; terrestrial human being (6:12); 77, 228
body armor; θώραξ, body armor, breastplate, chain-mail covering the chest, chest-armor, bullet-proof vest (6:14); 230, 246
body; σῶμα, governmental, organizational, administrative or associational body [in organizational contexts] (1:23; 2:16; 4:4, 12, 16[2x]; 5:23, 38, 30); 42, 79, 90, 140, 143, 144, 183, 188; the human body, a good state of bodily health [in individual contexts] (5:28); 187, 216
bond to; προσκολλάω, to bond to [someone psychologically, emotionally and spiritually] (5:31); 188, 220
bond; δέσμιος, bond (prisoner, i.e., one who is in bondage) or Bond [guarantee of the performance of a contract], (3:1; 4:1); 118, 119, 127, 130, 139, 150
bondage, 51
bones, 188, 223
boorishness, ἄγροικος, (insolence), 175, 198, 199
boots (to put on); ὑποδέω, to put on heavy gauge, sandal-type boots, including 'greaves,' i.e., armor plates strapped on to protect the leg and shin below the knee; to put on high-top military boots (6:15); 230, 248
boss(es), 46, 225, 242
breastplate, *see* body armor
brother; ἀδελφός, [lit. 'brother'] esteemed colleague, associate, fellow (6:10, 21); 227, 238, 241, 277
brothers, *see* colleagues
buffoonery; βωμολοχία, foolishness, [synonym of εὐτραπελία], 198-199
cultured insolence, εὐτραπελία, (5:4); 175, 198-199
build (a house); συνοικοδομέω, to build a house from a variety of divergent materials (2:22); 92, 117

build; ἐποικοδομέω, to build up, to build upon (2:20); 91, 116
build; κατοικητήριος, to build [make] a house into a home (2:22); 92
building; οἰκοδομή, (2:21; 4:12, 16); 92, 116, 143, 144, 156; constructive (4:29); 148, 169
business owners, 225, 242
business, economics and finance, 49
business (to put out of); καταργέω, to put out of commission, to put out of action (2:15); 90, 115
buy out, ἐξαγοραζω, buy up, purchase, acquire, obtain, procure (5:16); 180, 206-208

C

Caesar, 114, 259, 265
Caleb, 242
call; καλέω, to summon, to invite, to call (4:1, 4); 139, 140
calling, *see* lifework
calloused (to disregard and become indifferent to the welfare of other people), 146, 160
Calypso, Καλυψώ, ['she that veils,' from Homer's *Odyssey*, from καλύπτω, to cover, hide, conceal, veil – see ἀποκάλυψις]; 71
capital, 50
care; θάλπω, to warmly care for and gently comfort (5:29); 187, 220
Carolingian miniscule font, 43
Categories (Ten "Categories" of Aristotle), 213
challenge, *see* confront
chance, *see* gamble
charity, *see* love, gracious
Charlemagne, 43
cheat(ed), 146, 163
chest-armor, *see* body armor
chief leader, ἀρχή, [of the rebellious angels = Satan], (1:21, 2:2, 3:10, 6:12); 41, 75, 82, 121, 228
child, τέκνον, (5:1); 173, 189
Christ, *see* High King
Christendom, 111
chronology, 43, 128, 129, 252
Church; *see* Kingdom Apprenticeship Council, Lifework Council
Churchill, Winston; 58, 111

circumcision, περιτομή, (2:11); 88, 110
citizen (with); συμπολίτης, fellow citizen (2:19), 91
citizenship; πολιτεία, legal or political citizenship [esp. with accompanying economic rights to work and posession of legal rights] (2:12); 88
civil officials, 225
Civil War (American), 241
clear away; ἀρθήτω (aor pass imp - αἴρω), to 'clear away' [bad thoughts, attitudes, speech and behavior] (4:31); 149, 169
cleave, 188, 220
co-body members (co-administrators), 120, 131
co-heirs (equal heirs), 120, 131
colleagues (also associates, fellows, future kings) 227, 241
comfort (care for with tenderness and warmth, as well as vigorously and passionately protect and defend), 187, 220
Commander in Chief, κυρίος, (1:2, used 28 times in Ephesians, 26 to refer to Jesus in His present leadership role: 31, 45, 46; used twice in Ephesians to refer to human leaders, managers, business owners, bosses, entrepreneurs, military officers, civil or political officials [6:5, 9]; 46, 242
Commander, ἐπιστάτης, 46
Commanding Officer, (used twice to refer to human leaders in Eph. 6:5 and 6:9); 46, 225, 242
compassion; εὔσπλαγχνος, deep feeling for and understanding of misery or suffering and the concomitant desire to promote its alleviation (4:32); 149, 171
comply (refusal to); ἀπείθεια, obstinate refusal to comply with legitimate authority (2:2; 5:6); 83, 94, 176, 200
compound; περισσεύω, to go beyond, abound, to compound money through interest [in financial contexts] (1:8); 36, 50, 56
comprehensive understanding, ἐπίγνωσις (1:17; 4:13); 40, 143
con artist; πλάνης, [lit. 'wanderer'] transient, pirate [those that wander

English Index

from town to town to swindle or fool people], (4:14); 144, 155
conceal; λανθάνω, to cover-up, to escape notice, to be unknown, unseen, unnoticed (see ἀληθεύω), 62
concealed; λῆθος, unknown, unseen, unnoticed, (see ἀλήθεια), 62
confidence; εὐάρεστος, distinguished confidence or trust earned after being tested or proved [by a superior officer] (5:10); 178, 204
confidence; παρρησία, the ability to speak openly, freely and confidently in public (6:19); 237, 236
confront; ἐλέγχω, to confront, to challenge, to question, to expose, to refute, to resist, to arrest (5:11, 13); 178, 179, 205
confusion, 177, 204
consequence, 181, 208
con-sequence, 210
consistency, 177, 204
construction and building, 49, 50, 51, 81, 92, 106, 107, 116, 117, 137, 152, 156; (constructive), 92, 117, 148, 169
contact; ἀφή, enlightening relational contact [with other people or with the Spirit of God] (4:16); 145, 157
Contemporary era, xvi-xviii, xix-xx, xxxi-xxxviii, xl-xlix, 43, 66, 191, 213
contentment; ἀγαπητὸς, glad, cheerful contentment (5:1, 6:21); 173, 189-190, 238, 277
contextual setting, 46, 127-129
conversation (habitual public conduct and demeanor), 83, 100-102
convict (confront), 178, 205
cooperate, 181, 208
co-operate, 210
co-partnership (equal partners), 120, 131
Corinth, 128, 129, 251, 259, 260, 262
cornerstone; ἀκρογωνιαῖος, corner foundation stone (2:20), 91, 106
correcting, 178, 205
create; κτίζω, to create, form, shape, invent, forge (2:10, 15; 3:9; 4:24); 87, 106, 116, 147, 164
criminal view of love, 175, 194
cross, σταυρός, [Roman instrument of capital punishment] (2:16); 89, 112

crucifixion, 89, 112, 113, 114, 247, 248, 268
Cyclops, 211, 250
cynical resentment, 149, 169

D

darkened (to become spiritually); σκοτόω, [to become 'darkened,' i.e.,] to become dulled, enervated and stupefied in one's perception and understanding of reality, as well as in one's purposes and intentions [see darkness] (4:18), 145, 159
darkness (spiritual); σκότος, [lit. 'darkness'] fear and confusion or stubborn, willful ignorance that lead to deceitfulness, lack of confidence, indecisiveness – and ultimately to tragic, premature death (5:8; 6:12); 177, 204, 228, 244
David (King), 67, 211, 245, 246, 270
dead; νεκρός, dead, death, as good as dead (1:20; 2:1, 5; 5:14); 41, 75, 81, 84, 179
debt; ὀφείλημα, financial indebtedness, 55
debtor, ὀφειλέτης, 55
deceive, 148, 166
declare; λέγω, to declare, make a legal declaration (4:17); 145, 158
deference, 183, 212
Delilah, 246
deliver, deliverance, 38, 65, 102
demeanor (formation of); ἀναστρέφω, to have one's public demeanor formed for better or worse by one's habitual public associations (2:3); 50, 83, 100-102
demeanor; ἀναστροφή (see ἀναστρέφω), one's public demeanor, behavior and attitude formed by one's habitual public associations (5:22) 146, 162
demolish; λύω, to demolish, break up, destroy, put an end to, annul, dissolve (2:24); 90, 112
depraved, ἀκάθαρτος, (5:5); 176, 200
decadent; πόρνος, one who engages in sexual intercourse outside the bond of marriage (5:5); 176, 200

depravity; ἀκαθαρσία, ['uncleanness' in an ethical or moral sense] (4:19; 5:3); 146, 161, 175, 194
derisive humor, 175, 198
despair; ἀπαλγέω, to give up hope, to sink into despondency and despair (4:19); 51, 73, 134, 146, 160, 161
despair; ἐγκακέω, to slip into a pervasive dispirited and defeatist mood, leading to a cynical attitude of despair and the neglect of performing one's responsibilities (3:13); 123, 133
Devil, 148, 153, 166, 227, 241, 242, 247, 250, 270
devotion, 236, 278
dice playing, see gamble 144, 156
Dionysus, 78
discernment; φρόνησις, the skill of having the ability to habitually discern, think through and make good decisions about matters that affect the lives of others in society, (1:8); 36, 58
discover, see truth
disgusting; σαπρός, rotten, foul, disgusting or rancorous [speech] (4:29); 148, 169
disoriented; περιφέρω, to become disoriented due to having one's mind be spun around [lit. 'carried around'] in all directions by others (4:14); 144, 155
dispensation (see government)
distinguished confidence, 178, 204
distinguished; ἔνδοξος, special, dignified, distinguished, public recognition (5:27); 186, 216
disturbed; κλυδωνίζω, confused (4:14); 144, 155
divine secret, see Top Secret
Divine Spokesperson(s), 143, 306
down payment, 38, 50, 67
dress up; ἐνδύω, to 'dress up' [one's mind] (4:24; 6:11, 14); 147, 163, 227, 230, 243
drink (alcohol); μεθύσκω, to drink alcohol excessively, to become drunk, intoxicated (5:18); 181, 211
Druid, 63
drunk (intoxicated), 181, 211
due, 55
dysfunctional family, 240-241

E

earnest money; ἀρραβών, earnest money, down payment (1:14); 38, 67
Economics, ΟΙΚΟΝΟΜΙΚΩΝ [Treatise by Aristotle on administrative skills required for leadership over an estate or a government], 60-61
economy, see government
egoistic view of love, 175, 176
emotional estrangement, 35, 36
employee, δοῦλος, [lit. slave] employee, subordinate officer (6:5); 224, 241
English Nobles, 111
Enlighten(ed); φωτίζω, to be enlightened; realize, appreciate and act upon the spiritual duty to embrace leadership responsibility, see light (1:18; 3:9); 40, 121, 132
enlightening personal contacts, 145, 158
Enoch, 242
enterprise, 50, 52, 87, 107-109
entrepreneurs, 46, 87, 225, 242,
Epaphroditus, 192
Epictetus, 194
epoch, 78
equal heir; συγκληρονόμος, fellow heir (3:6), 120, 131
era; αἰών, era, epoch, age, (1:21; 2:2, 7; 3:9, 11, 21; 6:12); 41, 78, 82, 86, 121, 122, 127, 228
Esau, 246, 250
ethical skill; σοφία, the kind of knowledge that makes it possible to become competent, then gain mastery, then achieve superior leadership ability in living human life skillfully, especially in the ethical and political arenas (1:8, 17; 3:10; 5:15); 36, 40, 56-58, 121, 132, 180, 206
ethnocentric view of love, 175
eulogizer; εὐλογητὸς, [lit. Eulogizer] Keynote Speaker (1:3); 31, 47-48
eulogy (to deliver a); εὐλογέω, to deliver a eulogy or commendation speech (1:3); 31, 47-48
eulogy; εὐλογία, keynote address, proclamation, commendation speech (1:3); 31, 32, 47-48
Euripides, 103, 161, 192, 215

English Index

Eusebius, 268
examining, *see* confront
exasperation; παροργισμός, beside [oneself with] anger, exasperation (4:26); 147, 166
exchange, 188, 220-221
eye(s), 40

F

face; πρόσωπον, the face, especially the countenance or projection of one's attitude or mood by using one's facial expressions, 241
failure; ἁμαρτία, missed, failure, loss [of a goal or opportunity] (2:1), 55, 93, 173
faint, 134
fall, πίπτω, 56
fall to the side (of the road), 55-56, *see* sidetracked
fall short; ἁμαρτάνω, to miss or fall short [of a goal or opportunity], fail, lose (4:26); 55, 93, 147, 165-166, 173
fear, 35, 46, 72-73, 129, 178, 204, 225, 232, 235,
Felix, 127, 130, 265-266, 276
fellatio, 194
fellow member of a body; σύσσωμα, co-administrator, fellow member of a governmental, organizational, administrative or associational body (3:6); 120, 131
fellow human being; πλησίος, neighbor, (4:25); 147, 165
Festus, 127, 130, 265-267, 276
fight, *see* battle
fill; πληρόω, fill [a job position]; experience the full significance [of God's love, or of His Spirit] (1:23; 3:19; 4:10; 5:18); 42, 50, 79-80, 126, 142, 182
final cause (of Aristotle), the purpose, goal or end of something, 221, 275
financial indebtedness, *see* debt
fire; πυρόω, flaming (6:16); 231, 250
flaming [arrow-volleys], πεπυρωμένα, (6:16); 231, 232, 243, 250
focus; ὁσιότης (Lat. = aspecto), pay exclusive attention to (4:24); 147, 164
foolish words; μωρολογία, foolish, mythic fables that misrepresent God as petty, trivial, selfish or prejudiced (5:4); 175, 197-198
forbearance, 182, 183, 184, 187, 213, 215
force; ἰσχύς, military forces (6:10); 227, 243
forge(d), 90, 106, 111-112, 116, 169
forgiveness; ἄφεσις, forgiveness of a debt [esp. being released from the emotional estrangement, anger and resentment caused by the debtor being hopelessly in debt, due to the creditor releasing the debtor from his obligation to pay the debt] (1:7); 35, 50, 54
fornication, 193
found, θεμελιόω, lay the foundation of, found firmly (3:17); 125, 137
foundation, θεμέλιος, [of a building] (2:20); 91
founding, καταβολή, (1:4); 33, 51
frangrance; εὐωδία, fragrant smell (5:2); 174, 192-193
fraud; πανουργία, scoundrel, swindler (4:14); 144, 155
freeway, προσαγωγή, (2:18, 3:12); 91, 116, 122, 133
friendship, 199, 206; Aristotle on friendship, 190, 217-218,
fulfillment; πλήρωμα, fulfillment [of history]; completed [lifework], sense of fulfillment [in life], fully [mature human being] (1:10, 23; 3:19; 4:13); 37, 42, 126, 143
futile; ματαιότης, worthless (4:17); 145, 159
future kings, 63, 227, 238, 241

G

gamble; κυβεία, [the belief that] major decisions should be made by chance, a gamble or a mere 'roll of the dice' (4:14); 144, 156
gather together, *see* reorganize
gentile, *see* race
gift; δωρεάν, (3:7; 4:7); 120, 141; δῶρον, (2:8); 87
glory (Lat. = gloria), *see* Appearing
God, θεός, (used 32 times in Ephesians)
Goliath, 245, 269-270

good news, εὐαγγέλιον, wonderful message (1:13;3:6; 6:15,19); 38, 64, 120, 131, 230, 237, 249, 276
gospel, *see* good news
gossip, 178, 179
government; οἰκονομία, administration, government, economy (1:10; 3:2, 9); 37, 50, 61, 119, 121, 130
gracious; χάρις, [God's] graciousness, gracious [gift of a spiritual power or ability], gracious [benefit] (1:2, 6, 7; 2:5, 7, 8; 3:2, 7, 8; 4:7, 29; 6:24); 31, 34, 36, 84, 86 [2x], 119, 120 [2x], 141, 148, 238
greaves, *see* boots
greed; πλεονεξία, avarice, insatiable greed (4:19; 5:3); 146, 161, 175, 194
guarantee, *see* bond
guilt, ἔνοχος, 55

H

Hagar, 250
hand-made; χειροποίητος, made by hand, artificial (2:11); 88, 110
Hannibal, 206, 245
head; κεφαλή, the [head] leader (1:22, 4:15); 42, 144, 156
heart; καρδία, the ethical and moral decision making power of the soul (1:18, 3:17, 4:18, 5:19, 6:5, 22); 40, 72, 125, 136, 146, 160, 182, 224, 238, 246-248
helmet; περικεφάλαιος, that which goes around the head, helmet [in military context] (6:17); 233, 251
Hephaestus, 56, 78, 108, 168
Hera, 78
Herod the Great, 256
Herod Agrippa I; 129, 255, 256, 267, 268
Herod Agrippa II; 267
Herod Antipas; 253, 256, 267
High Emissary, ἀπόστολος, (1:1, 2:20, 3:5; 4:11); 29, 44, 91, 120, 142, 153
High King [of the future world], Χριστός, (this word occurs 46 times in Ephesians); 30 ff., 45
holy, *see* special, specially selected
Holy Spirit, *see* Specially Selecting Spirit

Homer, xxxix, xli, 57, 71, 75, 103, 170, 192, 194, 211, 215,
homosexuality, 175
honor(ed), 186, 216
hope for beforehand, προελπίζω, to place hope [in something] before it happens (1:12); 38, 62
house; οἶκος, house, home, any place where one might live; 117
household member; πάροικος, cabinet member, member of a governmental administration (2:19); 50, 91; *see* οἰκονομία
household; οἰκεῖος, household, home (2:19), 50, 91
humorist view of love, 175
hymn(s), 182, 258-259

I

idolater; εἰδωλολάτρης, [lit. idolater] one who trusts in and manipulates material objects as representations or vehicles in the attempt to satisfy desire (5:5); 176
ignorance (willful), *see* darkness (spiritual)
Iliad (by Homer), xxxix, 103, 249
illumination (of the mind),)177, 201, 204, *see* light
immersed; βάπτισμα, immersed under water (4:5); 140, 151
immortality, ἀφθαρσίᾳ, (6:24); 238, 277
implant; ῥιζόω, [lit. to 'root'] implant, embed (3:18), 125, 139
important, 180, 208, 236, 273
Im-port-ant, 210
in exchange for, ἀντὶ, (5:31); 188, 220-221
in order to; ἕνεκεν, for the purpose of, 220, 221
indecisive(ness), 177, 204
inherit, κληρόω, (1:11); 37, 50, 61, 67
inherit; κληρονομέω, to inherit [to obtain by lot (κληρόω) but also by law (νόμος), thus, to be legally appointed], 61
inheritance, κληρονομία, (1:14, 18; 5:5); 38, 40, 50, 67, 176, 200
Inigo Montoya, 108
insensitive; πώρωσις, [lit. a callous, i.e.,] a tough layer of habits gradually built

ENGLISH INDEX 349

up over time that decrease one's ability to sense or feel things – to disregard and become indifferent to the welfare of other people (4:18); 146, 160
intentional, 36, 58-59
interest (financial), 39, 50, 56, 67, 149
interests (the most valuable interests and concerns of life), 199-200
invest (investment), 35, 36, 49, 50, 208-209, 236, 273, 327
in-vest, (in-vest-ment), 210
investor, 49-50
Isaac, 75, 137, 242, 246, 250
Ishmael, 250
Israel, Ἰσραὴλ, (2:12); 88

J
Jacob, 48, 49, 75, 137, 242, 246, 250
James (the brother of John), 153, 253, 255-256, 267-268
Jeroboam, 251
Jerome, 46-47, 52, 53, 269-270,
Jesus, Ἰησοῦς, (1:1, 2, 3, 5, 15, 17; 2:6, 7, 10, 13, 20; 3:1, 9, 11, 14, 21; 4:21; 5:20; 6:23, 24)
John the Immerser (Baptist), 144, 240, 242, 253, 256, 267, 268
joining together with; συναρμολογέω, to fasten or join together carefully, harmoniously, and logically [as in assembling a ship's outer planking or in laying masonry] (2:21, 4:16); 92, 116, 144, 157
joint share-holders (to become), συγκοινωνέω, to become business partners or joint-shareholders with [someone] (5:11); 178, 205
Jonathan, 250
Joseph, 98, 242
Josephus, 51, 98-99, 100, 197, 245
Judas, 142

K
King David, *see* David, King
King Henry V, 273
King Henry VIII, xxviii-xxx, xliii
King John, 43, 111
King Saul, 245, 246, 250
king, βασιλεύς, 45
kingdom, βασιλεία, (5:5); 48, 176, 200

Kingdom Apprenticeship Council, ἐκκλησία, Lifework Council, (1:22; 3:10, 21; 5:23, 24, 25, 27, 29, 32); 42, 78, 122, 127, 132, 183, 185, 187, 188
know (comprehend), *see* comprehensive understanding
know; γινώςκω, to know by experience as well as by education, to be briefed by someone who knows from direct experience (3:19; 5:5; 6:22); 126, 176, 238
know (to come to know), *see* realize
Knox, John; 78

L
Langton, Stephen; 43, 111,
law, νόμος, rule; 60, 61, 67
lawless; ἄνομος, unlawful, 55
lead captive; ἠχμαλώτευσεν αἰχμαλωσίαν, "He led captives into captivity," ref. to Ps. 68:18 (Eph. 4:8); 142, 152-153
Lead Negotiator, πρεσβεύω, (6:20); 237, 277
leadership office, κυριότητος, (1:21); 41, 75
learn; μανθάνω, to learn and acquire the habits of a way of life by disciplined study, practice and experience (4:20); 146, 161
learners; μαθητής, pupils, apprentices, 162
least of all; ἐλαχιστότερος, less than the least (3:8); 120, 132
Lesbian, 194
lethargy (neglecting), 179
leverage, 210
Lewis, C.S., 190
liability; ὑπόδικος, legal liability, 55
liberal democracy(ies), 111
lie; ψεῦδος, a lie told to oneself or others, or giving in to the predisposition to acquiesce and accept falsehood (4:25); 147, 164
life; ζωή, qualitative spiritual and emotional life; vital, authentic and significant life (4:18); 145, 173
Lifework Apprenticeship Council; *see* Lifework Council, Kingdom Apprenticeship Council

Lifework Council; ἐκκλησία, or Kingdom Apprenticeship Council, Lifework Council, (1:22; 3:10, 21; 5:23, 24, 25, 27, 29, 32); 42, 78, 122, 127, 132, 183, 185, 187, 188

lifework; κλῆσις, life project, vocation, profession, occupation, job apprenticeship (1:18; 4:1, 4); 41, 73, 139, 140, 150,

lifeworld, xxvii, xxxii, xl, xliii, xliv, xlvi, , 59, 82, 84, 88, 89

light; φῶς, [lit. 'light' (of truth)]; living life in a publicly open way, showing sincere motives, honesty, vulnerability, mercy and legitimacy in order to lead others; illumination [of the mind] through continual learning and education; projecting one's public character with consistency and clarity (5:8, 13); 177, 179, 201-204

live in a home; κατοικέω, to land, plant a colony, then settle in, then live, and finally adminster and govern a new land (3:17); 124-125, 136

lobby, *see* petition

logic, *see* reason

long range archery, *see* arrow-volley

Lord, *see* Commander in Chief

Lord's Prayer, 55, 70

Lot, 250

love; ἀγάπη, self-sacrificial love (1:4, 15; 2:4; 3:17, 19; 4:2, 15, 16; 5:2; 6:23); 34, 52, 144, 150, 156, 174, 191, 251

loving, glad, cheerful and contented person, 190, 173, 238, 277

M

MacDonald, George; 190

Magna Carta, 43-44, 111

make; ποιέω, forge, build, create, conceive, produce, solve a problem, satisfy a condition (1:16; 2:3, 14, 15; 3:11, 20; 4:16; 6:6, 8, 9); 89, 105, 106, 111

Malta, 128, 129, 261, 267, 268, 276

manager(s), 46, 224, 225, 242

Marcinko, Richard, 249

Maro, son of Euanthes, 211

marriage relationship, 175, 183, 184, 185, 188, 189, 196, 213, 215, 222, 224,

Mary, 223, 242

masterwork; ποίημα, [lit. 'poem'] masterpiece, (2:10) 87, 105

mastery of the military arts, 227, 242

mature (spiritually), τέλειος, (4:13); 143

measure; μέτρον, measure [in both senses of laying out dimensions prior to construction, as well as evaluating and appraising value or performance after construction is completed] (4:7, 13, 16); 141, 143, 145, 152, 153, 158

Medieval era, xvii, xxiii-xxvii, xxxiv-xxxix, 43

Mediterranean Sea, xxi, xli, 34, 90, 91, 141, 253, 261, 267, 268

men's clubs, 175

merciful, 177

message of good news, *see* good news

Messiah, 45, 60, 95, 98, 141, 153, 235, 252, 253, 263

methods (of the Devil), *see* schemes

Milcom, 246

military service, 100, 168, 224, 225, 241, 242

military campaign or expedition, 229, 278, 230

military force(s), ἰσχύς, (6:10); 227, 228, 243

military command (military authority and its corresponding rank, earned and awarded as a result of mastering ascending levels of the practice of the military arts), xxi, 241-242

military equipment and weaponry; πανοπλία, soldier's military equipment, including belt, body armor, helmet, shield, boots, and sword (6:11, 13); 49, 226, 227, 228, 229, 242,

military fight, *see* battle

military officer, xxii, 46, 225, 242, 263, 264, 265

Military Quartermaster, 49, 51, 278

Millennial Kingdom, 48

Millennium, 48

mind (habits of); νόος, a formulated philosophical world view that is motivated by habits of feeling,

English Index

perceiving, understanding, and reasoned thinking; which is able to resolve purposes, intentions, plans and decisions about reality (4:17, 23); 145, 146, 159, 163

miser; πλεονέκτης, self-centered materialist (5:5); 176, 200

miss the mark, *see* fall short

Modern era, xvii, xx, xxxvi, xxxviii, 111

Morgenstern, 270

Moses, 48, 126, 137, 140, 158, 235, 242, 250, 258,

mystery, *see* Top Secret

N

naïve; νήπιος, naïve, purile, gullible and thus vulnerable (4:14); 144, 154

Navy "SEAL," 248, 249

Negotiator, *see* Lead Negotiator

neighbor, *see* fellow human being

Neoptolemus, 201-203

Nero, 127, 129, 130, 240, 261, 262

new; καινός, new, bright and fresh[ly outfitted] (2:15; 4:24); 90, 147, 163

Nicomachean Ethics (by Aristotle), 57, 100, 101, 190, 198, 206, 215, 217,

Noah, 242

nurture, *see* raise [children]

O

obtain, 207

ob-tain, 208

Ocean; i.e., deepest parts of the Ocean, 228, 244

Odysseus, 71, 164, 203, 211

Odyssey (by Homer), xxxix, 71, 103, 192, 211

OECONOMICA (by Aristotle), 60-61

offspring; παῖς, offspring, progeny, issue; 189

off-track, *see* sidetracked

old; παλαιός, foolish, acerbic, aged person [i.e., cynical "old folks"] (5:22); 146, 162

opening; τόπος, opportunity (4:27); 148, 167

opinion, 52-53

op-port-une, 210

opportunity; καιρός, history, proportion, important, relevant, investment, cooperation, consequence, season, time (1:10; 2:12; 5:16; 6:18); 37, 88, 180, 181, 208-210, 236, 273

organization; κόσμος, organized system of civilized government, organization, enterprise, or business (1:4; 2:2, 12); 33, 52

orgiastic view of love, 175

Origen, 268

ought; ὀφείλω, to be in debt, owe, ought, (5:28); 55, 56

outburst; κραυγὴ, blowing up in public outbursts of shouting, screaming or shrieking (4:31); 149, 170

owe, *see* ought

P

parental relationship, 183, 213, 222-224

partiality (to show); προσωπεῖον, putting on a mask [by deceitfully manipulating one's own facial expressions] (see προσωπολημψία), 241

partiality; προσωπολημψία, accepting uncritically at face value the fraudulent intentions of someone pretending to have good motives through the calculated and deceitful use of their facial expressions (6:9); 226, 241

partition; μεσότοιχος, partition wall, dividing wall (2:14); 89

partner (with); συμμέτοχος, fellow business partner, equal partner (3:6; 5:7); 120, 131, 176, 200

partner; μετόχος, partner, associate, colleague (see συμμέτοχος), 200

patience, *see* persistence

Patton, 274

Paul, Παῦλος, (1:1; 3:1); 29, 43, 118, 127; experiences of suffering and divine rescue, 128; eight major journeys, 129 (summary); 252-268 (detailed)

peace; εἰρήνη, [God of] Peace, P[p]eace[maker] (2:14; 6:15), 89, 110-111, 230, 249

perceive, *see* understand

persistence; προσκαρτερήσει, patience, persistence, diligence, devotion (6:18); 236, 274-275

Peter, 153, 247, 267, 268, 269,

petition; δέησις, lobbying or submitting official petitions to God to act in our behalf [because we recognize we need His assistance to accomplish an objective] (6:18); 70, 236, 248, 271, 273
Pharaoh, 51, 76, 136, 249
Pharisees, 97-100
Philoctetes (by Sophocles), 201-203
philosophical world view, *see* world view
philosophy, 93, 150, 158
Plato, 93, 190, 194
Plutarch, 249
political official, 26, 47, 128, 242
Politics (by Aristotle), 68, 69, 272
Polybius, 160-161, 206-207
polygamy, 175
polytheistic religion, 76, 78, 82, 84, 94, 103, 243
pornography, 174, 176, 193
Poseidon, 78, 162, 194
power; see gracious [gift of a spiritual power or ability], heart [ethical or moral decision making power of the soul], regime [political power], authority [official power]
pray(er); *see* request, petition, lobby
Predator, *see* Devil
predestine, *see* pre-survey
pre-finance, *see* pre-survey
prejudice, 175, 197-198
pre-mark out, *see* pre-survey
preplan, *see* pre-survey
preserve, 86, 126
pressure (psychological), *see* stress
pre-survey; προορίζω, preplan, pre-mark out, pre-survey, pre-finance, amortize (1:5, 11); 34, 37, 50, 52
prince, *see* authority
prisoner, *see* bond
proclamation; πρόθεσις, following sufficient planning and deliberation, to assert or publish in public an official case, proposition or statement (1:11, 3:11); 37, 61, 122, 133
procure, 207
Pro-cure, 208
Prophet, *see* Spokesperson(s) (Divine)
proportion, 58-59, 208, 273
Pro-portion, 208, 210

prostitution, 51, 146, 161, 175, 193
Providence, 124, 135, 209
provoke; παροργίζω, to provoke to anger (6:4); 223, 240
purchase, 54, 67, 207
Pur-chase, 207
put it all together, *see* well taught
put on and wear, *see* dress up

Q

qualifications, *see* qualify
qualified, *see* qualify
qualify; δοκιμάζω, to prove one's qualifications, to become qualified for high office (5:10); 178, 205
questioning, *see* confront

R

race (non-Jewish); ἔθνος, a member of any ethnic race or nation foreign to Judaism [whether a civilized Greek or an uncivilized Barbarian] (2:11, 3:1, 6, 8; 4:17); 88, 109, 118, 120, 130, 131, 145, 159
rage; θυμός, exploding in impulsive fits of fury or rage [that arise from suddenly aroused passions] (4:31); 149, 169
Rahab, 242
raise (children); ἐκτρέφω, to rear, to bring up, to raise properly, to educate, to nurture [children] (5:29; 6:4); 187, 219, 223, 240
rancorous, *see* disgusting
rank of authority; κράτος, military authority and its corresponding rank [earned and awarded as a result of mastering ascending levels of the practice of the military arts] (6:10); 227, 242
ransom, *see* redemption
realize; εἶδον (οἶδα) [Lat. = videre], to realize, to see, to come to know [the truth of something] (1:18; 6:8, 9, 21), 40, 57-58, 224, 225, 238
reason, λόγος, the ability to think intelligently and speak with a clear mind, using the best logical reasoning in public speaking, whether the forum be teaching, a public speech, debate or legal defense (6:19); 236-237, 275-276

ENGLISH INDEX

redeem, *see* redemption
redemption, ἀπολύτρωσις, (1:7, 14; 4:30); 35, 39, 50, 53, 149, 169
reflect; μνεία, the ability to think about and reflect upon something [or someone] and formulate specific plans do something about it [or for them] (1:16); 40, 68
refute, *see* confront
regime; ἀρχῆς καὶ ἐξουσίας καὶ δυνάμεως καὶ κυριότητος; [angelic] regime, hierarchy of authority, sovereign power and leadership office (1:21, 2:2, 3:10, 6:12); 41, 75, 82, 121, 228, 243
regimes (governmental), κοσμοκράτορας, (6:12); 228, 243
regimes; ἀρχάς …ἐξουσίας… κοσμοκράτορας… πνευματικὰ τῆς πονηρίας; [evil angelic] regimes… hierarchies of authority… [human] governmental regimes… [and the] evil [heirarchy of] spiritual beings [that control them] (6:12); 228, 243
Rehoboam, 251
relevant, 208-209
Re-lev-ant, 210
reorganize; ἀνακεφαλαιώσασθαι, to comprehensively reorganize an administration under a new authority structure (1:10); 37
request (to God); προσεύχομαι, to request information from God in order to discover sufficient essential facts necessary to make an important spiritual decision, to seek God's direction in the process of gaining a spiritual understanding or perspective in order to plan an important course of action for the future (1:16, 6:18); 39, 69, 236
rescue (to), σώζω, (2:5, 8); 84, 87, 102, 105
rescue; σωτηρία, rescue, deliverance (1:13); 38, 65
resist, *see* confront
resurrect(ed), resurrection, 34-35, 37, 39, 85, 87, 126, 143, 149, 186, 233
revive, ἀνανεόομαι, (4:23); 146, 163
Rhetoric (by Aristotle), 192, 199
rich; πλούσιος, rich, wealthy (2:4); 84

riches, *see* wealth
right; δικαιοσύνη, the right thing to do [legally, ethically and morally] (4:24); 147, 164
road; ὁδός, road, way, journey, [The Road, The Way, The Journey – a major metaphor describing the Christian's lifework quest] 95-97
Roman Catholic Church, xvii, xxi, xxv-xxx, xliii, 47
romantic view of love, 174-176
Rome, xxii-xxiv, xxix, xxxv, xlii, 42, 98, 100, 118, 123, 127, 237, 238, 259, 261, 264-269, 276, 277
root, *see* implant
ruler(s), *see* regime(s)
Runnymede, 111
Ruth, 242

S

saints, *see* specially selected recruits
salvation, *see* rescue, deliver, deliverance
Samson, 67, 246
Samuel, 242, 257
Sapphira, 247
Sarah, 242, 250
Satan, 50, 51, 54, 71, 76, 78, 82, 84, 94, 115, 121, 147, 148, 176, 227, 232, 235, 243, 244, 247, 248, 250, 263; *see* Devil, Slanderer
Saul (Paul), 95, 97, 121, 129, 162, 239, 247, 248, 252-257, 263
save, *see* rescue, deliver
savings account; περιποίησις, that which has been gained through acquisition and saved, savings account (1:14); 39, 67
schemes; μεθοδεία, [transliteration: methods] stratagems, schemes, maneuvers, feints, ambushes, snares, booby traps (4:14, 6:11); 144, 155, 227, 243
scream(ing), *see* outburst
screen wall; φραγμός, fence, partition, fortification wall (2:14); 89, 112
seal (to); σφραγίζω, to officially certify or authenticate [something that significantly affects the public health, safety and welfare], and signify legal responsibility for such by application

of a recognized stamp or symbol (1:13; 4:30); 38, 65, 149, 169
season, 208, 209
see (to come to know), *see* realize
select; ἐκλέγω, to single out, select, or choose someone or something for a special purpose [i.e., levying taxes, charging a toll, the selection of building materials and the selection of soldiers and their weapons] (1:4); 49, 50, 242
service; χρεία, to gain the ability to become useful, to provide a service [esp. 'providing a service' in business or 'going into the service' in the military] (4:28, 29); 148, 168, 169
service; χρηστός, service required to achieve the best and most beneficial outcome (4:31); 149, 170
sexual intercourse (immoral); πορνεία, consensual [albeit immature] sexual intercourse outside the bond of marriage (5:3); 174-175, 193
sexually degrading compulsion; αἰσχρότης, abnormal, degrading, violent, sexual compulsion [i.e., rape, sadism, masochism] that deforms the soul, leaving it distorted and hideously ugly (5:4); 175, 194-197
Shakespeare, xix, xxx, xxxi, xxxiv, xliii, 273
shame, *see* confront
shield (large rectangular); θυρεός (Lat. = scutum), oblong, rectangular, curved [Roman] shield, shaped like a door, covering the body from head to foot (6:16); 231, 249
shield (smaller oval); ἀσπίς, σάκος (Lat. = clipeus), 249-250
shout(ing), *see* outburst
shriek(ing), *see* outburst
sidetracked (to get); παραπίπτω, to fall to the side [of the road], to get sidetracked, 56
sidetracked; παράπτωμα, [e.g., from one's lifework] (1:7; 2:1, 5); 35, 55-56, 81, 83, 84, 95
Sidonians, 246
Simon the Leper, 193
Simon Peter, *see* Peter
Simon the Pharisee, 193

sin, *see* fall short, failure, sidetracked
sing(ing), 182, 258, 259
skill (ethical and moral), *see* ethical skill
sky, ἀήρ, (2:2); 82, 94
Slanderer, διάβολος [transliterated 'Devil'], Deceiver, Maligner, Accuser, Mocker, Scorner, Criticizer, Liar, Swindler, Fraud, Predator (4:27; 6:11); 148, 166, 227, 241, 247
slave, *see* employee
slavery, 241
sleep; καθεύδω, [lit. to sleep] to neglect, to lapse into a state of lethargy (5:13); 179, 206
smell (of frangrances), ὀσμή, (5:2); 174, 191
Sodom and Gomorrah, 250
soldier; ὁπλίτης, foot soldier, *see* πανοπλία
soldier's military equipment, *see* military equipment and weaponry
Solomon, King; 67, 126, 185, 215, 246, 251
song; ψαλμός, a spiritual song sung individually or as a group, accompanied by a musical instrument or instruments (5:19); 182, 212
Sophocles, xxxix, xli, 135, 196, 201-203, 215
sorcery, 232, 250
speak (openly and freely in public), *see* confidence
speak the truth; ἀληθεύω, to discover and speak what is true publicly (4:15); 144, 156
special (1:4, 2:21, 5:27); 33, 44, 92, 186
specially selected High Emissary (3:5); 45, 120
specially selected; ἅγιος(οι), as pl. n. specially selected recruits, (1:1, 15, 18; 2:19, 3:8, 18; 4:12, 5:3, 6:18); 30, 39, 41, 45, 91, 120, 125, 143, 174, 236; as pl. adj. specially selected ([High Emissaries] - 3:5); 120, as sg. adj. Specially Selecting ([Spirit] - 1:13; 4:30); 38, 45, 65, 148
Specially Selecting Spirit (1:13, 4:30); 38, 45, 65, 148
speech, *see* word (skillful public speech)
spikenard, 192

ENGLISH INDEX

spiritual (being); πνευματικὰ τῆς πονηρίας, evil [heirarchy of] spiritual beings (6:12); 228, 243

spiritual; πνευματικῇ, [disciplines, habits, attitudes, thoughts, demeanors and behaviors] (1:3); 33

Spokesperson(s) (Divine); προφήταις, [transliteration = 'prophet'] Official [Divine] Spokespersons (2:20); 131

stand (firm), στῆτε, [impv. of ἵστημι] never give up (6:14); 229, 245

steal; κλέπτω, steal, embezzle, run a confidence racket, smuggle (4:28); 148, 167

Stephen, 129, 162, 233, 239, 247, 248, 252, 254, 262, 268,

stewardship, 60, 207, 208; see government, procure

stratagems, see schemes

stress; θλῖψις, [psychological] pressure and resulting stress (3:13); 123, 134

strip-tease joints, 175

stubborn(ness), see darkness (spiritual)

stupefied, see darkness (spiritual)

submit; see defer(ence), forbear(ance)

subordinate; ὑποτάσσω, to subordinate; to develop the spiritual skill of adopting a cheerful and gracious attitude of deference and forbearance, trusting and supporting others, offering to help and enjoying the opportunity to gladly assist them in their efforts with a positive frame of mind (5:21, 22, 24);182-183, 212-215; see defer(ence), forbear(ance)

subordinate officer(s), see employee

suicide, 98, 232, 250, 258

superior officer(s), 122, 224

supply; ἐπιχορηγία, supply, provision, fortune [emph. of more common χορηγία = office or λητουργία of a χορηγός, one who is wealthy enough to pay for the cost of public choruses], (4:16); 145, 157

surrender, παραδίδωμι, [hand over a person to legal officials] (5:2); 174

survey; ὁρίζω, survey, mark out land, mark out with money, make a claim; 52

sword; μάχαιρα, short combat sword used by infantry (6:17); 233, 269

sword-belt, see arm (oneself for battle)

T

take off; ἀποτίθημι, to 'take off and leave outside' [one's former lifestyle and habitual way of viewing things] (4:22, 25); 146, 147, 162, 164

Tertullian, 268

testify (as a legal witness); μαρτύρομαι, to be summoned to testify as an official, legal witness [especially by a divinity] (4:17); 145, 159

The Foreign Wars (by Appian), 245

The Princess Bride (by Morgenstern), 270

thief (embezzler, con-artist, or smuggler), see steal

think; φρονέω, to be able to habitually discern, think through and make good decisions about matters that affect the lives of others in society, 58

Third (3rd) Army, 274

time, see opportunity

Top Secret; μυστήριον, Divine Top Secret Plan (1:9, 3:3, 4, 9, 5:32; 6:19); 36, 59, 119, 121, 130, 131, 188, 237

toward πρός, 69

tree, see truth

trespass (to); παραβαίνω, trespass (v.), encroach, infringe, intrude, 55

trespass; παράβασις, trespass (n.), infringement, intrusion, 55

trespasser; παραβάτης, intruder, 55

tricked; ἀπάτη, tricked, cheated (5:22); 146, 163

trustworthy; πιστοῖς, experienced, reliable, dedicated and dependable veterans (1:1); 30

truth [as uncovered, discovered or realized], ἀλήθεια, 1:13; 4:21, 24, 25; 5:9; 6:14), 38, 62, 146, 147,178, 229, 246

Twelve High Emissaries, 142, 153

Twelve Sons of Israel, 48

Tychicus, 237

U

Uncircumcised, 88, 110

uncircumcised, ἀκροβυστία, (2:11); 88, 110

un-conceal(ed), 62; see truth

uncover(ed), 62, *see* truth
understand; συνίημι, to deliberately face a dilemma and perceive what to do [about it] with understanding and composure of mind (5:17); 181, 211
unveil, ἀποκαλύπτω [a divine message] (3:5); 120, 131
unveiled, ἀποκάλυψις, [divine message] (1:17; 3:3); 40, 71, 119, 130
ureliable; ἄνεμος, unreliable, volatile [as a windstorm] (4:14); 144, 156
Uriah, 251

V
vehicle (extended metaphor), xlv, xlvi, 49, 106, 242, 271
venture capitalist, 49, 50
vocational relationship, 183, 213, 224
Vulgate, xxi, xxii, xxiv, 47, 281
vulnerable, *see* light

W
walk, *see* world view
waste(d); φθείρω, wasted, ruined, spoiled (5:22); 146, 163
watch; γρηγορέω, to watch, be on the lookout [synonym of ἀγρυπνέω], 273
watch; ἀγρυπνέω, to spend a sleepless night communicating with and intently petitioning God, and watching for an answer (6:18); 236, 273-274
wealth; πλοῦτος, riches (1:7, 18; 2:7; 3:8, 16); 35, 41, 86, 120, 124, 131
well taught; συμβιβάζω, to 'put it all together (in one's mind)' i.e., to be able, because of being taught well, to logically conclude the truth about something (4:16); 145, 157
width, length, height and depth; πλάτος καὶ μῆκος καὶ ὕψος καὶ βάθος, width and length and height [dimensions of the superstructure of a building] and depth [crucial dimension of the foundation of a building] (3:18); 125-126, 137
wine, οἶνος, [unmixed with water] (5:18); 181, 211
wisdom, *see* ethical skill

wish; εὔχομαι, to wish, desire, or hope for something to come about in the future, 69
wit, 57,
witch, 250
witty, *see* cultured insolence
witness, *see* testify (as a legal witness)
wives' tales, *see* foolish words
wizard, 57-58,
wonderful message, *see* good news
word (skillful public speech); ῥῆμα, the facility of using public speech to communicate skillfully and accurately (5:26; 6:17); 186, 216, 233, 210
word, *see* reason
work; ἐργάζομαι, work at a trade or business to earn an honest living (4:28); 148, 168
work; ἐργασία, work, trade or business in human vice or organized crime (4:19); 146, 161
work; ἔργον, enterprise, venture, endeavor, project, undertaking, business, industry, operation, work (2:9, 10; 4:12; 5:11); 87, 107
work; κοπιάω, hard labor [so as to make one exhausted by the end of the work day] (4:28); 148, 167
world view (to live according to a); περιπατέω, [lit. 'to walk around'] to deliberately and intentionally learn, practice and teach others a comprehensive philosophical world view (2:2, 10; 4:1, 17; 5:2, 8, 15); 82, 87, 93, 103, 109, 139, 145, 150, 159, 174, 177, 180, 191, 200, 201, 206
world, *see* government

X
Xenophon, 203, 204, 248, 269

Y
Yahweh, 32, 48, 206, 220, 235, 251
young man; νεανίης (Paul), 129, 239

Z
Zeus, 76, 77, 78, 82, 94, 110, 194, 195, 243

Greek Index and Glossary

A

ἄβυσσος, abyss, 244

ἀγάπῃ, self-sacrificial love (1:4, 15; 2:4; 3:17, 19; 4:2, 15, 16; 5:2; 6:23); 34, 52, 144, 150, 156, 174, 191, 251

ἀγαπητὸς, glad, cheerful contentment (5:1, 6:21); 173, 189-190, 238, 277

ἅγιος(οι), as pl. n. specially selected recruits, (1:1, 15, 18; 2:19, 3:8, 18; 4:12, 5:3, 6:18); 30, 39, 41, 45, 91, 120, 125, 143, 174, 236; as pl. adj. specially selected ([High Emissaries] - 3:5); 120, as sg. adj. Specially Selecting ([Spirit] - 1:13; 4:30); 38, 45, 65, 148

ἄγροικος, boorishness, 198, 199

ἀγρυπνέω, to spend a sleepless night communicating with and intently petitioning God, and watching for an answer (6:18); 236, 273-274

ἀδελφός, [lit. 'brother'] esteemed colleague, associate, fellow, future king (6:10, 21); 227, 238, 241, 277

ἀήρ, sky, (2:2); 82, 94

αἷμα, [lit. 'blood'] put to death by capital punishment (1:7, 2:13); 35, 89; terrestrial human being (6:12); 77, 228

αἰσχρότης, abnormal, degrading, violent, sexual compulsion [i.e., rape, sadism, masochism] that deforms the soul, leaving it distorted and hideously ugly (5:4); 175, 194-197

αἰτοῦμαι, to ask, (3:13); 123, 130, 133

αἰών, era, epoch, age, (1:21; 2:2, 7; 3:9, 11, 21; 6:12); 41, 78, 82, 86, 121, 122, 127, 228

ἀκαθαρσία, depravity ['uncleanness' in an ethical or moral sense] (4:19; 5:3); 146, 161, 175, 194

ἀκάθαρτος, depraved (5:5); 176, 200

ἀκροβυστία, uncircumcised (2:11); 88, 110

ἀκρογωνιαῖος, corner foundation stone (2:20), 91, 106

ἀλήθεια, truth [as uncovered, discovered or realized] (1:13; 4:21, 24, 25; 5:9; 6:14), 38, 62, 146, 147,178, 229, 246

ἀληθεύω, to discover and speak what is true publicly (4:15); 144, 156

ἁμαρτάνω, to miss or fall short [of a goal or opportunity], fail, lose (4:26); 55, 93, 147, 165-166, 173

ἁμαρτία, missed, failure, loss [of a goal or opportunity] (2:1), 55, 93, 173

ἀμήν, public recognition and wholehearted agreement to live according to the conclusive truths of a convincing line of reasoning (3:21; 6:24); 127, 138, 238, 277

ἀνακεφαλαιώσασθαι, to comprehensively reorganize an administration under a new authority structure (1:10); 37

ἀνανεόομαι, revive (4:23); 146, 163

ἀναστρέφω, to have one's public demeanor formed for better or worse by one's habitual public associations (2:3); 50, 83, 100-102

ἀναστροφή (see ἀναστρέφω), one's public demeanor, behavior and attitude formed by one's habitual public associations (5:22) 146, 162

ἄνεμος, unreliable, volatile [as a windstorm] (4:14); 144, 156

ἀνήκω, to rise to a higher level, to aspire to (5:4); 175, 199-200

ἄνομος, lawless, unlawful, 55

ἀντὶ, in exchange for (5:31); 188, 220

ἀπαλγέω, to give up hope, to despair (4:19); 146, 160

ἀπάτη, tricked, cheated (5:22); 146, 163

ἀπείθεια, obstinate refusal to comply with legitimate authority (2:2; 5:6); 83, 94, 176, 200

ἀπηλλοτριόω, to be alienated [from legal citizenship or status] (2:18; 4:18); 90, 145, 160

ἀποκαλύπτω, to unveil [a divine message] (3:5); 120, 131

357

ἀποκάλυψις, unveiled [divine message] (1:17; 3:3); 40, 71, 119, 130

ἀπολύτρωσις, redemption (1:7, 14; 4:30); 35, 39, 50, 53, 149, 169

ἀπόστολος, High Emissary (1:1, 2:20, 3:5 and 4:11); 29, 44

ἀποτίθημι, to 'take off and leave outside' [one's former lifestyle and habitual way of viewing things] (4:22, 25); 146, 147, 162, 164

ἀρθήτω (aor pass imp - αἴρω), to 'clear away' [bad thoughts, attitudes, speech and behavior] (4:31); 149, 169

ἀρραβών, earnest money, down payment (1:14); 38, 67

ἀρχή, chief leader [of the rebellious angels = Satan], (1:21, 2:2, 3:10, 6:12); 41, 75, 82, 121, 228

ἀρχῆς καὶ ἐξουσίας καὶ δυνάμεως καὶ κυριότητος; [angelic] regime, hierarchy of authority, sovereign power and leadership office (1:21, 2:2, 3:10, 6:12); 41, 75, 82, 121, 228, 243

ἀρχάς...ἐξουσίας....κοσμοκράτορας... πνευματικὰ τῆς πονηρίας; [evil angelic] regimes...hierarchies of authority...[human] governmental regimes...[and the] evil [heirarchy of] spiritual beings [that control them] (6:12); 228, 243

ἄφεσις, forgiveness of a debt [esp. being released from the emotional estrangement, anger and resentment caused by the debtor being hopelessly in debt, due to the creditor releasing the debtor from his obligation to pay the debt] (1:7); 35, 50, 54

ἀφή, enlightening relational contact [with other people or with the Spirit of God] (4:16); 145, 157

ἀφθαρσίᾳ, immortality (6:24); 238, 277

B

βάπτισμα, immersed under water (4:5); 140, 151

βασιλεύς, king, 45

βασιλεία, kingdom (5:5); 48, 176, 200

βέλος, arrow volley (6:16); 231, 250

βίος, biological life form, 173

βλασφημία, spouting blasphemous, irreverent speech against God (4:31); 149, 170

βωμολοχία, buffoonery, foolishness [synonym of εὐτραπελία], 198-199

Γ

γινώςκω, to know by experience as well as by education, to be briefed by someone who knows from direct experience (3:19; 5:5; 6:22); 126, 176, 238

γρηγορέω, to watch, be on the lookout [synonym of ἀγρυπνέω], 273

Δ

δέησις, lobbying or submitting official petitions to God to act in our behalf [because we recognize we need His assistance to accomplish an objective] (6:18); 70, 236, 248, 271, 273

δέσμιος, bond (prisoner, i.e., one who is in bondage) or Bond [guarantee of the performance of a contract], (3:1; 4:1); 118, 119, 127, 130, 139, 150

διάβολος [transliterated 'devil'], Slanderer, Deceiver, Maligner, Accuser, Mocker, Scorner, Criticizer, Liar, Swindler, Fraud, Predator (4:27; 6:11); 148, 166, 227, 241, 247

δικαιοσύνη, the right thing to do [legally, ethically and morally] (4:24); 147, 164

δοκιμάζω, to prove one's qualifications, to become qualified for high office (5:10); 178, 205

δόξα, Appearing, Appearance[of God] (1:6, 12, 14, 17, 18; 3:13, 16, 21); 34, 38, 39, 40, 41, 52, 123, 124, 127, 135

δοῦλος, [lit. slave] employee, subordinate officer (6:5); 224, 241

δωρεάν, gift (3:7; 4:7); 120, 141

δῶρον, gift (2:8); 87

E

ἐγκακέω, to slip into a pervasive dispirited and defeatist mood, leading to a cynical attitude of despair and the neglect of performing one's responsibilities (3:13); 123, 133

ἔθνος, a member of any ethnic race or nation foreign to Judaism [whether a

Greek Index and Glossary

civilized Greek or an uncivilized Barbarian] (2:11, 3:1, 6, 8; 4:17); 88, 109, 118, 120, 130, 131, 145, 159

εἰδωλολάτρης [lit. idolater], one who trusts in and manipulates material objects as representations or vehicles in an attempt to satisfy desire (5:5); 176

εἶδον (οἶδα), to realize, to see, to come to know [the truth of something] (1:18; 6:8, 9, 21), 40, 57-58, 224, 225, 238

εἰρήνη, [God of] Peace, P[p]eace[maker] (2:14; 6:15), 89, 110-111, 230, 249

ἐκκλησία, Kingdom Apprenticeship Council, Lifework Council, (1:22; 3:10, 21; 5:23, 24, 25, 27, 29, 32); 42, 78, 122, 127, 132, 183, 185, 187, 188

ἐκλέγω, to single out, select, or choose someone or something for a special purpose [i.e., levying taxes, charging a toll, the selection of building materials and the selection of soldiers and their weapons] (1:4); 49, 50, 242

ἐκτρέφω, to rear, to bring up, to raise properly, educate, nurture [children] (5:29; 6:4); 187, 219, 223, 240

ἐλαχιστότερος, less than the least (3:8), 120, 132

ἐλέγχω, to confront, to challenge, to question, to expose, to refute, to resist, to arrest (5:11, 13); 178, 179, 205

ἔνδοξος, special, dignified, distinguished, public recognition (5:27); 186, 216

ἐνδύω, to 'dress up' [one's mind] (4:24: 6:11, 14); 147, 163, 227, 230, 243

ἕνεκεν, for the purpose of, 220, 221

ἔνοχος, guilt, 55

ἐξαγοραζω, buy up, buy out, purchase, acquire, obtain, procure (5:16); 180, 206-208

ἐξουσία, [angelic] hierarchy of authority (1:21, 2:2, 3:10, 6:12); 41, 75, 82, 121, 228, 243

ἔπαινον, to recognize and then publicly and universally appreciate, acknowledge and express honor [to someone] (1:6, 12, 14); 34, 38, 39

ἐπίγνωσις, comprehensive understanding, (1:17; 4:13); 40, 143

ἐπιστάτης, Commander, 46

ἐπιχορηγία, supply, provision, fortune [emph. of more common χορηγία = office or λητουργία of a χορηγός, one who is wealthy enough to pay for the cost of public choruses], (4:16); 145, 157

ἐποικοδομέω, to build up, to build upon (2:20); 91, 116

ἐργάζομαι, work at a trade or business, earn an honest living (4:28); 148, 168

ἐργασία, work, trade or business in human vice or organized crime (4:19); 146, 161

ἔργον, enterprise, venture, endeavor, project, undertaking, business, industry, operation, work (2:9, 10; 4:12; 5:11); 87, 107

εὐαγγελίζομαι, announce good news, bring a wonderful message (2:17; 3:8); 90, 116, 120, 131

εὐαγγέλιον, good news, wonderful message (1:13;3:6; 6:15,19); 38, 64, 120, 131, 230, 237, 249, 276

εὐάρεστος, distinguished confidence or trust earned after being tested or proved [by a superior officer] (5:10); 178, 204

εὐλογέω, to deliver a commendation speech, eulogy, (1:3); 31, 47-48

εὐλογητὸς, [lit. Eulogizer] Keynote Speaker (1:3); 31, 47-48

εὐλογία, keynote address, proclamation, commendation speech, eulogy (1:3); 31, 32, 47-48

εὔσπλαγχνος, deep feeling for and understanding of misery or suffering and the concomitant desire to promote its alleviation (4:32); 149, 171

εὐτραπελία, cultured insolence [buffoonery] (5:4); 175, 198-199

εὔχομαι, to wish, desire, or hope for something to come about in the future, 69

εὐωδία, frangrance, fragrant smell (5:2); 174, 192-193

Z

ζωή, qualitative spiritual and emotional life; vital, authentic and significant life (4:18); 145, 173

Η

ἠχμαλώτευσεν αἰχμαλωσίαν, "He led captives into captivity," ref. to Ps. 68:18 (Eph. 4:8); 142, 152-153

Θ

θάλπω, to warmly care for and gently comfort (5:29); 187, 220
θεμέλιος, foundation [of a building] (2:20); 91
θεμελιόω, lay the foundation of, found firmly (3:17); 125, 137
θεός, God (used 32 times in Ephesians)
θλῖψις, [psychological] pressure and resulting stress (3:13); 123, 134
θυμός, exploding in impulsive fits of fury or rage [that arise from suddenly aroused passions] (4:31); 149, 169
θυρεός, oblong, rectangular, curved [Roman] shield, shaped like a door, covering the body from head to foot (6:16); 231, 249
θώραξ, body armor, breastplate, chain-mail covering the chest, chest-armor, bullet-proof vest (6:14); 230, 246

Ι

Ἰησοῦς, Jesus (1:1, 2, 3, 5, 15, 17; 2:6, 7, 10, 13, 20; 3:1, 9, 11, 14, 21; 4:21; 5:20; 6:23, 24)
Ἰσραὴλ, Israel (2:12); 88
ἰσχύς, military forces (6:10); 227, 243

Κ

καθεύδω, [lit. to sleep] to neglect, to lapse into a state of lethargy (5:13); 179, 206
καινός, new, bright and fresh[ly outfitted] (2:15; 4:24); 90, 147, 163
καιρός, history, proportion, important, opportunity, relevant, investment, cooperation, consequence, season, time (1:10; 2:12; 5:16; 6:18); 37, 88, 180, 181, 208-210, 236, 273
καλέω, to summon, to invite, to call (4:1, 4); 139, 140

Καλυψώ, Calypso ['she that veils,' from Homer's *Odyssey*, from καλύπτω, to cover, hide, conceal, veil - see ἀποκάλυψις]; 71
καρδία, heart; the ethical and moral decision making power of the soul (1:18, 3:17, 4:18, 5:19, 6:5, 22); 40, 72, 125, 136, 146, 160, 182, 224, 238, 246-248
καταβολή, foundation, founding (1:4); 33, 51
καταργέω, put out of business, put out of commission, put out of action (2:15); 90, 115
κατοικέω, to land, plant a colony, then settle in, then live, and finally adminster and govern a new land (3:17); 124-125, 136
κατοικητήριος, to build [make] a house into a home (2:22); 92
κεφαλή, the [head] leader (1:22, 4:15); 42, 144, 156
κλέπτω, steal, embezzle, run a confidence racket, smuggle (4:28); 148, 167
κληρονομέω, to inherit [to obtain by lot (κληρόω) but also by law (νόμος), thus, to be legally appointed], 61
κληρονομία, inheritance (1:14, 18; 5:5); 38, 40, 50, 67, 176, 200
κληρόω, inherit (1:11); 37, 50, 61, 67
κλῆσις, lifework, life project, vocation, profession, occupation, job apprenticeship (1:18; 4:1, 4); 41, 73, 139, 140, 150,
κλυδωνίζω, disturbed, confused (4:14); 144, 155
κοπιάω, hard work [so as to make one exhausted by the end of the work day] (4:28); 148, 167
κοσμοκράτορας, governmental regimes (6:12); 228, 243
κόσμος, organized system of civilized government, organization, enterprise, or business (1:4; 2:2, 12); 33, 52
κράτος, military authority and its corresponding rank [earned and awarded as a result of mastering

Greek Index and Glossary

ascending levels of the practice of the military arts] (6:10); 227, 242

κραυγὴ, blowing up in public outbursts of shouting, screaming or shrieking (4:31); 149, 170

κτίζω, to create, form, shape, invent, forge (2:10, 15; 3:9; 4:24); 87, 106, 116, 147, 164

κυβεία, [the belief that] major decisions should be made by chance, a gamble or a mere 'roll of the dice' (4:14); 144, 156

κυριότητος, leadership office (1:21); 41, 75

κυρίος, Commander in Chief (1:2, used 28 times in Ephesians, 26 to refer to Jesus in His present leadership role: 31, 45, 46; used twice in Ephesians to refer to human leaders, managers, business owners, bosses, entrepreneurs, military officers, civil or political officials [6:5, 9]; 46, 242

Λ

λανθάνω, to conceal, cover-up, to escape notice, to be unknown, unseen, unnoticed (see ἀληθεύω), 62

λέγω, to declare, make a legal declaration (4:17); 145, 158

λῆθος, concealed, unknown, unseen, unnoticed, (see ἀλήθεια), 62

λῆψις, to accept, to receive (see προσωπολημψία), 241

λόγος, the ability to think intelligently and speak with a clear mind, using the best logical reasoning in public speaking, whether the forum be teaching, a public speech, debate or legal defense (6:19); 236-237, 275-276

λύω, demolish, break up, destroy, put an end to, annul, dissolve (2:24); 90, 112

M

μαθητής, learners, pupils, apprentices, 162

μανθάνω, to learn and acquire the habits of a way of life by disciplined study, practice and experience (4:20); 146, 161

μαρτύρομαι, to be summoned to testify as an official, legal witness [especially by a divinity] (4:17); 145, 159

ματαιότης, futile, worthless (4:17); 145, 159

μάχαιρα, short combat sword used by infantry (6:17); 233, 269

μεθοδεία, stratagems, schemes, maneuvers, feints, ambushes, snares, booby traps (4:14, 6:11); 144, 155, 227, 243

μεθύσκω, to drink alcohol excessively, to become drunk, intoxicated (5:18); 181, 211

μεσότοιχος, partition wall, dividing wall (2:14); 89

μέτρον, measure [in both senses of laying out dimensions prior to construction, as well as evaluating and appraising value after construction is completed] (4:7, 13, 16); 141, 143, 145, 152, 153, 158

μετόχος, partner, associate, colleague (see συμμέτοχος), 200

μιμητής, actor, impersonator, imitator (5:1); 173, 189, 190-191

μνεία, the ability to think about and reflect upon something [or someone] and formulate specific plans do something about it [or for them] (1:16); 40, 68

μυστήριον, Divine "Top Secret" Plan (1:9, 3:3, 4, 9, 5:32; 6:19); 36, 59, 119, 121, 130, 131, 188, 237

μωρολογία, foolish, mythic fables that misrepresent God as petty, trivial, selfish or prejudiced (5:4); 175, 197-198

N

νεανίης, [Paul as a] young man, 129, 239

νεκρός, dead, death, as good as dead (1:20; 2:1, 5; 5:14); 41, 75, 81, 84, 179

νήπιος, naïve, purile, gullible and thus vulnerable (4:14); 144, 154

νόμος, law, rule; 60, 61, 67

νόος, a formulated philosophical world view that is motivated by habits of feeling, perceiving, understanding, and reasoned thinking; which is able to resolve purposes, intentions, plans and decisions about reality (4:17, 23); 145, 146, 159, 163

Ξ

ξένος, illegal alien [esp. economically, e.g., one who cannot get a job legally] (2:12, 19); 50, 88, 91

Ο

ὁδός, road, way, journey, [The Road, The Way, The Journey – a major metaphor describing the lifework quest of the Christian] 95-97

οἰκεῖος, household, home (2:19), 50, 91

οἰκοδομή, building, (2:21; 4:12, 16); 92, 116, 143, 144, 156; constructive (4:29); 148, 169

οἰκονομία, administration, government, economy (1:10; 3:2, 9); 37, 50, 61, 119, 121, 130

ΟΙΚΟΝΟΜΙΚΩΝ, *Economics* [Treatise by Aristotle on administrative skills required for leadership over an estate or a government]; 60-61

οἶκος, house, home, any place where one might live; 117

οἶνος, wine [unmixed with water] (5:18); 181, 211

ὄνομα, [lit. 'name'] the deliberate assigning, measuring out and keeping account or record of [something] (5:20); 182, 212

ὀνομάζω, to appoint (3:15); 124, 135

ὁπλίτης, foot soldier (see πανοπλία), 243

ὀργή, temperament, disposition, or habitual ascerbic mood of harboring anger and holding grudges (4:31); 149, 170

ὁρίζω, survey, mark out land, mark out with money, make a claim; 52

ὁσιότης, focus, pay exclusive attention to (4:24); 147, 164

ὀσμή, smell (5:2); 174, 191

ὀφειλέτης, debtor, 55

ὀφείλημα, financial indebtedness, debt, 55

ὀφείλω, to be in debt, owe, ought, (5:28); 55, 56

Π

παῖς, offspring, progeny, issue; 189

παλαιός, foolish, acerbic, aged person [i.e., cynical "old folks"] (5:22); 146, 162

πάλη, military fight, battle (6:12); 228, 243

πανοπλία, soldier's military equipment, including belt, body armor, helmet, shield, boots, and sword (6:11, 13); 227, 229, 243

πανουργία, scoundrel, swindler, fraud (4:14); 144, 155

παρά, to the side, beside; 56, 166

παραβαίνω, tresspass (v.), encroach, infringe, intrude, 55

παράβασις, tresspass (n.), infringement, intrusion, 55

παραβάτης, tresspasser, intruder, 55

παραδίδωμι, surrender [hand over a person to legal officials] (5:2); 174

παραπίπτω, to fall to side [of the road], to get sidetracked, 56

παράπτωμα, sidetracked [from one's lifework] (1:7; 2:1, 5); 35, 55-56, 81, 83, 84, 95

πάροικος, household member, cabinet member, member of a governmental administration [see οἰκονομία] (2:19); 50, 91

παροργίζω, to provoke to anger (6:4); 223, 240

παροργισμός, beside [oneself with] anger, exasperation (4:26); 147, 166

παρρησία, the ability to speak openly, freely and confidently in public (6:19); 237, 236

Παῦλος, Paul (1:1; 3:1); 29, 43, 118, 127

πεπυρωμένα, (perf part mid/pass neut nom pl of v. πυρόω), flaming (6:16); 231, 232, 243, 250

περιζωσάμενοι, to deliberately put a military sword-belt and sword upon one's body for the purpose of preparing for combat (6:14); 229, 245

περικεφάλαιος, that which goes around the head, helmet [in military context] (6:17); 233, 251

περιπατέω, [lit. 'to walk around'] to deliberately and intentionally learn, practice and teach others a comprehensive philosophical world view (2:2, 10; 4:1, 17; 5:2, 8, 15); 82, 87, 93, 103, 109, 139, 145, 150, 159, 174, 177, 180, 191, 200, 201, 206

περιποίησις, that which has been gained through acquisition and saved, savings account (1:14); 39, 67

περισσεύω, to go beyond, abound, to compound money through interest [in financial contexts] (1:8); 36, 50, 56

περιτομή, circumcision, (2:11); 88, 110

περιφέρω, to become disoriented due to having one's mind be spun around [lit. 'carried around'] in all directions by others (4:14); 144, 155

πικρία, bitter mood of cynical resentment (4:31); 149, 169

πίπτω, to fall, 56

πιστοῖς, experienced, reliable, dedicated and dependable veterans (1:1); 30

πλάνης, [lit. 'wanderer'] transients, pirates, con artists [those that wander from town to town to swindle or fool people] (4:14); 144, 155

πλάτος καὶ μῆκος καὶ ὕψος καὶ βάθος, width and length and height [dimensions of the superstructure of a building] and depth [crucial dimension of the foundation of a building] (3:18); 125-126, 137

πλεονέκτης, self-centered miser or materialist (5:5); 176, 200

πλεονεξία, avarice, insatiable greed (4:19; 5:3); 146, 161, 175, 194

πληρόω, fill [a job position], experience the full significance [of God's love, or of His Spirit] (1:23; 3:19; 4:10; 5:18); 42, 50, 79-80, 126, 142, 182

πλήρωμα, fulfillment [of history], completed [lifework], sense of fulfillment [in life], fully [mature human being] (1:10, 23; 3:19; 4:13); 37, 42, 126, 143

πλησίος, fellow human being (4:25); 147, 165

πλούσιος, rich, wealthy (2:4); 84

πλοῦτος, wealth, riches (1:7, 18; 2:7; 3:8, 16); 35, 41, 86, 120, 124, 131

πνευματικὰ τῆς πονηρίας, evil [heirarchy of] spiritual beings (6:12); 228, 243

πνευματικῇ, spiritual [disciplines, habits, attitudes, thoughts, demeanors and behaviors] (1:3); 33

ποιέω, make, forge, build, create, conceive, produce, solve a problem, satisfy a condition (1:16; 2:3, 14, 15; 3:11, 20; 4:16; 6:6, 8, 9); 89, 105, 106, 111

ποίημα, [lit. 'poem'] masterwork, masterpiece, (2:10) 87, 105

πολιτεία, legal or political citizenship [esp. with accompanying economic rights to work and posession of legal rights] (2:12); 88

πορνεία, consensual [albeit immature] sexual intercourse outside the bond of marriage (5:3); 174-175, 193

πόρνος, one who engages in sexual intercourse outside the bond of marriage (5:5); 176, 200

πρεσβεύω, to be Lead Negotiator (6:20); 237, 277

προελπίζω, to place hope [in something] before it happens (1:12); 38, 62

πρόθεσις, following sufficient planning and deliberation, to assert or publish in public an official case, proposition or statement (1:11, 3:11); 37, 61, 122, 133

προορίζω, preplan, pre-mark out, pre-survey, pre-finance, amortize (1:5, 11); 34, 37, 50, 52

πρός, to toward, 69

προσαγωγή, freeway (2:18, 3:12); 91, 116, 122, 133

προσεύχομαι, to request information from God in order to discover sufficient essential facts necessary to make an important spiritual decision, to seek God's direction in the process of gaining a spiritual understanding or perspective in order to plan an important course of action for the future (1:16, 6:18); 39, 69, 236 προσκαρτερήσει, patience, persistence, diligence, devotion (6:18); 236, 274-275

προσκολλάω, to bond to [someone psychologically, emotionally and spiritually] (5:31); 188, 220

προσωπεῖον, putting on a mask [by deceitfully manipulating one's own facial expressions] (see προσωπολημψία), 241

προσωπολημψία, accepting uncritically at face value the fraudulent intentions of someone pretending to have good motives through the calculated and deceitful use of their facial expressions (6:9); 226, 241

πρόσωπον, the face, especially the countenance or projection of one's attitude or mood by using one's facial expressions, 241

προφήταις, [transliteration = 'prophet'] Official [Divine] Spokespersons (2:20); 131

πυρόω, fire, flaming (6:16); 231, 250

πώρωσις, [lit. a callous, i.e.,] a tough layer of habits gradually built up over time that decrease one's ability to sense or feel things – to disregard and become indifferent to the welfare of other people (4:18); 146, 160

P

ῥῆμα, the facility of using public speech to communicate skillfully and accurately (5:26; 6:17); 186, 216, 233, 210

ῥιζόω, [lit. to 'root'] implant, embed (3:18); 125, 139

Σ

σαπρός, rotten, foul, disgusting or rancorous [speech] (4:29); 148, 169

σκότος, [lit. 'darkness'] fear and confusion, or stubborn, willful ignorance that lead to deceitfulness, lack of confidence, indecisiveness – and ultimately to tragic, premature death (5:8; 6:12); 177, 204, 228, 244

σκοτόω, [to become 'darkened,' i.e.,] to become dulled, enervated and stupefied in one's perception and understanding of reality, as well as in one's purposes and intentions [see σκότος] (4:18), 145, 159

σοφίᾳ, the kind of knowledge that makes it possible to become competent, then gain mastery, then achieve superior leadership ability in living human life skillfully, especially in the ethical and political arenas (1:8, 17; 3:10; 5:15); 36, 40, 56-58, 121, 132, 180, 206

σταυρός, cross [Roman instrument of capital punishment] (2:16); 89, 112

στῆτε, [impv. of ἵστημι, lit. 'stand (firm)'] never give up (6:14); 229, 245

συγκληρονόμος, equal heir, fellow heir (3:6), 120, 131

συγκοινωνέω, become joint shareholders or business partners with [someone] (5:11); 178, 205

συμβιβάζω, to 'put it all together (in one's mind)' i.e., to be able, because of being taught well, to logically conclude the truth about something (4:16); 145, 157

συμμέτοχος, fellow business partner, equal partner (3:6; 5:7); 120, 131, 176, 200

συμπολῖτης, fellow citizen (2:19), 91

συναρμολογέω, to fasten or join together carefully, harmoniously, and logically [as in assembling a ship's outer planking or in laying masonry] (2:21, 4:16); 92, 116, 144, 157

συνεζωοποίησε...καὶ συνήγειρε καὶ συνεκάθισεν, He has made us alive with...and He has resurrected us with and He has seated us with (2:5-6), 85, 103-104

συνίημι, to deliberately face a dilemma and perceive what to do [about it] with understanding and composure of mind (5:17); 181, 211

συνοικοδομέω, to build a house from a variety of divergent materials (2:22); 92, 117

σύσσωμα, co-administrator, fellow member of a governmental, organizational, administrative or associational body (3:6); 120, 131

Greek Index and Glossary

σφραγίζω, to seal, i.e., to officially certify or authenticate [something that significantly affects the public health, safety and welfare], and signify legal responsibility for such by application of a recognized stamp or symbol (1:13; 4:30); 38, 65, 149, 169

σώζω, rescue (2:5, 8); 84, 87, 102, 105

σῶμα, governmental, organizational, administrative or associational body [in organizational contexts] (1:23; 2:16; 4:4, 12, 16[2x]; 5:23, 38, 30); 42, 79, 90, 140, 143, 144, 183, 188; the human body, a good state of bodily health [in individual contexts] (5:28); 187, 216

σωτηρία, rescue, deliverance (1:13); 38, 65

T

τέκνον, child (5:1); 173, 189

τέλειος, [spiritually] mature (4:13); 143

τίκτω, to give birth, 189

τόπος, opening, opportunity (4:27); 148, 167

Y

υἱοθεσία, adoption as a son (1:5); 34, 50

ὑποδέω, to put on heavy gauge, sandal-type boots, including 'greaves,' i.e., armor plates strapped on to protect the leg and shin below the knee; to put on high-top military boots (6:15); 230, 248

ὑπόδικος, legal liability, 55

ὑποτάσσω, to subordinate; to develop the spiritual skill of adopting a cheerful and gracious attitude of deference and forbearance, trusting and supporting others, offering to help and enjoying the opportunity to gladly assist them in their efforts with a positive frame of mind (5:21, 22, 24); 182-183, 212-215

Φ

φθείρω, wasted, ruined, spoiled (5:22); 146, 163

φραγμός, screen wall, fence, partition, fortification wall (2:14); 89, 112

φρονέω, to be able to habitually discern, think through and make good decisions about matters that affect the lives of others in society, 58

φρόνησις, the skill of having the ability to habitually discern, think through and make good decisions about matters that affect the lives of others in society, (1:8); 36, 58

φῶς, [lit. 'light' (of truth)]; living life in a publicly open way, showing sincere motives, honesty, vulnerability, mercy and legitimacy in order to lead others; illumination [of the mind] through continual learning and education; projecting one's public character with consistency and clarity (5:8, 13); 177, 179, 201-204

φωτίζω, to be enlightened; realize, appreciate and act upon the spiritual duty to embrace leadership responsibility [see φῶς] (1:18; 3:9); 40, 121, 132

X

χάρις, [God's] graciousness, gracious [gift of a spiritual power or ability], gracious [benefit] (1:2, 6, 7; 2:5, 7, 8; 3:2, 7, 8; 4:7, 29; 6:24); 31, 34, 36, 84, 86 [2x], 119, 120 [2x], 141, 148, 238

χειροποίητος, made by hand, artificial (2:11); 88, 110

χρεία, to gain the ability to become useful, to provide a service [esp. 'providing a service' in business or 'going into the service' in the military] (4:28, 29); 148, 168, 169

χρηστός, service required to achieve the best and most beneficial outcome (4:31); 149, 170

Χριστός, High King [of the future world] (this word occurs 46 times in Ephesians); 30 ff., 45

Ψ

ψαλμός, a spiritual song sung individually or as a group, accompanied by a musical instrument or instruments (5:19); 182, 212

ψεῦδος, lying to oneself or others, or giving in to the predisposition to acquiesce and accept falsehood (4:25); 147, 164

SCRIPTURE INDEX

Genesis, 112
  2:18-25   118, 220
  6:5,   72
  6:6,   72
  18,   250
  19,   250
  27:41,   246
  49,   48

Exodus
  3,   158
  3:11-15   48
  7:3-4,   72
  8:15,   72
  14,   151
  14:5,   246
  20:12,   239

Leviticus
  25:29,   53

Numbers
  20,   250

Deuteronomy
  5:16,   239
  8:3,   270
  15:19,   45
  30:12-14,   244

Joshua
  3,   151
  7:5   250

Judges
  16:16-17, 246

1 Samuel
  17:51,   270
  28:5, 7;   246
  31,   250

2 Samuel
  11,   251
  18,   251
  24,   251

1 Kings
  11:4, 6;   246
  11-12,   251

2 Kings
  5,   151

Job 1-2,   244, 250
  33:24   163

Psalms
  2:7   257
  16:10   257
  4:1-4,   147, 165
  45:6-7,   131
  45:7,   200
  68:18,   141, 142, 152, 242
  90:10,   239
  91:11-12,   235, 270
  104:14-15, 211

Song of Solomon
  4:2,   215

Isaiah,
  26:19,   206
  40:3,   95
  60:1,   206

Daniel
  9,   69
  10,   243

Zechariah
  8:16,   147, 165
  9:9,   96

Matthew
  3:1-12,   151
  3:3,   95
  3:13-17,   152
  4:1-4,   270
  4:4,   270
  4:5-7,   270
  4:8-11,   270
  5:8,   72
  5:28,   72

Matthew
  5:32,   193
  6:9-13,   70
  6:12,   55
  6:21,   73
  7:24-27,   137
  12:34,   73
  13:18-23,   137
  13:44-46,   207
  15:19,   72
  19:19,   165
  21:8,   96
  22:36-40,   73
  25:14-31,   49, 153
  26: 6-13,   66, 193
  27:41,   247
  28:19-20   151

Mark 1:1-8,   151
  1:2-3,   96
  1:9-12,   152
  4:12,   54
  11:8,   96
  13:33,   273
  14:3-9,   193
  14:61,   47
  16:15-16,   151

Luke 2:75,   164
  3:1-18,   151
  3:4,   96
  3:21-22,   152
  4:27,   151
  6:13   135
  7:36-50,   193
  8:23-24   46, 47
  8:26-39,   244
  18:1,   134
  19:11-26,   153, 154
  19:23-40,   261
  19:36,   96
  21:36,   273
  22:21-34,   248

SCRIPTURE INDEX

23:34, 247

John
1:19-34, 151
1:23, 96
2:1-12, 211
4:1-2, 152
8:13, 44; 247
12:1-8, 193
12:7, 193
13:2, 247
14:4-6, 96
18:28-37, 112-114
19:12-22, 114-115

Acts, 128-129
1:13-26, 153
2, 158
2:28, 97
5:1-5, 247
6:15-7:1, 247
7, 129
7:54-60, 239
7:57-8:1, 247
7:58, 129, 162, 239, 247
8:1, 3; 247
9, 95
9:1-2, 97, 247
9:2, 97
9:3-19, 252
9:17, 97
9:20-22, 252
9:23-27, 253, 254
9:27, 97
9:28-30, 254
10:36, 165
11:19-26, 254
11:27-30, 255
12:1-23, 255
12:25, 255
13-28, 252
13:1-3, 255
13:4-52, 256-257
13:10, 97
14:1-6, 258
14:2, 95
14:19-20, 258
14:28, 258
15:1-29, 110
15:30-35, 258

16:16-40, 258-259
16:17, 97
Acts
17:5, 95
17:5-10, 259
17:13-15, 259
17:16-34, 94
17:26-27, 135
18, 94
18:1-3, 259
18:9-11, 67, 259
18:12-16, 260
18:18, 24; 260
18:19-21, 68
18:25, 26; 97
19:1, 260
19:9, 95
19:9, 23; 97
19:10, 68
19-20, 94
20:31, 68
20:31, 35; 260
20:32, 131
22:4, 97
22:17-21, 252
23-26, 276
23:6, 97, 247
23:11, 276
24:14, 22; 97
26:5, 247
26:5-11, 97
26:9-11, 247
28:30-31, 277

Romans, 51, 52, 55, 56, 68, 72, 127, 130, 262
1:4, 52
1:9, 68
1:13-14, 109
1:25, 47
2:7, 277
2:28-29, 110
3:24, 54
5:2, 116
8:23, 54
8:38-39, 76
9:5, 47
10:7, 244
10:10, 73
11:13, 153
11:29, 74

1 Corinthians, 52, 55, 59, 60,
1:26, 74
1:30, 54
2:7-8, 59
6:1-3, 132
7:18-20 110
7:20, 74
10:1-4, 151
11:23-33, 252
11:30, 251
13: 4-8, 191
13:13, 191
15:24-25, 76
15:42-54, 277

2 Corinthians, 127, 244, 261, 262, 263
2:15, 192
5:1-4, 104-105
6:5, 273
11, 128
11:7, 260
11:23-27, 261, 263
11:27, 273
11:32-33, 253-254
12:7-9, 244, 263
12:1-10, 244
12:14-16 260

Galatians, 51, 67, 127, 253, 254, 262
1:15-19, 252
1:21-23, 254
5:6; 110
6:15; 110

Philippians, 51, 59, 127, 130, 239, 262
1:4, 271
1:19, 157, 271
1:20-25, 239
2:5, 59
3:5, 247
3:14, 74
3:20, 101
4:6, 271
4: 6-8, 72
4:18, 192

Colossians, 51, 59, 60, 67, 127, 130, 262
- 1:14,   54
- 1:16,   77
- 2:10,   77
- 2:15,   77
- 3:6,   95
- 3:11,   110

1 Thessalonians, 127, 262
- 2:7,   220
- 5:1-10, 251
- 5:8,   251

2 Thessalonians, 127, 262
- 1:11,   74

1 Timothy, 127
- 6:14-15 45

2 Timothy, 127, 130, 240, 262
- 1:8-11, 74
- 1:9,   74
- 1:10,   277
- 4:6-8,   240

Titus, 127, 262
- 2:7,   277
- 3:1-2,   77

Philemon, 127, 130, 262

Hebrews
- 1:9,   131, 200
- 1:13,   104
- 3:18,   95
- 4:6, 11, 95
- 6:6,   56

Hebrews
- 10:11-13, 104
- 11,   242
- 11:8-10   75
- 11:31,   95

James
- 1:17,   204

1 Peter
- 1:15,   101
- 2:6,   49

1 John
- 1:5-10, 203

Revelation, 244
- 19-22,   153
- 20:1-3, 153
- 20:2-7, 48

COMING SOON!

PHILIPPIANS
PAUL'S TREATISE ON MATURE CHRISTIAN THINKING

A New Basic Explanatory Translation
With
A New Extended Interpretive and Expositional Translation

Into
Professional (Non-Ecclesiastical)
Contemporary (Non-Medieval)
American (Non-British)
English

From
The Greek Text

Additional Publications by this Author currently being edited,
revised and improved for republication in 2006 by Authorhouse:

- *Ethics: Ancient and Medieval*
- *Ethics: Modern and Contemporary*
- *Metaphysics: Ancient and Medieval*
- *Metaphysics: Modern and Contemporary*
- *Professional Intentional Leadership for Entrepreneurs and CEOs* – 26 Leadership Principles derived from Winston Churchill's *History of the English Speaking Peoples* (Unabridged Classic Four Volume Set of Churchill's Historical Lifework)
- *Professional Intentional Leadership for Managers, Supervisors and Administrators* – 10 Leadership Principles derived from Navy SEAL Commander Richard Marcinko's *Leadership Secrets of the Rogue Warrior*

To contact us or find out about additional publications by this author,
visit our website:

I L I
The Intentional Leadership Institute
www.intentionalleadershipinstitute.com